The Archaeology of Inequality

THE INSTITUTE FOR EUROPEAN AND MEDITERRANEAN ARCHAEOLOGY
DISTINGUISHED MONOGRAPH SERIES

Peter F. Biehl, editor-in-chief
Sarunas Milisauskas and Stephen L. Dyson, editors

The Magdalenian Household: Unraveling Domesticity
Ezra Zubrow, Françoise Audouze, and James G. Enloe, editors

Eventful Archaeologies: New Approaches to Social Transformation in the Archaeological Record
Douglas J. Bolender, editor

The Archaeology of Violence: Interdisciplinary Approaches
Sarah Ralph, editor

Approaching Monumentality in Archaeology
James. F. Osborne, editor

The Archaeology of Childhood: Interdisciplinary Perspectives on an Archaeological Enigma
Güner Coşkunsu, editor

Diversity of Sacrifice: Form and Function of Sacrificial Practices in the Ancient World and Beyond
Carrie Ann Murray, editor

Climate and Cultural Change in Prehistoric Europe and the Near East
Peter F. Biehl and Olivier P. Nieuwenhuyse, editors

Water and Power in Past Societies
Emily Holt, editor

Coming Together: Comparative Approaches to Population Aggregation and Early Urbanization
Attila Gyucha, editor

The Early Bronze Age in Western Anatolia
Laura K. Harrison, A. Nejat Bilgen, and Asuman Kapuci, editors

The Archaeology of Inequality
Orlando Cerasuolo, editor

THE ARCHAEOLOGY
OF INEQUALITY

Tracing the
Archaeological Record

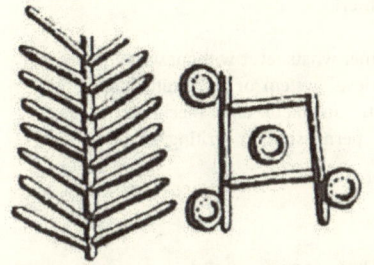

IEMA Proceedings,
Volume 10

EDITED BY
Orlando Cerasuolo

STATE UNIVERSITY OF
NEW YORK PRESS

Logo and cover/interior art: A vessel with wagon motifs from Bronocice, Poland, 3400 B.C. Courtesy of Sarunas Milisauskas and Janusz Kruk, 1982, Die Wagendarstellung auf einem Trichterbecher aus Bronocice, Polen, *Archäologisches Korrespondenzblatt* 12: 141–144.

Published by
State University of New York Press, Albany

For information, contact
State University of New York Press, Albany, NY
www.sunypress.edu

Library of Congress Cataloging-in-Publication Data

Name: Cerasuolo, Orlando, 1977– editor.
Title: The archaeology of inequality : tracing the archaeological record /
  [edited by] Orlando Cerasuolo.
Description: Albany : State University of New York Press, 2021. | Series:
  SUNY series, The Institute for European and Mediterranean Archaeology
  distinguished monograph series | Includes bibliographical references and
  index.
Identifiers: LCCN 2021024197 | ISBN 9781438485133 (hardcover : alk. paper) |
  ISBN 9781438485140 (ebook)
Subjects: LCSH: Equality—History. | Social classes—History. | Social
  archaeology.
Classification: LCC HM821 .A73 2021 | DDC 305.5/1—dc23
LC record available at https://lccn.loc.gov/2021024197

10 9 8 7 6 5 4 3 2 1

Contents

PART IV
BIOARCHAEOLOGY OF HISTORICAL INEQUALITY

Illustrations

FIGURES

TABLES

CHAPTER ONE

Archaeological Perspectives on Inequality

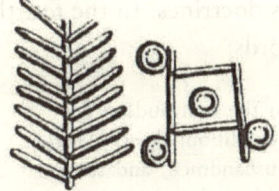

Orlando Cerasuolo

In contemporary society we continuously experience the existence, the threat, and the consequences of inequality. It happens every day on both global and personal scales, affecting individual lives as well as groups and societies. In modern times, the debate on inequality is mostly focused on the economic distortions within the society, the differences in income, and their social outcomes. Examples of such climates can be found in recent history, as part of the worldwide 99% and Occupy movements.

Current journalism looks at ancient inequalities, projecting the modern situation onto the ancient one, in a rather naive way.[1] The result is major confusion for both students and the general public. There is a series of scholars, from Gherard Emmanuel Lenski (1966) to Milanovic and colleagues (2010), who believe that economic inequality reached its peak before the Industrial Revolution. Milanovic and colleagues argued that there is less inequality nowadays than in the past, since today the ruling elite are "extracting" less income from their citizens. As a matter of fact, it is hard to compare modern and ancient situations without taking into account the substantial differences between the social and economic structures of the societies. As a consequence, a fruitful comparison between present and past should be very carefully thought-out.

Without such a hypermodern economic view, inequality reveals itself through the presence of unbalanced relationships and can result (and usually does) in uneven relations between genders and ages, but also in terms of ethnicity, religion, freedom, and so on. Social and political divisions within communities were a common feature in past civilizations all around the world. In many ancient cultures there were several discrimination strategies; social boundaries, economic concentrations, and exclusions were typical aspects of many ancient communities, in a way that is not different to the modern world (Giddens 2007:61–71; Khan 2012). Social inequality in antiquity is a complex issue that is often contentious among prehistorians and anthropologists, while it is taken for granted or not considered at all by most of the classical archaeologists (Price and Hayden, this volume). Much contention revolves around how to interpret the available archaeological and historical records, or the cultural models for societies and interactions.

The study of ancient inequality began well before the modern archaeological approach. In fact, several philosophers and thinkers had addressed the issues of human relationships as determining the social structures of communities, and where the origins of the inequalities are rooted. For the greater part of human history, the existing order was regarded as a natural feature of the society, and the intellectual task was mainly to explain or justify this order in terms of religious or quasi-religious doctrines. In the fourth century BC, Aristotle addressed the issue with the following words:

> In the first place we see that all states are made up of families, and in the multitude of citizen there must be some rich and some poor, and some in a middle condition; the rich are heavy-armed, and the poor not. Of the common people, some are husbandmen, and some traders, and some artisans. There are also notable differences of wealth and property—for example, in the number of horses which they keep, for they cannot afford to keep them unless they are rich. . . . Besides differences of wealth there are differences of rank and merit, and there are some other elements. (Aristotle, Politics IV.3)

It was only with the Enlightenment that a critical "rhetoric of equality" emerged in opposition to the civil and legal advantages of the aristocracy and other privileged groups. The declaration expressed by J.-J. Rousseau in *The Social Contract* (1762), "[M]an is born free, and yet we see him everywhere in chains," is the best example of this approach.

Nowadays, there is much attention paid to understanding the nature, the origin, and the evolution of inequalities among human beings, but when it comes to defining what inequality is, there is much debate and, as a result, there are many ways in which inequality can be conceptualized. To better analyze ancient inequalities, both on the social and the individual level, archaeology and anthropology take advantage of approaches and findings borrowed from many other disciplines, such as ethnography, sociology, economy, demography, physical anthropology, geography, and so on. Current approaches often elaborate on the works of modern sociologists and thinkers (M. Weber, V. Pareto, G. Mosca, P. Bourdieu, T. Veblen, J. Pakulski, A. Giddens, etc.).

That part of archaeology that focuses on relationships within communities is often called *social archaeology* (Renfrew and Bahn 2007:141; Wason 1994; Meskell and Preucel 2004; Ames 2008; Haas 2001; Paynter 1989; Smith 2012; Hodder 1982; Shanks and Tilley 1982). Since material culture is fundamentally inherent in the process of self-representation as well as in the configuration of social time and space, this approach focuses on the materiality of human existence, from conceptualization, to making and use, to discard and reuse. For archaeologists, some classes of evidence are more revealing than others, such as burial customs, decorative styles, settlement hierarchy, food consumption, household arrangements, or pottery (Ames 2008; Wason 1994), but the inquiry on inequality can be operated on almost every aspect of the archaeological evidence. Nevertheless, every type of evidence requires some premises that must be tested only under a careful analysis. The strength and reliability of the documentation is enhanced if coupled with other types of evidence, and a diachronic analysis might shed light on potential changes over time.

Following the strong IEMA tradition of interdisciplinarity, this book aims to present and debate different aspects of social boundaries, by comparing several approaches and methods for the analysis of archaeological data, as well as actual case studies. The 19 international scholars that were involved in the two-day conference at Buffalo explored practical methods of analysis as well as the theories about ancient inequality, how these are culturally shaped and reflected in the material culture.

The contributions collected in this conference proceedings are devoted to the Mediterranean, Europe, and North America, from the Neolithic to the Roman Imperial time and the 20th century CE. Their focuses and approaches are varied, as well as the case studies they discuss, ranging from settlement analysis to funerary evidence, from physical anthropology to demography, from architecture to epigraphy and iconography, from theory to the presentation of new finds. As we are aware of the complexity of the topic of the conference we did not want to cover all the aspects, but, rather, to present a variety of approaches from different disciplines at different levels of the theoretical framework.

The different essays collected in this book aim to present the results of past studies together with some novel investigations. It is appropriate to summarize some of the main archaeological approaches and the contribution to the topic made by the essays presented to the reader. In addition to the chronological and geographical order followed in the book, it is possible to highlight some alternative trajectories connecting the different papers, from the relation among individuals of a single community, to the wider territorial perspective. This volume addresses how the archaeological evidence is varied and rich in information about the social structure, but at the same time how it sometimes provides unclear data, often difficult to understand.

THE PROCESS OF DIFFERENTIATION: FROM NATURAL DIFFERENCES TO SOCIAL STRATIFICATION

Human beings are alike, but differ in personalities, intelligence, interests, skills, and other individual characteristics that by nature define horizontal, fair categories. On the other hand, divisions are socially constructed, and their precise forms vary over time from community to community. Differences become inequalities when they are invested with cultural and social meanings, or unequal access to resources and shares, or to knowledge. In the progressive development of the social structure, social categories and roles assume different values and are perceived—or practiced—in a stratified ranking, marking the passage from social divisions to social stratifications.

Among the major elements that describe social inequalities, there are status, gender, age, and ethnicity (Price and Feinman 2010). Those elements, today as in the past, are deeply connected to each other and often overlapping. Every identity is constituted at the same time by a multiplicity of attributes, a condition that is sometimes referred to as "intersectionality" (Meskell and Preucel 2004:121–141; Preucel and Mrozowski 2010:284).

While archaeological methods of investigating ancient inequalities vary, the common threads are the analyses of differential access to basic resources and prestige, production and surplus, elite control, and the nature of structural power (Hayden 1995; Price and Feinman 2010; Wolf 1999; Price and Brun this volume). Each level of this multifaceted system is a challenge for scholars, given that each requires specific methods of inquiry in a continuous relation with the limits and fragmentary nature of the archaeological record. The major sources for archaeologists are administrative evidence, burial analysis and wealth differentiation, monuments and public works, means and forms of production, settlement analysis and demography, material culture, iconography, warfare, land ownership, written records, and ethnography (Ames 2008; Wason 1994).

As long as social inequalities can be defined in terms of differences in power and status, distribution and access to resources, within and between societies, such inequalities are created and maintained by those in powerful positions via social processes and institutions. The dynamics of power relationships, domination, and resistance have also been partially investigated in recent years (Paynter and McGuire 1991:1–27). Moreover, the powerful affirmation of even (egalitarian) or uneven (hierarchical) social organization is a controversial topic often given as a key factor in determining the relative success (or not) of ancient societies (Westgate this volume).

Many variations can be found among historical—as well as modern—societies. However, these variations, even when showing different degrees of social complexity, should not be seen as evolutionary steps in a continuous development. It is even true that in the initial stages of the process of development it can stop and move back, as a result of social negotiation and dominance mitigation (Hayden 1995; Price, Parkinson, and Brun this volume). In past decades, several efforts have been made to identify and describe general trends within this range of variations (Brun this volume). The most popular is the one designed by Service in the 1960s, and later criticized and further developed, that makes a distinction between band, tribe, chiefdom, and state (Service 1962; Kristiansen 1998; Drennan, Peterson, and Fox 2010; Peregrine 2012; Peterson and Drennan 2012; Drennan Peterson 2012). Using a simpler model, we can recognize egalitarian, ranked, and stratified societies, each characterized by the different access that people had to basic resources, prestige, and power positions. The model can be sketched as follows:

	basic resources	**prestige position**	**structural power**
Egalitarian	equal access	equal access	absent
Ranked	equal access	differential access	sometimes
Stratified	differential access	differential access	common

From the structuralist to the cognitive, from the functionalist to the interactionist, every school of interpretation highlights different triggering factors for the development of inequality in early communities and the development of cultural complexity: population pressure, risk management, social or ideological factors, social or geographical circumscription, ritual values, external threats, resources control and management, feastings and debts, demographic imbalance, storage management, environmental conditions (Hayden 1995; Hendon 2000). The emergence of potential leaders and social struggles seems to appear in every human group that is larger than 50–100 people (Hayden 1995) and a stratified level of power and administration occurs in every complex society. In terms of economic functioning, the development of private property and binding contracts are critical elements in the establishment of structured power, resulting in further levels of social restraint.

The first chapters of this book deal with the emergence of social inequality from different points of view and shed light on its economic foundations. The paper presented here by Price provides a thorough analysis of differences between early gatherers and more structured hunter-gatherers. The latter show some degree of social complexity and organization, but only some groups seem to have institutionalized inequalities. On the other hand, gatherers have customs and social strategies to limit individual attitudes and to guarantee egalitarian behaviors. As a conclusion to his extensive survey, Price argues that the beginning of social inequality lies within the changes associated with the origins of agriculture, together with the earliest forms of hereditary status differentiation. Surplus, wealth, feasting, prestige technologies, corporate and network strategies are the main factors involved in the emergence of inequality, though they are affected by issues of visibility of their material correlates. During the Neolithic, when some individuals or social groups gained power and wealth, the many ceded their egalitarian status for benefits in terms of reliable food and greater security.

In his chapter, Hayden summarizes his past research and highlights the early signs of complexity and inequality among the transegalitarian societies of hunter-gatherers of the American Northwest Plateau, an environmental area with great diversity in natural resources. Both ethnographically and archaeologically, the major centers on the plateau exhibited pronounced wealth, sedentism, large communities, inequalities, but also a coexistence of corporate and more egalitarian groups. The area studied by Hayden exhibits relevant cultural similarities with Near Eastern Late Mesolithic cultures, such as the Natufian, and contributes to the development of more general explanatory models for the emergence of inequality, also taking advantage of relatively detailed ethnographic accounts available for the Northwest Plateau. Hayden criticizes some theoretical concepts followed by others, such as the institutionalized inequalities and the hyper-heterarchical approach, offering a coherent view of the archaeological evidence. He provides evidence for a strong correlation between the distribution of prestige items and the best fish procurement sites and discusses other classes of evidence such as burials and houses. Following a political ecology approach, Hayden rejects a stress-driven theory while supporting a surplus-and-aggrandizer model as the base for an economically based inequality. In Hayden's view, transegalitarian societies are based on privately owned surplus production, and a variety of competitive aggrandizer strategies are meant to increase self-interests and benefits.

Parkinson in this volume addresses the origins of institutionalized hereditary political and economic inequality within early agricultural villages of southeastern Europe, from the

Neolithic to the Bronze Age. In this area, patterns of landscape occupation and changes in material culture style characterize the long period between the establishment of sedentary agricultural villages and the emergence of societies with institutionalized hereditary ranking and hierarchy. His peculiar approach stresses how the archaeological perspective on the emergence of social inequalities is skewed by success stories that Parkinson considers exceptional with respect to human history. He focuses on what he calls "false starts" that never experienced political and economic complexity and did not persist over time, but that can be extremely useful in order to understand the reason for great historical changes. False starts occur in social contexts that are precocious and cannot support a certain social process. In his area, for example, massive settlements dating back to the Neolithic were abandoned and only reoccupied later, when both the historical situation and social life had changed. During this new phase, the previous large households were replaced by smaller houses with storage facilities, denoting a change in the family structure. These new social conditions were likely more suitable for the development of permanent inequalities.

Similar trends of cyclic evolution and crisis are presented in Brun's chapter, which describes the social changes that occurred in France through five distinct stages during the Iron Age. Giving an explanation for the cultural oscillation in Iron Age France, Brun seems to follow an environmental model, where climate improvements correspond to political and economic growth. Migration of groups involved the entire area, causing further turbulence but also new contacts with external people, such as the Etruscans and the Greeks. Also, the technical development of iron tools caused an increase in agropastoralism and supported the gradual formation of large political entities, from simple to complex chiefdoms. At the end of this process, the political centers were managed by political institutions such as magistrates, oligarchs, and judges, while small and large armies defended the cities. Coins and writing were introduced and functioned as administrative tools for these new political entities. At the same time, the funerary evidence does not present signs of significant social stratification, so perhaps religion and ideological customs were masking the stratified structure of the society.

HOUSEHOLD, GENDER, AGE, AND THE BODY

Other forms of discrimination are based on age and gender, and have different outcomes in different types of societies. In more egalitarian societies (i.e., hunter-gatherers), the social categories of age and gender do not take on rigid and determining qualities; all voices provide some contribution to the community decision making (Gilchrist 2004). In these "simple" societies, status and roles are not based on economic production and resource management (Hayden this volume). In hierarchical societies, in which access to inherited property is crucial for economic well-being, age and gender criteria are frequently quite rigid and strongly sanctioned. An example is the textile production and specialization of the advanced Iron Age communities in central Italy: early female burials show several tool sets associated with different phases of spinning and weaving, the sort of activities that were likely performed by females of different ages (Gleba 2008).

In different cultures and times, the social roles of gender and age were also affected by the concept of the household. The household is in fact a social arena for economic organization, structure, power, and agency, but also, as the place for everyday experience and practice, it is crucial for the construction of social identity (Hendon 2004).

Of course, it is necessary to be aware that roles exercised in a social group based on cultural divisions are not constant, but may change over time; and sometimes this phenomenon makes it very difficult to analyze the material evidence and extract meaningful information. An example is the variation in the status value of men and women during the course of a lifetime: in many ethnographic cases, women's status improves once menopause has released them from reproductive roles, and they achieve a senior place within the family through institutionalized roles of grandmothers or mothers-in-law (Gilchrist 2004). A woman's influence grows with age, since her power over kin and household increases until she dominates more generations of the family. Men, in contrast, achieve greater public power, but hold this authority for a shorter period, with influence decreasing with age and the termination of military activity.

Children and the young have different consideration and status in egalitarian and hierarchical societies, and their productive role can change as well. Their involvement in social life is often marked by stages (each with specific roles and tasks) that may vary in different cultures. Young girls and boys can have separate and complex pathways to adulthood, as shown by L. Beaumont (2000) for fifth century Athens. Moreover, the young usually have funerary practices and tomb locations separated from the rest of the community, in isolated burial grounds or within the settlements (Gilchrist 2004).

The paper by Bagnasco investigates the relationship between men and women in terms of social polarity, both in the archaeological and the textual evidence. It is still hard to define Etruscan women's condition through the lens of the archaeological and literary record but recent analyses can shed new light on the topic. For example, the series of painted tombs found at Tarquinii show women taking part in banquets and feasting over more than three centuries, but it is not easy to understand how much this representation reflects the actual condition of females and how it changed over time, even in restricted aristocratic circles. Epigraphic evidence is somehow elusive too, but a relevant presence of inscriptions with women's names, rather than men's, is clearly documented. Furthermore, the most ancient texts mention women and female goddesses. Textile production—a typically female activity—is a symbolic action connected by Bagnasco to the social role of bringing together what is socially parted, as if threads of a fabric. And it is significant that the earliest epigraphic evidence in Etruscan archaeology comes from textile evidence. Bagnasco also stresses how early literacy is related to women, as a system of "organizing signs." Bagnasco highlights how the role of women was also central to some cult activities, for example, at the "monumental complex" of Tarquinii. As a matter of fact, onomastics shows that the Etruscan woman had some relevant legal rights, but the condition of women and their role within society had also changed over time.

A completely different approach to inequality is offered in this volume by Muller, who introduces the potential impact of inequalities on the physiology of the human body, as recorded in skeletal remains. The evidence discussed by her belongs to impoverished and marginalized peoples from the recent past, but has broader applications. The paper constitutes a great contribution to the theme of the book because it proposes a point of view that is far from the traditional archaeological perspective, but whose integration is beneficial. In particular, Muller clarifies how in addition to cultural and social outcomes of inequality, specific sets of behavior, biology, and psychology could impact the material dimension of humans, both positively and/or negatively. Analytical study of the micro- and macroscopic evidence preserved in bones can result in the recovery of the causes of death, such as violence or the social and environmental conditions at the time of death.

THE UNEQUAL DEATH

The evidence from the necropolis is somehow more revealing. Although the funerary contexts can be strongly characterized by customs influenced by religion and ritual practices, the tombs are usually a well-preserved context, providing multiple levels of information about society, ideology, and religious beliefs (Wason 1994). In many ancient societies, funerary rituals constituted a public arena where social structure was reaffirmed. Thus, from an archaeological perspective, the analysis of the variation in the disposal treatments and patterns of association can help identify the position of the deceased within the social framework.

In this volume, Hanks presents a case study from the Southern Ural Mountains region, where archaeological evidence suggests relevant social, economic, and political change during the second and first millennia BC. Special focus is given to the complex picture of mortuary practice and symbolism in the area that is greatly changing thanks to modern research and analyses. The burial record is varied and several intriguing cases are discussed by Hanks, showing how some complex evidence can bear multiple meanings. In particular, the high degree of variability of some burial contexts encourages a more nuanced understanding of mortuary rituals and their relationship with social practices and organization. While cemeteries revealed the disposal of select members of the community and special burial customs, contemporary settlements have not revealed any clear difference in terms of house structures and associated material finds. Moreover, the use of cemeteries sometimes continues long after the abandonment of the related settlement, denoting different social functions as well as the crucial role of the tombs as a way of legitimizing access and control over environmental resources.

The complete analysis of a necropolis can show major changes in burial customs, sometimes related to changes in the right to a formal burial. Different trajectories of burial practices in ancient Greece have been widely explored (Morris 1992; Whitley 1996), but similar trends can also be found in other areas. For instance, if we look at the prominent urban center of Cerveteri in Etruria during the Iron Age and the early Archaic period, a marked drop is evident in the number of burials at the end of the eighth century BC, at a time when the city went through a major political expansion, when new monumental burials were erected and new economic and power systems were established. While a demographic decrease is very questionable, it seems likely that this phenomenon represents a deep change in civic burial rights (Cerasuolo 2016). The illusory disappearing of a part of the community, or its invisibility in the archaeological record, must emphasize the idea that most of the time only a part of the society left a durable evidence, while the rest of the community is also marginalized in terms of the archaeological record.

Marginalization is surely at the base of the development of social inequalities, and in its extreme forms led to slavery. It is one of the goals of the ruling class to create and maintain the marginalization of part of its community, as well as of other communities. The ruler eases the marginalization, for example dislocating manpower to build monuments, fostering the specialization of craftsmen (that are by nature not self-sufficient), or conditioning the economy (for example, by organizing communal feasts or redistributing prestige goods). Furthermore, aspiring rulers used the social imbalance caused by marginalization to act as advisors and negotiators, thus increasing their power (Hayden 1995).

The so-called deviant burials are often attributed to individuals of lower social status. An interesting project devoted to late prehistoric Italy is presented here by Saracino and colleagues. They collected burial data from cemeteries and settlements in order to understand whether abnormal mortuary practices (special rites, body treatment, lack of grave goods, isolated location, etc.) and osteological characteristics might be connected to the "marginal" social situations of specific individuals. Burial findings from settlements and natural locations seem to be related to specific ritual activities typical of liminal areas. The funerary variability has been connected by Saracino and colleagues to changes in the ritual practices and the economy of this region, and might have expressed changing perspectives on social inclusion and exclusion.

In antiquity, a common selective process, perhaps testifying to status and age marginalization, was that a part of the community, sometimes the great majority, never received a formal burial. The Dalsoglio chapter discusses a pattern of differentiation among the Transitional and Protogeometric burials in the Kerameikos cemetery at Athens through quantitative and qualitative analyses as well as the measurement of the energy expenditure. The sample is small but significant. During that period, burials became selective, and likely only the higher part of society received a formal burial, even if there was a strong egalitarian ideology and self-representation (Morris 1987; Whitley 1991). The number of burials is inversely proportional to the quantity of pottery and metal objects found in them; a few graves (about 20 percent) stand out among all the others, which contain precious and rare items. There are male burials with and without weapons, while female burials can be divided into rich and poor depositions; higher tombs being generally female. Thus, the grave hierarchy based on gender and status constitutes a further differentiation among an already selected group, while most of the community did not receive a formal burial.

The funerary custom of ancient Greece is a crucial topic, and two more papers analyze the Iron Age evidence for male (D'Onofrio) and female (Vlachou) burials. D'Onofrio focuses on the complex evidence of weapons in the funerary set of the protohistoric

Athens and provides a comprehensive dataset. Weapons, together with personal ornaments, are present in only about 20 percent of the male burials and are clearly a marker
of (engendered) rank selection, as is also highlighted by their presence in adolescent
graves. Weapons are buried in a few tombs and distributed regularly in intervals of
decades, suggesting, in the framework of a strong continuity of use of burial plots, the
presence of single-armed males for every generation (perhaps the subsequent masters of
the *oikos*). The distribution of these graves in the necropolis suggests that they pertain
to local, corporate descent groups. Ritual damage to the weapons is common and the
presence of swords, in particular, carries significant symbolic meanings, as in the use of
wrapping it around the neck of the cinerary urn in a sort of long-lasting embrace. In a
few fortunate cases, particular tombs show a combination of local and foreign elements
together with a marginal location within the necropolis. For example the case of tomb
PG2N, where local pottery is associated with one of the most ancient swords found at
Athens, recalls an Argive custom.

As we move to the female burials, Vlachou provides an updated and in-depth
analysis. From her point of view, Attica offers an important perspective for the study of
the role of women in Greek society. The funerary record reveals significant inequalities in
burial treatments and sheds light on the representation of wealth, status, age, and gender
both vertically and horizontally. A long-term view allows for an analysis of the constant
negotiation of an individual's role within the broader social context. In the framework
of funerary customs, burial practices and the selection of specific classes of items serve as
ritual choices. Some hints of the representation of relatively lower classes are also recovered
from the archaeological record. Patterns in the distribution of burial gifts demonstrates
that wealthier burials tend to incorporate personal items of value as well as ritual options
exercised by the relatives during the funeral. The evidence is complex and there are trends
that cross vertical distinctions of wealth. Female burials, especially young females, seem
to represent the major social arena for aristocratic families, with more complex funerary
sets and rituals. The lavishness of items and their quantity, or in some cases just their
presence, may constitute an indicator of rank. The careful analysis made by Vlachou
points out which items are personal (those burned on the pyre together with the dead
body) and which are added during the interment (that is, outside the urn). The latter
perhaps might be connected to family choices, in the light of social display of power.

An interesting approach is the one proposed by Borbonus in his paper, which
discusses inequality more in terms of political dynamics than of social injustice, marking an important difference between modern and ancient perceptions of inequality. The
author analyzes a distinctive form of organized collective burial, used by urban slaves and
freed slaves, starting from a dataset of funerary epitaphs and the characteristics of the
architectonic monuments—the *colombaria*. It is an interesting case study because of the
nature of the relationship that binds the individuals, which is not familial but socially
selective, structured and regulated by specific customs. Beyond the funerary aspects, the
collegia created complex networks of relation supporting the members and creating new
levels of interactions, which also worked as a "social pressure valve."

ECONOMY AND SUBORDINATION

All of the evidence of economic activity and resource management might result in a formative condition of status. At least since the Chalcolithic period, the evidence of hunting, as well as animal raising and management has been interpreted as a means of communicating social position, status, and group membership inside and outside the household (i.e., Arbuckle 2012). The social use of food in feasting and other communal activities is a powerful tool in the hand of the ruling individuals and groups, and represents "gastro-politics," as defined by Appadurai (1981).

Classical historians have addressed the issues of economy size and income distribution in the Roman world, as the available sources are more abundant. For the Roman Empire period, several attempts have been made to assess the Gross Domestic Product based on the expenditure, income, and the supposed consumption of wheat (Scheidel and Friesen 2009). These analyses are mostly focused on the wealthy classes, while the data about subordinates are more faint and difficult to recover.

A robust analysis of the historical and archaeological sources related to the servants in the last phases of the Etruscan civilization is undertaken by †Torelli in this volume. The object of his study is to understand the dynamics of emancipation and the character of the subordinate classes before and after the definition of a new social role at a crucial historical turning point. The analysis highlights a far-reaching network of cultural connections and local developments, demonstrated by historical accounts and archaeological finds. The social dimension of slavery is part of major economic activities, such as metal production and landscape management. Servants, both men and women, have also a central role in ritual, as the evidence from sanctuaries clearly shows. But the historical reconstruction, through the sequence of political claims and social achievements, suggests also the chain of priorities felt by the Etruscan servants, which are ultimately directed toward reshaping the social order.

Zelnick Abramowitz, in this volume, discusses levels of social status in classical Athens. They were demarcated by administrative boundaries (born citizens, naturalized citizens, metics, slaves, etc.), not always matching with individual economics resources. These statuses entailed access to different civil rights, but ambiguity was common, since in the relatively big city of Athens a person's status could be questioned on a few occasions. The privileges and social rights were also affected by temporary situations, that is, noncitizens could take part in some religious celebrations together with citizens, as equals, while being separated for the rest of everyday life. How one's political condition was socially visible in ancient Greece is still hard to say, as different sources of information give different pictures of citizenship attributes.

De Ligt offers the reader a complete synthesis of many aspects of inequality in the Roman world from a long-term perspective. The evolution of major developments related to funerary practice, social organization, politics, and dissent as well as the economic bases are discussed in depth thanks to a robust theoretical framework.

The chapter by Fentress provides an account of an exceptional discovery of slave barracks in the area of a large Roman Imperial residence. The similarity between the excavated building and the military barracks is evident and perhaps reflects a logic of optimization of functions and spaces. The analysis of the findings provides an interesting range of data about life, work, material culture, diet, health condition, death, and many other aspects of the people living in the barracks. For the author of the paper it is also a chance to gather the rare evidence of similar housing for the constrained labor force in other areas. The examples seem to highlight complex and articulated structures, conceived in order to keep workforces relatively comfortable, though productive. A general comparison between a similar situation between the Late Republic and Early Empire suggests a worsening of the conditions of slaves over time.

The contribution by McCallum addresses the issue of measuring inequality in the Roman countryside of Italy, based on the evidence for an imperial estate and its structured economy. By the end of the first century AD, these estates were collectively the most important land property in the empire and constituted a complex economic and social reality that was managed directly by imperial agents or tenant farmers. Thanks to literary sources, epigraphy, and archaeological remains, McCallum attempts the first analysis of both the internal organization of the estate and the broader economic interaction of imperial estates and other land properties. The imperial estates, though largely variable, were complex infrastructures, with diversified functions and spaces, as well as an articulated material culture. Available data allows a general comparison of slave organization—mostly productive—both within the single context and in its association with representative and residential elements. The distribution of the different types of estates and their relation to resources and services are also explored in the paper. In general, the imperial estate could be seen as a self-sufficient and market-oriented community, located at crucial nodes of multilevel networks, differentiated in relation to their political and natural landscape. Thus, the economic dynamics echo inequality at a landscape level. At such a large scale, to fully understand the evidence under discussion, it is necessary to develop a holistic approach, for which McCallum poses a first systematic operational scheme.

INEQUALITY AND SPATIAL RELATIONS

Within archaeological studies, spatial analysis began to develop in the 1950s (Wason 1994:128–138). Spatial approaches have been used in different ways by different generations of archaeologists, but the general trend has changed from "how people are conditioned by the landscape" to "how people interact with the landscape" to "how people shape the landscape." Since these approaches are not contradictory, today's trend is to put them together, in a more comprehensive, multidimensional analysis.

Spatial analysis considers any pattern of distribution of elements (settlements or building) as useful for defining hierarchy and rank. This is based on the assumption that higher characteristics are material expressions of individuals or groups with leadership functions controlling part or the entirety of the economic process. Consequently, the idea is that we can infer spatial hierarchy and social inequality from any evidence of personal status. Of course, the direct correlation between the ranking of individuals and spatial ranking is not always accurate, and it must be proven case by case.

At the broader landscape level, the social basis for the stratification among sites is the centralization of certain activities. This results in the concentration both of the physical structures used directly for these activities (palaces, archives, etc.), and of the material correlates of their presence. Of course, the character of residences might be affected by a large number of factors external to the social or economic organization: environment, history, utilitarian consideration, social factors, and religious beliefs.

At the level of a single settlement, structure, plan, and architecture may indicate functional differentiation among buildings, implying specialization and role division among residents (Wason 1994:134). Other features usually listed among the evidence of nonegalitarian settlements (although none are in themselves sufficient) are the presence of major residence size differentials and the presence of nonresidential constructions. These are considered as direct evidence of different statuses, although not necessarily of different ranking (Renfrew 1972). Organization and planning can say a lot about the social organization of the communities, since planning requires leadership and capacity to exercise power.

There are a series of elements that seem to be important to verify the existence of social differences; major differences among them point toward qualitative differences in status. The house of the ruling family might be larger than the other houses because the leaders would require more space to house crafts, food, and equipment, and since it would serve additional purposes or accommodate different activities (social, public meeting space, etc.) in contrast to a normal household. In many civilizations, the houses of the chiefs were important to the religious/ritual system and were used for feasts. If we look in more detail at the structure of the dwellings, we might also derive hints about the social relationships among the members of the household (Blanton 1995; Morris 1999; Westgate 2007; Goldberg 2013; Hayden this volume).

The case of the earliest Greek domestic architecture is very illustrative. Morris (1999) identifies changes in the use of domestic space in the eighth century BC and suggests that the contrast between Homer and later sources does indeed represent an important diachronic shift in gender ideologies in the central parts of Greece. Before 800 BC, attitudes toward gender were much more flexible than those we see in archaic and classical literary sources; but, by 700, the outlines of the classical model, with a more segregated role of women, were starting to become visible. Parallel changes can be seen in the domestic architecture: for example at Oropos and Zagora, the huts belonging to the eighth century were built in open spaces and all the domestic activities were performed outdoors, where everyone could see each other. Later, the huts were surrounded by precincts, where all activities were done inside a courtyard, in a more private environment. And this exceptional transformation occurred within the space of a single human lifetime.

The number of architecturally discrete spaces in the houses and the pattern of connections between the spaces tend to reflect social relations linking the members of the community (Westgate 2007; Blanton 1994). The patterns of circulation within the houses also define different degrees of privacy and interactions between the individuals living in the houses.

The contribution by Westgate in this book further develops the issue of domestic characteristics and organization in the framework of social relations. Through a clear theoretical setting and the available literary sources, she highlights how the analysis of ancient Greek houses could be meaningful, though not straightforward, in determining wealth, political, and status differentiation. To Westgate, the traditional view of large or elaborate households as belonging to rulers is far too simplistic. An analytic analysis might reveal a more complex reality. She considers a range of variables that are potentially linked to inequality, including size and prominence of the house, differences in plan and specialization of the spaces, finishing, decoration, and architectural features. At least until the archaic period, differences in house size was limited, and major buildings seem not to offer any preserved evidence of socially strong functions (such as banquets) formally shaped in the house. In the Classical period, although it has been argued that housing indicates a relatively high degree of equality in wealth as a reflection of a more democratic political organization, the variation between houses is greater than before, with larger and more elaborate buildings at the top end of the scale. In Hellenistic times, a period of rulers with near-absolute power, the differences become even larger. Some of the royal palaces partially survived and even without the evidence of perishable adornments they still preserve paintings and mosaics of superior quality. In light of Westgate's research, it is evident that a great part of the social self-representation is not preserved in the house architecture alone and could only be inferred through a multilevel analysis of the entire range of evidence.

ARTIFACTS AND INEQUALITY

To infer the value of status or rank from artifacts (i.e., pottery or architecture) is a delicate operation subject to strong interpretation and uncertainty; general rules are hard to find, and meanings are most of the time culture- or context-based.

Material culture is definitely involved in practices designed to accomplish social goals. Consumption is a social process, and is part of how people define themselves and their identities. As Hodder argued in his seminal work in 1986, material culture should be read as a text. The study of material culture displays the relationship between structure and context, and the object's meanings need to be built up through a difficult contextual consideration of similarities and differences.

Even though most of the chapters of this book consider different aspects of material culture, only a few really deal with it systematically. In general, two points can be made about the relationship between artifacts' variety and the social complexity. First, the greater the variation and complexity in the status system, the greater the variety in artifacts. In fact, hierarchical societies need more items, especially nonutilitarian artifacts, to display differences in status, than do nonhierarchical ones; and greater variety in style generally has a positive correlation with social articulation (Rice 1981). Second, higher-status individuals will acquire a greater variety and number of objects than those of lower status, as some artifacts are restricted to the higher status people (Wason 1994; Rice 1989).

CONCLUSION

Ancient communities, like modern ones, are not uniform and should not be characterized as such. As the papers collected here will show, there is no single or simple way to define inequality. In general, social inequality manifests itself in different ways within and between communities, often changing over time due to many causes. When examining inequality, it is fundamental to use a combination of several sources and measurements, with a holistic approach, in order to test the research hypothesis. A diachronic perspective and large-scale analysis greatly assist in identifying the major historical processes of our past.

The extremely broad cross-cultural view proposed in this book is meant to cover many different regions and periods and to offer a variety of approaches to the topic through case studies grounded in archaeological evidence as well as epigraphy and historical data. Every piece of evidence discussed in these chapters contributes to the general picture of ancient inequality, and a number of the papers in this book provide a fine introduction to the theoretical debates on social inequality and recent perspectives. While studies of slavery, gender, and ethnicity are relatively common, the IEMA conference explored them as intersecting areas of study within the larger framework of inequality that exemplify to what degree archaeologists can identify and analyze different patterns of inequality. Nevertheless, it seems impossible to develop a general theory of inequality in antiquity since the causes and results of social articulation are affected by cultural and environmental factors, and as such, they exist specific to both time and local scale. Still, it is possible to define wide-ranging strategies for the archaeological analysis of inequality, in relation to social and economic complexity. We hope this collective work will constitute a valuable contribution to the development of the study of inequality in antiquity and support the interdisciplinary trend in social archaeology.

ACKNOWLEDGMENTS

My deepest thanks to all the contributors to the book, who agreed to take part to the lively conference and the following debate, presenting their theories and recent finds in a format accessible to students. I would also like to thank the graduate and undergraduate students who helped in organizing and running the conference. Special thanks are due to the two graduate representatives to IEMA at the time, Alexander Mazurek and Darren Poltorak. Finally, very warm thanks to professors Peter Biehl and Stephen Dyson, and the whole IEMA Board for the continuous support and advice that made my residence at the University at Buffalo so valuable and formative.

NOTE

1.   For example: Tim Dechant, "Income Inequality in the Roman Empire," *Per Square Mile*, December 16, 2011; Gillian Berman, "U.S. Income Inequality Higher Than Roman Empire's Levels: Study," *The Huffington Post*, December 19, 2011; Michael E. Smith, "Inequality—the 99% in ancient times," *Wide Urban World*, May 22, 2012.

REFERENCES

Ames, K. 2008 The Archaeology of Rank. In *Handbook of Archaeological Theories*, edited by R. A. Bentley, H. D. G. Maschner, and C. Chippindale, pp. 487–513. Rowman and Littlefield, Lanham, Maryland.

Appadurai, A. 1981 Gastro-Politics in Hindu South Asia. *American Ethnologist* 8:494–511.

Arbuckle, B. 2012 Animals and Inequality in Chalcolithic Central Anatolia. *Journal of Anthropological Archaeology* 31:302–313.

Beaumont, L. 2000 The Social Status and Artistic Presentation of "Adolescence" in Fifth Century Athens. In *Children and Material Culture*, edited by J. S. Derevenski, pp. 39–47. Routledge, London.

Blanton, R. E. 1994 *Houses and Households. A Comparative Study*. Springer, New York.

Blanton, R. E. 1995 The Cultural Foundations of Inequality in Households. In *Foundations of Social Inequality*, edited by T. D. Price and G. M. Feinman, pp. 105–127. Plenum Press, New York.

Cerasuolo, O. 2016 The Orientalizing Period at Caere—Cultural and Material Connections. In *Caere—An Etruscan city*, edited by N. de Grummond and L. Pieraccini, pp. 136–178. University of Texas Press, Austin.

Drennan, R. D., and C. E. Peterson 2012 Challenges for Comparative Study of Early Complex Societies. In *The Comparative Archaeology of Complex societies*, edited by M. E. Smith, pp. 62–85. Cambridge University Press, Cambridge.

Drennan, R. D., C. E. Peterson, and J. R. Fox 2010 Degrees and Kinds of Inequality. In *Pathways to Power*, edited by T. D. Price and G. M. Feinman, pp. 45–76. Springer-Verlag, New York.

Giddens, A. 2007 *Europe in the Global Age*. Polity Press, Cambridge.

Gilchrist, R. 2004 Archaeology and the Life Course: A Time and Age for Gender. In *A Companion to Social Archaeology*, edited by L. Meskell and R. W. Preucel, pp. 142–160. Blackwell, Malden, MA.

Gleba, M. 2008 *Textile Production in Pre-Roman Italy*. Oxbow Books, Oxford.

Goldberg, M. Y. 2013 Spatial and Behavioural Negotiation in Classical Athenian City Houses. In *The Archaeology of Household Activities*, edited by P. M. Allison, pp. 142–161. Routledge, New York.

Haas, J. 2001 Cultural Evolution and Political Centralization. *From Leaders to Rulers*, edited by J. J. Haas, pp. 3–17. Kluwer Academic, New York.

Hayden, B. 1995 Pathways to Power. Principles for Creating Socioeconomic Inequalities. In *Foundations of Social Inequality*, edited by D. T. Price and G. M. Feinman, pp. 15–86. Plenum Press, New York.

Hendon, J. A. 2000 Having and Holding: Storage, Memory, Knowledge, and Social Relations. *American Anthropologist* 102(1):42–53.

Hendon, J. A. 2004 Living and Working at Home: The Social Archaeology of Household Pro-
    duction and Social Relations. In *A Companion to Social Archaeology*, edited by L. Meskell
    and R. W. Preucel, pp. 272–286. Blackwell, Malden, MA.

Hodder, I. 1982 *Symbolic and Structural Archaeology*. Cambridge University Press, Cambridge.

Hodder, I. 1986 *Reading the Past*. Cambridge University Press, Cambridge.

Khan, S. R. 2012 The Sociology of Elites. *Annual Review of Sociology* 38:361–77.

Kristiansen, K. 1998 Chiefdom, States, and Systems of Social Evolution. In *Social Transformations
    in Archaeology*, edited by K. Kristiansen and M. Rowlands, pp. 236–259. Routledge, London.

Lenski, G. E. 1966 *Power and Privilege. A Theory of Social Stratification*. University of North
    Carolina Press, Chapel Hill.

Meskell, L. and R. W. Preucell (eds.) 2004 *A Companion to Social Archaeology*. Blackwell, Mal-
    den, MA.

Milanovic, B., P. H. Lindert, and J. G. Williamson 2010 Pre Industrial Inequality. *The Economic
    Journal* 121:255–272.

Morris, I. 1987 *Burial and Ancient Society. The Rise of the Greek City-State*. Cambridge University
    Press, New York.

Morris, I. 1992 *Death Ritual and Social structure in Classical Antiquity*. Cambridge University
    Press, Cambridge.

Morris, I. 1999 Archaeology and Gender Ideologies in Early Archaic Greece. *Transactions of the
    American Philological Association* 129:305–317.

Paynter, R. 1989 The Archaeology of Equality and Inequality. *Annual Review of Anthropology*
    18:369–399.

Paynter, R. and R. H. MacGuire (eds.) 1991 *The Archaeology of Inequality*. Blackwell, Oxford.

Peregrine, P. 2012 Power and Legitimation. Political Strategies, Typology, and Cultural Evolution.
    In *The Comparative Archaeology of Complex societies*, edited by M. E. Smith, pp.165–191.
    Cambridge University Press, Cambridge.

Peterson, C. E., and R. D. Drennan. 2012 Patterned Variation in Regional Trajectories of Com-
    munity Growth. In *The Comparative Archaeology of Complex societies*, edited by M. E. Smith,
    pp. 88–137. Cambridge University Press, Cambridge.

Preucel, R. W., and S. A. Mrozowski 2010 *Contemporary Archaeology in Theory: The New Prag-
    matism*. John Wiley and Sons, Malden, MA.

Price, T. D. and G. M. Feinman 2010 *Pathways to Power*. Springer-Verlag, New York.

Renfrew, C., and P. Bahn 2007 *Archaeology: Theories, Methods, and Practice*. Thames and Hudson,
    London.

Scheidel, W., and S. J. Friesen 2009 The Size of the Economy and the Distribution of Income
    in the Roman Empire. *The Journal of Roman Studies* 99:61–91.

Service, E. 1962 *Primitive Social Organization: An Evolutionary Perspective*. Random House, New
    York.

Shanks, M., and C. Tilley 1982 *Social Archaeology and Theory*. Polity Press, Cambridge.

Smith, M. E. 2012 What It Takes to Get Complex. In *The Comparative Archaeology of Complex
    Societies*, edited by M. E. Smith, pp. 44–61. Cambridge University Press, Cambridge.

Wason, P. K. 1994 *The Archaeology of Rank*. Cambridge University Press, Cambridge.

Westgate, R. 2007 House and Society in Classical and Hellenistic Crete: A Case Study in Regional
    Variation. *American Journal of Archaeology* 111(3):423–457.

Whitley, J. 1991 *Style and Society in Dark Age Greece. The Changing Face of a Pre-literate Society,
    1100–700 B.C.* Cambridge University Press, New York.

Whitley, J. 1996 Gender and Hierarchy in Early Athens. The Strange Case of the Disappearance of the Rich Female Grave. *Métis. Anthropologie des mondes grecs anciens*, 11:209–232.

Wolf, E. R. 1999 *Envisioning Power: Ideologies of Dominance and Crisis*. University of California Press, Oakland.

PART I

Pathways of Early Social Inequality

CHAPTER TWO

The Emergence of Social Inequality in Prehistory

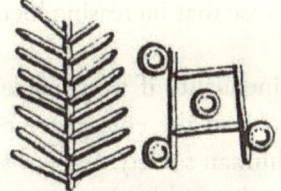

T. Douglas Price

Abstract *Inequality is an inherent characteristic in many species of animals. Nonetheless, human hunter-gatherers in the later Pleistocene created mechanisms that overrode tendencies toward dominance and chose egalitarian behavior as a means to structure social, economic, and political organization. Here I argue that those egalitarian constraints were relaxed at the end of the Pleistocene with the beginnings of surplus production and storage, which created a basis of wealth and an increasingly important role for dominance behavior and inequality. The almost simultaneous emergence of domestication and social differentiation speaks strongly for the relationship between these two aspects of human adaptation at the origins of agriculture. This essay elaborates on the argument.*

INTRODUCTION

Social inequality is a major problem in many modern societies. The rich and powerful become more so at the expense of the rest of us. Such a situation is of benefit only for the elite—most of us lose ground as social, political, and economic structures weaken and falter. This needs to be fixed. In such times, the emergence of social inequality in ancient human society is a matter of substantial interest. It is also a very thorny question that remains largely unresolved in archaeology. One of the reasons for that, I believe, is that the archaeologists who consider the problem do so through the lenses or blinders of their own experience with the past. Thus, the emergence of inequality has been said to take place in almost every major time period from the Paleolithic to the Iron Age.

Inequality has two meanings for archaeologists. On the one hand, the term refers to unequal rights and privileges among members of the same society, a situation that often leads to abuse and exploitation, and has a negative connotation. On the other hand, social inequality is one of the major organizing principles of human society, creating hierarchy and adding structure to human social organization. Institutionalized inequality is associated with ascribed status, assigned at birth, and usually expressed in ranked or class structure. One's role, rights, and status in society are determined on the basis of membership in rank, class, or caste. Such institutionalized social inequality creates hierarchy in human society and greatly enhances the flow of material, energy, and information. Modern society would not function without some form of hierarchical structure. It is the case that increasing hierarchy is a corollary of more complex social organization.

I believe we can be more specific about the emergence of inequality if we consider several related issues such as the appearance of "hunter-gatherers" and the emergence of equality, the visibility of inequality, and the role of inequality in human society. I will discuss these issues and argue that the beginnings of social inequality lie within the changes associated with the origins and spread of agriculture, beginning around 10,000 BC in the Old World. One of the many caveats associated with such an exercise is the fact that the beginnings of almost anything in the past are clouded by time, the limited survival of information, and the few subtle hints that have been recovered by archaeologists. Thus, my essay is somewhat speculative, but based on rather robust assumptions.

Equality

To try to better understand inequality, we need to consider the concept of equality. The diaspora of anthropologists to remote parts of the planet after World War II led to many new and revealing studies of hunter-gatherers on five continents. The plethora of ideas and information that emerged from those studies culminated in the *Man the Hunter* conference held in Chicago in 1966 (Lee and DeVore 1968). As Rowley-Conwy (2001) has pointed out, small groups of highly mobile, egalitarian hunter-gatherers came to be seen as the baseline for all subsequent social evolution. Prestige was ephemeral and achieved; power and wealth were limited or nonexistent.

It was precisely those concepts that were challenged in the following years—emphasizing larger numbers, less mobility, and greater complexity among hunter-gatherers. Marshall Sahlin's discourse on *Stone Age Economics* (1972) and his description of an original affluent society substantially revised thinking about the harshness and simplicity of foragers' lives. It became generally agreed that hunter-gatherers were not just small and mobile.

Aspects of the wide variation present among hunter-gatherer societies were the subjects of a volume called *Prehistoric Hunter-gatherers: The Emergence of Cultural Complexity* that I edited with Jim Brown in 1985. Some of the hallmarks of complexity among foragers we suggested included features such as higher population numbers and density, sedentism, territoriality, storage, elaborate technologies, intensive subsistence practices, long distance trade, among others (Price 1985; Rowley-Conwy 1999). Status differentiation and social inequality were also listed among these characteristics (e.g., Hayden 1995a, 2001; Price and Brown 1985).

Status differentiation and social inequality have frequently been attributed to more complex foragers. This is appropriate for certain ethnographically or historically known hunter-gatherers, especially for groups along the western coast of North America (e.g., Ames and Maschner 1999; Matson and Coupland 1994). Social complexity, however, is not dependent on institutionalized inequality. I would argue that institutionalized social inequality is rare among hunter-gatherers, particularly in prehistory, and only in the context of reliable food surpluses (per Hayden 2001). This evidence suggests that we must be very cautious in attributing institutionalized inequality to most groups of hunter-gatherers in the past.

On the other hand, some form of inequality is inherent in many species, as documented in pecking orders, dominance behavior, and alpha males. Most primate groups exhibit distinctively hierarchical social organization (DeVore 1965; de Waal 1998; Perry 2006). It is, also clear that both egalitarian and nonegalitarian relations are present in all societies, along dimensions of sex, age, ability, health, and the like (Boehm 2001; Cashdan 1980; Flanagan 1989; Lee 1978). Thus, the emergence of status differentiation in and of itself is not an issue. Most ethnographically known societies of hunter-gatherers, however, exhibit evolved mechanisms for dampening dominance behavior in favor of the sharing of food and property, care of kin, and egalitarian relationships (e.g., Wiessner 1996; Wiessner and Schiefenhovel 1996). The suppression of dominance behavior and sharing must have been important aspects of the success of early groups of hunter-gatherers (e.g., Boehm 1993, 2001; Price 1995).

There is an archaeological maxim, found in numerous textbooks and edited volumes, that more than 99 percent of our human past was spent as hunter-gatherers. But is that really true? Have humans always been hunter-gatherers? When did egalitarian behaviors emerge? These questions are related to the development of self-awareness, the recognition of kinship, and the emergence of human society.

We haven't always been hunter-gatherers. Our earliest ancestors started on the path to being biologically human more than six million years ago. But when did the groupings of our ancestors take on a recognizably human form—when did we change from being simply social animals to members of human society? The archaeological remains of our earlier ancestors through the Middle Paleolithic are remarkably unstructured. Little patterning can be observed in the distribution of artifacts and occasional features at these places of residence or feeding. The term *gatherings* was coined by Clive Gamble (1999) to describe the concentrations of remains—the archaeological sites—and the groupings of early humans in this murky period of the human past, before we became hunter-gatherers.

When did we make the transition from roving, foraging groups to egalitarian bands of hunter-gatherers integrated into human-like societies? Such societies are defined by kin-structured social relationships. Food, property, and information were shared. Status was ephemeral and earned through achievement, held only by the individual who gained it and not mandatorily passed to offspring. Non-kin relationships were maintained by the exchange of goods or foodstuffs. It is these aspects of social organization that truly distinguish the emergence of hunter-gatherers. Kuhn and Stiner (2001) have argued that the transition to life as hunter-gatherers took place during the Upper Paleolithic. Evidence such as the appearance of regularly patterned materials and distributions at archaeological sites, distinctions between residence and procurement locations, exchange of exotic materials, and technological solutions to seasonal or regional differences supports their argument.

RECENT CONSIDERATIONS

If we accept that egalitarian behavior is an artificial construct created by small scale hunter-gatherer societies as a means of maintaining social relationships and reducing the transaction costs of exchange, then the emergence of inequality is perhaps not such a remarkable development but rather a result of the relaxation of the norms and constraints that enforced equality. In this sense we do not need to explain where dominance behavior comes from, but rather consider other aspects of the emergence of inequality. Several studies from the last 15 years or so shed more light on this question and some of the important factors involved.

SURPLUS

Weissner's (2002) classic study of egalitarian structures and the institutionalization of inequality among the precolonial Enga in Papua New Guinea provides a number of insights. Her study focuses on a period of some 250 years after the introduction of the sweet potato, during which widespread exchange networks developed and hierarchical inequalities began to be institutionalized. Population grew and subsistence changed from shifting taro horticulture and hunting and gathering to a surplus economy based on sweet potato cultivation and intensive pig husbandry.

Surplus was essential to the changes that took place in social organization. Distributed power among hunters, traders, warriors, ritual experts, and managers took on a hierarchical form, with leaders directing the economy (Weissner 2002). Weissner's study emphasizes that changes came about when there was consensus among leaders and the people regarding the benefits of new practices.

A number of authors have recognized the role of surplus in the emergence and maintenance of inequality. Gerhard Lenski's (1966) theory on the origins of social inequality invoked the role of economic surplus, derived from technological and environmental advantages, in creating demographic, productive, and political contexts that are responsible for the extent of inequality in material wealth. Lenski suggests that in societies with a reliable surplus, some households can accumulate larger shares as long as others can obtain the minimum needed to survive. He further argues that this surplus makes larger settlements possible, facilitates occupational specialization, and brings about the control of decision making by a few. Testart (1982a, b) argued that surplus and food storage were fundamental aspects of social inequality among hunter-gatherers. Hayden's (2001) comment on the production of surplus as a condition for the emergence of inequality is worth repeating.

As Wiessner described the situation among the Enga (2002:234), "Quantitative economic gains are applied to bring about alterations in the social order."

WEALTH

Another very useful distinction has been made regarding different kinds of wealth by Smith et al. (2010) who argued that inheritance of wealth is the mechanism for increasing inequality in small-scale societies. They describe three kinds of wealth: material, relational, and embodied. Material wealth is what we commonly think of in terms of land, livestock, slaves, jewelry, and other objects. "Relational" wealth involves an individual's place in society in social networks, including the number of connections they have. What Smith et al. call "embodied" wealth involves personal conditions and abilities—health, strength, endurance, intelligence, knowledge, skills. One of the reasons that the early emergence of inequality may be so difficult to identify is that these other, nonmaterial forms of wealth may have been predominant. As Ames (2007) has pointed out, "The archaeology of egalitarianism is based on negative evidence. Evidence for inequality is primarily material wealth."

FEASTING

Brian Hayden (1995a, 1997, 2014), among others, has had a lot to say about the emergence of inequality and social change. Hayden points to feasting as a major mechanism in the process of creating change. Large, competitive feasts are occasions for the display of surplus, the consumption of rare and valuable foods, and they often involve gift giving. Such competitive feasting can also be understood as a mechanism for subverting the egalitarian practice of sharing food and property by creating alliances and debts among members of the same group. Dietler and Hayden (2001) document feasting practices in a wide range of societies.

PRESTIGE TECHNOLOGIES

Hayden (1995b, 1998) has distinguished practical and prestige technologies on the basis of the intended use of the materials that are produced. Practical technologies produce functional objects used for various purposes in everyday life. The purpose of creating prestige artifacts is not to perform a practical task, but to display wealth, success, and power. Their purpose is to solve a social problem or accomplish a social task such as attracting productive mates, labor, and allies or bonding members of social groups together via displays of success. The appearance of prestige technologies may be synonymous with the rise of social inequality.

CORPORATE AND NETWORK STRATEGIES

The distinction between corporate and network modes of organization (Blanton et al. 1996) involves group versus individual strategies for achieving and maintaining power in society (Feinman 2000). The network strategy is exclusionary; political actors endeavor to consolidate and monopolize sources of power. This is the direction pointed to by Bender (1978) in her essay "Gatherer-hunter to Farmer: A Social Perspective," and Hayden (1990) in "Nimrods, Piscators, Pluckers and Planters: The Emergence of Food Production." In the corporate strategy, power is shared and divested in different groups or social segments. The exceptional archaeological manifestations of institutionalized social inequality—rich burials with impressive offerings, elaborate residences for leaders, monumental constructions—are associated with the network mode and individual power, while the alternate corporate mode is also hierarchical but produces much less conspicuous archaeological evidence (Drennan et al. 2010).

Chaos

A recent publication on the origins of agriculture (Price and Bar-Yosef 2010) reports an interesting phenomenon that involved variation, not pattern. In the one or two places around the globe where data on the transition to farming are relatively rich, there appears to be a period of chaos (Goring-Morris and Belfer-Cohen 2011), a "zone of variability," at the time of the origins of agriculture (Weiss, Kislev, and Hartmann 2006). Smith and Yarnell (2009) have described this as a period for the auditioning of many possible new options in human adaptation.

Visibility

The emergence of social inequality is a difficult issue in large part because the evidence is poorly visible, uncommon, and contentious. There are a number of reasons why institutionalized inequality is difficult to detect in its early stages. Different pathways to differentiation (e.g., Drennan et al. 2010; Feinman 2000; Hayden 1995a) mean that the material expression of emergent inequality may be different in various places/times. In the same vein, emerging inequality is not likely to be a linear process. In other words, an individual, family, lineage, or group may achieve wealth or power for a period of time and lose that status as conditions change or others gain advantage. Such oscillation is reported in various archaeological (e.g., Anderson 1994; Marcus 1992) and ethnographic cultures (Leach 1954).

Smith et al. (2001) suggested three different kinds of wealth—material, relational, and personal. As Ames (2007) has noted, archaeology has relied on material wealth as evidence for social inequality. If material wealth is not important in social relations, then inequality will be difficult to detect archaeologically. This point follows closely on the distinction of corporate versus network strategies for gaining and holding power. Corporate strategies may rely on relational wealth and not produce elaborate manifestations of prestige goods or labor.

Another factor that might make the recognition of emerging inequality difficult concerns the conditions of chaos or variability at the time of the transition to agriculture noted above. An absence of patterning or repeated occurrence will mean a lack of clarity in the evidence available. These limitations outlined here are above and beyond the normal opacity of archaeological data, particularly from periods in the distant past.

Origins of Agriculture and Inequality

I have argued elsewhere that institutionalized, hereditary status differentiation probably begins with the Neolithic (Price 1995; Price and Bar-Yosef 2010). I believe that the consensus of norms and sanctions that maintained equality among hunter-gatherers began to unravel with the growing surplus of foods that were a result of farming. Following a brief discussion of some of the relevant factors involved in the origins of agriculture and the rise of institutionalized social inequality, I offer a scenario for the emergence of inequality and some of the evidence that we might look for in order to document this process.

Current thinking suggests that the search for causality in terms of the adoption of agriculture should focus on the realm of human choice, rather than forcing models involving changes in climate, environment, or population growth. At the same time, the almost worldwide synchronicity of the origins of agriculture requires some global impetus. Changes in levels of carbon dioxide are argued here to provide such a driver. Several points from recent studies are reiterated as they provide useful insight regarding the rise of inequality and the origins of agriculture. The importance of surplus as the funding for social, economic, and political change seems essential. The distinction of material, relational, and embodied wealth may help us to understand the shortage of evidence in the early part of the Neolithic for inequality.

The Neolithic meant the production of surpluses based on domesticated plants and animals and involvement in both local and long-distance exchange that intensified economic production. The reasons that hunters became farmers likely had more to do with access to new goods, ideas, and organization than new ways of obtaining food. It seems most reasonable to suggest a scenario in which interaction through exchange networks among foragers and farmers involving people, ideas, and materials fostered the adoption of agriculture, participation in new forms of social and economic organization, and the rise of hierarchical leadership in society (Price and Bar-Yosef 2010).

The emergence of agriculture and social inequality likely took place together although surplus would have been necessary as a basis for wealth. A 30–50 percent increase in atmospheric carbon dioxide occurred at the end of the Pleistocene (Sage 2006). Shakun and colleagues (2012) demonstrated that rising temperatures were correlated with, and generally lagged behind, increasing levels of CO_2 at the end of the Pleistocene. Cunniff et al. (2010) found experimentally that both the C3 and C4 plants responded positively to increased CO_2 levels from the glacial to post-glacial with vegetative biomass nearly doubling and a yield increase of 50 percent in the C3 species.

Plants, of course, metabolize carbon dioxide to grow and produce tissue. An increase in atmospheric CO_2 would have resulted in larger plants and denser vegetation in many areas. Agriculture originated in regions where resources were relatively abundant, and an increase in plants would certainly have brought more attention to their use as food, particularly for the cereals. Cereal grains are an almost perfect food for storage as they are designed to survive for long periods with a hard shell protecting a rich carbohydrate package. The domestication of wild cereals likely took place as these valuable, storable resources were cultivated outside their natural habitat. Animals were no doubt domesticated as a source of protein, but it is important to remember that these fauna provided grain storage on the hoof.

In this context of the increasing availability of storable food surplus, dominance behavior likely reemerged in human society as egalitarian mores relaxed. Surplus and storage permitted the acquisition of wealth and prestige; inheritance may have permitted the accumulation of wealth across generations. The paucity of material evidence for the accumulation of material wealth in the Neolithic suggests that corporate strategies may have been operating to create hierarchical organization in human society. Wealth may have been largely in a relational form involving connections and group decision making rather than individual control. Feasting may well have been one of the mechanisms used to emulate food sharing while in fact creating prestige and power for the hosts.

In spite of the paucity of strong evidence for inequality in the Early Neolithic there are a number of indicators. Drennan et al. (2010) mentioned three categories of evidence that provide information on inequality: burials, household artifact assemblages, and public works. Elaborate burials, especially of children, are often taken as diagnostic of status differentiation (e.g., Ames 2007; Peebles and Kus 1977). Differences between the assemblages of artifacts recovered from different household units are taken to reflect differences in social status, wealth, and economic and other activities (Hirth 1993; Smith 1987). Other kinds of evidence have also been proposed, including feasting and prestige goods production.

In the ancient Near East from the time of the origins of agriculture there are a number of curious new phenomena that likely pertain to the rise of social inequality. This evidence, as expected, is rather vague and tenuous and can be interpreted in other ways. At the same time, the newness of these places and things and their almost simultaneous appearance argues for a substantial change in social and economic organization in human society. Much of this argument has been made previously in Price (1995) and Price and Bar-Yosef (2010) and will only be summarized briefly here.

The evidence for storage and surplus begins to accumulate in the Epipaleolithic in the ancient Near East as the collection and possible cultivation of wild cereals increased (Kuijt and Finlayson 2009). The use of storage facilities increased dramatically after domestication (Kuijt 2008, 2009). Storage features are reported at a number of Early Neolithic sites including Netiv Hagdud in the Jordan Valley (Bar Yosef et al. 1991), at Dhra' in the southern Jordan Valley (Kuijt and Mahasneh 1998), at 'Ain Ghazal in Syria (Rollefson 1984), and many other places.

There are very good indications of feasting activities at a number of Epipaleolithic and Early Neolithic sites (e.g., Benz 2006; Munro and Grosman 2010; Twiss 2008), including in Turkey Göbekli Tepe, including possible beer production (Dietrich et al. 2012; Schmidt 2000, 2010), and Hallan Çemi (Rosenberg and Redding 2000), among many other places.

There are hundreds of human burials from the Natufian. Hayden (2004), following Bar-Yosef 2000; Byrd and Monahan 1995; Wright 1978, and others, argues that ancestor worship, formal cemeteries, and secondary burials all point to the existence of corporate groups that controlled important resources. The burial evidence from the Pre-Pottery Neolithic has been summarized in the literature (Belfer-Cohen 1995; Kuijt and Goring-Morris 2002). Although the number of burials from the Early Neolithic is limited (Kuijt 1996), the evidence is convincing. There are several places that suggest that status differentiation is manifested among the interred individuals. In particular, the site of Kfar HaHoresh, Israel, provides intriguing documentation of status differences among the burials (Eshed et al. 2009; Goring-Morris 2005). Goring-Morris argues that the distribution of material culture remains at Kfar HaHoresh, along with age and sex data, provides evidence of both ascribed and achieved status. At Tell Halula in Syria, Guerrero et al. (2008, 2009) report that interments show distinctive differences in treatment and contents that crosscut age and sex distinctions and likely reflect social inequality. Numerous other examples exist.

Early PPNA villages were 10 times larger than Natufian hamlets with populations on the order of 250–500 people (Byrd 1994; Goring-Morris and Belfer-Cohen 2013; Price and Bar-Yosef 2005). Davis (1998) argues for social differentiation at the early Neolithic village of Çayönü, Turkey, on the basis of house size and burial patterns. Monumental public works began to appear in the Early Neolithic, highlighted by the wall and tower at Jericho (Bar-Yosef 1986; Naveh 2003). Göbekli Tepe not only contains evidence for feasting but the most spectacular public works from the entire Neolithic. The construction of a total of perhaps 20 large circular structures with massive t-shaped decorated pillars and the deliberate filling of these features were monumental tasks involving a substantial labor force and coordinated logistics and supervision (Schmidt 2000).

The production of prestige items is another aspect of social inequality and likely documented among the trade items moving around the ancient Near East during the Early Neolithic. Among the better-known items were obsidian, chlorite bowls, asphalt, cinnabar, marine shells, and more (e.g., Aurenche and Kozlowski 1999; Bar-Yosef Mayer 2005; Rosenberg 1998). The extraction, preparation, and transport of these materials over long distances probably meant high costs and ownership may well have provided enhanced status.

CONCLUSION

The evidence for the almost simultaneous origins of agriculture and social inequality from my perspective is very convincing. Moreover these data emphasize the social and economic aspects of the agricultural revolution. It is possible to envision the process as one in which the richer vegetation caused by increases in atmospheric CO_2 at the end of the Pleistocene resulted in large crops of wild cereals, which could be cultivated and stored and permitted the relatively easy accumulation of surpluses. In the context of growing population, these surpluses would have provided a source of wealth and status differentiation. Social norms must have changed as sanctions for nonegalitarian behavior relaxed and wealth and power grew among families and lineages in these larger settlements of the Early Neolithic. As higher-status groups or individuals emerged, their role in social life is seen in increasing long-distance trade in more exotic and valuable items, the appearance of monumental constructions, differences in house size and contents within communities, and burial patterns reflecting different groups of people in society. The origins of agriculture were about much more than new foods. This transition was about new ways of organizing society and economy that required social differences among the individuals involved and the emergence of hierarchical social relations. Some individuals gained authority and wealth; many ceded their equality to the few for benefits that may have been experienced as more reliable sources of food and greater security.

References

Ames, K. M. 2007 The Archaeology of Rank. In *Handbook of Archaeological Theories*, edited by R. A. Bentley, H. D. G. Maschner, and C. Chippendale, pp. 487–513. Alta Mira Press, Lanham, Maryland.

Ames, K. M., and H. D. G. Maschner 1999 *Peoples of the Northwest Coast: Their Archaeology and Prehistory*. Thames and Hudson, New York.

Anderson, D. G. 1994 *The Savannah River Chiefdoms*. University of Alabama Press, Tuscaloosa.

Aurenche, O., and S. K. Kozlowski 1999 *La naissance du néolithique au Proche Orient*. Editions Errance, Paris.

Bar-Yosef O. 1986 The Walls of Jericho: An Alternative Interpretation. *Current Anthropology* 27:157–162.

Bar-Yosef, O. 2002 The Natufian Culture and the Early Neolithic—Social and Economic Trends. In *Examining the Farming/Language Dispersal Hypothesis*, edited by P. Bellwood and C. Renfrew, pp.113–126. McDonald Institute Monographs, Cambridge.

Bar-Yosef, O., A. Gopher, E. Tchernov, M. E. Kislev 1991 Netiv Hagdud: An Early Neolithic Village Site in the Jordan Valley. *Journal of Field Archaeology* 18:405–424.

Bar-Yosef Mayer, D. E. 2005 The Exploration of Shells as Beads in the Palaeolithic and Neolithic of the Levant. *Paléorient* 31:176–185.

Belfer-Cohen, A. 1995 Rethinking Social Stratification in the Natufian Culture: The Evidence from Burials. In *The Archaeology of Death in the Ancient Near East*, edited by S. Campbell and A. Green, pp. 9–16. Oxbow, Oxford.

Bender, B. 1978 Gatherer-hunter to Farmer: A Social Perspective. *World Archaeology* 10:204–22.

Benz, M. 2000. *Die Neolithisierung im Vorderen Orient. Theorien, archäologische Daten und ein ethnologisches Modell.* ex Oriente, Berlin.

Blanton, R. E., G. M. Feinman, S. A. Kowalewski, and P. N. Peregrine 1996 A Dual-Processual Theory for the Evolution of Mesoamerican Civilization. *Current Anthropology* 37:1–14.

Boehm, C. 1993 Egalitarian Behavior and Reverse Dominance Hierarchy. *Current Anthropology* 34:227–254.

Boehm, C. 2001 *Hierarchy in the Forest: The Evolution of Egalitarian Behavior*. Harvard University Press, Cambridge.

Byrd, B. 1994 Public and Private, Domestic and Corporate: The Emergence of the Southwest Asian Village. *American Antiquity* 59:639–666.

Byrd, B., and C. Monahan 1995 Death, Mortuary Ritual, and Natufian Social Structure. *Journal of Anthropological Archaeology* 14:251–287.

Cashdan, E. A. 1980 Egalitarianism among Hunters and Gatherers. *American Anthropologist* 82:116–120.

Cunniff, J., M. Charles, G. Jones, and C. P. Osborne 2010 Was Low Atmospheric CO_2 a Limiting Factor in the Origin of Agriculture? *Environmental Archaeology* 15:113–123.

Davis, M. K. 1998 Social Differentiation at the Early Village of Çayönü, Turkey. In *Light on Top of the Black Hill*, edited by G. Arsebük, M. J. Mellink, and W. Schirmer, pp. 257–266. Ege Yayinlari, Istanbul.

de Waal, F. 1998 *Chimpanzee Politics: Power and Sex Among Apes*. Johns Hopkins University Press, Baltimore.

DeVore, I. 1965 *Primate Behavior: Field Studies of Monkeys and Apes*. Holt, Reinhart and Winston, New York.

Dietler, M., and B. Hayden (eds.) 2001 *Feasts: Archaeological and Ethnographic Perspectives on Food, Politics, and Power*. Smithsonian Institution Press, Washington, District of Columbia.

Dietrich, O., M. Heun, J. Notroff, K. Schmidt, and M. Zarnkow 2012 The Role of Cult and Feasting in the Emergence of Neolithic Communities. New Evidence from Göbekli Tepe, South-eastern Turkey. *Antiquity* 86:674–695.

Drennan, Robert D., C. E. Peterson, and J. R. Fox 2013 Degrees and Kinds of Inequality. In *Pathways to Power: New Perspectives on the Emergence of Social Inequality*, edited by T. D. Price and G. M. Feinman, pp. 45–75. Springer, New York.

Eshed, V., I. Hershkovitz, and A. N. Goring-Morris 2009 A Re-evaluation of Burial Customs in the Pre-Pottery Neolithic B in Light of Paleodemographic Analysis of the Human Remains from Kfar Hahoresh, Israel. *Paléorient* 34:91–103.

Feinman, G. M. 2000 Corporate/Network: New Perspectives on Models of Political Action and the Puebloan Southwest. In *Social Theory in Archaeology*, edited by M. B. Schiffer, pp. 31–51. University of Utah Press, Salt Lake City.

Flanagan, J. 1989 Hierarchy in Simple "Egalitarian" Societies. *Annual Review of Anthropology* 18:245–66.

Gamble, C. 1999 *The Palaeolithic Societies of Europe*. Cambridge University Press, Cambridge.

Goring-Morris, A. N. 2005 Life, Death, and the Emergence of Differential Status in the Near Eastern Neolithic: Evidence from Kfar HaHoresh, Lower Galilee, Israel. In *Archaeological Perspectives on the Transmission and Transformation of Culture in the Eastern Mediterranean*, edited by J. Clarke, pp. 85–109. Council for British Research in the Levant and Oxbow Books, Oxford.

Goring-Morris, A. N., and A. Belfer-Cohen 2011 Neolithization Processes in the Levant. The Outer Envelope. *Current Anthropology* 52(4):195–208.

Goring-Morris, A. N., and A. Belfer-Cohen 2013 Houses and Households: a Near Eastern Perspective. In *Tracking the Neolithic House in Europe*, edited by D. Hofmann and J. Smyth, pp. 19–28. Springer Science+Business Media, New York.

Guerrero, E., S. Naji, and J-P. Bocquet-Appel 2008 The Signal of Neolithic Demographic Transition in the Levant. In *Neolithic Demographic Transitions*, edited by J.-P. Bocquet-Appel and O. Bar-Yosef, pp. 57–80. Springer, New York.

Guerrero, E., M., Molist, I. Kuijt, and J. Anfruns 2009 Seated Memory: New Insights into Near Eastern Neolithic Mortuary Variability from Tell Halula, Syria. *Current Anthropology* 50:379–391.

Hayden, B. 1990 Nimrods, Piscators, Pluckers, and Planters: The Emergence of Food Production. *Journal of Anthropological Archaeology* 9:31–69.

Hayden, B. 1995a Pathways to Power. In *Foundations of Social Inequality*, edited by T. D. Price and G. M. Feinman, pp. 15–86. Springer, New York.

Hayden, B. 1995b The Emergence of Prestige Technologies and Pottery. In *The Emergence of Pottery*, edited by W. Barnett, and J. Hoopes, pp. 257–266. Smithsonian Institution Press, Washington, District of Columbia.

Hayden, B. 1997 Feasting in Prehistoric and Traditional Societies. In *Food and the Status Quest*, edited by P. Wiessner and W. Schiefenhövel, pp. 127–147. Berghahn Books, Providence, Rhode Island.

Hayden, B. 1998 Practical and Prestige Technologies: The Evolution of Material Systems. *Journal of Archaeological Method and Theory* 5:1–55.

Hayden, B. 2001 Richman, Poorman, Beggarman, Chief: The Dynamics of Social Inequality. In *Archaeology at the Millennium: A Sourcebook*, edited by G. Feinman, and T. D. Price, pp. 231–272. Kluwer Academic/Plenum, New York.

Hayden, B. 2004 Sociopolitical Organization in the Natufian: A View from the Northwest. In *The Last Hunter-Gatherer Societies in the Near East*, edited by C. Delage, pp. 263–308. BAR International Series, Oxford.

Hayden, B. 2014 *The Power of Feasts. From Prehistory to the Present.* Cambridge University Press, Cambridge.

Hirth, K. G. 1993 The Household as an Analytical Unit: Problems in Method and Theory. In *Prehispanic Domestic Units in Western Mesoamerica: Studies of the Household, Compound, and Residence*, edited by R. S. Santley and K. G. Hirth, pp. 21–36. CRC Press, Boca Raton, Florida.

Kuhn, S. L., and M. C. Stiner 2001 The Antiquity of Hunter-Gatherers. In *Another Day, Another Camp: An Interdisciplinary View of Hunter-Gatherers*, edited by C. Panter-Brick, R. H. Layton, and P. A. Rowley-Conwy, pp. 99–142. Cambridge University Press, Cambridge.

Kuijt, I. 1996 Negotiating Equality through Ritual: A Consideration of the Late Natufian and Pre-Pottery Neolithic A Period Mortuary Practices. *Journal of Anthropological Archaeology* 15:313–336.

Kuijt, I. 2008 Demography and Storage Systems during the Southern Levantine Neolithic Demographic Transition. In *The Neolithic Demographic Transition 287 and Its Consequences*, edited by J.-P. Bocquet-Appel and O. Bar-Yosef, pp. 287–313. Springer, New York.

Kuijt, I. 2009 What Do We Really Know about Food Storage, Surplus, and Feasting in Preagricultural Communities? *Current Anthropology* 50:641–645.

Kuijt, I., and H. Mahasneh 1998 Dhra': An Early Neolithic Village in the Southern Jordan Valley. *Journal of Field Archaeology* 25:153–161.

Kuijt, I, and N. A. Goring-Morris 2002 Foraging, Farming, and Social Complexity in the Pre-Pottery Neolithic of the Southern Levant: A Review and Synthesis. *Journal of World Prehistory* 16:361–440.

Kuijt, I., and B. Finlayson 2009 Evidence for Food Storage and Predomestication Granaries 11,000 Years Ago in the Jordan Valley. *Proceedings of the National Academy of Science* 106:10966–10970.

Leach, E. R. 1954 *Political Systems of Highland Burma.* Harvard University Press, Cambridge.

Lee, R. B., and I. DeVore 1968 *Man the Hunter.* Aldine, Chicago.

Lee, R. B. 1978 Politics, Sexual and Non-Sexual in an Egalitarian Society. *Social Science Information* 17:871–895.

Lenski, G. 1966 *Power and Privilege: A Theory of Social Stratification.* McGraw-Hill, New York.

Marcus, J. 1992 Dynamic Cycles of Mesoamerican States. *National Geographic Research Explorations* 8:392–411.

Matson, R. G., and G. Coupland 1994 *Prehistory of the Northwest Coast*. Left Coast Press, Walnut Creek, California.

Munro, N. D., and L. Grosman 2010 Early Evidence (ca. 12,000 BP) for Feasting at a Burial Cave in Israel. *PNAS* 107:15362–15366.

Naveh, D. 2003 PPNA Jericho: A Socio-political Perspective. *Cambridge Archaeological Journal* 13:83–96.

Peebles, C. S., and S. Kus 1977 Some Archaeological Correlates of Ranked Societies. *American Antiquity* 42:421–448.

Perry, S. E. 2006 What Cultural Primatology Can Tell Anthropologists about the Evolution of Culture. *Annual Review of Anthropology* 35:171–90.

Price, T. D. 1985 Affluent Foragers of Mesolithic Southern Scandinavia. In *Prehistoric Hunter-Gatherers. The Emergence of Cultural Complexity*, edited by T. D. Price and J. A. Brown, pp. 341–363. Academic Press, New York.

Price, T. D. 1995 Agricultural Origins and Social Inequality. In *Foundations of Social Inequality*, edited by T. D. Price and G. M. Feinman, pp. 129–151. Plenum Press, New York.

Price, T. D., and J. A. Brown 1985 Aspects of Hunter-Gatherer Complexity. In *Prehistoric Hunter-Gatherers*, edited by T. D. Price and J. A. Brown, pp. 3–20. Academic, Orlando.

Price, T. D., and O. Bar-Yosef 2010 Traces of Inequality at the Origins of Agriculture in the Ancient Near East. In *Pathways to Power. New Perspectives on the Origins of Social Inequality*, edited by T. D. Price and G. M. Feinman, pp. 147–168. Springer, New York.

Price, T. D., and O. Bar-Yosef 2011 The Origins of Agriculture: New Data, New Ideas. *Current Anthropology* 52(4):163–174.

Rollefson, G. O. 1984 'Ain Ghazal: An Early Neolithic Community in Highland Jordan, near Amman. *Bulletin of the American Schools of Oriental Research* 255:3–14.

Rosenberg, M. 1998 Cheating at Musical Chairs. Territoriality and Sedentism in an Evolutionary Context. *Current Anthropology* 39:653–684.

Rosenberg, M., and R. W. Redding 2000 Hallan Çemi and Early Village Organization in Eastern Anatolia. In *Life in Neolithic Farming Communities. Social Organization, Identity, and Differentiation*, edited by I. Kuijt, pp. 39–61. Kluwer Academic/Plenum, New York.

Rowley-Conwy, P. 1999 Economic Prehistory in Southern Scandinavia. In *World Prehistory: Studies in Memory of Grahame Clark*, edited by J. Coles, R. M. Bewley, and P. Mellars 125–159. University Press, Oxford.

Rowley-Conwy, P. C. 2001 Time, Change, and the Archaeology of Hunter-Gatherers: How Original Is the Original Affluent Society? In *Hunter-Gatherers: An Interdisciplinary Perspective*, edited by C. Panter-Brick, R. H. Layon, and P. Rowley-Conwy, pp. 39–72. Cambridge University Press, Cambridge.

Sage, R. F. 2006 Was Low Atmospheric CO_2 during the Pleistocene a Limiting Factor for the Origin of Agriculture? *Global Change Biology* 1(2):93–106.

Sahlins, M. 1972 *Stone Age Economics*. Aldine, Chicago.

Schmidt, K. 2000 Göbekli Tepe, Southeastern Turkey: A Preliminary Report on the 1995–99 excavations. *Paléorient* 26:45–54.

Schmidt, K. 2010 *Sie bauten die ersten Tempel. Das rätselhafte Heiligtum der Steinzeitjäger*. Verlag C. H. Beck, München.

Shakun, Je. D., P. U. Clark, F. He, S. A. Marcottt, A.C. Mix, Z. Liu, B. Otto-Bliesner, A. Schmittner, and E. Bard 2012 Global Warming Preceded by Increasing Carbon Dioxide Concentrations during the Last Deglaciation. *Nature* 484:49–54.

Smith, B. D., and R. A. Yarnell 2009 Initial Formation of an Indigenous Crop Complex in Eastern North America at 3800 B.P. *Proceedings of the National Academy of Science* 106:6561–6566.

Smith, E. A., K. Hill, F. W. Marlowe, D. Nolin, P. Wiessner, M. Gurven, S. Bowles, M. B. Mulder, T. Hertz, and A. Bell 2010 Wealth Transmission and Inequality among Hunter-Gatherers. *Current Anthropology* 51:19–34.

Smith, M. 1987 Household Possessions and Wealth in Agrarian States: Implications for Archaeology. *Journal of Anthropological Archaeology* 6:297–335.

Testart, A. 1982a *Les chasseurs-cueilleurs, ou l'origine des inégalités.* Société d'ethnographie, Paris.

Testart, A. 1982b The Significance of Food Storage among Hunter-Gatherers: Residence Patterns, Population Densities, and Social Inequalities. *Current Anthropology* 23:523–537.

Twiss, K. C. 2008 Transformations in an Early Agricultural Society: Feasting in the Southern Levantine Pre-Pottery Neolithic. *Journal of Anthropological Archaeology* 27:418–442.

Weiss, E., M. E. Kislev, and A. Hartmann 2006 Autonomous Cultivation before Domestication. *Science* 312:1608–1610.

Wiessner, P. 2002 The Vines of Complexity. *Current Anthropology* 41:233–269.

Wiessner, P. and W. Schiefenhovel 1996 *Food and the Status Quest.* Berghahn Books, Oxford.

Wright, G. 1978 Social Differentiation in the Early Natufian. In *Social Archeology: Beyond Subsistence and Dating*, edited by C. Redman, pp. 201–223. Academic Press, New York.

CHAPTER THREE

Transegalitarian Societies on the American Northwest Plateau

Social Dynamics and Cultural/Technological Changes

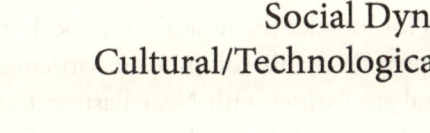

Brian Hayden

Abstract   *The American Northwest Plateau is an ideal area for investigating the origins of inequality due to archaeological continuity with ethnographic groups and variability between groups. However, there are major disagreements about the conditions and timing of the appearance of inequality on the plateau, with one school emphasizing stressful conditions leading to inequality and another school emphasizing conditions of abundance and surpluses. This chapter argues for conditions of abundance and surplus as leading to initial inequalities.*

If we want to find the origins of inequality, it is to complex hunter/gatherers that we must turn, and areas with ethnographic accounts of these societies are particularly valuable in understanding prehistoric social dynamics of groups that first exhibit signs of complexity and inequality. While great attention has been focused on the complex hunting/gathering/fishing cultures of the American Northwest Coast, relatively little recognition has been accorded the complex cultures of the Northwest Interior Plateau. However, the Northwest Plateau exhibited a range of complexity and socioeconomic inequality among its various ethnic groups that makes it an excellent region to investigate the origins of inequality. Both ethnographically and archaeologically, the major centers on the plateau exhibited pronounced wealth accumulations, sedentism, large communities, inequalities, and large corporate groups while other groups were more egalitarian. The Northwest Plateau is an ideal area to research the origins of inequality not only because of its rich and varied ethnographic documentation but also because of the considerable diversity in environments, which enables researchers to examine the role of environment and resources in the emergence of inequality.

On the British Columbian Plateau, where I work, inequality has become a contentious topic. Even in the most productive salmon regions, contemporary bands have fiercely egalitarian views of the present and the past, which contrast with some of the historically documented class differences between hereditary chiefs, commoners, and slaves, as well as with the ownership of the best fishing sites. Much contention revolves as well around how to interpret the archaeological and historical records. One school, which I will refer to as using the "stress model," argues that inequalities developed very late (c. 1200 cal. BP) due to subsistence stresses. Another school, referred to as using the "surplus and aggrandizer model," argues that significant inequalities existed much earlier (c. 2,000+ cal. BP) emerging from the efficient exploitation, storage, and use of salmon in surplus-based aggrandizer strategies. A more recent school, which I will refer to as using the "hyper-heterarchical model," maintains that all large villages were egalitarian throughout their history.

The implications for broader theoretical issues both in the region and cross-culturally are considerable (compare Price this volume). In particular, the Northwest Plateau exhibits a number of cultural similarities with Near Eastern Late Mesolithic, or Epipaleolithic, cultures that display early inequalities, such as the Natufian (Hayden 2004). Thus, a study of the origins of inequality in the Northwest Interior may be relevant to developing more general explanatory models. However, in contrast to other regions such as the Near East, the Northwest Interior has the key advantage of having relatively detailed ethnographic accounts of what complex hunter-gatherer cultures were actually like. It can be argued that the basic cultural dynamics and strategies documented ethnographically in the Northwest were the result of prehistoric developments of complexity among hunter-gatherers that persisted until European contact and were similar to developments in other parts of the world. However, definitions are critical for engaging with any of the basic models. Thus, the following section provides a few critical notes on definitions.

DEFINITIONS OF INEQUALITY AND COMPLEXITY

While it is frequently pointed out that hunter-gatherers are not truly egalitarian since there are usually inequalities based on gender, age, abilities, and specialized roles (e.g., shamans, warriors, raid organizers, resident custodians of territories), these kinds of inequalities are *not* what is generally referred to by archaeologists who use the rubric *egalitarian* societies. Certainly, this is not what I mean by egalitarian or "simple" foragers. Rather, I use the term *egalitarian* to refer to communal control over resources and production that is held in common by all residents of communities and is enforced via obligatory sharing of resources and products. Typically, personal private property is not even given much importance, while the amassing of surpluses for personal or competitive uses is universally considered anathema. Simple egalitarian hunter-gatherers may have gender and age inequalities and specialized roles or statuses, but acquisition of these attributes or statuses is not based on economic production, the private ownership of resources, or the competitive use of economic produce. Thus, age, gender, abilities, and special role differences constitute a kind of baseline of equality and complexity; that is, all human societies have these characteristics. Any greater degrees of egalitarianism are rarely, if ever, achieved in traditional societies. What most archaeologists refer to as "inequality" and "complexity" is something significantly more than these standard, more or less universal, inequalities.

Inequalities beyond the universal baseline are largely represented by increasing disparities in wealth, control of resources, and/or power, which usually result in larger and more complex settlements and polities. Most frequently, increasing socioeconomic disparities in these domains are associated with differential production of goods (especially food), control of key resources such as water (Wittfogel 1957), or control of trade (e.g., Leach 1954). Notwithstanding this strong pattern, there are some ethnographers who claim that political power in some groups like the Pueblos in Southwestern United States was based only on the control of ritual knowledge and not on economic control. However, this is a very controversial position (see discussion by Ware 2014:52) and if it really was the case, it begs the question of why such control could not have been exercised much earlier to create complex village and tribal societies.

The use of the term *institutionalized inequality*, widely employed by Prentiss et al. (2005, 2007, 2008), has up until the present lacked an operational definition or justification. It is not clear why inequalities must be institutionalized to be important—in fact, many of my publications have argued the opposite, notably, that major inequalities emerge in transegalitarian societies whether these inequalities are "institutionalized" or not (Hayden 2014). Nor have there been any efforts to indicate how "institutionalized" inequality can be identified archaeologically or to justify possible criteria. In fact, in regard to one archaeological indicator often used to infer "ascribed status," I have shown that subadult burials with lavish grave goods are *not* indexical of stratified societies such as chiefdoms but that they occur in transegalitarian societies without any "institutionalized" inequalities. Thus, I propose that use of the term *institutionalized inequalities* be abandoned and other measures of inequality, such as Gini coefficients, be used instead (per Schulting 1995; Hayden 1997, 2000a).

In addition, the attempt by some archaeologists and ethnographers to blur the distinction between egalitarian and nonegalitarian societies by invoking heterarchical differences of status and multiple types of status under an egalitarian umbrella may be compared to Boas's attempts to discredit early evolutionary cultural paradigms by showing that "primitive" peoples supposedly at the low (hunting and gathering) end of the evolutionary ladder were actually "complex" societies as demonstrated by their complex language, rituals, myths, symbolism, dances, art, and kinship. This is the same tactic currently being used by the new "hyper-heterarchical" school (Crumley 2005; Furniss 1995, 2004; Harris 2012), and I suspect it is driven by the same relativistic agenda.

The wider heterarchical concept of multiple, more or less equal, centers of power in communities certainly has an important role to play, as we shall see, but not as the hyper-heterarchical advocates would have it, by throwing out the role of economic production, prestige items, power, and internal hierarchies within corporate groups, and replacing them with the communitarian consensus decision making of egalitarian groups led by chiefs whose main role was promoting the common good. In contrast to the hyper-heterarchical view, the political ecology approach, which I prefer, focuses instead on: the importance of establishing claims to private ownership of property, produce, and resources, as well as the competitive use of surplus production via a number of different strategies to promote organizers' self-benefits.

THE MID-FRASER LARGE VILLAGES

All archaeologists who have worked in the Mid-Fraser region generally agree that there was a period from about 1600–1000 BP when unusually large nucleated winter pithouse villages were active and that the large villages were subsequently abandoned sometime between 800–1200 BP. Some researchers who support the surplus and aggrandizer model, like myself, think that large village formation began earlier (c. 2000–2500 cal BP) and that abandonment was relatively rapid. Other researchers, who support stress scenarios, see somewhat later agglomerations of communities (c. 1700 cal. BP) purportedly the result of a reduction in salmon runs forcing groups to coalesce around the best fishing localities, followed eventually by protracted abandonments—responses to further reduced salmon runs (Prentiss et al. 2003). Thus, the stress versus surplus models differ in terms of the conditions that were conducive to the establishment of large villages: resource scarcity versus resource abundance. Key considerations involve environmental variables in relation to: land and aquatic food resources (especially salmon, ungulates, and roots); the size of settlements; the degree of investments in structures; the formation of corporate groups; the production of prestige items of copper, bone, stone, and shell; long-distance procurement of prestige items; the breeding and domestication of dogs; large-scale storage; and the emergence of ritual societies.

NECESSITY VERSUS THE PROMOTION OF SELF-INTERESTS

In order to evaluate the stress versus the surplus-and-aggrandizer models, one can take two approaches. First, one can take a synchronic approach by examining the association of relative complex societies with various resources throughout geographic regions among contemporaneous occupations. Second, one can take a diachronic approach by examining climate changes over time together with associated cultural changes.

THE SYNCHRONIC APPROACH

A number of studies have demonstrated that political and social complexity was strongly associated with resource productivity in the area. On the Northwest Coast, the size of salmon-bearing streams was directly related to political complexity (Donald and Mitchell 1975; Mitchell and Donald 1988:321). The prehistoric distribution on the Northwest Plateau of wealth or prestige items such as copper, pipes, and nephrite adzes shows a similar association with locations that were known ethnographically to have been the most productive salmon procurement sites (Hayden and Schulting 1994, 1995). Along the Columbia River, these locations included: The Dalles, Kettle Falls, and the confluence with the Snake River. On the Fraser River, the most important locations were around Lillooet and the Chilcotin canyon. The ethnographic communities in these locations were notable for being unusually complex, replete with substantial amounts of dried surplus salmon for exchange and pronounced socioeconomic inequalities, even including the sacrifice of slaves upon the death of their owners (e.g., in The Dalles, Thompson, Lillooet, and some Shuswap areas—Schulting 1994:131).

The largest and most productive location of all, The Dalles, was also renowned as a major trading location where many goods including slaves could be bought and sold (Schulting 1995). Historically, the population of the main settlement approached 1,000 people. In 1805, Lewis and Clark saw 10,000 pounds of stored dried salmon at this location, while historic catch rates reached up to 100,000 pounds per day (Spier and Sapir 1930:178–179; Hunn 1990:133). A lesser, but still very productive fishing location on the Northwest Plateau along the Fraser River near Lillooet, in British Columbia, was known to early fur traders as a breadbasket, and a place where one "could not suffer for want" (Kennedy and Bouchard 1992:318; Hayden 1992:530; 2000b:276).

Schulting (1994:128) observed that, historically, the most complex localities on both the Columbia and British Columbia plateaus had the best salmon resources and were located in strategic trading locations between the coast and the interior with considerable wealth accruing from these activities. Similarly, in California, Gamble (2008:298) has shown that the three most politically complex regions had very productive fish resources resulting in large fish surpluses, the production of huge numbers of shell beads used as wealth, the establishment of large settlements with hundreds or thousands of people, pronounced socioeconomic inequalities (with several burials accompanied by c. 30,000 shell beads), the establishment of secret societies, and in the case of the Chumash and Patwin, chiefdom political organizations. The political economies of the Chumash region were established several thousand years ago, presumably based on the surplus production of that area (Gamble 2008:201). It is a truism that social inequality and complexity as exemplified by chiefdoms require high levels of food production in order to sustain the political structures and thus can only occur where environments can be made productive at high levels (Rambo 1991:Fig. 10.3; Hayden 2014). Tellingly, Gamble (2008:277–278) observes that stress arguments for the emergence of inequalities cannot be credibly used for the Chumash coast around Santa Barbara because of the abundance of resources there.

The Diachronic Approach

Under the stress model proposed by Prentiss et al. (2005, 2007, 2008), village agglomeration was supposed to have followed the same sequence of village amalgamation reported for the Southwestern United States in which deteriorating (drying) climatic conditions were associated with increased settlement nucleation at a few well-watered, agriculturally productive refugia. However, it can be observed that in contrast to subsistence agriculturalists, most hunter-gatherers, such as the Bushmen, appear to disperse under conditions of scarcity (Hayden 1981). Prentiss et al. (2003, 2005, 2007, 2008) argue that with fewer salmon in dry periods, groups would gather together near the best salmon procurement locations. Prentiss et al. have therefore attempted to tie the emergence of large villages and large residential corporate groups to periods of increased dryness. In their view, residential corporate groups controlled the best fishing locations, but nevertheless managed to remain egalitarian.

However, the data used to argue for a climatic stress around 1700 cal. BP as a key factor in large village formation has been questioned. Even Harris (2012:160, 228), one of the co-authors in Prentiss et al. 2007, has admitted, after a thorough review of the climate data, that early large residential corporate groups and villages did *not* exhibit any scalar stresses, and that there was no significant environmental change that occurred when Prentiss predicted this should have occurred. Hayden and Mathewes (2009) have similarly challenged Prentiss's climate reconstruction from this period as inaccurate. In fact, studies of fish abundances in the Northeast Pacific Ocean during the late Holocene are replete with conflicting interpretations of increased salmon spawning in Alaskan lakes from 1150–100 BP (Finney et al. 2010:320,324) when salmon were supposed to be in decline in the Northeast Pacific according to Prentiss et al. However, there is no real data on salmon abundance from marine sources. Herring abundance displayed virtually *no* change from 4000–1000 BP in the Northeast Pacific (Tunnicliffe 2001:203; Wright et al. 2005:381). And in general, Finney et al. (2010:321) note that there have been modern oceanic climatic conditions in the area from about 2800 BP to the present. While they note some likely relationships between climate and fish abundance, they also emphasize that the relationship between fish abundance and environmental factors is quite complex (ibid. 325).

At the end of the Mid-Fraser sequence of large villages, Prentiss and coauthors have suggested that abandonment of the large villages was due to another, more severe climatic period of drought c. 1100–700 BP This can be more convincingly tied to the Medieval Warm Period widely documented in the Northern Hemisphere. In both Prentiss's scenario and my own, the reason for the abandonment of large villages was the collapse of the principal food resource base: salmon. I had earlier postulated that a massive landslide may have blocked salmon runs up the Fraser River, but it matters little to me what the proximate cause of the failure of salmon runs may have been or how rapidly it occurred. Thus, I have little to argue about in this respect with Prentiss et al. They may very well be correct that a severe climate change might have greatly reduced salmon runs in the Fraser River at this time and, in general, on the West Coast. However, this remains to be definitively demonstrated, especially since the claimed subsistence shift in the villages away from salmon to land mammals toward the end of their occupations (Prentiss et al. 2007; Harris 2012) is based on very biased samples and categorization of fauna. Moreover, there is conflicting data (such as the fish abundance data) and a complete lack of taphonomic considerations, as well as a lack of any supporting evidence from carbon isotope analyses. In fact, the faunal trends that Prentiss et al. purport to see in their data (from reliance on salmon to reliance on deer or even dogs) is belied by a relatively constant intake of salmon of about 60–70 percent throughout *at least* the last 2,000 years on the Plateau, with no increase in the consumption of land mammal protein apparent over the last 2,000 years (Chisholm 1986; Lovell et al. 1986; Stryd and Rousseau 1996; Schwarcz et al. 2014). There are no data for the preceding two millennia. A similar, even higher, very consistent intake of almost exclusively marine protein is recorded for the British Columbia Coast over the past 5,000–6,000 years to historic times, which Schwarcz et al. (2014) note does not support the inferences of increasing land mammal use on the coast by faunal analysts. In addition, the isotopic analyses that have been conducted from two much earlier burials on the plateau (dated to 4950 BP) indicate that even at that early date, almost 40 percent of the protein consumed came from salmon. This implies some level of effective storage (evidenced at the contemporaneous Baker site by storage pits) and hence probable surpluses. In any case, as far as I am concerned, the reasons for the abandonment of the large Mid-Fraser villages constitute a separate, unrelated, issue of when and why significant inequalities emerged in the region.

In order to maintain the credibility of the stress model for the emergence of inequalities, Prentiss et al. have manipulated the sampling of housepits so as to emphasize late occupations, and they have repeatedly ignored good early dates from within large housepits and ritual structures. In terms of sampling, Prentiss et al. have only placed relatively small test pits in the floors of housepits at the Bridge River site (usually one or two 50 x 50 cm. test pits). Since many, if not most, housepit floors on the plateau were regularly cleaned out and the contents deposited outside the structures on their rims, all the early deposits are in the rims in many structures, while the floor deposits usually only represent the last occupation, or last few occupations, of a long series. Prentiss et al. only sampled floors, so they strongly biased their results toward the last occupation period of their site and recovered little or nothing from the early occupations of long-lived households (which most structures were). The early history of these structures lies still untouched and unknown in the rim middens surrounding the structures. Moreover, the faunal and artifactural assemblages obtained from small testpits (usually less than a square meter) did not reliably represent the household assemblages—an aspect that Harris (2012:129) has demonstrated—even for the few larger floor excavations of four or five square meters. These two facts (biased sampling and inadequate sample sizes) bring into question all of the so-called demographic histories, subsistence changes over time, and constructs that Prentiss et al. have generated from their data base.

Prentiss et al. have steadfastly refused to accept evidence for early occupations of large structures or large occupations at the Keatley Creek site. Yet, according to a number of radiocarbon dates from articulated dog skeletons in storage pits in one large structure, ritual structures, and large corporate housepit rims, the founding of large villages and corporate residences predates any period of possible climatic stress episodes by at least several hundred years if not considerably more (Hayden and Mathewes 2009).

Prentiss and coauthors have also refused to recognize any ritual activity or the existence of prestige objects as being important prior to their postulated climatic downturn c. 1200 BP, which they think produced the first significant inequalities due to control of access to increasingly difficult-to-obtain salmon resources. Yet, there are very good examples of ritual structures and ritual objects (including what appears to have been a button blanket) at the Keatley Creek site dating to c. 2000 BP (Hayden and Adams 2004). According to Prentiss et al. (2007:308-9321-2; 2008:77), prior to 1200 BP, large communities were supposedly egalitarian, without wealth disparities or hierarchical control either within corporate groups or within settlements or via exclusive ritual organizations. While it is certainly true that prestige items, inequalities, and population levels appear to have increased over time from 2000–1200 BP, I think it is unreasonable to maintain that there were no significant inequalities before this time and that village societies were egalitarian. Archaeological data indicating inequalities come from burials, house construction, prestige objects, village locations, control over resources, storage, and evidence of aggrandizer strategies.

BURIALS

On the British Columbia Plateau, very few burials have been recovered prior to 2400 BP, and no burials have been found dating to the critical period from 2400–1500 BP (Schulting 1994, 1995). Thus, the sample is inadequate for making any reliable inferences about inequality based on grave goods prior to 1500 BP. However, the occurrence of substantial grave goods throughout the Plateau from 1500 BP onward is ample testimony of the existence of socioeconomic inequalities well before the 1200 BP date when Prentiss et al. argue inequality first appeared. The existence of significant inequalities in grave goods on the Columbia Plateau at least from 3000 BP (Schulting 1994), and on the Northwest Coast c. 4000 BP involving burials with up to 350,000 stone beads (!) (Mackie 2012, Coupland et al. 2016), provide further grounds for thinking that such inequalities probably also existed on the British Columbia Plateau well before 2000 BP. Schulting (1994, 1995) has even quantified the relative degree of inequality in the grave goods from different assemblages and time periods using Gini coefficients, where 0 equals perfect equality and 1 equals complete inequality. The values for the earliest burials on the Columbia Plateau (c. 3000 BP) were 0.30 and increased over time to a maximum value in one assemblage of 0.77 (the overall average was 0.55). To put this into perspective, Schulting notes that the Gini index for incomes in the United States in 1980 varied according to state from 0.32 to 0.44.

HOUSE CONSTRUCTION

From the beginning of large village occupations (c. 2000+ BP), the existence of very large corporate housepit residences (up to 20 meters in diameter) together with contemporaneous small housepit residences (no more than six or seven meters in diameter) leads to expectations of inequalities within villages. Ethnographically, in cultures where large corporate groups exist, they exert far more power within villages than residents of small independent households (Hayden 2012, 2014). In addition, the considerable effort involved in building large corporate residences, not the least of which involved procurement of timbers, implies substantial planning, authority, and hierarchical control over labor, especially since the wood supply for fuel and construction would have become exhausted in the areas immediately surrounding large villages after several generations of site occupation. The division of floor areas in large houses into one half with large hearths and large storage pits versus an opposing half of the house with small hearths and small or no storage pits also indicates major inequalities within residential corporate groups, presumably reflecting owner families versus client families (Hayden 1997, 2000b).

PRESTIGE GOODS

The occurrence of prestige objects in large villages and throughout the region attests to inequalities existing much earlier than Prentiss and coauthors postulate. For instance, the Baker site (near Kamloops), dated to 4950 BP, yielded a number of prestige objects including: the presence of domesticated dogs, tooth pendants, eagle claw pendants, and shell beads from the Coast, eyed needles, and the use of hawk, loon, and eagle parts. These are good indications that inequalities existed by c. 5000 BP, well before Prentiss's date of 1200 BP. Obsidian found near Lillooet from more than 4,000 years ago, but sourced to Oregon, indicates exchange in exotic materials. Exotic materials from the coast and Oregon required extra travel efforts to procure as well as the surplus wealth to acquire such items via exchange. In addition, prestige animals such as dogs required surpluses to feed and breed, and only the rich would ordinarily be able to afford such luxuries. Throughout the region, Darwent (1998:22, 24) has demonstrated that nephrite adzes were prestige items that began to be made and circulated from about 3000 BP, coeval with similar developments on the Columbia Plateau and along the British Columbia Coast (see also Richards and Rousseau 1987).

On the basis of comparative ethnographies, I have argued that prestige items were developed and functioned as part of several aggrandizers' strategies to concentrate control in their own hands and increase surplus production (Hayden 1998). Other archaeologists similarly use prestige objects as indicators of the existence of a "political economy" (Earle 1978; Gamble 2008:201). Thus, the presence of a variety of prestige objects (often procured from distant sources) in housepit occupations such as the Baker site dating to the beginning of the Plateau Housepit Tradition (5000 BP) is not consistent with Prentiss's position that "wealth-based inequality" only emerged c. 1200 BP. Exactly why Prentiss and coauthors are loathe to accept inequalities as existing before 1200 BP is far from clear. There appears no logical reason for this interpretive position, especially since they posit stress as the causal factor in the emergence of inequalities and envisage stress conditions well before 1200 BP.

Harris (2012) has argued that there are no clear differences between large corporate residences and other structures in terms of prestige objects, which she thinks should occur if there were wealth-based inequalities. However, as she and I have noted, the frequency of prestige or wealth items is not high enough in housepit deposits to make any meaningful statistical assessment of differential occurrences. Most prestige items appear to have been deposited in graves. Moreover, in the ethnographic transegalitarian societies that I have studied, prestige objects tend to be widely dispersed among households rather than concentrated in a few hierarchically controlling households (Hayden 2014). This is because these items are promoted by aggrandizers as required paraphernalia to transact all important social relationships such as marriages, funerals, and alliance formations. Thus, like the fine china sets of most contemporary middle-class households, every "respectable" family in ethnographic transegalitarian societies had to "buy into" the acquisition of prestige objects, and it seems highly likely that the situation was the same in the prehistoric past. Aggrandizers could profit from the social requirements for prestige objects since they often controlled the sources of them, and poorer families often had to go into debt to acquire them by borrowing from the more wealthy families. This situation easily leads to exploitation and becomes a major driver of inequality by itself. Such exploitation involving required prestige items for funerals, marriages, and other important events was loudly lamented by some missionaries in Sulawesi, and undoubtedly many other places (Hayden 2014).

SITE LOCATION

Another feature that is inconsistent with the stress model for the formation of large villages is that the largest site of the region, Keatley Creek, is not actually located near any good fishing rock locations (Hayden 2000b:258–259). By far, the best fishing locations are formed by bedrock outcrops jutting out into the Fraser River creating exceptionally productive back eddies. The best of these are located seven to 15 kilometers downstream at the Ten-Mile and Six Mile fisheries which were undoubtedly controlled by residents of the large Bell and Bridge River sites adjacent to these fisheries and contemporaneously occupied with Keatley Creek. Similarly, the moderately lucrative fishing locations above the mouth of Pavilion Creek (six kilometers upstream from Keatley Creek) would undoubtedly have been under the direct control of residents occupying the prehistoric Pavilion village site. The stretch of river where Keatley Creek is located, from the Ten-Mile fishery to the confluence with Pavilion Creek, is almost devoid of favorable fishing sites. This is a major disconformity with the stress model of village formation in which large villages coalesced around the best fishing locations due to reductions in salmon availability.

Clearly, the residents of Keatley Creek must have been getting salmon from some source in the region, but this does not appear to have been from fishing locations in their immediate village territory. Exactly how the residents managed to procure the necessary salmon—whether through trade, intermarriage, charging transit fees, or other means—is still unresolved. However, it is interesting to note that the largest mainland settlements of the Chumash complex hunter-gatherers in Southern California were optimally placed to control the flow of goods between the interior and the coast, and that this control over trade facilitated the development of wealth and power among a limited number of individuals (Johnson 2004). The same situation may explain the large size of Keatley Creek, especially if the residents were able to erect a bridge across the Fraser River at the nearby Camelsfoot constriction, a location where the river is unusually narrow.

CONTROL OF RESOURCES

There is also good evidence that key resource procurement sites were owned by residents of the large corporate residences. Control over productive resources is generally viewed as a major means of establishing socioeconomic inequalities. Control over access to the most important salmon resources at Keatley Creek has been demonstrated by Kevin Berry (2000) who showed that salmon vertebrae assemblages from small housepits exclusively represented two-year-old, weak-swimming salmon that could be caught from gravel shorelines of the Fraser River. These were the least desirable types of salmon ethnographically. In contrast, significant amounts of three-to-five-year-old salmon vertebrae were recovered from large corporate housepit structures (in some cases representing three quarters of the salmon remains), indicating privileged access to the larger, more desirable types of salmon (whether via intermarriage privileges, special arrangements with neighboring villages controlling fishing sites, trade, fees, or other means). Ethnographically, the larger salmon were stronger swimmers and only could be procured from special fishing rocks jutting out into the river, and these rocks were owned by specific families. It appears that this kind of ownership was only tolerated by other community members under conditions of relative abundance when the majority of community members could be assured of access to enough food for their own needs (Hayden 1994).

Ed Bakewell (2000) similarly demonstrated that the residents of different large corporate houses used different hunting and root-gathering areas in the mountains, from which they brought back distinctive types of tool stones for use in their winter villages. Each large corporate house at Keatley Creek focused on a different type of tool stone that was used throughout the life of the structure. Presumably, residents had some territorial or ownership claim over the mountain areas that they used as their exclusive terrain. Such control of resource areas would have provided the basis for increased inequalities of food, wealth, and power within the winter village communities.

DISCUSSION AND CONCLUSION

On the Northwest Plateau, we have an important case of independent development of complex hunter-gatherers exhibiting the first signs of inequality and complexity, as defined at the outset of this chapter. The timing and necessary and sufficient conditions for this development are still debated between the advocates of the stress model and the advocates of the surplus-and-aggrandizer model. From my perspective, the surplus-and-aggrandizer model fits the data best and seems consistent with similar developments in the Near East as presented by Price (this volume). Synchronic analysis of the most complex and nonegalitarian societies in the area shows that developments of inequalities are associated with the most productive localities. Diachronic perspectives indicate that salmon achieved major importance in Interior diets c. 5,000 years ago (reaching a maximum use by *at least* 2,000 years ago) and that important elements of the prestige economy had begun to appear around 5,000 years ago as well (Stryd and Rousseau 1996). Elements of the prestige economy included: the use of shells from the coast; nephrite adzes; domesticated dogs; imported obsidian; the use of hawk, loon, and eagle appendages; and sculpted pieces of bone, antler, or stone. The mere existence of these prestige items indicates the accumulation of surpluses and wealth. Comparative ethnographies indicate that these objects would have been used in competitive strategies to promote the self-interests of aggrandizers (Hayden 1998, 2014). Such objects, together with large storage pits associated with individual domestic hearths within corporate structures, attest to the existence of private property norms.

The existence of large-scale storage by at least 2000 BP at Keatley Creek can also be linked to the creation of surpluses (due to overcompensation for potential losses), the development of strategies to use the resulting surpluses to advance self-interests, and the emergence of inequalities as documented elsewhere by Halstead (1989, 1990; also Hayden 2014). Six large storage pits, with volumes approaching a cubic meter, existed in the large corporate residence excavated at Keatley Creek (Housepit 7). Significant use of storage can be inferred from at least 4950 BP on the basis of early storage pits (at the Baker site) and two skeletons found to the north of Keatley Creek, both of which obtained almost 40 percent of their protein from salmon (Stryd and Rousseau 1996:193–196). Such a high level of salmon consumption could not have happened unless they relied for much of the year on dried salmon since the salmon runs in this region occur for only a few weeks of the year. Even more extreme consumption of marine resources has been isotopically documented from the coast, where almost all protein was consistently derived from marine sources for at least the last 5,000, if not 6,000 years (Schwarcz et al. 2014). This strongly indicates that storage technology was probably well established by that time on the coast and was probably well known by interior groups as well. Thus, there are good grounds for expecting the foundations of economically based inequality to have been laid by 5000 BP, including private ownership, surplus production, storage, and the use of prestige items. Differential occurrences of grave goods on the Columbia Plateau c. 3000 BP display the existence of very marked inequalities by this time (Schulting 1995).

Thus, although socioeconomic inequalities may not have taken the form of sociopolitically stratified chiefdoms or exhibited "institutionalized inequalities" (whatever that may mean), there are many indications that substantial socioeconomic inequalities existed from c. 5000 BP to historic times on the Canadian Plateau, at the very least in the form of aggrandizers-cum-big men using various strategies to promote their own self-interests. Some of these strategies make no sense as responses to resource stresses, but make perfect sense as strategies to create inequalities. These include feasting, high costs of marriages and funerals, and claims of restricted access to supernatural power. How might the burial of individuals with surprising amounts of wealth items be a response to resource stress? If people did not have enough food, why would they devote some of their efforts and food to produce or procure wealth items that they subsequently essentially destroyed by burying? Such scenarios do not make sense. I refer to the types of sociopolitical organizations on the plateau that engage in these and the other aggrandizer strategies as "transegalitarian" societies, and I have steadfastly maintained that they provide the best model for understanding sociopolitical organizations and inequality during the occupation of the large villages.

Transegalitarian societies are based on privately owned surplus production and its use in a variety of competitive aggrandizer strategies devised to increase self-interests and benefits. These surplus (wealth)-based strategies include: ownership of the most productive resource locations (shown at Keatley Creek in the different types of salmon and raw materials used in corporate residences); feasting (evident at Keatley Creek from large roasting pits—Hayden and Mossop 2004); acquiring spouses on the basis of wealth payments and investing surplus in augmenting the marriage value of children (evident in the region from subadult burials with lavish grave goods—Schulting 1995); the development of prestige items required for marriages, funerals, alliances, and other socially important events (evident in grave goods and from the presence of prestige items); and the development of restricted access to supernatural forces (indicated at Keatley Creek by the presence of small early ritual structures only large enough for a few select individuals).

Other indicators of inequality consist of: the existence of regional exchange networks that restricted access to prestige items; the existence of major differences in the sizes of residences and the division within corporate residences between domestic areas of privileged owners versus clients; the keeping and breeding of dogs as part of a prestige economy; differential access to better versus poorer types of salmon; differential access to mountain hunting and geophyte areas; and the differential burial of wealth in graves, including rich child burials (Schulting 1995). Large villages such as Keatley Creek, far from being the utopian egalitarian societies that some researchers envisage (e.g., Harris 2012), were more likely magnets of wealth that drew people to the surpluses and power that were concentrated there, much like the dynamics of contemporary and historic urban centers. Sociopolitical inequalities and complexity must have increased in tandem with these developments, and this is reflected in the establishment of large residential corporate groups and exclusive ritual associations at sites like Keatley Creek, probably beginning well before 2000 BP Invoking subsistence stress to account for the formation of large villages and the view that societies in the region were egalitarian until the last gasp of large village life are interpretations not supported by most of the available data.

As for the hyper-heterarchical models, it is difficult to take their proponents seriously when they create Rousseauian visions in which everyone is equal and respectful of each others' rights, there are no disputes, wealth does not play an important role in inequalities or power, people are generous and give wealth away simply to gain some vague social status, extra effort does not translate into special objects of value, large villages are the most egalitarian expression of the settlement variability, chiefs rule over large villages magnanimously, no one pursues their own self-interests or tries to exploit others, everyone shares equally in the running of corporate groups, and ethnographies cannot be trusted as bases for interpreting the past. Such views are presented as the "true understanding" of complex hunter-gatherer social organization (Harris 2012:239). Hyper-heterarchical models also must develop explanations for why large multifamily residences should develop and why prestige items appear in the archaeological record and how they should be defined. These aspects are currently lacking.

In sum, starting from an initial state of egalitarian bands, I doubt that subsistence stresses ever resulted in the development of inequalities. Among egalitarian bands, subsistence stress is much more likely to result in dispersals and increased assertions of egalitarian rights to all resources within territories (Hayden 1981). However, once principles of private property, contractual debts, enforcement, and other nonegalitarian norms became established, I think it was possible for those in secure positions of power to profit from conditions of resource stress and exploit individuals who were less powerful, thereby enhancing socioeconomic inequalities in societies, as documented in some cases historically (Hayden and Gargett 1990; Hayden 1994).

ACKNOWLEDGMENTS

I would like to thank Orlando Cerasuolo for the opportunity to explore these issues in greater depth. I am indebted to the Social Sciences and Humanities Research Council of Canada, to the Simon Fraser University Small Grant Fund for supporting excavations at Keatley Creek and my comparative ethnographic research. The Sir John Templeton Foundation has generously provided support for continuing this research.

REFERENCES

Bakewell, E. 2000 Classification and Distribution of Debitage at the Keatley Creek Site. In *The Ancient Past of Keatley Creek*. Vol. 1: Taphonomy, edited by B. Hayden, pp. 267–298. Archaeology Press, Burnaby, British Columbia.

Berry, K. 2000 Prehistoric Salmon Utilization at the Keatley Creek Site. In *The Ancient Past of Keatley Creek*, Vol. 2: Socioeconomy, edited by B. Hayden, pp. 135–142. Archaeology Press, Burnaby, British Columbia.

Coupland, G., D. Bilton, T. Clark, J. S. Cybulski, G. Frederick, A. Holland, B. Letham and G. Williams 2016 A Wealth of Beads: Evidence for Material Wealth-Based Inequality in the Salish Sea Region, 4000–3500 Cal B.P. *American Antiquity* 81:294–315.

Crumley, C. 1995 Heterarchy and the Analysis of Complex Societies. In *Heterarchy and the Analysis of Complex Societies*. Vol. 6, edited by E. Ehrenreich, C. Crumley, and J. Levy, pp. 1–5. Archaeology Papers of the American Anthropological Association, Washington, District of Columbia.

Darwent, J. 1998 *The Prehistoric Use of Nephrite on the British Columbia Plateau*. Archaeology Press, Burnaby, British Columbia.

Donald, L., and D. Mitchell 1975 Some Correlates of Local Group Rank among the Southern Kwakiutl. *Ethnology* 14:325–346.

Earle, T. 1978 *Economic and Social Organization of a Complex Chiefdom*. Vol. Anthropology Paper No. 63, University of Michigan Museum of Anthropology, Ann Arbor.

Finney, B., J. Alheit, K-C Emeis, D. Field, D. Gutierrez, and U. Struck 2010 Paleoecological Studies on Variability in Marine Fish Populations. *Journal of Marine Systems* 79:316–328.

Furniss, E. 1995 *The Burden of History*. University of British Columbia Press, Vancouver.

Furniss, E. 2004 Cycles of History in Plateau Sociopolitical Organization. *Ethnohistory* 51:137–170.

Gamble, L. 2008 *The Chumash World at European Contact*. University of California Press, Berkeley.

Harris, L. 2012 *Heterarchy and Hierarchy in the Formation and Dissolution of Complex Hunter-Gatherer Communities on the Northern Plateau of Northwestern North America, ca. 2000–300 B.P.* Ph.D. thesis, University of Toronto, Toronto.

Hayden, B. 1992 Conclusions: Ecology and Complex Hunter/Gatherers. In *A Complex Culture of the British Columbia Plateau*, edited by B. Hayden, pp. 525–564. University of British Columbia Press, Vancouver.

Hayden, B. 2000a The Opening of Keatley Creek. In *The Ancient Past of Keatley Creek*. Vol. 1: Taphonomy, edited by B. Hayden, pp. 1–34. Archaeology Press, Burnaby, British Columbia.

Hayden, B., and R. Adams 2004 Ritual Structures in Transegalitarian Communities. In *Complex Hunter-Gatherers*. edited by W. Prentiss and I. Kuijt, pp. 3–22. University of Utah Press, Salt Lake City.

Hayden, B., and S. Mossop 2004 The Social Dimensions of Roasting Pits in a Winter Village Site. In *Complex Hunter-Gatherers,* edited by W. Prentiss and I. Kuijt, pp. 140–154. University of Utah Press, Salt Lake City.

Hayden, B. 1981 Subsistence and Ecological Adaptations of Modern Hunter/Gatherers. In *Omnivorous Primates: Gathering and Hunting in Human Evolution,* edited by G. Teleki and R. Harding, pp. 344–421. Columbia University Press, New York.

Hayden, B., and R. Gargett 1990 Big Man, Big Heart? A Mesoamerican View of the Emergence of Complex Society. *Ancient Mesoamerica* 1:3–20.

Hayden, B. 1994 Competition, Labor, and Complex Hunter-Gatherers. In *Key Issues in Hunter-Gatherer Research,* edited by E. J. Burch and L. Ellanna, pp. 223–239. Berghahn, Oxford.

Hayden, B. 1997 *The Pithouses of Keatley Creek.* Harcourt Brace, Fort Worth.

Hayden, B., and R. Schulting 1997 The Plateau Interaction Sphere and Late Prehistoric Cultural Complexity. *American Antiquity* 62:51–85.

Hayden, B. 1998 Practical and Prestige Technologies: The Evolution of Material Systems. *Journal of Archaeological Method and Theory* 5:1–55.

Hayden, B. 2012 Traditional Corporate Groups in Southeast Asia: An Ethnographic Study with Archaeological Implications. *Asian Perspectives* 50:1–23.

Hayden, B. 2014 *The Power of Feasts.* Cambridge University Press, Cambridge.

Hunn, E. S. 1990 *Nch'i-Wana "The Big River" Mid-Columbia Indians and Their Land.* University of Washington Press, Seattle.

Johnson, J. 2004 Social Responses to Climate Change among the Chumash Indians of South-Central California. In *Prehistoric California: Archaeology and the Myth of Paradise.* edited by L. M. Raab and T. Jones, pp. 149–160. University of Utah Press, Salt Lake City.

Kennedy, D., and R. Bouchard 1992 Stl'atl'imx (Fraser River Lillooet) Fishing. In *A Complex Culture of the British Columbia Plateau,* edited by B. Hayden, pp. 266–354. University of British Columbia Press, Vancouver.

Leach, E. 1954 *Political Systems of Highland Burma.* Beacon Press, Boston.

Lovell, N., B. Chisholm, E. Nelson, and H. Schwarcz 1986 Prehistoric Salmon Consumption in Interior British Columbia. *Canadian Journal of Archaeology* 10:99–106.

Mackie, Q. 2012 Bead-Rich Human Burials in Shíshálh territory. Electronic Document, http://qmackie.com/2012/08/31/bead-rich-burials-in-shishalh-territory/; accessed June 21, 2017.

Mitchell, D., and L. Donald 1988 Archaeology and the Study of Northwest Coast Economies. In *Prehistoric Economies of the Pacific Northwest Coast,* edited by B. Isaac, pp. 293–351. JAI Press, Greenwich, Connecticut.

Noah, A. 2005 *Household Economies: The Role of Animals in a Historic Period Chiefdom on the California Coast.* Ph.D. diss. University of California, Los Angeles, Los Angeles.

Patterson, R., A. Prokoph, A. Kumar, A. Chang, and H. Roe 2005 Late Holocene Variability in Pelagic Fish Scales and Dinoflagellate Cysts along the West Coast of Vancouver Island, NE Pacific Ocean. *Marine Micropaleontology* 55:183–204.

Prentiss, A., M. Lenert, T. Foor, N. Goodale, and T. Schlegel 2003 Calibrated Radiocarbon Dating at Keatley Creek: The Chronology of Occupation at a Complex Hunter-Gatherer Village. *American Antiquity* 68:719–736.

Prentiss, A., M. Lenert, T. Foor, and N. Goodale 2005 The Emergence of Complex Hunter-Gatherers on the Canadian Plateau. *American Antiquity* 70:175–180.

Prentiss, A., N. Lyons, L. Harris, M. Burns, and T. Godin 2007 The Emergence of Status Inequality in Intermediate Scale Societies. *Journal of Anthropological Archaeology* 26:299–327.

Prentiss, A., G. Cross, T. Foor, M. Hogan, D. Markle, and D. Clarke 2008 Evolution of a Late Prehistoric Winter Village on the Interior Plateau of British Columbia. *American Antiquity* 73:59–81.

Rambo, A. T. 1991 Energy and the Evolution of Culture: A Reassessment of White's Law. In *Profiles in Cultural Evolution,* edited by A. T. Rambo and K. Gillogly, pp. 291–310. University of Michigan, Ann Arbor.

Richards, T., and M. Rousseau 1987 *Late Prehistoric Cultural Horizons on the Canadian Plateau.* Archaeology Department, Simon Fraser University, Burnaby, British Columbia.

Schulting, R. 1994 (published version in 1995) An Investigation of Mortuary Variability and Socioeconomic Status Differentiation on the Northwest Plateau. Unpublished Ph.D. diss. Simon Fraser University, Burnaby, British Columbia.

Schulting, R. 1995 *Mortuary Variability and Status Differentiation on the Columbia-Fraser Plateau.* Archaeology Press, Burnaby, British Columbia.

Schwarcz, H., B. Chisholm, and M. Burchell 2014 Isotopic Studies of the Diet of the People of the Coast of British Columbia. *American Journal of Physical Anthropology* 155:460–468.

Spier, L., and E. Sapir 1930 *Wishram ethnography.* Vol. 3, University of Washington Publications in Anthropology, Seattle.

Stryd, A., and M. Rousseau 1996 The Early Prehistory of the Mid Fraser-Thompson River Area. In *Early Human Occupation in British Columbia,* edited by R. Carlson and L. D. Bona, pp. 177–204. University of British Columbia Press, Vancouver.

Tunnicliffe, V., J. O'Connell and M. McQuoid 2001 A Holocene Record of Marine Fish Remains from the Northeastern Pacific. *Marine Geology* 174:197–210.

Ware, J. 2014 *A Pueblo Social History.* School for Advanced Research, Santa Fe.

Wittfogel, K. 1957 *Oriental Despotism.* Yale University Press, New Haven.

Wright, C., A. Dallimore, R. Thomson, R. Patterson, and D. Ware 2005 Late Holocene Paleofish Populations in Effingham Inlet, British Columbia, Canada. *Palaeogeography, Palaeoclimatology, and Paleoecology* 224(4):367–384.

CHAPTER FOUR

The Emergence of Social Inequality in Southeastern Europe

A Long-Term Perspective

William A. Parkinson

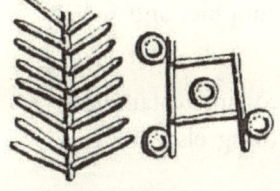

Abstract *Many recent models of the emergence of institutionalized hereditary inequality emphasize the role of individuals who were capable through various means (e.g., long-distance travel and trade) of transforming their social environment from a basically egalitarian or "tribal" system to one predicated upon inherent social inequalities and ascribed ranking. Such models, which tend to privilege the role of human agency over that of social structure, do not deal well with those instances when incipient complexity began to emerge but did not "catch on." An examination of these cultural "false starts" suggests that some forms of social organization are more amenable to the emergence of social inequality over the long-term.*

As the chapters in this book demonstrate, the issue of social inequality is a huge topic. I would argue that it also is one of the most important aspects of contemporary human social organization that we, as archaeologists, potentially can shed light upon. Those of us here in the United States are acutely aware that wealth inequalities and income disparities are the greatest they have been since the Great Depression (see, for example, Saez and Zucman 2016), and this trend shows no signs of changing any time soon. Although most modernist economists attribute this to very recent developments in the capitalist political economy, as the other chapters in the volume demonstrate, the trend we are seeing today began thousands of years ago. By studying the development of inequality over the long-term, we stand to glean a better understanding of how we got where we are, and hopefully where we are going.

Unlike many of the chapters in this book, which deal with social inequalities in bureaucratic states and empires, my chapter, like those by Price, Hanks, and Hayden, deals with the other end of the spectrum—the emergence of social inequalities. More specifically, this paper is about *how we study* the origins of institutionalized hereditary political and economic inequality within early agricultural villages.

My goal here is to convince the reader of the following, which I discuss with reference to the emergence of inequalities, but which also apply more broadly to our study of prehistoric social processes.

- Our archaeological perspective on the emergence of social inequalities is skewed by success stories, which give us a biased view of the past.

- To properly study the origins of inequality, or other transformative social processes, we need to incorporate multiple temporal, geographic, and social scales into our analyses.

- Diffusionist arguments are never, in and of themselves, adequate explanations for the emergence of institutionalized inequality, or anything else, for that matter.

- To understand why hereditary inequality became institutionalized in some social contexts and not in others, it is helpful to examine the accumulation and modification of cultural features over the long-term.

I discuss these issues in light of the long-term trajectory of social change in southeastern Europe, during the Neolithic, the Copper Age, and the Bronze Age, focusing specifically upon my own collaborative research on the Great Hungarian Plain (see, for example, Gyucha 2015; Gyucha et al. 2014; Gyucha et al. 2015; Parkinson 2006; Parkinson et al. 2010). Although a lot of effort has been dedicated to understanding the process of Neolithization in this part of the world (Banffy 2013), relatively little effort has been spent trying to model the variable processes that occurred within sedentary agricultural villages once they were established at the beginning of the Neolithic. This period between the establishment of sedentary agricultural villages during the seventh millennium BC and the emergence of societies with institutionalized hereditary ranking and hierarchy in the second millennium BC is characterized by patterns of village aggregation and dispersal throughout the Neolithic, Copper Age, and earlier Bronze Age. These changes in settlement patterns are associated with patterns of regionalization and homogenization in material culture. These shifting patterns, which I have called "tribal cycling" (Parkinson 2002) occurred for several thousand years before we begin to see evidence of ascribed ranking during the Bronze Age (Duffy 2014). And it is precisely those social dynamics, which created the framework for the emergence of institutionalized hereditary inequality that for the first time transcended age and gender (Siklósi 2004), that we need to understand.

SUCCESS STORIES AND "FALSE STARTS"

The archaeological record is almost exclusively a record of social successes. It is composed primarily of the material signature of those social processes that actually caught on. It records those social processes that "worked" and established an archaeologically identifiable social trajectory. We are less good at identifying those instances when there were incipient steps toward a social trajectory that did not work out, which was far more often the case than not. By focusing only on the success stories, it is difficult to identify what about those particular social situations was exceptional and, by contrast, to model why things did not work in another time and place.

This idea builds upon something that my colleagues Rick Yerkes, Attila Gyucha, and I discussed in an SAA paper in 2010 (Yerkes et al. 2010), when we compared the long-term trajectories of southeastern Europe to those of the southeastern United States. In both cases, we identified what we called false starts, or initial steps toward economic and political complexity that never became formalized or institutionalized and did not persist over time. In both parts of the world, the formalization and institutionalization of complexity occurred only after a full cycle of village nucleation and dispersal.

For those who do not waste several weekends a year watching American football, a "false start" occurs when all the players are lined up at the line of scrimmage and someone jumps too soon, or does something else that is not permitted. Then the play is reset and everyone has to go back to the line and try again. False starts also occur in other sports, such as track and swimming, when participants begin to move too early. The analogy of a false start reflects a cultural precociousness wherein certain social processes, such as ascribed ranking or village nucleation, occur but do not become institutionalized because the social context within which the process occurs cannot support it. We argued that prehistoric "false starts" toward complexity can be just as helpful in elucidating cross-cultural patterns as those instances when the play was well executed, the touchdown scored, and the "chief came to power" (Earle 1997).

Throughout the later prehistory of southeastern Europe there are several examples of false starts—flickerings of complexity that just didn't catch on and become institutionalized. These include the Cucuteni-Tripolye "Megasites" of the fourth millennium BC, which frequently were larger than 200 hectares and occasionally even larger than 400 hectares (Chapman et al. 2013; Chapman et al. 2014). Many of these sites have more than a thousand structures laid out in planned concentric circles, but there is no clear evidence of institutionalized hereditary ranking or persistent hierarchy. Even earlier, in the fifth millennium BC there are the well-known cemeteries of Varna and Durankulak, with marked achieved status differentiation and incipient ascribed ranking. But those too were short-lived flashes in the pan that, despite all the gold, never turned into hierarchical chiefdoms (Bailey 2000; Chapman et al. 2007).

Some of my own research has focused on the Great Hungarian Plain, where, almost a thousand years after the establishment of agricultural villages at the end of the seventh millennium BC, large, tell-centered villages were established during the latter half of the sixth millennium BC. Some of these sites, such as the one at Szegahalom-Kovácshalom in the Körös Region, exceeded more than 100 ha in areal extent (Gyucha et al. 2015). Although they are not as large or as formally arranged as those fourth-millennium Cucuteni-Tripolye sites, these Late Neolithic Tisza sites were inhabited nearly a thousand years earlier, and constitute some of the earliest proto-urban centers in Europe.

These later Neolithic tell-based systems on the Great Hungarian Plain bear many of the hallmarks commonly associated with economic and political complexity, including a clear settlement hierarchy centered around tells, settlement nucleation and fortification, economic intensification, and incipient ranking of social status marked in burials (Parkinson 2002). The tell sites were central nodes within clusters of Neolithic settlements. More figurines, burials, communal areas, and items acquired via long-distance exchange occur in the tells than at contemporaneous "flat" sites. This suggests that the tells may not have been established only to facilitate the redistribution of goods and services, but also to isolate the residences of the emergent leaders of these Neolithic societies and to serve as central foci for the performance of rituals, exchanges, and social interactions.

But the later Neolithic tell-based systems did not lead to the emergence of hierarchical chiefdoms (Parkinson and Gyucha 2012a, 2012b). Instead, these large, nucleated centers were abandoned at the end of the Neolithic. The Copper Age is characterized by a dispersed settlement pattern with smaller settlements more randomly distributed across the land-scape. Hierarchically organized societies did not emerge in the region until the later Bronze Age, when there was a return to a more nucleated settlement pattern centered again around fortified tells (Duffy et al. 2013).

The Late Neolithic was effectively a false start toward political and economic complexity in this region. But in the long-term, many of the social changes that occurred at the end of the Neolithic may have been essential for the emergence of institutionalized hierarchy in the Bronze Age (Parkinson 2006).

MULTIPLE SCALES OF ANALYSIS

To study these processes effectively, it is useful to adopt a theoretical perspective that incorporates multiple scales of analysis. This is especially a problem with European prehistory, which is historically schizophrenic. Ever since the publication of John Lubbock's *Pre-Historic Times* in 1865, European prehistorians have adored the age-old tradition of writing grand syntheses of the entire continent. But most syntheses were based almost exclusively on the narrow perspective offered through excavations at individual sites. While such macroscale syntheses are essential for the discipline of archaeology, they need to be tethered to specific regional and microregional studies, which, thanks to the explosion of archaeological survey in the last forty years, now are widely available in many parts of the continent (Parkinson and Galaty 2009; Parkinson and Gyucha 2012b).

By being explicit and deliberate about how social processes that occurred at different temporal and geographic scales relate to different kinds of archaeological evidence—from individual features on archaeological sites to microregions to archaeologically defined cultural groups to continental-scale phenomena such as the Bronze Age—we are better positioned to create a more nuanced reconstruction of the social processes that created those material datasets, and which ultimately laid the groundwork for the emergence of novel social institutions, such as institutionalized hereditary inequality (see Galaty et al. 2014).

By incorporating multiple scales of analysis, we can take full advantage of the breadth and depth of the archaeological record, as well as keep ourselves—and our models—honest.

INTERACTION, INTEGRATION, AND DIFFUSION

The importance of incorporating multiple scales of analysis really hits home when considering the origins of institutionalized hereditary inequality in European prehistory, which have since the time of V. Gordon Childe (1925) been attributed to diffusion from the Near East. But even though Colin Renfrew demonstrated almost a half-century ago, using both absolute and traditional chronologies, that many technological and social innovations occurred just as early—if not earlier—in southeastern Europe as they did in the Near East (Renfrew 1970), diffusionist models persist even in very recent European syntheses. For example, Kristiansen and Larsson (2005) have argued that the emergence of Bronze Age chiefs in Northern Europe can be explained through the long-distance selective transmission of ideas (what we used to call stimulus diffusion) through Central Europe and the Aegean, ultimately from Egypt and the Near East. This is a good example of why broad, macroregional, syntheses need to articulate with regional datasets (see Galaty et al. 2014). When Mike Galaty and I held an SAR seminar on Archaic State Interaction in the Eastern Mediterranean, we were unable to find solid evidence of Mycenaean interaction up into Albania, let alone into Central or Northern Europe (Parkinson and Galaty 2009). But my point here is not to attack this—actually very good—synthesis of the European Bronze Age, but rather to make the point that diffusion alone is itself never a sufficient causal explanation, because interaction alone can never itself cause something like the emergence of hereditary inequality. In the same way that Renfrew (1972) demonstrated that, even if there is evidence for indirect interaction between Crete and the Near East, this in and of itself is not enough to explain the emergence of the Minoan Palaces, and thus long-distance interaction cannot alone explain the emergence of Bronze Age chiefs.

I have found it helpful to model social organization along two separate but intimately intertwined dimensions—integration and interaction (Parkinson 2002, 2006). Integration refers to processes that incorporate individuals into specific organizational units (e.g., families, households, communities). Interaction, on the other hand, refers to those processes that operate between individuals and social units. Although primarily heuristic, these dimensions crosscut the false theoretical dichotomy that frequently is drawn between human agents and social structures. Ultimately, the origins of hereditary inequality created new integrative units within society that cannot be attributed to processes of interaction alone.

THE LONG-TERM PERSPECTIVE

Finally, there is an ironic tendency in European prehistory to neglect the *longue durée*. Many models attribute the development of novel social institutions—such as the emergence of hereditary inequality—to historical reactions to specific social contexts (see, for example, Kristiansen and Larsson 2005). But we also need to consider the accumulation of those cultural processes that developed over generations, or even millennia, through dynamic processes of social integration and interaction and perhaps the occasional false start—to create those exceptional social contexts that permitted the emergence of novel social institutions.

In addition to comparing similarly organized societies *in different regions,* it also is productive to compare different societies that occurred in the same region *at different times.* This permits us to ask the question, "Why, when faced with similar social contexts, did people sometimes choose to 'vote with their feet' and disperse, while at other times, they chose to develop systems of hierarchy?" Historical contingencies clearly play a critical role in answering these questions. No one can dispute that the horse, the sword, the chariot, and the dagger were critical elements in the establishment of elites in Bronze Age Europe. Human agents clearly manipulated these new elements and modified their symbolism to create something truly new. But just as important as historical contingencies are the specific social contexts into which those new elements were incorporated. Models that seek to understand the emergence of political and economic complexity must take into account the social structures that human agents and historical contingencies operated within and, in turn, influenced, reproduced, and changed.

If we look at the prehistory of the Great Hungarian Plain, for example, we can ask the questions: "Why did institutionalized hereditary inequality occur here during the Bronze Age and not during the Late Neolithic? What changed during the interceding three thousand years that created an environment that permitted hereditary inequality to become institutionalized here in the Bronze Age but not during the Late Neolithic?" During the Late Neolithic we find massive tell sites that functioned as the centers of ritual and trade within a multiple-tiered settlement hierarchy. During this period of nucleation, regional cultures with discrete, actively maintained social boundaries developed in areas where diffuse and permeable boundaries had existed previously. The Late Neolithic is characterized by three discrete cultural complexes, each with very different ceramic traditions, settlement layouts, house forms, and economic systems. These cultural complexes were incorporated into broader networks of interregional exchange that linked the Carpathian Basin to Little Poland and the Adriatic. And although we see flashes of incipient hereditary inequality in burials, it never became institutionalized. Hierarchical chiefdoms did not emerge. Instead, the tell sites were abandoned when the farming communities on the plain chose to live in smaller, more dispersed settlements throughout the Copper Age (Parkinson and Gyucha 2012a).

During the Bronze Age, there again was a return to nucleation, and to a clustered settlement system centered around fortified tell sites. This complex, multiple-tiered, nucleated system of settlement organization last occurred in the region during the Late Neolithic. Similar to that period, this pattern in the Bronze Age also was associated with increasing regionalization, and more discrete, actively maintained social boundaries at the regional scale. The Bronze Age regional systems were incorporated into continent-wide networks of trade and exchange that linked central Europe to southwestern Asia and the Mediterranean.

It was during this Bronze Age nucleation cycle that institutionalized hereditary inequality emerged in some parts of the Great Hungarian Plain (Parkinson and Gyucha 2012b; Duffy 2014).

One critical change that might have contributed to the institutionalization of social differentiation in the Bronze Age was the reorganization of the household within the settlement, which seems to have occurred sometime during the Copper Age (Parkinson 2006; Gyucha 2015). Extended corporate groups that lived in the large, multiroomed structures and longhouses at Late Neolithic sites probably pooled their labor and resources communally within partitioned sections of the settlements. When they dispersed to smaller, scattered settlements during the Early Copper Age sites, each site may have been occupied by a single, smaller social unit. This would have created greater autonomy for each Copper Age family group, and declining interdependence and cooperation with kinfolk. When these farmers returned to the tells during the Bronze Age, they no longer lived in large multiroomed structures. Instead, they resided in tightly packed, smaller houses, each with its own storage facilities.

These changes in household organization coincided with other significant developments in the Bronze Age, including the introduction of horses, the widespread use of secondary products, and of course bronze tools, weapons, and jewelry. The intersection of these multiple vectors and cycles in the social trajectory of the agricultural societies of this region ultimately provided a social context that permitted the institutionalization of hereditary inequality and the emergence of regional hierarchical polities—or hereditary chiefdoms—at least in some parts of the Plain (see Duffy 2014).

CONCLUSION

My goal was to discuss how we study the origins of social inequality in a cross-cultural framework. By highlighting the long-term dynamics of village dynamics at multiple scales, we can begin to ask even bigger cross-cultural questions. In addition to comparing distantly related regional trajectories within Europe, for example, we also can begin to ask even broader questions that cross the continent, such as: Why did it take several thousand years for hereditary inequality to become institutionalized in southeastern European farming villages, but in some places, like Mesoamerica, hierarchical regional polities quickly emerged within a few generations of the establishment of sedentary villages (see Clark and Cheetham 2002)?

The term *false start* is far from perfect. It carries with it teleological and neo-evolutionary connotations that I do not intend. Nevertheless, I believe that until we examine why some social contexts did *not* lead to the emergence of institutionalized hereditary inequality, as they did in the Bronze Age in southeastern Europe, our perspective will continue to be skewed by those rare, exceptional, circumstances when some communities committed to living in a world with inherent hereditary inequalities.

Although the world we live in today is to a large extent defined by hereditary inequalities, the world was not always like this. But once hereditary inequality became institutionalized within different communities, hierarchy tended to spread in a predatory manner not dissimilar to how archaic state bureaucracies spread. But that is a topic for a different article.

ACKNOWLEDGMENTS

I thank Orlando Cerasuolo for inviting me to participate in the conference. I also thank everyone at the Institute for European and Mediterranean Archaeology at the University of Buffalo, especially Peter Biehl, for creating the opportunity for people like Orlando to have a postdoctoral position that permits him to organize conferences like this.

REFERENCES

Bánffy, E. 2013 *The Early Neolithic of the Danube-Tisza Interfluve, Southern Hungary.* Central European Series 7. BAR International Series. Archaeopress, Oxford.

Bailey, D. 2000 *Balkan Prehistory.* Routledge, London.

Chapman, J., T. Higham, V. Slavchev, B. Gaydarska, and N. Honch 2007 Social Context of the Emergence, Development, and Abandonment of the Varna Cemetery, Bulgaria. *European Journal of Archaeology* 9(2):157–181.

Chapman, J., N. Burdo, M. Videiko, and B. Gaydarska 2013 Houses in the Archaeology of the Tripillia-Cucuteni Groups. In *Tracking the Neolithic House in Europe Sedentism, Architecture, and Practice,* edited by D. Hofmann and J. Smyth, pp. 95–116. Springer Verlag, New York.

Chapman, J., M. Y. Videiko, D. Hale, B. Gaydarska, N. Burdo, K. Rassmann, C. Mischka, J. Müller, A. Korvin-Piotrovskiy, and V. Kruts 2014 The Second Phase of the Trypillia Mega-Site Methodological Revolution: A New Research Agenda. *European Journal of Archaeology* 17(3):369–406.

Childe, V. G. 1925 *The Dawn of European Civilization.* A. A. Knopf, New York.

Clark, J. E., and D. Cheetham 2002 Mesoamerica's Tribal Foundations. In *The Archaeology of Tribal Societies,* edited by W. A. Parkinson, pp. 278–339. International Monographs in Prehistory, Ann Arbor.

Duffy, P. R. 2014 *Complexity and Autonomy in the European Bronze Age.* Prehistoric Research in the Körös Region, Volume I. Archaeolingua, Budapest.

Duffy, P. R., W. A. Parkinson, A. Gyucha, and R. W. Yerkes 2013 Coming Together, Falling Apart: A Multiscalar Approach to Prehistoric Aggregation and Interaction on the Great Hungarian Plain. In *From Prehistoric Villages to Cities: Settlement Aggregation and Community Transformation,* edited by J. Birch, pp. 44–62. Routledge, New York.

Earle, T. 1997 *How Chiefs Come to Power: The Political Economy in Prehistory.* Stanford University Press, Stanford.

Galaty, M. L., H. Tomas, and W. A. Parkinson 2014 Bronze Age European Elites: From the Aegean to the Adriatic and Back Again. *Cambridge Handbook of the Mediterranean World in the Bronze-Iron Ages,* edited by B. Knapp and P. van Dommelen, pp. 157–177. Cambridge University Press, Cambridge.

Gyucha, A. 2015 *Prehistoric Village Social Dynamics: The Early Copper Age in the Körös Region.* Prehistoric Research in the Körös Region, Volume II. Archaeolingua, Budapest.

Gyucha, A., P. Duffy, and W. A. Parkinson 2014 Prehistoric Human-Environmental Interactions on the Great Hungarian Plain. *Anthropologie* (Prague) LI/2:157–168.

Gyucha, A., R. W. Yerkes, W. A. Parkinson, N. Papdopoulos, A. Sarris, P. R. Duffy, and R. B. Salisbury 2015 Settlement Nucleation in the Neolithic: A Preliminary Report of the Körös Regional Archaeological Project's Investigations at Szeghalom-Kovácshalom and Vésztő-Mágor.

In *Neolithic and Copper Age between the Carpathians and the Aegean Sea. Chronologies and Technologies from the 6th to the 4th Millennium BCE. International Workshop Budapest 2012*, Archäologie in Eurasien 31, edited by S. Hansen, P. Raczky, A. Anders, and A. Reingruber, pp. 129–142. Verlag Dr. Rudolf Habelt, Bonn.

Kristiansen, K., and T. Larsson 2005 *The Rise of Bronze Age Society: Travels, Transmissions, and Transformations.* Cambridge University Press, Cambridge.

Kristiansen, K., and T. Larsson 2006 *The Social Organization of Early Copper Age Tribes on the Great Hungarian Plain,* BAR International Series 1573. Archaeopress, Oxford.

Parkinson, W. A. 2002 Integration, Interaction, and Tribal 'Cycling': The Transition to the Copper Age on the Great Hungarian Plain. In *The Archaeology of Tribal Societies,* edited by W. A. Parkinson, pp. 391–438. International Monographs in Prehistory, Ann Arbor.

Parkinson, W. A., and M. L. Galaty 2009 Introduction: Interaction and Ancient Societies. In *Archaic State Interaction: The Eastern Mediterranean in the Bronze Age*, edited by W. A. Parkinson and M. L. Galaty, pp. 3–28. School for Advanced Research Press, Santa Fe.

Parkinson, W. A., and A. Gyucha 2012a Long-Term Social Dynamics and the Emergence of Hereditary Inequality: A Prehistoric Example from the Carpathian Basin. In *Beyond Elites: Alternatives to Hierarchical Systems in Modeling Social Formations,* The Proceedings of an International Conference at the Ruhr-Universität Bochum, Germany, October 22–24, 2009, edited by T. Keinlin, pp. 243–250. Ruhr-Universität, Bochum.

Parkinson, W. A., and A. Gyucha 2012b Tells in Perspective: Long-Term Patterns of Settlement Nucleation and Dispersal in Central and Southeast Europe. In *Tells: Social and Environmental Space,* Proceedings of the International Workshop "Socio-Environmental Dynamics over the last 12,000 Years: The Creation of Landscapes II," March 14–18, 2011, Kiel. Volume 3, edited by R. Hoffman, F.-K. Moetz, and J. Müller, pp. 105–116. Verlag Dr. Rudolf Habelt, Bonn.

Parkinson, W. A., R. W. Yerkes, and A. Gyucha 2010 The Social Dynamics of Emerging Complexity: A Long-Term Perspective on Middle Range Societies in the Prehistoric Carpathian Basin and the Eastern Woodlands. Invited paper presented in a symposium entitled *Trajectories to Complexity in Woodland Environments: Eastern North America and Temperate Europe Compared*, organized by D. Gronenborn and D. G. Anderson, at the 75th Annual Meeting of the Society for American Archaeology, St. Louis, April 14–18, 2010.

Parkinson, W. A., R. W. Yerkes, A. Gyucha, A. Sarris, R. Salisbury, and M. Morris 2010 Early Copper Age Settlement Organization on the Great Hungarian Plain: The Körös Regional Archaeological Project, 2000–2006. *Journal of Field Archaeology* 35(2):164–183.

Renfrew, C. 1970 The Autonomy of the South East European Copper Age. *Proceedings of the Prehistoric Society (New Series)* 35:12–47.

Renfrew, C. 1972 The *Emergence of Civilization: The Cyclades and the Aegean in the Third Millennium BC.* Oxbow Books, Oxford.

Saez, E., and G. Zucman 2016 Wealth Inequality in the United States since 1913: Evidence from Capitalized Income Tax Data. *Quarterly Journal of Economics* 131(2):519–578.

Siklósi, Z. 2004 Prestige Goods in the Neolithic of the Carpathian Basin: Material Manifestations of Social Differentiation. *Acta Archaeologica Scientiarum Hungaricae* 55(2004):1–62.

Yerkes, R. W., A. Gyucha, and W. A. Parkinson 2009 A Multi-Scalar Approach to Modeling the End of the Neolithic on the Great Hungarian Plain Using Calibrated Radiocarbon Dates. *Radiocarbon* 51:1071–1109.

CHAPTER FIVE

Long-Term Trends in Social Organization and Inequality in the Late Prehistoric Eurasian Steppes

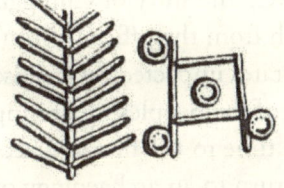

Bryan K. Hanks

> One day, at the time of his first rising to power . . . he drew an arrow from his
> quiver and gave it to [his sons]. Clearly it required no great strength to break it. He
> made the number two and so continued till there were fourteen, and even athletes
> were unable to break them. "So it is," he said, "with my sons also. So long as they
> tread the path of regard one for the another they shall be secure from the evils of
> events and shall be free to enjoy the fruits of their kingdom."
>
> —Story attributed to Chinggis Khan by Juvaini,
> "History of the World Conqueror"

INTRODUCTION

In studies of the ancient cultures of the Eurasian steppes one name routinely stands out as representing one of the most powerful rulers the world has known, Chinggis Khan (*Temüjin*). His rise to power is a remarkable example of a political career that did not rely on family ties and traditional lines of kinship but rather set out a completely new social order extended directly from organization of his household to the farthest reaches of his Empire. This political institution emphasized the strength of allegiance through deeds of honor and valor in combat and close personal relationships known as *anda* (blood brothers) and *nöker* (sworn followers). As David Christian notes, Chinggis Khan's *keshig* (imperial guard) initially included 70 day guards and 80 night guards but by AD 1206 it had grown to 10,000 men that were recruited from the junior lines of other tribes (1998:395–396). This provided the Khan with an exceptionally effective structure that tied representatives of tribal groups directly to his "household" and what was, in effect, the very hub of the Mongolian Empire.

As the narrative above portrays, the meteoric rise of Chinggis Khan's political power was founded on the remarkable ability to secure and maintain both personal and political relationships in a manner that in some ways departed substantially from those strategies of powerful rulers and polities that had preceded him. There is no question that this was effective, as the Mongolian Empire has been considered to represent the very pinnacle of pastoralist power in the Eurasian steppes in terms of consolidation of resources within Inner Asia and ability to exert physical and political force on powerful neighboring polities. In recent years, scholars have sought the antecedents of steppe pastoralist sociopolitical organization and power through archaeological study of Bronze Age and Iron Age groups that occupied the central and eastern steppes in the second and first millennia BC. The story of Chinggis Khan is richly detailed, largely as a result of historical sources both from the official chronicle of his reign and accounts from the multitude of peoples and states impacted by the rise and expansion of the Mongol Empire. Yet, these textual accounts of the peoples inhabiting the steppe lands fade quickly as we journey further back through time to the first and second millennia BC. Largely lacking in historical sources, we must turn to an archaeology of those periods in an attempt to answer questions surrounding social, political, and economic organization and how these institutions developed through time and, as the example of Chinggis Khan illustrates, changed remarkably in the space of a single individual's lifetime.

Scholars have long recognized that shifting patterns of material culture in the late prehistoric Eurasian steppes reflect vibrant transformations in social leadership, inequality, and status that also were intertwined with shifting patterns of subsistence, craft production and trade, conflict and violence, and new attitudes concerning death and burial as seen through elaborate funerary monument construction. To examine such processes over a temporal span of centuries and millennia, representative of a *longue durée* historical perspective, is archetypal of archaeological interpretation. This view, when considered in the context of Eurasian steppe pastoralist societies, effectually emphasizes multiple trajectories of social development and acknowledges that many of these emerged and declined due to diverse sets of socionatural variables. However, the identification, and physical nature, of archaeological evidence differs substantially in many regions. For example, settlement and mortuary evidence is relatively well identified for the second millennium in many regions of the steppes. However, clear settlement patterns are less observable by the first millennium BC, as conventional explanations posit that pastoralist communities utilized greater levels of spatial mobility that became seasonally conditioned. This "invisibility" of mobile pastoralist populations has been widely discussed by scholars and it seems clear that occupation evidence does exist but that new methods of field survey and targeted excavation will need to be employed to gain a clearer identification and understanding of such patterns of movement and occupation. The important point here, however, is that the relationship of settlement and mortuary evidence to interpretive understandings of social organization of late prehistoric pastoralist communities must engage with how these patterns relate to social institutions that have long-term duration as opposed to those that reflect momentary events and episodes of collective action. Settlements, on the one hand, frequently reflect the rather abstract accumulation of patterned human action over several generations. Cemeteries can provide such information as well, but are more definable in terms of representing singular events of ritual action through interment of individual social members. Our ability, therefore, to address specific questions about the nature of social organization and inequality in these early societies must contend with how such institutions are represented across temporal scales of human action through the archaeological evidence we may recover from such sites.

As this paper examines, an understanding of social organization and inequality in the late prehistoric Eurasian steppes must work toward more effective understandings of long-term diachronic change as a composite of *episodic transitions* and significant *events* that reflect historical social processes and material conditions. To explore these issues, a case study from the Southern Ural Mountains region of the Russian Federation will be discussed against the background of broader temporal patterns from the second and first millennia BC.

Archaeological evidence suggests that this region experienced tremendous social, economic, and political change during late prehistory, including the appearance of new forms of nucleated settlement and spoke-wheeled chariot technology by 2100 BC. By approximately 1200 BC, demographic disaggregation and a trend toward mobile pastoralism seem to have been well under way, and previous social institutions changed significantly. However, before moving into a more detailed presentation of this case study, it is useful to consider some of the recent theoretical approaches to inequality and social organization in prehistory and the variety of methods being employed to index these important social phenomena.

RECENT APPROACHES TO INEQUALITY IN THE PAST

The Seventh IEMA Visiting Scholar conference in 2014 focused attention on interdisciplinary investigations of inequality in the ancient world. One of the key goals of this symposium was to work out whether a general theory of inequality could be established for antiquity and to what degree interdisciplinary perspectives would aid in this effort. As an anthropological archaeologist, I have considered the subject of inequality as deeply embedded within the topic of social complexity and long-term trajectories of social and political change and development. Recent scholarship continues to highlight the necessity of comparative, cross-culture studies of these important processes and it is clear that there is still much to learn from the myriad ways by which inequality becomes manifest within human societies and the variety of pathways this takes in terms of long-term social change (Flannery and Marcus 2012; Smith 2012; Vaughn et al. 2009).

Comparative studies, such as these, commonly focus on small-scale and middle-range societies and key variables of human behavior linked to decision making beyond the household and kin group levels, access to and control of material wealth and other resources, and the institutionalization of multigenerational leadership and inequality (Vaughn et al. 2009). The study of such issues has been a key element of comparative processual approaches within archaeology for several decades (Johnson and Earle 2000). In recent years, a reinvigoration of such approaches has appeared and some scholars have devoted considerable energy toward the discussion of improving comparative approaches to the study of social complexity through more effective uses of primary data sets from multiple regions of the world (Smith 2012).

There also have been efforts to bridge the emphasis on structure, process, and authority, common to processual approaches within archaeology, with trends that are more post-processual in nature that highlight individual agency, social identity, and materiality. For example, in a recent comparative study of European Bronze Age societies, Earl and Kristiansen suggest that such multiscalar approaches might "capture the active linkages in societies among economy, identity, and politics—linkages that help us understand how human action results in broad social transformations" (2010:4).

Even though the subject of "inequality," as a key element of social organization in early societies, has been a widely discussed theme, theoretical and methodological approaches to inequality are being revitalized in thought-provoking ways. Certainly, postmodernist shifts across the social sciences and humanities over the past three decades have brought about more nuanced theoretical approaches to the dynamics of societies and individuals in archaeological practice (Hodder 2001; Hodder and Hutson 2003). At the same time, resurgence in the comparative study of early societies is making use of decades of detailed archaeological research, and multiple strands of social and environmental data, from around the world, in an attempt to produce more empirically grounded models of social change in the human past. Such approaches seek to account for the emergence of larger, more centralized communities that led to early states and, in some cases, to the nation-states that largely define the world of today. New approaches to modeling socionatural dynamics through the use of computer simulation also have been advanced and are providing novel ways of exploring the multivariate nature of human dynamics and their relationship to local and regional environmental variables (Kohler and Gumerman 2000; Barton et al. 2012).

Fortunately, case studies from the Eurasian steppes are becoming increasingly a part of such comparative treatments, and this has helped to bring important new perspectives into the study of early steppe societies in addition to stimulating greater awareness to the value of this region of the world and its influence on perceptions of world prehistory. As an archaeologist specializing in the study of the Eurasian steppes, I have spent the past two decades working in many regions that were formerly a part of the Soviet Union. Opportunities to do so have increased rapidly since 1991, and the archaeology and prehistory of this vast region of the world has become more accessible and of much greater significance to current understandings of world prehistory. Certainly for later prehistory, the Eurasian steppes have been traditionally viewed as rather peripheral to the rise of early civilizations within China, the Near East, and Europe. This view is beginning to change as knowledge of this immense region becomes more widely disseminated in multiple languages and as scholars have considered more carefully the fascinating trajectories of social, cultural, and political development for the region (Anthony 2007; Frachetti 2008; Hanks and Linduff 2009; Honeychurch 2015).

Social Organization and Inequality:
A Case Study from the Urals

In this section of the paper, I wish to examine some key developments in the southeastern Ural Mountains and adjacent regions. This geographical area represents the eastern pene-plain zone of the Urals and contains a variety of environmental resources that were crucial for early populations including: timber, grassland, water, and copper and other mineral resources. Since 2007, I have been co-directing the Sintashta Collaborative Archaeology Research Project (SCARP), which has examined evidence relating to social, economic, and political change from approximately 2100–1500 BC. Regional-scale pedestrian survey, in addition to geochemical and geophysical surveys and targeted excavations at identified settlements and cemeteries, have produced diverse archaeological data ranging from as early as the Paleolithic through to the early Soviet Period. While focused on research questions connected with key transitions in the first half of the second millennium BC, the project also has yielded a unique view of long-term transitions in subsistence economies, settlement patterning, cultural contact and trade, and funerary monument construction and use (Hanks and Doonan 2009; Johnson and Hanks 2012; Doonan et al. 2014). We have made progress toward answering many of the original questions we set out to investigate and in the process of doing so, as is inevitably the case, a variety of fascinating new ones have emerged.

The Sintashta archaeological culture has become internationally well known in recent years, and a variety of theories have been put forth to account for this development (Jones-Bley and Zdanovich 2002; Hanks and Linduff 2009). Initial studies by Soviet archeologists identified a rather unique pattern of 22 nucleated settlements situated in the northern steppe zone of the Southeastern Urals on tributaries of the Ural and Tobol rivers. The identification and study of these sites benefited directly from advances in the methods of air photo interpretation during the late Soviet Period (Batanina and Hanks 2013). Sintashta settlements frequently have associated cemeteries, although additional cemeteries producing Sintashta-type artifacts have been reported in the southwestern Urals and just across the border to the east in Kazakhstan. Radiocarbon dating has provided a date range of 2100–1750 cal. BC for these sites (Hanks et al. 2007).

Nucleated settlements vary in size, but most range from approximately 1.5 to 3.5 hectares and are constructed in a circular and/or rectangular fashion. Most exhibit one to four phases of construction that appear to represent diachronic growth in households. Rectangular house structures appear to be contained within the confines of the enclosure ditch and bank and are placed immediately adjacent to one another in either a concentric fashion (within circular settlements) or linear rows (rectangular). Floor areas of house structures range from 100 to 250 square meters (Koryakova and Epimakhov 2007).

Cemeteries have yielded fascinating finds that include evidence of spoke wheeled chariots and related horse harnessing gear, copper alloy weaponry, and animal sacrifice. In almost all cases, the cemeteries are comprised of multiple burials placed within low relief burial mounds. Some burial complexes include shallow surrounding ditches and additional deposits of animal remains in small pits. The eponymous cemetery site *Sintashta*, located along the Sintashta River, is the only site known to date that yielded evidence of distributed burial pits not clustered under mound features.

David Anthony has argued that several factors, including a shift in climate, nucleated settlement patterning, long-distance trade, and the development of new forms of warfare technology such as the chariot, coalesced at the end of the third millennium BC and brought about the "genesis" of the Sintashta archaeological pattern (Anthony 2007; 2009). Sintashta cemeteries, with their lavish animal sacrifice with frequent deposits of weaponry and chariots and/or partial horse carcasses and harnessing accouterments, reflected the emergence of elites within these societies. He further argues that the scale of animal sacrifice in some of the graves and larger kurgan complexes represents chiefly feasts that brought together hundreds if not thousands of people from the immediate region as part of sociopolitical processes including funerary constructions and elite aggrandizement (Anthony 2009:62–63).

Kristiansen and Larsson, in the context of discussing the European Bronze Age and the transmission of prestige symbols, also have underscored the complexity of Sintashta societies and chiefly elites and warfare technology, in particular, the chariot (2005). These views are consistent with a long-term trend in archaeological interpretation that has placed emphasis on the search for evidence of rank and inequality within early societies and how variability in mortuary evidence reflects this (Binford 1971; Brown 1981; Chapman 1987; Gilman 1981).

Some regional scholars in Russia, however, have taken a more conservative view of Sintashta funerary remains and have suggested that the funerary evidence does not provide a clear pattern of social status and hierarchy when considering factors such as spatial layout, tomb elaboration, and specific categories of grave goods (Epimakhov 2002:144; Vinogradov 1995; 2003:274). A survey by Andrei Epimakhov (2002) of five of the most significant Sintashta cemeteries indicates that of 242 individuals, 181 contained artifacts and of these 65 contained weaponry in the form of bronze knives, bronze or stone projectile points and bronze axes. Interestingly, only 79 of the 242 individuals were adults and of these only 43 had weaponry. Of these 43 adults, only 13 were assigned a gender and of these 11 were biologically sexed as male. What is important in terms of these general characteristics is that nearly half of all recovered Sintashta-period individuals are adolescents and children and of the adult burials very few of them have been reliably sexed. While chariot burials and weaponry are noteworthy for this region, the inclusion of such material culture hints at a much more complex picture of mortuary practice and symbolism.

For example, a recent book by Elena Kupriyanov (2008) has focused on dress, ornamentation, and grave goods connected specifically with women and female gender in Sintashta-Petrovka period societies (Middle Bronze Age, 2100 to 1750 BC) and Late Petrovka and Alakul' societies (Late Bronze Age, 1750 to 1550 BC). This research has indicated that the emphasis on male elite warriors by many foreign scholars has overshadowed more nuanced understandings of gender, age, status, and social identity among Bronze Age communities in this region of the steppe and how social identities may have changed during this period (Kupriyanova 2008). An interesting example of this is grave pit 17 in the Stepnoye VII cemetery in the Southern Urals of Russia. This burial, attributed to the early phase of the Petrovka culture (possibly synchronous with the Sintashta phase), was excavated in 1990 and yielded the remains of three individuals, two of which were buried together and posed in an embrace with arms interlocked. This couple, both aged between 15–17 years of age, was biologically sexed with the male on the western side of the grave pit and the female in the center. The third individual, placed in the eastern side of the grave pit and posed facing the embraced couple, was aged between 35–55 years and was biologically sexed as a female. Aside from the intriguing positioning of the skeletons, the young couple represents a very interesting pattern in terms of their associated grave goods. The "male" on the western side was dressed in what is presumed to be female dress and ornamentation, with highly ornate bronze medallions that were likely part of a face covering, a long ornamented headdress, and a bronze battle axe that was placed in "his" extended left hand. In general, it should be noted that male burials in this region rarely contain evidence of metal ornamentation. The "female" in the middle was not buried with any metal ornamentation. While the biological sexing of these subadults might be inaccurate due to their age, the fact that the "male" buried with "female" ornamentation was placed with a battle-axe is very unusual. Even if the biological sexing is incorrect and this is a female individual, it is very unusual to see a combination of weaponry (copper alloy axe) with ornamentation typically found with adult females.

There are instances where adult males have been recovered with female-style ornamentation from Bronze Age graves in the southern Urals and northwestern Kazakhstan. These include the site of Bestamak 1, grave pit 21 (adult male aged 50+ years), Krivoe Ozero, kurgan 10, burial 1 and burial 3 (two adult males aged 25–30 years and 50–55 years respectively) and the cemetery of Tanabergen 2, wherein burial 36 in kurgan 7 contained the remains of a male 30–36 years with finger rings and small ornaments (Kupriyanova 2008:155).

Another interesting Sintashta burial recovered from kurgan 2 (burial pit 8) at the Kamennyi Ambar 5 cemetery complex (located near the Kamennyi Ambar settlement) yielded evidence for the inclusion of a chariot, sacrificial animals (cattle and horses), bone cheek pieces associated with the harnessing of horses, and weaponry in the form of two stone mace heads and stone projectile points. Individuals placed in the grave pit include a male approximately 27 years of age with three children: one approximately nine years, one between four and five years, and a neonate. A recent physical anthropological analysis of the human remains from three kurgan complexes at the Kamennyi Ambar 5 cemetery, including burial pit 8, indicated that the older male showed no evidence of paleotrauma, significant bone robusticity or notable musculoskeletal stress markers. In a society where social mobility has been interpreted as based on achieved status in warfare and the control and display of wealth, the actual "osteobiography" of this individual provides no clues as to a particularly eventful life in terms of stressful activities or episodes of trauma (Judd et al. 2008). Furthermore, his interment in a peripheral burial within the kurgan complex with three children impedes our appeal for a straightforward interpretation of what such burials could, or should, signify. Certainly one can consider such burials as signs of possible elite status, although the high degree of variability of such burials during the Sintashta period

encourages us to look for more nuanced understandings of mortuary ritual and their connection with changing social practices and organization. This includes the deposit of weaponry and other "high-status" grave goods (Hanks et al. 2015).

The Sintashta development has persisted as one of the most vibrant case studies within
discussions of social complexity within the steppes during the late prehistoric period. However, archaeological teams working in the region have begun to document an intriguing way
of life at this time when the rhythms of the seasons, the complex nature of human-animal
and human-environmental relationships, and long-term transitions in the demographic and
social organization of populations changed in the second half of the second millennium
BCE. The work of the SCARP team, in conjunction with previous work by Russian colleagues at the Sintashta settlement of Ust'ye, and associated cemetery of Solntse II, has
begun to document such changes. Geophysical surveys, additional excavation, and radiocarbon dating have illustrated demographic growth at the settlement over three major cultural
phases, spanning the Middle to Late Bronze Age: Phase I (Sintashta) 2030–1770 cal. BC;
Phase II (Petrovka) 1880–1740 cal. BC; Phase III (Alakul'-Srubnaya) 1670–1500 cal. BC
(Vinogradov 2013; Hanks et al. 2007; Hanks et al. 2013). This settlement, like others,
has not revealed any clear patterning of social inequality through the excavation of house
structures and associated material finds. Quite the contrary, Sintashta-period settlements
reflect great similarity in the size of houses, and spatial positioning relative to others. This
stands in contrast to cemeteries, which appear to indicate the disposal of select members of
the community.

The Solntse II cemetery, located directly across the river to the north from the Ust'ye
settlement, reveals an incredible history of use ranging from the Sintashta period all the
way up to the present day as a contemporary Muslim population in the neighboring village
of Solntse continues to bury their deceased at this site. The cemetery, therefore, represents
nearly 4,000 years of use with Bronze Age, Iron Age, Medieval, and contemporary populations using this location to inter their dead. What is particularly fascinating is that the
prehistoric component of the cemetery is not large in terms of number of burial complexes
or burials. Rather, it appears that the placement of a few members of the societies was
important. Geophysical surveys throughout the prehistoric features within the cemetery
have indicated that additional burials are not present between the mound complexes. One
might argue that the cemetery was reserved only for elite members of the societies, and
that may have indeed been the case. However, just as important, it appears that placement
of these individuals also represents an appropriation of the location through time, with
larger Iron Age mound complexes being built, in some cases, directly over earlier Bronze
Age mounds. In fact, the placement of the historical, fenced Muslim cemetery was placed
directly over two or more prehistoric burial mounds. Excavation and dating at the Ust'ye
settlement indicates that the settlement was occupied through the Middle and Late Bronze
Age but then was abandoned in the last centuries of the second millennium BC. The cemetery, in contrast, witnessed continued use for several thousands of years.

As discussed above, populations by the Late to Final Bronze Age became more dispersed and likely more conditioned by an annual cycle that included greater seasonal mobility with their domestic herds. Settlement evidence within the valley is not known for the

Iron Age, however, burial mounds from this period dot the landscape and were placed in strategic locations that might have been important in terms of marking ancestral rights and appropriation of important resources for watering and grazing herds. Evidence today would seem to support that view, as contemporary herders from the Solntse village construct a summer seasonal camp for cattle directly adjacent to their fenced cemetery area within the Solntse II mortuary complex. It is intriguing to consider the power of this place through time and use of the dead as a way of legitimizing access and control over crucial environmental resources.

In regions farther to the east, the Iron Age is well represented by prominent tombs that have been interpreted as representing the emergence of powerful new tribes and chiefdoms in the first millennium BC. It is worthwhile to consider some of this evidence here and to identify key material patterns relating to social organization and representations of inequality.

THE EARLY IRON AGE

The transition from the Final Bronze Age to the Early Iron Age (approximately 1200 to 800 BC) represents a radical change within many areas of the Eurasian steppes. Such change includes a general decrease in permanent settlement sites, the appearance of new, large-scale funerary monuments and what has been seen as a transition to more institutionalized mounted warfare. While some scholars continue to debate the earliest evidence for horse domestication and riding, many scholars agree that mounted warfare really took shape only in the first centuries of the first millennium BC (Hanks 2003; Koryakova 1996; Renfrew 1998).

It is important to note that an interesting pattern also emerges in the central Eurasian steppes region, encompassing parts of present day Russia, Western Siberia, Mongolia, and Kazakhstan. It is in this region that we see some of the earliest large-scale monument constructions, such as Arzhan I with its 160 sacrificed horses and complex wood and stone architecture (dating to the ninth century BC), and the more recently excavated Arzhan II (dating to the seventh century BC) (Chugunov et al. 2004). It is also within the Altai Mountains that the famed Pazyryk frozen tombs have been investigated with the chance preservation of a rich array of organic remains. These include felt and textile carpets and patterned cutouts, wood carvings, preserved human bodies, sacrificed horses and accompanying riding equipment (e.g., headdresses and other flamboyant accessories) (Gryaznov 1950; Rudenko 1953; 1970). Such materials provide a rare opportunity in terms of preservation to see how objects and decorative symbolism were intertwined in unique ways. Such a view might be somewhat biased, since such preservation is for the most part absent for other periods of the Iron Age. Nevertheless, these burials provide a unique view of the material vibrancy of these groups and must be considered in terms of understanding changing attitudes toward social inequality and power.

The Eurasian steppe Iron Age has been characterized as the "Scythian Epoch" and has been traditionally concerned with the ethnogenesis and migration of what are thought to be the historical Scythians as discussed by Herodotus (1996). Such interpretations frequently focus on what is termed the "Scythian triad," which is perceived as a widespread mortuary pattern that yields objects decorated with animal-style art, weaponry, and horse riding accessories. Rather than highlighting the diversity associated with the inclusion of such objects within burials, the general pattern of interpretation has been used to infer movements of Scythian tribes within the western Eurasian steppe region. Some scholars have criticized the connection of this very broad pattern of martial symbolism with specific ethno-genetic theories (Yablonsky 2000:3–4). This is an important trend and one that emphasizes much greater variety of social and cultural change connected with Iron Age groups in the vast Eurasian steppe zone, including the eastern steppe zone and Mongolia, and the variety of ways in which grave goods were placed with the deceased during this time (Yablonsky 2000).

In recent years, several important research projects have brought to light important Late Bronze Age to Early Iron Age developments in these regions (Allard and Erdenebaatar 2005; Bayarsaikhan 2005; Fitzhugh et al. 2005). One of the most important facts to emerge has been the recent dating and exploration of several large monumental complexes known as *khirigsuurs* in the Mongolian region. These large monumental sites are comprised of stone central mounds (some with human and animal remains) with surrounding square or rectangular "fences" made of surface stones and peripheral cist features containing sacrificed animal parts (often horse skulls and metapodials). The large khirigsuur site known as *Urt Bulagyn* contains nearly 1,700 such cist features with horse skulls and metapodial elements (Allard and Erdenebaatar 2005). The appearance of such monuments has been discussed in terms of how they connect with regional integration, new forms of ritual practice, and an overall trend in greater levels of social complexity (Houle 2009). Another important aspect of these sites is that they date closely to, or in some cases predate (BP 2970–2780 and BP 2980–2770—Houle 2009:365), some of the earliest Iron Age tombs in the Altai region of Russia (Arzhan I and II noted above).

Khirigsuur complexes also occasionally contain stelae known as "deer stones," which yield some of the earliest evidence for iconographic and figurative engravings. However, research has also shown that deer stone complexes, either single stones or groups of stones within a larger ritual complex, are relatively contemporaneous with the emergence of khirigsuurs. Previous scholarship assumed that deer stones postdated the Scythian development, although recent dating programs have now overturned this understanding and it has been proven that they predate early Iron Age monuments such as Arzhan I by several hundred years (Fitzhugh 2009). Deer stones and Khirigsuur complexes, therefore, represent an extremely important horizon of development in terms of large-scale monument building and the creation and use of stone markers. Deer stones are understood as having much deeper roots in Eurasian cosmology and provide an important example of how a particular form of material culture changed through time as it was appropriated and rearticulated within new cultural contexts (Hanks 2010; Jacobson 1983; 1993).

An important feature associated with the use of deer stones is a notable change in engraving from symbolic iconography (e.g., stylized cervid figures with elongated noses that appear birdlike, a tripartite scheme with discs and other symbols near the top, etc.) to more anthropomorphic forms that co-opt the tripartite structure and infer a neckline and beltline.

These frequently represent attached or associated weaponry in the form of bows, swords, axes, daggers, and whetstones. It has been argued that, in conjunction with the excavation of the preserved male from Pazyryk Barrow 2, which yielded a complex variety of tattooed imagery, such iconography might have been connected with tattooing of warriors and elites during the Early Iron Age (Jettmar 1994). Such developments suggest that attitudes to the body, particularly in the case of warriors and associated materiality, had deep historical roots within the Eurasian region but that attitudes surrounding the body as a nexus for violence and status began to evolve in new ways (Hanks 2008). The broader historical nature of these developments is something that has often been overlooked in the scholarship of the region, as emphasis is placed on ethnocultural interpretations.

The period of time that spans the emergence of khirigsuur monuments and deer stones in the Mongolian Late Bronze Age, to the construction of the large Arzhan I and II tombs in the Early Iron Age, to the Pazyryk tombs that date from the third to second centuries BC, all indicate important historical shifts in cultural attitudes surrounding the body and its connection to martial symbolism and efficacy. From an initial focus on large scale monument constructions, which indicate corporate or network structured sociopolitical events, to greater individuality in terms of burial trappings and the utilization of various themes including animal-style art, suggest that the construction of social identity and personhood developed in important new directions. It is particularly the development of animal-style art that indicates several stages of development from initial traditional motifs encompassing the stag and early deer stones, perhaps from Mongolia, and what have been seen as the large stone tomb and ritual complexes called khirigsuurs. Animal-style art themes then become incorporated and rearticulated in new ways, with the Arzhan I tomb indicating some of the earliest animal-style themes with accompanying deer stones and a large feline plaque that is believed to have formed part of a breastplate for a horse (Bokovenko 1995). Within approximately 500 years from the first Arzhan tomb we begin to see the use of animal-style art by Pazyryk groups in vibrant new ways. For example, a variety of motifs emerge that include hybrid animals connected with tattooing on individuals and predator-prey compositions connected with horse masks and costumes.

When viewing this region of the Eurasian steppe for the Late Bronze Age to Early Iron Age, it seems that we have several clear horizons of development connected with traditional forms of cosmological symbolism and the appropriation and (re)articulation of such practices into new forms of material agency linked to individual identity construction and in some cases martial efficacy and power. Koryakova has noted several important patterns for the Urals and the Western Siberian plain, whereby large kurgan complexes with singular burials, usually adult males or adult males with females, give way to smaller kurgan complexes with multiple burials (Koryakova 1996). Such a transition may reflect a general shift in emphasis from the high status of singular leaders to kinship groupings and an overall general stabilization of the region after a period of territorial conflict and sociopolitical growth.

These later mortuary complexes contain more burials and offer an important opportunity to look at patterns of deposition connected with grave goods, animal sacrifice, tomb construction, and spatial layout of grave pits. What is particularly interesting during this time are burials connected with what may be perceived as important age grade transitions within these early societies. Such burials contain subadults with weaponry and riding accessories and may be considered important markers in terms of age grades. Interestingly, such burials have often led to intense discussion over female Amazon warriors within the steppe region, particularly connected with the Sauro/Sarmation period in the Southern Urals of Russia and parts of present-day Ukraine (Davis-Kimball 2002). Unfortunately, the unreliable sexing of subadult skeletons has led to the problematic interpretation of "warrior" burials. A good example of this is the burial of a 12-year-old subadult at the Sarmatian period cemetery of Pokrovka in Southern Urals Russia. This individual was interpreted as a "warrior-priestess" as a result of the accompanying grave goods, which included 40 bronze arrowheads, a quiver, iron dagger, and animal tooth amulet (Davis-Kimball 2002). Such an interpretation is based on a direct reading of the included grave goods as the property of the deceased with little acknowledgment of the agency of the living in the mortuary process. The problem of understanding such patterning in terms of its relationship to social structure and agency has been discussed recently for Iron Age burials in Europe (Arnold 1995; 2001).

In the Pokrovka case, the problem is not whether males or females were warriors but rather how we as archaeologists interpret the meaning surrounding the deposit of weaponry with the deceased. It is a fact that very few burials in the steppe region contain what might be considered a standard "kit" or assemblage for Iron Age warriors. Rather, objects that we might include within the category of weaponry might have had multiple meanings, and therefore the deposit of such items may have much more to say about familial status as well during periods of less intense conflict. This issue in conjunction with how the deposit of weaponry co-varies with age and sex and other grave good items, is something that requires a great deal more analysis and thought in the future.

Conclusion

In this paper, I have emphasized long-term patterns of historical change connected with warfare, weaponry, and the unique symbolism and "value" that surround the role of such materiality in the creation of individual identities and inequality. The narrative of Chinggis Khan introduced at the beginning of the paper emphasized the need for scholars to recognize that long-term social institutions and inequality can suddenly rupture and be reworked in completely new ways. As archaeologists working on such issues in prehistory, we are challenged by such dynamic transformations within our efforts to tease patterns from multiple strands of data.

The discussion in this chapter has reviewed some of these patterns known from the central Eurasian steppes. When viewed over the *longue durée*, it is clear that social inequality played an important role in the organization of societies in the first and second millennia BC. Yet, the nature of this inequality took on many different forms in concert with changing historical conditions. Comparative studies of inequality in early societies are helpful in considering more effectively what role such sociopolitical dynamics may have played within these societies but this author is doubtful that a "general theory of inequality" can be utilized. Rather, it is important to work steadfastly toward greater contextual, and historically situated, understandings of power, inequality, and social identity and how such phenomena might be materially represented through archaeological study.

In terms of how this would integrate with future studies of such issues in the context of the prehistoric Eurasian steppes, I believe it is helpful to consider more thoughtfully the publication of the very first IEMA conference in 2008, which focused on the application of historical analysis to the duration of long-term structures and the significant role of "events" in contributing to this (Bolender 2010).

The material record of the late prehistoric Eurasian steppes is robust when considering eventful archaeology—with the multitude of earthen and stone funerary monuments that mark the passing of such events and their representation within the landscape and in the minds of people dwelling within those regions. Such markers are a powerful reminder of the collective efforts of communities and so too of the social power of the individuals interred within these monuments. In some ways, the emphasis on mortuary archaeology has presented a rather skewed view of the past in these regions, as more detailed excavation and interpretation of settlements will provide a deeper understanding of the rhythms and tempos of early life in these regions. Such an archaeological record of human life and patterned agency stands in contrast to the abrupt markers of death and commemoration surrounding highly visible burial monuments. The construction of such monuments was in many cases a statement of historically situated sociopolitical power but also was intertwined within the social memory of future generations in new ways. Such patterns represent an important relationship between how individual identity and memory were constructed within these early societies and ultimately how communities chose to commemorate their dead and rearticulate social meaning and structure.

ACKNOWLEDGMENTS

I would like to thank the organizers of the IEMA conference for their kind invitation to participate and for their patience in the preparation of this contribution. I would also like to thank all of the team members of SCARP for their hard work and dedication over the years. It has been a remarkable journey.

REFERENCES

Allard, F., and D. Erdenebaatar 2005 Khirigsuurs, Ritual and Mobility in the Bronze Age of Mongolia. *Antiquity* 79:547–563.

Anthony, D. 2009 The Sintashta Genesis: The Roles of Climate Change, Warfare, and Long-Distance Trade. In *Social Complexity in the Eurasian Steppe: Monuments, Metals, and Mobility*, edited by B. Hanks and K. Linduff, pp. 47–73. Cambridge University Press, Cambridge.

Anthony, D. 2007 *The Horse, the Wheel, and Language. How Bronze Age Riders from the Eurasian Steppes Shaped the Modern World.* Princeton University Press, Princeton.

Anthony, D., and N. Vinogradov 1995 Birth of the Chariot. *Archaeology* 48:36–41.

Arnold, B. 2001 The Limits of Agency in the Analysis of Elite Iron Age Celtic Burials. *Journal of Social Archaeology* 1(2):210–224.

Arnold, B. 1995 Honorary Males or Women of Substance? Gender, Status, and Power in Iron-Age Europe. *Journal of European Archaeology* 3(2):153–168.

Barton, M. C., I. I. T. Ullah, S. M. Bergin, H. Mitasova, and H. Sarjoughian 2012 Looking for the Future in the Past: Long-term Change in Socioecological Systems. *Ecological Modelling* 241:42–53.

Batanina, N., and B. Hanks 2012 Soviet Period Air Photography and Archeology of the Bronze Age in the Southern Urals of Russia. In *Archaeology from Historical Aerial and Satellite Archives*, edited by William S. Hanson and Ioana A. Oltean, pp. 199–219. Springer, London.

Bayarsaikhan, J. 2005 Shamanistic Elements in Mongolian Deer Stone Art. In *The Deer Stone Project: Anthropological Studies in Mongolia 2002–2004*, edited by W. Fitzhugh, J. Bayarsaikhan, and P. Marsh, pp. 41–53. Smithsonian Institution, Washington, District of Columbia.

Binford, L. 1971 Mortuary Practices: Their Study and Their Potential. *American Antiquity* 3(2):6–29.

Bokovenko, N. 2006 The Emergence of the Tagar Culture. *Antiquity* 80(310):860–879.

Bokovenko, N. 1995 Scythian Culture in the Altai Mountains. In *Nomads of the Eurasian Steppes in the Early Iron Age*, edited by J. Davis-Kimball, V. Bashilov, and L. Yablonsky, pp. 285–295. Zinat Press, Berkeley.

Bolender, D. J. (ed.) 2010 *Eventful Archaeologies: New Approaches to Social Transformation in the Archaeological Record*. State University of New York Press, Albany.

Brown, J. 1981 The Search for Rank in Prehistoric Burials. In *The Archaeology of Death*, edited by R. Chapman, I. Kinnes, and K. Randsborg, pp. 25–37. Cambridge University Press, Cambridge.

Chapman, R. 2003 *Archaeologies of Complexity*. Routledge, London.

Christian, D. 1998 *A History of Russia, Central Asia and Mongolia: Volume I, Inner Eurasia from Prehistory to the Mongol Empire*. Blackwell, Oxford.

Chugunov, K., H. Parzinger, and A. Nagler 2004 Arzhan 2: la tombe d'un prince scythe en Sibérie du Sud. Rapport préliminaire des fouilles russo-allemandes de 2000–2002. *Arts Asiatiques* 59:5–29.

Davis-Kimball, J., with M. Behan 2002 *Warrior Women: An Archaeologist's Search for History's Hidden Heroines*. Warner Books, New York.

Doonan, R., and B. Hanks 2014 Metals, Society, and Economy in the Late Prehistoric Eurasian Steppe. In *Archaeometallurgy in Global Perspective: Methods and Syntheses*, edited by B. W. Roberts and C. P. Thornton, pp. 755–784. Springer, New York.

Epimakhov, A. 2002 Complex Societies and the Possibilities to Diagnose them on the Basis of Archaeological Data: Sintashta Type Sites of the Middle Bronze Age of the Trans-Urals. In *Complex Societies of Central Eurasia from the Third to the First Millennia BC: Regional Specifics in the light of global models, Vol. 1*, edited by K. Jones-Bley and D. Zdanovich, pp. 139–147. Institute for the Study of Man, Washington, District of Columbia.

Epimakhov, A. 2005 *Ranniye Kompleksniye Obshyestva Severa Tzentral'noi Evrazii (po materialam mogil'nika Kamennyi Ambar-5), Kniga 1*. Nauk, Chelyabinsk.

Earle, T. 1997 *How Chiefs Come to Power: The Political Economy in Prehistory*. Stanford University Press, Stanford.

Earle, T., and K. Kristiansen 2010 *Organizing Bronze Age Societies: The Mediterranean, Central Europe, and Scandinavia Compared.* Cambridge University Press, Cambridge.

Fitzhugh, W., J. Bayarsaikhan, and P. Marsh (eds.) 2005 *The Deer Stone Project: Anthropological Studies in Mongolia 2002—2004.* Arctic Studies Center, Washington, District of Columbia.

Flannery, K., and J. Marcus 2012 *The Creation of Inequality: How our Prehistoric Ancestors Set the Stage for Monarchy, Slavery, and Empire.* Harvard University Press, Cambridge.

Frachetti, M. D. 2008 *Pastoralist Landscapes and Social Interaction in Bronze Age Eurasia.* University of California Press, Berkeley.

Gilman, A. 1981 The Development of Social Stratification in Bronze Age Europe. *Current Anthropology* 22:1–23.

Gryaznov, M. 1950 *Pervyi Pazyrykskii Kurgan (The First Pazyryk Kurgan.)* Cresset Press, London.

Gryaznov, M. 1980 *Arzhan: tsarskiy kurgan ranneskifskogo vremeni (Arzhan: A Royal Kurgan of the Early Scythian Period).* Nauk, Leningrad.

Hanks, B., R. Doonan, D. Pitman, E. Kupriyanova, and D. Zdanovich 2015 Eventful Deaths—Eventful Lives? Bronze Age Mortuary Practices in the Late Prehistoric Eurasian Steppes (2100–1500 BC). In *Death Shall Have no Dominion,* edited by C. Renfrew, M. Boyd, and I. Morley, pp. 328–347. Cambridge University Press, Cambridge.

Hanks, B., I. Chechushkov, R. Doonan, D. Pitman, B. Music, I. Medaric, and M. Mori 2013 Noveishiye rezul'taty i perspektivy issledovanii mikroraiona drevnego rasseleniya Ust'ye i doliny reki Nizhnii Toguzak. In *Ust'ye,* edited by N. B. Vinogradov, pp. 393–416. Arbis, Chelyabinsk.

Hanks, B. 2010 Agency, Hybridity, and Transmutation: Theorizing Human-Animal Symbolism among Early Eurasian Steppe Societies. In *Master of Animals in Old World Iconography,* edited by D. Counts and B. Arnold, pp. 175–191. Archaeolingua, Budapest.

Hanks, B. 2009 Modeling Early Metallurgical Production and Societal Organization in the Bronze Age of North Central Eurasia. In *Social Complexity in Prehistoric Eurasia: Monuments, Metals, and Mobility,* edited by B. Hanks and K. Linduff, pp. 146–167. Cambridge University Press, Cambridge.

Hanks, B., and R. Doonan 2009 From Scale to Practice: A New Agenda for the Study of Early Metallurgy on the Eurasian Steppe. *Journal of World Prehistory* 22:329–356.

Hanks, B., and K. Linduff (eds.) 2009 *Social Complexity in Prehistoric Eurasia: Monuments, Metals, and Mobility.* Cambridge University Press, Cambridge.

Hanks, B. 2008 Reconsidering Warfare, Status, and Gender in the Eurasian Steppe Iron Age. In *Are All Warriors Male? Gender Roles on the Ancient Eurasian Steppe,* edited by K. Linduff and K. Rubinson, pp. 15–34. AltaMira Press, New York.

Hanks, B., A. Epimakhov, and C. Renfrew 2007 Towards a Refined Chronology of the Bronze Age of the Southern Urals, Russia. *Antiquity* 81:333–367.

Herodotus 1996 *Herodotus: The Histories.* John Marincola revision of the translation by Aubrey De Selincourt. Penguin Books, London.

Hodder, I. (ed.) 2001 *Archaeological Theory Today.* Polity Press, Oxford.

Hodder, I., and S. Hutson 2003 *Reading the Past: Current Approaches to Interpretation in Archaeology,* 3rd Edition. Cambridge University Press, Cambridge.

Honeychurch, W. 2015 *Inner Asia and the Spatial Politics of Empire: Archeology, Mobility, and Culture Contact.* Springer-Verlag, New York.

Houle, J.-L. 2009 Social Integrative Facilities and the Emergence of Societal Complexity on the Mongolian Steppe. In *Social Complexity in Prehistoric Eurasia: Monuments, Metals, and Mobility*, edited by B. Hanks and K. Linduff, pp. 358–377. Cambridge University Press, Cambridge.

Jacobson, E. 1983 Siberian Roots of the Scythians: Stag Image. *Journal of Asian History* 17:68–120.

Jacobson, E. 1993 *The Deer Goddess of Ancient Siberia: A Study in the Ecology of Belief.* Brill, Leiden.

Jettmar, K. 1994 Body-Painting and the Roots of the Scytho-Siberian Animal Style. In *The Archaeology of the Steppes: Methods and Strategies*, edited by B. Genito, pp. 3–15. Instituto Universitario Orientale, Naples.

Johnson, J., and B. Hanks 2012 Society, Demography, and Community: Reassessing Bronze Age Sintashta Populations in the Southern Urals, Russia (2100–1700 BCE). In *Beyond Elites: Alternatives to Hierarchical Systems in Modelling Social Formations, Teil 2*, edited by T. L. Kienlin and A. Zimmermann, pp. 355–367. Aus dem Institut für Archäologische Wissenschaften der Universität Bochum Fach Ur- und Frühgeschichte Band 215, Bochum.

Johnson, A. W., and T. Earle 2000 *The Evolution of Human Societies: From Foraging Group to Agrarian State, Second Edition.* Stanford University Press, Stanford.

Jones-Bley, K. and D. B. Zdanovich (eds.) 2002 *Complex Societies of Central Eurasia from the 3rd to the 1st Millennium BC: Regional Specifics in Light of Global Models* (Journal of Indo-European Studies Monograph series 45). Institute for the Study of Man, Washington, District of Columbia.

Judd, M., M. E. Kovacik, D. Rajev, B. Hanks, and A. Epimakhov 2008 Unpublished Bioarchaeology Report on Kamennyi Ambar 5 Cemetery. Report held by B. Hanks at the University of Pittsburgh, Department of Anthropology.

Kohl, P. 2007 *The Making of Bronze Age Eurasia.* Cambridge University Press, Cambridge.

Kohler, T. A., and G. J. Gumerman (eds.) 2000 *Dynamics in Human and Primate Societies: Agent-Based Modeling of Social and Spatial Processes.* Santa Fe Institute Studies in the Sciences of Complexity. Oxford University Press, Oxford.

Koryakova, L. 1996 Social Trends in Temperate Eurasia during the Second and First Millennia BC. *Journal of European Archaeology* 4:243–280.

Koryakova, L. N., and A. V. Epimakhov 2007 *The Urals and Western Siberia in the Bronze and Iron Ages.* Cambridge University Press, Cambridge.

Kristiansen, K., and T. B. Larsson 2005 *The Rise of Bronze Age Society: Travels, Transmissions, and Transformations.* Cambridge University Press, Cambridge.

Kupriyanova, E. (ed.) 2008 *Ten' Zhenshiny: zhenskii kostum epokhi bronzy kak "tekst" [po materialam nekrpoloei Yuzhnogo Zaural'ya I Kazakhstana].* Avto Graf, Chelyabinsk.

Merrony, C., B. Hanks, and R. Doonan 2009 Seeking the Process: The Application of Geophysical Survey on Some Early Mining and Metalworking Sites. In *Metals and Societies. Studies in Honour of Barbara S. Ottaway*, edited by T. K. Kienlin and B. W. Roberts, pp. 421–430. (Universitätsforschungen zur prähistorischen Archäologie) Habelt, Bonn.

Renfrew, C. 1998 All the King's Horses. In *Creativity in Human Evolution and Prehistory*, edited by S. Mithen, pp. 260–284. Routledge, London.

Rudenko, S. I. 1953 *Kultura naselenia gornogo Altaya v skifskoe vremya* [*The Culture of the Altai Mountain Population during the Scythian Period*]. Nauka, Moskva-Leningrad.

Rudenko, S. I. 1970 The *Frozen Tombs of Siberia.* Dent, London.

Smith, M. E. 2012 *The Comparative Archaeology of Complex Societies*. Cambridge University Press, Cambridge.

Vaugh, K. J., J. W. Eerkens, and J. Kantner 2009 *The Evolution of Leadership: Transitions in Decision Making from Small-Scale to Middle-Range Societies*. School for Advanced Research Press, Santa Fe.

Vinogradov, N. B. (ed.) 2013 *Ust'ye*. Arbis, Chelyabinsk.

Vinogradov, N. 2003 *Mogil'nik bronzovogo veka Krivoe Ozero v Yuzhnom Zaural'ye*. Yuzhno-Ural'skoe knizhnoe izd-vo, Chelyabinsk.

Yablonsky, L. 2000 "Scythian Triad" and "Scythian World." In *Kurgans, Ritual Sites, and Settlements: Eurasian Bronze and Iron Age,* edited by J. Davis-Kimball, E. Murphy, L. Koryakova, and L. Yablonsky, pp. 3–8. BAR International Series 890. Archeopress, Oxford.

Zdanovich, G. B., and I. Batanina 2002 Planography of the Fortified Centers of the Middle Bronze Age in the Southern Trans-Urals According to Aerial Photography Data. In *Complex Societies of Central Eurasia from the Third to the First Millennia BC: Regional Specifics in the Light of Global Models,* Chelyabinsk, Russian Federation/Journal of Indo–European Studies Monograph series, edited by K. Jones-Bley and D. G. Zdanovich, pp. 121–147. Institute for the Study of Man Chelyabinsk State University, Washington, District of Columbia.

Zdanovich, G. B., and I. Batanina 2007 *Arkaim—Strana Gorodov*. Krokus, Chelyabinsk.

Zdanovich, G. B., and D. Zdanovich 2002 The "Country of Towns" of Southern Trans-Urals and Some Aspects of Steppe Assimilation in the Bronze Age. In *Ancient Interactions: East and West in Eurasia,* edited by K. Boyle, C. Renfrew and M. Levine, pp. 249–263. McDonald Institute Monographs, Cambridge.

Chapter Six

The Unequal Dead

Bronze and Iron Age Evidence from Veneto and Trentino-South Tyrol

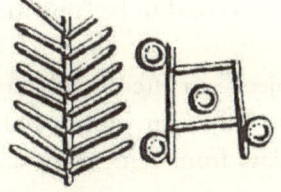

Massimo Saracino, Elisa Perego,
Lorenzo Zamboni, Vera Zanoni

Abstract   *This chapter explores social marginality and practices of potential ritual marginalization through the analysis of burial data from Bronze and Iron Age cemeteries and settlements of Northeast Italy. To date, our research project (called "IN or OUT") has mainly consisted in sampling and reevaluating already published burial data in order to understand whether the adoption of abnormal mortuary treatments might have been motivated by social diversity, social exclusion, and/or the dead's anomalous or "marginal" social standing. As for the geographical and chronological contexts of our analysis, we have initially focused on Veneto (Phase 1) where several cases of funerary deviancy are documented from the Bronze to the Late Iron Age (c. 2300–200 BC). More recently, our work on Trentino-South Tyrol has focused on the Iron Age, with preliminary research on the Bronze Age period (Phase 2).*

Overall, the funerary evidence analyzed has allowed us to address some crucial issues involving the organization of these ancient communities. On the one hand, the data available seem to reflect a social organization based on an unequal access to the resources and/or a hierarchical structuring of social roles and statuses. On the other hand, we have noted the existence of different forms and degrees of social integration (or social exclusion) based, for example, on the age, physical development or, potentially, the health status of the buried individual. While these patterns are clearer for Veneto, our preliminary analysis of the evidence from Trentino-South Tyrol has been made more difficult by this region's smaller sample size and peculiarity in terms of burial practices.

Introduction

The issue of ancient inequality has been tackled by our research group in some preliminary work (e.g., Perego 2012; 2014; Perego et al. 2015; Saracino 2009; Saracino and Zanoni 2014; Saracino et al. 2015, 2017; Zamboni and Zanoni 2010; Zanoni 2011) that proposed an in-depth socio-anthropological analysis of a sample of abnormal inhumation burials from northeast Italy between the Final Bronze Age (FBA) and the early Roman period (ERP) (c. 1200–25 BC). The so-called "deviant" burials—known as *Sonderbestattungen* in the German literature (Lauermann 1992)—are often attributed to individuals of lower social standing, or whose conditions of life and death were perceived to be "unnatural" (Murphy 2008).

Our research subsequently merged into the "IN or OUT Project," an interdisciplinary effort exploring social exclusion and marginality in late prehistoric Italy. Our work mainly consists in collecting and reevaluating already published burial data from cemeteries and settlements in order to understand whether the adoption of abnormal mortuary treatments might be motivated by social diversity, social exclusion, and/or the dead's anomalous or "marginal" social standing. Among the burial features that might characterize an abnormal deposition in the study area, we considered: any abnormality or differentiation in funerary rite (e.g., inhumation where cremation was normative or vice versa) and body treatment (e.g., postmortem skeletal manipulation); the lack or scarcity of grave-goods where their interment was the norm, and/or the adoption of any burial practice potentially indicative of lower energy expenditure (Tainter 1978) vis-à-vis the rest of the buried community; the adoption of anomalous tomb structures and/or burial locations (e.g., settlement burial instead of formal cemetery burial); the adoption of rare or anomalous burial postures (e.g., prone burial) and/or practices aimed at constraining or degrading the corpse (e.g., postmortem abuse of the cadaver); and the evidence of peri-mortem violence potentially indicative of homicide, ritual killing, and the like. Furthermore, we believe that focusing on bio-archaeological data is crucial to uncover information on the dead's biological sex, age at death, health status, and cause of death (Waldron 2009; Walker 2001), and explain their abnormal mortuary treatment. Additionally, the recurrence of several deviant attributes in one burial may point to a greater degree of perceived difference than deviation from the norm for a single parameter; the adoption of several deviant burial practices at once, therefore, may indeed be motivated by extreme social exclusion.

Initially focused on Iron Age (IA) Veneto, our research later explored the funerary record of this region from the Early Bronze Age (EBA) (IN or OUT Phase 1) and recently expanded to Trentino-South Tyrol (Phase 2) (Figure 6.1). This chapter, therefore, critically resumes the results of Phase 1 and introduces some methodological issues and sample data from Phase 2. Overall, we investigated some underrated aspects of social organization in late prehistoric Italy, such as marginality, and tackled any potential reflection of inequality and social exclusion in the funerary record of the study area. Additionally, we aimed to construct an appropriate methodological approach to uncover the underlying reasons for the burial occurrences of diversity, abnormality, and even "resistance" identified in the archaeological record.

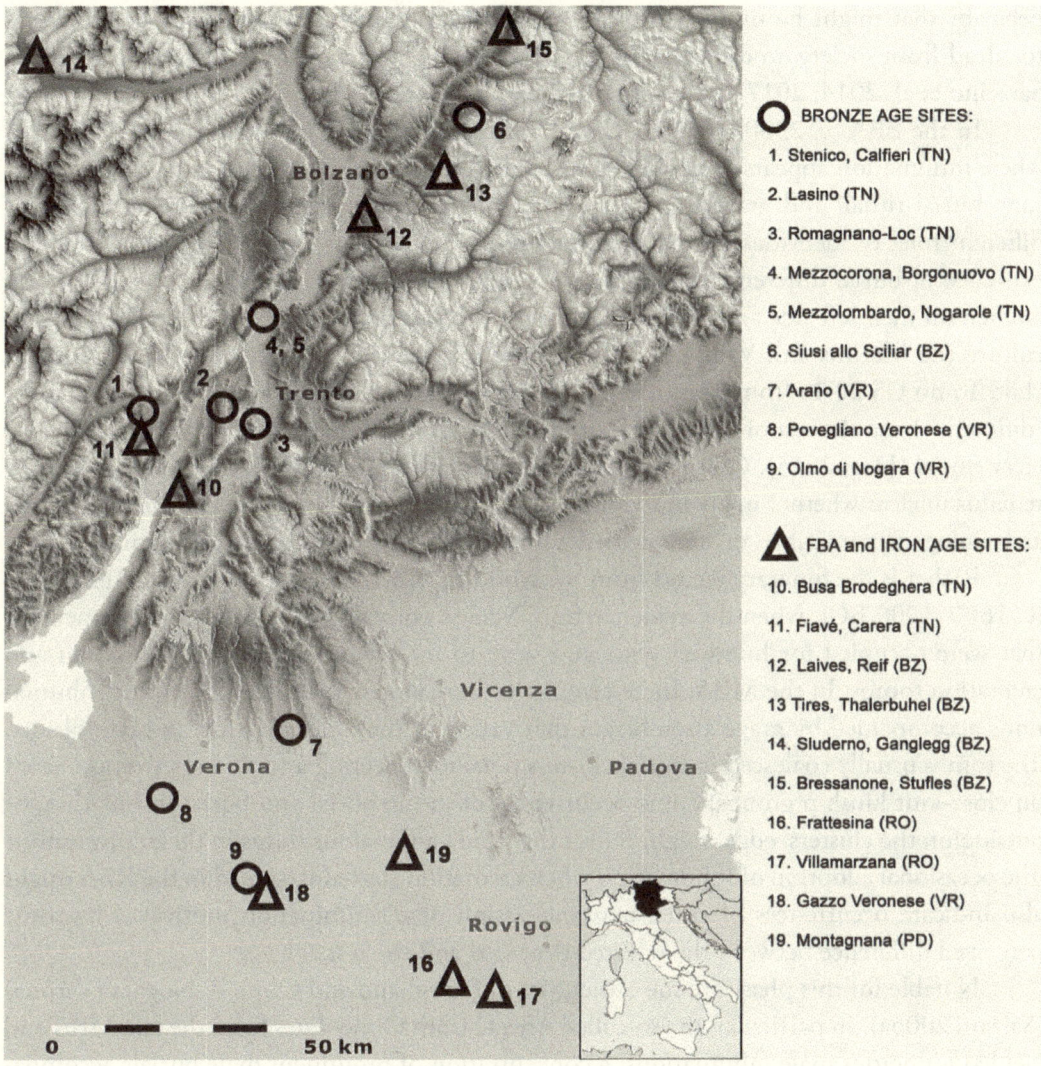

BRONZE AGE SITES:

1. Stenico, Calfieri (TN)
2. Lasino (TN)
3. Romagnano-Loc (TN)
4. Mezzocorona, Borgonuovo (TN)
5. Mezzolombardo, Nogarole (TN)
6. Siusi allo Sciliar (BZ)
7. Arano (VR)
8. Povegliano Veronese (VR)
9. Olmo di Nogara (VR)

FBA and IRON AGE SITES:

10. Busa Brodeghera (TN)
11. Fiavé, Carera (TN)
12. Laives, Reif (BZ)
13. Tires, Thalerbuhel (BZ)
14. Sluderno, Ganglegg (BZ)
15. Bressanone, Stufles (BZ)
16. Frattesina (RO)
17. Villamarzana (RO)
18. Gazzo Veronese (VR)
19. Montagnana (PD)

FIGURE 6.1. Map of Veneto and Trentino-South Tyrol with main sampled sites (elaboration by L. Zamboni).

BACKGROUND AND RESULTS OF PHASE 1

The work presented here (2013–2015) has mainly investigated marginality and marginalization, and their visible archaeological and bio-archaeological correlates. We initially focused on Veneto for the numerous cases of funerary deviancy documented. Until recently, such burials were either disregarded in favor of richer tombs displaying sophisticated burial practices, or generically attributed to low-ranking individuals or foreigners (Saracino 2009). Overall, our analysis of BA (c. 2300–900 BC) and IA (c. 900–200 BC) Veneto reexamined both evidence of social differentiation at death and occurrences of abnormal mortuary behavior that might be motivated by forms of ritual marginalization aimed at excluding the dead from society, to different degrees. The results of this research (Perego et al. 2015; Saracino et al. 2014; 2017) are summarized and developed below.

In the EBA (c. 2300–1650 BC), only rare cemeteries are known from the Po Valley, where inhumation appears to be the main visible funerary rite. Variation in the tomb structure, burial ritual, and grave furnishing from this area may indicate the construction of different roles or identities for the dead, in a society defined as "tribal" (Peroni 1996). The existence of burial differentiation based on gender might relate to the custom of burying women on their left side and men on their right side, ascribable to the previous Bell Beaker culture (de Marinis and Valzogher 2013). Rare occurrences of settlement burial, such as child Tomb US 20-1a from Arano, may indicate that some individuals were perceived to be "different" from the rest of the buried community and might have been denied formal cemetery burial (Dori 2014). Given the scanty funerary evidence from this period, however, it remains unclear whether many individuals might have received funerary treatments that are archaeologically invisible, or were denied a funeral for their incomplete social integration.

Richer is the funerary record from the Middle (MBA) and Recent Bronze Age (RBA) (c. 1650–1200 BC), when the evidence from Veneto comes from large bi-ritual cemeteries that were occupied for hundred years and were to include hundreds of inhumation and cremation tombs. In the MBA, these cemeteries were largely composed of supine inhumations accompanied by grave assemblages that varied in their composition and complexity. The tombs usually coalesced in burial clusters possibly reflecting a social organization based on close-knit kinship groups. Some occurrences of prone burial and burial in isolation, or outside/on the clusters' edge, might reflect the dead's anomalous status in their community. The occasional adoption of inhumation when cremation started to spread in the RBA might also indicate occurrences of ritual marginalization or discrimination motivated by some perceived difference between the selected deceased and the rest.

Notable for this phase are the cemeteries of Povegliano and Olmo di Nogara (Verona) (Salzani 2005a). In particular, the so-called Area C from Olmo dates from the late MBA and yielded numerous male inhumations; a concentration of prominent male burials accompanied by a sword appeared in the northern segment of Area C (C1), where some child and rich female inhumations also emerged. The southern segment of Area C (C2) dates instead to the RBA and yielded more numerous cremations, often with no grave-goods; the lack of weaponry further indicates a change in the ideological and socioeconomic structuring of the burying community (Bietti Sestieri et al. 2013; Cupitò and Leonardi 2005; de Marinis and Salzani 2005). It is indeed from the MBA2 to the RBA that cremation started to spread in Emilia, Lombardy, and Veneto as the main burial rite. This transformation in burial practice was related to the spread of the so-called *Urnenfelderkultur* and to potential changes in these communities' religious views: the dead, cremated with their personal furnishings, might have been consecrated to the deity through the action of fire. Subsequently, the bones were placed in pottery vases (or other perishable containers) and deposited in simple pits, either with or without some grave-goods and the remains of the objects burned on the pyre. The pits generally coalesced in dense clusters probably indicative of kinship plots. This apparent uniformity in burial practice has been interpreted as an ideological choice to mask any evidence of social inequality, in communities characterized by evolving social differentiation (Cupitò and Leonardi 2005). Cremation was to remain the main visible burial rite in Veneto also in the FBA and IA, with rituals that "*si consolidano, vengono via via formalizzati e codificati, acquistano spesso in complessità*" (Peroni 1996:581–582).

In the FBA and beginning of the IA (c. 1200–900 BC), cremation is the only funerary rite attested at cemeteries such as Garda and Angarano (Salzani 2013). Notable, however, is the sporadic appearance of inhumations in the cemeteries surrounding settlements such as Frattesina (Salzani and Colonna 2010), Gazzo Veronese (Salzani 2005b), and Montagnana (Bianchin Citton et al. 1998) (Figure 6.2).

Accompanied by extremely scanty grave assemblages, or no grave-goods at all, these depositions sometimes displayed other abnormal burial features, such as prone burial or burial in isolation (or on the edge of the mounds where most cremations coalesced). Notable is also the presence of some inhumations in settlements including Montagnana (Bianchin Citton et al. 1998) and Villamarzana (Salzani and Consonni 2005). Usually deprived of any grave-goods, these burials were sometimes marked by evidence of palaeopathology and/or the adoption of anomalous treatments, such as prone burial.

The presence of inhumations outside formal cemeteries characterized Veneto also during the IA (Michelini 2005; Saracino 2009). In most cases involving adults, these burials displayed other deviant attributes such as the prone posture, and evidence of paleopathology and physical abuse, including, presumably, human sacrifice. For the entire IA, inhumation remained a minority burial rite in Veneto, where cremation was accounting for

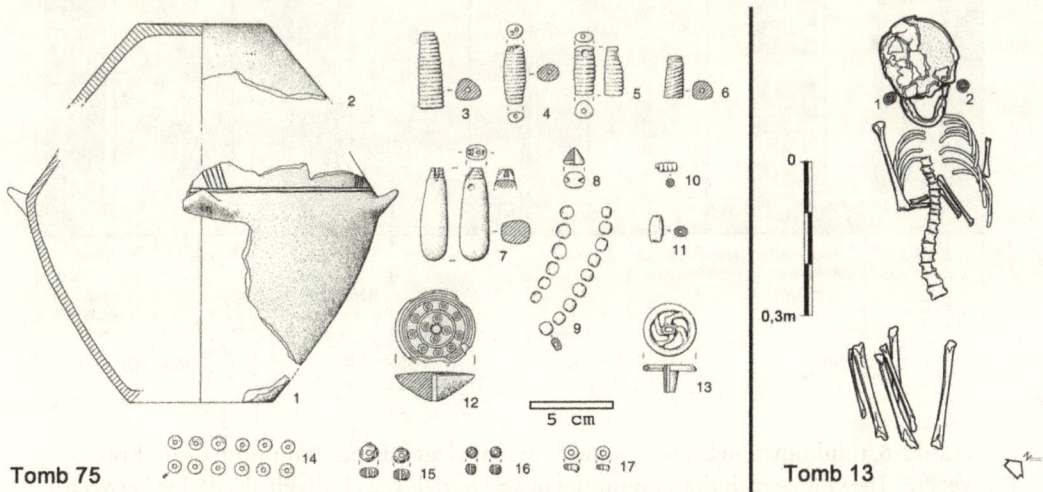

Tomb 75   Tomb 13

FIGURE 6.2. Reconstruction of two FBA graves from Narde II cemetery of Frattesina, Sector I: ceramic urn (1–2) and grave-goods (3–11: amber beads, 12–14: horn/bone objects, 15–17: vitreous material beads) from cremation Tomb 75 (left); child prone inhumation burial from Tomb 13 with two bronze rings used (1–2) to hold the plait (right) (elaboration by M. Saracino after Salzani and Colonna 2010).

up to 85–100 percent of all the thousands of burials attested (with variability in different sites and chronological phases). While most inhumations deposited in formal cemeteries might not display striking deviant features possibly indicative of extreme social exclusion, many yielded only poor grave assemblages (or no grave-goods) and were located in marginal cemetery areas or on the edge/outside the clusters where most cremations coalesced. It remains unclear whether inhumation in IA Veneto was a marker of social exclusion per se, or some might have occasionally adopted it to underline some cultural difference between them and those practicing cremation. Notably, cremations were similarly characterized by marked variability in their tomb structure, grave assemblage, and the like; this variation was presumably connected to the dead's role, gender, age, rank, and affiliation (Figure 6.3).

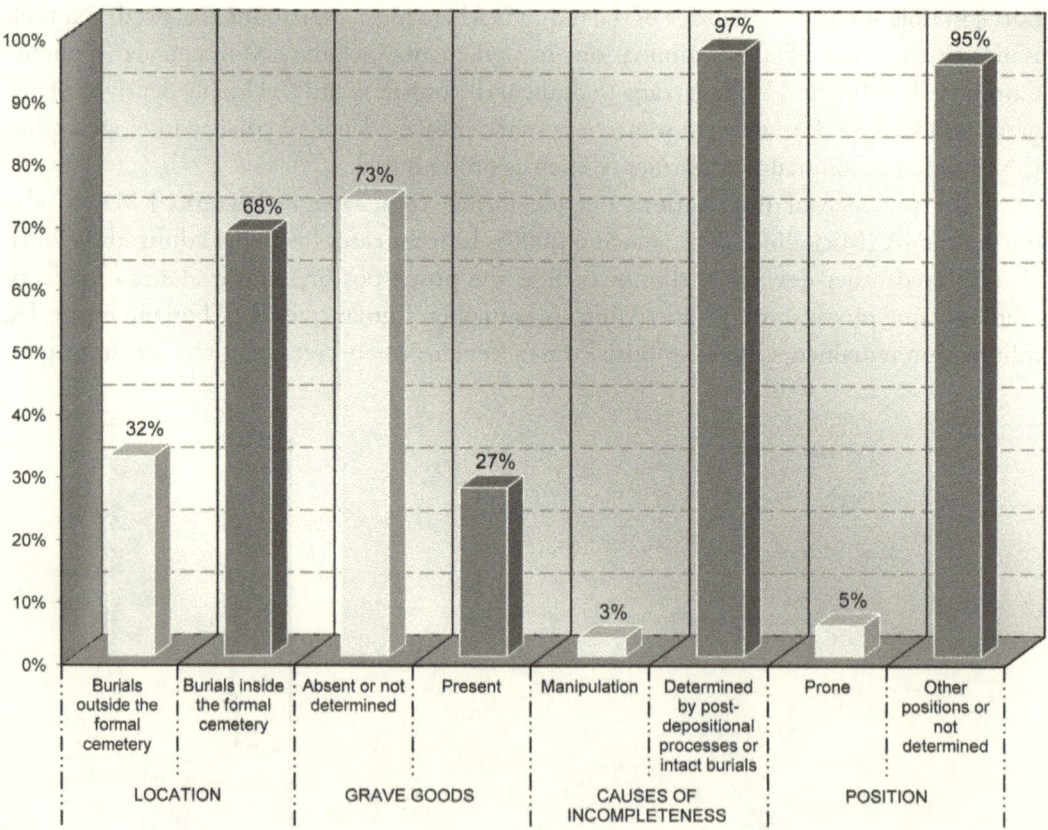

Figure 6.3. Inhumation burials (%) with potential anomalous traits from proto-historic Veneto. The sample includes a minimum of 280 burials (i.e., individuals) dating between the Final Bronze Age and the late first millennium BC. The majority of burials deposited outside the formal cemetery are infants or children buried in the settlement; other cases (n = *c.* 20/280) are represented by scattered bones brought to the settlement for ritual or practical purposes (i.e., to be used as tools or offerings). Some burials displayed two or more anomalous traits at once (elaboration by M. Saracino and E. Perego after Perego 2012 and 2014).

PHASE 2: TRENTINO-SOUTH TYROL

Our work on Trentino-South Tyrol focused on the IA, with preliminary research on the BA period (2014–2015). For the latter, significant data seems to concentrate in the EBA, when notable is the regional peculiarity of some funerary rites, and their continuity with the Copper Age (c. 3300–2300 BC).

Most EBA burial sites emerged in the Adige Valley, where the dead were often deposited in small caves, rock shelters, or clefts (Nicolis 2001). Most burials were single, isolated inhumations covered with small stone mounds and accompanied by scanty grave-goods, usually ornaments. No clear differentiation based on gender or rank is evident in burial. The only members of the buried community clearly displaying different treatments were fetuses and neonates; these were deposited in ceramic pots subsequently placed in pits covered with stone slabs (e.g., Tomb 4 from Mezzocorona-Borgonuovo and Tombs 1 and 2 from Mezzolombardo-Nogarole 3: Nicolis 2004).

The presence in the EBA and MBA of inhumation burials whose skulls may be dislocated has been linked by some scholars to practices of intentional skeletal manipulation and/ or skull veneration, with potential relations to the presence of human crania or skull bones in some contemporaneous Northern Italian settlements (Cavazzuti 2008–10; de Marinis 2003; Tecchiati 2011). For BA Trentino-South Tyrol, notable are: (a) the juvenile cranium with evidence of porotic hyperostosis placed under a stone mound and a fortification at Siusi (BZ); (b) the skull found under a stone mound at Lasino (TN), in a context that might have been a settlement or a seasonal shelter; (c) the skull accompanied by grave-goods in the Romagnano Loc cemetery (TN); (d) the female skeleton deprived of the skull from the Stenico-Calfieri *tumulus* (TN); (e) the female skeleton from La Vela (TN), placed on a furnace and with possible evidence of skull dislocation.

This evidence finds comparisons in similar practices of skeletal manipulation, involving skull removal, from Piedmont (Alba), Emilia Romagna (Poviglio, Montata, Montecchio, Marendole, Castione dei Marchesi, presumably S. Eurosia) and Veneto (Bovolone, Padua, Lozzo Atestino, Este-Morlungo, Este-Canevedo), dating between the EBA and EIA. Cavazzuti (2008–10) suggested that the presence of some MBA-IA Northern Italian cremations deprived of skull bones might indicate the persistence of such old practices after the spread of incineration. In discussing the ritual deposition of skull bones in MBA Padua and S. Rosa di Poviglio, Cremaschi et al. (2012) suggested that the removal of the skull, followed by the relocation of skull bones in the settlement, might have been practiced on individuals who held peculiar statuses/roles in their group, in occasion of rituals delimiting the community space. Hence, there is no evidence that such individuals, granted different funerary rites vis-à-vis the rest of their community, were the victims of ritual marginalization: indeed, the opposite might be true.

IA Trentino-South Tyrol is characterized by the so-called Luco-Meluno and Fritzens-Sanzeno cultural complex, which roughly covers the provinces of Trento, Bozen, and the Engadin and presents significant intrasite variability, with external cultural influences. There, the funerary evidence cannot be compared to the Venetic one, as rarer are the cemeteries that have been the focus of in-depth archaeological and osteological analysis. Therefore, we preliminarily tackled the issue of social exclusion from this region by reviewing occurrences of settlement burial and burial in geographical contexts that may be defined as *natural places of significance* (Knapp-Ashmore 1999:2).

The presence of human remains in locations such as hilltops, ravines, and bogs includes: (a) scattered human bones in some of the so-called *Brandopferplätze*, sacrificial sites attested in Northern Italy and the circum-Alpine area from the BA to the ERP; while we cannot develop further this line of enquiry here, we note that the precise meaning of these depositions remains unclear; (b) the so-called Hunter from Busa Brodeghera, a juvenile skeleton recovered from a niche in a ravine near Nago-Torbole (TN, fifth century BC). While the burial was initially interpreted as an accidental fall, the possibility that the ravine was chosen to remove the deceased from formal burial is compounded by evidence of physical malformation on the skeleton (bilaterally ankylosed hips), while a cranial lesion might indicate the cause of death (Corrain 1983); (c) seven human skulls radiocarbon-dated to the fourth–second century BC from the peat bog context of Fiavè-Carera (TN); evidence of trauma compatible with scalping, and the presence of weaponry in the bog, might indicate that the skulls belonged to the victims of violence, possibly as enemies or war prisoners. Notably, at both Nago-Torbole and Fiavè-Carera deposition in liminal, secluded sites may

Figure 6.4. Double settlement prone burial from Bressanone-Stufles, Via Elvas, Room B (elaboration by M. Saracino after Feltrin et al. 2009).

reflect the dead's liminal or abnormal social status; (d) the ritual site of Tires-Thalerbühel (BZ), which yielded a child's skull; Tires-Thalerbühel, located 1,100 m above sea level, had been the focus of long-term occupation before this first-century-BC deposition.

Settlement burial in IA Trentino-South Tyrol often involved the deposition of infants in houses or ruined structures, with at least one exception. Some notable occurrences are: (a) the fetus found at Bressanone-Stufles (BZ), in the Via Elvas settlement context, datable from the fifth century BC onward (House 1, Room A); the same site yielded an "infant" femur, found in House 2, Room B (Feltrin et al. 2009); (b) the supine neonate found in a corner of House 1 from Laives-Reif (BZ, third century BC), where the burial pit was probably signaled by a stone on the floor (Zanoni 2011:32); (c) the neonatal remains found in a corner of House D1 from Sluderno-Ganglegg (BZ, first century BC); there, the bones emerged from the layers pertaining to a "floor" covered with clay, and were close to bronze fragments and a pit containing a "worked stone" (Steiner 2007); (d) the double adult burial from Via Elvas, House 2, Room B, at Bressanone-Stufles; the deceased—buried in the same pit—were two men approximately aged 40 at death. Both were prone and the second partially overlays the first deposited in the pit. One or both might have been tied up before burial. The presence of a cranial lesion on one skeleton, coupled with the abnormal treatment and place of burial, suggested they may have been prisoners or outcasts, killed and deposited outside a cemetery as a form of capital punishment (Feltrin et al. 2009; Tecchiati 2011) (Figure 6.4).

DISCUSSION AND CONCLUSION

We reviewed the methodology and preliminary results of the "IN or OUT" Project, an interdisciplinary effort exploring funerary deviancy, marginality and inequality in proto-historic Italy. While our research to date focused on EBA to early Roman Veneto, we more recently started a review of funerary data from Trentino-South Tyrol, covering the same time period.

Our analysis of data from Veneto in the *longue durée* showed that (1) a notable variability in burial practice is attested; this variability is presumably connected to changes in the economic, socioritual and sociopolitical structuring of this region, and may have expressed changing notions of social inclusion and exclusion; (2) the adoption of deviant funerary practices is attested for the entire period considered, with an apparent increment between c. 1200–500 BC; overall, some occurrences of extreme ritual marginalization seems indeed indicative of the dead's abnormal social standing, or their social exclusion; more difficult to interpret remain other instances, such as the supine inhumations with grave-goods from the formal cemeteries of IA Veneto; (3) inequality and differentiation at death can be recognized in the burial record of Veneto for the whole period considered, with different degrees of visibility: for example, the relative uniformity in burial practice at the onset of the *Urnenfelderkultur* might indicate the conscious adoption of rites aimed at masking the extent of existent inequality; by contrast, inequality becomes more outright in some IA phases, when striking differences can be noted between some extremely rich Venetic cremations, and the abnormal inhumations deposited outside formal cemeteries; (4) while gender was a factor in determining funerary differentiation (with variability in different sites and chronological phases), there is no evidence that it might have motivated social exclusion per se: both women and men of different ages were among those granted either normative or abnormal mortuary treatments; (5) further research is needed on funerary representativity; while the proven absence of certain age- or gender-groups from the funerary population in some contexts might simply indicate the adoption of alternative burial rituals, other individuals may have been denied formal burial to exclude them from society; this might be the case of infants in some funerary contexts (e.g., Cavazzuti 2008–10).

Our preliminary analysis of funerary data from Trentino-South Tyrol showed that (1) with exceptions such as the Vadena necropolis, relatively scanty are the cemetery data from this region, where significant are the burial findings from settlements and natural locations that might have been frequented for ritual/cultic reasons; this hampers any direct comparison with Veneto; however, intersite and intrasite variability and change in burial practice over time characterized both regions; (2) the Trentino-South Tyrol sample size also hampers the identification of clear patterns in funerary deviancy and marginalization; one of the clearest examples of funerary marginalization might be the double settlement burial from Bressanone-Stufles—possibly the outcome of capital punishment or sacrifice; (3) settlement burial, therefore, might have been an abnormal practice underlying the dead's incomplete social integration, as also suggested by the settlement infant burials from late-first-millennium BC South-Tyrol; (4) neonates seem indeed to have received peculiar burial rites in both regions (albeit with intersite, intrasite, and chronological variability), possibly because of their premature death; (5) unclear remains the socioritual meaning of interment in *places of natural significance* such as the *Brandopferplätze* sacrificial sites; similarly, we cannot demonstrate whether practices of bone manipulation, often involving skull removal, represented forms of skull veneration, ritual exploitation/reuse of human remains, or ritual violence.

Overall, the evidence uncovered from late prehistoric northeast Italy seems to reflect a social organization based, on the one hand, on unequal access to resources and/or a hierarchical structuring of social roles and statuses, or, on the other, on the existence of different forms and degrees of social integration based, for example, on the age, physical development, or health status of the individual. While this pattern is clearer for Veneto, our preliminary reading of the Trentino-South Tyrol evidence is blurred by the regional peculiarity and relative scarcity of the sample from this region, also potentially motivated by the harsh terrain characterizing this (largely) mountainous area.

Acknowledgments

We thank the organizers of the IEMA conference for accepting our contribution. The original draft of this paper had been conceived and written by the authors in 2015, and submitted and received in 2016, with only minor further bibliographical updates. We also thank the anonymous reviewers who provided us useful feedback for improving the final text.

References

Bianchin Citton, E., G. Gambacurta, and A. Ruta Serafini (eds.) 2008 ". . . *presso l'Adige ridente. . . .*" *Recenti rinvenimenti archeologici da Este a Montagnana*. ADLE, Padova.

Bietti, Sestieri, A. M., L. Salzani, C. Giardino, and G. Verly 2013 Ritual Treatment of Weapons as a Correlate of Structural Change in the Italian LBA Communities: The Bronze Hoard of Pila del Brancon (Nogara, Verona). *Rivista di Scienze Preistoriche* LXIII:155–169.

Cavazzuti, C. 2008–10 Aspetti rituali, sociali e paleodemografici di alcune necropoli protostoriche a cremazione dell'Italia Settentrionale. Unpublished PhD dissertation, Università di Ferrara.

Corrain, C. 1983 Ricerche antropologiche su resti umani antichi del Trentino nel decennio 1972–1982. In *Beni Culturali nel Trentino-interventi dal 1979 al 1983—Contributi all'archeologia*, edited by G. Ciurletti, pp. 23–28. Provincia autonoma di Trento, Assessorato alle attività culturali, Trento.

Cremaschi, M., A. Mutti, M. Bernabò Brea, L. Salvadei, C. Ottomano, and E. Maini 2012 L'area sepolcrale della terramara di S. Rosa di Poviglio (RE). Contesto, materiali, riti. *Rivista Scienze Preistoriche* LXII:265–294.

Cupitò, M., and G. Leonardi 2005 Proposta di lettura sociale della necropoli di Olmo di Nogara. In *La necropoli dell'età del bronzo all'Olmo di Nogara*, edited by L. Salzani, pp. 488–494. Museo Civico di Storia Naturale, Verona.

de Marinis, R. C., and L. Salzani 2005 Tipologia e cronologia dei materiali. In *La necropoli dell'età del bronzo all'Olmo di Nogara*, edited by L. Salzani, pp. 391–448. Museo Civico di Storia Naturale, Verona.

de Marinis, R. C., and E. Valzolgher 2013 Riti funerari dell'antica età del Bronzo in area padana. In *L'età del Rame: la pianura padana e le Alpi al tempo di Ötzi*, edited by R. C. de Marinis, pp. 545–559. Ed. Euroteam, Brescia.

Dori, I. 2014 *Storie sepolte: paleobiologia della popolazione di Arano (Illasi, VR). Studio antropologico di una comunità del Bronzo Antico*. Unpublished PhD dissertation, Università di Firenze.

Feltrin, M., S. Marconi, M. I. Pezzo, J. Rizzi Zorzi, and U. Tecchiati 2009 Indagini dendrocronologiche su alcuni edifici dell'età del Ferro recentemente scavati a Stufles (Bressanone, Prov. Bolzano). Via Elvas 12 e 16. Campagne di scavo 2007 e 2008. *Annali del Museo Civico di Rovereto* 24:95–122.

Knapp, B. A., and W. Ashmore 1999 Archaeological Landscapes: Constructed, Conceptualized, Ideational. In *Archaeologies of Landscape: Contemporary Perspectives*, edited by B. A. Knapp and W. Ashmore, pp. 1–32. Blackwell, Oxford.

Lauermann, E. 1992 Sonderbesttungen der frühen Bronzezeit im Weinviertel Niederösterreichs. *Praehistorische Zeitschrift* 67(2):183–200.

Marconi, S., and U. Tecchiati 2006 La fauna del villaggio della prima età del Ferro del Thalerbühel di Tires (Bz). Economia, uso del territorio e strategie insediative tra II e I millennio a.C. In *Proceedings of the International Conference Animali tra uomini e dei. Archeozoologia del mondo preromano*, edited by A. Curci, and D. Vitali, pp. 11–26. Ante Quem, Bologna.

Michelini, P. 2005 Via S. Massimo 17-19-Angolo via S. Eufemia. In *La città invisibile. Padova preromana: trent'anni di scavi e ricerche*, edited by M. De Min, M. Gamba, G. Gambacurta, and A. Ruta Serafini, pp. 157–159. Tipoarte, Bologna.

Murphy, E. M. (ed.) 2008 *Deviant Burial in the Archaeological Record*. Oxbow Books, Oxford.

Nicolis, F. 2001 Il culto dei morti nell'antica e media età del Bronzo. In *Storia del Trentino*, edited by M. Lanzinger, F. Marazatico, and A. Pedrotti, pp. 337–365. Il Mulino,Trento.

Nicolis, F. 2004 Le evidenze funerarie dell'antica età del Bronzo in Italia settentrionale. In *Graves and Funerary Rituals during the Late Neolithic and the Early Bronze Age in Europe (2700–2000 B.C.)*, edited by M. Besse and L. Desideri, pp. 111–145. BAR IS 1284, Oxford.

Perego, E. 2012 The Construction of Personhood in Veneto (Italy) between the Late Bronze Age and the Early Roman period. Unpublished PhD dissertation. University College London.

Perego, E. 2014 Anomalous Mortuary Behaviour and Social Exclusion in Iron Age Italy: A Case Study from the Veneto Region. *Journal of Mediterranean Archaeology* 27(2):161–185.

Perego, E., M. Saracino, L. Zamboni, and V. Zanoni 2015 Practices of Ritual Marginalization in Late Prehistoric Veneto: Evidence from the Field. In *Death Embodied: Archaeological Approaches to the Treatment of the Corpse*, edited by Z. L. Devlin and E. J. Graham, pp. 129–159. Oxbow Books, Oxford.

Peroni, R. 1996 *L'Italia alle soglie della storia*. Laterza, Bari-Roma.

Salzani, L. (ed.) 2005a *La necropoli dell'età del bronzo all'Olmo di Nogara*. Museo Civico di Storia Naturale, Verona.

Salzani, L. 2005b La necropoli protostorica di Ponte Nuovo a Gazzo Veronese. *Notizie Archeologiche Bergomensi* 13:7–112.

Salzani, L. (ed.) 2013 *La necropoli di Desmontà (Veronella-Albaredo d'Adige. Verona). Scavi 1982–2011*. vol. 56, SAP, Mantova.

Salzani, L., and C. Colonna (eds.) 2010 *La fragilità dell'urna. I recenti scavi a Narde necropoli di Frattesina (XII–IX sec. a.C.)*. Catalogo della mostra, Rovigo.

Salzani, L., and A. Consonni 2005 L'abitato protostorico di Villamarzana-Campagna Michela (RO). Scavi 1993. *Padusa* XLI:7–55.

Saracino, M. 2009 Sepolture atipiche durante il Bronzo Finale e la seconda età del Ferro in Veneto. *Padusa* XLV:65–71.

Saracino, M., E. Perego, L. Zamboni, and V. Zanoni 2014 Investigating Social Exclusion in Late Prehistoric Italy: Preliminary Results of the "IN or OUT" Project (PHASE 1). *Papers from the Institute of Archaeology* 24(1)12:1–14.

Saracino, M., and V. Zanoni 2014 The Marginal People of the Iron Age in North-Eastern Italy: A Comparative Study. i.e., The Iron Age Written by the Losers. In *Actes de XXXVIe Colloque International AFEAF*, pp. 535–550. Revue archéologique de l'Est, 36e supplément.

Saracino, M., V. Zanoni, E. Perego, and L. Zamboni 2017 "Funerary deviancy and social inequality in protohistoric Italy: what the dead can tell." *Preistoria Alpina* 49:73–83.

Steiner, H. 2007 Die Bronze- und urnenfelderzeitliche Siedlung. In *Die befestigte Siedlungam Gangleggim Vinschgau-Südtirol. Ergebnisse der Ausgrabungen 1997–2001 (Bronze-/Urnenfelderzeit) und natur-wissenschaftliche Beiträge*, edited by H. Steiner, pp. 17–394. Forschungenzur Denkmalpflege in Südtirol-Band 3, Bozen.

Tainter, J. A. 1978. Mortuary Practices and the Study of Prehistoric Social Systems. In *Advances in Archaeological Method and Theory*, vol. 1, edited by M. B. Schiffer, pp. 105–141. Academic Press, San Diego.

Tecchiati, U. 2011 Sepolture e resti umani sparsi in abitati della preistoria e della protostoria dell'Italia settentrionale con particolare riferimento al Trentino-Alto Adige. *Notizie Archeologiche Bergomensi* 19:49–63.

Waldron, T. 2009 *Paleopathology*. Cambridge University Press, Cambridge.

Walker, P. L. 2001 A Bioarchaeological Perspective on the History of Violence. *Annual Review of Anthropology* 30:573–596.

Zamboni, L., and V. Zanoni 2010 Giaciture non convenzionali in Italia settentrionale durante l'età del Ferro. In *Atti della giornata di studi Sepolture Anomale. Indagini archeologiche e antropologiche dall'epoca classica al Medioevo in Emilia Romagna*, edited by M. G. Belcastro and J. Ortalli, pp. 147–160. All'Insegna del Giglio, Firenze.

Zanoni, V. 2011 *Out of Place. Human Skeletal Remains from non-Funerary Contexts. Italy during the 1st Millennium B.C.* BAR IS 2036, Oxford.

CHAPTER SEVEN

Inequality during the Iron Age in France

Tracing the Archaeological Record

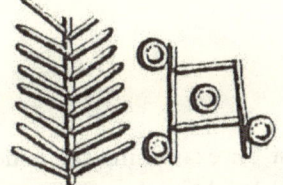

Patrice Brun

Abstract   *Research in comparative primatology has shown that from chimpanzees to humans, all societies are segmented into groups based on age and sex and that adult males are generally dominant. From the emergence of Homo Sapiens onward, we can detect arbitrarily defined groups, which are socially constructed from ethnicity, nationality, caste, class, religion, etc., and have differences in social positions (political authority, power, wealth, status privileges, main material resources, better conditions for education and health). In arbitrary groups, hierarchical positions are more responsive to changing circumstances and context. The main cause of the presence of an arbitrary group system would seem to be the opportunity to generate an economic surplus facilitating differentiation of social roles and leading to the formation of a monopolistic political authority (professional army, police, administration, etc.), that is, according to Weber's definition of the State, the monopoly of legitimate violence.*

The Iron Age (730–125 BC) in France is of particular interest for examining the issue of inequality because societies evolved over seven centuries through a process of nonlinear complexity, from simple chiefdoms to archaic states. These are politically autonomous entities, which marked strong social distinctions through the wealth of funerary deposits and monumental tombs. As we know, burial practices are not a true reflection of social organization; we must include the evidence for settlement hierarchy. Spectacular results have been achieved over the last thirty years due to extensive fieldwork, at last enabling the proper study of large settlements of this period, from simple farms to urban areas.

These archaeological data complement the information provided by Greek and Latin textual sources which describe various organization strategies: social elites, ordinary free people and slaves, age- and gender-based categories in different groups, accumulation of economic surplus, and exclusion. I describe in detail how we can interpret the archaeological record in terms of social status and try to identify the perspectives emerging from the application of new biological, physico-chemical and electromagnetic methods of investigation.

I intend to conclude with a proposed theory of the growth of inequality before and during the emergence of the State. My basis for this is not only the development of organizational complexity, but also the political regimes that we are beginning to better perceive in the archaeological record.

INTRODUCTION

The Iron Age (730–125 BC) in France is of particular interest for examining the issue of inequality because societies evolved over these seven centuries through a nonlinear process of nonlinear complexity, from simple chiefdoms to archaic states. These were politically autonomous entities, which marked quite strong social distinctions through the wealth of funerary deposits and more or less monumental tombs. As we know, burial practices are not true reflections of social organization; we must also include the evidence for settlement hierarchy. Spectacular results have been achieved over the last thirty years due to extensive fieldwork, at last enabling the proper study of large settlements of this period, from simple farms to urban areas.

The archaeological data complement the information provided by Greek and Latin textual sources that describe various organization strategies: social elites, ordinary free people and slaves, age- and gender-based categories in different groups, accumulation of economic surplus, and exclusion. A brief description of the history of ideas on the evolution of inequality helps us to understand the current state of the debate, the mainstream ideas of which have fluctuated between evolutionist and anti-evolutionist approaches since the eighteenth century. Challenging new perspectives on this issue clearly favor an evolutionary perspective. Archaeology has provided an impressive amount of data studied with more efficient methods of analysis, which suggest processes of unequal growth that are better documented than before. The theoretical implications are drawn to finish highlighting a blind spot of research on stateless societies: the question of forms of political regimes.

BRIEF HISTORY OF IDEAS ON THE EVOLUTION OF INEQUALITY

In the mid-eighteenth century primarily, reflections on the causes of increased social inequalities multiplied. We find in most of these works a similar evolutionary pattern emphasizing a fundamental tension between the limited environmental resources and the universal conquering nature of the human psyche (Rousseau 1755; Helvetius 1759; Ferguson 1767). This constant insecurity would have stimulated the capacities of technical innovations that enabled the increase in production and, therefore, the increase in population. It would have resulted in more numerous and more serious conflicts, which would have required coordinated ways of policing, thus, greater political complexity. From the start, there are two opposing interpretations to explain the process of increasing complexity: one offers a consensual process, the community accepting the authority of one or a few for a better management for the benefit of all (Helvetius 1759), the other a contentious process imposed to consolidate the gains made by a few (Rousseau 1755). This conception, free from metaphysical beliefs, was strengthened by Charles Darwin's theory, which gave an overall powerful materialist logic to the evolution of living things and, indirectly, of human societies (Darwin 1859). Major works synthesizing the history of mankind, suggesting the first social typologies and obviously necessary for any comparative work, were completed. Two of the most notable of these were Morgan's three stages of increasing complexity: (1) savagery, (2) barbarism, and (3) civilization (Morgan 1877); and Engels's five types of societies: (1) hunter-gatherers with egalitarian economies, (2) pastoralists with kind leaders, (3) farmers and metallurgists with surplus labor and social classes, (4) specialized warriors and craftsmen in tribal confederations, and (5) States (Engels 1884).

Between 1890 and 1930, evolutionary approaches generated a strong outcry from the believers whose intimate religious convictions and conservative political movements were shaken, and who were very concerned about the social criticisms formulated by K. Marx and F. Engels, who worked from an explicitly evolutionary approach (Marx 1869; Engels 1884). In the academic world too, the mainstream line of thought required adhering to description and classification, and banishing any speculation. Among social anthropologists, evolutionism was rejected on all sides in the Western world. Some felt that it established a hierarchy among peoples and, therefore, supported racist attitudes (Boas 1897). Those who collaborated with the colonial administrations reckoned it offered nothing (Radcliffe-Brown 1922).

An evolutionist current reaffirmed itself in the United States under the leadership of Leslie White, and then Julian Stewart. The main advances of this neo-evolutionism are the inclusion of the environmental dimension and the demonstration of perfectly compatible multilinear approaches (White 1949; Stewart 1955), in contrast to the rigid caricature of unilinear and mechanical perspectives denounced by opponents. The archaeologist V. Gordon Childe continued an evolutionary approach by borrowing elements of Marxism without falling into Stalinist dogma (Childe 1942). He highlighted the revolutionary importance of the adoption of a production economy by humanity, and then of urban organization, by treating western Asia and Europe integrally. Evolutionism found itself at the same time, validated by the discovery of the genetic structure of the living (DNA). The result was that random mutations and natural selection do not operate at the individual level, but on that of genes (Huxley 1942). The evolutionary sequence of neo-evolutionists, however, has not fundamentally changed compared to those generated by their predecessors (Fried 1960; Service 1962). It was mainly enriched by details of the evolutionary sequence's continuation by insisting on a growing complexity of task specialization and on processes of the diffusion and expansion of social innovations. Clarifications were also proposed for the factors of change. On the growth of resources, great importance was always given to technical innovation, but also to the effects of climate change. On the internal conflicts that might lead to the disintegration of societies, diverging economic interests between the dominant and the dominated, according to Engels, remained a force, but was now combined with other factors. According to R. Carneiro, the name *environmental area* emphasized the critical importance of war and the submission of conquered populations (Carneiro 1970). Various means for legitimizing social hierarchy have been proposed based on concrete examples from archeology or anthropology: a privileged relationship with the supernatural, control of resources, trade and/or work, the formation of alliances, information processing, risk management, intersocietal domination. The systemic perspective has become commonplace, accompanied by a positive feedback effect. It is, as it turns out, often caused by the possibilities offered by a more hierarchical and better-coordinated organization, which is able to overcome resource limitations (conquest of new lands, major development work, etc.). In general, the conceptual evolution is then characterized by the growth of the temporal, spatial, and demographic dimensions of social groups, which should be taken into account in order to be more relevant and not to remain focused on highly localized communities anymore (Binford and Binford 1968; Clarke 1968; Dunnel 1971, 1978). Additionally, some authors have stressed the benefit of ethology and asserted the idea of a nature/culture co-evolution (Moscovici 1972; Morin 1973). The intellectual debate, however, escalated sharply in this regard with the 1975 publication of *Sociobiology, The New Synthesis*, by Edward O. Wilson. In it, this entomologist borrowed promising theories from several researchers: William D. Hamilton's kin theory (1964), Robert Trivers's theory of reciprocal altruism (1971), and John Maynard Smith and George R. Price's game theory in dynamic populations (1973). Wilson devoted his last chapter to human societies; hence the scandal. Reading the text carefully, without excessive prejudices, we found that he unambiguously affirmed that selective and environmental pressures had led to an "additional mental growth and a social organization that had made hominids cross the threshold leading to a more interesting autocatalytic phase of evolution," and that mental and social change came to depend more on an internal reorganization and fewer direct responses to environmental characteristics. Social change, in short, acquired its own engine.

In 1982, Ian Hodder's *Symbols in Action* launched a new movement in archaeology called postprocessualism. Designed in opposition to the new archeology, this movement was the archaeological version of postmodernism, which stood against the desire to draw general laws of social change, against the belief in truly objective theories, independent of the context, and against the importance of ecological factors. This conceptual nebula is characterized by two basic principles. The first is a philosophical skepticism and even a fundamental metaphysical doubt about the existence of the world outside our sensations—it would only be the product of our imagination, our representations—relying on the assumption of an absence of universal reality; current knowledge is considered a matter of perspective. Then, there is a further critique of Western society by means other than Marxism and structuralism, by isolating new structures of oppression: race, gender, culture, affirming that there is no unique truth in the past, only stories developed to gain more power in the present. These principles rejected big universalizing theories, and all those considered politically incorrect (e.g., the barbarians' dependence on Mediterranean civilizations, or a pre-state centralized and hierarchical political organization), and declared the preference for religious and symbolic dimensions of culture, local education, microsocial dimensions, prominence of the individual actor, plurality of meanings, and relativism. Until around 2000, this mainstream movement dominated the human sciences, resulting in sterilized research by enclosing the majority of researchers in the deconstruction perspective; however, to deconstruct to the extreme leads to the dissolution of the studied object, and therefore to a total loss of significance and widespread confusion. In *Theory and Practice in Archaeology* (1992), Hodder tried to advocate a more nuanced approach, avoiding binary oppositions, but the damage was done. Postmodernism was the mainstream movement the conventional majority of the archaeological community followed.

New Perspectives on the Evolution of Inequality

Around 2000, evolutionary approaches again became dominant after making very significant progress, supported by the achievements of cognitive science and ethology. For our purposes, they led to the answer to a crucial question that had previously been unexplored: How do humans manage to cooperate, within large political entities, with thousands of unrelated individuals? Two mechanisms led to a better understanding of the cooperative evolution trend among an animal species: kin selection (Hamilton 1964) and reciprocal altruism (Axelrod 1984). The first is the fact that natural selection acts on genes and not on individuals, and a behavior that might contribute to the transmission of genes has been selected, even if it might affect the survival of the individual, especially when it comes to saving an offspring or siblings. But we also found evidence for cooperative behavior between unrelated individuals among humans and many primates. Robert Axelrod has shown that cooperation can be established between unrelated individuals if they repeatedly interact. Individuals can cooperate conditionally, that is to say, until their partners become uncooperative (Axelrod 1984). They may not, however, establish trusting relationships with a large number of members, because they have a limited memory and a limited time.

Samuel Bowles and Herbert Gintis proposed a solution to this problem with the theory of strong altruism. Cooperation with many unrelated individuals implies a willingness not only to cooperate conditionally, but also to punish uncooperative behavior, even if it involves costs for the individual and lack of future gain. The higher the proportion of strong reciprocal altruism there is in a group, the more caution is required toward opportunistic individuals. If the species evolved in a context of competition between groups for the same ecological niche, groups with a higher proportion of strong reciprocal altruism could flourish more and impose themselves in the population through a group's selection process. The arguments are mainly derived from game theory (Bowles and Gintis 2003). However, strong reciprocal altruism does not explain why the formation of larger human societies, with village or urban agglomerations, was necessarily accompanied by greater social differentiation and political centralization. Weak or strong, altruism is sensitive to group size, as noted by Benoît Dubreuil (2006) in response to Robin Dunbar's observation according to which the average group size in primates is proportional to the relative size of the neocortex, that is to say, the ability to store information on "who's who" and "who did what to whom" (Dunbar 1998). He took up the idea that language is a form of "remote grooming," an economical way to stay abreast of "who did what to whom" (Dunbar 1996). The size of the human neocortex, compared to that of other primates, leads one to suppose that we should form groups of about 150 members. It is likely that human groups reach an optimal size, pushed up by the benefits associated with increased social pressure, but tend to peak due to difficulty for humans to monitor the actions of their peers in too big groups. Group size would be subject to a cap because of rising costs associated with social sanction; the emergence of villages and towns would be made possible by the creation of institutions that allowed a tight control of costs related to the punishment of deviant behaviors.

Christopher Boehm examined the behavior of chimpanzees and bonobos to better understand ancient human societies and, specifically, their apparent resistance to the emergence of very heightened inequalities (Boehm 1993, 1999). He derived from these comparisons the idea that archaic humans had also lived in small exogamous groups of individuals capable of selfishness, aggression, and nepotism. Their social behavior was governed by rules and standards such as the priority given to some, for the access to food, by their implicitly subordinate companions. These rules potentially benefited all members of these groups, as they imposed a social order and prevented chaos. Alpha males of archaic human groups were suitably equipped to ensure that subordinate members adhere to the rules. But at this level of reasoning there arose, he said, a fundamental question: How had these dominant males been led to resist the temptation to intimidate the subordinate members of the group or to monopolize, in excess, the resources for themselves?

He assumed that mechanisms had existed for subordinate group members to put pressure on the controlling behavior of Alpha males. He thought that, as in primate groups, subordinate members of archaic human groups might form coalitions and unite against Alpha men to limit their power and access the resources. He concluded that hunter-gatherers were engaged mainly in altruistic behavior for sharing meat, rejecting tyrannical individuals, and repressing free riders, cheats, and disloyal members. They defended equality and fairness carefully through promoting and implementing sanctions. Social deviants, bullies, and fraudsters were reprimanded, excluded, stigmatized, and often murdered. To explain this peculiarity, he stressed that the most important differences between chimps and humans were the hunter-gatherers' language skills. Language allowed humans to limit selfishness and reward altruism by acting on the reputation of members of their groups through gossip. These people were not good or bad by nature; like us today, they were both. Although humans are naturally willing to give free rein to their selfish interests by cheating and parasitizing, they are also naturally disposed to dominate these drives when they expect they might produce side effects, such as corporal punishment and damage to their reputation. From many examples, the anthropologist has shown, moreover, that the amount of generosity and selfishness in hunter-gatherer societies is correlated with the abundance of food and other resources. Satiety promotes altruism. In times of moderate scarcity, nepotism worsens.

And in the case of famine, it becomes every man for himself. It is the specific skills of language, reasoning, and planning that would have allowed early humans to establish contracts and social norms, identify deviants, and agree on ways to punish them.

This idea seems compatible with the major theories of social anthropology and historical data on the global evolution of societies toward greater inequality. Village societies of hundreds of individuals all came to create complex kinship structures (often hierarchical), with sanctioned divisions of labor: in a lineage or clan special duties are assigned to punish relatives, often to meet a higher standard of preserving honor (honor killing). Societies of hundreds of thousands of individuals have experienced a universal differentiation between a political center and a periphery accompanied by the appearance of chains of command where the cost of punishment was controlled by a hierarchy. A process of bureaucratization, militarization, and monopolization of political power accompanied the appearance of the primary state everywhere (Mesopotamia, Egypt, China, India, Peru, and Mexico). Cognitive constraints do not account for all the reasons these institutions appear, but explain the correlation between demography and social organization (Boyd et al. 2003).

Along with the integration of knowledge about our cognitive system, the need was felt again imperiously to expand the vision beyond the local, regional, and national areas to embrace the scale of a globalized world. In line with the work of Immanuel Wallerstein (1974) and Fernand Braudel (1979), with their respective concepts of world system and world economies, global history has turned the page from the hostile postmodernist interlude to broader comparative approaches, to grand narratives necessarily considered accomplices of capitalism and imperialism. Christopher Bayly, in *The Birth of the Modern World 1780–1914*, rightly notes that "postmodern work generally ignores the 'metanarrative' specific that underlies them, which is both political and moralistic by its origins in its implications. Thus, many of these works seem starting from the idea that a change towards a better world could emerge if the historical engines generators of domination phenomena such as the unifying State, patriarchy, or even the rationalism of Western Enlightenment were not as powerful" (Bayly 2004). This comprehensive history examines transfers between different cultural zones in a systemic and comparative manner. He freed the constrictions that had been placed on the long-term macrohistorical prospects over vast areas articulating societies of unequal developmental levels, such as Southwest Asia and Europe.

THE GROWTH PROCESSES OF INEQUALITY

In Europe, the growth in inequality is made visible by traversing the sequence of social organization types proposed by Allen W. Johnson and Timothy Earle (1987) (Figure 7.1). As elsewhere in the world, this trajectory has followed linear growth neither in time nor in space. Besides the importance of these fluctuations, it should be noted that Neolithic, urban, and state appearances were systematically secondary processes in Europe, proceeding as inhabitants, goods, and ideas extended from the Near and Middle East. For Europe, strictly speaking, it is necessary to distinguish three distinct areas where political complexity and growing inequality have developed in a very staggered manner by answering different combinations of factors. The adoption of a state organization is generally considered the transition to a higher level of social inequality.

1. The emergence of Minoan states around 2000 BC and Mycenaean toward 1600 BC, continued by primarily borrowing an Oriental organizational model facilitated by the same type of Mediterranean bioclimatic environment, the same palatial organization policy, and participation in the same system of economic relations around the eastern Mediterranean basin; a system in which the general collapse of the twelfth century BC led to the disintegration of the Aegean States.

2. The Greek and Etruscan city-states, formed in the eighth century BC, quickly spread their political organization in the form of settlements and trading posts along the Mediterranean and Black Sea coasts. Their trading partners in the European hinterland accentuate their own level of organizational complexity, but do not to take the form of state organization outside the Mediterranean climate zones. This suggests that, in humid temperate regions, agro-pastoral farming techniques were not able to produce sufficient amounts regularly enough to supply urban areas that state organizations require.

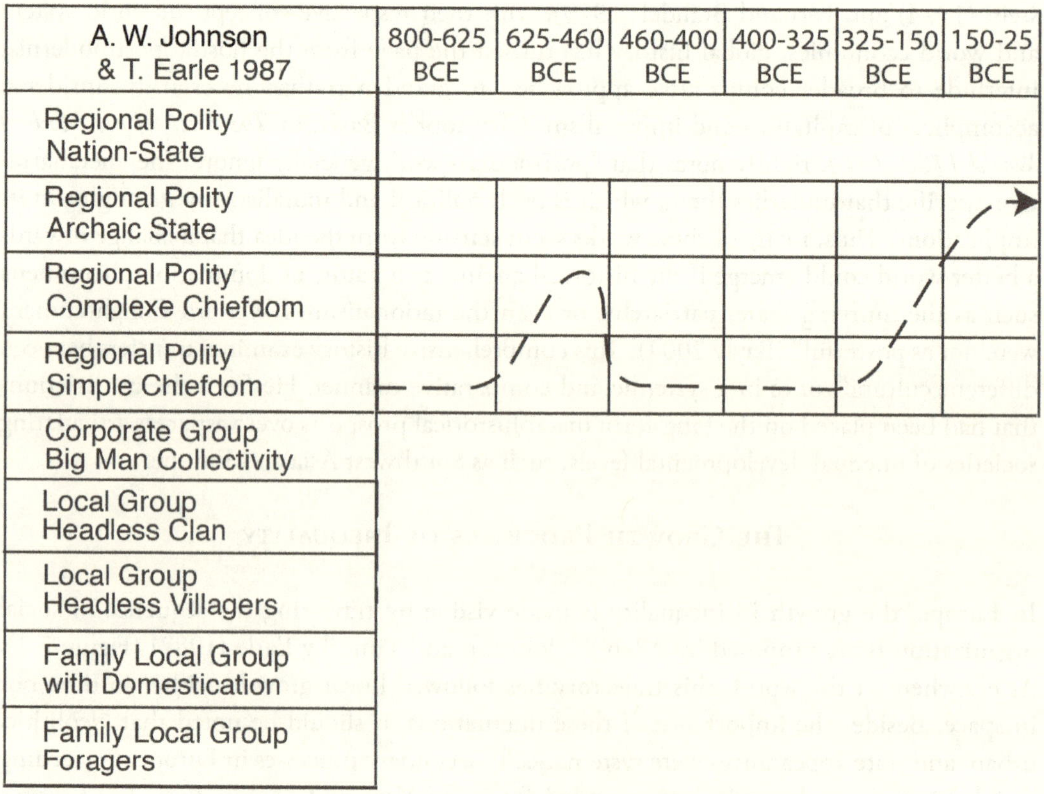

A. W. Johnson & T. Earle 1987	800-625 BCE	625-460 BCE	460-400 BCE	400-325 BCE	325-150 BCE	150-25 BCE
Regional Polity Nation-State						
Regional Polity Archaic State						
Regional Polity Complexe Chiefdom						
Regional Polity Simple Chiefdom						
Corporate Group Big Man Collectivity						
Local Group Headless Clan						
Local Group Headless Villagers						
Family Local Group with Domestication						
Family Local Group Foragers						

FIGURE 7.1. Sawtooth evolution of organizational complexity during the Iron Age in France, according to the typology of Johnson and Earle (1987).

3. The emergence of more extensive states in humid temperate zones and steppes, took place in the second century BC promoting their integration into the economic system run by Rome and an intensification of agricultural production made possible by the widespread use of iron tools.

4. The emergence of states in Denmark and around the Baltic, that is, in the northern areas of the humid temperate European hinterland, farther from the Mediterranean, took place in the eighth century through an increase of maritime contacts with the southern most states that had previously been integrated into the Roman Empire during the first four centuries of the Common Era (Viking colonies).

Europe adopted technical and organizational innovations, including the state, developed in the Middle East. This secondary process cannot, however, be explained using a simple diffusion model. Specific difficulties had to be resolved for states to appear across the whole of Europe. Various combinations of factors, adapted to local social and environmental conditions, had to be implemented. They give us precious keys to understand the general issue of growing inequality. It is considered that the Iron Age began in Western Europe, thus in France, around 800 BC. Social change has occurred here in five distinct stages.

800–730 BC (Gündlingen level) and 730–625 BC (Hallstatt C)

Compared to the end of the Bronze Age, around 800 BC, changes appear to have mainly resulted from economic factors; what we have called a "new deal" (Brun and Ruby 2008; Brun et al. 2009). The main centers of power have indeed changed location, favoring the most topographically remote areas, but closer to dense forests (for fuel), and deposits of iron and rock salt, and where it was also possible to develop a breeding program to produce exportable cured meats (pigs, cattle) and luxury textiles (woolly sheep). This new situation may have resulted from climatic degradation and disorganization of the bronze exchange networks to which the answer would have been the transfer of economic investment to the best assets, including other resources. However, no structural change is noticeable politically; the picture is blurry because it is composed of contradictory elements. Some elements suggest a fundamental continuity (no major break in material culture, sustainability of the basic agropastoral occupation with scattered farms and hamlets, continuation and even an increase in the practice of individual burial mounds for male elites). Other elements point to significant evidence of rupture (a break in the practice of terrestrial hoards, abandonment of many fortified and unfortified agglomerated settlements). Simple chiefdoms probably continued, a dominant chief or a council controlling local networks (lineages) and external exchange networks. The rapidly growing number of rich funerary deposits compared to nonfunerary deposits reproduced the change, first demonstrated in Denmark (Kristiansen 1978), but that proves quite general between these two deposition categories. This alternation suggests that there were cultural choices expressing two different political ideologies: one favoring unity and solidarity of the group by more egalitarian burial practices and the ceremonial expenditure of wealth in form of votive deposits, and the other showing the distinction of elites in a more or less ostentatious and individualized manner.

628–460 BC (HALLSTATT D)

During Hallstatt D, more extensive attempts at political and hierarchical integration occurred in some areas. Complex chiefdoms were formed, as a result of agropastoral productivity, which benefited from improved weather conditions and intensified connections via external exchange networks. These local and global factors combined to provide the means of enriching and developing power, taking particularly conspicuous forms during the sovereign's funeral. This strengthening of social hierarchy has long been demonstrated in burial data. This political and economic complexity is largely confirmed by the prioritization and diversification of institutions. Through an increase of field operations on larger surfaces than before—made possible by preventive archeology, especially in the Paris Basin—we have data that reflect much more reliably the level of complexity of ancient societies than grave data alone.

The top-level sites suggest fifty-kilometer radius modules for politically autonomous territories between western Bavaria and Berry. The climax of this phenomenon, traditionally called "princely," lasted about three generations (530–460 BC). During this period, settlement typologies diversified, with family farms being open, enclosed, or fortified and larger or smaller in size. Agglomerated settlements were open or fortified and of various dimensions, culminating with the famous "princely residences," some of which, such as Hundersingen "Heuneburg," Vix "Mont Lassois," and perhaps Bourges, have even approached an urban pattern. This growth in political and economic complexity has been confirmed in recent years in the group of southwestern cultures of the North Alpine cultural complex (Brun and Chaume 2013). This test of urban and state organization has nevertheless remained unfinished, the scale and the level of integration regaining the previous dimensions; those simple chiefdoms were very constrained by a difficult threshold of a day's walking distance back and forth, that is, in politically autonomous territories of about 25 to 30 kilometers on flat land. Beyond this dimension, the cost incurred in travel time and energy for the chief and his escort made centralized management and control more difficult and fragile, requiring the ability to relay supreme power in more remote areas. However, the loyalty or fidelity of these subordinate leaders has always been a major problem for the unity of such political entities. Even territorial states larger than city-states have long been threatened by defections of great vassals, which constantly called their unity into question.

460–325 BC (LA TÈNE A-B1)

Disintegration of politically complex chiefdoms was accompanied by a decrease in ostentatious display. Even in the western margins such as Berry, Middle Loire, Aisne-Marne, Saarland, Hunsrück-Eifel and Hesse, the richest tombs, many containing Etruscan bronze vessels, are less impressive than the Ha D princely grave. Their monumentality is inferior, their funerary deposits are less impressive, and corresponding settlements are less rich and monumental. Rich tombs at corresponding institutions show a very different geographical distribution of previous "princely" centers: more dispersed with much shorter distances to the nearest neighbor. Despite maintaining privileged relationships with networks of northern Italy, it seems that the size of political entities remained equivalent to simple chiefdoms where a leader could intervene anywhere in half a day to regain control, conduct arbitration, and restore order.

The reasons for the disintegration of great Hallstatt D "principalities" remain difficult to explain. As with most things, it's probably a combination of factors that triggered collapse. Active exchange networks with the Etruscans might have become substitutes for Greek partners, upsetting established alliances with "princely" elites. In addition to this are the effects of a less favorable climate and increasingly controversial social relations, with the peasantry supporting too-despotic potentates with greater difficulty.

It seems that the solution to these difficulties of continuity was finally found in the organization of orderly migration, as suggested by textual sources from the beginning of La Tène B, around 400 BC. These migratory movements continued for a little more than a century, aiming for more southern areas. Climatic degradation might have accentuated this heliotropism, but the most striking of these movements lies in the attraction of North Alpine Celts for the more developed societies with which they previously entered into indirect contact. They clearly sought to invest in zones that put them in direct contact with Etruscans in northern Italy and Greece, through the Balkans, along the Black Sea, and to the Greek cities of Asia Minor, by crossing the Dardanelles Strait.

325–150 BC (LT B2-C)

Networks of cross-cultural exchange of prestige goods were most likely interrupted by migratory turbulence. Intercultural systemic relationships have, however, continued. They have changed in nature. Trade and diplomatic relations, during Ha D, with Etruscan and Greek city-states were made very attractive to the North Alpine Celts, for example, due to the orientation of their migration in northern Italy, in the Carpathian basin, in the Balkans between the Black Sea and Asia Minor's Greek cities, and to their massive presence in mercenary armies recruited by the various Mediterranean countries (Péré-Nogues 2013).

At the end of fourth century BC, simple chiefdoms of the North Alpine Celtic world show signs of reconstruction, including constructed shrines, with a major role as territorial markers. They illustrate increased importance for members of these political entities and their neighbors, a more sustainable symbol of their collective identity. Social cohesion, promoted and celebrated regularly in and around these sanctuaries, seems to have been additionally cemented by frequent military conflicts between competing chiefdoms; battles with weapons; and even vanquished corpses proudly displayed in these religious monuments. Deterioration of the previous level of political complexity, which had been characterized by authoritarian centralization and autonomous territories of unprecedented size, probably created a stimulus for economic competition.

We note that from the end of fourth century BC (LT B2) major technological changes occurred in the iron and steel field. One of the most important was the production of iron agricultural tools, especially plowshares (Nillesse 2009). Widespread use of iron in the ordinary tools of the peasantry implies a sharp rise in raw material production. This is a crucial qualitative and quantitative leap, well attested by the discovery of large iron mines, as in La Bazoge "Petites Rouilles" (between Normandy and Touraine) (Langlois 2008) and in the rapid increase in the number of forge sites in the Paris Basin (Bauvais and Fluzin 2007). This, logically, resulted in a strong intensification of farming production. An increase in technical efficiency, enabled by the use of iron for plowing, facilitated the opportunity for more agricultural productivity. There is, indeed, by the evidence of aerial surveys and the excavations preceding the construction of highways and railway tracks, the habit to investigate general areas previously unoccupied, especially uplands (Malrain et al. 2002). This gain in productivity, probably supported by continuous global warming, could give growers more confidence, as suggested by the gradual abandonment of the practice of planting two or three different species in the same plot. The adoption of monospecificity in this period was discovered by Matterne (2001) while analyzing the composition of grain reserves in the Paris Basin. This is also based on the assurance of having a broad and well-organized solidarity; further indicative of organizational complexity in net growth.

We note, finally, the appearance of villages in the third century BC. We expect more specific publications, but it seems that on the surface of several dozen hectares, fairly small and densely occupied enclosures were identified. Various indications of craft production are concentrated, but internal organization, the composition of resident groups, and the chronology of their development are difficult to grasp. An increase in productivity, however, occurred. It was also logically accompanied by other technological improvements such as the rotating grinding wheel.

150–25 BC (LA TENE D)

In the middle of the second century BC, a new attempt at social complexity reached its fulfillment with city and state emergence. Spatial organization quite clearly illustrates social organization. These are, in fact, significantly hierarchical networks that appear as archaeological finds. Economic and political integration levels are logically structured by distance, that is to say, the length and difficulty of moving. At the head of these networks is the capital city. At lower levels, there are towns and villages, and finally hamlets and farms. Two types of networks are combined within each politically autonomous formation:

- Settlements with a primarily agropastoral function, which come in several hierarchical levels, depending on their area and the investment level required for their construction, which likely reflect strong inequalities in land ownership.

- Settlements with more diversified economic functions, controlled by the family that owns land on which they were located.

Open cities, which began to grow in the third century BC, grew and multiplied in the first half of the next century. The very pronounced aristocratic and military characteristics of these societies suggest that local aristocracy owned the land in question, exercised patronage on these large villages or concentrated on handicraft production, to ensure minimum safety. The trend emerges gradually, and suggests a meeting or merger of major branches of these two types of networks to form large fortified settlements. This merger took place, it seems, by the fortification of a wide area around the original lowland village, or by transferring the population of the original town from a nearby point, also with fortifications, such as Levroux (Buchsenschutz et al. 2000). In many, cases, this fortified urban area was created on a site where there was also a quadrangular ditch sanctuary, such as Gournais-sur-Aronde (Metzler 2008). Thereafter, for about a century, during the period from LT D1 to LT D2a, most low-lying fortified settlements were gradually abandoned in favor of new fortified towns on hills, for example, Villeneuve-Saint-Germain in favor of Pommiers (Brun et al. 2000).

These very large towns fulfill all the criteria of urbanization (Brun and Chaume 2013). Their urbanized societies also have characteristics of archaic states. The main archaeological criteria are the use of a currency and writing. A combination of the two became common in the first century BC with bronze coins bearing the name of a king or chief magistrate. This implies that at least a fraction of the population had the ability to read these names. Several styles have also been discovered in different materials. Gauls certainly did not have lapidary inscriptions, however, they wrote on wooden tablets coated with wax. Caesar also refers to these, unambiguously stating that, on the one hand, writing was outlawed within the religion, but, on the other, that 368,000 migrants, soldiers, women, children, and old people (263,000 Helvetii, 36,000 Tulingi, 14,000 Latovices, 23,000 Rauraci, 32,000 Boii) he stopped at the beginning of the Gallic Wars carried tablets on which were displayed their full civil status in the Greek alphabet (Caesar DBG XXIX). Writing was therefore used for administrative management necessitated by the organizational complexity of any state-level political entity.

Assuming that there is little doubt that medieval dioceses had recorded the areas of the Gallic *civitates,* then we should be able to see changes in the size of integrated territories compared to previous periods. Eight *civitates* were part of a circle with a 25 to 30 km radius (2500–3600 km²), that is to say, a difficult threshold for managing simple chiefdoms, which became widespread in the mid-second millennium BC. It was logically the average size of *pagi*, these subsets of *civitates*. A second category of around 28 *civitates* had about a fifty kilometers radius (10,000 km²) and consisted therefore of federations of three or four *pagi*; this was the average size of complex chiefdoms during the sixth and fifth centuries BC, traditionally called "principalities." A third category consisted of 16 *civitates* within 75 km (22 500 km2), thus uniting 6 to 12 *pagi* (Figure 7.2); Caesar said, however, that the Helvetii State consisted of four "cantons," which would correspond to an average *pagi* with a 37 km radius, that is to say, a little larger than a day of walking round trip. Several signs suggest that apparent discrepancies between the sizes of certain medieval dioceses and those of previous *civitates* resulted from the integration of some *pagi* into different *civitates*. There is nothing surprising here, as states are historically full of variations of this kind; territorial subsets often follow a strategy to promote their own interests first. And this might explain the surprising attachment of the Mandubii, with Alesia as their capital, to Aedui State, in defiance of logic related to topographic and spatial factors, rather than their likely integration into the *civitas* of Lingons; the power of Aedui could have led them to expect a higher profit in terms of economic benefits and military alliance. Some *pagi* felt, conversely, that their interest was to resume their political independence in the course of the first century BC, as in the case of the Meldi separating from the Suessiones (Brun 2002). The best strategy for *pagi*, as for *civitates*, was based on various factors, likely including their cultural history and geostrategic location, as suggested by their mapping. The larger archaic states were juxtaposed within a wide band barring Gallic space diagonally from northeast to west-central, while most smaller states lined up along a strip parallel to the Channel. This bipartition strongly echoes the previous cultural millennium during which the respective Atlantic and North Alpine cultural complexes faced each other while maintaining a marked contrast in artifact styles, in residential building forms, or in burial practices. Smaller states also tend to be found along the boundaries between different sets of political and economic levels: firstly, the boundary between the Roman world, Narbonensis, and central Gaul, then that between the most integrated Gallic states and those who were less so, where aligning states are the size of single chiefdoms, a *pagus* or an average city-state (Eburovisques, Parisii, Meldi, Viromanduens).

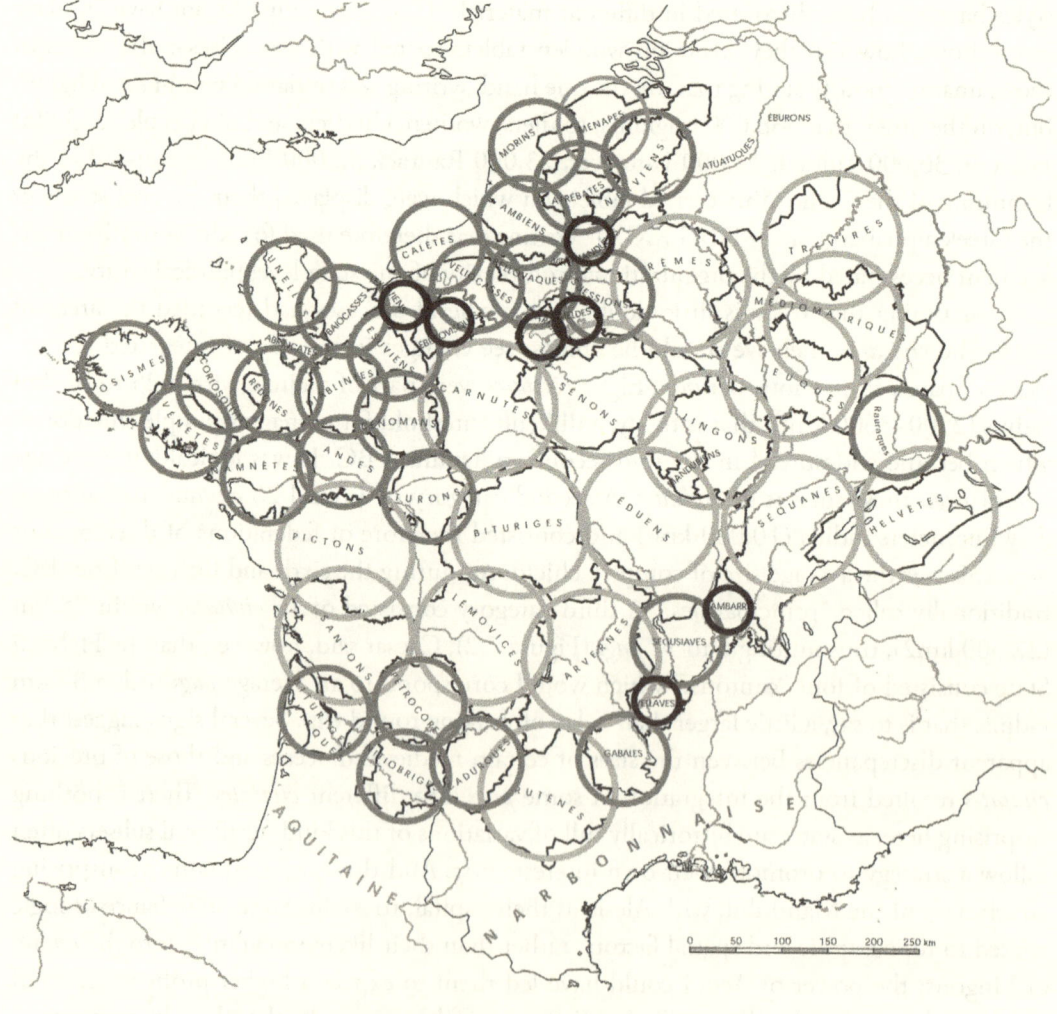

FIGURE 7.2. Map of the Gallic *civitates* (archaic states) LT D (150–25 BC) with a mapping of policy integration across three territorial radiation classes; black line: Circle of 25 to 30 km radius, line dark gray means: circle of about 50 km radius, light gray lines: a circle of 75 km radius and over (S. Fichtl base map).

THEORETICAL IMPLICATIONS

The changing scale of territorial integration during the Iron Age in humid temperate Europe accords with what happened all over the world. This fluctuating type of integration scale has been clearly demonstrated in various regions in central Mexico between 800 BC and AD 1700, in the Andes between 1400 BC and AD 1700, in Mesopotamia between 4500 and 1500 BC, or in Egypt between 3700 and 300 BC (Marcus 1998). These developments are interspersed with sometimes drastic phases of disintegration, followed by stages of growth that always end, overall, by exceeding the highest level previously achieved. This fundamentally nonlinear change is a universal feature of globalization, at least since the Neolithic; a condition that is nearing completion today.

In Europe and elsewhere, various factors have combined to cause the collapse of this level of integration, which logically include climate changes. To avoid confusion, the subtitle of Jared Diamond's book about societal collapse driven by climate change should be: *How Societies Choose to Fail or Succeed* (Diamond 2005). These are, indeed, social organizations that are traditionally incompetent, blind, and focused on short-term management and are incapable of changing their lifestyle to adapt better to hazards. It was probably the same during the Iron Age. Climate improvements clearly correspond to the stages of growth of the scale of political integration (Figure 7.3).

Another factor played a major role in these changes: technological progress. Among them, the most crucial were, of course, those which were likely to increase agropastoral productivity; the level must be sufficient to maintain communities where many residents do not produce their own food. Perhaps it was not a failed urbanization attempt in the middle of the first millennium BC, which would explain, in part, its ephemeral nature. Dramatic growth in steel production, which transformed agricultural tools and made them available to all users, most likely provided the means for subsequent urban and state development. This implies some correct conclusions from the valuable *History of World Agriculture. Neolithic to the Contemporary Crisis* (Mazoyer and Roudart 1997). It focuses, however, for far too long on slash-and-burn farming systems, and ignores the widespread use of the iron plow, coulter, and scythe from the third century BC. The authors do not distinguish between uncultivated systems and light animal traction, and those in fallow and plow culture, where there was a fundamental stage of development that led to social changes of great magnitude. They called the "agricultural revolution of the Middle Ages" the adoption of the moldboard plow, which is considered the most significant attribute of plow culture. There are many reasons to believe that iron agricultural tools had already created conditions for revolution through agrarian economy by the beginning of the last quarter of the first millennium BC.

Another factor has been underestimated or even ignored: the change of political regimes. It is, moreover, one of the shortcomings of social typologies, such as that of Johnson and Earle (1987). Relevant foundations have been laid by Greek and Roman thinkers from antiquity. Thus, the theory of Anacyclosis by Polybius proposed a six-phase cycle of political regimes: monarchy, tyranny, aristocracy, oligarchy, democracy, and ochlocracy within which there would be a wait for the right man who would renew the monarchy. Behind the cyclical, very mechanical aspect of the proposal lies a relevant structure that distinguishes

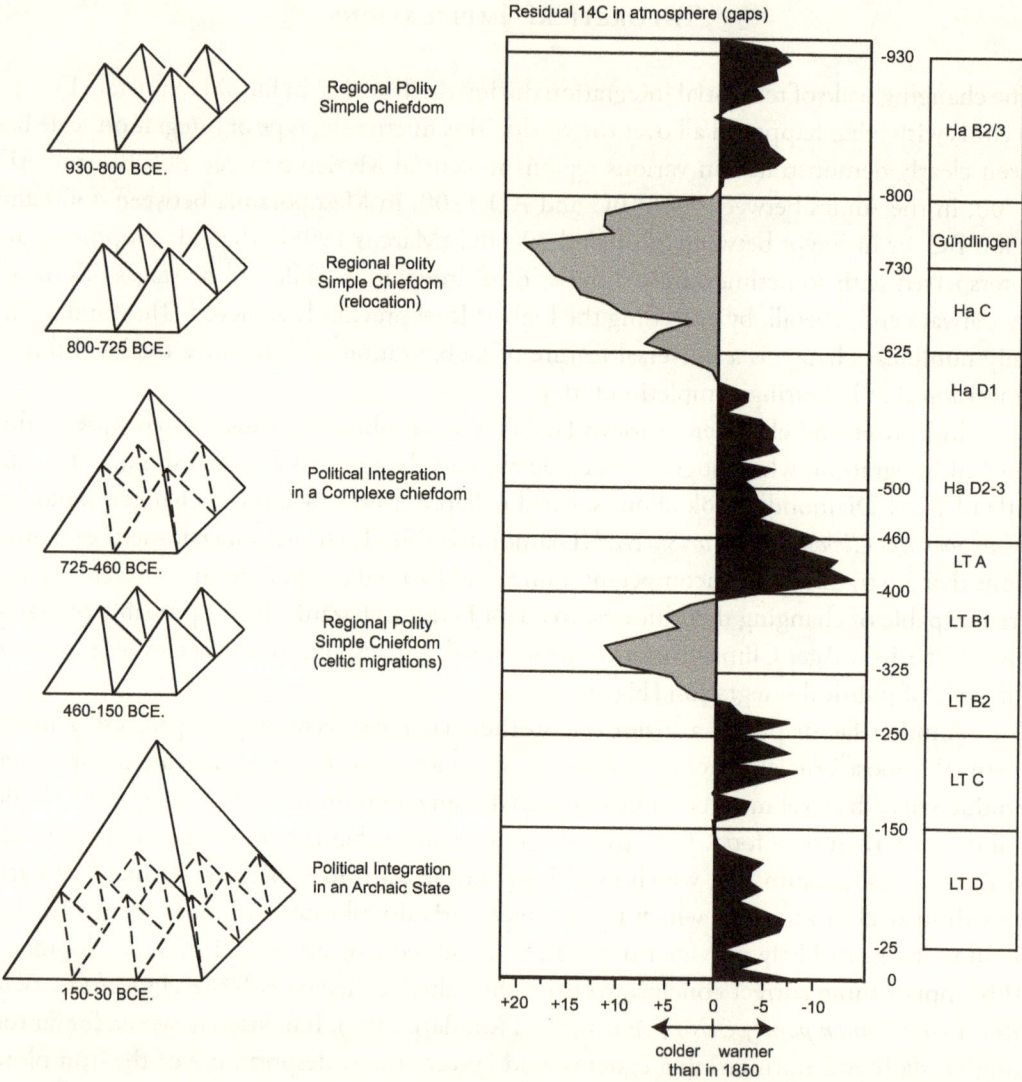

FIGURE 7.3. Comparative evolution of the level of political integration—each autonomous political unit (solid lines) or integrated (dashed) are represented in a pyramid shape—and residual 14C in the atmosphere well correlated with climatic oscillations.

three types of government: government of one, government of several (or minority), and government of all (or a majority). Three types might have two forms each: one just concerned with the public interest guided by reason—respectively, monarchy, aristocracy, and democracy—the other deviant, subject to the special interests and passions—respectively, tyranny, oligarchy, and ochlocracy (Figure 7.4). It seems that the evolution of political systems in Europe, from the eighth century BC does not conform only to Johnson and Earle's typology in terms of organizational complexity, but also to the typology of political regimes. In terms of simple chiefdoms, the head is a small monarch, a wren, which can already only

political regimes	Right form: mind the general interest oriented reason	Deviant form: subject to the special interests and passions
Government of one	monarchy	tyranny
Government of many (or minority)	aristocracy	oligarchy
Government of all (or a majority)	democracy	ochlocracy

FIGURE 7.4. Political regimes and forms of exercise of power, according to Polybius: right or deviant.

exercise power. At the level of complex chiefdoms, a king may be more inclined to rule in a despotic, even tyrannical, manner. And this risk is even higher in archaic states. Over the course of these eight centuries, the textual sources clearly demonstrate such changes. Julius Caesar stated that the Gallic hereditary kings tended more and more to make room for judges elected among aristocrats in each archaic state, but in an extremely tense political atmosphere; until the outbreak of revolutions similar to those that overthrew and expelled the Tarquin in Rome or Codrides in Athens. These tyrannical deviant monarchies were transformed into the "aristocracy."

The Arverni renounced their royal family in 121 BC. It is likely that the Aedui state was suspicious of monarchy even earlier; it seems that, for the Gauls, royalty was most unfavorable, and that they took the most exacting provisions against tyranny. The Aedui had accurate and skillful laws, which Polybius might have found to be as good as those in Roman law. In peacetime, the Aedui people obeyed a single magistrate, elected annually, that the Celts called *vergobret*: he was very like a dictator or consul of primitive times, for he had, except in title and duration, all the royal authority. He was a sovereign judge, who held the power of life and death. His power was likely to become even more dangerous, in that one would not have hesitated to attract to this sovereign position young, bold, and ambitious persons. But many precautions were taken against institutionalizing the *vergobret*: his magistracy lasted only one year; he could not cross borders of state; he could not appear at the head of armies, unless he was out of office: if he gave them orders, it was as a minister of war who would not fight, and his authority was as a commissioner, during campaigns, to one or more military commanders of infantry or cavalry. The Aedui shared with all Greco-Roman towns fear of a coup d'état and suspicion of tyranny (Jullian 1907).

Some salient points can be made in conclusion. First, and in general, it is confirmed that protohistorical societies were more complex, economically and politically, than expected and that their jagged evolution corresponds to a standard of universal history, as had plainly been seen by Stewart with his multilinear evolution and cultural ecology approaches (Stewart 1955). Then, during the eighth and seventh centuries BC, a progressive rupture occurred, marked by a relocation of many high-level settlements, but despite the still too rare documentation, it seems that the political integration module did not change after 800 BC. It experienced a strong growth in the sixth and early fifth centuries BC, especially in the southwestern part of the north-alpine zone. The model of "princely residences" is indeed validated broadly; some princely capitals have even proven much larger than expected, although they did not reach the urban stage. There is a decline in social complexity from the middle of the fifth century BC, the causes of which remain poorly understood. Of these cases, the military seat of power and the exceptionally ostentatious funeral practices of ruling dynasties, related to their power to install a woman of their family on the throne, suggest that despotic management might have caused a spike in revolts. A reprisal of the political complexity appeared from the third century BC on a more solid economic base. It led to a further growth of the integration scale among unstable federations of *pagi*, allowing the spread of what Caesar has called *civitates*, meaning, archaic states, including Northwestern Gaul, that reached the territorial dimension of principalities from the previous four centuries, while those located farther southeast and nearer to the Roman world reached significantly larger territorial dimensions. More complex in their political organization, these states were also places with great social inequalities. Caesar cited powerful Gallic aristocrats with a clientele of thousands of people, and even a hired army. Currently available funerary data, however, does not demonstrate strong social inequalities; they are significantly less ostentatious than during the "princely phenomenon" in the middle of the first millennium BC; however, the major agropastoral areas uncovered recently by preventive archeology operations leave no doubt about the degree of inequality of these societies. This paradox is due to the fact that the funerary practices fail to accurately reflect not only the social hierarchy—if the monumentality and the rich funerary deposits unambiguously reveal a hierarchical society, uniformly simple graves do not necessarily indicate an egalitarian society—but also the fundamental difference between political inequality and economic inequality. It has long been assumed that the inequalities of law and resources tended to grow correspondingly in human societies until the adoption of democracy, with which the link weakens. This was a mistake. It should now be considered that at all levels of organizational complexity, societies might vary between forms of political regimes oriented toward the general interest, on one side, to the special interests of the powerful, on the other. There is a growing number of indications that human societies have always been aware of the risks of abuse and the violation of freedoms by rulers, who have always been potentially tempted by despotism and tyranny. Social evolution, as made perceptible by archeology, during the Iron Age in France shows that among the factors that combined to explain the observed changes, political regimes probably played a major role.

REFERENCES

Axelrod, R. 1981 The Evolution of Cooperation. *Science* 211:1390–1396.

Bauvais, S., and P. Fluzin 2007 Réflexion sur l'organisation technico-sociale des activités de forge à La Tène finale dans l'Aisne (02). *Revue d'Archéométrie* 30.

Bayly, C. A. 2004 The Birth of the Modern World 1780–1914. Blackwell, Oxford.

Binford, S. R., and L. Binford (eds.) 1968. *New Perspectives in Archaeology*. Aldine, Chicago.

Boas, F. 1896 The Limitations of the Comparative Method in Anthropology. *Science* 4:901–908.

Boehm, C. 1993 Egalitarian Behavior and Reverse Dominance Hierarchy. *Current Anthropology* 34(3):227–253.

Boehm, C. 1999 *Hierarchy in the Forest: The Evolution of Egalitarian Behavior*. Harvard University Press, Cambridge.

Bowles, S., and H. Gintis 2003 The Origins of Human Cooperation. In *Genetic and Cultural Evolution of Cooperation*, edited by P. Hammerstein, pp. 429–443. MIT Press, Cambridge.

Braudel, F. 1979 *Civilisation matérielle, Economie et Capitalisme, XV–XVIIIe siècle*. Armand Colin, Paris.

Brun, P. 1993 La complexification sociale en Europe moyenne pendant l'âge du Fer : essai de modélisation. In *Fonctionnement social de l'âge du Fer: opérateurs et hypothèses pour la France*, Actes de la Table ronde de Lons-le-Saunier, 24–26 Oct. 1990, edited by A. Daubigney, pp. 275–290. Cercle Girardot, Lons-le-Saunier.

Brun, P. 1995a From Chiefdom to State Organization in Celtic Europe. In *Celtic Chiefdom, Celtic State Symposium*, edited by B. Arnold and B. Gibson, pp. 13–25. Cambridge University Press, Cambridge.

Brun, P. 1995b Oppida and social "complexification" in France. In *Different Iron Ages: Studies on the Iron Age in Temperate Europe*, edited by J. D. Hill and C. G. Cumberpatch, pp. 121–128. BAR International Series 602, British Archaeological Reports, Oxford.

Brun, P. 2002 Territoires et agglomérations chez les Suessiones. In *Territoires celtiques. Espaces ethniques et territoires des agglomérations protohistoriques d'Europe occidentale*, Actes du XXIVe colloque de l'AFEAF, Martigues, juin 2000, edited by D. Garcia and F. Verdin, pp. 306–314. Errance, Paris.

Brun, P., N. Buchez, S. Gaudefroy, and M. Talon (with the collaboration of I. Le Goff, F. Malrain, and V. Matterne) 2005 Protohistoire ancienne en Picardie. In *La recherche archéologique en Picardie : bilans et perspectives*, pp. 99–126. *Revue Archéologique de Picardie* 3–4:99–126.

Brun, P., M. Chartier and P. Pion 2000 Le processus d'urbanisation dans la vallée de l'Aisne. In *Les processus d'urbanisation à l'âge du Fer*, edited by V. Guichard, S. Sievers, and O. Urban, pp. 83–96. Centre archéologique européen du Mont-Beuvray, H. Glux-en-Glenne.

Brun, P., and B. Chaume (eds.) 1997 *Vix et les éphémères principautés celtiques. Les Vie–Ve siècles av. J.-C. en Europe centre-occidentale*. Actes du colloque international de Châtillon-sur-Seine, octobre 1993. Errance, Paris.

Brun, P., and B. Chaume 2013 Une éphémère tentative d'urbanisation en Europe centre-occidentale durant les Vie et Ve siècles av. J.-C.? *Bulletin de la Société Préhistorique Française* 110(2):319–349.

Brun, P., B. Chaume, L. Dhennequin, and B. Quilliec 2009 Le passage de l'âge du Bronze à l'âge du Fer . . . au fil de l'épée. In *De l'âge du Bronze à l'âge du Fer en France et en Europe occidentale (Xe–VIIe siècle av. J.-C.)*. Actes du XXXe Colloque International de l'AFEAF, mai 2006, St-Romain-en-Gal/Vienne, pp. 477–486. Revue archéologique de l'Est, Dijon.

Brun, P., and P. Ruby 2008 *L'âge du Fer en France. Premières villes, premiers États celtiques*. La Découverte, Paris.

Buchsenschutz, O., A. Colin, and G. Firmin 2000 Le village celtique des arènes à Levroux. Supplément à la Revue archéologique du centre de la France 19, FERAC-ADEL, Levroux.

Carneiro, R. L. 1970 A Theory of the Origin of State. *Science* 169:733–738.

Chaume, B., and C. Mordant (eds.) 2011 *Le complexe aristocratique de Vix. Nouvelles recherches sur l'habitat, le système de fortification et l'environnement du mont Lassois*. Ed. universitaires de Dijon, 2 vols. (Art, archéologie et Patrimoine), Dijon.

Childe, V. G. 1942 *What Happened in History*. Penguin Books, Harmondsworth.

Clarke, D. L. 1968 *Analytical Archaeology*. Methuen, London.

Darwin, C. R. 1859 *On the Origin of the Species, by Means of Natural Selection or the Preservation of Favoured Races in the Struggle for Life*. Murray, London.

Diamond, J. 2005 *Collapse. How Societies Choose to Fail or Succeed*. Viking Penguin, New York.

Dubreuil, B. 2006 L'origine de l'État et la nature de la coopération. *Eurostudia* 2(2).

Dunbar, R. I. M. 1996 *Grooming, Gossip, and the évolution of Language*. Harvard University Press, Cambridge.

Dunbar, R. I. M. 1998 The Social Brain Hypothesis. *Evolutionary Anthropology* 7:178–190.

Dunnel, R. 1971 *Systematics in Prehistory*. The Free Press, New York.

Engels, F. 1884 *Origin of the Family, Private Property and the State*. Verlag der Schweizerischen Volksbuchhandlung, Hottingen Zürich.

Ferguson, A. (1767) 1996 *Essay on the History of Civil Society*. Cambridge University Press, Cambridge.

Fried, M. 1960 On the Evolution and Social Stratification and the State. In *Culture in History*, edited by S. Diamond, pp. 269–282. Columbia University Press, New York.

Hamilton, W. D. 1964 The Genetic Evolution of Social Behaviour. *Journal of Theorical Biology* 7:1–52.

Hansen, M. H. 2006 Polis. *An Introduction to the Ancient Greek City-State*. Oxford University Press, Oxford.

Härke, H. 1983 Höhensiedlungen im Westhallstattkreis. Ein Diskussionsbeitrag. *Archäologisches Korrespondenzblatt*, 13(4):461–477.

Härke, H. 1989 Transformation or Collapse. Bronze Age to Iron Age Settlement in West Central Europe. In *The Bronze Age–Iron Age Transition in Europe, Aspects of continuity and change in European societies c. 1200 to 500 B.C.* BAR International Series 483, edited by M. L. Stig SØrensen and R. Thomas, pp. 184–203. British Archaeological Reports, Oxford.

Helveticus, C.-A. 1759 *De l'Esprit*. Mortjens, La Haye.

Hodder, I. 1982 *Symbols in Action*. Cambridge University Press, Cambridge.

Hodder, I. 1992 *Theory and Practice in Archaeology*. Routledge, London.

Huxley, J. 1942 *Evolution: The Modern Synthesis*. Allen and Unwin, London.

Johnson, A. W., and T. Earle 1987 *The Evolution of Human Societies*. Stanford University Press, Stanford.

Kristinsen, K. 1978 The Consumption of Wealth in Bronze Age Denmark. A Study in the Dynamics of Economic Processes in Tribe Societies. In *New Directions of Economic Processes in Tribe Societies*, edited by K. Kristiansen and C. Paludan-Muller, pp. 158–191. National Museum Press, Copenhagen.

Langalois, J.-Y. 2008 Le minerai de fer et son extraction de la Protohistoire au XIXe siècle dans l'ouest de la France. Présentation des quatre mines fouillées sur le tracé de l'A2. *Archéopages* 22:24–27.

Malrain, F., V. Matterne, and P. Méniel 2002 *Les paysans gaulois (IIIe siècle–52 av. J.-C.)*. Editions errance—Inrap, Paris.

Marcus, J. 1998 The Peaks and Valleys of Ancient States: An Extension of the Dynamic Model. In *Archaic States*, edited by G. M. Feinman and J. Marcus, pp. 59–94. School of American Research Press, Sante Fe.

Matterne, V. 2001 *Agriculture et alimentation végétale durant l'âge du Fer et l'époque gallo-romaine en France septentrionale*. Editions monique mergoil, Montagnac.

Maynard-Smith, J., and G. R. Price 1973 The Logic of Animal Conflict. *Nature* 246(5427):15–18.

Mazoyer, M., and L. Roudart 1997 *Histoire des agricultures du monde. Du néolithique à la crise contemporaine*. Seuil, Paris.

Metzler, J. 2008 Du Titelberg à Trèves. De l'oppidum gaulois à la ville romaine. In *Topographie sacrée et rituels. Le cas d'Aventicum, capitale des Helvètes. Actes du colloque international d'Avenches*, 2–4 novembre 2006, pp. 155–165. Archéologie suisse, Bâle.

Morgan, L. H. 1877 *Ancient Society*. Holt, New York.

Morin, E. 1973 *Le paradigme perdu: la nature humaine*. Seuil, Paris.

Moscovici, S. 1972 *La Société contre-nature*. Seuil, Paris.

Nillesse, O. 2009 Activités, métiers, vie quotidienne dans les établissements ruraux de l'Ouest de la France à travers l'instrumentum (Hallstatt D/début du Haut-Empire). In *Habitats et paysages ruraux en Gaule et regards sur d'autres régions du monde celtique*, Actes du XXXIe colloque de l'AFEAF, Association des Publications chauvinoises, Mémoire XXXV:254–261.

Pare, C. 1991 *Swords, Wagon-graves, and the Beginning of the Early Iron Age in Central Europe*. Philipps-Universität, Marburg.

Pere-Nogues, S. 2013 Aux limites de l'interprétation: mercenariat et mobilité au second âge du Fer. In *L'âge du Fer en Aquitaine et sur ses marges. Mobilité des hommes, diffusion des idées, circulation des biens dans l'espace européen à l'âge du Fer*, 35ᵉ colloque international de l'AFEAF, Bordeaux, 2–5 juin 2011, Bordeaux 2013, edited by A. Colin and F. Verdin. Fédération Aquitania, Bordeaux.

Polibius 1878 *De la République*. trad. Villemain. Larousse, Paris.

Radcliffe Brown, A. R. 1922 *The Andaman Islanders; A Study in Social Anthropology*. The University Press, Cambridge.

Roymans, N. 1991 Late Urnfield Societies in the Northwest European Plain and the Expanding Networks of Central European Hallstatt Groups. In *Images of the Past. Studies on Ancient Societies in Northwestern Europe*, edited by N. Roymans and F. Theuws, pp. 9–89. Instituut voor Pre- en Protohistorische Archeologie, Amsterdam.

Rousseau, J.-J. [1755] 1992 Discours sur l'origine et les fondements de l'inégalité parmi les hommes; discours sur les sciences et les arts. Flammarion, Paris.

Salac, V. 1990 Zu Untersuchungen über ein latènezeitliches (LT C2-D1). Produktions und Distributionszentrum in Lovosice. *Archeologické Rozhledy* 42:609–639.

Service, E. R. 1962 *Primitive Social Organization. An Evolutionary Perspective*. Random House, New York.

Steward, J. H. 1955 *Theory of Culture Change: The Methodology of Multilinear Evolution*. University of Illinois Press, Urbana.

Testart, A. 2005 *Eléments de classification des sociétés*. Errance, Paris.

Thomas, A. H. 2009 *Historical dictionary of Denmark*. The Scarecrow Press, Toronto.

Treuil, R., P. Darcque, J.-C. Poursat, and G. Touchais (eds.) 1989 *Les Civilisations égéennes du Néolithique et de l'âge du Bronze*. Presses Universitaires de France, Paris.

Trivers, R. 1971 The Evolution of Reciprocal Altruism. *The Quarterly Review of Biology* 46(1):35–57.

Wallerstein, I. 1974 *The Modern World-system* volume 2. Academic Press, New York.

White, L. 1949 *The Science of Culture: A Study of Man and Civilization*. Farrar, Straus, and Giroux, New York.

Wilson, E. O. 1975 *Sociobiology: The New Synthesis*. Belknap/Harvard University Press, Cambridge.

PART II

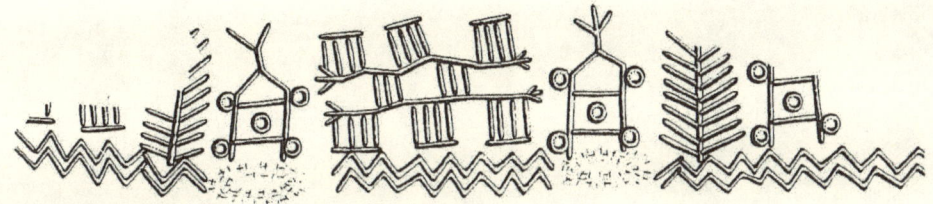

Inequality in Early Greece and Etruria

CHAPTER EIGHT

The Protogeometric Graves of the Kerameikos Cemetery at Athens

Is There Inequality?

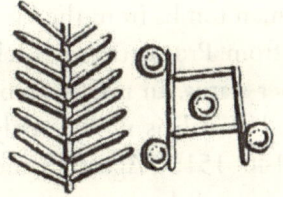

Simona Dalsoglio

Abstract   *According to I. Morris's theory of "formal burial," in Attica during the Dark Age the "access to the formal cemeteries was limited on the basis of rank." The aim of this work is to analyze the Transitional and Protogeometric graves (c. 1050–900 BC) of the Kerameikos necropolis at Athens using a quantitative approach and integrating it with the qualitative data, in order to find traces of inequalities among the burials.*

The tombs have been divided according to the number of their grave gifts from the grave equipment and the pyre refuse. The majority of the burials contain fewer than five items, while only a few graves contain more than ten objects; moreover, there is a positive correlation between the "wealth" of the burial and the presence of metals. The number of items in the graves has been also analyzed in relation to the gender of the dead and to the chronology. The analysis confirms that the female burials are richer than the male ones in terms of number and variety of objects; in the case of the male graves sometimes the presence of few distinctive objects, such as weapons, was enough to state a high status.

In conclusion, there are several levels of differentiation in the selection of the grave-goods, related, for example, to the status, the gender, the age of the deceased: the material evidence shows us some tombs standing out for their burial rite and reflecting an inequality among the restricted group of people who had access to the formal burial stated by Morris.

QUANTITATIVE APPROACH TO THE
GRAVE GOODS OF THE ATHENIAN FORMAL BURIAL

The aim of this paper is to determine the existence of a pattern of differentiation among the grave goods of the Transitional and Protogeometric burials in the Kerameikos cemetery at Athens (c. 1050–900 BC). First the quantitative data will be taken into account, as the measurement of the energy expenditure in the funerary rites; this will be integrated with the qualitative data, in order to get a more complete overview.

According to I. Morris's theory of "formal burial," the Athenian tombs from the Protogeometric to the Middle Geometric, together with the ones from Protoattic to Black Figure, represent a restricted range of adults belonging to a higher status. In this chronological span only *"agathoi"* are represented in the cemeteries and wealth is more evenly distributed than in the other periods (Morris 1987:93, 99–109, 140–151; d'Agostino and D'Onofrio 1993:41–51). J. Whitley, taking into account the richness of the graves, wrote that in the Protogeometric stage there are not "the disparities in wealth characteristic of Submycenaean" (Whitley 1991:111). According to the author, this phenomenon can be explained by a change in the form of ideological collective self-representation rather than a real change in the social organization (Whitley 1991:115). The analysis of the grave-goods will help us demonstrate that the presence of a group of graves belonging to a selection of people who have access to formal burial does not mean that these burials are without differences.

The Early Iron Age in Greece was a period of great change; in Athens, the most significant were the adoption of iron to make tools and weapons, the emergence of a new pottery style, and the use of cremation as the main burial ritual instead of inhumation. In the majority of cases the material evidence for this period comes from the burials. Scattered Protogeometric tombs have been found in several areas of Athens, while three extensive burial grounds have been excavated: in the Kerameikos, in the later Agora, and near Leophoros Vassilias Sophias. The graves of the Kerameikos necropolis, well documented and fully published, allows us to develop some statistical analyses with reliable results.

I have taken into account the graves found in the three burial areas of the Kerameikos site including tombs of this period: the Pompeion (Kraiker and Kübler 1939; Ruppenstein 2007), the one situated south of the Eridanos River (Kraiker and Kübler 1939; Kübler 1943), and the Sacred Road (Schlörb-Vierneisel 1966). The majority of the burials show the same rituals: they are "trench-and-hole" secondary cremations; the grave consists of a rectangular trench, into which often the debris of the pyre is thrown, containing a hole with the cinerary vase, almost always an amphora, sometimes together with other grave-goods. The only exceptions are represented by a few cases of cremation without cinerary urn, such as tombs PG 1 and PG E, and a few inhumations, likely recalling the previous Submycenaean tradition.

NUMBER OF OBJECTS FOUND IN THE GRAVES

The first step of this research is an analysis of the graves according to the number of objects given to the dead. Regarding the cremations, the urn and all the items (that are found in the cinerary vase, in the hole with the urn, and in the shaft along with the debris of the pyre) have been examined. In his analysis, J. Whitley considered only the objects found in the urn and in the surroundings (the grave equipment), but not those from the upper trench (the pyre refuse). In my opinion the remains of the objects put on the pyre or employed during the ritual have to be considered since they were part of the destruction of wealth that took place during the funeral.[1]

Moreover, I have taken into account all the classes of object found in the grave: pottery (82 percent, mostly vases but also beads, spindle whorls, and idols), metal objects (17 percent, weapons, jewelry, tools), glass and faience items (1 percent only). Twenty-four tombs that were disturbed have not been taken into consideration, because in these cases the number of the objects found in the burials is not reliable. Nevertheless, I have included in this study six disturbed graves because of their high number of objects (PG 4, PG 9, PG 13, PG 33, PG 37, PG 40), which make them useful for a first quantitative analysis.

The graves have been organized into four groups: the tombs with 0 to 5 objects, the ones with 6 to 10 items, the graves in which 11 to 15 items were found, and the ones with more than 15 objects (Figure 8.1). The majority of the tombs in the Kerameikos cemetery contain fewer than five items as grave goods, while only 10 graves have more than 10 objects. The result is that the number of burials is inversely proportional to the quantity of objects contained in them and the few graves with a high number of objects stand out among all the others.

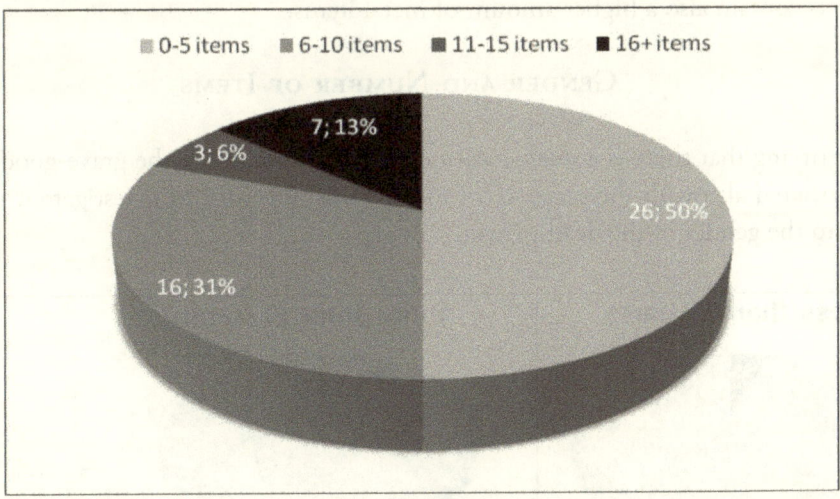

FIGURE 8.1. Relative frequency of items quantitative intervals for the Transitional and Protogeometric graves of the Kerameikos cemetery.

METAL OBJECTS FOUND IN THE GRAVES

Is it possible to consider the quantitative data alone, as an indicator of inequality among these graves? The quantity of items in the tombs gives us a rough indicator of the social differentiation but considered alone it may mislead. In fact, in some cases burials with more objects, made of poorer materials, appear to be wealthier than other ones with fewer items, but made of precious materials. The quantitative data should be then integrated by the qualitative one.[2] For this reason I have taken into account also the incidence of metal items.

J. Whitley (Whitley 1991:183) and H. van Wees (van Wees 1998:342) investigated the presence of metals in the Athenian Iron Age graves, but their tables didn't take into account the whole number of items found in each burial.

The most common metal objects are pins; among the ornaments we have also fibulae, rings, golden hair-spirals. Some male graves are characterized by weapons and tools: swords, daggers, spearheads, arrowheads, shield bosses, knives, chisels.[3] In a couple of graves the archaeologists found also a bronze bowl and the remains of some metal decorations, including a bird head.

Is the presence of metal objects and their number related to the quantity of grave-goods found in each tomb? To simplify the analysis I have divided the number of the items found into the burials into two main groups: the first with the burials that have up to 10 objects and the second with the graves with more than 10 items (Figure 8.2). The graves with more than two metal objects constitute 9 percent of the tombs with up to10 items and 40 percent of the ones with more than 10 items; the percentage of graves with a high number of metal objects is significantly greater in the burial group with more than 10 items.

In these burials the presence and the number of metal items has a positive correlation with the number of grave gifts: the graves that we can define as wealthiest for the quantity of objects contain also a higher amount of metal items.

GENDER AND NUMBER OF ITEMS

After verifying that there is a quantitative differentiation among the grave-goods, and that it is associated also with the presence of metal items, we want to investigate if it might be related to the gender of the dead person.

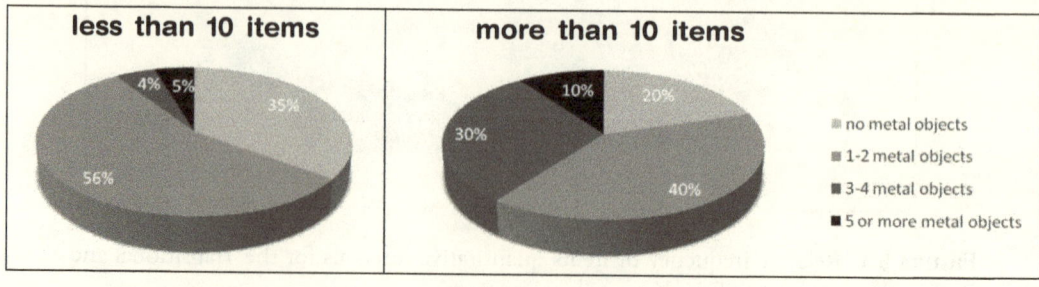

FIGURE 8.2. The percentage of the graves with up to or more than 10 items that include metal objects.

In Athens, some Iron Age female graves stand out for their wealth, and in general the female burials are characterized by a higher number of objects compared to the male ones (Strömberg 1993:53, 108–109; Whitley 1996:209–232). The gender of the graves taken into consideration has been determined by osteological analysis[4] and, in case of lack of analysis, by examination of the grave-goods.[5] Nevertheless, in some cases it is not possible to determine if the buried was male or female.

For 10 burials of the first group (0–5 items) it is not possible to establish the gender. In another 10 cases we are able to say that the dead was male, and in six cases that the remains belonged to a female. In the second group (6–10 items) we have 12 female burials and only three males. In one case it is not possible to establish the gender of the dead. In the third group (11–15 items) we have two female graves and one male, while in the last group six burials are female and one is male. As we can see from the graph (Figure 8.3), the male burials prevail in the tombs with a lower number of objects, while in the other three groups the female graves outnumber. It is worth noting that almost all the graves with more than 10 items are female; a significant exception is PG 40, a male burial (according to Breitinger's osteological analysis, Kübler 1943:2), in which the high number of grave goods is added to the presence of metal items.

In general, the quantity of objects prevails in the female graves, but wealth is not exclusive to women. It is necessary to point out that the wealthiest male grave, PG 40, counts 20 objects while the two wealthiest female graves, PG 39 and PG 48, count respectively 51 and 149 items;[6] the maximum numbers of grave-goods among the female burials much exceed the maximum amounts of items among the male ones.

In some cases, the wealthiest burials stand out also for the redundancy of such objects as the *lekythoi* (nine in PG 40), the *oinochoai* (16 in PG 48), the cups (nine in PG 37), the

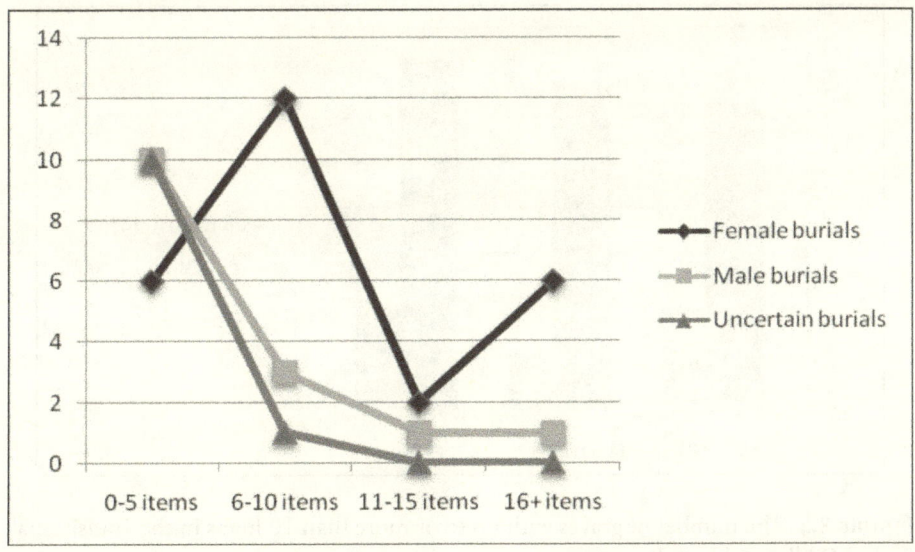

Figure 8.3. Absolute frequency of items quantity intervals for burial gender.

spindle whorls (21 in PG 48), or the clay beads (15 in PG 39 and 80 in PG 48). Nevertheless, wealth is not indicated only by the number but also by the variety of the items. In the tombs with a higher number of grave-goods it is possible to find special objects that occur quite rarely in the other burials of the necropolis. An example is given by the golden spirals, occurring in only four graves, two of them with more than 10 items, or even by flasks and *askoi,* found in another four graves, three of which contain more than 10 objects. The ring flask is even rarer (found in tombs SM 146 and PG 48, both very wealthy) as well as the clay cauldrons (found in tombs PG 4 and PG 39). Finally, special objects occur in only one grave, such as the bronze bowl along with the clay stands in PG 48, or the multiple vase in PG 1. In the case of vessels we could argue that the content, rather than or together with the container, was rare and precious or had a particular significance for the burial rite.

In the most of cases these rare objects have been found in the female burials, while the elements that characterize the male graves are weapons and metal tools.

CHRONOLOGY

Is the variability in the number of objects in the graves related to chronology? In this study I have taken into account the Transitional together with the Protogeometric period. The latter is traditionally divided into three phases: Early, Middle, and Late. The Early Protogeometric and the Middle Protogeometric, whose duration is still not well defined (c. 980–960 BC),[7] are shorter than the Late Protogeometric and, due to the low number of graves that belong to these earlier phases, I considered them together. Late Protogeometric phase is considerably longer and with a higher number of tombs.

As we can observe from the graph (Figure 8.4), the tombs that belong to the group with up to 10 items prevail in all the ages (Transitional, Early and Middle Protogeometric,

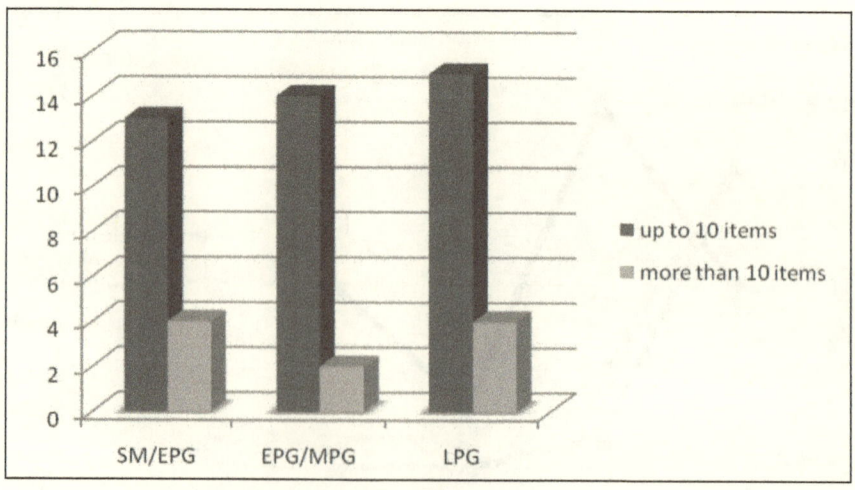

FIGURE 8.4. The number of graves with up to or more than 10 items in the Transitional, Early-Middle, and Late Protogeometric periods.

and Late Protogeometric); the number of the graves belonging to the second group (more than 10 items) is almost constant. Data confirm that the variability in the quantity of the items in the burials is not related to chronology, but covers all the periods taken into account.

CONCLUSIONS

All the analyses of the content of the graves show an uneven distribution in the number of objects as well as in the presence of metal items. In all the chronological phases from the Transitional to the Late Protogeometric we can observe a low number of burials (not more than four in each phase) standing out among all the others for the quantity of their grave-goods and/or the energy expenditure during the funerary rite. The number of these richer graves is almost always constant in time and it is worth noting that the majority of these burials are female. Their wealth is indicated by a higher number of grave-goods, the presence of metal goods, and a greater variety of items, including some rare objects. The last step in verifying the existence of a nonegalitarian distribution in the grave-goods is to demonstrate that there is a group of burials in which wealth is not so evident. This group can be identified with the graves that present fewer than five items and have no metal objects: they constitute a distinctly lower level, in opposition to the higher one previously described. Even if the sample is small, it is necessary to underline that there are no empty tombs: in a couple of cases the amphora-urn is the only artifact, while usually there is at least one other object in addition to the ashes container.

Does this data reflect a social inequality? It is known that a cemetery is not the faithful mirror of a society but just the image that the latter wants to give of itself.[8] I. Morris's theories state that the graves of this period belong to a limited group of people selected by rank (*agathoi*). In this case, access to the formal burial itself should be considered a proof of a social unbalance. Moreover, even if the wealth is considered more equally distributed in this period than in the previous one, the grave-goods are far from being egalitarian; this constitutes a further difference among an already selected group.

The choice and the arrangement of the grave-goods is the result of a social process, but the criteria on which this selection is based are not always self-evident. The burial ritual indicates the relations between the deceased and society, showing horizontal or vertical stratifications. In the funerary context there is the representation of the social identities that persons reached or had to reach during their life. But the material evidence gives us only a partial view of this system of relations, and the anthropological dimension of the burials can only be traced in the main lines. The differences in the quantity and quality of the objects in the tombs might be the result of an unevenness related to the status, the gender, the age, or other. Moreover, not all the social roles deserved to be represented through the grave-goods (d'Agostino 1985:47–58; Bartoloni 2003:13–21; Laneri 2011:91–97).

In the case of the Kerameikos Protogeometric burials, the higher numbers of items do not necessary correspond to a greater wealth in the lifetime. The tombs that stand out for their richness are usually female, so the quantity of objects can be linked to gender; since we have also female burials with a lower quantity of goods, this could be interpreted as the existence of differentiated social positions. On the other hand, the "poorer" graves, with a low number of objects, are usually male. In some cases, they are characterized by distinctive items, weapons, and metal tools, the presence of which was enough to bring up these burials among the others. Weapons are considered male gender indicators but do not occur in all the male tombs, so it is plausible that they were used also to stress the social position of the buried.[9]

From this analysis we can observe that the differences in the distribution of the grave goods are related to gender and status.

It is worth noting that in this period children's graves are not attested in the Kerameikos cemetery, so this category was excluded from the formal burial. Probably further differentiations in the selection and combination of grave gifts were related to the age of the buried, but the osteological data are not so detailed, and only in a very few cases do we have this information. For example, in the case of the tomb SM 146, a wealthy female grave that belonged to an adolescent (13–24 years old, Lagia 2007:30–35, 277),[10] or PG A, a double burial with the remains of an adolescent and a young man (15–16 and 20–22 years old, Kraiker and Kübler 1939:100–103), containing weapons. In both cases, the association of wealthy funerary equipment, including gender indicators, with a young person allows us to consider the grave-goods not only related to gender differentiation; in this case we have a selection related to age, which was advanced enough to permit access to the formal burial, and another related to rank: the wealth of their funerary goods and their high social position was indicated by their family status. Unfortunately, we do not have more data about the age of the deceased, so a comparison with the other graves of the necropolis and the elaboration of any theory related to this argument are not possible.

Concluding, in these graves we can observe several levels of selection. According to the current theory, the access to the formal burial itself was restricted by status (*agathoi*) and age (adults). Within the limits of the evidence examined, a further differentiation in the number, quality, and variety of the grave-goods has been made on the basis of gender. The age of the dead of these burials remains largely unknown, so it is not possible to recognize subadult, young, mature, and aged people; presently, the unevenness in the grave-goods points to the identification of a few individuals within the wider group of those "formally buried," who received an extraordinary burial rite: we interpret this data as a marker of inequality. Inequality is a "value" that plays a role at many levels of exclusion, and this paper shows that the funerary arena is one of the social contexts where it played a great role, as we can demonstrate in spite of the previously described limits.

NOTES

1.   For the analysis of the objects from the different areas of the "trench-and-hole" graves and the reconstruction of the funerary rite see Dalsoglio 2018 and Dalsoglio and D'Onofrio 2016.

2.   For the methods for assessing the wealth of grave-goods assemblages see Alekshin et al. 1983:141–142.

3. To deepen the argument see D'Onofrio's contribution in this volume.

4. The osteological analyses were made by Breitinger and Apostulopulos (Breitinger 1939; Kraiker and Kübler 1939; Kübler 1943) and Lagia (Lagia 2007).

5. Strömberg 1993: cat. A-B; the author used the "exclusion principle" to "produce a number of probably male and female graves gifts which may be used as sex indicators," treating the Submycenaean, the Protogeometric, and the Geometric periods separately due to the great differences in types of objects between these phases

6. The wealth of these female graves has been underlined also by Vlachou's contribution in this volume.

7. According to Desborough 1952:294; for the relative sequence of the burials and the problems related to the chronology see Dalsoglio 2014.

8. As for example D'Onofrio demonstrates in her contribution in this volume: in the case of the male graves with weapons the creation of a social persona did not necessary mirror the biography of the dead.

9. For the Athenian Early Iron Age burials with weapons see D'Onofrio 2011:645–674.

10. Lagia 2007:30–35, 277; the exceptional burial rite of this young female grave is stressed also by the presence of two kraters, one used as lid of the urn and one fragmentary (see Dalsoglio and D'Onofrio 2016).

REFERENCES

Alekshin, V. A. et al. 1983 Burial Customs as an Archaeological Source. *Current Anthropology* 24(2):137–149.

Bartoloni, G. 2003 *Le società dell'Italia primitiva. Lo studio delle necropoli e la nascita delle aristocrazie.* Carocci, Roma.

Breitinger, E. 1939 Die Brandreste aus den protogeometrischen Amphoren. In *Kerameikos. Ergebnisse der Ausgrabungen, I. Die Nekropolen des 12. bis 10. Jahrhunderts*, edited by W. Kraiker and K. Kübler, pp. 256–261. Walter de Gruyter, Berlin.

D'Agostino, B. 1985 Società dei vivi, comunità dei morti: un rapporto difficile. *Dialoghi di Archeologia* 1:47–58.

D'Agostino, B., and A. M. D'Onofrio 1993 Review of I. Morris, *Burial and Ancient Society. The Rise of the Greek City-State. Gnomon* 65:41–51.

Dalsoglio, S. 2014 The Relative Sequence of the Earlier Kerameikos Burials (ca. 1100–900 BC): a methodological approach. In *Newsletter di Archeologia CISA* 5:39–57 Università degli Studi di Napoli "L'Orientale" (http://www.unior.it/ateneo/11491/1/volume-5-anno-2014.html).

Dalsoglio, S. 2018 L'analisi spaziale degli oggetti nelle sepolture per la ricostruzione del rituale funerario: il caso delle cremazioni protogeometriche del Kerameikos di Atene. In *Archeologia e Antropologia della morte, Atti del III Incontro di Studi di Archeologia e Antropologia a confronto*, edited by V. Nizzo, pp. 677–689. Arbor Sapientiae, Rome.

Dalsoglio, S., and A. M. D'Onofrio 2016 Associazioni di vasi e pratiche conviviali nelle sepolture ateniesi della prima età del Ferro: un riesame delle evidenze dal Transizionale al Geometrico medio. In *Atti del convegno Archeotipico: l'archeologia come strumento per la ricostruzione del paesaggio e dell'alimentazione antica*, edited by G. M. Di Nocera, A. Guidi, and A. Zifferero, pp. 209–226. RSA 56.

D'Onofrio, A. M. 2011 Athenian Burials with Weapons: The Athenian Warrior Graves Revisited. In *The "Dark Ages" Revisited: Acts of an International Symposium in Memory of William D. E. Coulson*, 2, edited by A. M. Ainian, pp. 645–674. University of Thessaly Press, Volos.

Kraiker, W., and K. Kübler 1939 *Kerameikos. Ergebnisse der Ausgrabungen, I. Die Nekropolen des 12. bis 10. Jahrhunderts*. Walter de Gruyter, Berlin.

Kübler, K. 1943 *Kerameikos. Ergebnisse der Ausgrabungen, IV. Die Nekropolen des 11. bis 10. Jahrhunderts*. Walter de Gruyter, Berlin.

Lagia, A. 2007 The Human Skeletal Remains. In *Kerameikos. Ergebnisse der Ausgrabungen, XVIII. Die Submykenische Nekropole: Neufunde und Neubewertung*, edited by F. Ruppenstein, pp. 273–281. Hirmer, München.

Laneri, N. 2011 *Archeologia della morte*. Carocci, Roma.

Langdon, S. 2005 Views of Wealth, a Wealth of Views: Grave Goods in Iron Age Attica. In *Woman and Property in Ancient Near Eastern and Mediterranean Societies*, edited by D. Lyons and R. Westbrook, pp. 1–27. Harvard Center for Hellenic Studies, Cambridge.

Morris, I. 1987 *Burial and Ancient Society. The Rise of the Greek City-State*. Cambridge University Press, New York.

Ruppenstein, F. 2007 *Kerameikos. Ergebnisse der Ausgrabungen, XVIII. Die Submykenische Nekropole: Neufunde und Neubewertung*. Hirmer, München.

Schlörb-Vierneisel, B. 1966 Eridanos-Nekropole I. Gräber und Opferstellen hS 1-204. *Mitteilungen des Deutschen Archäologischen Instituts*, Athenische *Abteilung* 81:4–111.

Strömberg, A. 1993 Male or Female? A Methodological Study of Grave Gifts as Sex-Indicators in Iron Age burials from Athens. *Studies in Mediterranean Archaeology and Literature* 123, Paul Åströms Förlag, Jonsered.

van Wees, H. 1998 Greeks Bearing Arms. In *Archaic Greece: New Approaches and New Evidence. Proceedings of a Conference Held at Aberdare Hall, Cardiff, 19–21 September 1995*, edited by N. R. E. Fisher and H. van Wees, pp. 333–378. Duckworth with The Classical Press of Wales, London.

Whitley, J. 1991 *Style and Society in Dark Age Greece. The Changing Face of a Pre-literate Society, 1100–700 B.C.* Cambridge University Press, New York.

Whitley, J. 1996 Gender and Hierarchy in Early Athens. The Strange Case of the Disappearance of the Rich Female Grave. *Mètis. Anthropologie des Mondes Grecs Anciens* 11:209–232.

Chapter Nine

Diversities and Inequality

The Male Burials in Early Iron Age Athens

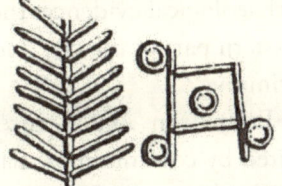

A. M. D'Onofrio

Abstract *Burials constitute the main evidence for existence of Athenian society during the Early Iron Age and are distributed all around the Acropolis, in close proximity to the space of the living, within a kinship-based society. The paper deals with the burials that have been attributed to male individuals on the basis of the anthropological determination of their gender, and highlights those features that can be connected with their rank. The distribution of the weapon burial ritual (centered on the sword bearer) and the weapon ritual (including the killing of the weapon) are discussed in detail. The paper focuses on the Kerameikos evidence and on the gender strategies enacted there. The analysis follows two trajectories: on one hand, a local and generational perspective; on the other hand, within a wide comparative approach, looking to the European prehistory. The main characteristics of the social dimension of burials are investigated in order to discover the strategies of discrimination and distinction enacted with regard to the male members of the Athenian community and to test their durability.*

EARLY ATHENS: CLUSTERS OF DWELLINGS AND FAMILY GROUPS OF BURIALS

Early Athens is a multi-stratified site centered on the well-known Acropolis. The Eridanos and the Ilissos water courses (which today run below the street level) were a relevant feature of the ancient settlement and a vital resource. The archaeological finds attest to Athens's long history as an attractor of population since the Late Neolithic; it flourished in the Late Bronze Age, reaching its typical structure with a Mycenaean fortified citadel on the Acropolis and the sparse traces of a lower city—the *asty*—growing around it.[1] Due to the lack of adequate stratigraphical documentation, it is not possible to follow the story of the Acropolis site before the dawn of the Orientalizing period, when it commenced a long history of religious practice.[2] The extent of the city in the Early Iron Age is not clear, either, and what can be assumed is detectable through discontinuous occupation layers and a network of scattered tombs, burial grounds, and organized necropoleis. According to the archaeological record, the early Athenians settled in small and more or less scattered homesteads around the Acropolis,[3] which have been brought to light over a long history of archaeological excavations, partly due to scientific research projects, more often to the needs of the modern urban development.[4] Since Mycenaean times, according to the archaeological evidence, the Western slopes of the Pnyx attracted more inhabitants than the Eastern part of the city and the urban infilling in the subsequent Iron Age is evident and continuous.[5]

Comparing the overall phenomenon of urbanization in Early Iron Age Greece, Mazarakis-Ainian classified Athens into a category of sites inhabited by communities that were organized in several small family clans, "which accepted burials within or in close proximity to the space of the living or a more loose organization of the cemeteries according to the clusters of dwellings, into 'family groups'" (Mazarakis Ainian 2008:386–389n4). According to the author, these sites withstood well the changes that ended in the formation of the historical *polis*. Such a peculiar social structure can explain why Athens became a powerful attractor for people coming from other communities: it corresponds to a densely nucleated settlement pattern with formal cemeteries, which is more subject to break off under the pressure of internal conflict.[6] How these *oikiai* (which were, apparently, kinship-based groups settled in small and scattered homesteads or clustered around the Acropolis) were organized and related to each other is a matter of debate: certainly these households had a potentially broader structure in comparison with contemporaries, typical mononuclear families.[7] The Homeric *oikos,* like the Iron Age burying group, is "often conceived as an extended group three generation deep" and "might be built up through alliances, with subsidiary individuals and households becoming apparently attached to more powerful households in patron-client relationship, expressed by the poet in the language of kinship" (Morris 1987:91).

THE FUNERARY EVIDENCE AND THE FORMAL BURIAL THEORY: INEQUALITY AT DEATH

The publications about early Athens mostly deal with the funerary evidence, focusing on the grave-goods, while rarely on the human remains. The physical anthropologists (sometimes just medical doctors) examined the inhumed or cremated bones in a minimal percentage of cases,[8] and it is difficult to restudy them, either because they went lost or because the bones have been packed in the deposits and their retrieval is a complicated matter, or—to be honest—because their study is not yet on the agenda.[9] Argive mortuary evidence has been fruitfully reexamined in light of the anthropological data. There, the overall picture of the biological quality of life based on the skeletal remains points toward high levels of health status among the male individuals buried in the so-called warrior graves (Pappi and Triantaphyllou 2011:719).

Burials, in spite of the limitations of the available documentation, remain a basic source for investigating the discrimination strategies that led to the aristocratic leadership of the early city-state of Athens.[10] The funerary rites are subject to the variability of the social behavior and can be classified as "social rationing"; I. Morris's book *Burial and Ancient Society* (1987), puts forward the theory of selectivity of the formal burial, with an opposition between formal and informal disposal of the dead. According to Morris, in some periods of the Greek history, only the *agathoi*—those who enjoyed full membership in the community—were buried in an archaeologically visible manner. On the other hand, the *kakoi*—the many—did not receive the honor of a ritual mortuary treatment, and their memory was not kept alive in the consciousness of their kinship-based group and of the community.[11] The energy expenditure of the funeral rite, measured through the mortuary variability (the differences among burials within a coherent funerary area), has been taken as the basic measure of inclusion or exclusion related to a position of social relevance or irrelevance—that is, inequality related to ranking.[12] When a society adopts this kind of strategy as regards the burial practice, there is no direct correspondence between the graves (number and age classes as well) and its demographic layout.[13]

For Athens, we dispose of high-quality evidence only for a few intact graves in context that have been published, and scarce data regarding many burials that occurred during the transition between two different phases, whose duration was highly variable. Further factors that hamper an effective treatment of the archaeological record by applying quantitative as well as qualitative analysis include limitations imposed by the randomness of the excavations, the poor state of the evidence (usually badly damaged by the later phases), and the tentative chronology given in the preliminary reports. For age and sex determination of the graves the situation is even worse, due to the abovementioned limitations of the anthropological studies.

Thanks to the interplay of different aspects and categories of the funerary record and in spite of the abovementioned limitations, I shall present some thoughts about inequality at the dawn of the city-state, focusing on male members of the Athenian society as they were commemorated in the burial ritual, examined under a diachronical perspective. The process of engendering (as regard to male/female polarization) the grave assemblages and more generally the burial rites, has been presented in relation to the use of the funerary arena for the establishment of the mechanisms of privilege and exclusion.[14]

THE MALE COMMUNITY: MEN BEARING WEAPONS AND OTHERS

In Late Bronze Age Athens and Attica burial of weapons in multiple graves was highly restricted, and there is a dearth of evidence from the whole Attic region in LH IIIC, the only exceptions being the "Warrior burial" on the Southern slopes of the Athenian Acropolis dated LH IIIC Early, which yielded a remarkable pair of bronze oval greaves with a fine, punch decoration Balkan origin[15] and Tomb 38 of the cemetery of Perati, on the Attic Eastern coast.[16]

The Iron Age represents an increase in the frequency of the weapons given to the dead, but still this custom cannot be considered as common.[17] The concentration of weapon deposition in Athens (Figure 9.1) in specific burial grounds, as well as their variable distribution through time, calls for a more refined analysis. Figure 9.2[18] shows that the earliest post-Mycenaean burials with weapons appeared on the outskirts of the Northern sector of the city (Kerameikos and Kriezi, with a possible occurrence in the unpublished cemetery beside Vasilissis Sophias Avenue).[19] From the Late Protogeometric onward, the phenomenon extended to the Agora and to other sites in the Southern city. The second half of the eighth century BC, when the Kerameikos cemetery ceased to contribute after a long series of occurrences, represents the last period of the practice. The weapon burial rite is then traceable in the Asty through the whole period, from c. 1100 to c. 700 BC, with a higher density in the Protogeometric; sometimes it is stated that it faded out in MG II (Wecowski 2014:282n 95), but in the so-called Dipylon cemetery the custom lasted until 760–720 BC,[20] when the well-known vases from the same necropolis show elitist figured scenes centered on the warriors' exploits.[21]

The relative paucity of metal objects in the graves and their inherent value compared with pottery lead archaeologists to treat them as markers of wealth.[22] Among them, weapons are universally recognized as the major male gift in the Athenian burials, and no exception has been reported so far. Many male graves are identified as such only on the basis of the grave equipment.[23] On the other hand, weapons were not given to every male adult individ-

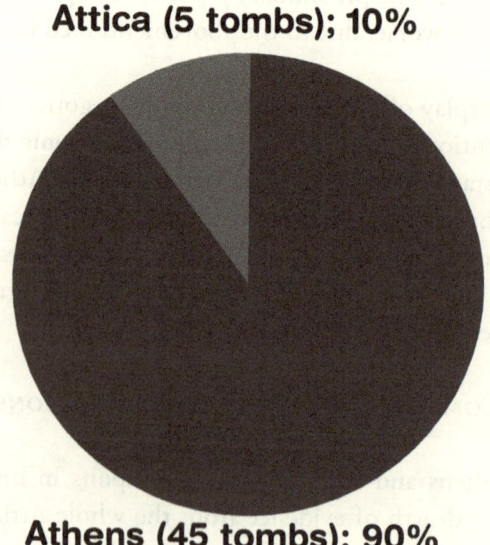

Attica (5 tombs); 10%

Athens (45 tombs); 90%

FIGURE 9.1. Burials with weapons from Athens and Attica, from the Submycenaean to the Late Geometric period.

	Kerameikos North riverbank	Kerameikos South riverbank	Kriezi	Sites in Asty North	Agora and Areopagus slopes	Sites in Asty South
SM/Tr 1125/1085-1070/40 B.C. **EPG** 1070/40-1000 B.C.	128 N PG 2 N PG A double gr. PG B	PG 24	Gr. LXX Gr. LXXIX	Vasilissis Sophias av., T. 51		
MPG 1000-950 B.C.	PG E	PG 6 PG 17 PG 34	T. X			
LPG 950-900 B.C.		PG 28 PG 32 PG 40 PG 43		Metropolitan church, double gr.	N 16:4	Erechtheiou st., gr. Gamma (?)
EG I-II 900-850 B.C.	G 74	G 2 G 38		Ag. Markou st., double gr.	AR II D 16:4 R 20:1	Mitsaion/Zitrou st., gr. 1
MG I-II 850-760 B.C.		G 13 G 23 hS 109	T. II T. VII		AR V	Erechtheioust., gr. VI Kavalotti st., gr. Delta
LG I-II 760-700 B.C.			T. XXVI	Dipylon gr. IV Dipylon gr. V Dipylon gr. XVII		Dimitrakopoulou st. 110, gr. XVIII Kynosarges Hill, gr. II

FIGURE 9.2. Burials with weapons in Athens.

ual (Figure 9.3). In the Kerameikos cemetery, 12 out of 50 osteologically determined male burials of the period under scrutiny bear weapons; in the Agora burial ground, one out of 8.[24] From these premises, I consider weapons in the Athenian graves to have been subject to social rationing, and any other aspects of the weapon ritual—including those related to

with weapons (14 tombs); 23%

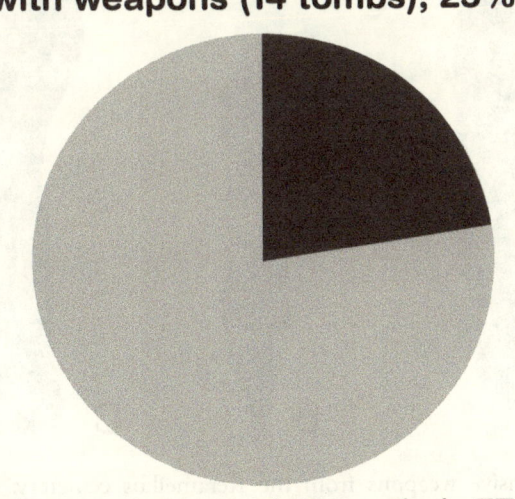

without weapons (48 tombs); 77%

FIGURE 9.3. Osteologically determined male graves: the percentage of graves with and without weapons.

personhood and agency or material entanglements—should be investigated bearing this circumstance in mind (Whitley 2002 and 2015 are crucial to the topic).

The most common weapon in the Athenian burials is the iron sword[25] (for about one-third of cases it is the only weapon in the grave), followed by the spearhead (in bronze or iron, usually associated with the sword or the dagger) (Figure 9.4) and a few iron daggers.

FIGURE 9.4. Offensive weapons from the Kerameikos cemetery. (A) Iron sword in wooden scabbard. L. 48 cm. From gr. PG2N. (B) Dagger with iron blade and bone pommel. L. 21 cm. From gr. PGB. (C) Iron spearhead. L. 32 cm. From gr. G2. Photo by the Author. Ephorate of Antiquities of Athens—Kerameikos Museum. Copyright Hellenic Ministry of Culture and Sports—Archaeological Receipts Fund.

	DEPOSITION	SWORD	DAGGER	SPEARHEAD
inhumation	Near the right arm.	**PG2N** in the scabbard, intact. **Hs109** in the scabbard, in pieces.		
	Near the right leg.			**Hs109** damaged, heavily restored.
	Near the head.			**Gr. 128** intact.
cremation	On the trench floor: simple cremation, ashes not inurned.	**PGE** in the scabbard, in pieces, slightly bent, struck at the hilt.		
	On the trench floor, beside the urn.	**G13** in pieces, struck at the hilt, burnt.		
	On the trench floor, beside the urn, together with the complex pottery set and animal bones.			**G2** broken tip, burnt.
	From the stone packing around the urn.			**PG17** burnt.
	By the neck and shoulder of the urn, with the drinking set.	**G38** killed, U-shaped tip missing, burnt.		**G38** damaged blade, burnt.
	Bent around the urn.	**PG6** killed (loosely bent), missing tip, burnt. **PG28** killed (bent), burnt.		
	In the urn, with the cremated remains.		**PGA1** broken blade (inferior part missing) and damaged pommel. **PGB** kept in linen cloth, blunt tip, broken hilt, damaged pommel.	**PGA1** damaged in early restoration. **PGA2** damaged in early restoration. **PGB** damaged in early restoration. **PG34** burnt, with an adhering bone fragment. **PG32** missing tip. **G23** burnt, broken.
	In the pyre refuse.	**G74** only hilt and tip.		**G74** only a fragment, burnt (currently lost).

FIGURE 9.5. The ritual treatment of the weapons in the Kerameikos graves.

A few bronze shield-bosses[26] and some knives complete the picture.[27] Lethal weapons rather than warrior attributes are a couple of iron arrowheads[28] The sword is a personal object, custom made and representing both a fundamental war implement and an attribute related to the social sphere; it points to the specific identity of the warrior.[29] In the Late Bronze Age the sword wearer was identified as the aristocratic war chieftain, commanding a particular territory from which his companions were, assumedly, recruited.[30] In the Early Iron Age, the rationing of the ritual over the burial grounds sparse in the Asty attests to the maintenance of its role within the sphere of the household (oikia). Crucial for understanding of the Athenian funerary performance is the great variety of the ritually disposed-of swords and spearheads—mostly hit, broken, burnt, or bent—always denoting the high symbolic value attributed to these objects, undergoing the ritual of conspicuous consumption (Figure 9.5) (D'Onofrio 2011a; Cf. Wecowski 2014; Whitley 2015). The overwhelming importance of the sword as a war implement and as a prestige gift has a lasting tradition in Greek culture, as well as in the broader European prehistoric and protohistoric context, as Kristiansen remind us, quoting Homer and the gift of a precious sword made to Odysseus by King Alcinous.[31] The epics are a fundamental source for exploring the ideology of the aristocrats and of the male-dominated social elites of the Early Iron Age, but the relationship between the text and the archaeological record is far from self-evident and needs to be tested within an adequate theoretical frame.

A fruitful comparison between text and images has been proposed by H. van Wees, who cites the representations of weapons wielded in action in the *Iliad* and on Attic Geometric vase paintings. His conclusion demonstrates the preponderance of the spear in the *Iliad* and of the sword in the iconography: the author explains this diversity in combat tactics by suggesting that the usage of weapons in the Homeric text does not correspond to Geometric, but to early-seventh-century practice, that is, to the rise of the phalanx.[32] On the other hand, the same author suggests that the absence of defensive equipment in the Athenian graves—in contrast with Argos where a limited group of 11 burials brought to light an arsenal of three helmets, two cuirasses as well as 19 weapons[33]—would allude to the daily attire of men, who usually went around the city furnished with their offensive weapons but not fully armed, as they were in war. Then van Wees considers the burial custom as a direct result of Homeric daily behavior: "The poet [Homer] treats weapons as a regular item of male apparel . . . the right to carry a sword and spear in public is not the preserve of an elite, but extends to all independent and physically fit men who know how to use them."[34] This interpretation of the mortuary evidence is based on the theory that the burials reflect the daily life and do not constitute "material repositories of social obligations."[35] But for the social archaeologists, the quantity and quality of the material deposited in the grave, along with the entangled objects, contribute to the articulation of the social identity of the deceased. This aspect of these burials, in fact, by emphasizing a warrior's status without displaying his actual fighting equipment (including helms and shields), does not involve the absence of the process theorized by van Wees. On the contrary, they take on a new meaning for understanding the elitist mechanism of engendering the society of Early Iron Age Athens.

Weapons, indeed, in the examined context are associated with other rare (and often neglected in Greek protohistory) objects, for instance, tools for working wood and metals, such as axes or adzes, chisels, knives. Such a hybridization of symbols related to war and carpentry is well known in the European *koine* of the Early Iron Age, culminating in the eighth century BC, when the new urban organization emerges. At this advanced chronological stage, the presence of tools should not be considered the mark of low rank but, on the contrary, a status symbol coherent with the elitist ideology of the time.[36]

Necklaces, bracelets, pins, fibulae, rings have been found not only and more obviously in female graves but also in male graves at Athens, Lefkandi, Argos, and elsewhere (D'Onofrio 2017). At Athens, after the Submycenaean period—when the pattern of metal adornment is comparable for both sexes—fibulae and pins produced by male graves are restricted to those with weapons, showing the high level of distinction of these individuals.[37] Other type of items, such as gold and silver bands or metal rings, also occur—though rarely—in male graves without arms, but more frequently in those with.[38] Warriors indeed worried about their physical appearance, which was intended to mirror their warlike qualities (Harding 2008:194), and personal adornments represented a sign of *charis*—polysemic word alluding to grace, a supreme quality that brings human beings near to the divine—and contributed to distinguishing these *agathoi andres* from the others. It was a long-term phenomenon, destined to decline in the mature Archaic period: adorned bands and necklaces still occur on early funerary *kouroi*.[39]

Finally, the exceptional recovery of a couple of bronze razors from a Geometric cremation, with an iron sword and spearhead in Southern Athens, known only from a preliminary report and then unnoticed until now,[40] recalls the evidence from Late Mycenaean warrior tombs, where razors can be associated with tweezers and combs,[41] all items attributable to warriors' obsession for grooming, beautifying, and presenting the body, coinciding with a wider archeological record from prehistoric Europe, as well as in the Aegean.[42]

The grave-goods of the male burials without weapons in the Protogeometric through the Geometric period show a minor variety of items in comparison with those with weapons, and a total lack of personal adornments. In the Middle Geometric, a banqueting set of skyphos and oinochoe recurs more frequently in this group. The same set becomes the most relevant feature in the Late Geometric male grave assemblages, when weapons are abandoning the funerary scene, although, due to the lack of adequate knowledge regarding the equipment carried by the weapon bearers of this period, the comparison is not possible.[43] M. Wecowski has developed a groundbreaking study of the rise of the aristocratic banquet, drawing attention to the phenomenon of the emergence of a consistent series of material "tracer elements" that can be analyzed in terms of the function of the rising symposion, as well as communal, turn-taking drinking, interpreted as a practice designed to manage the resolution of social tensions.[44] It seems from an overall consideration of the burial customs that this phenomenon involved both the weapon bearers and the others, and future development of the research might better explain the role played by both "parties" in the change toward a more egalitarian society.[45]

Finally, at the lower end of the mortuary energy expenditure scale, there are a few simple graves without grave-goods. Empty male graves occur more frequently in the Submycenaean period. The skeleton from Gr. 142/144 (the provenance is doubtful) of the Pompeion cemetery, a young man whose age at death was 12–24 years, presents vertebral lesions of a type "generally related to strenuous physical activities that possible involve lifting of heavy loads."[46] The custom of giving no offerings to the dead is not attested in Protogeometric time. A possible candidate, PG 42, is empty, but disturbed (Kübler 1943:42). A male Geometric inhumation (G 61) devoid of any offerings (Figure 9.6), was found on the edge of the so-called Plattenbau plot, gathering a dozen "moderately rich" burials dated c. 750–730 BC: both Bouzek and Coldstream speak of "a family slave,"[47] though it seems to me that it would be safer to attribute his identity to a lower status individual, eventually a servant but not necessarily a slave (the property of his owner).[48] In contrast with the Classical times, when the mortuary evidence from the Laurion mining district is largely represented by graves without grave-goods, which have been tentatively attributed to slaves,[49] empty graves known from

Figure 9.6. Kerameikos. Plattenbau plot. The empty grave G61 (on the right, in the foreground). Courtesy of the German Archaeological Institute at Athens, Neg. D-DAI-ATH-Kerameikos 2764.

this early period are extremely rare: when grouped with the others with grave-goods in formal burial grounds, as in the Plattenbau case, they represent the lowest scale of the formal burial. A simple cist-grave of an inhumed man, cut into the rock in the NW edge of the Agora, represents a further example of an EIA empty grave (Blackman 1997:6, fig. 2).

A very special case is represented by the inhumation in the fill of a well (Agora U-V 19:1), of a man considered a social outcast, probably dated EG II, made notable by the presence of a cup given as sole *kterisma*.[50]

THE BURIALS WITH WEAPONS WITHIN A KINSHIP-BASED BURYING PRACTICE: A GENERATIONAL PERSPECTIVE

The burials with weapons concentrate in the Asty area (45 burials), within a radius of about one kilometer from the Acropolis, as shown in Figure 9.2.[51]

There is a strong clustering of weapons (20 occurrences) in the Kerameikos cemetery, which extends to the northwestern outskirts of the inhabited area of the city and became over time the favorite burial site for the aristocratic and wealthy families (D'Onofrio 2014). Here, different burial grounds developed on both sides of the Eridanos River: the Submycenaean necropolis on the northern bank of the stream (the so-called Pompeion cemetery), which survived into the early Geometric; and the cemetery of Hag. Triada on the southern bank, splitting into two main early burial grounds, with only scant evidence dated to the Submycenaean or Transitional, most of the graves being Protogeometric and Geometric.[52] The Kerameikos site is the better candidate for a contextual approach, due to its extension, frequency of burials, and available published data, though the lack of microstratigraphy, along with the relative rarity of overcutting the graves, make the burial sequence debatable, as well as their organization in rows and/or in plots.[53]

The earliest weapons have been found in the Pompeion burial ground on the north river bank. Here a bronze spearhead ascribable to a shape characteristic of the LH IIIC has been found in cist grave 128 (Submycenaean, probably "Stufe III," Phase III), a disturbed inhumation dug above an earlier cremation grave 127 (Submycenaean, "Stufe I"), which gave back only this weapon. Therefore, it remains questionable, in my opinion, whether it is the earliest "warrior's grave" in the Kerameikos cemetery, even though it seems the most probable hypothesis.[54] An alternative candidate for inaugurating the weapon series is PG2N, which lies at some distance west of the Pompeion necropolis, along with the female (?) grave PG1N, attributed to the Transitional phase ("Stufe IV").[55] The iron sword attributed to the mature inhumed man is one of the earliest examples of this type in Greece. It falls within Kilian-Dirlmeier's Type I of the iron full-grip sword and compares to the short sword or dagger from the exceptional tomb XXVIII at Tyrins (which includes also a second weapon, a helmet, and a shield-boss), whose redundancy in war equipment is typical of the Argive costume.[56] The peripheral location of the Kerameikos plot suggests newcomers' status for the people buried there, and it is worth noting the phenomenon of the marginality of these burials associated with the technological innovation of the iron weapon,[57] though the small lekythoi with handmade concentric semicircles, found as grave gifts in PG2N as well as in PG1N, do speak an Athenian language.

The other burials with weapons on the Eridanos north bank (PGA, PGB, PGE, G74) all lie on the SW edge of the Pompeion cemetery and show a variety of types as well as of burial rites. Those belonging to the Transitional phase (PGA double grave and PGB) are plotting together, equipped with daggers and other weapons of excellent manufacture which do not fit easily in the current typological series. Not far from them, the proximity of the Protogeometric grave PGE and the Early Geometric G 74 points again to the adoption of the weapon burial ritual in another family plot, here with a major interval of at least two generations, preceding the abandonment of the interment ground.

Turning to the Eridanos's southern riverbank, and looking again for the relative chronological sequence of burials with weapons, the evidence fits a generational model, as the northern river bank: following the isolated occurrence in the SM/Tr phase of a bronze shield-boss in the tomb PG 24—corresponding to the first funerary activity in this part of the Kerameikos site—the weapons make their appearance in the Middle Protogeometric phase (PG6, PG17, PG34), then in the Late Protogeometric (PG28, 32, 40, 43), with a noticeable variety of rites and only one sword in each group.[58] Interestingly, the whole burial sequence is concentrated within a few rows of adult female and male graves, with some cases of overcutting:[59] this particular behavior is attested to in the eastern part of the burial ground, where a high number of burials lean against each other. Some of the wealthy female graves illustrated by my colleague Vlachou in this volume (PG 37, PG38, PG39, and PG48) are located here; then it is interesting to compare the distribution of engendered female and male tombs within the same community. It is worth noting the unequal visibility of genders, the result of giving, or not, to the dead some special objects that distinguish a few individuals within a single social group of adults.[60]

The later development of the custom of burying with weapons in this sector is represented by two graves that follow in short order in the Early Geometric phase: G2 (EGI c. 900–875 BC, with a spearhead) and G38 (EG II c. 875–850 BC, with a sword, a spearhead, and a big curved knife), which lie beside an earlier, extraordinarily rich female grave PG48.[61] Of these, grave G2 cuts into (and destroys) PG46.[62] Does this overcutting mean a deliberate offense to the earlier burial? Or does it, on the contrary, prove attachment to the communal burying site and represent the need to stay on the same ground as the community's ancestors, maybe linked to a "special" ancestor? [63] This hypothesis seems suitable in the case of the rich female graves PG38 and PG 37, both with vase-sema, commented on by Vlachou (this volume). Further Geometric burials took place beside the Protogeometric ones; among them, two burials with weapons dated to the Middle Geometric: G13 (MGI c. 850–800 BC, with a sword) and G23 (probably MGII c. 800–760 BC, with a spearhead), and they represent the last occurrences on the site.

The coeval inhumation Sacred Street Grave 109 (MGI), a man with a long iron sword and a spearhead, lies in a distant plot.[64]

In summary, the practice started in the peripheral northwest sector of Athens, in the Kerameikos cemetery as well as in the nearby cemetery excavated in Kriezi Street.[65] In the Late Protogeometric the custom spread to the near Agora site, where the Mycenaean graves had once attested to the rite. Afterward, burials with weapons appeared in other parts of the Asty, contributing the impressive evidence of the type. In the few other Athenian locations where these burials form a series (i.e., Kriezi St., Agora), they show the same tendency toward generational disposal distributed at intervals of decades, reaching a peak in the Kerameikos south bank burial ground, with a series of four Late Protogeometric graves whose equipment is diverse and not comparable (PG28, PG32, PG40, PG43) (I refer to my catalogue in D'Onofrio 2011a and D'Onofrio 2015). This means that the ritual of giving weapons had been considered for a long time as a special reward for a restricted elite of males in each kinship-based elite group. The diversity found among the funerary rites and types of equipment alludes to a complex tradition of weapon ritual (Figure 9.5).[66]

I would conclude noticing that, among the few individuals that have been attributed to a class based on age, there are some cases of adolescents (PGA$_2$, PGB; G13).[67] The performing of the rite for a minority of immature male individuals, adolescents or the very young, can be explained in terms of rank selection: this was the way most of the burying groups honored their best men or, exceptionally, their *aoroi* heirs.[68]

THE KILLED WEAPON AND THE BODY OF THE MAN OF EXCELLENCE

The ritual of weapon burial, centered on the sword, can be explained as a tribute to a select group of men, whose roles and/or biographies, as well as potential deeds (in case of adolescents or children), required a special honor.[69] From Late Protogeometric period, in Athens, a minority of these men of excellence were honored at their funerals by a rare rite, the sword's blade bent and put round the shoulder of the urn-vase (Figure 9.7). Cases

FIGURE 9.7. The urn-amphora from the double burial in Ag. Markou st., with the killed weapon on the urn's shoulder. After V. Kallipolitis, Archaiologikon Deltion 19:B1, 1964, pl. 51a. Copyright Hellenic Ministry of Culture and Sports—Archaeological Receipts Fund.

of killed weapons—otherwise "de-functionalized" but not wrapped around the urn—are known from a number of Greek sites of early age, and mostly from Lefkandi in Euboea, but the Athenian rite remains unique.[70]

An experimental test has been lately carried on to verify the technical processes used to U-bend the swords from the hoard of Pila del Brancon, an Italian Late Bronze Age collection; the bronze swords underwent a specific metallurgical conditioning such as the technique known as "reverse quenching."[71] Archaeometric analysis of the Athenian material has not been undertaken, and the poor state of preservation of the iron objects, which are heavily corroded, hampers the investigation. Nevertheless it seems highly probable that the "killing" was obtained, as in the abovementioned case, by expert smiths with a specific metallurgical training.

M. Lloyd has proposed a choice of alternative explanations of the phenomenon, within a reductive perspective: either the funerary swords were ceremonial, structurally weaker exemplars made on purpose for the rite, or "some may have identified the fact that weapons in their possession were made of poorer quality iron, and have chosen to deposit these items into the grave of a recently deceased associate."[72] An even more speculative hypothesis advanced by the same author—untenable in the specific historical context—is that "perhaps these are the swords of men who lost duels, retired from combat, or killed unlawfully or sacrilegiously, and thus needed cleansing or taking out of use." Lloyd's thesis of the funerary blades as damaged in the process of "discarding" them, being inferior in value to those left whole, is not supported by the scholarly traditions of both Greek and wider European prehistory: similar reductive approaches to the weaponry that ended their honorable life in graves or in other ritualized contexts have been definitely disproven by recent research with extensive use of archaeometrical data.[73]

Apart from the Kerameikos series, a few other examples of this typical Athenian practice have been found, the most renowned being the "Areopagus Warrior tomb" (Agora Tomb 27);[74] most recently, evidence of the rite has been detected at Kanakia, in the Attic island of Salamis, just off the Athenian coast (a double grave, exhibited in the Piraeus Museum) (Dekoulakou 1991; D'Onofrio 2011a:662, 669, fig. 5.d).

This special ritual creates a symbolic representation of strong impact: the urn-vase recalls/embodies the dead man, his weapon embracing him—buried forever in a lasting *symplegma*—alluding to an inimitable, unique destiny. In Hellenistic time, the silver hydria-urn of the "Prince's tomb" in Vergina, crowned by a golden wreath, stands for a royal version of the symbolic practice centered on the urn-vase.[75]

CONCLUSION: RANKING IN THE EIA ATHENIAN MORTUARY RECORD

Bearing or not bearing arms in death corresponds to a binary coding structurally elaborated (Leach 1977) by the social groups dwelling in the early Athenian city: the burials with weapons represent a long-term phenomenon of ranking by birth and are restricted to a minor part of the population. When gender visibility fades, in the course of the eighth century BC, the attribute of the weapon disappears with it. In the same period, probably under the pressure of a significant demographic increase leading to the structural revolution of the eighth century and to the so-called internal colonization of Attica, the kinship groups achieve a wider representation of their members in the mortuary record.[76] This major, twofold change in the self-representation of the members of the households (themselves contributing the wider Athenian community) seems to me the main cause for abandoning this traditional custom. We lack any direct information source on the economy of the period in the Attic region, either of the change that might have been produced in both the economic as well as the social sphere during the four centuries that constitute the horizons of this paper, but something is sure to have happened to inspire the new communal drinking practices of the rising aristocratic banquet, which promoted successfully a new ideal of equality.[77]

According to the archaeological evidence, the weapon ritual was reserved to a selected group of male individuals of different age-class and does not (necessarily) mirror the biography of the dead (Whitley 2002); the variability in the grave equipment and the specific context of each grave suggests different roles and stories, where the honor imparted by including weapons might have been given for various reasons (e.g., premature death, primogeniture, inheritance, war excellence, the ruler's role within the *oikos* or beyond its boundaries). The weapon itself was an entangled object and became a supreme gift for the dead (*geras thanonton*).[78]

Generally, grave equipment shows a clear reason to emphasize gender attributes, construct roles for dead people who were treated as "special," and demonstrate social inequality.[79] It is a long-term, transcultural pattern, and in Greece it represents a heritage from the preceding period, but in the Early Iron Age the ritual achieved a new frequency, with a peak in the tenth and ninth centuries BC. It seems to have been destined to designate the master of the household (*oikos*), or his young son and/or heir who could not fulfill the role, usually taking place at generational intervals within the same burying group. The ritual states that the group itself has got its own relevance and legitimacy within the wider community of early Athens, and this legitimacy is attested by sharing a portion of the burial ground whose visible memorials constitute the community's sacred memory place. The high variability in terms of equipment and rites observed in these graves[80] was a response to the need for individual behavior not to contrast with the social relevance of the warlike honored dead. It is also worth noting that in Athens the *exotica* do not concur to the competition package among the male elite, while ornaments and tools do, because they allude to their virtues of *charis* and ability.

What about the other males, those not bearing arms in their graves? Though their inclusion in the family plot, destined to keep the memory of the descent group within the network of the settlement sites around the Acropolis, they betray the hallmark of inequality. Rare male graves devoid of any *kterismata* may represent the lowest degree of ranking: inclusion in the family plot but devoid of any particular visibility inside the group.

The decline of the weapon ritual coincides with the end of the local ruler's social system and the adoption of new funerary rites and cult patterns, which can be observed in the Early Archaic evidence, a time when the rise of the city-state had become a historical fact (D'Onofrio 2011a:657–59).

ACKNOWLEDGMENTS

I would like to express my best thanks to Orlando Cerasuolo for his kind invitation, which gave me the opportunity to deepen a topic which constitutes a key argument for the comprehension of the EIA archaeological record and its historical background. Before delivering this paper for print, I had the opportunity to held a conference on "The Burials with Weapons in the Early Iron Age Kerameikos: A Reappraisal of Ritual Aspects" at the German Institute at Athens, February 11, 2015: I am most grateful to the director, Katja Sporn, for her kind invitation, and to Jutta Stroszeck, field director of the Kerameikos site, for her useful observations. The director of The Kerameikos Museum, Ephorate of Athens, Leonidas Bournias, has granted me through the years his invaluable help in conducting my study. Many ongoing critical conversations contributed to improving this article, and it is not possible to make a list here, but I owe a special debt to Annarita Doronzio and Simona Dalsoglio, who patiently read one draft after another, until the final version. Florian Ruppenstein helpfully offered me a supplement of information about the stratigraphy of the Pompeion cemetery: our perspectives on "plots" remain partly different, but his volume stands as a fundamental source for researches on the early Kerameikos cemetery. Last but not least I am grateful to my colleague Vicky Vlachou, who gave me the opportunity to exchange our presentations and discuss together some of the topics we dealt with.

NOTES

1. See Lemos 2006:506, for the LH IIIB enceinte the Acropolis and the doubtful evidence of a palace. For a survey of Athens in antiquity see Etienne 2004.

2. The funerary use of the rock was carried on in prehistoric times as well as in the Submycenaean period; W. Gauss and F. Ruppenstein deduced the existence of Geometric graves from funeral scenes on fragmentary pottery whose provenance from the Acropolis is highly doubtful (Mazarakis Ainian 2008, 387, n. 77; Coulié 2013, 63).

3. This settlement pattern predates the Early Iron Age, and according to P. Mountjoy, "The location of the LH IIIC Late and SM graves in central Athens suggests they belong to different farms or hamlets" (Mountjoy 1995, 73).

4. The German Institute excavated the Kerameikos cemetery and the American School of Archaeology in the Agora. Rescue excavations have been regularly carried on and reported in the *Archaiologikon Deltion* and other periodicals. Extraordinary finds come from the digs for the new metro line by the Greek Ephorates (Parlama and Stampolidis 2000).

5. Mountjoy 1995 (site maps). A survey for the Late Helladic to Protogeometric evidence is in Lemos 2006. For the 10th–7th c. BC settlement pattern see Whitley 1991a, 61–64; D'Onofrio 2008, with map on p. 442, Fig. 1.

6. A fundamental reappraisal of the category of mobility (which substitutes the old migration model) is offered by Mazarakis Ainian 2008; see also Morgan 2009:48–52, and Papadopoulos 2014:187–188.

7. Kinship ties are generally not based on anthropological data but on the groupings of the burials. I do not share a reductive definition of the *oikos* as a mononuclear family, eventu-

ally including the grand-fathers and grand-mothers (Duplouy 2006:19). Both literary and archaeological contexts call for a wider meaning with diachronic adaptations. For example, "The age and sex profiles of the Pompeion cemetery are what one would expect from a loosely based, non-exclusive kin-grouping" (Whitley 1991a, 97). A fundamental approach to the pseudo-kinship groupings of early Athens and to the sense of shared ancestry developed through this kinship pattern ("The state itself was known as *Athenai*") is offered by Whitley 1991a, 58. A heritage from the Greek family is the difficult management of bastardy (Ogden 1996).

8. Whitley 1991a:64–65. Langdon 2005:2 and n3. Alexandridou 2016:348. My paper is largely based on the anthropological evidence systematically reported by Strömberg 1993.

9. For Athens, Strömberg 1993 is still useful. See now the full edition of the Agora graves (Papadopoulos and Smithson, 2017). A new study of the SM skeletal remains from the Pompeion cemetery has been announced (Lagia 2007:273).

10. The term *aristocracy* to indicate a hereditary class of privileged men and women and their households (*oikoi*) ruling the middle-scale EIA society of Athens has proven inadequate (Duplouy 2006). A most useful approach is offered by Whitley (1991a:136, 182), who discerned a pattern of hereditary chiefdom or "monarchy." He also points to the ninth century for the earliest establishment of an Athenian aristocracy (see Kalaitzoglou 2010; Whitley 2015:112–113; and Morris 1987, 1). I follow M. Wecowski and others (Wecowski 2014:23, 318–336; Morgan 2009; Morris 2009, Rabinowitz 2015) in using the conventional term *aristocracy* for the élite, in spite of the unstable character of aristocratic status. Furthermore, my use of the term *aristocracy* follows the way prehistorians describe pre-state societies, e.g., the war-aristocracies of LBA Europe (Kristiansen 1999; Vandkilde 2013).

11. Duplouy 2006, 25 f., on the terminology *agathoi* and *kakoi*, borrowed from Pareto, see Morris 1987, 1. Still under debate is the "full membership of the community" of these *agathoi*, and their rights as citizens within the *polis* (*contra* Wecowski 2014:250).

12. Morris 1987:216, "From the early Dark Age to the mid-eighth century, formal burial was in many places restricted to a group of agathoi." On the debate inspired by Morris 1987, see Papadopoulos 1993; Morris 1993; Morris 1998; d'Agostino and D'Onofrio 1993:41–51; Laneri 2011:80–85. In my opinion the social-anthropological approach of the Cambridge school remains fundamental.

13. Morris 1987, 72. The author has been accused of neglecting the horizontal divisions of the burying groups (Alexandridou, 2016:354). The research on burial customs has widely proceeded since the '80s (see Langdon 2005), but I maintain that the EIA burials before the eighth century BCE mirror a society where ranking and the vertical dimension are overwhelming (Morgan 2009; Whitley 2015); then, a population increase occurred, as well as a parallel major change in the social organization (Morris 2009; cf. Wecowsky 2014:320).

14. Langdon 2005. Dalsoglio in this volume addresses the rich female burials in Transitional and Protogeometric times within a similar theoretical frame, while Vlakou deals with the EIA female graves stressing individual behavior and agency.

15. Mountjoy 1984; Mountjoy 1995:51 f., 72. Mountjoy rejected the hypothesis by Snodgrass (2000, 333) to consider the context as a re-use of a Mycenean grave. See also Privitera 2013:49 and 72.

16. Privitera 2013:42–43 and 44. In his Table IV the eight occurrences from Athens predates LH IIIC, and all but one come from the Agora excavations. The abovementioned LH IIIC

"Warrior Grave" with the greaves is not included in Table IV due to the absence of offensive weapons. His Table IV lists tombs with weapons considered by Privitera as belonging to hunters rather than to warriors (I am grateful to Privitera for his kind clarification). At Perati, the sword of Tomb 38 (late LH IIIC) is preceded by weapons of the Tombs 12 and 123, dated to middle LH IIIC (D'Onofrio 2011a:647).

17. For distribution, see Fig. 9.2. After Strömberg 1993:40, on 625 SM and LG/PA graves (c. 1100–675 BC), only 125 are sex-determined by bone analysis, 57 of them being male. The 34 SM or SM/EPG burials in the Pompeion cemetery (Lagia 2007:273–281) do not change that proportion: one adult male (Gr. 142/144) and two likely males (Graves 114 and 148). Of the sex-determined burials presented by Strömberg, ten are empty (one from Agora; 7 SM from Kerameikos; one PG cremation is disturbed).

18. The evidence of uncertain chronology is not included in the table. For the chronology of the Transitional and EPG series, I follow Ruppenstein 2009. I made a preliminary choice here, but a more refined study of the whole sequence is forthcoming (see D'Onofrio 2011a:661).

19. Gr. 51 (EPG?) at 2 Herodou Attikou Street (better known as "Vasilissis Sophias cemetery"), with a broken and incomplete blade within the urn. I am most grateful to Marilena Kontopanagou, PhD candidate at the University of Peloponnese, Department of History, Archaeology, and Cultural Resources Management, who is studying this large cemetery, for the information she kindly provided. A few other weapons come from this cemetery and she will publish them.

20. Coulié 2013:62 quotes E. Conze's report from 1870 about the earliest excavations on the site, mentioning the alternation of cremations and inhumations "les uns et les autres ayant uniformément auprès d'eux une lourde épée à poignée de bois, un couteau effilé et deux pointes de javelots," as well as gold bands variously decorated that were sewn on textiles or curled around their heads. Unfortunately, the grave-goods have been dispersed. In my Fig. 9.2, I refer to a few graves from Stais's excavations in 1891–1892 with a fixed chronology and context.

21. According to Snodgrass (2008:23–24), a series of iconographic themes on the vases from this cemetery (lions, battle-chariots, and others) evoke "a different world," producing "social exclusion": in fact "the main viewing group" sets itself against "the marginal bystanders."

22. The peripheral region of Macedonia represents a conspicuous exception (Chemsseddoha 2014). For the metal finds in tombs from Athens, Knossos, Argos, Lefkandi, see Whithey 1991a:181–194. For the Transitional and Protogeometric evidence at the Kerameikos see Dalsoglio, this volume.

23. D'Onofrio 2011a (Catalogue:659–663) and 2014 (Appendix, 110–112). Add the cremation grave XVIII from Dimitrakopoulou Str. 110, discussed above (Alexandri 1970, 57; cf. Nikopoulou 1970:177, Figs. 12–13) and finds from Kephisia near Athens (Schilardi 2011; cf. Alexandridou 2016:350).

24. Lagia 2007 and Strömberg 1993. A complete list of items is not available yet. The project "Atlas of the Funerary Evidence of Athens (11th–7th c. B.C.)," has been developed since 2014 by Dr. Annarita Doronzio under my direction and in collaboration with the University of Paris 1 Panthéon-Sorbonne and the Ephorate of Athens, the Ministry of Culture and Sport will soon provide an analytic database to scholars.

25. The crucial debate on the origin of iron technology for weapons cannot be discussed here. See Snodgrass 2000:211–239 and Molloy 2010.

26. The bronze discs with a protruding spike should have been attached to a shield with perishable material (Bouzek 1969, 93, 118–119; Bouzek 1997, 91, with bibliography). The finds are listed in D'Onofrio 2011a, 660 (PG24, PG40, PG43).

27. The typology and size of the knives calls for further study: the larger are those that came from Kerameikos graves PG 28 (L. 27 cm. ritually killed, as the sword: Kübler 1943, 34–35), and G 38 (L. 23,4 cm. Kübler 1954, 234–235).

28. The arrowhead of Kerameikos Gr. 147 caused the death of the child (Lagia 2007, 277). Since the arrowhead from Kerameikos gr. PG28 comes from the urn (while the sword and a big knife were killed around it), it could be the cause of death as well.

29. Kilian-Dirlmeier 1993:152–153; cf. Blandin 2007:112–113; D'Onofrio 2011a:650; Molloy 2010, 97 (on the exclusive war function of the sword). The personal aspect does not conflict with the symbolic value (Whitley 2004). Langdon 2005, 5. About Homeric warriors accompanying a leader of high descent, see Vandkilde 2006. For ritual use see Vandkilde 2015, 609–611.

30. Kristiansen 2002; Vandkilde 2013:49. Their study focuses on the Late Bronze Age but they trace a long-term analysis that is valid also for the Early Iron Age. About weaponry circulation between Mycenaean Greece and Late and Final Bronze Age Italy, see Jung, Mehofer 2013.

31. Homer, *Odyssey* Book 8:400–405; Kristiansen 2002:330: "The earliest tales and myths in European history, from the Iliad, the Odyssey and Beowulf to the Celtic and Nordic sagas, all contain evidence about the role of famed swords and spears, often with names." Cf. Jung, Mehofer 2013: "To use a Homeric term—which fits quite well despite of the chronological difference—a sword would have been a praised ξείνιον of highest esteem in a time when weapon burials ranked among the richest grave assemblages both in RBA 2-FBA 2 Italy and in LH IIIC-Submycenaean Greece."

32. Van Wees 1994:143–146, with Table 1. Van Wees 1998:352–358, on the spear in Archaic art and society.

33. Van Wees 1998:339, and n. 24: "Easily the highest proportion of pieces of armor in any set of central Greek graves is found in Argos, where eleven 'warrior' burials between them produced three helmets and two cuirasses, as well as nineteen weapons."

34. The author comes back to Helbig's theory: not warriors but "men in peace-time costume, yet with spears and swords" (van Wees 1998:334–336, 340). Nevertheless, "when we occasionally encounter burial groups in which *most* of the dead are accompanied by arms, therefore, we may safely conclude that these represent cemeteries used exclusively by members of the elite." Van Wees 1998:338–340 and note 27. For distribution of weaponry in the graves, see D'Onofrio 2011a:662—663.

35. Whitley 1991a, 96–97: commenting on the SM evidence, the author stresses the quantity of material deposited rather than its quality, noting that in the Kerameikos cemetery, "the rich graves are distributed evenly across the cemetery." For an entangled object theory see Whitley 2015 and Voutsaki 2010.

36. The best representative of this association is the Early Geometric grave of "warrior and craftsman" from the Areopagus slopes (Blegen 1952). I deal in depth with the argument in

"Armi, strumenti da lavoro, pissidi e gioielli: genere, età e rango nelle tombe con armi della Prima Età del Ferro ad Atene e Lefkandi (c. 1050–800 a.C.)," presented at the conference *Investigating Gender in Mediterranean Archaeology*, organized by the Royal Netherlands Institute in Rome May 31 and June 1, 2012. The volume should have been edited by G. Saltini Semerari and N. Sojc. An English version of the paper is D'Onofrio 2017.

37.   Single and paired pins and rings have been found in male and female SM graves (Strömberg 1993:42, 52–53), while the Pompeion cemetery yielded a sole weapon of this period (a spearhead from grave 128). About the metal adornments from the burials with weapons, see D'Onofrio 2011a:649, 657; D'Onofrio 2012, 146–148. See also van Wees 1998:338–339, Table 1 where the lack of metal adornment in the burials without weapons is not commented on.

38.   van Wees 1998, Table 1. D'Onofrio 2011a, 649 ("warrior graves" with fibulae, pins, rings as well as gold bands, in many cases not fully published). D'Onofrio 2012, 146–148.

39.   Earrings and elaborated necklaces are a specific attribute of the rich female graves (Langdon 2005). A pair of bronze earrings comes from the grave known as the "Warrior Trader" in the Toumba cemetery (cf. D'Onofrio 2012:147n72, with bibliography).

40.   Dimitrakopoulou St. 110, Grave XVIII (Alexandri 1970:57; cf. Nikopoulou 1970:177, Figs. 12–13) with an iron sword, an iron spearhead, and fragments of two bronze razors as well as a bronze shallow bowl (*lopas*) used as lid for the urn vase. A couple of razors/cleavers has been found in the so-called Warrior Grave from the Southern Slopes of the Acropolis (see above). These kinds of objects did belong to the end of the Mycenaean civilization (Mountjoy 1984, 140), so the items from Grave XVIII should be *keimelia*. The date proposed in the preliminary report is the end of the eighth century BC. I am grateful to A. Doronzio for directing my attention to that.

41.   Deger-Jalkotzy 2006:172–173: "[T]weezers, combs and razors seem to indicate that personal grooming befitted a warrior as it befitted other male members of the leading social ranks. In contrast, for prestige objects such as jeweler, antiques and exotica warrior burials were frequently surpassed by other elite burials. Clearly this does not indicate that warriors were less prosperous than members of social elite. It only shows that for a warrior burial the military equipment was the decisive element."

42.   References are plenty; see Treherne 1995; Vandkilde 2013:48 (Urnfield-period warriors from the Late Bronze Age). For the Aegean, see D'Agata 2014.

43.   This is based on Strömberg 1993, but more discussion is needed. Fragmentary knowledge about the Dipylon cemetery and graves at Kriezi Street hampers the comparison between groups with and without weapons. I can only observe that the set is a standard offering for burials without weapons. For a survey of the ninth-century graves see Kalaitzoglou 2010; for the eighth century see Alexandridou 2015. For a review of the vase associations see Wecowski 2014, 271–294; Dalsoglio, and D'Onofrio 2016.

44.   Wecowski 2014:249–301. The beginning of such process is marked by the monumental craters and amphoras functioning as *sema*. The end of the ninth century BC shows the initial convergence of a wide range of sympotic patterns, evident in MG II. Nonetheless, a further theoretical discussion is needed.

45.   I do not share Wecowski's opinion about the marginal role of the EIA warriors soon after the beginnings of the Dark Ages (Wecowski 2014:323). Murray's theory of the *Männerbunde* at the origin of the Greek symposium as discussed on p. 238, with bibliography. On the

role of warriors in EIA Crete and the figured crater from Sybrita with a male dancing group, see D'Agata 2014. About the chronology of the last Athenian burials with weapons, see previous note.

46. Empty SM male graves: Strömberg 1993 cat. 36, 40, 44, 46, 48, 51. The young man (12–24 yrs.) from Kerameikos empty Gr. 142/144 (the provenance is doubtful) of the Pompeion cemetery presents vertebral lesions of a type "generally related to strenuous physical activities that possible involve lifting of heavy loads" (Lagia 2007:275–276).

47. Kübler 1954:253, Beil. 2 (G 61), and Coldstream 1977:136 f. and footnote 73, consider the three empty graves from the Plattenbau plot as belonging to family slaves, following Bouzek's suggestion (Bouzek 1969:182, Fig. 72; cf. Marchiandi 2014:1360 and fig. 857).

48. Morris 1987:173–179, regarding serfs, peasants, and slaves in EIA Greece: "The exclusion of the *kakoi* from formal cemeteries might then be a justification for seeing their relationship with the *agathoi* as one of serfdom." In Morris's view, the *kakoi* of the Dark Age enjoyed the usufruct of the land, although the *agathoi* may have "owned" it, and had some right to evict a household of *agathoi* (ibid., 175).

49. Morris 2010:180–187. According to Morris's calculations, in the Laureotika seventy percent of the intact adult graves and eight percent of the intact child graves held no grave-goods at all. This behavior is explained as an archaeological correlates of slavery: "[T]he slave was kinless, stripped out of his or her old social identity in the process of capture, sale and deracination, and denied the capacity to forge new bonds of kinship through marriage alliance" (ibid., p. 176).

50. Little and Papadopoulos 1998: "Close examination of the skeletal remains reveals that the individual buried in tomb U-V 19:1a sustained severe cranial trauma during life; as a result, he may have suffered from some type of post-traumatic neurologic impairment. It is suggested here that the "life events" evident in the bones may have contributed to the unusual burial treatment and thus that tomb U-V 19:1a represents an expression of social role and deviancy in mortuary behavior" (ibid., 379). No certain grave-goods were associated with the burial, but the cup (P 26434, Fig. 3; Pl. 66:b), found near the feet of the skeleton, seems likely. It was the only complete vessel in the well and to be considered as a *kterisma*. Papadopoulos examined other cases of "rejects" burials and discussed the visibility of "deviance" (Papadopoulos 2000, with bibliography).

51. Fig. 2 omits burials whose chronology cannot be fixed in a specific period. For a concise catalogue of burials see D'Onofrio 2011a:659–662 (Athens and Attica); D'Onofrio 2014:110–112 (Kerameikos cemetery). I omit here grave Kerameikos 147 because its arrowhead caused the death of the young boy (I thank A. Lagia, who kindly drew my attention to the case; see Lagia 2007, 277).

52. Mountjoy 1995:73, the author suggests that the new flat cemetery of Kerameikos was contributed by new settlers who migrated into the area from another Attic site or from the neighborhood. About mobility cf. above note 7.

53. Cf. Papadopoulos 1993 and Morris 1993. For "Grabgruppen" in the Pompeion cemetery see Ruppenstein 2007:245–247. Cf. Dalsoglio 2014:43–44; Snodgrass 2016, 195.

54. The skull of the corpse buried in grave 128 had fallen down in the cavity of cremation 127 (Ruppenstein 2007, 16 f.; 239). About Submycenaean cremations, Stufen I-III, all dislocated in the North and East sectors of the necropolis, ibid. 252 f. One cannot exclude that the spear—the sole finds from the grave—was a "keimelion" or had been used for a long time.

For a discussion of the bronze spearheads from the graves in the Pompeion cemetery see ibid., 200–202. Ruppenstein's chronological sequence remains the most probable.

55.   Graves PG1N and PG2N, deposit PG3N: Kerameikos IV, p. 43; cf. D'Onofrio 2014:104. On cremation PG3N see Ruppenstein 2007:253.

56.   Verdelis 1963: the burial was reused, and it yielded a second inhumation. For both weapons, see Kilian-Dirlmeier 1993:106.

57.   On the diffusion of weaponry technology from central Europe see Jung 2009; Jung, Mehofer 2013.

58.   The swords come from graves PG 28 and PG 6. Graves PG 43 and PG 40 contained a shield-boss (in PG 40 associated with a bronze axe and an iron tool). The other burials contained only spearheads. The "dagger" of PG 17 is a knife indeed.

59.   Male grave PG 40—with shield-boss and tools—cuts PG46 (undetermined) and is cut on turn by male graves PG42 and PG41, probably female and of the same chronology. A similar behavior recurs in the case of PG38 (female), which cuts PG37 (female): both graves are female with amphoras as *semata* (Vlachou, this volume), while the last one is cutting PG 35 and PG36 (both undetermined). The overcutting of seemingly coeval graves is a remarkable feature, see Dalsoglio 2014:44, 46 and 47; fig. 3. The stratigraphical sequence has been sketched out by Krause 1975, vol. II, tab. 30.

60.   A phenomenon investigated in the Vergina Iron Age cemetery thanks to a contextual approach (Chemsseddoha 2014).

61.   For female cremation PG 48, with extraordinary grave assemblage, see Vlachou in this volume.

62.   Kübler 1954:210–212. On the pottery assemblage, see D'Onofrio and Dalsoglio 2016:214–215 (fig. 5 and 6), 223.

63.   In the seventh-century BC Kerameikos cemetery, within the same burial clusters, funerary offering-trenches perform the ritual on the same spot, destroying the traces of the previous rites (D'Onofrio 1993; cf. Marchiandi 2014:1361).

64.   Sacred Street Grave 109 (see Schlörb-Vierneisel 1966:7–8). For the possible defunctionalization of the sword, found broken in pieces, see D'Onofrio 2011a:652. For the topographic relationship between the Hag. Triada cemetery and the burial ground north of it, where this grave was, see Marchiandi 2014:1358, fig. 854.2.

65.   On the early chronology of the Kriezi St. cemetery, not far from the so-called Dipylon graves, see Mountjoy 1995:59; on p. 64 and note 245, she comments upon burial with weapons.

66.   Details will be treated in a volume in preparation dedicated to the Kerameikos evidence, thanks to the kind permission of the German Archaeological Institute at Athens and of the Ephorate of Athens, to whom I am most indebted for the courtesy.

67.   Double burial PGA_2: age 15–16 (Kraiker and Kübler 1939:101). PGB: adolescent, likely male (Kraiker and Kübler 1939:103). G13: a female adult according to Breitinger 1939, 259, a male adolescent according to Krause 1975, I, 86 and II, Tab. 22, or "probably man" after Strömberg 1993, 138. Only a comprehensive reexamination of the human remains could prove the validity of these outdated age and sex determinations. I deal with the grave assemblage in D'Onofrio, 2017.

68.   Pomadère 2011: in the Homeric *epos* the children are essentially defined according to their descent; male children will preserve the durability of the *oikos* and are represented as par-

ticipating with the men at the banquet (which has been identified as "un des instruments de la reproduction sociale des élites" [Deplouy 2006]). Cf. Wecowsky 2014, 315 on the father introducing his son to the banquet. Therefore, "les hiérarchies sociales et la différence de sexe impliquent des enfances multiples" (Deplouy 2006:569–71).

69. About the sword as rank signifier, archaeologically visible even in a negative way, like in the terramare area of Northern Italy, cf. Jung, Mehofer 2013:98.

70. For the assimilation of the rites, see Coldstream 2007; a discussion in D'Onofrio 2011a, 651.

71. Bietti Sestieri et al. 2013. "[A] certain degree of respect to the sword is indicated both by the attention paid to preserving its wholeness, and by the markedly individualizing treatment given to each piece. Neither of these two conditions applies to the spearheads. Apparently, the sword was a prestige marker, also carrying a specific symbolic value. As such, it was an important correlate of vertical role (*sensu* Goodenough 1965)" (p. 162).

72. Lloyd 2015. K. Harrell, who investigates the correlation between fragmentation of the weapons and social worth in the Mycenae Shaft Graves, shares the idea that the killing of the iron blade required "the honed technical abilities of an expert, as well as a smith's toolkit," rejecting Lloyd's thesis (Harrel 2015:144–145).

73. Vandkilde 2015, with references. Kristiansen 2002. See also Harrell 2015. For the meaning of the funerary rites of destruction see, among others, Whitley 2015:112–113 and fig. 3 (on the role of breaking and burning in the gender polarity of EIA burials). See also Wecowsky 2014:284 (breaking and burning weapons and banqueting services in the Kerameikos cemetery, with bibliography).

74. Blegen 1952. On the topic, see D'Onofrio 2011a, 651–653; 669, fig. 5 (a collection of the urns with "wrapped" weapons). In some cases, such as the "Cathedral grave" (Dontas, 1953–54) or the Kerameikos grave PG 28 (Kübler 1943, 34), the bending (S-shaped, or U-shaped) does not repeat this exclusively Athenian ritual.

75. The urn was put on a marble table (Andronikos 1980, 212 and fig. 165, p. 203). In this case the golden wreath of oak leaves and acorns alludes to the Macedonian banquet ideology and the hydria to the achievement of *athanasia* (the Nymphs extinguish Herakles's pyre by drawing water with the hydriae on Late Classical Attic and Italian vases): this suggestion cannot be deepened in this paper.

76. See Whitley 1991a:57–61, with bibliography. On the age structure of Attic cemeteries, see Morris 1987, 57–62 (fig. 16); 219. V. Vlachou in this volume highlights some correlates of the structural revolution of the eighth century (the definition is by A. M. Snodgrass) as regards the mortuary evidence. Cf. Alexandridou 2016:354.

77. Whitley 1991a, 158–59. Wecowski's view of a long-term, stable, and uniformly dominant agricultural Dark Ages economy remains conjectural (Wecowski 2014:319–323). I would call major attention on regional diversities *sensu* Whitley 1991b.

78. Cerchiai 1984. The funerary performance is called *geras thanonton* in *Il.* XVI, 456–57 = 674–675; *Il.* XXIII, 9; *Od.* IV, 195–98. On the function of the praised gift of the sword in the epics, see above.

79. For the social competition where the aristocrats use "graves as the prime medium of investment" in the EBA Europe and the social change related to warfare in Southern Europe, see Randsborg 1999:199 and 200–202. The author emphasizes an alleged paucity of weapons in the Aegean Iron Age (p. 201), which does not correspond to the archaeological record.

80.   Figure 9.6 illustrates the variety of rites for weapon deposition at the Kerameikos site. The topic will be developed in further contributions in relation to the whole grave assemblages (see above; a first insight in Dalsoglio and D'Onofrio 2016).

REFERENCES

Alexandri, O. 1970 C Athens Classical Antiquities, Athens. *Archaeological Bulletin 25, Chronicles* B1:40–91.

Alexandridou, A. 2016 Funerary Variability in Late Eighth-Century B.C.E. Attica (Late Geometric II). *American Journal of Archaeology* 120(3):333–360.

Andronikos, M. 1984 *Vergina: The Royal Tombs and the Ancient City*. Ekdotike Athenon, Athens.

Banou, E. S., and L. K. Bournias 2014 *Kerameikos*. John S. Latsis Public Benefit Foundation, Athens.

Bietti Sestieri, A. M., L. Salzani, C. Giardino, and G. Verly 2013 Ritual Treatment of Weapons as a Correlate of Structural Change in the Italian LBA Communities: The Bronze Hoard of Pila del Brancon (Nogara, Verona). *Rivista di Scienze Preistoriche* LXIII:155–169.

Blackman, D. 1997 Archaeology in Greece 1996–97. *Archaeological Reports* 43:1–125.

Blandin, B. 2007 *Les pratiques funéraires d'époque géométrique à Érétrie. Espace des vivants, demeures des morts*. 2 vols. Ecole Suisse d'Archéologie en Grèce, Athènes.

Blegen, C. B. 1952 Two Athenian Grave Groups of about 900 B.C. *Hesperia* 21:279–294.

Bouzek, J. 1969 *Homerisches Griechenland im Lichte der Archäologischen Quellen*. Universita Karlova, Praha.

Bouzek, J. 1997 *Greece, Anatolia, and Europe: Cultural Interrelations during the Early Iron Age*. Paul Åströms Förlag, Jonsered, Sweden.

Breitinger, E. 1939 Die Brandreste aus den protogeometrischen Amphoren. In *Kerameikos. Ergebnisse der Ausgrabungen, 1. Die Nekropolen des 12. bis 10. Jahrhunderts*, edited by W. Kraiker and K. Kübler, pp. 256–261. Walter de Gruyter, Berlin.

Cerchiai, L. 1984 Geras Thanonton: note sul concetto di "Belle Mort." *Annali di Archeologia e Storia Antica* VI:39–69.

Chemsseddoha, A.-Z. 2014 Quelques observations sur les thématiques funéraires en Macédoine à l'âge du Fer: le cas de la nécropole de Vergina. *Pallas* 94:63–86.

Coldstream, J. N. 1968 *Greek Geometric Pottery: A Survey of Ten Local Styles and Their Chronology*. Revised second ed. Liverpool University Press, Liverpool.

Coldstream, J. N. 2003 *Geometric Greece: 900–700 BC*. 2nd ed. Taylor and Francis, London.

Coldstream, J. N. 2007 Foreigners at Lefkandi? In *Oropos and Euboea in the Early Iron Age: Acts of an International Round Table, June 18–20, 2004*, edited by A. Mazarakis Ainian, pp. 135–139. University of Thessaly Press, Volos.

Coulié, A. 2013 *La céramique grecque aux époques géométrique et orientalisante (xie–vie siècle av. J.-C.)*. Picard et Epona, Paris.

D'Agata, A. L. 2014 Guerra, guerrieri e protopoleis a Creta tra la fine dell'Età del Bronzo e gli inizi dell'Età del Ferro. In *Guerra e memoria nel mondo antico*, edited by E. Franchi and G. Proietti, pp. 127–151. Università degli Studi di Trento, Dipartimento di Lettere e Filosofia, Trento.

D'Agostino, B., and A. M. D'Onofrio 1993 Review of Morris 1987. *Gnomon* 65(1):41–51.

Deger-Jalkotzy, S. 2006 Late Mycenaean Warrior Tombs. In *Ancient Greece: From the Mycenaean Palaces to the Age of Homer*, Edinburgh Leventis Studies 3, edited by S. Deger-Jalkotzy and I. S. Lemos, pp. 151–179. Edinburgh University Press, Edinburgh.

D'Onofrio, A. M. 1993 Le trasformazioni del costume funerario ateniese nella necropoli pre-soloniana del Kerameikos. *Annali di Archeologia e Storia Antica* 15:143–171.

D'Onofrio, A. M. 2008 Gli Ateniesi dell'Asty: l'abitato della prima età del ferro attraverso il record archeologico. In *Sepolti tra i vivi : evidenza ed interpretazione di contesti funerari in abitato : Roma, 26–29 aprile 2006: atti del convegno internazionale*, edited by G. Bartoloni and M. G. Benedettini, pp. 437–460. Dipartimento di scienze storiche, archeologiche e antropologiche dell'antichità, Roma.

D'Onofrio, A. M. 2011a Athenian Burials with Weapons: The Athenian Warrior Graves Revisited. In *The "Dark Ages" Revisited: Acts of An International Symposium in Memory of William D. E. Coulson*, edited by A. Mazarakis Ainian, pp. 645–673. University of Thessaly Press, Volos.

D'Onofrio, A. M. 2011b *I cittadini e i loro antenati: sulle tracce dei rituali nei contesti archeologici ateniesi della prima età del ferro e il primo arcaismo (ca. 1075–600 a.C.)*, contributo presentato alla Riunione Scientifica "Cibo per gli uomini cibo per gli dei. Archeologia del pasto rituale," Piazza Armerina, 4–8/5/2005. *OPAR*, 2011; http://opar.unior.it/1337/.

D'Onofrio, A. M. 2012 Kouroi e opliti: sulle tracce della charis maschile. In *L'Olpe Chigi. Storia di un agalma*, Atti del Convegno Internazionale, Salerno 3–4 giugno 2010, edited by E. Mugione and A. Benincasa, pp.135–149. Pandemos editore, Paestum-Salerno.

D'Onofrio, A. M. 2014 The Weapon Burial Ritual in the Early Iron Age Kerameikos Cemetery: A Research Project. *Newsletter di Archeologia (CISA)*, 5:99–122. http://www.unior.it/ateneo/11491/1/volume-5-anno-2014.html.

D'Onofrio, A. M. 2017 Working Tools, Toilet Implements, and Personal Adornments in Weapon Burials at Early Iron Age Athens and Lefkandi, *Studi Micenei ed Egeo-Anatolici Nuova Serie* 2017:27–52.

Dalsoglio, S. 2014 The Relative Sequence of the Earlier Kerameikos Burials (ca. 1100–900 B.C.): A Methodological Approach. *Newsletter di Archeologia (CISA)* 5:39–57. http://www.unior.it/ateneo/11491/1/volume-5-anno-2014.html.

Dalsoglio, S., and A. M. D'Onofrio 2016 Associazioni di vasi e pratiche conviviali nelle sepolture ateniesi della prima età del Ferro. In *ArcheoTipico: l'archeologia come strumento per la ricostruzione del paesaggio e dell'alimentazione antica*, Atti del convegno, 16 ottobre 2015, Università degli Studi della Tuscia, Viterbo, edited by G. M. Di Nocera, Alessandro Guidi, Andrea Zifferero, pp. 209–226. Rivista di Storia dell'Agricoltura.

Dekoulakou, I. 1991 Salamis. *Archaeological Bulletin* 46(B1):71.

Dontas, G. S. 1953–54 Excavation under the Sanctuary of the Metropolis of Athens. *Archaeological Effect* 92/93:89–97.

Duplouy, A. 2006 *Le prestige des élites. Recherches sur les modes de reconnaissance sociale en Grèce entre les Xe et Ve siècle avant J.C.* Les Belles Lettres, Paris.

Etienne, R. 2004 *Athènes, espaces urbains et histoire: des origins à la fin du IIIe siècle ap. J.–C.* Hachette, Paris.

Harding, A. 2008 Razors and Male Identity in the Bronze Age. In *Durch die Zeiten . . . ; Festschrift für Albrecht Jockenhövel zum 65. Geburtstag*, edited by V. von Frank et al., pp. 191–195. Rahden/Westf., Leidorf.

Harrell, K. 2015 Piece Out: Comparing the Intentional Destruction of Swords in the Early Iron Age and the Mycenae Shaft Graves. In *THRAVSMA. Contextualising the Intentional Destruction of Objects in the Bronze Age Aegean and Cyprus*, edited by K. Harrel and J. Driessen, pp. 143–153. UCL Presses Universitaires de Louvain, Louvain.

Jung, R. 2009 I "bronzi internazionali" ed il loro contesto sociale fra Adriatico, Penisola balcanica e coste levantine. In *Dall'Egeo all'Adriatico: Organizzazioni sociali, modi di scambio e interazione in età postpalaziale (XII–XI sec. a.C.)*, Atti del Seminario internazionale (Udine, 1–2 dicembre 2006), edited by E. Borgna and P. Càssola Guida, pp. 129–157. Ateneo, Roma.

Jung, R., and M. Mehofer 2013 Mycenaean Greece and Bronze Age Italy: Cooperation, Trade or War? *Archäologisches Korrespondenzblatt* 43(2):175–187.

Kalaitzoglou, G. 2010 Adelsgräber des 9.Jhs.v. Chr. in Athen und Attika. In *Attika: Archäologie einer "zentralen" Kulturlandschaft: Akten der internationalen Tagung vom 18.–20. Mai 2007 in Marburg*, edited by H. Lohmann and T. Mattern, pp. 47–72. Harrassowitz, Wiesbaden.

Kilian-Dirlmeier, I. 1993 *Die Schwerter in Griechenland (ausserhalb der Peloponnes) Bulgarien und Albanien*, PBF IV, 12. Franz Steiner Verlag, Stuttgart.

Kistler, E., and Ulf, C. 2005 Athenische "Big Men"—ein "Chief" in Lefkandi? Zum Verhältnis von historischen und archäologischen Aussagen vor dem Hintergrund der Bedeutung anthropologischer Modelle. In *Synergia: Festschrift für Friedrich Krinzinger*, edited by B. Brandt, V. Gassner, and S. Ladstätter, vol. II, pp. 271–277. Phoibos-Verlag, Vienna.

Kraiker, W., and K. Kübler 1939 *Kerameikos. Ergebnisse derAusgrabungen, 1. Die Nekropolen des 12. bis 10. Jahrhunderts*. Walter de Gruyter, Berlin.

Krause, G. 1975 *Untersuchungen zu den ältesten Nekropolen am Eridanos in Athen*, I–II, Helmut Buske Verlag, Hamburg.

Kristiansen, K. 1999 The Emergence of Warrior Aristocracies in Later European Prehistory and Their Long-Term History. In *Ancient Warfare: Archaeological Perspectives*, edited by J. Carman and A. Harding, pp. 175–189. Stroud, Sutton.

Kristiansen, K. 2002 The Tale of the Sword—Swords and Swordfighters in Bronze Age Europe. *Oxford Journal of Archaeology* 21(4):319–332.

Kübler, K. 1943 *Kerameikos. Ergebnisse der Ausgrabungen, 4. Die Nekropolen des 11. bis 10. Jahrhunderts*. Walter de Gruyter, Berlin.

Kübler, K. 1954 *Kerameikos, Ergebnisse der Ausgrabungen 5.1. Die Nekropole des 10. bis 8. Jahrhunderts*. Walter de Gruyter, Berlin.

Lagia, A. 2007 The Human Skeletal Remains. In *Kerameikos. Ergebnisse der Ausgrabungen, 18. Die submykenische Nekropole: Neufunde und Neubewertung*, edited by F. Ruppenstein, pp. 273–281. Hirmer, München.

Laneri, N. 2011 *Archeologia della morte*. Carocci editore, Roma.

Langdon, S. 2005 Views of Wealth, a Wealth of Views: Grave Goods in Iron Age Attica. In *Women and Property in Ancient Near Eastern and Mediterranean Societies, August 2003*, edited by D. Lyons and R. Westbrook, pp. 1–27. Center for Hellenic Studies, Harvard University, Cambridge.

Leach, E. R. 1976 *Culture and Communication: The Logic by Which Symbols Are Connected. An Introduction to the Use of Structuralist Analysis in Social Anthropology*. Cambridge University Press, Cambridge.

Leach, E. R. 1977 A View from the Bridge. In *Archaeology and Anthropology: Areas of Mutual Interest*, edited by M. Spriggs, pp. 161–176. British Archaeological Reports, Oxford.

Lemos, I. S. 2002 *The Protogeometric Aegean: The Archaeology of the Late Eleventh and Tenth Centuries BC.* Oxford University Press, Oxford.

Lemos, I. S. 2006 Athens and Lefkandi: A Tale of Two Sites. In *Ancient Greece. From the Mycenaean Palaces to the Age of Homer*, edited by I. S. Lemos and S. Deger-Jalkotzy, pp. 505–530. Edinburgh Leventis Studies 3. Edinburgh: Edinburgh University Press.

Little, L. M., and J. K. Papadopoulos 1998 A Social Outcast in Early Iron Age Athens. *Hesperia* 67:375–404.

Lloyd, M. 2015 Death of a Swordsman, Death of a Sword: The Killing of Swords in the Early Iron Age Aegean (ca. 1050 to ca. 690 B.C.E.). In *Ancient Warfare: Introducing Current Research Volume I*, edited by G. Lee, H. Whittaker, and G. Wrightson, pp. 14–31. Cambridge Scholars Publishing, Newcastle upon Tyne.

Marchiandi, D. 2014 I monumenti lungo la via Sacra. In *Topografia di Atene. Sviluppo urbano e monumenti dalle origini al III secolo d.C.*, edited by E. Greco, pp. 1339–1396. Pandemos, Atene-Paestum.

Mazarakis Ainian, A. 2008 Buried among the Living in Early Iron Age Greece: Some Thoughts. In *Sepolti tra i vivi: evidenza ed interpretazione di contesti funerari in abitato: Roma, 26–29 aprile 2006: atti del convegno internazionale*, edited by G. Bartoloni and M. G. Benedettini, pp. 365–398. Dipartimento di scienze storiche, archeologiche e antropologiche dell'antichità, Roma.

Molloy, B. 2010 Swords and Swordsmanship in the Aegean Bronze Age. *American Journal of Archaeology* 114:403–428.

Morgan, C. 2009 The Early Iron Age. In *A Companion to Archaic Greece*, edited by Kurt Raaflaub and Hans van Wees, pp. 43–63. Wiley Blackwell, Malden, Massachusetts.

Morris, I. 1987 *Burial and Ancient Society. The Rise of the Greek City-State.* Cambridge University Press, Cambridge.

Morris, I. 1993 The Kerameikos Stratigraphy and the Character of the Greek Dark Age. *Journal of Mediterranean Archaeology* 6:207–221.

Morris, I. 1998 Burial and Ancient Society after Ten Years. In *Nécropoles et pouvoir : idéologies, pratiques et interprétations, Actes du colloque Théorie de la nécropole antique, Lyon 21–25 janvier 1995*, edited by S. Marchegay, M.-T. Le Dinahet, and J.-F. Salles, pp. 21–35. Travaux de la Maison de l'Orient, Lyon.

Morris, I. 2009 The Eighth-Century Revolution. In *A Companion to Archaic Greece*, edited by K. Raaflaub and H. van Wees, pp. 64–80. Wiley Blackwell, Malden, Massachusetts.

Morris, I. 2010 Archaeology and Greek slavery. In *The Cambridge World History of Slavery*, edited by K. Bradley and P. Cartledge, pp. 176–193. Cambridge University Press, Cambridge.

Mountjoy, P. A. 1984 The Bronze Greaves from Athens. A Case for a LHIIIC Date. *Opuscula Atheniensia* XV:135–146.

Mountjoy, P. A. 1995 *Mycenaean Athens.* Studies in Mediterranean Archaeology 127, Jonsered.

Nikopoulou, Y. 1970 Νεκροταφείον παρά την προς Φάληρον οδόν. *Archaeological Analysis of Athens* 3:171–179.

Ogden, D. 1996 *Greek Bastardy: In the Classical and Hellenistic Periods.* Clarendon Press, Oxford.

Papadopoulos, J. K. 1993 To Kill a Cemetery: The Athenian Kerameikos and the Early Iron Age in the Aegean. *Journal of Mediterranean Archaeology* 6:175–206.

Papadopoulos, J. K. 2000 Skeletons in Wells: Towards an Archaeology of Social Exclusion in the Ancient Greek World. In *Madness, Disability, and Social Exclusion: The Archaeology of "Difference,"* edited by J. Hubert, pp. 96–118. Routledge, London.

Papadopoulos, J. K. 2014 Greece in the Early Iron Age: Mobility, Commodities, Polities, and Literacy. In *The Cambridge Prehistory of the Bronze and Iron Age Mediterranean*, edited by A. B. Knapp and P. van Dommelen, pp. 178–195. Cambridge University Press, Cambridge.

Papadopoulos, J. K., and E. L. Smithson 2017 In *The Early Iron Age*. Part. 1, *The Cemeteries. Athenian Agora* 36. American School of Classical Studies at Athens, Princeton.

Pappi E., and S. Triantaphyllou 2011 Mortuary Practices and the Human Remains: A Preliminary Study of the Geometric Graves in Argos, Argolid. In *The "Dark Ages" Revisited: Acts of An International Symposium in Memory of William D. E. Coulson*, edited by A. Mazarakis Ainian, pp. 717–732. University of Thessaly Press, Volos.

Parlama, L., and N. Stampolidis 2000 *Athens: The City beneath the City: Antiquities from the Metropolitan Railway Excavations*. Greek Ministry of Culture, N. P. Goulandris Foundation-Museum of Cycladic Art, Athens.

Pomadère, M. 2011 "Un Héritier choyé d'innombrables biens" (Il. IX,482): les enfants de l'élite sociale au début de l'Âge du Fer. In *The "Dark Ages" Revisited: Acts of An International Symposium in Memory of William D. E. Coulson*, volume II, edited by A. Mazarakis Ainian, pp. 569–577. University of Thessaly Press, Volos.

Privitera, S. 2013 *Principi, Pelasgi e pescatori. L'Attica nella Tarda Età del bronzo*. SATAA 7, Pandemos, Atene-Paestum.

Randsborg, K. 1999 Into the Iron Age: A Discourse on War and Society. In *Ancient Warfare: Archaeological Perspectives*, edited by J. Carman and A. Harding, pp. 191–202. Sutton, Stroud.

Ruppenstein, F. 2007 *Kerameikos. Ergebnisse der Ausgrabungen, 18. Die submykenische Nekropole: Neufunde und Neubewertung*, Kerameikos XVIII. Hirmer, München.

Ruppenstein, F. 2009 The Transitional Phase from Submycenaean to Protogeometric: Definition and Comparative Chronology. In *LH III C Chronology and Synchronisms III: LH III C Late and the Transition to the Early Iron Age. Proceedings of the International Workshop held at the Austrian Academy of Sciences at Vienna*, February 23 and 24, 2007 (Wien 2009), edited by S. Deger-Jalkotzy and A. E. Bächle, pp. 327–343. Verlag der Österreichischen Akademie der Wissenschaften, Wien.

Schilardi, D. 2007 Geometric Period Necpropolis in Kifisia. In *The "Dark Ages" Revisited: Acts of An International Symposium in Memory of William D. E. Coulson*, volume II University of Thessaly, Volos, 14–17 June 2007, edited by A. Mazarakis Ainian, pp. 675–695. University of Thessaly Press, Volos.

Schlörb-Vierneisel, B. 1966 Eridanos-Nekropole, I. Gräber und Opferstellen hS 1-204. *Mitteilungen des Deutschen Archäologischen Instituts, Athenische Abteilung 81:*4–111.

Snodgrass, A. 2008 Descriptive and Narrative Art at the Dawn of the Polis. In *Alba della città, alba delle immagini?: da una suggestione di Bruno d'Agostino*, edited by B. d'Agostino, pp. 21–30. Scuola archeologica italiana di Atene, Atene.

Snodgrass, A. 2010 *The Dark Age of Greece: An Archaeological Survey of the Eleventh to the Eighth Century BC.* 2nd ed. Edinburgh University Press, Edinburgh.

Snodgrass, A. 2016 Putting Death in Its Place: The Idea of the Cemetery. In *Death Rituals, Social Order and the Archaeology of Immortality in the Ancient World: 'Death Shall Have No Dominion,'* edited by C. Renfrew, M. J. Boyd, I. Morley, pp. 187–199. Cambridge University Press, Cambridge.

Strömberg, A. 1993 *Male or Female? A Methodological Study of Grave Gifts as Sex Indicators in Iron Age Burials from Athens*. Studies in Mediterranean Archaeology 123, Paul Åström Förlag, Jonsered.

Treherne, P. 1995 The Warrior's Beauty: The Masculine Body and Self-Identity in Bronze-Age Europe. *Journal of European Archaeology* 3:105–144.

van Wees, H. 1994 The Homeric Way of War: The "Iliad" and the Hoplite Phalanx (II). *Greece and Rome,* Second Series, 41/2:1–18, 132–155.

van Wees, H. 1998 Greeks Bearing Arms: The State, the Leisure Class, and the Display of Weapons in Archaic Greece. In *Archaic Greece: New Approaches and New Evidence,* edited by N. Fisher and H. van Wees, pp. 333–378. The Classical Press of Wales, London.

Vandkilde, H. 2006 Warfare and Gender According to Homer: An Archaeology of an Aristocratic Warrior Culture. In *Warfare and Society. Archaeological and Social Anthropological Perspectives,* edited by T. Otto, H. Thrane, and H. Vandkilde, pp. 477–490. Aarhus University, Aarhus.

Vandkilde, H. 2013 Warfare in Northern European Bronze Age Societies: Twentieth-Century Presentations and Recent Archaeological Research Inquiries. In *The Archaeology of Violence: Interdisciplinary Approaches,* edited by S. Ralph, pp. 37–62. State University of New York Press, Albany.

Vandkilde, H. 2015 Conflict and War, Archaeology of: Weapons and Artifacts. In *The International Encyclopedia of Social and Behavioral Sciences,* 2nd ed., edited by J. D. Wright, pp. 607–613. Elsevier, Oxford.

Verdelis, N. M. 1963 Neue geometrische Gräber in Tyrins. *AM* 78:1–62.

Voutsaki, S. 2010 Agency and Personhood at the Onset of the Mycenaean Period. *Archaeological Dialogues* 17:65–92.

Wecowski, M. 2014 *The Rise of the Greek Aristocratic Banquet.* Oxford University Press, Oxford.

Whitley, J. 1991a *Style and Society in Dark Age Greece: The Changing Face of a Pre-Literate Society 1100–700 BC.* Cambridge University Press, Cambridge.

Whitley, J. 1991b Social Diversity in Dark Age Greece. *Annual of the British School at Athens:*341–365.

Whitley, J. 2002 Objects with Attitude: Biographical Facts and Fallacies in the Study of Late Bronze Age and Early Iron Age Warrior Graves. *The Cambridge Archaeological Journal* 12:217–232.

Whitley, J. 2013 Homer's Entangled Objects: Narrative, Agency, and Personhood. In and Out of Iron Age Texts. *Cambridge Archaeological Journal* 23(3):395–416.

Whitley, J. 2015 *Agency, Personhood and the Belly-Handled Amphora: Exchange and Society in the Ninth-Century Aegean.* In *Pots, Workshops, and Early Iron Age Society: Function and Role of Ceramics in Early Greece,* edited by V. Vlachou, pp. 107–126. Centre de Recherches en Archeologie et Patrimoine Universite Libre de Bruxelles, Bruxelles.

CHAPTER TEN

Tracing Inequality in Early Attica

Wealthy and Deprived, Ladies and Maidens

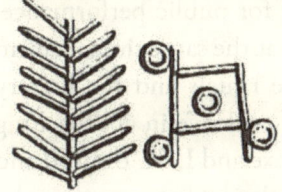

Vicky Vlachou

Abstract   *The best area to study inequality in Early Iron Age Greece is by far the necropoleis and especially those of Attica. In this paper a case study is undertaken on the Attic female burials focusing on the use and function of certain classes of material culture and burial treatments. It is argued that embodied inequalities in the funerary record might relate to a larger variety of cultural and social variables than was once appreciated. Variability in the funerary rituals and the seemingly irregular patterning of material culture in contemporary burials reveal sharp differences even within the same burial grounds, which may not be entirely understood as simply reflecting the competing strategies of the local elites. Female burials from Athens and Attica of the Protogeometric and Geometric periods (covering largely from the tenth to the late-eighth centuries BC) serve as the main body of evidence of the assumed or expected differences within the established funerary ideology.*

Despite the notable differences among concurrent funerary practices, visibility of inequality in the archaeological record may still be claimed in relation to certain prestige and symbolic items, mainly related to the personal adornment of the deceased female. Such discrepancies, when observed in the funerary record, pinpoint the importance of the individuals and their personal standings within the family and the community.

How is inequality expressed and what can our approach to the material record reveal about the choices facing the families and the communities that allowed or even encouraged such discrepancies among contemporaneous burials? The use and function of the giant pitchers interred with the dead body are further discussed. A symbolic and gender-linked function of the vessel in the funerary context is argued. Nonetheless, the use of such items in rich burials should not automatically and exclusively equate gender marking with social class and rank. Putting aside past considerations on the exclusivity of the upper classes in formal burial treatments, and beyond patterned behaviors in the burial treatments, the comparisons between contemporaneous burials demonstrate that we should no longer focus on prominent groups alone, but rather on broader class strata.

INTRODUCTION

In many societies, funerary rituals constitute a central moment for public performance, providing an occasion for the living both to honor the dead and at the same time reaffirm social structure. For past societies, the material remains of those rituals and the literary sources, whenever those are available, serve as the main corpus of evidence in approaching funerary ideology and beliefs. The arguments originally set by A. Saxe and L. R. Binford and the reformulations discussed by L. Goldstein[1] placed a direct correlation between the roles a person held in life and the energy invested in the burial of the individual. This perspective has offered a dominant interpretative framework for discussing mortuary assemblages. Within a different theoretical approach, the arguments presented by I. Hodder (Hodder 1982, 1989, 1991; Cannon 1989; Parker Pearson 1999; Silverman and Small 2002) highlighted the importance of the cultural context, when dealing with the mortuary record. Funerary rituals offer a powerful medium to the living for negotiating social distinctions and thus serving as agents of cultural change.

Honoring the dead by means of the proper rites (*ta nomizomena*) was the common practice in ancient Greece throughout its history (Kurtz-Boardman 1971:142–161; Harisch-Schwarzbauer, Hermary, and Jaeggi 2011; Vlachou 2012). The range of the funerary record has offered possibilities of contextual and interpretative approaches and has largely served in detecting patterned funerary expressions. However, burial rites present a much richer and more complex variety in the Early Iron Age; they frequently are expressed in ways not attested in the material record later than the Archaic period (Morris 1987; Whitley 1991a, 1991b, 1996:231–219; Dickinson 2006:183–195). Distinguishing features, such as social status and rank, wealth and land property have been discussed as key indicators in this social-stratification system in an attempt to better approach and understand it. In the introduction to his book on women in Classical Greece, P. Brulé notes: "*Être née femme diminue prodigieusement les chances de laisser une trace dans l'histoire. Et ce handicap est cumulatif : tant et si bien que si l'on ajoute la pauvreté, l'exclusion politique et le statut d'inférieur, cela condamne au néant*" (Brulé 2001:9). On the contrary, female burials in early Attica offer an important perspective for the study of women through varied lenses.

Attica, and specifically Athens, represents a rare case in the Greek world, one where burials and material culture accordingly have attracted an unrivaled share of the scholarship concerned with the Early Iron Age burials (eleventh–seventh centuries BC) (Morris 1987, 1992; Whitley 1991:23–34; 1996; Papadopoulos 1993; Strömberg 1993, 1998; Langdon 2005; Kalaitzoglou 2010; Kourou 2011). One basic theme in the archaeological analysis has been the variation in the disposal treatments and the potential association of these rituals with the social standing of the deceased, which ultimately determined the acts and duties of the living. In a period with an apparent absence of legal institutions regulating excess in funerary rituals (Garland 1989; Morris 1992–93), the lavishness or lack of material accompaniment to the burials has been seen as reflecting the unequal social status of either the individuals or of the social groupings. Yet, quantitative and qualitative reconstructions of the distribution of the various artifacts in the burial contexts of the Early Iron Age have been mainly concerned with social stratification in the Athenian upper class.[2]

A second issue that was raised apropos the diversity of the funerary assemblages concerned the differential treatment of males and females, mainly on the basis of their material accompaniments. The regular placement of certain categories of material culture with male and female burials demonstrates that sex differentiation was one among several factors affecting the choice of the grave-goods. A change in how this binary approach, male or female, is viewed has been introduced by the integration of gender dynamics as a structuring principal in the processes of social construction. Gender archaeology has offered a wide range of approaches and tentative interpretations of the funerary record, thus fueling discussions and responses related to the cultural and social construction of the deceased.[3] Beyond gender issues, and inspired by the poststructuralist approaches regarding the communicative values of material culture, the exploration of issues of polysemy, concerning the biographical and cultural meaning of artifacts, has underlined the active role played by context and material culture in discussing social structures (Landgon 2001; Vlachou 2016b).

It becomes evident that embodied inequalities in the funerary record might relate to a larger variety of cultural and social variables than once appreciated.[4] Yet, in addressing the concern with inequality in the archaeological record of the Early Iron Age, one inevitably asks, inequality with regard to what? It is thus essential to define those variables that may help us respond to the question. A Sen and S. Babić (Babić 2005:74–76; Sen 1992) highlighted human diversity as one variable of inequality, defined both by internal characteristics, such as age, gender, etc., and by external circumstances. Building on this theoretical framework, it is possible to critically revisit a number of burials from Athens and Attica from throughout the Geometric period, and to concentrate on their assumed or expected differences within the established funerary ideology. Female burials from Athens and Attica will serve as the main body of evidence in discussing the reasons for the selection of specific classes of material culture and of burial treatments. How is inequality expressed and what can our approach to the material record reveal about the choices facing the families and the communities that allowed or even encouraged such discrepancies among contemporaneous burials?

THE VISIBILITY OF SOCIAL INEQUALITY: WEALTHY OR DEPRIVED?

Early Iron burial grounds have long been viewed as containing only a certain proportion of those actually available to be buried. I. Morris (Morris 1987, 1992, 1999) has associated this skewed mortuary record with class divisions in Athens; he argued in favor of a social stratification within the upper class that is reflected in the burials down to the later eighth century BC. Formal burial has been considered as a practice carried out by the highest-ranked individuals of the Athenian society from the Protogeometric to Middle Geometric and then again in the Archaic period. However, is visibility in the archaeological record by itself enough evidence to establish social status and rank? Although this may be true for a number of burials in Athens and Attica, not all the cases involved conform entirely to this one model. Variability in the funerary ritual and the seemingly irregular patterning of material culture in the contemporary burials reveal sharp differences even within the same burial grounds that may not be entirely understood as just reflecting the competing strategies of the local elites.

In the small burial plot on Erechtheion Street, by the south slope of the Acropolis, burials were modestly furnished (Brouskari 1980). Tomb H was a simple pit, inside which the cremation amphora, an oinochoe, and two more fragmentary vessels were deposited. The single object that may be considered as a personal possession was a steatite conical spindle whorl. The burial, dated around the middle of the tenth century BC (MPG period),[5] was the latest among a small group of burials that, despite their simple form, were enclosed by a wall approximately two centuries later, in the eighth, which was restored again in the fourth century BC. The construction of the enclosure wall that defined and marked the space of rituals addressed to the deceased was interpreted by the excavator M. Brouskari as a *heroon* (Brouskari 1980:16–19, 29–31; Lemos 2002:154). Whether a *heroon*, where ancestors were venerated as heroes, or an enclosure delimiting the space of a family burial and presumably also of the funerary rituals to honor the deceased, any assertion of a direct link with rank and hierarchy remains quite vague and open to doubt.

When dealing with differing expressions by Athenian families within the framework of the prevailing funerary ideology, the determining factors are themselves quite diverse and change over time. The findings from Tomb H could be compared with the contemporary tomb PG15, from the burial plot at the south bank of the Eridanos at the Kerameikos.[6] The Athenian lady that was cremated and then buried in tomb PG5 from the same burial ground was accompanied by the standard set of a trefoil oinochoe and a skyphos, but also by an amphora, a storage vessel that usually serves as a container for cremated remains and is rarely offered as a burial gift (Strömberg 1993:56 table 2.4; Kalaitzoglou 2010:table 1), and also by two golden spirals and two iron pins. Inequality in the range and nature of the accompanying burial gifts demonstrates that beyond the quantitative and qualitative approaches, wealthier burials tend to incorporate personal items of value, possibly a reflection on the wealth of the deceased.

By the late tenth century BC, women's burials were marked by changing forms of mortuary differentiation. The area of burials PG 38 and PG 37 at Kerameikos burial ground on the south bank of the Eridanos was marked by the placement of an amphora over each grave.[7] Both amphorae were found *in situ* (Figure 10.1): they probably served a double function as both honorary offerings to the deceased and the indication of the tomb proper. The vessels are among the earliest burial markers in the Athenian funerary record; indeed, the act of marking a grave remained quite rare until the eighth century BC.[8] Yet, despite the

FIGURE 10.1. Burial markers *in situ* over burials PG 37 and PG 38, Kerameikos. Courtesy of the German Archaeological Institute. Photograph: K. Kübler, DAI-ATH-Kerameikos 4486.

care taken in distinguishing the location of those burials among their contemporaries, the burial gifts that were collected from inside the grave merely consisted of a few clay vessels and two iron pins, items that occur in most burials of the time. On the other hand, different shapes of vases have been chosen for each of the tombs: a set of nine cups and two oinochoae, accompanied by a coarse jug, an incised pyxis, and two iron pins were deposited in PG 37, all showing traces of fire, while just a skyphos and a bowl, accompanied by a coarse jug and two iron pins, were placed in PG 38.

Some meters to the west of burials PG 37 and 38, the contemporary burial PG 48 contained the inurned cremation of a woman, sealed with a bronze bowl (Kübler 1943:44–46; Breitinger in Kübler 1943:2; Strömberg 1993:126 no. 89). Although no burial marker was found in the area, the richness of the other burial gifts with her is seen not only in the quantity, but also the quality and variety of the different materials. No fewer than thirty-nine clay vessels were collected from the area of the pyre: nine oil containers, mainly lekythoi and two flasks, one small pyxis, two skyphoi, a kantharos and sixteen oinochoae (probably used for the libations of liquids to the funerary pyre by the family and the relatives). The rest of the burial offerings consisted of loom weights, clay bowls and beads with incised decoration, two Incised-Ware dolls and two clay stands with fine decoration, that were collected from

the pit around the urn and the layer of the deposited cremated remains. Two fibulae probably once attached to the clothing of the deceased were found inside the burial amphora. The
range of the ceramic assemblage and the presumed function of the two clay stands for the
display of certain objects or even vessels[9] show the special care taken by the family and kin
of the deceased during the funeral. The contrast to burial PG 29[10] from the same burial plot
is striking. Here, apart from the cremation amphora and a small skyphos that functioned
as its lid, only some fragments of iron pin(s) were found, presumably once attached to the
clothing or the shroud of the deceased.

In discussing the unequal distribution of the categories of material culture among contemporary female burials it becomes evident that certain patterned behaviors do emerge. The
regular use of belly and shoulder-handled amphorae as the cremation urns, and more rarely
as the burial markers, seems almost exclusively associated with female burials.[11] Pins, and to a
lesser degree fibulae, are usually placed inside the amphorae with the cremated remains, most
probably representing the personal possessions of the deceased used to adorn or to fix the
burial cloth. However, most of the clay vessels used as oil and/or perfume containers and the
number of the drinking sets, compiled of oinochoae and skyphoi, are better assigned to the
family, the relatives or the people that attended the funerals and participated in the rituals.
Thus, no direct associations may be claimed between them and the individual interred.

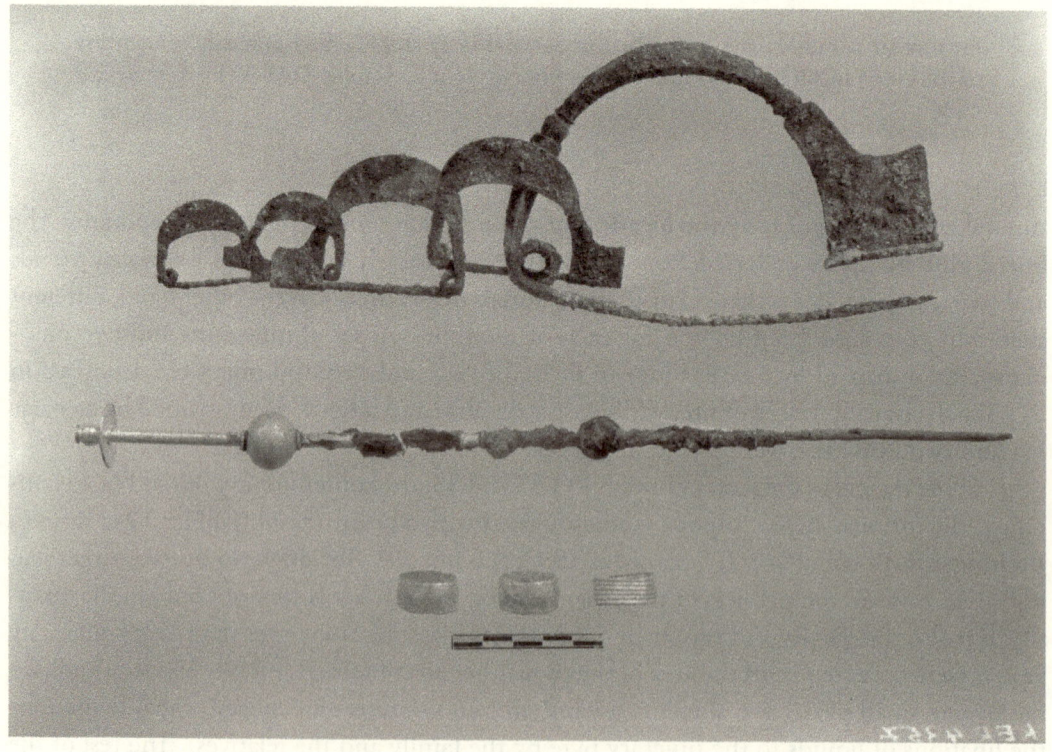

FIGURE 10.2. Selection of jewelry from burial G 41, Kerameikos. Courtesy of the German Archaeological Institute. DAI-ATH-Kerameikos 4407.

During the ninth century BC, amphorae remain the standard urns for the secondary deposition of the adult cremation burials, thus maintaining a long Athenian funerary tradition. Amphorae with horizontal arched handles attached to the belly and decorated in the prevailing circle style served as the cremation urns in some of the wealthiest female burials of this period, again revealing a patterned funerary behavior. Inequality, in the cases of grave H16:6 (also known as the burial of the Rich Lady of the Areopagus),[12] grave 41 from the Kerameikos (Kübler 1954:235–236; Breitinger in Kübler 1943:208), graves V, XII, and XIV from Kiezi Street (Alexandri 1968), and grave II from Anavyssos (Vedelis and Davaras 1966:97–98, pls. 94a-b; Coldstream 2003:58), is mainly expressed in the mass of gold and gold-plated jewelry and bands offered alongside the rest of the funerary gifts (Figure 10.2). A comparable set of three golden fibulae, two gold-plated pins and a golden band (41 cm long and decorated with an animal frieze) were placed with burial XIX from the Kynosarges burial ground (Alexandri 1972:173–175). In contrast to the inurned cremations common in this cemetery, this was an inhumation burial. A few other clay vessels accompanied all the burials, apart from the Areopagus and Anavyssos cases that contained as large a collection of clay vessels as it had artifacts.

The reexamination of the cremated remains of the Areopagus burial by M. A. Liston and J. K. Papadopoulos revived interest in this celebrated burial. It threw some new light on the circumstances of her death, as possibly occurring during pregnancy or from premature childbirth (Liston and Papadopoulos 2004). The extraordinary quantity of burial gifts, consisting of imported objects of luxury materials, jewelry, seals, terracotta models of granaries and openwork baskets, Attic Dark Age Incised Ware, and a variety of clay finely decorated vessels, all leave no doubt as to the social standing, the wealth, and presumably also the property owned by her family. At the same time, the physical anthropology of the deceased revealed in an explicit way the complexities involved in considering funerary assemblages. The reanalysis and discussion of tomb H16:6 touches upon the reasons lying behind the choice of certain objects or the treatment of the body, and in this it goes beyond the processual model, based on social status and the energy invested in the tomb.

On the north slopes of the Areopagus and the area of the later Agora (Smithson 1974), ritual discrepancies can be traced in the funerary practices: inurned cremations are far from usual. Among the burials of the ninth century BC, some have been considered female burials on the basis of the type of the material accompaniments alone. Pieces of personal ornament were rare or completely absent, while the regular use of a single shape—the pyxis—ritually consecrated in the fire, displays a symbolic and presumably ritual function attaching to this shape and possibly also to its contents during the funerals. No fewer than nine clay vessels, almost exclusively pyxides, were collected from the cremated remains of each of the burials I 18:2 and AR III/IV, the later also containing 25 clay beads with incised decoration.

Despite the notable differences among concurrent funerary practices, visibility of inequality in the archaeological record may still be claimed in relation to certain prestige and symbolic items, mainly related to the personal adornment of the deceased female. It can be argued that those items, such as jewelry, pins, fibulae, necklaces (also frequently found in pairs), should be understood as the personal possessions of the deceased ladies used to adorn them in death and subsequently buried with them. The varying degrees of luxury expressed by those items and their varying numbers in concurrent burials may constitute a reliable indicator of inequality, embedded in the social rank and hierarchy of their possessors.

J. Whitley and S. Langdon have discussed certain symbolic items that were almost exclusively associated with Athenian female burials (Whitley 1996; Langdon 2005:7–14). Some may be viewed as personal possessions of the deceased that could have had an equally practical use in daily life, such as jewelry, beads, seals, and possibly also some clay containers such as kalathoi or pyxides. Other artifacts such as wheel-made animal figurines, and "Attic Dark Age" incised dolls, granary and boot models, or even clay pomegranates, would seem to be rather symbolic depositions for the grave, presumably also associated with cultic and religious beliefs beyond the funerary practices. They may even have been obtained in the event of the funerals, to be offered to the deceased. These symbolic objects tend to accompany only some of the wealthier Attic burials: thus, it is not their quality or quantity that might serve as an indicator of social inequality, but rather simply their presence or absence. The presence of those objects would seem to have been regulated by their symbolic function and ritual or cultic associations, and so to be associated with another form of social inequality related to the gender of the deceased.

Assessing Gender Inequality: Ladies and Maidens

The importance of gender as a culturally created identity in the construction of the social persona has been explored for various different periods (Sørensen 2000, 2007; Díaz-Andreu 2005). Gender has regularly been assigned based on material culture. Athens and Attica remain exceptional cases, where gender disparities seem especially pronounced in the mortuary record and "gender-exclusive symbolic grave assemblages" have been isolated and discussed (Whitley 1996; Langdon 2006). Anna Maria D'Onofrio discusses in this volume the deposition of weapons in male burials, a phenomenon closely associated with gender and social rank. In addition to such exclusive funerary gifts, the selection of the cremation urn seems to have been equally gender-based. N. Kourou[13] has demonstrated that for approximately two centuries the Attic amphorae with two loop handles attached to the shoulder were used as the cremation urns in female burials, mainly for those of a younger age.

Although shoulder-handled amphorae were favored as cremation urns in the burials of younger females, this choice does not seem to have been regulated by social distinctions: the vessel is found equally with both poor and more lavishly furnished burials. The amphora from burial O in the burial ground on the south slopes of the Acropolis (Charitonidis 1973:26–27 [LPG], pls. 16c-d) had a small pyxis as a lid. The only other finds were collected from the interior of the amphora, and consisted of two bronze fibulae and at least two pins, probably from the clothing of the deceased. The amphora of burial 4 from the same cemetery (Charitonidis 1973:24 [EG I], 15a-b) was sealed with the conical foot of a small krater, and only a fragmentary pin was found with the cremated remains. Burial G 14 from the Kerameikos burial ground (Kübler 1954:220 [EG II]; Strömberg 1993:127 no. 97) contained nothing more than a skyphos. By contrast, Kerameikos burial PG 39[14] was one of the wealthiest cremation burials of the LPG period. The jewelry that would have adorned the deceased was placed in the cremation amphora (fragments of bronze and iron fibulae, 2 iron pins and 3 bronze finger rings), while a number of clay vessels, mainly lekythoi, loom weights, clay beads with incised decoration, and a wheel-made figurine of a deer (Figure 10.3) were included among the offerings. Likewise, the EG I tomb D16:2 at the Areopagus (Young 1949) contained no fewer than 20 clay vessels, two bronze pins, two bronze fibulae, an iron knife, some more jewelry, among which were two rare electrum spirals, and two pairs of clay boots (Figure 10.4).

Cremation burials in shoulder-handled amphorae of the MG period,[15] dating largely from the middle of the ninth to the middle of the eighth centuries BC, never display the lavishness of contemporary female burials in belly-handled amphorae, as discussed above. Pins and fibulae are regularly found mingled with the cremated remains, while a few clay vessels accompany the burial amphora. In this sense, both burials PG 39 from Kerameikos and D16:2 from the Areopagus are distinguished among contemporary burials for the addition of some exceptional artifacts. The clay wheel-made deer and the pairs of clay boot models are some of the objects discussed and convincingly associated with gender marking (Haentjens 2002; Langdon 2006:13, 2008:136; Kourou 2011:192–193). Unsurprisingly, these objects were recovered from wealthy furnished burials, and are to be associated with elite expressions in the funerary record.

Yet, while the presence of the wheel-made animal figurines may be discussed with reference to the function and use of such symbolic artifacts from the Late Bronze Age onward,

FIGURE 10.3. Wheel-made painted deer from burial PG 39, Kerameikos. Courtesy of the German Archaeological Institute. DAI-ATH-Kerameikos 4357.

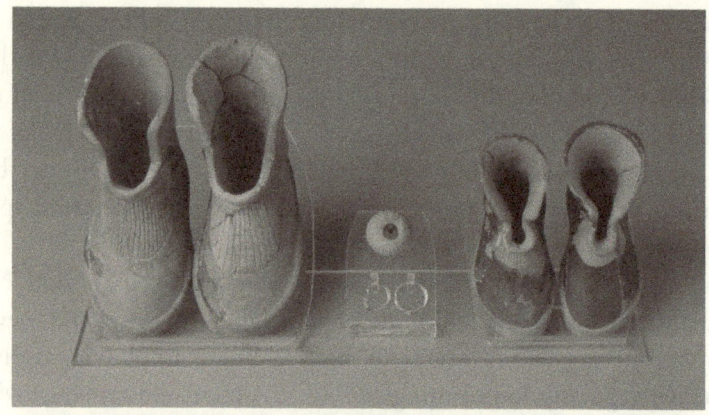

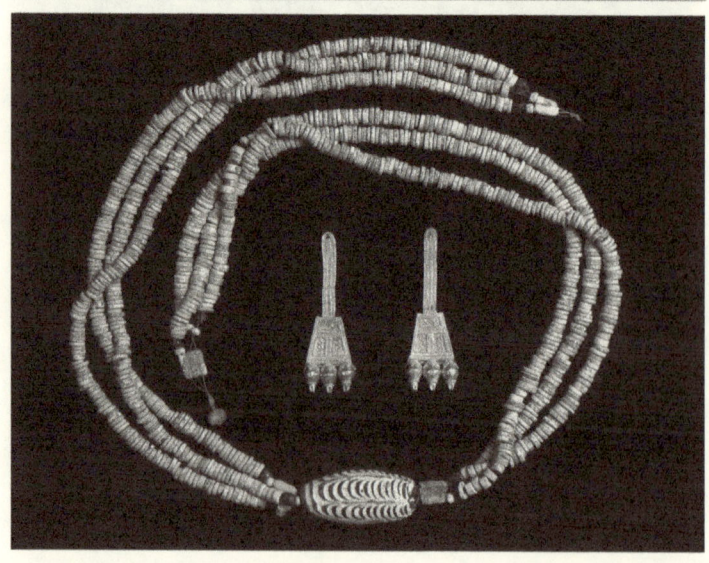

Figure 10.4. Burial D16:2, Areopagus. American School of Classical Studies at Athens: Agora Excavations.

the pairs of clay boot models that appear during this period embody specific funerary beliefs, and ones that can be equally discerned beyond the regional boundaries of Attica. Furthermore, their presence in both cremation and inhumation burials demonstrate that their symbolic function was valid in the burial record irrespective of differences in the funerary practice. This argues for the importance of those artifacts within the more widely accepted funerary ideology. Among the most discussed maiden's burials in Attica are two from Eleusis (Skias 1898:76–122; Coldstream 2003²:56–57). The so-called Isis grave was named after the most unusual among the numerous burial offerings, a faience figurine of this Egyptian deity. The burial was furnished with no less than 68 clay vessels, a clay model granary, and some fine jewelry, including two necklaces of faience and amber beads, three faience scarabs, an ivory pin, a pair of lunate golden earrings, finger rings, bracelets, and fibulae. The small, and indeed miniature, size of most of the clay vessels offered at this burial usually indicate children's graves. They support the identification of this burial as that of a young individual. The unusual variety of jewelry and the unique Isis statuette that accompanied the burial have been mainly viewed as indications of the social status and personal standing of the deceased within the family and the local community. The distinctive character of the Isis burial, as well as that of the contemporary burial A, places it apart from the rest of the burials from the same necropolis: this fact led the excavator Skias to view these females as possible priestesses at the early sanctuary. Burial B from Kavalloti Street to the south of the Athenian Acropolis (Stavropoulos 1965:78 pls. 45b, 46a-c) contained an almost equal number of burial offerings, among which was a small Egyptian statuette that has been identified as a depiction of Goddess Mehit (Mehyt) by the inscription on its reverse.

Even so, the symbolic use of certain gender-linked items in rich burials should not automatically and exclusively equate gender marking with social class and rank. We might argue that contemporary elites made use of the existing ideologies and beliefs that were available to all, but whose material expression is archaeologically more visible to us when the very wealthy are involved. Such objects may be understood only when the prevailing customs allow for such rare and symbolic items to be deposited and so become conspicuously available to us. Not all contemporary burials received such objects, though, despite the richness of other offerings that accompanied them. The inhumation of a young female around 14 years old from the burial plot at the Areopagus north slopes (gr. I 18:1) (Smithson 1974:352–359) is singled out from the rest there as it was furnished with around 20 clay vessels, two iron pins, and a small stone plaque, most probably a pendant or amulet (Figure 10.5). The inhumation burial from the south slopes of the Acropolis (Θ2)[16] remains one of the richest Athenian burials of this period: it contained no fewer than 83 clay vessels, some of which were already decorated with newly introduced figured scenes.

MADE TO IMPRESS? OVERSIZED PITCHERS AND SOCIAL COMPLEXITY IN LG ATTICA

Oversized clay vessels had been introduced into the Attic funerary record by at least the early ninth century BC. Amphorae and pedestaled kraters served both as cremation urns and burial markers, demonstrating thus a specific funerary tradition and the special care taken by certain families while honoring their dead (Smithson 1961; Bohen 1997). By the early eighth century BC, pedestaled kraters and belly-handled amphorae grew considerably in size: they were placed over the graves of certain individuals of aristocratic origin, first in the Kerameikos burial ground and soon afterward in the so-called Dipylon cemetery (Brükner and Pernice 1893:73–156; D'Agostino 2008). Their imposing size puts the emphasis on the commemoration of the deceased; they were probably acting both as ritual utensils and burial markers of the chosen few. Figured decoration applied on their surfaces from around the middle of the eighth century BC emphasized their funerary character, albeit enhanced with mythic overtones.

Around the same period, oversized pitchers appear in inhumation burials from Athens and Attica (Vlachou 2016a). Unlike the monumental burial markers or the oversized funerary urns, the use of oversized pitchers in the burials illustrates a different funerary practice, one that saw the regular interment of vessels exceptional in their size and quality with the deceased. It is probable that these vessels were used during the funerary rituals, and in fact some of them have their bottoms pierced. This process of deforming the object in such a way as to remove any regular usage is well known in funerary and ritual contexts. It constitutes a negation of the practical aspect and the value of the object (Kübler 1954:33–34; Boardman 1988:176–177; Luce 2003:60–61; Luce 2011:57), though simultaneously in these contexts the habit bestows a ritual one (the pot can act as a libation vessel now).

FIGURE 10.5. Burial I 18:1, Athenian Agora. American School of Classical Studies at Athens: Agora Excavations.

The usual size of the LG pitchers was fixed between 40 and 55 cm. They became very popular in Athens and Attica during the Late Geometric period, being placed evenly with both male and female burials irrespective of social discrepancies of status. Nonetheless, only a few pitchers, no more than 25 in number, stand out: they are significantly taller, reaching almost one meter in height.[17] Those vessels were selectively placed with burials in Athens and Attica. Although the sex of the deceased cannot be determined with certainty for most, it is possible to argue for a gender-based Attic funerary behavior biased toward young females.

The earliest examples were found at the so-called Dipylon cemetery by the later Eriai Gates, under the modern Eleutherias Square, where amphorae and kraters monumental in size were used during the same period to mark the graves of the chosen few.[18] Dipylon graves 13, 14, and 7 all contained a large-sized pitcher placed either at or by the feet of the deceased (Figures 10.6–10.8). Dipylon grave 14[19] contained a large-size pitcher and an equally large oinochoe placed in the internment of a female. In Dipylon grave 7[20] the large pitcher was accompanied by a skyphos decorated with an oriental-inspired figured scene, a high-rimmed skyphos, a small round aryballos, a cup, and a few pieces of jewelry. Dipylon grave 13,[21] again an inhumation burial, contained, along with the large pitcher, an equally large amphora and five oversized high-rimmed skyphoi, two faience lion figurines, a few more bone objects, and the unique collection of five ivory female statuettes.

The Dipylon burials are not isolated examples in eighth-century Athens (Figure 10.9): oversized pitchers accompanied one burial from the Kerameikos burial ground, two burials

FIGURE 10.6. Giant pitcher from Dipylon grave 14, National Archaeological Museum, Athens inv. 814. Reproduced with permission of the National Archaeological Museum, Athens. © Hellenic Ministry of Culture and Sports / Archaeological Receipts Fund.

FIGURE 10.7. Giant pitcher from Dipylon grave 7, National Archaeological Museum, Athens inv. 782. Photo by the author, reproduced with permission of the National Archaeological Museum, Athens.

FIGURE 10.8. Giant pitcher from Dipylon grave 13, National Archaeological Museum, Athens inv. 771. Photo by the author, reproduced with permission of the National Archaeological Museum, Athens.

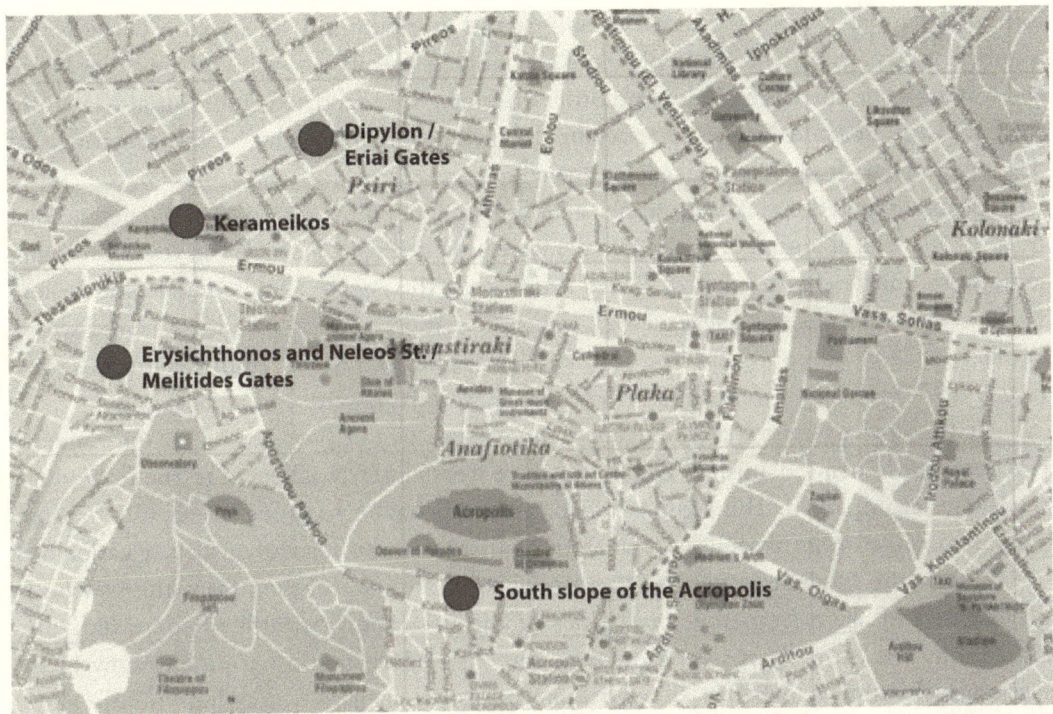

Figure 10.9. Distribution map of the Athenian giant pitchers.

in the small burial plot on the north slopes of the Hill of the Nymphs in the area of the later Melitides Gates, and a much-disturbed burial on the south slopes of the Acropolis.[22] Similar pitchers have been found with burials elsewhere in Attica—at Anavyssos, Spata, and Marathon, areas with strong Athenian affinities.[23] Yet more giant pitchers of excellent preservation exist today in museums and collections and follow the monumental size established by the Dipylon Painter.

The use of the pitcher, the *prochous,* for pouring water appears already in the Homeric epics.[24] Although pitchers serve for washing before important events or feasts, the crucial function of water in funerary rituals may provide a reason for the consistent presence of such vessels in LG burials. However, we may also argue that this specific class of pottery, the large-sized pitchers, was inextricably associated with Attic gender-based funerary behavior, presumably embodying the individual social standing of the deceased. This suggestion is further strengthened by the high selectivity in the use of oversized pitchers in Athens and Attica.

Nonetheless, there are two points that deserve further consideration. First, although most of the burials that contained an oversized pitcher included other objects of intrinsic and high value, this was not the rule for all burials furnished with such a fine vessel. All three Dipylon graves contained some rare vessels and items along with the pitchers: an equally large oinochoe was placed in grave 14, a skyphos with a unique ritual scene of oriental influence depicting dancing females before a seated figure was found in grave 7, while five ivory female statuettes were collected from grave 13, along with some more valued artifacts. In addition, burial VI from the area at the junction of the modern Erysichthonos and Neleos

Streets and tomb 3 from the small burial ground at Spata both included a considerable number of clay vessels and some pieces of fine golden jewelry as well. On the other hand, and leaving aside the large pitcher, no other offerings were reported from burial XIV from the Erysichthonos and Neleos Streets plot. Likewise, only a few clay vessels accompanied the large pitchers from Kerameikos and Spata.

Secondly, and despite the presumed gender-based function of large-sized pitchers among Attic burials, not all burials of young females were provided with such a lavish vessel, although some were quite richly furnished. Burial XVII from the Agora Tholos burial plot (Young 1939:76–87) was offered no less than 22 clay vessels, most of them pyxides, together with a number of pieces of bronze and iron jewelry. Equally, burial VADK1 from Kerameikos (Von Freytag 1974) received a total of 43 vessels, two seals, some jewelry and an iron knife.

It becomes evident that those lavish items that would have served in the funerary practices before being deposited inside the grave were closely connected to the individuals they once accompanied. This significantly patterned behavior has gone largely unremarked, possibly because of the absence of clear signs of aristocratic exclusivity in their selection and use. Yet the use of these vessels may be understood and approached from the viewpoint of gender, and again from the specificities of the lives and/or deaths of those individuals. Among the earliest large-sized pitchers with figured decoration, a pitcher now in the National Museum at Athens[25] shows female mourners in a row, drawing attention thus to its funerary intent (Figure 10.10). In the late eighth century BC, two fine decorated

Figure 10.10. Giant pitcher from Agia Paraskevi, National Archaeological Museum, Athens inv. 16022. Photo by the author, reproduced with permission of the National Archaeological Museum, Athens.

pitchers draw their inspiration from contemporary hydriae, being decorated with female dancers, horses, and a centaur.[26] And although no specific archaeological context exists for those vessels, a huge pitcher from Marathon was the only specimen in the burial of a young female, as established by osteological analysis.[27] Here, though, the original and rich figured decoration that covers almost entirely the surface of the pitcher alludes to nuptial celebrations. The theme is in marked contrast to its placement inside the tomb: it could thus be an early example of a *loutrophoros*.[28] Such discrepancies, when observed in the funerary record, pinpoint the importance of the individuals and their personal standings within the family and the community: they are easily and often overlooked in favor of patterned behaviors. The individual's circumstances in play at pivotal points in their lives will have an important impact, when we consider both the inequalities expressed in their having had access to various categories of materials and the treatment of those persons in the funerary record.

CONCLUSIONS

Tracing forms of inequality brings about a renewed perspective when forming questions concerning social structure and evolution. The funerary record of Athens and Attica reveals significant disparities among the burial treatments and the demonstrations of wealth, status, age, and gender during the Early Iron Age. Our survey of certain Athenian and Attic female burials dating from around the late tenth to the late eighth centuries BC reveals discrepancies with regard mainly to the funerary practices and the access and distribution of certain classes of material culture, both vertical (hierarchical) and horizontal. In assessing such matters in the Early Iron Age societies, we should consider the extent to which the funerary record can be interpreted in terms of social exclusivity and inequality. The high degree of variation that exists may be understood as the outcome of the families' involvement in the funerary arrangements, while the persistence of certain repeated choices and behaviors allows the development of a comparative framework for further discussion. Past considerations on the exclusivity of the upper classes in formal burial treatments must be put aside, now that comparisons between contemporaneous burials demonstrate that we should no longer focus on prominent groups alone, but rather on broader class strata.[29]

In considering the Attic funerary record from around the late tenth century BC, there is an increasing complexity discernable in the funerary practices that may not be fully understood as the result of competing strategies amongst the *eupatrid* families. Class complexity matches economic complexity. In this view, the progressive "disappearance" of poor graves in Athens and Attica may be considered through the lens of a constant negotiation of how individuals and their families were perceived within the social and also funerary context. We may thus argue that manifestations of social inequality increase in complexity in keeping with the progressive transformation of human societies into more complex structures. In this way, the obvious distinctions between rich and poor graves, drawn on the basis of the funerary arrangements and grave goods, progressively fade away as broader-based class and social groups embrace similar behaviors and symbolic expressions. A visible outcome of such transformations in the archaeological context of Attica after the mid-eighth century BC is illustrated by a more balanced distribution of those manifestations of material wealth that had been previously viewed as an expression of *isonomia* (Morris 1985; also Whitley 1991a:171–183).

Although only a token number of burials are considered in this paper, namely, those of Attic females, they look to form a good point to start from when identifying those alterations and variations in the funerary record that may parallel phenomena on a social level. Attica has been considered as an "unusual case," in that imported goods and exotic material culture were far less favored in the funerary context than in other regions such as Knossos or Euboea (Whitley 1991; Strömberg 1993; Duplouy 2006:151–183). On the other hand, Attic pottery, had reached most of the Aegean regions by the late ninth century BC, and, soon afterward, the shores of Cyprus and the Eastern Mediterranean, thus displaying "a common artistic language for most of the Greek world," according to Coldstream (Coldstream 1983:18). During the same period, an economic boost is revealed in the use of valued bronze, silver, and golden artifacts, most of them of local manufacture, and a few more imported goods that were deposited in the tombs. The role of the Laurion mines in the local economy should not be underestimated. These steady developments call for the mobility of objects, people and ideas, by which were enabled important reactions and outcomes affecting the economy and social structures. Craftsmen, peasants, and other broader social groups could accumulate wealth, despite the hierarchical nature of Athenian society, and so embrace a traditional and socially accepted way of representing themselves in life and death.[30]

By the middle of the eighth century BC, the increasing complexity of funerary practices and beliefs and the emergence of pronounced attitudes that placed an emphasis on developing a ritual-symbolic system related to the *oikos* (Langdon 2006, 2008), can be taken as an expression of the constant social negotiations in the coming to be of the broader class strata. From this angle, the dynamics of social mobility, as has been discussed by N. Purcell and recently emphasized in the work of A. Duplouy (Purcell 1992; Duplouy 2006), might contribute in tracing and forming a better understanding of the inequalities expressed in the material record of the Early Iron Age Aegean.

ACKNOWLEDGMENTS

My warmest thanks go to Orlando Cerasuolo and the director of the IEMA Peter F. Biehl, for their hospitality during our stay in Buffalo and for putting together so many stimulating papers. I have benefited from discussions with Anna Maria D'Onofrio during the conference, working on the Attic funerary record of the Early Iron Age. For language editing my thanks are due to Dr. Don Evely. My research on Early Iron Age Attic necropoleis was funded by the F.R.S.-FNRS as part of an individual postdoctoral project at CReA-Patrimoine, ULB (Brussels).

NOTES

1. Saxe 1970; Binford 1971; 1972, 208–243; Goldstein 1980; 1981; Morris 1991; for an overview cf. Rakita and Buikstra 2005; Babić 2005, 71–73.

2. Morris 1987; 1992; 1999, for critical reviews of this theory, cf. Garland 1989; d'Agostino and D'Onofrio 1993.

3. Gibbs 1987; Sørensen 1991; 2007; Arnold 2007. For the Athenian female burials of the Geometric period, cf. Whitley 1996; Langdon 2005; De Polignac 2007.

4. According to Shanks and Tilley, social contradictions could have been denied or masked, as well as being demonstrated or emphasized, in the funerary practices. Shanks and Tilley 1982; Sjögren 2010.

5. I use the following chronological abbreviations:
    PG: Protogeometric (ca. 1050/25–900 BC)
    EG: Early Geometric (EG I ca. 900–875, and EG II ca. 875–850 BC)
    MG: Middle Geometric (MG I ca. 850–800, and MG II 800–760 BC)
    LG: Late Geometric (LG I ca. 760–735, and LG II 735–700/690 BC)

6. Kerameikos PG 5: Kraiker and Kübler 1939, 97; Strömberg 1993, 120 no. 57; Lemos 2002, pl. 21.1–6. Kerameikos PG 15: Kraiker and Kübler 1939, 189; Strömberg 1993, 122 no. 64; Lemos 2002, pl. 22.

7. Kübler 1943, 38–39 (PG. 37), pls. 2, 33 inv. 1074, and inv. 1089; Kurtz and Boardman 1971, 38; Strömberg 1993, 124 no. 80–81; Lemos 2002, 152–153.

8. Grave markers take a variety of forms in the Early Iron Age that change over time; they range from a small mound of earth to a rough stone or clay vase. Johansen 1951, 65–71; Smithson 1961, 150–155, Pyre A; Smithson 1968, 87 no. 28; Kurtz and Boardman 1971, 38, 56–57; Bohen 1997; Vlachou 2012, 378–379. For a Mycenaean hydria used to mark a Protogeometric tomb on Naxos, cf. Lambrinoudakis 1988; Antonaccio 1995, 199–207; Hägg 1983; for an interpretation of the large Attic amphora and the krater found in the filling layers of the Toumba building at Lefkandi, as sémata for the burials of the "royal couple," cf. Coldstream 2011, 802–803; Catling and Lemos 1990, pls. 50, 54.

9. It is possible that small and medium-sized clay stands were used to hold clay vessels during the funerals and deposited later in the tombs. For a stand and a kantharos possibly from a single funerary assemblage and now in Tubingen, cf. Paoletti 2012, 103–104 Appr.13–14. For an Attic stand and a tankard found at Corinth, cf. Shoe 1932, 63–65, fig. 9.

10. Kübler 1943, 35; Breitinger, in Kübler 1943, 2; Strömberg 1993, 123 no. 76. Compare also PG 22 and PG 23. Kübler 1943, 32; Strömberg 1993, 122–123 nos. 70–71.

11. Boardman 1988; Whitley 1991a, 110–114, 132–135; Kourou 2001. For exceptions, cf. a double cremation burial in a belly-handled amphora from tomb Erechtheiou Street, Brouskari 1980, 29–31; Kourou 2011, 197 no. 4.

12. Smithson 1968; Coldstream 1995; Liston and Papadopoulos 2004. For alternative interpretations of the intriguing fine decorated terracotta model with a set of five granaries that accompanied the burial, cf. Cherici 1989; Williams 2000; Langdon 2005.

13. Kourou 2011. The latest of the shoulder-handled amphora date to the LG Ia/b period. Trachones Tr 296 from grave A 36 (LG Ia): Geroulanos 1973, 39, pl. 26.2. Basel inv. Lg SCHL.D 01 (LG Ib, assigned to the Hirschfeld Workshop): Latacz et al. 2008, 302–303 no. 19; Vlachou 2015.

14. Kübler 1943, 39–41 (LPG); Breitinger in Kübler 1943, 2; Strömberg 1993, 124–125 no. 82; Xagorari 1996, 18–20, 53, 84–85 no. 30, pl. 18; Kourou 2011, 192. See also the analysis of Dalsoglio on the grave goods from the PG graves at Kerameikos in this volume.

15. For a catalogue of the graves, cf. Kourou 2011, 197–198 notes 13–16. G12 from the Kerameikos seems to have been the only known burial of this type to have received an amphora and a stone stele that acted as burial markers. Kübler 1954, 216–218 (MG I/II).

16. Brouskari 1979. The sex of the deceased remains inconclusive due to the absence of the osteological material. The excavator G. Meliadis noted that the well-preserved skeleton of a young female was found, while M. Brouskari, who studied and published this burial, concluded that this should have been a male burial, on the basis of the pottery and figured scenes depicted on certain pots.

17. For a catalogue of the pitchers with bibliographical references and further analysis, cf. Vlachou 2016a.

18. For the burial ground formerly associated with the Dipylon Gate, cf. Kavvadias and Lagia 2009, 74–75; Coulié 2013, 61–63.

19. Brückner and Pernice 1893, 131–132. Giant pitcher, Athens National Museum, NM 812: Coldstream 1968, 30 no. 6, pl. 7e;

20. Brückner and Pernice 1893, 112–113; Giant pitcher, Athens National Museum (NM 782): Wide 1899, 206–207, fig. 75; Coldstream 1968, 66 no. 4. From the same burial, one skyphos with high lip (Athens National Museum, NM 783): Wide 1899, 214, fig. 97 middle; a smaller skyphos decorated with a unique ritual scene on the interior surface (Athens National Museum, NM 784): Brückner and Pernice 1893, 113, fig. 10; Borell 1978, 8, cat. no. 24, pl. 20; Langdon 2008, 170–171; a small round aryballos and a cup are also mentioned from the same burial, as well as three spiral ornaments with a rosette at one end, lost by the time of the publication.

21. Brückner and Penice 1893, 128; Giant pitcher, Athens National Museum (NM 771): Wide 1899, 206–207, fig. 74; Davison 1961, fig. 144a-b; Coldstream 1968, 66 no. 2. From the same burial are the amphora (Athens National Museum, NM 770): Wide 1899, 190–191, fig. 48; three oversized skyphoi with high lip similar to the skyphos from grave 7 and two more smaller ones (Athens National Museum, NM 772–775); a collection of small bone and faience objects and figurines (Athens National Museum, NM 780–781, 2604) among them an unparalleled set of ivory statuettes modeled after Syrian prototypes (Athens National Museum, NM 776–779): Schweitzer 1971, pls. 147–148; Carter 1985, 1–7, 40; Zosi 2012.

22. Kerameikos cemetery, grave 51 (inv. no. 1314): Kübler 1954, 245–247, pl. 113, 140. Erysichthonos and Nileos str., graves VI and XIV: Tzahou-Alexandri 1967, 80, pls. 80d and 81d. South Slopes of the Acropolis (ΓΜ26), Pit burial IX: Charitonides 1973, 14, pls. 7a-c.

23. Spata, graves 1, 3 and 4: Philadelfeus 1920–1921. Anavyssos: Kastriotis and Philadelfeus 1911, 122 figs. 20 and 21; Coldstream 1968, 73, no. 1, pl. 13c.

24. *Od.* 1.136, 7.172, 15.135,17.91; *Il.* 24.301.

25. Athens National Museum (NM16022) from Agia Paraskevi. Coldstream 1968, 67 no. 5, pl. 12d.

26. Athens National Museum (NM 29838): Tölle 1964, pl. 10; Coldstream 1968, 59 no. 24. Providence (Museum of Art Rhode Island School of Design 15006): CVA (USA 2) Providence Museum of the Rhode Island School of Design 1, pl. 8.2.

27. Marathonos Avenue by the former American naval communications base, Grave 15, Marathon Museum inv. no. (K 2207). For the archaeological context of the tomb, cf. Mazarakis Ainian 2011, 711, figs. 9–10; For a detailed presentation of the pitcher, see Vlachou 2016b.

28. For the clay loutrophoros, a vessel that held a prominent place as the carrier of water for ritual bathing, both during the wedding and funerary rituals, cf. Mösch 1988; Sabetai 1993, 129–174; Oakley and Sinos 1993, 6–7, 15–16, 32; Mösch-Klingele 1999; Smith 2005, 3–9; Sabetai 2009. For the origins of the clay loutrophoros already in the LG period, cf. Walter-Karydi 1963, 90–92; Boardman 1988, 175–178; Sabetai 1993, 132–136; Vlachou 2016a and 2016b.

29. In an overview of the LG II burials in Athens and Attica, A. Alexandridou (2016, 354–355) concludes that funerary variability is the visible outcome of "horizontal divisions on the burial rites" that she further interprets in the context of kinship.

30. For wealth associated with the markets, cf. Tandy 1997. The discussion by A. Snodgrass on the different opinions supporting an egalitarian or stratified structure of the Early Iron Age society remains essential, Snodgrass 1993. For recent discussion on the issue, Rose 2012, 60–92. For the interpretation of certain burial offerings in view of the sympotic patterns that distinguish local aristocracies in Attica and Euboea, cf. Wecowski 2014, 249–288.

References

D'Agostino, B. 2008 Alba della città, alba delle immagini?. In *Alba della città, alba delle immagini Tripodes* 7, edited by B. D'Agostino, pp. 9–20. Scuoloa Archaeologica Italiana di Atene, Athens.

D'Agostino, B., and A. M. D'Onofrio 1993 Review of Morris 1987. *Gnomon* 65(1):41–51.

Alexandri, O. 1968 Trench Digging at Night along Kriezis Street. *AAA* 1:20–30.

Alexandri, O. 1972 Geometric Graves at Kynosarges. *AAA* 5(2):165–176.

Alexandridou, A. 2016 Funerary Variability in Late Eighth-Century B.C.E. Attica (Late Geometric II). *AJA* 120(3):333–360.

Antonaccio, C. M. 1995 *An Archaeology of Ancestors. Tomb Cult and Hero Cult in Early Greece.* Rowman and Littlefield, London.

Arnold, B. 2007 Gender and Archaeological Mortuary Analysis. In *Women in Antiquity: Theoretical Approaches to Gender and Archaeology*, edited by S. M. Nelson, pp. 107–140. Alta Mira Press, Lanham, Maryland.

Babić, S. 2005 Status Identity and Archaeology. In *The Archaeology of Identity: Approaches to Gender, Age, Status, Ethnicity, and Religion*, edited by M. Díaz-Andreu, S. Lucy, S. Babić, and D. N. Edwards, pp. 67–85. Routledge, London.

Binford, L. R. 1971 Mortuary Practices: Their Study and Their Potential. *Memoirs of the Society for American Archaeology* 25:6–29.

Boardman, J. 1988 Sex Differentiation in Grave Vases. *AION* 10:171–179.

Bohen, B. 1997 Aspects of Athenian Grave Cult in the Age of Homer. In *New Light on a Dark Age. Exploring the Culture of Geometric Greece*, edited by S. Langdon, pp. 44–55. University of Missouri Press, Columbia.

Borell, B. 1978 *Attisch Geometrische Schalen, eine Spätgeometrische Keramikgattung und ihre Beziehungen zum Orient, Keramikforschungen* II. P. von Zabern, Mainz am Rhein.

Brouskari, M. 1980 A Dark Age Cemetery in Erechtheion Street. *The Annual of the British School at Athens* 75:13–31.

Brouskari, M. 1979 *From the Athenian Kerameikos of the 8th Century BC.* The Athenian Archaeological Society, Athens.

Brükner, A., and E. Pernice 1893 Ein attischer Friedhof. *Athenische Mitteilungen* 18:73–191.

Brulé, P. 2001 *Les femmes grecques à l'époque classique.* Hachette, Paris.

Cannon, A. 1989 The Historical Dimension in Mortuary Expressions of Status and Sentiment. *Current Anthropology* 30:437–458.

Carter, J. B. 1985 *Greek Ivory-Carving in the Orientalizing and Archaic periods*. Garland, New York.

Catling, R. W. V., and I. S. Lemos 1990 *Lefkandi II,1. The Protogeometric Building at Toumba, Part I*, The Pottery. The Annual of the British School at Athens Suppl. 11, Oxford.

Charitonidis, S. I. 1975 Evremata Protogeometrikis kai Geometrikis epochis tis anaskafis notios tis Akropoleos. *Archaiologikon Deltion* 28, Meletai, Athens.

Cherici, A. 1989 Granaî o Arnie? Considerazioni su una classe fittile attica tra IX e VIII sec. A.C. *Atti dell' Academia nazionale dei Lincei. Rendiconti* 44:215–230.

Coldstream J. N. 1968 *Greek Geometric Pottery. A Survey of Ten Local Styles and their Chronology*. Methuen, London.

Coldstream, J. N. 1983 The Meaning of the Regional Styles in the Eighth Century B.C. In *The Greek Renaissance of the Eighth Century B.C. Tradition and Innovation. Proceedings of the Second International Symposium at the Swedish Institute in Athens, 1–5 June, 1981*, edited by R. Hägg, pp. 17–25. Svenska institutet i Athen, Stockholm.

Coldstream, J. N. 1995 The Rich Lady of the Areiopagos and Her Contemporaries. A Tribute in Memory of Evelyn Lord Smithson. *Hesperia* 64(4):391–403.

Coldstream, J. N. 2003 *Geometric Greece* (second edition). Routledge, London.

Coldstream, J. N. 2011 Geometric Elephantiasis. In *The "Dark Ages" Revisited. Acts of an International Symposium in Memory of W. D. E. Coulson, University of Thessaly, Volos, 14–17 June 2007*, vol. II, edited by A. Mazarakis Ainian, pp. 801–807. University of Thessaly Press, Volos.

Coulié, A. 2013 *La céramique grecque aux époques géométrique et orientalisante (XIe–VIe siècle av. J.-C.)*. Picard et Epona, Paris.

Davison, J. M. 1961 *Attic Geometric Workshops*. Yale University Press, Rome.

Díaz-Andreu, M. 2005 Gender Identity. In *The Archaeology of Identity. Approaches to Gender, Age, Status, Ethnicity, and Religion*, edited by M. Díaz-Andreu, S. Lucy, S. Babić, and D. N. Edwards, pp. 13–42. Routledge, London.

Dickinson, O. 2006 *The Aegean from Bronze Age to Iron Age: Continuity and Change between the Eighth and Twelfth Centuries BC*. Routledge, London.

Duplouy, A. 2006 *Le prestige des élites*. Les Belles Lettres, Paris.

von Freytag, B. 1974 Ein spätgeometrisches Frauengrab vom Kerameikos. *Athenische Mitteilungen* 89:1–25.

Garland, R. 1989 The Well-Ordered Corpse: An Investigation into the Motives behind Greek Funerary Legislation. *Bulletin of the Institute of Classical Studies* 36:1–15.

Geroulanos, J. 1973 Grabsitten des ausgehenden geometrischen Stils im Bereich des Gutes Trachones bei Athen. *Athenische Mitteilungen* 88:1–54.

Gibbs, L. 1987 Identifying Gender Representation in the Archaeological Record: A Contextual Study. In *The Archaeology of Contextual Meanings*, edited by I. Hodder, pp. 79–89. Cambridge University Press, Cambridge.

Goldstein, L. 1981 One-dimensional Archaeology and Multi-dimensional People: Spatial Organization and Mortuary Analysis. In *The Archaeology of Death*, edited by R. W. Chapman, I. Kinnes and K. Randsborg, pp. 53–69. Cambridge University Press, Cambridge.

Haentjens A. M. E. 2002 Ritual Shoes in Early Greek Female Graves. *L'antiquité classique* 71:171–184.

Hägg, R. 1983 Funerary Meals in the Geometric Necropolis at Asine? In *The Greek Renaissance of the Eighth Century B.C.: Tradition and Innovation, Proceedings of the Second International*

Symposium at the Swedish Institute in Athens, 1–5 June, 1981, edited by R. Hägg, pp. 189–193. Svenska institutet i Athen, Stockholm.

Harich-Schwarzbauer, H., A. Hermary, and O. Jaeggi 2011 1.e. Tod und Bestattung in der griechischen Welt. In *Thesaurus Cultus et Rituum Antiquorum 6, Occasions et circonstances des activités cultuelles et rituelles*, edited by A. Hermary and B. Jaeger, pp. 111–139. Getty, Los Angeles.

Hodder, I. (ed.) 1982 *Symbolic and Structural Archaeology*. Cambridge University Press, Cambridge.

Hodder, I. 1989 *The Meanings of Things: Material Culture and Symbolic Expression*. Unwin Hyman, London.

Hodder, I. 1991 Interpretative Archaeology and its Role. *American Antiquity* 56(1):7–18.

Johansen, K. F. 1951 *The Attic Grave-Reliefs of the Classical Period. An Essay in Interpretation*. Ejnar Munksgaard, Copenhagen.

Kalaitzoglou, G. 2010 Adelsgräber des 9. Jhs. v. Chr. in Athen und Attika. In *Attika: Archäologie einer "zentralen" Kulturlandschaft, Akten der internationalen Tagung vom 18.–20. Mai 2007 in Marburg, Philippika, Marburger altertumskundliche Abhandlungen 37*, edited by H. Lohmann and T. Mattern, pp. 47–72. Harrassowitz, Wiesbaden.

Kastriotis, P., and A. Philadelfeus 1911 Anaskafai Anavyssou. *Praktika* 1911:111–31.

Kavvadias, G. G., and A. Lagia 2009 New Light on Old Finds: Two Classic Tombs from the Plot of Sapoutzaki on Piraeus Street. In *Athenian Potters and Painters* II, edited by J. H. Oakley and O. Palagia, pp. 73–89. Oxbow Books, Oxford.

Kourou N. 2011 Attica Young Girls' Ashtrays: Around an Amphora and a Mineralized Cloth of the Early Geometric Age. In *Epainos Luigi Beschi, Mouseio Benaki 7*, edited by A. Delivorrias, G. Despinis, and A. Zarkadas, pp. 189–200. Mouseio Benaki, Athens.

Kourou, N. 2001 An Attic Geometric Amphora from Argos. The Legacy of Protogeometric Style. In *Studies in Honor of D. Tzouhou-Alexandri*, edited by I. Leventi, and A. Alexandri, pp. 51–68. Athens.

Kraiker, W., and K. Kübler 1939 *Kerameikos: Ergebnisse der Ausgrabungen* I. *Die Nekropolen des 12. Bis 10. Jahrhunderts*. de Gruyter, Berlin.

Kübler, K. 1943 *Kerameikos: Ergebnisse der Ausgrabungen* IV. *Neufunde aus der Nekropole des 11. U. 10. Jahrhunderts*. de Gruyter, Berlin:.

Kübler, K. 1954 *Kerameikos: Ergebnisse der Ausgrabungen* V. *Die Nekropolen des 10. Bis 8. Jahrhunderts*. de Gruyter, Berlin.

Kurtz, D. C., and J. Boardman 1971 *Greek Burial Customs*. Thames and Hudson, London.

Lambrinoudakis, V. 1988 Veneration of Ancestors in Geometric Naxos. In *Early Greek Cult Practice*, edited by N. Marinatos and R. Hägg, pp. 235–246. Svenska institutet i Athen, Stockholm.

Langdon, S. 2001 Beyond the Grave: Biographies from Early Greece. *American Journal of Archaeology* 105(4):579–606.

Langdon, S. 2005 Views of Wealth, a Wealth of Views: Grave Goods in Iron Age Attica. In *Women and Property*. Conference organized in 2003 at the Center for Hellenic Studies, Harvard University, edited by D. Lyons and R. Westbrook; http://zeus.chsdc.org/chs/files/women_property_langdon.pdf.

Langdon, S. 2006 Maiden Voyage: from Abduction to Marriage in Late Geometric Art. In *Pictorial Pursuits. Figurative Painting on Mycenaean and Geometric Pottery, Papers from Two Seminars at the Swedish Institute at Athens in 1999 and 2001*, edited by E. Rystedt and B. Wells, pp. 205–215. Svenska institutet i Athen, Stockholm.

Langdon, S. 2008 *Art and Identity in Dark Age Greece, 1100–700 B.C.E.* University of Cambridge, Cambridge.

Latacz J., T. Greub, P. Blome, and A. Wieczorek (eds.) 2008 *Homer: Der Mythos von Troia in Dichtung und Kunst, Antikenmuseum Basel und Sammlung Ludwig.* Hirmer, Munich.

Lemos, I. S. 2002 *The Protogeometric Aegean, The Archaeology of the Late Eleventh and Tenth Centuries BC.* Oxford University Press, Oxford.

Liston, M. A., and J. K. Papadopoulos 2004 The "Rich Athenian Lady" was Pregnant: The Anthropology of a Geometric Tomb Reconsidered. *Hesperia* 73(1):7–38.

Luce, J.-M. 2003 Le banquet, l'amour et la mort, de l'époque géométrique à l'époque classique. In *Symposium; Banquet et représentations en Grèce et à Rome, Colloque International, Université de Toulouse-Le Mirail, mars 2002, Pallas* 61, edited by J. C. Carrière and C. Orfanos, pp. 55–69. Presses Universitaires du Mirail, Toulouse.

Luce, J.-M. 2011 From Miniature Objects to Giant Ones: The Process of Defunctionalisation in Sanctuaries and Graves in Iron Age Greece. In *The Gods of Small Things, Pallas* 86, edited by A. C. Smith and M. E. Bergeron, pp. 53–73. Presses Universitaires du Mirail, Toulouse.

Mazarakis Ainian, A. 2011 A Necropolis of the Geometric Period at Marathon: The Context. In *The "Dark Ages" Revisited, Acts of an International Symposium in Memory of W. D. E. Coulson, University of Thessaly, Volos 14–17 June 2007*, edited by A. Mazarakis Ainian, pp. 703–716. University of Thessaly Press, Volos.

Morris, I. 1987 *Burial and Ancient Society. The Rise of the Greek City-state.* Cambridge University Press, Cambridge.

Morris, I. 1991 The Archaeology of Ancestors: The Saxe/Goldstein hypothesis revisited. *Cambridge Archaeological Journal* 1(2):147–169.

Morris, I. 1992 *Death-ritual and Social Structure in Classical Antiquity.* Cambridge University Press, Cambridge.

Morris, I. 1992–93 Law, Culture and Funerary Art in Athens, 600–300 B.C. *Hephaistos* 11/12:35–50.

Morris, I. 1999 Iron Age Greece and the Meanings of "Princely Tombs." In *Les Princes de la Protohistoire et l'Émergence de l'État*, edited by R. Pascal, pp. 57–80. Centre Jean Bérard, Naples.

Morris, S. P., and J. K. Papadopoulos 2004 Of Granaries and Games: Egyptian Stowaways in an Athenian Chest. In *XARIS: Essays in Honor of Sara A. Immerwahr, Hesperia* Suppl. 33, edited by A. P. Chapin, pp. 225–242. American School of Classical Studies at Athens, Athens.

Mösch, R. M. 1988 Le marriage et la mort sur les loutrophores. In *La Parola, l'Immagine, la Tomba, Atti del Colloquio Internazionale di Capri, AION* 10, edited by B. D'Agostino, pp. 117–139. Dipartimento di Studi del Mondo Classico e del Mediterraneo Antico, Napoli.

Mösch-Klingele, R. 1999 Loutra und loutrophoros im Totenkult. Die literarischen Zeugnisse. In *Proceedings of the XVth International Congress of Classical Archaeology, Archaeology towards the Third Millennium: Reflections and Perspectives, Amsterdam, 12.-17.7.1998*, edited by R. Docter and F. E. M. Moormann, pp. 273–275. Allard Pierson Museum, Amsterdam.

Oakley, J. H., and R. H. Sinos (eds.) 1993 *The Wedding in Ancient Athens.* University of Wisconsin Press, Madison.

Paoletti, O. 2012 *Ceramica geometrica greca nel Museo archeologico nazionale di Firenze.* All'Insegna del Giglio, Florence.

Papadopoulos, J. K. 1993 To Kill a Cemetery. The Athenian Kerameikos and the Early Iron Age in the Aegean. *Journal of Mediterranean Archaeology* 6:175–206.

Parker Pearson, M. 1999 *The Archaeology of Death and Burial.* Sutton, Stroud.

Philadelfeus, A. 1920–21 Anaskafi para to chorio Spata. *Archaiologikon Deltion* 6:131–38.

Polignac, F. de 2007 Sexe et genre dans les rites funéraires grecs: quelques aperçus. In *Pratiques funéraires et société: nouvelles approches en archéologie et en anthropologie sociale: actes du colloque interdisciplinaire de Sens, 12–14 juin 2003*, edited by L. Baray, P. Brun, and A. Testart, pp. 351–358. Editions universitaires de Dijon, Dijon.

Rose, P. W. 2012 *Class in Archaic Greece*. Cambridge University Press, Cambridge.

Price, T. D., and G. M. Feinman (eds.) 2010 *Pathways to Power. New Perspectives on the Emergence of Social Inequality*. Springer-Verlag, New York.

Purcell, N. 1992 La mobilité et la *polis*. In *La cité grecque d'Homère à Alexandre*, edited by O. Murray and S. Price, pp. 43–76. La Découverte, Paris.

Rakita G. F. M., and J. E. Buikstra 2005 Introduction. In *Interacting with the Dead. Perspectives on Mortuary Archaeology for the New Millennium*, edited by G. F. M. Rakita, J. E. Buikstra, L. A. Beck, and S. R. Williams, pp. 1–11. University Press of Florida, Gainesville.

Sabetai, V. 1993 *The Washing Painter: A Contribution to the Wedding and Genre Iconography in the Second Half of the Fifth Century B.C.*, Unpublished thesis, University of Cincinnati.

Sabetai, V. 2009 Marker Vase or Burnt Offering? The Clay loutrophoros in Context. In *Shapes and Uses of Greek Vases (7th–4th centuries B.C.)*, *Études d' Archéologie* 3, edited by A. Tsingarida, pp. 291–306. ULB—CReA-Patrimoine, Brussels.

Saxe, A. 1970 Social Dimensions of Mortuary Practices, dissertation, University of Michigan.

Saxe, A. 1971 Social Dimensions of Mortuary Practices in a Mesolithic Population from Wadi Halfa, Sudan. *Memoirs of the Society for American Archaeology* 25:39–57.

Sen, A. 1992 *Inequality Reexamined*. Russel Sage Foundation, New York.

Shanks, M., and C. Tilley 1982 Ideology, Symbolic Power, and Ritual Communication: A Reinterpretation of Neolithic Mortuary Practices. In *Symbolic and Structural Archaeology*, edited by I. Hodder, pp. 129–161. Cambridge University Press, Cambridge.

Shoe, L.T. 1932 A Box of Antiquities from Corinth. *Hesperia* 1:56–89.

Silverman, H., and D. B. Small 2002 *The Space and Place of Death*. Archaeological Papers of the American Anthropological Association 11, Arlington, Va.

Sjögren, K.-G. 2010 Anonymous Ancestors? The Tilley/Shanks Hypothesis Revisited. In *Monumental Questions: Prehistoric Megaliths, Mounds, and Enclosures*, edited by D. Calado, M. Baldia, and M. Boulanger, pp. 111–118. BAR International Series 2122, London.

Skias, A. 1898 Ancient Eleusinian Necropolis. *Archaiologike Ephemeris* 76–122.

Smith, A. C. 2005 The Politics of Weddings at Athens: An Iconographic Assessment. *Leeds International Classical Studies* 4(1):1–32.

Smithson, E. L. 1961 The Protogeometric Cemetery at Nea Ionia, 1949. *Hesperia* 30:147–178.

Smithson, E. L. 1968 The Tomb of a Rich Athenian Lady, ca. 850 B.C. *Hesperia* 37:77–116.

Smithson, E. L. 1969 The Grave of an Early Athenian Aristocrat. *Archaeology* 22:18–25.

Smithson, E. L. 1974 A Geometric Cemetery on the Areopagus: 1897, 1932, 1947, with Appendices on the Geometric Graves Found in the Dorpfeld Excavations on the Acropolis West Slope in 1895 and on Hadrian Street ("Phinopoulos' Lot") in 1898. *Hesperia* 43:325–390.

Snodgrass, A. 1993 The Rise of the Polis: the Archaeological Evidence. In *The Ancient City State: Symposium on the Occasion of the 250th Anniversary of the Royal Danish Academy of Science and Letters*, edited by M. G. Hansen, pp. 30–40. Mogens Herman Hansen, Copenhagen.

Sørensen, M. L. S. 1991 The Construction of Gender through Appearance. In *The Archaeology of Gender, Proceedings of the Twenty-Second Annual Conference of the Archaeological Association of the University of Calgary*, edited by D. Walde and N. D. Willows, pp. 121–129. University of Calgary, Canada.

Sørensen, M. L. S. 2000 *Gender Archaeology*. Polity Press, Cambridge.

Sørensen, M. L. S. 2007 Gender, Things, and Material Culture. In *Women in Antiquity: Theoretical Approaches to Gender and Archaeology*, edited by S. M. Nelson, pp. 75–105. Alta Mira Press, Lanham, Maryland.

Stavropoulos, F. 1965 Odou Kavalotti. *Archaiologikon Deltion* 20:75–80.

Strömberg, A. 1993 *Male or Female? A Methodological Study of Grave Gifts as Sex-indicators in Iron Age Burials from Athens*. Paul Astöms Förlag, Jonsered.

Schweitzer, B. 1971 *Greek Geometric Art*. Phaidon, London.

Tandy, D. 1997 *Warriors into Traders. The Power of the Market in Early Greece*. University of California Press, Berkeley.

Tzahou-Alexandri, O. 1967 Erysichthonos kai Nileos. *Archaeologikon Deltion* 22(B1):79–83.

Verdelis, N., and K. Davaras 1966 Anaskafes Anavyssou. *Archaeologikon Deltion* 21(B1):97–98.

Vlachou, V. 2012 Death and Burial in the Greek World. In *Thesaurus Cultus et Rituum Antiquorum* VIII, *Death and Burial* (Addendum to vol. VI), edited by A. Hermary and B. Jaeger, pp. 363–384. J. Paul Getty Museum, Los Angeles.

Vlachou, V. 2015 From Pots to Workshops: The Hirschfeld Painter and the Late Geometric I Context of Attic Pottery Production. In *Pots, Workshops, and Early Iron Age Society. Function and Role of Ceramics in Early Greece, Proceedings of the International Conference, Brussels 14–16 November 2013, Études d' Archéologie* 8, edited by V. Vlachou, pp. 49–74. ULB—CReA-Patrimoine, Brussels.

Vlachou, V. 2016a Nuptial Vases in Female Tombs? Aspects of Funerary Behavior during the Late Geometric Period in Attica. In *An Archaeology of Prehistoric Bodies and Embodied Identities in the Eastern Mediterranean*, edited by M. Mina, S. Triantafyllou, and Y. Papadatos, pp. 96–103. Oxbow Books, Oxford.

Vlachou, V. 2016b Image and Story in Late Geometric Attica: Interpreting a Giant Pitcher from Marathon. In *The Consumer's Choice: Uses of Greek Figure-Decorated Pottery, AIA Monographs Series, Selected Papers in Ancient Art and Archaeology*, edited by T. Carpenter, E. Langridge-Noti, and M. D. Stansbury-O'Donnell, pp. 125–151. Archaeological Institute of America, Boston.

Walter-Karydi, E. 1963 Schwarzfigurige Lutrophoren im Kerameikos. *Athenische Mitteilungen* 78:90–103.

Wecowski, M. 2014 *The Rise of the Aristocratic Banquet*. Oxford University Press, Oxford.

Whitley, J. 1991a *Style and Society in Dark Age Greece, The Changing Face of a Pre-literate Society 1100–700 BC*. Cambridge University Press, Cambridge.

Whitley, J. 1991b Social Diversity in Dark Age Greece. *The Annual of the British School at Athens* 86:341–365.

Whitley, J. 1996 Gender and Hierarchy in Early Athens. *Metis* 11:209–232.

Wide, S. 1899 Geometrische Vasen aus Griechenland. *Jdl* 14:188–215.

Williams, D. 2000 Of Geometric Toys, Symbols, and Votives. In *Periplous: Papers on Classical Art and Archaeology Presented to Sir John Boardman*, edited by G. R. Tsetskhladze, A. J. N. W. Prag, and A. M. Snodgrass, pp. 388–297. Thames and Hudson, London.

Xagorari, M. 1996 *Untersuchungen zu frühgriechischen Grabsitten: figürliche plastische Beigaben aus geschlossenen Grabfunden Attikas und Euböas des 10. bis 7. Jhs. v. Chr.* P. von Zabern, Mainz.

Young, R. S. 1949 An Early Geometric Grave near the Athenian Agora. *Hesperia* 18:275–97.

Young, R. S. 1939 *Late Geometric Graves and a Seventh Century Well in the Agora*. Hesperia suppl. 2.

Zosi, E. 2012 An Enigmatic Female Burial. In *"Princesses" of the Mediterranean in the Dawn of History*, edited by N. C. Stampolidis, pp. 146–157. Museum of Cycladic Art, Athens.

CHAPTER ELEVEN

Etruscan Women and Social Polarity

Two Case Studies for Approaching Inequality

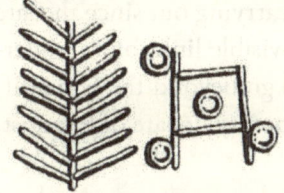

Giovanna Bagnasco Gianni

In memory of the scholarship of Antonio Aloni

Abstract   *This contribution discusses the possibility that gender polarity does not represent opposition in the Etruscan culture, against the current belief that the biological and physical aspects of gender are always a core theme, being innate and implying hierarchy.*

Two case studies belonging to the Orientalizing and Late Archaic–Classical periods are considered. The first study includes a group of inscribed weaving and spinning instruments, consisting of some female funerary equipment of the Orientalizing period, and in female goddesses' sanctuaries of the seventh century BC (Tarquinia, Veio, Satricum). They seem to support the idea that the activity of weaving was not "a women's job" but a skill that could go beyond the production of textiles, making it possible to connect things that were originally separated. This might be the reason why women had such a prominent position in the dissemination of the alphabetical knowledge in Etruscan society, since they were aware of the need of conceptual tools to bring together what was separated in origin. In other words, the pragmatic content of letters and threads challenges the ability to bring them to the condition of being a text(ile) and to identify patterns.

The second case study belongs to the Late Archaic–Classical periods and approaches material evidence in Etruscan mirrors by means of iconography. It focuses on the recurrence of sets of objects that have to do with catoptromancy and the concept expressed by the feminine entity Munθuχ. We touch upon women's skill in bringing order in the semantic sphere of the contact with the gods.

If we accept this argument, the novel effect would be to contextualize the Etruscan woman in the semantic sphere of order, in areas that might have been complementary to men's. Complementarity is more likely than hierarchy, due to the all-inclusive sphere in which women acted. In addition to this, it seems relevant

*to the idea of "equality," with which we have been long acquainted in literary
reviews about the Etruscans.*

Introduction

The two case studies I am going to present might support the idea of a complementarity
of skills and behaviors within the Etruscan society, at least in some sectors, and make
it possible to evaluate the relationship between men and women in terms of social polarity.
The key images I selected belong to ongoing research I have been carrying out since the late
1980s. What I tried to do at that time was begin to extract the invisible links of an underlying rationale from the material evidence that, to my eyes, could go beyond the basic difference between male and female that is at the root of the contemporary debate of feminist,
gender, and queer archaeology.[1]

The topic that I would like to point out for discussion is whether we are now ready to
take advantage, in our studies of the organization of the Etruscan society, of positions that
have been ripening during the last century and can be considered alongside structural analysis, which is mainly focused on a dualistic separation between men and women. In trying
to measure social gender polarity in the Etruscan civilization it is impossible to overlook the
literature reviews about Etruscan women, considering their position in respect to the classical world and contextualization in the wider framework of archaeology devoted to women.

In other words, besides the belief shared in the literary review concerning a common
ground for men and women as it is depicted in the Etruscan imagery, we have a number
of hints addressing a possible multifaceted concept of the relationship between men and
women in the Etruscan society.

Prior Studies of Etruscan Inequality

The debate on women's status in the Etruscan society, started long ago with J. J. Bachofen's
statement on the Etruscan "tyranny of women." Focusing on one of the women connected
to the Etruscan kings of Rome, Tanaquil, the wife of the first Tarquinius, Bachofen develops
his thesis of an ancestral Mediterranean *Mutterrecht* that had survived in the Etruscan civilization. His thesis was immediately challenged (Bonfante 1973:91; Foxhall 2013:8–10),
but literary sources referring to this period are currently used to show the degree of freedom
Etruscan women had in comparison to their Greek or Roman counterparts.[2] However,
Dominique Briquel pointed out that these powerful and politicized women are described
by Roman literary sources and must be considered issuing more from that tradition than
from a real Etruscan one. On the other hand, as "historicized avatars of their ancient gran-
deur," these "hypostases of divine characters" were considered alien to the Roman mentality
of the beginnings of the Republic when these stories were created (Briquel 1998). We shall
encounter Briquel's position later on for his focus on these women's sacred power that could
extend beyond their feminine nature, as it happened in ancient Mediterranean societies

(Near East, Egypt, Crete etc.), and in which women were also at the root of royal power and gave men their supremacy as "*faiseuses de rois.*"

At the end of the 1950s, J. Heurgon (Heurgon 1961) pointed out a number of aspects that are still crucial for the evaluation of women's status in the Etruscan civilization in general, such as their participation in banquets and entertainment together with men and the use of the metronymic. His important article also focuses on a crucial issue: what is true for one city in one period is not necessarily true for the same city in other periods, or for other Etruscan cities in general. For example, in the case of *Caere*, he pointed out the extraordinary richness of the Regolini Galassi tomb (mid-seventh century BC) belonging to a woman (Heurgon 1961:141–143) whose precious silver funerary equipment is marked by the controversial homonymic genitive of the name *Larthia* that could suit both the feminine *Larthi* and the masculine *Larth* (Bonfante 1973:101; Bagnasco Gianni 1996:351–352). Its female or male belonging is further complicated by the discovery of a silver *patera* inscribed with a second name *Velthurus* in which we could recognize both the genitive of the masculine *Velthur* or a gamonimic.[3] However, there is no doubt about the high ranking level of this feminine deposition at *Caere* around the middle of the seventh century BC. As in later periods (sixth and fifth centuries BC), Heurgon also noticed a relevant presence of inscriptions with women's names, rather than men's, at *Caere* (Heurgon 1961:143–149), and a conscious selection of the architectonic features of women's funerary beds. It is an imitation of a sarcophagus that includes a bed and precedes the choice of the later house-shaped *cippi* to indicate women's presence in tombs. Heurgon's question about the meaning of this choice remains open, even if he claims that women received, in death, a double protection in order to underline the inviolability and sacredness of their burial and, in some cases, the idea of venerability and divinization (Heurgon 1961:149–160).

The epigraphic review of the Etruscan onomastics, carried out by Helmut Rix in the early 1970s (Rix 1972:706 and 756), confirmed Heurgon's statement about the early presence of the metronymic alongside the patronymic due to the structure of the Etruscan family, which was different from that of the Roman, as it was more centered on the *pater familias.*

Heurgon's paper led to additional reflections on epigraphic and archaeological aspects of Etruscan women that were presented by Larissa Bonfante in the volume of *Arethusa* (6.1, 1973) devoted to women in Antiquity. It was published in the United States as a consequence of the "widespread discovery of women in antiquity in the Anglo-American world" (1970s and 1980s) "following on the rise of the women's movement in the late 1960s and early 1970s in the atmosphere of the so-called 'second-wave' feminism" (Foxhall 2013:6–7). However, Bonfante's article did not depend on this perspective, since, as mentioned above, evidence of an outstanding status of Etruscan women had already been acknowledged. Her use of the term *equality* between men and women, for a nuanced idea of Etruscan "matriarchy" (Bonfante 1973:91), is particularly suitable for the present Conference on Inequality and represents an important keyword to build on here.

In 1981, M. Sordi offered a thorough account of ancient Greek and Roman literary sources focused on the special status of Etruscan women, and reinforced the importance of the metronymic, after G. Colonna's review of two very ancient Etruscan inscriptions belonging to the end of the seventh century BC: the stele of Vetulonia and the *dolium* from *Rusellae* (Colonna 1977:189–191; Bagnasco Gianni 1996:numbers 237, 233).

Metronymic actually implies kinship acknowledged in the female and the principle of matrilinearity so that, according to Sordi, in Etruria motherhood was enough to legally recognize children and assure them almost all civil rights. Onomastics shows that the Etruscan woman was a legal person, different from the Roman, who was conceived as part of her *gens* without personal name (her name corresponding to that of her *gens*) or legal capacity, since her legal protection shifted from that of her father to her husband's. This kind of freedom and independence probably explain the Greek historian Theopompus's scandalized remark about the Etruscan habit of bringing up all children, even those born out of wedlock. Moreover, the Etruscans refused to accept so-called honor killings and the exposition of children, which was frequent in the rest of the Classical world (Sordi 1981:53 and 56). With this evidence, Sordi compares the current Etruscan depiction of men and women banqueting and feasting together on the same bed to a number of historical sources and explains this habit as a peculiar aspect of Etruscan family management inspired by "a confident intimacy unknown in the Greek world" (Sordi 1981:54 and 57–58).

In spite of strong criticism (Martelli 1991), the collection of essays edited by A. Rallo in 1989 fills the gap of interest in scholarship about women in Etruria, in comparison to other sectors of the classical world, after the cultural climate brought on by the Anglo-American feminist movements (Rallo 1989:7).

Shortly after, B. d'Agostino (d'Agostino 1993) pointed out the need to distinguish between different phases and areas of the Etruscan civilization and, returning to Heurgon's position, attempted to focus on the historical framework. He recognized a gap in women's status when a political timocratic structure, based on commerce and extensive agriculture, took over the preceding gentilitial organization at the end of the sixth century BC when the Etruscan polis took place. The diminishing status of women was nevertheless short-lived when in the middle of the fifth century BC, after the Etruscans were defeated by the Syracusans at Cuma (474 BC), the system of the Etruscan *polis* faded away.

CURRENT RESEARCH

Throughout Etruscan history it is hard to find consistent collections of testimonies showing ruptures and continuity in women's status (Nielsen 1998; Nielsen 1999; Rathje 2007; Haynes 2005:XVI–XVIII). For example, the series represented by the painted tombs of Tarquinia show women involved in banqueting and feasting over more than three centuries (Marzullo 2017:105–106), but do not aid us in understanding to what extent this kind of conviviality was shared. Women depicted in tombs, even if they may represent only a sector of the Etruscan society, mirror the same condition that the abovementioned literary sources portray.

In addition to iconography, attempts to read the archaeological record and perceive male and female presence in funerary equipment are focused on the first phases recognized as the Etruscan civilization across the Italian Peninsula during the Villanovan and Orientalizing periods.[4] All contributions focus on raw data and are oriented to reconstructing the relationship between objects, or sets of objects, and corresponding duties in funerary equipment.

Evidence from our excavations at Tarquinia, based on the ceremonial remains, might show that there was a woman, next and equal to the *rex-sacerdos,* involved in the act of dedicating the 'monumental complex' to the main Etruscan goddess *Uni* (Bonghi Jovino 2005).

The results of this scholarship provides a solid background for research based on specific sectors of evidence. Material evidence can be observed from a phase preceding the crystallization of duties, as we usually expect them from their Greek and Roman counterparts. We barely know how duties were recognized, selected, and distributed in the Etruscan society, what capacities and/or skills actually made it possible to carry out particular duties, or to whom such duties were assigned.

Research on the relationship between tools and duties is now crucial in order to get a more complete picture of Etruscan women and touch upon the coverage of their formal autonomy. The two case studies I present here aim at investigating these aspects of social polarity from the point of view of effective agency.

L. Foxhall recently claimed that in Greek and Roman societies the household was "[t]he locus of social, and ultimately political entitlement. A mother, a sister, a nurse or slave girl was not just a 'woman,' rather she was a woman entitled to undertake specific roles defined to a large extent by her place in and relationship to one or more households and the kin groups with which they were entangled" (Foxhall 2013:44). But this situation does not necessarily indicate formal autonomy in social choice or management.

In the case of Etruscan men and women, the attempt to reconnect the two aspects of research, theoretical approach and raw data analysis, shows degrees of reliability often not in accordance with the condition of the surviving data. For example, the interpretation of the gender of the abovementioned inscriptions of the Regolini Galassi tomb remains uncertain, but the lady buried there is unambiguously a woman.

Moreover, considering grammatical gender L. Agostiniani claims that "Etruscan does not have a grammatical distinction of gender. . . . Nouns belong to two semantically motivates classes, animate and inanimate." (Agostiniani 2013:474). This situation might mirror the results of M. Cristofani's research on the shifting of gender in a number of iconographic representations of the anthropomorphization of Etruscan gods and the personification of particular aspects of life conditions and natural forces. This evidence is evaluated by means of comparing and contrasting their development to the corresponding Greek repertoire (Cristofani 1997:214; Krauskopf 2013:517). In a number of cases, in the Etruscan language the distinction between animate and inanimate entities is more relevant than those between male and female, aside from the fact that polarity of gender is currently expressed by the lexicon (for example, used to indicate pairs: *clan / sech* "son / daughter," *apa / ati* "father / mother").

R. Lazzeroni suggested, according to E. Rosch's scholarship following the late Wittgenstein, that in a number of languages and in some situations gender opposition implies a grammatical expression and is used as a metaphor of polarity. This aspect of language is not always necessarily shared: we may define by means of the lexicon, conceived as a semantic relationship, and as a scalar category, instead of as distinct (Lazzeroni 1993:8–14).

Is the absence of gender-polarity opposition in the Etruscan language consistent with specific cultural traits? The examples collected by M. Cristofani show that the emphasis is on the concepts of animate and inanimate entities. If these remarks are correct, gender polarity does not represent opposition in the Etruscan culture, contrary to the current belief that the biological and physical aspects of gender are always a core theme, being innate and implying hierarchy (Héritier 2002:IX–XXIV). On the other hand, we have already pointed out the risk of generalization before checking data and acknowledging that "the very existence of those biological elements of gender, whatever precisely they turn out to be, constructs a dimension of apparent continuity between ourselves and people in the past, however differently gender might have operated in these societies" (Foxhall 2013:3).

This crucial aspect of research goes beyond the limits of Etruscan culture and leads to consideration of the dualities that are extracted from the materiality of evidence by means of thorough analyses of recurrent associations of objects that address a difference between men and women. The issue is to contextualize the result of such analyses within a given society in terms of duties or skills that produce a multifaceted sequence of actions but do not show the nature of social polarity. Was it focused on equality or hierarchy? From this point of view, the quality of the relationship between men and women is the next crucial step to complete.[5]

In the case of the Etruscans, equality from the point of view of women is a seemingly easy aspect to examine, since we have been introduced to it already. Women are indeed more well-known than men (Bonfante 2013), but as mentioned, we are uncertain about what level of equality was shared within all of Etruscan society. What can be considered broadly recognized and what belonged to a limited environment, notwithstanding diachronic and territorial differences?

This background is crucial in dealing with data and daring to interpret them from the point of view of polarity. Let's now examine the key images of the abovementioned case studies related to the phenomenon of the acquisition of writing and the use of mirrors by women.

CASE STUDY 1

- Texts on the most ancient inscribed objects, included in funerary equipment (end of the eighth century BC) and sanctuaries (first quarter of the seventh century BC), address women and female goddesses (Bagnasco Gianni 1999, 99–100; Colonna 2009)

- The most ancient inscribed objects (end of the eighth century BC) are spindle-whorls and bobbins that recall the activity of weaving (Bagnasco Gianni 1996:351–352).

Weaving, "the women's job,"[6] is a powerful tool for bringing together what is separate in origin: threads, originally separate themselves, challenge the ability to put them in the right order and create a textile. This thought has been one of the major pillars in the field of anthropology since M. Griaule's studies (Griaule 1948:25–26). J. Scheid and J. Svenbro built on this thesis in their essay on the myth of weaving in the classical world (Scheid and Svenbro 1994).

Their skill with weaving could have been the reason why women had a prominent position in the dissemination of alphabetical knowledge in the Etruscan society: letters, which are originally separate, challenge the ability to bring them together to form text (Bagnasco Gianni 1999). This activity fits well with women's educational tasks and is not inconsistent with the role of "mother" (Pitzalis 2011:259, 265–266; Bonfante 2013:439). However the twofold evidence of the very beginning of writing in Etruria, spindle-whorls and bobbins and women's tombs, is not enough to support a direct link between the ability to handle a system of signs (in this case, writing) and the female component of society. Men might have actually inscribed all of the objects that were included in women's funerary equipment. On the other hand, the corresponding antiquity of inscribed objects dedicated in sanctuaries devoted to female goddesses[7] supports the idea of the importance of women in the dissemination of writing, at the very least, at the time of its introduction in Etruria. In written sources, Etruscan writing was introduced by Damaratus of Corinth in the second half of the seventh century BC. Nowadays, it is clear that the story of Damaratus represents a step in the development of Etruscan writing toward an institutional reform, fixing the Etruscan identity through the selection of specific forms of letters, *litterarum formas*. Damaratus's role is consistent with that of a *protos euretes*, who was involved with writing in Etruria, as Tacitus refers to it in his account on the introduction of writing by a number of outstanding characters in several Mediterranean populations (*Annales*:XI, 14, 3). However, the much later chronology of his intervention is more in accord with that of the graphic reform that actually took place in the Etruscan writing during the last decades of the seventh century BC. (Bagnasco Gianni 1999:89–92).

In conclusion, both series of testimonies, epigraphic and literary, support the thesis of a male intervention during a second period, when the management of writing was definitively included in the political organization of the Etruscans.

Later on, the impression of consistency with other series of evidence was reinforced by research on the Etruscan mirrors that in the United States is being fruitfully carried out by L. Bonfante and N. de Grummond (Bonfante 2000; de Grummond 2006a). In particular, de Grummond's studies on catoptromancy (de Grummond 2000) motivated me to carry out a research project for approaching a qualitative and quantitative evaluation of sets of tools depicted on Etruscan mirrors that may refer to different actions. Combining investigations on the recurrent association of objects, potentially reflective or reflecting, depicted as details of scenes on more than 650 mirrors with investigations of the different contexts in which such recurrent associations appear made it possible to recognize a difference between the purpose and the use of these objects within different sectors of activity (Bagnasco Gianni et al. 2012).

The result of our work on this series, certainly belonging to women, contains meaningful information and clues for considering a possible clash between women depicted as being solely interested in cosmetics and their actual role as subjects involved with divination, through catoptromancy, in the social organization of the Etruscans.

CASE STUDY 2

- Targeted analyses made it possible to assess a number of sets containing potentially reflective or reflecting objects (mirrors, eggs, *alabastra*), also combined in sets with drapes used to direct the light,[8] in the presence of a recurrent character connected to divination, the goddess Menerva (Bagnasco Gianni et al. 2012:294)

- *Munθuc* is one of the supernatural entities surrounding a woman doing her makeup (Jucker 2001, number 38), end of the fourth century BC.

- The Etruscan linguistic root *mun-* , that means "to put in order," is connected to the Latin noun *mundus* "the vault of heaven," and the adjective "tidy, clean," reaffirmed by the Etruscan *munθ-* "to put (well) in order" (Facchetti 2003:211).

The impressive similarity between the Etruscan and Latin series—*Munθuχ, mundus*—on the one hand, and the Greek—*kosmesis, kosmos*—on the other, has long been acknowledged in the literary review (Dognini 2002; Govi 2015:116–119). G. M. Facchetti has recently claimed that the contact point is the concept of "order": the root *mun-* is used to indicate private and public sacred areas, similar to those areas that for Roman law were not available and non-tradable (Facchetti 2012:153). C. Dognini, while assessing a different meaning for the very first Greek etymology, shares a similar approach for the series *kosmos, kosmesis*: the concept of "physical order, ornamentation" might have developed given the degree of abstraction of "order," also considered as a composition of structures and words organized according to a system, a rule (Dognini 2002:84–85).

Such a similarity between the two series makes it possible to depart from the linguistic information and move to the lowest common denominator of "order, rule" as one of the pillars of ordinary and supernatural relationships in the Etruscan society (Bagnasco Gianni 2011). We have already encountered women's skill in organizing signs, for example, through weaving or writing. G. Colonna perceived, by means of epigraphic evidence, the possibility of having one of them ruling, as a master, an atelier of pottery production as early as the seventh century BC (Colonna 1993). Now, through catoptromancy and the concept expressed by the feminine entity *Munθuχ*, we should consider women's skill in bringing order into the semantic sphere of contact with the gods. Von Eles claimed that a group of women, buried in the necropolis of Verucchio (second half of the eighth and beginning of the seventh century BC), could be identified as priestesses due to the presence of a peculiar vase decorated with an impressive handle, which alludes to the semantic sphere of *kosmos* and its partitions (von Eles 2007; Pitzalis 2011:265–266). At the beginning of the seventh century BC, a similar situation can be recognized for the woman buried in the Bocchoris tomb (Tarquinia), in which the set formed by an *olla*, its lid, and the *holmos*, which rises to a level under the viewer's eye, inspires comparisons with the abovementioned iconography and the related behaviors and actions concerning organization of space (Bagnasco Gianni 2014).

Furthermore, the role of women in cult practices seems to have been unchanged until more recent periods of Etruscan history, at least in the case of *hatrencu*,[9] probably connected to the abovementioned cosmological aspects.[10]

If we accept this argument, the novel effect would be to contextualize the Etruscan woman in the semantic sphere of order, in areas that might have been complementary to men's. Complementarity is more likely than hierarchy, due to the all-inclusive sphere in which women acted, which all the more touches upon the idea of "equality," with which we have been long acquainted in literary review.

In conclusion, I believe that the materiality of evidence suggests shifting to a different understanding of the use of a number of objects in Etruscan contexts and assessing a basic complementarity of skills within the Etruscan society (Sordi 1981). Such a complementarity might have produced a number of different roles that could have gone beyond the mainstream dualistic interpretation.

NOTES

This paper corresponds to the paper sent to the editor in 2017.

1.   In the extensive bibliography: Whitehouse 1998; Nelson 2006; Cintas Peña 2012; M. Cuozzo, in Cuozzo and Guidi 2013, pp. 24–37; Foxhall 2013.

2.   Heurgon 1961; Sordi 1981; d'Agostino 1993. For a recent overview of this theme: Amann 2000:185–194; Meyers 2016.

3.   Buranelli and Sannibale 2001:361; Sannibale 2008:344, with bibliography including Pallottino's statement about goods possibly belonging to a man who inserted them in his consort's funerary equipment, followed by a number of scholars listed in: Bagnasco Gianni 1996, pp. 79–81.

4.   Bartoloni and Grottanelli 1984; d'Agostino 1993, pp. 63–66; Bagnasco Gianni 1996, pp. 351–352, 445; Toms 1998; von Eles 2007; Bartoloni 2008, pp. 23–29; Pitzalis 2011.

5.   Before Héritier's attempt, described by the title of her book (2002), Ivan Illich worked on replacing the sexual distinction and completion implied in the idea of *homo oeconomicus*, which involves need and scarcity within a given society (Illich 1982, pp. 9–15), with a more complex system of analysis focused on "vernacular values" (Illich 1982, pp. 67–89, in particular footnotes 56–57). His theory of a difference between sex and gender is well known, and the Italian translation of his famous book "Gender" (1982) is introduced by the idea that Illich's work is currently experiencing a "now of readability" (Agamben 2013, p. 7). Even if the term *gender* was first introduced by this scholar (Illich 1982:3), his name is absent from the vast literature produced after the theoretical shift from biological sex to construction of sexual identity that took place when in American universities gender studies took over women studies (it is amazing that in recent literature reviews, concerning these themes in the Ancient world, Illich keeps to be ignored). The reason is probably embedded

in his wider perspective of "conviviality," a set of "timeless human practices and aspirations" forming the core of the cultural heritage of a given culture, which was misinterpreted as a theoretical tool to escape from current "musts" of the feminist movements (Agamben 2013, p. 9; Milana 2013, pp. 246–247). On Illich's theory of complementarity: Wilson 1989, pp. 8, 32–33.

6.   For an interesting survey of the primary archaeological evidence for the intersection between elite Etruscan women and the production of ceremonial garments: Meyers 2016.

7.   A habit continuing later on in sanctuaries of other cultures, such as that of Reitia (Este) (Bagnasco Gianni 1999).

8.   The female figure on the lefthand side of the mirror (Lambrechts 1995, number 12) holds a peculiar object, in which it is possible to recognize the reproduction of a bronze liver (Bagnasco Gianni et al. 2012:292). It cannot be compared to the knots held by a number of characters belonging to mirrors of different ateliers (Bagnasco Gianni et al. 2012:298–299) because the mirror hereof includes three details that are to be definitively considered as *unica*: (1) the shape of the object is ovoid and is divided in two parts by a curvilinear line pointing opposite from the character, whereas the knot represented on a mirror belonging to the same production (Sassatelli 1981, number 4) is depicted with three concentric lines pointing toward the hand of the character holding it, exactly as it happens on a number of other mirrors belonging to other productions; (2) the way in which the left arm of the character holding the object is bent closer to the body; (3) the position of the head of the character, whose eyes are attentively pointing toward the object. For more details see S. Zanni in Bagnasco Gianni et al. (2012), p. 300.

9.   For an interpretation of this term as "priestess" see de Grummond 2006b:38–39; Krauskopf 2012, 186–187; for further bibliographical references and a discussion of the different shades of meaning and their contextualization in Vulci see Lundeen 2006:57–58.

10.   I am grateful to G. M. Facchetti for informing me about his forthcoming study on the possibility of better circumscribing this feminine role as devoted to marking positions during rituals.

REFERENCES

Agamben, G. 2013 Introduzione. In *Genere. Per una critica storica dell'uguaglianza*, Italian translation edited by I. Illich and F. Milana, pp. 7–17. Neri Pozza, Vicenza.

Agostiniani, L. 2013 The Etruscan Language. In *The Etruscan World*, edited by J. Macintosh Turfa, pp. 457–477. Routledge, London.

Amann, P. 2000 *Die Etruskerin. Geschlechterverhältnis und Stellung der Frau im frühen Etrurien (9.–5. Jh. v. Chr.)*. Verlag der österreichischen Akademie der Wissenschaften, Wien.

Bagnasco Gianni, G. 1996 *Oggetti iscritti di epoca orientalizzante in Etruria*. Leo S. Olschki, Firenze.

Bagnasco Gianni, G. 1999 L'acquisizione della scrittura in Etruria: materiali a confronto. In *Scritture mediterranee tra il IX e il VII secolo a. C. Atti del Seminario di Studio* (Milano 23–24 febbraio 1998), edited by G. Bagnasco Gianni and F. Cordano, pp. 80–105. Edizioni ET, Milano.

Bagnasco Gianni, G. 2011 Lettere e immagini: esempi etruschi di parola ispirata. In *Corollari. Scritti di antichità etrusche e italiche in omaggio all'opera di Giovanni Colonna. Promossi da Gilda Bartoloni, Carmine Ampolo, Maria Paola Baglione, Francesco Roncalli, Giuseppe Sassatelli*, edited by D. F. Maras, pp. 185–192. Fabrizio Serra Editore, Pisa-Roma.

Bagnasco Gianni, G. 2014 Presenza/assenza di mura: implicazioni storico-culturali. Il caso di Tarquinia. *Scienze dell'Antichità* 19(2–3):429–453.

Bagnasco Gianni, G., M. Marzullo, S. Zanni, and V. Zenti 2012 Tra uomini e dei: funzione e ruolo di alcuni oggetti negli specchi etruschi. In *Kulte–Riten–religiose Vorstellungen bei den Etruskern und ihr Verhaltnis zu Politik und Gesellschaft, Akten der 1. Internationalen Tagung der Sektion Wien/Osterreich des Istituto Nazionale di Studi Etruschi ed Italici* (Wien 2008), edited by P. Amann, pp. 287–314. Verlag der Österreichische Akademie der Wissenschaften, Wien.

Bartoloni, G. 2008 Le donne dei principi nel Lazio protostorico. In *Aspetti dell'Orientalizzante nell'Etruria e nel Lazio. Giornata di studio* (Milano 6 marzo 2006), *Aristonothos. Scritti per il Mediterraneo Antico* 3, edited by F. Cordano and G. Bagnasco Gianni, pp. 23–45. CUEM, Milano.

Bartoloni, G., and C. Grottanelli 1984 I carri a due ruote nelle tombe femminili del Lazio e dell'Etruria. *Opus* III:383–410.

Bonfante (Warren), L. 1973 The Women of Etruria. *Arethusa* 6(1):91–10.

Bonfante, L. 2000 Alcuni specchi etruschi nel Metropolitan Museum of Art. In *Aspetti e problemi della produzione degli specchi etruschi figurati. Atti dell'Incontro internazionale di studio* (Roma, 2–4 maggio 1997), edited by M. D. Gentili, pp. 13–26. Aracne, Roma.

Bonfante, L. 2013 Mothers and Children. In *The Etruscan World*, edited by J. Macintosh Turfa, pp. 426–446. Routledge, London.

Bonghi Jovino, M. 2005 Tarquinia. Monumenti urbani. In *Dinamiche di sviluppo delle città nell'Etruria meridionale. Veio, Caere, Tarquinia, Vulci, Atti del XXIII Convegno di studi etruschi ed italici. Roma-Veio-Cerveteri-Pyrgi-Tarquinia-Tuscania-Vulci-Viterbo* 2001, edited by O. Paoletti, pp. 309–322. Istituti editoriali e poligrafici internazionali, Pisa-Roma.

Briquel, D. 1998 Les figures féminines dans la tradition sur les rois étrusques de Rome. *Comptes rendus des séances de l'Académie des Inscriptions et Belles-Lettres*:397–414.

Buranelli, F., and M. Sannibale 2001 Caere. *Rivista di Epigrafia Etrusca* 64:357–366.

Cintas Peña, M. 2012 Género y Arqueología: un esquema de la cuestión. *Estrat Critic* 6:177–187.

Colonna, G. 1993 Ceramisti e donne padrone di bottega nell'Etruria arcaica. In *Indogermanica et Italica, Festschrift für Helmut Rix zum 65. Geburtstag*, edited by G. Meiser, pp. 61–68. Institut für Sprachwissenschaft der Universität Innsbruck, Innsbruck.

Colonna, G. 1997 Nome gentilizio e società. *Studi Etruschi* XLV:175–192.

Colonna, G. 2009 *Picentia* (Pontecagnano). *Rivista di Epigrafia Etrusca* 73:359–361.

Cristofani, M. 1997 Masculin-féminin dans la théonymie étrusque. In *Les plus religieux des hommes. Etat de la recherche sur la religion étrusque. Actes du colloque international* (17–19 novembre 1992), edited by F. Gaultier and D. Briquel, pp. 209–219. La Documentation Française, Paris.

Cuozzo, M., and A. Guidi 2013 *Archeologia delle identità e delle differenze*. Carocci, Roma.

d'Agostino, B. 1993 La donna in Etruria. In *Maschile/femminile. Genere e ruoli nelle culture antiche*, edited by M. Bettini, pp. 61–73. Laterza, Bari.

de Grummond, N. 2000 Mirrors and *Manteia*: Themes of Prophecy on Etruscan and Praenestine Mirrors. In *Aspetti e problemi della produzione degli specchi etruschi figurati. Atti dell'Incontro internazionale di studio* (Roma, 2–4 maggio 1997), edited by M. D. Gentili, pp. 27–67. Aracne, Roma.

de Grummond, N. 2006a *Etruscan Myth, Sacred History, and Legend*. University of Pennsylvania Museum of Archaeology and Anthropology, Philadelphia.

de Grummond, N. 2006b Prophets and Priests. In *The Religion of the Etruscans*, edited by N. T. de Grummond and E. Simon, pp. 27–44. University of Texas Press, Austin.

Dognini, C. 2002 Kosmos e mundus due concezioni a confronto. In *Kosmos. La concezione del mondo nelle civiltà antiche*, edited by C. Dognini, pp. 81–98. Edizioni dell'Orso, Alessandria.

Facchetti, G. 2003 Note Etrusche. *Archivio Glottologico Italiano* 87:203–220.

Facchetti, G. 2013 Diritto nel mondo etrusco. In *Thesaurus Cultus et Rituum Antiquorum (ThesCRA)* VIII, pp. 151–159. Getty, Los Angeles.

Foxhall, L. 2013 *Studying Gender in Classical Antiquity. Key Themes in Ancient History*. Cambridge University Press, Cambridge.

Govi, E. 2015 Una nuova iscrizione dal tempio urbano di Tinia a Marzabotto. *Studi Etruschi* LXXVII:109–147.

Griaule, M. 1948 *Dieu d'Eau: entretiens avec Ogotemmeli*. Chene, Paris.

Haynes, S. 2005 *Etruscan Civilization: A Cultural History*. Getty, Los Angeles.

Héritier, F. 2002 *Dissolvere la gerarchia. Maschile/ femminile II*. Raffaello Cortina Editore, Milano.

Heurgon, J. 1961 Valeurs féminines et masculines dans la civilisation étrusque. *Mélanges de l'Ecole française de Rome. Antiquité* 73:139–160.

Jucker, I. 2005 *Corpus speculorum Etruscorum. Schweiz, 1, Basel, Schaffhausen, Bern, Lausanne*. Stämpfli Verlag, Bern.

Koloski-Ostrow A. O., and C. L. Lyons (eds.) 1997 *Women, Sexuality, and Gender in Classical Art and Archaeology*. Routledge, London.

Krauskopf, I. 2012 Die Rolle der Frauen im etruskischen Kult. In *Kulte–Riten–religiose Vorstellungen bei den Etruskern und ihr Verhaltnis zu Politik und Gesellschaft, Akten der 1. Internationalen Tagung der Sektion Wien/Osterreich des Istituto Nazionale di Studi Etruschi ed Italici* (Wien 2008), edited by P. Amann, pp. 185–197. Verlag der Österreichische Akademie der Wissenschaften, Wien.

Krauskopf, I. 2013 Gods and Demons in the Etruscan Pantheon. In *The Etruscan World*, edited by J. Macintosh Turfa, pp. 513–538. Routledge, London.

Lambrechts, R. 1995 Corpus speculorum Etruscorum. *Stato della Città del Vaticano 1, Città del Vaticano. Museo profano della Biblioteca apostolica vaticana. Roma. Collezione di antichità dell'Abbazia di San Paolo fuori le mura*. L'Erma di Bretschneider, Roma.

Lazzeroni, R. 1993 Il genere indoeuropeo. Una categoria naturale?. In *Maschile/ femminile. Genere e ruoli nelle culture antiche*, edited by M. Bettini, pp. 3–16. Laterza, Bari.

Lundeen, L. E. 2006 In Search of the Etruscan Priestess: A Re-examination of the hatrencu. In *Religion in Republican Italy*, edited by C. E. Schultz and P. B. Harvey, pp. 34–61. Cambridge University Press, Cambridge.

Martelli, M. 1991 Review of Rallo 1989. *Rivista di Filologia e Istruzione Classica* 119:337–346.

Marzullo, M. 2017 *Spazi Sepolti e Dimensioni Dipinte nelle tombe etrusche di Tarquinia* (Tarchna supplemento 5). Ledizioni, Milano.

Meyers, G. E. 2016 Tanaquil. The Conception and Construction of an Etruscan Matron. In *A Companion to the Etruscans*, edited by S. Bell and A. A. Carpino, pp. 305–320. John Wiley and Sons, Hoboken.

Milana, F. 2013 Nota al testo. In I. Illich, *Genere. Per una critica storica dell'uguaglianza*, Italian translation edited by F. Milana, pp. 227–249. Neri Pozza, Vicenza.

Nelson, S. M. 2006 *Handbook of Gender in Archaeology*. AltaMira Press, Lanham, Maryland.

Nielsen, M. 1998 Etruscan Women: A Cross-Cultural Perspective. In Aspects of Women in Antiquity. *Proceedings of the First Nordic Symposium on Women's Lives in Antiquity, Göteborg,12–15 June 1997 (Studies in Mediterranean Archaeology and Literature 153)*, edited by L. Larsson Lovén, A. Strömberg, pp. 69–84. Paul Åströms, Jonsered.

Nielsen, M. 1999 Common Tombs for Women in Etruria: Buried Matriarchies? In *Female Networks and the Public Sphere in Roman Society*. Institutum Romanum Finlandiae, Roma.

Pitzalis, F. 2011 *La volontà meno apparente*. L'Erma di Bretschneider, Roma.

Rallo, A. (editor) 1989 *Le donne in Etruria*. L'Erma di Bretschneider, Roma.

Rathje, A. 2007 Etruscan Women and Power. In Public Roles and Personal status: Men and Women in Antiquity. *Proceedings of the Third Nordic Symposium on Gender and Women's History in Antiquity, Copenhagen, 3–5 October 2003 (Studies in Mediterranean Archaeology and Literature 172)*, edited by L. Larsson Lovén, A. Strömberg, pp. 19–34. Paul Åströms, Sävedalen.

Rix, H. 1972 Zum Ursprung des römischmittelitalischen Gentilnamensystems. In *Aufstieg und Niedergang der römischen Welt, Geschichte und Kultur Roms im Spiegel der neueren Forschung*, edited by H. Temporini, Band I/ 2, pp. 700–758. Walter de Gruyter, Berlin.

Sannibale, M. 2008 Gli ori della Tomba Regolini-Galassi: tra tecnologia e simbolo. Nuove proposte di lettura nel quadro del fenomeno orientalizzante in Etruria. *Mélanges de l'Ecole française de Rome. Antiquité* 120(2):337–367.

Sassatelli, G. 1981 Corpus speculorum Etruscorum. *Italia 1, Bologna, Museo Civico* 2. L'Erma di Bretschneider, Roma.

Sheid, J., and J. Svenbro 1994 *Le métier de Zeus: mythe du tissage et du tissu dans le monde gréco-romain*. Editions La Découverte, Paris.

Sordi, M. 1981 La donna etrusca. In *Misoginia e maschilismo in Grecia e a Roma*, pp. 49–67. Istituto di Filologia classica e medievale, Genova.

Toms, J. 1998 The Construction of Gender in Early Iron Age Etruria. In *Gender and Italian Archaeology. Challenging the Stereotypes*, edited by R. Whitehouse, pp. 157–179. Accordia Research Institute, London.

von Eles, P. 2007 Le ore del sacro. Il femminile e le donne, soggetto e interpreti del divino? In *Le ore e i giorni delle donne. Dalla quotidianità alla sacralità tra VIII e VII secolo a.C.*, edited by P. von Eles, pp. 149–156. Pazzini Stampatore Editore srl, Verucchio.

Whitehouse, R. (ed.) 1998 *Gender and Italian Archaeology. Challenging the Stereotypes*. Accordia Research Institute, London.

Wilson, H.T. *Sex and Gender: Making Cultural Sense of Civilization*. Brill, Leiden.

PART III

Inequality in Classical Archaeology

CHAPTER TWELVE

History and Archaeology of the Etruscan *Servitus*

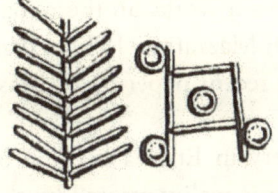

†Mario Torelli

Abstract   *Ancient literary sources are analyzed through the lenses of archaeology and epigraphy to define Etruscan slaves and incidence of* servitus *in terms of production processes.*

A text from Zonara mentions the stages of self-emancipation of the servants after the terrible defeat suffered by Volsinii against Rome: first, the aministration of the temple's cash; second, becoming part of the city army; third, the right to marry aristocratic women; then, the right to inheritance; finally, access to the senate. The evidence from the sanctuary of Gravisca confirms this process, showing how during the sixth and fifth centuries BC Etruscan servants and Greek douloi *were the real actors in the sanctuary. They were involved in craftsmanship and prostitution, but also performed ritual offerings. At the end of the fifth century the sanctuary was largely renewed, thanks to a higher economic capacity.*

The origin of the Etruscan dependency seems rooted in the Iron Age colonization, when the process of subjugation of close communities started. Servants and slaves were used for manual labor, especially in agricultural activities, as evidenced by the settlements in the territories of Vulci and Tarquinii. Since the mid-fifth century BC the complete or partial emancipation of the servants is combined with a regular distribution of land between clientes *and former servants.*

The recent publication of a collective volume, written by the cream of the second and third generation of Italian Etruscan archaeologists, celebrates the seventieth anniversary of the glorious "Etruscology" by Massimo Pallottino. In more than 450 pages, the book offers an articulate image of every aspect of the culture and the society of the Etruscans. I have read with interest and curiosity the entire volume, drawing inspiration from it. Nevertheless, to the topic of the Etruscan *servitus* (which is very close to my heart), only twenty lines have been devoted on pages 130–131, giving just a vague description of the phenomenon. What I get from that book is that this interest of mine in the subordinate classes in Etruria is by no means shared by these young colleagues. They are seduced more by French anthropology or by the Anglo-Saxon new archaeology approaches, rather than by economic and social history. I guess we are expiating the aftereffects of the binge of economic history of the ancient world celebrated in symposia and university classes during 1970s and 1980s. At that time, everyone sided with primitivists or modernists, and talk about slavery and means of production was a must. As a matter of fact, the last relevant works on these topics date to the 1950s and 1960s (Frankfort 1959; Heurgon 1959; Mazzarino 1957; Lotze 1959; M. Finley 1963–64; Harris 1971). The only exception is a recent paper by A. Mastrocinque (1996), which will be discussed later.

I'm sure that a dark curtain dropped on the issue of slavery in Etruria because of that saturation and due to an unconscious removal of the economic reality created by the burdens of the financial economy. I have to admit that it does not benefit a modern understanding of the Etruscan world. To settle for accepting only the little that the ancient sources tell us about Etruscan slaves, statutes, and incidence of *servitus* in the framework of production processes, without making any effort to understand its role by reading the sources through the lenses of archaeology and epigraphy and without any attempt to find in the archaeological evidence the traces of it, is like writing the history of Sparta while removing the Helots. To anticipate critics, I also make a *mea culpa* because I have had new data available that I have been thus far unable to understand.

Instead of recalling well-known texts (such as Dionysius IX.5.4) to bring the old comparison between Etruscan and Thessalian slavery back up, I consider it useful to start with a passage from Zonaras, which is less famous and, curiously, not exploited enough, reporting the servants' uprising at Volsinii. His epitome comes from Cassius Dio, who—as is well known—has good sources. The passage is crucial because while recording the stages of self-emancipation of the servants it also shows the limits of their freedom. The chronology of the events is not stated, but we will try to define it later. The text (Zon. VIII, 7.4–8) is as follows:

Ὡς δ' ἐχειρώθησαν, αὐτοὶ μὲν ἐξώκειλαν εἰς ἁβρότητα, τὴν δὲ διοίκησιν τῆς πόλεως τοῖς οἰκέταις ἐπέτρεψαν, καὶ τὰς στρατείας δι᾽ ἐκείνων ὡς τὸ πολὺ ἐποιοῦντο· καὶ τέλος ἐς τοῦτο προήγαγον σφᾶς, ὡς καὶ δύναμιν τοὺς οἰκέτας καὶ φρόνημα ἔχειν, καὶ ἐλευθερίας ἑαυτοὺς ἀξιοῦν. Προϊόντος δὲ τοὺς χρόνου καὶ ἔτυχον ταύτης δι᾽ ἑαυτῶν, καὶ τὰς σφῶν δεσποίνας ἠγάγοντο, καὶ τοὺς δεσπότας διαδέχοντο, καὶ εἰς τὴν βουλὴν ἐνεγράφοντο καὶ τὰς ἀρχὰς ἐλάμβανον, καὶ αὐτοὶ τὸ σύμπαν κῦρος εἶχον, καὶ τά τε ἄλλα καὶ τὰς ὕβρεις τὰς ὑπὸ τῶν δεσποτῶν αὐτοῖς γινομένας ἰταμώτερον εἰς αὐτοὺς ἐκείνους ἀνταπεδείκνυντο.

[(The aristocracy of Volsinii) after the defeat, being felt in a state of effeminacy, left the administration of the city to the servants, to whom left the army too. At this point the servants felt pushed to free themselves. After some time, they also obtained that; then they got the right to marry the women of the aristocracy, to inherit from their past masters, to be admitted in the senate, and to get the magistratures.]

It is worth noting that, in addition to the usual mention to the *abrosyne/tryphé* (that for the Greeks was the root of all evil of the Etruscan society), Cassius Dio/Zonaras put the beginning of the servants' emancipation in the aftermath of the Roman defeat of Volsinii. The annals tradition and the *Fasti Triumphales* provide two potential dates: the victory and relative triumph *de Volsonibus* of 294 BC (*Fast. Triumph. ad a.* 294: A.Degrassi, in *Inscr.It.* XIII, 1, 544), attributed to both L. Postumius Megellus and M. Atilius Regulus, or the triumph *de Vulsiniensibus et Volcientibus* by Ti. Coruncanius dating to 280 BC (*Fast. Triumph. ad a.* 280: A. Degrassi, in *Inscr.It.* XIII, 1, 545). I believe it is likely the 294 BC date, for which the tradition records as many as 2,800 Volsinians dead (Liv. X, 37, 1–2.). Let's examine more closely the sequence of achievements of the *oikétai*. The first stage of this path is the διοίκησις τῆς πόλεως, to be translated as "the administration of the temple's cash," since political systems in the ancient world did not allow unfree people to manage the funds of the state. We must think of the cash of the temple of Ceres, Liber, and Libera, managed by the *aediles,* known also in other Latin cities, responsible for the cash of the *aedes,* with whom plebeians identify themselves. Also in this case, the birth of an autonomous religious *foyer* is the first step of an emancipation process. It was made long before by the Roman plebs and it is parallel to the one started by the Etruscan servants—even given the many differences in condition of the two classes. From the text of Zonaras it seems possible to deduce that concessions of autonomous administration of temple cash and demands to be part of the city army—which was the second step in the process—went together. The two measures taste like a *do ut des,* absolutely justifiable in the aftermath of the terrible defeat suffered by Volsinii in 294 BC. The great losses, proudly recorded by the Roman sources, were enormous if we consider the proverbial *oliganthropía* of the Etruscan political systems based on the oligarchy, of which Volsinii were also a part, and the military forces of that city in comparison to Rome. We can also imagine that the concession was made later, in the aftermath of the new defeat of the Volsinii in 280 BC, when the management of the Volsinian army had to have been completely exhausted. In that case, it is easy to understand the long hesitation of the local aristocracy to follow that direction: the local aristocracy surely had evaluated the risk inherent in putting the army in the hand of those who had been dominated and downtrodden from time immemorial. The same formulation of the passage (*"the servants felt pushed to free themselves"*) proposes that the concession of arms had raised their class consciousness—as was usual to say in the past—and stimulated the servants to ask for *eleuthería*. The latter to be understand not only as a general *manumissio* but also what in the ancient political system was inherent to *eleuthería,* which is the *ius suffragi ferendi* (the right to vote). At this point, the analogies between the status of the Roman plebs at the moment of its secession and the status of the servants of Volsinii after 294 BC (if that was the starting date for the process) almost become identitical. *Plebei qui gentem non habent,* as the Roman patricians scornfully reproached their natural plebeian adversaries; but in Rome no one ever had doubts that the Plebeians had to serve the army.

After that, Zonaras/Cassius Dio clearly marks the subsequent stages of the emancipation: first, the concession of *ius connubi* with the women of the aristocracy (a close parallel to the Roman *lex Canuleia* of 444 BC); then the achievement of the right to inheritance, a statute that in the Etruscan world was also connected to the *connubium*; finally, the achievement of the *ius honorum,* with its related access to the senate. The continuation of the story—the secret request of the aristocrats for a Roman intervention; the former servants discovering the deceit; the following slaughter of the *nobiles;* the Roman intervention and suppression of the uprising—is beyond our interest here. As we will see soon, what is relevant is the chance to determine the original statute of the Etruscan *servitus* and the stages to gaining freedom, even if the servants from each *poleis* obtained that in different ways and times.

Let us now try to verify such a reconstruction by moving to the archaeological evidence, starting from the case of Gravisca, which is well known to me—and from which comes the *mea culpa* made before (Fiorini and †Torelli 2010). Long ago, I highlighted the epigraphic evidence of the Greek inscription Johnston 117,[1] in which a certain Pat[—], perhaps a Pat[roklos], offers an Attic band cup of the mid-sixth century BC bearing the following formula:

Πατ[ροκλος - - - ἀνέθηκε *vel sim.* τ]ο δολο κατ<τ>άξαντος.

The dedicant Pat[roklos], who is clearly absent, entrusted the duty of offering the *anáthema* to his *doulos*. The entrustment to the servile element to the transport, the deposit of the *tithe,* and even the execution of the libation to the deity explains many aspects of these emporic sanctuaries. First, the very modest level of the chapels sacred to Aphrodite at Naukratis and Gravisca; second, the equally modest appearance of the *anathémata;* and finally, the practice of the *asylia,* common in many Mediterranean sanctuaries with high servile attendance. In its tangible materiality, the ritual exchange is made through the hand of subordinate elements, free middlepersons (similar to the traditional *kápeloi*), and above all *douloi,* slaves. These subordinates, who settled the *empórion* and ensured its existence, give to the daily life of the sanctuary a well-defined character, which includes (and I did not recognize this before) a multitude of indigenous elements, subordinates as well, attested by Etruscan inscriptions. All of them are characterized by *Individualnamen* e, therefore to be referred to servants. There is no single sure dedication of a free man or woman. Also the inscription CIE 10378 (*mi velθurus f<e>lnas*) cannot be considered, as it is painted on bucchero before the firing of the vase, and then made before and without any particular relationship with the final destination.[2] The list of *Individualnamen* totals ten men and three women. Between the sixth and fifth century BC the following men: a [—]*aretu* (*CIE* 10256), a [—]*nuzu* (*CIE* 10278), a [—? *ar*]*nza* (*CIE* 10295), a [—? *l*]*arza* (*CIE* 10369), a *paiθe* (*CIE* 10310), a *pav(e)* or *pav(a)* (*CIE* 10279); in the fourth century BC: a *tit*[*e*] (*CIE* 10263), a *kuru* (CIE 10353), a *veru* (*CIE* 10261) and a *v(e)θe* (*CIE* 10303). The women, not by chance identified by a Greek-like name, counts in the sixth century BC a *zui*—Greek *Zoe* (*CIE* 10260) and a *lai*—Greek *Lais* (*CIE* 10344); and in the fourth century BC another *lai* (*CIE* 10283). Moreover, the *pav(a)* of *CIE* 10279 could correspond to the Greek πάϜις, Latin *puer,* in this case meaning "slave" (†Torelli 1988:115).

All of these people, Etruscan servants and Greek *douloi,* along with prostitutes, are the real mediators of the exchange. At Naukratis, after about a century of life of the only sanctuary of Aphrodite,[3] the major *poleis* had built temples of great architectonic quality and attracted high-status people to the city (from the brother of Sappho to Herodotus). On the contrary, at Gravisca the extreme exiguity of the buildings attests that no high-status Greek ever arrived who used, as we said, *douloi*, slaves. In conclusion, we can easily affirm that Gravisca flood of people of servile status. We have to bear this in mind in order to fully understand the later developments.

Further advancement to the understanding of the real meaning of the Tarquinian emporium has been made thanks to a recent discovery by L. Fiorini, the current director of the excavation (Fiorini and †Torelli 2007): he found that around the chapel of Aphrodite and for the entire archaic phase of the sanctuary more than twenty furnaces were in use (for the Elban iron, and bronze) (Figure 12.1). They are verified by crucibles and by melting-pits

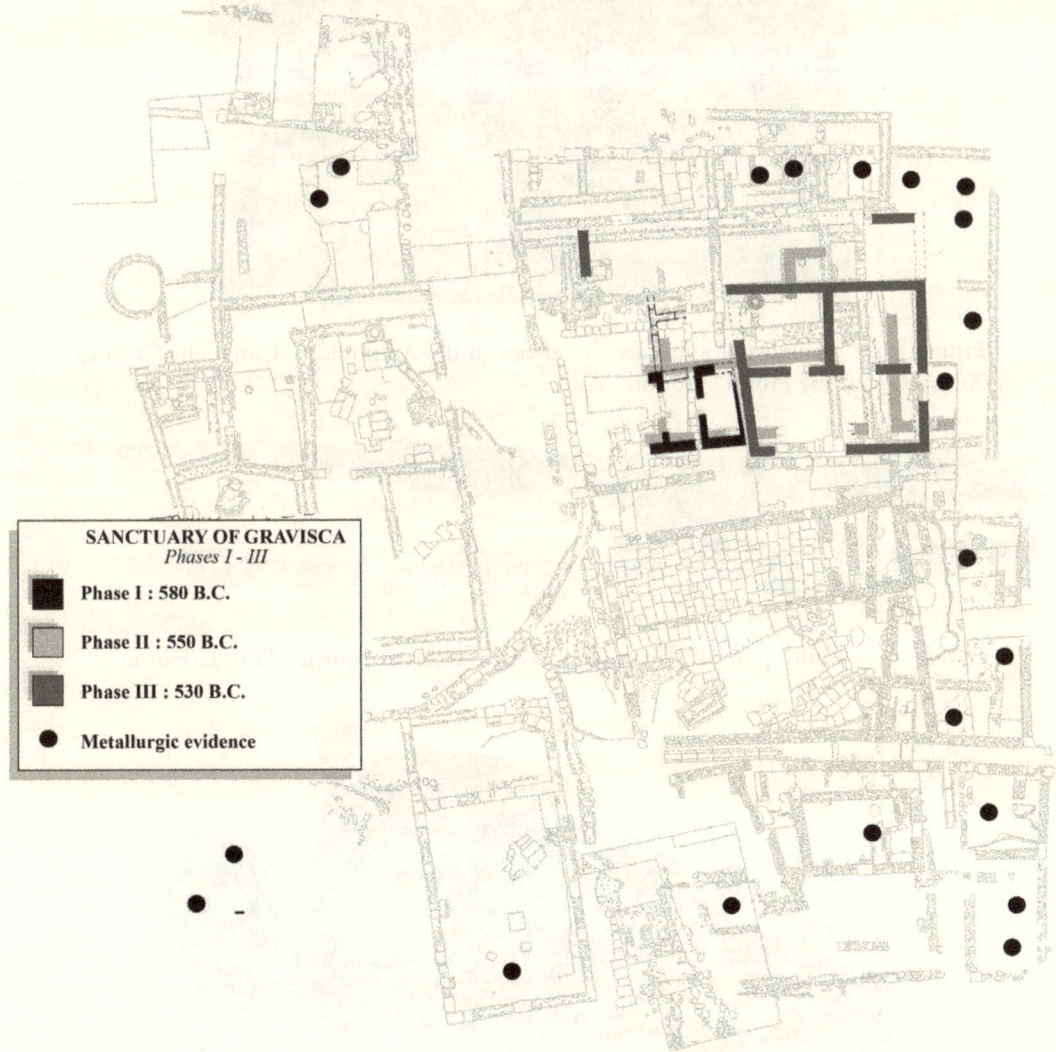

FIGURE 12.1. Gravisca. Distribution of archaic furnaces. Copyright Gravisca Archives, courtesy Prof. L. Fiorini.

(Figure 12.2), slags and fire tools (Figure 12.3), and by objects such as a metal plowshare (Figure 12.4). The *douloi* of the great *emporoi* in eastern Greece and Aegina were bringing the precious trade goods requested by the Etruscans and bringing back the finished, semi-worked metal items, while the Etruscan servants were operating their usual activities of metal melting. At the same time, the *servae* (like *zui* and *lai,* who left epigraphic evidence), were offering their services ἄφετοι ὄντες τοῖς ἐντυχοῦσιν, "moving toward who was passing there," to recall the expression used by Clearchus of Soloi[4] for the *ierodule* of Locri Epizefirii.

FIGURE 12.2. Remains of a furnace found east of the Aphrodison. Copyright Gravisca Archives, courtesy Prof. L. Fiorini.

FIGURE 12.3. Smith pincers. Copyright Gravisca Archives, courtesy Prof. L. Fiorini.

FIGURE 12.4. Metal plowshare, perhaps a production waste. Copyright Gravisca Archives, courtesy Prof. L. Fiorini.

Their services had to supply the wealth of the sanctuary as much as the metallurgy did. The same was happening, at a different scale, with the women put up in the twenty rooms of the *temenos* of Uni at Pyrgi (*contra* Gentili 2015). All of that explains the very low level of the buildings in the sanctuary during the sixth and fifth centuries, lacking any decorations and made with poor techniques. The cult complex has to be considered first and foremost a workshop located close to the landing place at the lagoon of the current saltworks. As is beautifully illustrated by the eponymous cup of the Foundry Painter, the furnace devoted to the microfusions to join different parts of the bronze statues (that were made in different pieces and are depicted all around the furnace) was under the magic protection of a small cult place decorated with votive *pinakes,* apotropaic horns, and two tablets with heads of the two deities of the sanctuary, viewed from the front, Aphrodite and Hephaestus.

The two large areas of the sanctuary were founded c. 530 BC (Figure 12.5), the southern one sacred to the cults of Aphrodite-*Turan*, Demeter-*Vei*, and Hera-*Uni* and character-

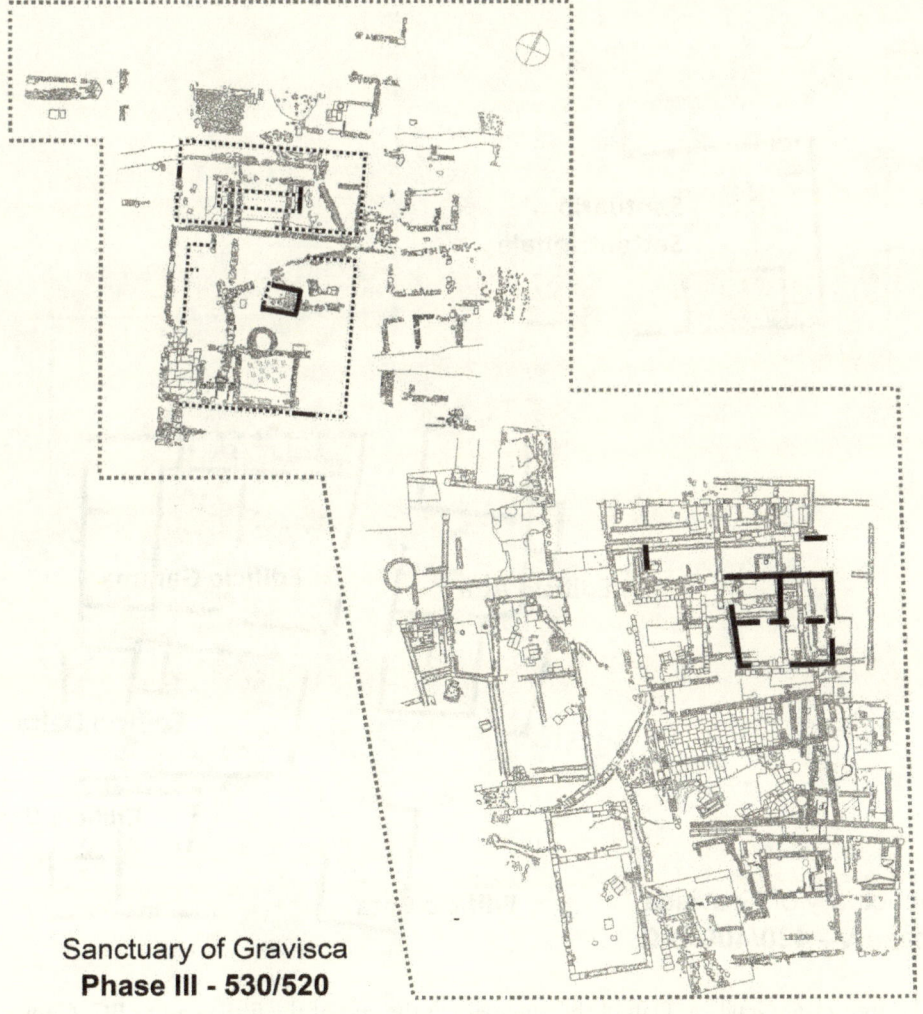

Sanctuary of Gravisca
Phase III - 530/520

Figure 12.5. Gravisca. Plan of the sanctuary in 530/520 BC. Copyright Gravisca Archives, courtesy Prof. L. Fiorini.

ized by the presence of Ionic and Aeginetic merchants, and the northern one with the cult of *Śuris* and *Cavatha*, frequented by Siceliotes. Suddenly and seemingly simultaneously, around 410–400 BC, the two areas underwent a radical change. The new architectonic project was very ambitious: the old altars and buildings erected during the sixth century BC were abandoned and robbed of the best materials, while a new sole complex, unified and compact, was built (†Torelli 1997a) (Figure 12.6). It is crossed by the road that, since the fifth century BC, connected the landing point in the lagoon to the actual settlement. The same general plan of the sanctuary reveals that it was conceived following a clear ritual logic, putting together all the altars of the cult buildings, abiding by the augural tradition. The renovated sanctuary, now with a uniform appearance, was made of four cult buildings,

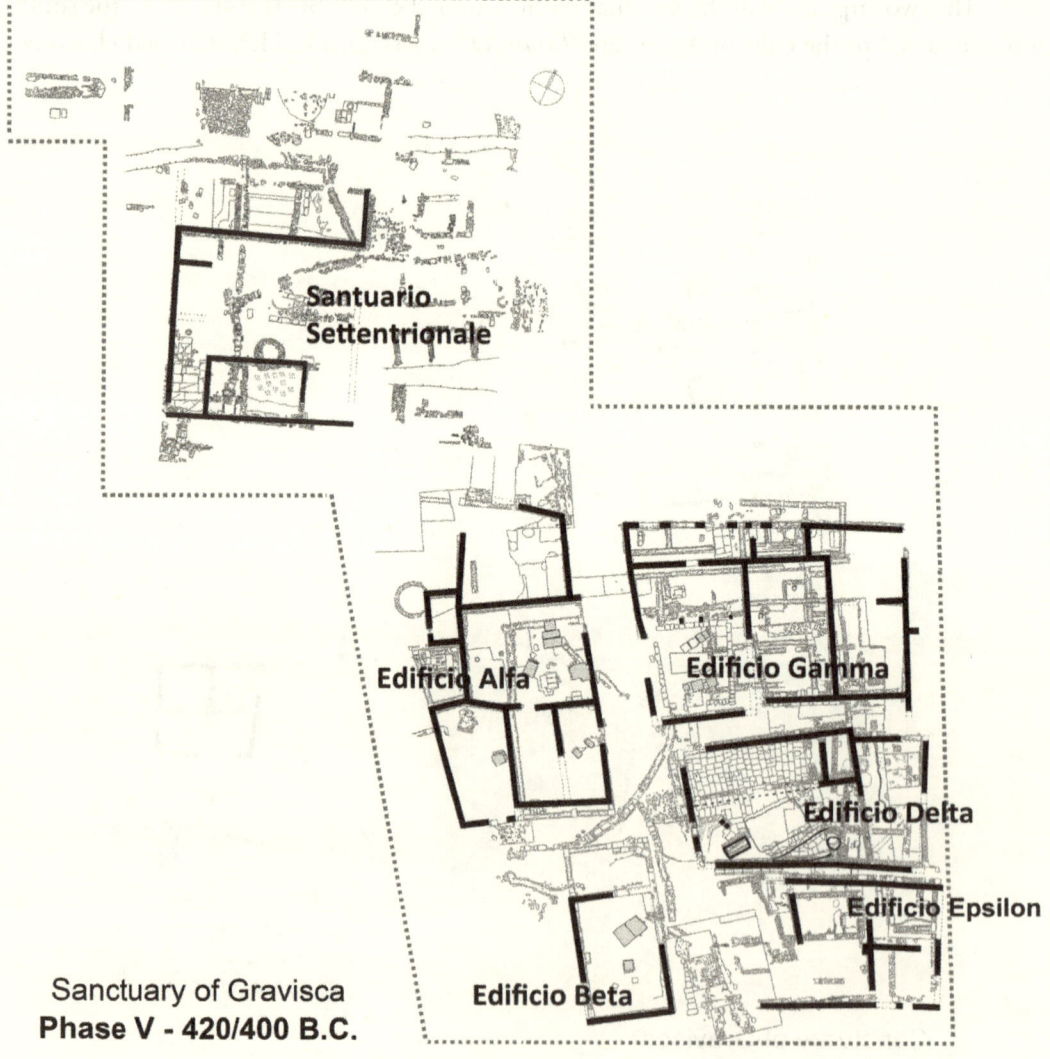

FIGURE 12.6. Gravisca. Plan of the sanctuary at the end of the fifth century BC. Copyright Gravisca Archives, courtesy Prof. L. Fiorini.

each with one or more altars, and two open spaces south of the buildings. The open space to the west was devoted to Demetriac feasts and had a circular altar of Sicilian type; the space to the east, dedicated to the feasts for Adonis, hosted the ancient coffin for the ritual deposition of the deity. Such a project, which is the clear result of a communication plan, denotes a high self-consciousness, which in modern terms could be called a strong political will. It is worth noting that these buildings express full autonomy from the official models, which are clearly alien to the entire design of the sanctuary. They ignore magniloquent and expensive *podia*, as well as demanding terracotta revetments. On the one hand, every new building is far from the official models of sacred architecture, but on the other hand they carefully follow ritual prescriptions and the same complex project. All these elements show an elevated level of religious culture and a relatively high economic capacity.

In other words, it seems correct to read the situation as a tangible expression of the διοίκησις τῆς πόλεως cited in the Zonaras text, as transferred to the Tarquinian *polis*. If the chronology I proposed is right, it would have happened a century before the servant emancipation at Volsinii mentioned by Zonaras. Nevertheless, we must take into account the classic work by H. Rix on the *Vornamengentile*, where the German scholar recovered the traces of the process of social integration of the *oikétai* class. Rix proved how the ways and times of servants' emancipation were different at Perusia and Clusium (two cities for whom the epigraphic evidence is large enough). The chronology of these measures dates back to the late third century BC, as suggested by the events at Volsinii that were halted by Aulus Spurinna (†Torelli 1975), and also by the *servilia bella* that began tormenting Arretium during the fourth century BC and were resolved by M. Valerius Corvus in 302 BC (Liv. X.5,13). They also attest to the existence of different formulas to free the *servi*: at Perusia, emancipation was followed by the concession of the *ius connubi*; at Clusium, this right seems to have been denied, while the archaeological evidence shows that the manumission was coupled with a massive division of the lands all over the ample *ager Clusinus*. The latter seems not to have been realized in the case of Volsinii, but it is clear in the case under analysis of Tarquinii.

As is well known, the process of the subjugation of minor settlements by major ones started as soon as the dawn of the Etruscan, as well as of the Latin, civilization. It is a phenomenon at the origin of the Etruscan *servitus*. This gigantic effort toward expansion, required the subjugation of a large number of allogenes, not much different from what happened for the creation of forms of dependency in Greece, labeled by Pollux as μεταξὺ ἐλευθέρων καὶ δούλων, the Spartan Helots, the *klarotai* at Crete, the *penestai* in Thessaly, the *marandynoi* at Heraclea Pontica, to limit ourselves to the most popular ones (see the classic Lotze 1959). Recently, in the case of the Sicels of Locri Epizefirii, D. Musti had talked of "forms of Doric dependency," so that we can refer to forms of Etruscan dependency. But the subjugation must also concern large groups of Etruscans, involved in the long-lasting struggle between close communities. This phenomenon is evident in the progressive desertification of the city territories at the end of the sixth century BC, when the borders between the historical city-states became essentially fixed. In other words, the great Villanovan (that is Iron Age) colonization is realized against the background of the creation of the Etruscan *servitus* of the historical period. It cannot be, as suggested by A. Mastrocinque, an exclusively public *servitus* (but it is reasonable to think of forms of public "propriety" of servants in Etruria alongside the usual private dependency), as long as every source (i.e., the Zonaras we started from) talks about servants of private ownership. In addition, the exceptional epigraphic document found at the Fanum Voltumnae and belonging to the fifth century BC (Stopponi 2009) clearly shows the emancipation of a servant woman, named *Kanuta,* made by a private individual or family from Volsinii, the *Larecenas.* As mentioned in the dedication, *Kanuta,* who is going to be married to a freedman named *Aranθ Pinies,* will become a *lauteniθa,* using a label that in later times would be used for the classical *liberti.* In Etruria, all evidence points toward a form of dependency bound to the land or controlled by private ownership, as we have seen for the subordinates of Doric type. The same is true concerning the eminent role given to Etruscan women, misinterpreted by the modern scholars as *Mutterrecht,* similar to the function given to the Spartiates women, which is the right to inherit the *kleros* and to transmit it. I have directed my attention many times to the eminent monuments of that custom (†Torelli 1997b:52–86), such as the throne of Verucchio, the female canopic urn of Sarteano, or the so-called tintinnabulus from the Tomb of the Gold Jewelry at Bologna (which is actually a reproduction of an ax, a well-known symbol of power). It seems that these suggestions have not been embraced by the current large bibliography on the Etruscan women.

As everywhere in the ancient world, the manual labor and the servants (both the Etruscan and the Greek *douloi*) were an inseparable duo. We have evidence of this around the furnaces at Gravisca, but it is also largely common on the shores of Populonia at the house of the local industrial quarter for the transformation of the Elban pyrite, as recorded by Strabo (Strabo V, 223). Thanks to past excavations made by A. Minto and M. Martelli (1981:162–172), we have several inscriptions from this area: at least 20 out of 41 are related to servants.[5] They are in charge of artifact production, and even painting as the *aranth heracanasa* (that is, a servant named *aranth* owned by a *heracana*),[6] known to be the master of the painted Tomb of the Jugglers at Tarquinii (530 BC); or the potter from the Micali Painter Workshop, who signs as *kape mukaθesa* (a servant named *kape,* owned by a *mukaθe*). These cases refer to the domestic sphere, where frequently the servants dressed in luxury clothes (as the modern butlers do), but even more often we can imagine them busy preparing sumptuous banquets, as in the scene painted on the walls of the Tomb Golini I at Orvieto (Steingräber 1986), or as their definition in Greek has it: *oikétai* and *therápontes.* But it is in agricultural activities that we have to imagine the majority of the Etruscan servants. It is the case of the Vulci territory (regrettably, not yet investigated with modern techniques), where there are large fortified settlements (Firmati 2012), as Ghiaccioforte, lacking of any formal temple (Talocchini 2007) but with copious evidence of popular cults, as witnessed by the bronze votive statuettes depicting farmers; or small settlements such as Rofalco,[7] again with defensive walls. These centers constitute the servile population of the countryside, but also the chain of *oppida* defending the territory. Still, it is hard to understand how these defensive systems, which are often very advanced, reconcile with the condition of *inermes,* which is typical of the *servi.* We can speculate that the same δεσπόται/ *domini* organized the defense recruiting their own workers, first of all the free *clientes.* Literary evidence of that might be found—if the annals are trustworthy—in the passage that records free *clientes* forming the *auxilia* sent from some Etruscan cities to Veii around 480 BC, to support the city attacked by Rome (Harris 1971:120).

In Etruria, Tarquini provides the best evidence of the emancipation process of the servants. At the mid fifth century BC, soon after the awakening of the servants at Gravisca, old archaic settlements (such as Tuscania, Acquarossa-Ferento) were reoccupied in order to populate the vast territory controlled by the city, or new sites were founded (as Musarna or Castel d'Asso) (Gros and †Torelli 2007:75–78, fig. 10). In the Roman world, all the *coloniae civium Romanorum*, which are conceived as *imagines simulacraque parva urbis*, have their own polyadic temples, shaped on the model of the *Urbs*. Similarly, the minor centers in the territory of Tarquinii, as actual colonies, replicate the polyadic temple of the city found at Ara della Regina. In fact, the famous relief depicting the winged horses pulling the chariot was copied—at one-third of the original size—at the colony of Blera, likely for the local polyadic temple. These small cities were always under the control of the major Tarquinian families, which left in the territories their imposing sepulchers enriched by sarcophagi and lavish goods. A typical example is represented by the three tombs of the *Curunas* family found at Tuscania (Moretti and Sgubini Moretti 1983), connected to another tomb in Tarquinii owned by the same family.[8] To put it simply, the complete or partial emancipation of the servants is combined with a regular distribution of land between *clientes* and former servants, under the vigilant supervision of the *nobiles* relocated in the countryside.

A renowned passage by Diodorus (Diod.Sic. V, 40), that he deduced from Posidonius, describes with surprise the houses of the Etruscan servants, adding as a personal comment that they are richer and larger than the ones belonging to the free people. Without considering the spirit of the comment (which recalls the early 1900s bourgeois remarking the farmer women with silk hose), two aspects are worth noting: the first is the confirmation of the peculiar condition of the Etruscan *servitus*, which was allowed to own property; the second is that in Posidonius's times, that is, between the second and first century BC, the old *servitus* was still alive.

In addition to the transition moving forward at a different pace in all the Etruscan cities, it is also likely that it did not happen universally within each city, especially if the emancipation decrees were not *erga omnes*. Once again, Tarquinii provides some crucial hints to understanding. From the votive deposit at the Ara della Regina, comes an ex voto offered by a *Vel Tiples* who is clearly a Greek person translating his personal name Δίφιλος with the *Vornamengentile Tiples*, with whom one associates the usual Etruscan prename *Vel*. The Greek origin of the individual could suggest that only the *oikétai* bonded to the land were emancipated, and not the metics. At the same time, at Gravisca a dedication to *Turan* (*CIE* 10337) was offered around the mid-fourth century BC by one of the many women frequenting the site before the Roman conquest. Her name was *Ramtha Venatres*, which is *Ramtha* slave of a *Venatre*. This dedication gives us the chance to touch the (somehow fatal) introduction of classical slavery into a context that for centuries had seen the confrontation of the different statutes of Etruscan servants and Greek *douloi*. At that time, the Mediterranean world had truly become one.

Notes

1.   The inscription is found in A. Johnston-M. Pandolfini, *Le iscrizioni*, 22, n. 117, I refer to it in PP 1982 cit., 321.
2.   *CIE* 10378 = M. Pandolfini, *Iscrizioni etrusche*, in A. Johnston-M. Pandolfini, *Le iscrizioni* cit., 72, n. 397; I do not know how to interpret *CIE* 10296 = M. Pandolfini, *Iscrizioni etrusche*, in A. Johnston-M. Pandolfini, *Le iscrizioni* cit., 72, n. 393: [—]*al zeriniie.*
3.   The bibliography about "sacred" prostitution is endless (see the recent Scheer and Lindner 2009) and ises almost entirely against the literary, epigraphic, and archaeological evidence that refer to *ierodulia* as usual. In general, the (wrong) classicist view wants the sacred world immaculate and pure, forgetting that within the archaic economic systems (see Musti 1981) the sanctuaries performed almost all the major finance functions, as shown, for example, by the archival tablets of Zeus Olympian at Locri Epizefiri (Musti 1978). Furthermore, it is easy to imagine that the economic contribution to the treasures of the temple by this form of *servitium* had to be very high.
4.   Clearch.Sol. fr.6 ap Athen 12,11 = fr. 43a Wehrli.
5.   I refer to *mam(erkes)* (*ET* Po 2.1), *la* (*ET* Po 2.2), *vel* (*ET* Po 2.3), *vepe* (*ET* Po 2.4), *[—] nzas* (*ET* Po 2.13), *vipi* (*ET* Po 2.14), *alepu* (*ET* Po 2.15), *sesa* (*ET* Po 2.18), *venel* (*ET* Po 2.19), *larces* (*ET* Po 2.20), *paites* (*ET* Po 2.22), *larizas ET* Po 2.23), *arnzas* (*ET* Po 2.24), *venu* (v *ET* Po 2.25), *laru* (*ET* Po 2.26), *laris* (*ET* Po 2.27), *lar* (*ET* Po 2.29), *vel* (*ET* Po 2.30), *saltu* (*ET* Po 2.33), *apiu* (*ET* Po 2.36).
6.   On the signs of the Etruscan craftsmen see Colonna 1975.
7.   Cerasuolo and Pulcinelli 2018.
8.   I refer to the tomb published in *Notizie degli Scavi di Antichità 1900*, 83–87, with the sarcophagus of *zilath Seθre Curunas* (*ET* Ta 1.35).

References

Cerasuolo, O., and L. Pulcinelli 2018 *The Etruscan Fortress of Rofalco. Twenty Years of Excavation and Outreach Activities.* In *Proceedings of the 7th Conference in Italian Archaeology*, Galway, Ireland:172–180. Archeopress, Oxford.

Colonna, G. 1975 Firme arcaiche di artefici nell'Italia centrale. *Mitteilungen des Deutschen Archäologischen Instituts, Römische Abteilung* 82:181–192.

Finley, M. I. 1963–64 Between Slavery and Freedom. *Comparative Studies in Society and History* 6:233–249.

Fiorini, L., and †M. Torelli 2007 La fusione, Afrodite e l'emporion. *Facta* I:75–106.

Fiorini, L., and †M. Torelli 2010 Quarant'anni di ricerche a Gravisca. *Annual Papers on Mediterranean Archaeology (BABesch Supplement 16)*:29–49.

Frankfort, T. 1959 Les classes serviles en Etrurie. *Latomus* 18:3–22.

Firmati, M. 2012 *Le mura di Ghiaccio Forte, presidio etrusco nella Valle dell'Albegna.* In Quarto Seminario Internazionale sulle mura poligonali. Attri del Convegno Alatri 7–10 ottobre 2009, Alatri, 171–177.

Gentili, M. D. 2015 *Thefarie Velianas e l'edificio delle Venti Celle*, in L.Michetti (ed.), *Le lamine d'oro a cinquant'anni dalla scoperta. Dati archeologici su Pyrgi nell'epoca di Thefarie Velianas e rapporti con altre realtà del Mediterraneo.* In Atti del Convegno, Roma, 30 gennaio 2015:101–112.

Gros, P., and †M. Torelli 2007 *Storia dell'urbanistica. Il mondo romano*. Laterza, Rome.

Harris, W. V. 1971 *Rome in Etruria and Umbria*. Oxford University Press, Oxford.

Heurgon, J. 1959 Les pénestes étrusques chez Denys d'Halicarnasse (IX, 5, 4). *Latomus* 18:713–723.

Lotze, D. 1959 Μεταξὺ ἐλευθέρων καὶ δούλων: *Studien zur rechtsstellung unfreier Landbevölkerungen in Griechenland bis zum 4. Jahrhunfert v.Chr*. Akademie-Verlag, Berlin.

Martelli, M. 1981 *Scavi di edifici nella zona industriale di Populonia*, in *L'Etruria mineraria*. Atti del XII Convegno di studi etruschi e italici, Firenze, 16–20 giugno.

Mastrocinque, A. 1996 Servitus publica a Roma e nella società etrusca. *Studi Etruschi* 62:249–270.

Mazzarino, S. 1957 Sociologia del mondo etrusco e problemi della tarda etruscità. *Historia* 6:98–122.

Moretti, M., and A. M. Sgubini Moretti 1983 *I Curunas di Tuscania*. De Luca Editore, Roma.

Musti, D. 1981 *L'economia in Grecia*. De Luca Editore, Roma.

Musti, D. (ed.) 1978 *Le tavole di Locri. Atti del Colloquio, Napoli 1977*. Arte Tipografica, Napoli.

Stopponi, S. 2009 Campo della Fiera di Orvieto: nuove acquisizioni. *Annali Fondazione Faina* XVI:425–478

Scheer, T. S., and M. Lindner (eds.) 2009 *Tempelprostitution im Altertum. Fakten und Fiktionen*. Verlag Antike, Berlin.

Steingräber, S. 1986 *Catalogo ragionato della pittura etrusca*. Jaca Book, Milano.

Talocchini, A. 2007 *Ghiaccio Forte, un oppidum nella Valle dell'Albegna*, in *La città murata in Etruria*. Atti del XXV Convegno di studi etruschi e italici, Chianciano Terme, Sarteano, Chiusi, 30 marzo–3 aprile 2005, Pisa-Roma, 373–387.

†Torelli, M. 1975 *Elogia Tarquiniensia*. Sansoni, Firenze.

†Torelli, M. 1988 'Etruria principes disciplinam doceto.' *Il mito normativo dello specchio di Tuscania*. In *Studia Tarquiniensia*, edited by †M. Torelli and F.-H. Massa-Pairault, pp. 109–118. Bretschneider, Roma.

†Torelli, M. 1997a *Les Adonies de Gravisca. Archéologie d'une fête*. In *Les Etrusques, les plus religieux des hommes. Etat de la recherche sur la religion étrusque*. Actes du Colloque international, 17–19 novembre 1992, Paris, 233–291.

†Torelli, M. 1997b *Il rango, il rito e l'immagine*. Electa, Milano.

CHAPTER THIRTEEN

Housing and Inequality in Ancient Greece

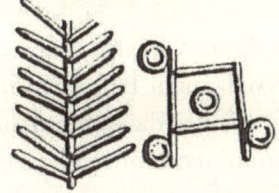

Ruth Westgate

Abstract   *This paper evaluates the relationship between housing and inequality in Greece and the Aegean, in light of recent arguments that use the remains of houses as evidence for inequalities in wealth, power, and status. Through a series of case studies from the Archaic, Classical, and Hellenistic periods, it demonstrates that the relationship between housing and inequality is complicated by problems of archaeological visibility and by the existence of different activity patterns and prestige strategies in different periods and places. It is suggested that in some communities, variation in housing may be the product of competition for status or power, and is thus an indication of the potential for mobility within the hierarchy, rather than of inequality per se.*

Equality is central to our understanding of Greek history: debates about the development and functioning of the polis often revolve around questions about the extent of equality, and a recent study (Ober 2015) argues that an exceptional degree of political and economic equality was a major factor in the extraordinary economic and cultural efflorescence of Classical Greece. Housing has featured prominently in these debates, either as evidence for political inequality or as an index of economic equality. This paper examines the relationship between housing and inequality in Greece from the eighth to the first century BC, and suggests that it is more complex than is generally acknowledged.

I will focus on three dimensions of inequality between households, though houses were also shaped by inequalities within the household, between men and women, and free and slave (Westgate 2015). Variation between houses is obviously related to inequality in wealth, and house sizes have been used as an index of wealth distribution in several recent studies (de Callataÿ 2012; Kron 2014; Ober 2010; 2015). Variation in housing can also be linked to political inequality: particularly large or elaborate houses are often seen as belonging to rulers (e.g., Mazarakis Ainian 1997; Nielsen 1999), and conversely it has been argued that the relatively narrow range of variation between houses in some Classical settlements reflects the democratic ideal of political equality (Hoepfner and Schwandner 1994). Finally, differences in housing may reflect inequality in social status. Status is a complex and much-debated concept; for the purposes of this paper, I use it to mean prestige or social standing, rather than legal status.[1] These three types of inequality are distinct, but not necessarily independent of each other: social status may depend on wealth, and wealth or high standing may help individuals to achieve political power, which may further enhance their status and generate opportunities for acquiring more wealth.

I will examine variation between houses in Greece and the Aegean in the Archaic, Classical, and Hellenistic periods, and ask how the patterns observed might be related to each of these dimensions of inequality. I will consider a range of variables that are potentially linked to inequality (Wason 1994:136–145): the size and prominence of the house; differences in plan, such as the number of rooms and the presence of specialized rooms; and the quality of construction and finish, including decoration and architectural features. For each period, I will start with a brief survey of the whole range of surviving houses, but I will focus on case studies of individual sites, to minimize the effect of variations due to local differences in topography, materials, and values or customs. The evidence used is thus inevitably selective, because only a few sites have enough well-preserved houses to give a reliable impression of the range of variation, but my aim here is only to identify general issues and problems. Testing the relationship between housing and inequality systematically would require a much fuller, quantitative study of a large sample of houses—if it is possible at all. Even a basic statistical analysis of house areas or numbers of rooms quickly runs into problems, because it is often not clear where one house ends and the next starts, or whether there was an upper floor, and if so, how large it was. For this reason, the areas and numbers of rooms given below should be taken as approximate. Where no published figures are available, the areas are rough estimates for the ground floor only, measured from plans and including exterior walls and enclosed unroofed spaces such as courtyards.

The argument will make use of two key ideas. The first is Alain Duplouy's concept of *modes de reconnaissance sociale* (Duplouy 2006). Duplouy argues that in Greek communities from the tenth to the fifth century BC, elite status was not inherited or fixed: there was no "aristocracy" in any formal or legal sense, and social status had to be constantly acted out. He explores some of the strategies that were used to lay claim to prestige, such as marriages, burials, sculpture dedications, and the acquisition of oriental objects, and argues that these were not simply symbols of elite status, but also served to generate it. These strategies varied in different places and periods, and not all of them are archaeologically visible. The second key idea is Amos Rapoport's theory of systems of activities and systems of settings (Rapoport 1990). He points out that in any society, the house is only part of a system of settings for a system of related activities, and we cannot consider it in isolation from the rest of the system, as activities that take place in the house in one culture may be distributed across a range of settings in another; thus, in order to make comparisons between different societies, it is necessary to consider the whole system of settings, not just the house. Using these two ideas, I will show that the relationship between housing and inequality is not straightforward, and highlight some of the problems raised by recent attempts to use houses as an index of equality.

HOUSING AND INEQUALITY IN THE
LATE GEOMETRIC AND ARCHAIC PERIODS

In the Late Geometric and Archaic periods (eighth to early fifth centuries BC), there is a relatively limited range of variation in housing, although the number of excavated houses is small. Most houses from this period fall within a range from c. 15 to 150 m^2 (figures from Lang 1996:78–103; Nevett 2010:22–42), although some of the smallest structures may have been part of larger compound-houses consisting of several free-standing buildings in an enclosure; the most complete of these compounds, in the Central Quarter at Oropos, covers an area of roughly 220 m^2, including the open space within the compound (Mazarakis Ainian 2007:158, fig. 17.2). The most common size is one room, and only a few houses have more than four rooms. There are a handful of larger structures, with areas of up to 500 m^2 and as many as 11 rooms, but it is not certain that the largest ones are domestic (e.g., Building F in Athens and the building at Kopanaki in Messenia, both dating to the sixth century: Lang 1996:96–97). Building materials vary in quality and permanence, from wattle-and-daub to mud-brick to stone, but this is largely the product of local differences in the availability of materials. Similarly, local rather than social factors may have determined the choice of roofing materials, which range from mud to thatch to tiles, although tiles may be an indication of wealth, as they were more typically used for public and religious buildings (Lang 1996:111–113). Some Archaic houses might have been distinguished by decorated terracotta fittings on the roof (Lang 1996:112–113), but there is no evidence for permanent interior decoration.

The only settlements with enough excavated housing to serve as case studies were occupied in the early part of the period, during the eighth and seventh centuries. At Zagora on Andros (Figure 13.1), the houses in their final state range from one room of c. 25 m^2 (F1) to six rooms covering up to 325 m^2 (H19-H21-H22-H23-H28-H29),[2] though it is not always clear which spaces constituted a single house (Cambitoglou et al. 1988, 1992; Cambitoglou 1972; Westgate 2015:54–56). At Emporio on Chios (Figure 13.2), the houses have one or two rooms and range in area from about 21 to 125 m^2 (Boardman 1967:31–51). The top of the range is smaller than at Zagora, but the figures may not be directly comparable, as the areas quoted for Zagora include internal courtyards, whereas the houses at Emporio are free-standing and we do not know how much outdoor space each household controlled. At Emporio the largest houses have a more regular plan than the smaller houses, with a porch in front, and are built of better-quality masonry (Boardman 1967:35–37), but there is no evidence at either site for additional differentiation in the form of architectural elaborations or decoration.

How might this pattern of variation in housing be related to the different types of inequality defined above? It must relate to wealth inequality at some level, because only households with more resources could afford a larger house, but as there is no independent evidence for wealth distribution in the Archaic period, we have no way of testing the correlation. Similarly, there is no way of judging the relationship of housing to social

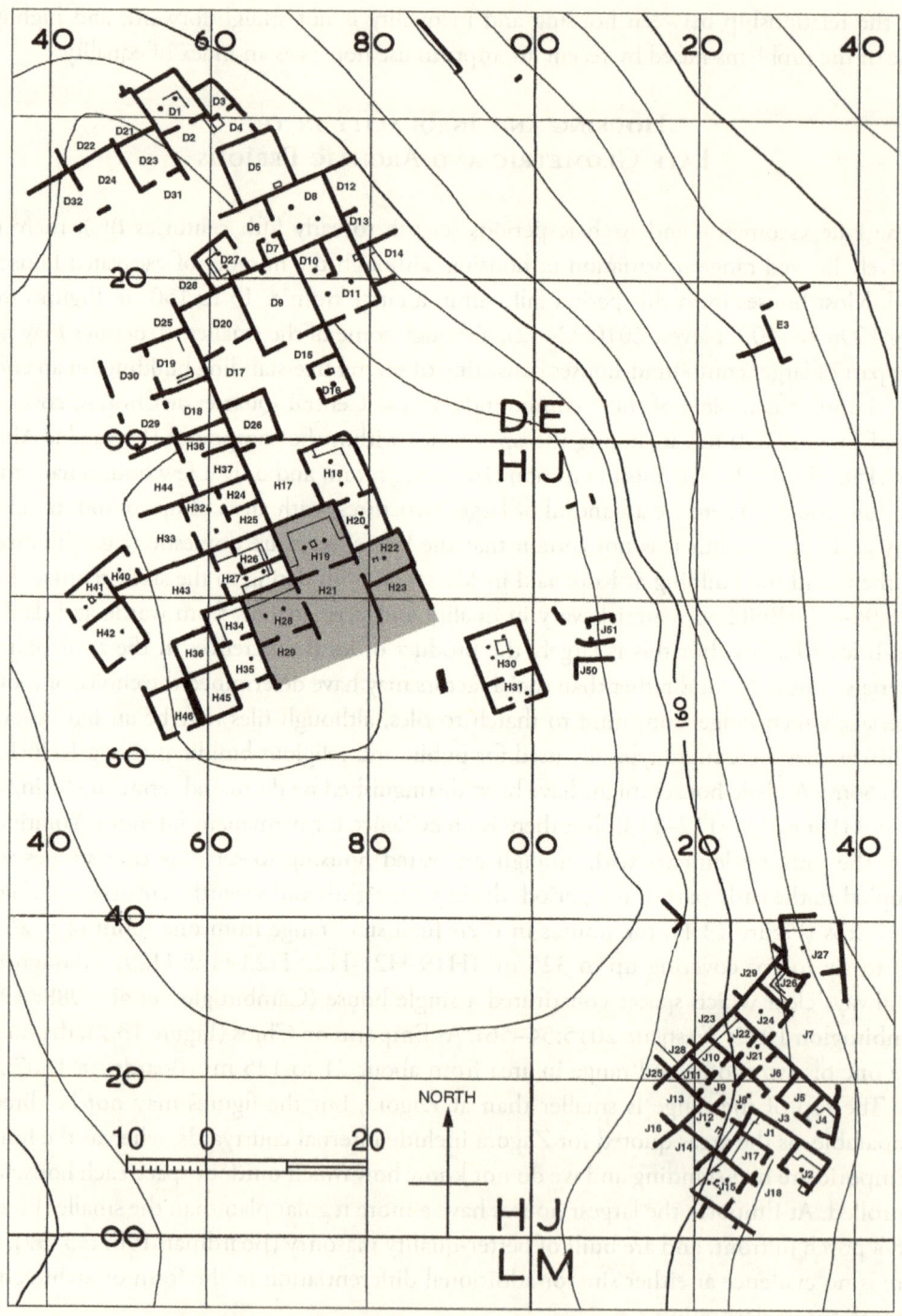

FIGURE 13.1. Zagora, plan of areas D/H and J, with the "ruler's house" shaded (after Cambitoglou 1972:260, fig. 261; courtesy A. Cambitoglou).

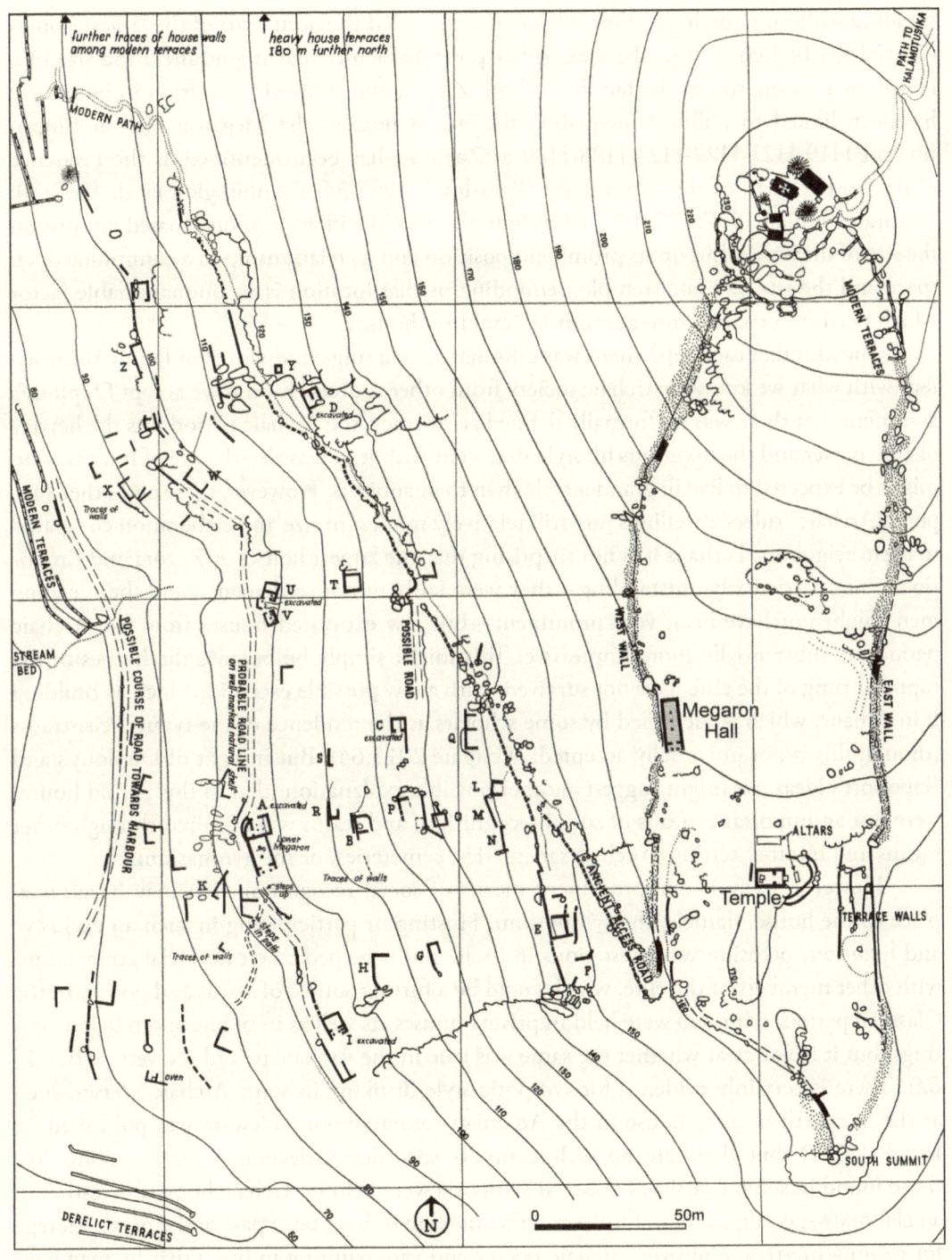

FIGURE 13.2. Emporio, with the Megaron Hall shaded (after Boardman 1967:fig. 4; courtesy British School at Athens).

standing without resorting to the circular argument that the occupants of the largest houses enjoyed the highest status. There are other possible factors that might affect the size of a house, such as the size of the family. At both Zagora and Emporio, variation in house size has been linked to political inequality: the largest house—the Megaron Hall at Emporio and H19-H21-H22-H23-H28-H29 at Zagora—has been identified as the residence of the leading man of the community (Boardman 1967:34; Cambitoglou et al. 1992:30; Mazarakis Ainian 1997:175–176, 198). In both cases, the identification is based not just on the size of the house, but on its prominent position and its relationship to a communal open space and the site of a later temple, reminding us that location is an unquantifiable factor which needs to be taken into account in "ranking" houses.

The idea that each settlement was dominated by a single individual or family is consistent with what we know of Archaic society from other sources. Even if we accept Duplouy's argument that there was no formally defined aristocracy, the Archaic period was the heyday of elite power and the luxurious lifestyle that went with it; it was also the age of tyrants, who might be expected to live in grander style than their subjects. However, these and other supposed Archaic "rulers' dwellings" are still relatively modest in size and elaboration compared to their neighbors. Perhaps it is not surprising that the largest houses at Zagora and Emporio are not particularly outstanding—they were fairly minor settlements, and their leading men might not have been very prominent—but few excavated houses from the Archaic period are substantially more impressive. This might simply be because the homes of the topmost rung of the elite have not survived, with a few possible exceptions such as Building F in Athens, which is identified by some scholars as the residence of the tyrant Peisistratos (though this is not universally accepted: Westgate 2015:64). But in light of Duplouy's and Rapoport's ideas, we might suggest another possible explanation: that in this period houses were not an important means of social recognition, and status was acquired through other means and in other settings, such as sanctuaries, cemeteries, or the gymnasium.

However, there is one prominent means of social recognition that may have taken place in the house, namely, the symposium. Hosting or participating in such an exclusive and luxurious occasion was prestigious in itself, and it helped to create social connections with other members of the elite, which could be a further source of status and power. In the Classical period, symposia were held in private houses, as well as in public and religious settings, but it is not clear whether the same was true in the Archaic period (Nevett 2010:43–62). There is certainly evidence for sympotic-style drinking in some Archaic houses, such as the late-sixth-century house in the Athenian Agora whose tableware was published by Lynch (2011), but there are no architecturally specialized, decorated dining rooms like those found in some Classical houses. If symposia were held in Archaic houses, investing in an elaborate specialized room for them does not seem to have been part of the host's strategy for gaining prestige. However, Archaic poetry and vase painting indicate that he may have acquired prestige from the non-fixed and perishable elements of the setting, such as expensive furniture, precious metal tableware, textiles, perfume, and flowers, and both he and his guests might have laid claim to status through their performances at the event, such as singing or reciting poetry, taking part in learned or witty conversations, and winning games of skill and dexterity—none of which is visible in the archaeological record.[3]

The existence of alternative strategies and settings for achieving social recognition means that the relatively narrow range of variation in early Archaic housing may not be a reliable index of inequality in wealth, status, or power. Both Zagora and Emporio were abandoned in the seventh century, and there are no later Archaic sites with such large samples of excavated houses, so it is difficult to judge how the range of variation in housing changed as a result of the profound social and political changes that took place during the following centuries.

THE CLASSICAL PERIOD: THE AGE OF EQUALITY?

By the Classical period, the elite in many cities had ceded power to a wider group of citizens, and it has been suggested that an ideology of equality between male citizens is reflected by relatively egalitarian housing (Hoepfner and Schwandner 1994). It has also been argued that Classical housing indicates a relatively high degree of equality in wealth (Kron 2014; Ober 2015:90). However, variation between houses is much greater than in the Archaic period. The range of sizes is much wider: the bottom end of the scale was probably still a single room, as it was in the Archaic period, but the top end is much larger. Houses in planned cities such as Olynthos or Piraeus typically have 7–10 rooms and cover about 200–300 m² (Hoepfner and Schwandner 1994:305–307, figs. 293, 294), and the largest known house, House II at Eretria, has 24 rooms and an area of 1225 m² (Reber 1998:95).[4] Moreover, as Classical houses are generally more substantially built than Archaic ones, many now had an upper story with additional rooms, which widens the gap between the smallest and the largest still further, although it is impossible to determine the size of the upper floors. Most houses were built of mud-brick on rubble footings, with a flat or tiled roof, but a few were marked out by ashlar masonry on the facade or in the dining room (Nevett 2009). Also, from the late fifth century we start to see other forms of differentiation between houses: architectural elaborations, especially columns around the courtyard; architecturally specialized rooms, such as dining rooms and bathrooms (Westgate 2015:71–77); and permanent decoration in the form of painted wall-plaster and decorated mosaic floors, as well as semi-fixed or portable decorations such as statues and terracotta appliqués (Walter-Karydi 1994; Westgate 1997–98).

Literary evidence from democratic Athens forms the basis for most arguments about egalitarian ideals in the Classical period. However, despite the rhetoric about equality, the range of house sizes in Athens and Attica was probably as wide as anywhere else (Figure 13.3). The smallest identifiable house is probably a unit of two or three rooms in a block behind the South Stoa, which covers about 60 m² (Figure 13.3a, southwest unit: Thompson 1959:99–103), but this is unlikely to be the very bottom of the range. There are many one- or two-room shops or workshops, either attached to houses or in purpose-built blocks, which could have doubled as homes; finds of domestic pottery are reported in at least one

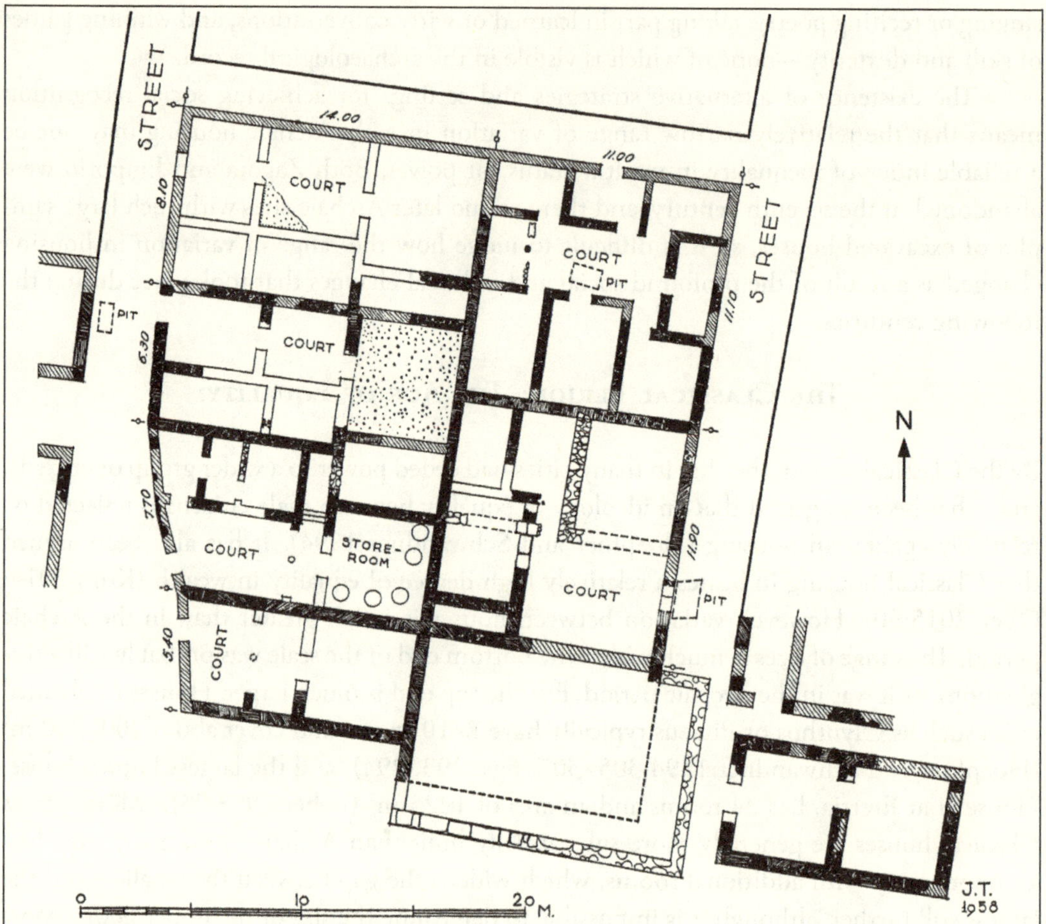

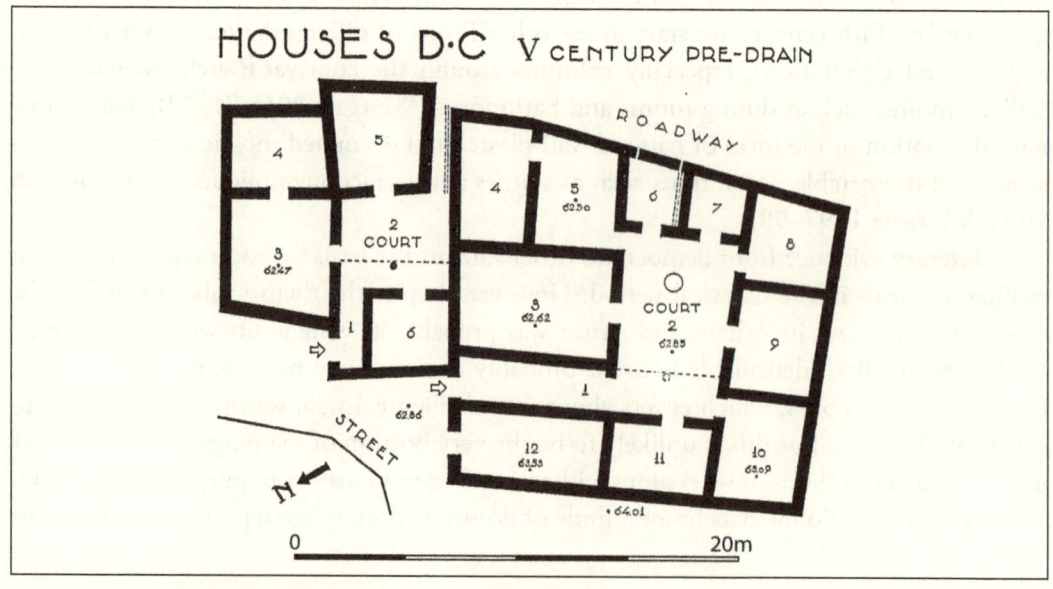

HOUSES D·C V CENTURY PRE-DRAIN

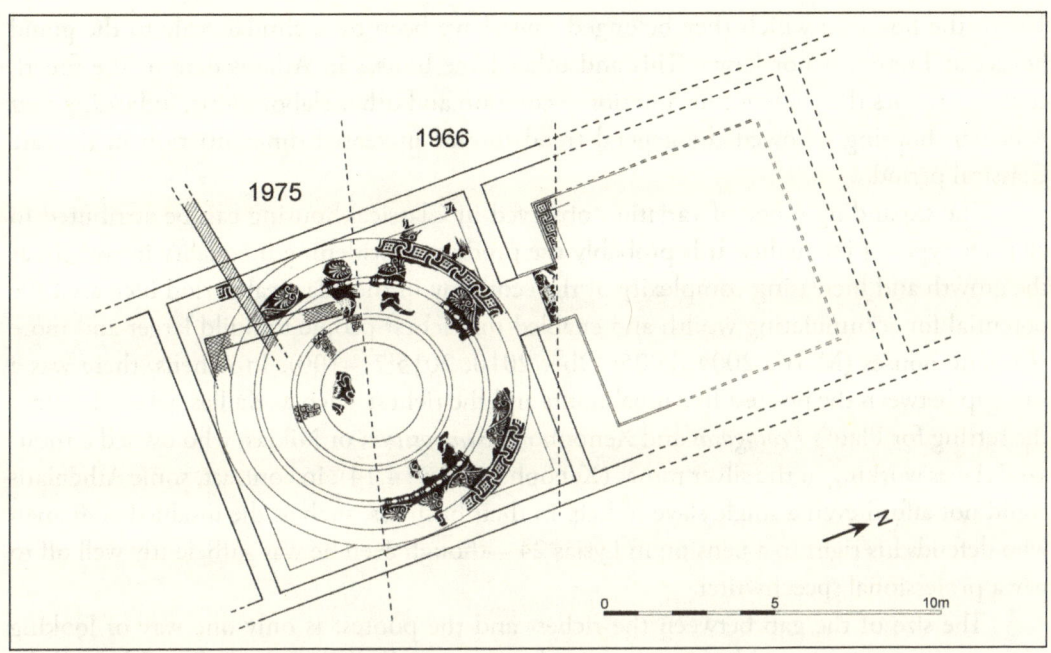

FIGURE 13.3. Athens, Classical houses: a. (top of opposite page) Block of houses behind the South Stoa, restored as in the fourth century BC (Thompson 1959: pl. 17; courtesy American School of Classical Studies at Athens); b. (bottom of opposite page) Houses C and D, period 1, first half of the fifth century BC (Young 1951:204, fig. 11; courtesy American School of Classical Studies at Athens); c. (above) Anteroom and dining-room of a fourth-century house on Odos Menandrou (drawing R. Westgate, after Alexandri 1967: pl. 92; 1975:26, fig. 5).

case, a block of shops east of the Agora (Shear 1975:360–361). Moreover, Athenian writers mention various types of low-status housing that have never been conclusively identified in the archaeological record (Ault 2005), such as the *synoikia,* or multiple dwelling (Aischines 1.124, Isaios 6.19–21), and the *kleision,* perhaps an outhouse or shed, which must have been very humble indeed, as the term can also refer to accommodation for animals (Lysias 12.18, Demosthenes 18.129, Pollux, *Onomastikon* 4.125, quoting Antiphanes fragment 22: Kassel and Austin 1991). At the other end of the scale, the largest houses whose areas can be estimated with any confidence cover up to 450 m².[5] But the pattern of excavation in Athens means that the evidence is probably biased toward the smaller end of the scale: systematic excavations have focused on the center, where space was limited, but farther out, toward the city walls, rescue excavations have revealed parts of much larger houses. For example, a dining room and anteroom found on Odos Menandrou occupied an area of at least 170 m², greater than any of the houses in the South Stoa block (Figure 13.3c: Alexandri 1967;

1975); the house to which they belonged must have been on a similar scale to the grand houses at Eretria, if not larger. This and other large houses in Athens date to the fourth century, as does the evidence for interior decoration and other elaborations, indicating that Athenian housing followed the general trend toward increased differentiation in the late Classical period.

The expanding range of variation observed in Classical housing can be attributed to all three types of inequality. It is probably the product of widening inequality in wealth, as the growth and increasing complexity of the economy in the Classical period increased the potential for accumulating wealth and enabled the richest people to build larger and more elaborate houses (Morris 2004, 2005; Ober 2010, 2015:71–100). In Athens, there was a vast gap between the poorest free inhabitants and the richest, such as Kallias, whose house is the setting for Plato's *Protagoras* and Xenophon's *Symposium*, or Nikias, who owned a thousand slaves working in the silver mines (Xenophon, *Poroi* 4.14); in contrast, some Athenians could not afford even a single slave to help in their business, such as the disabled craftsman who defends his right to a pension in Lysias 24—though even he was sufficiently well off to pay a professional speechwriter.

The size of the gap between the richest and the poorest is only one way of looking at inequality: it is also important to consider the overall distribution of wealth, and for Classical Athens we do have an attempt to generate a Lorenz wealth distribution curve, using literary and epigraphic evidence (Kron 2011). This suggests a relatively egalitarian distribution of wealth compared to other historical societies, though by no means equal. Unfortunately, too little Athenian housing survives to produce a meaningful pattern that we could compare with Kron's statistics. Instead, Kron (2014, followed by Ober 2015:90) uses the distribution of house sizes at Olynthos to back up the picture of Classical Greece as a relatively equal society, where a large segment of the population enjoyed a high standard of living in comparison with many later societies, notably England in 1831. However, using house sizes as a proxy for wealth distribution may exaggerate the egalitarianism of Classical Greece, for several reasons.

Firstly, as the case study of Athens suggests, housing at the lower end of the range is difficult to recognize in the archaeological record, which skews the size distribution toward the middle. Even at Olynthos, the housing is not as equal as it looks at first glance (Figure 13.4). It is true that in the most extensively excavated part of the city, the grid-planned area on the North Hill, the range of house sizes is relatively narrow, from c. 140 to 450 m², with most houses occupying a standard plot of c. 290 m², which, taken in isolation, appears relatively egalitarian because the sample is dominated by medium-sized houses (Kron 2014:129, table 2).[6] However, this impression of equality would be less pronounced if the analysis included the South Hill, where limited excavations revealed parts of smaller, more irregular structures, at least some of which were houses (Robinson 1946:272–308). There were probably smaller living units on the North Hill too, which are not easily recognizable. Some of the "standard" houses might have been divided into smaller units, such as C –x 7, which has been reconstructed as four dwellings of 28–61 m²;[7] other houses could have been subdivided in ways that have left no visible trace.

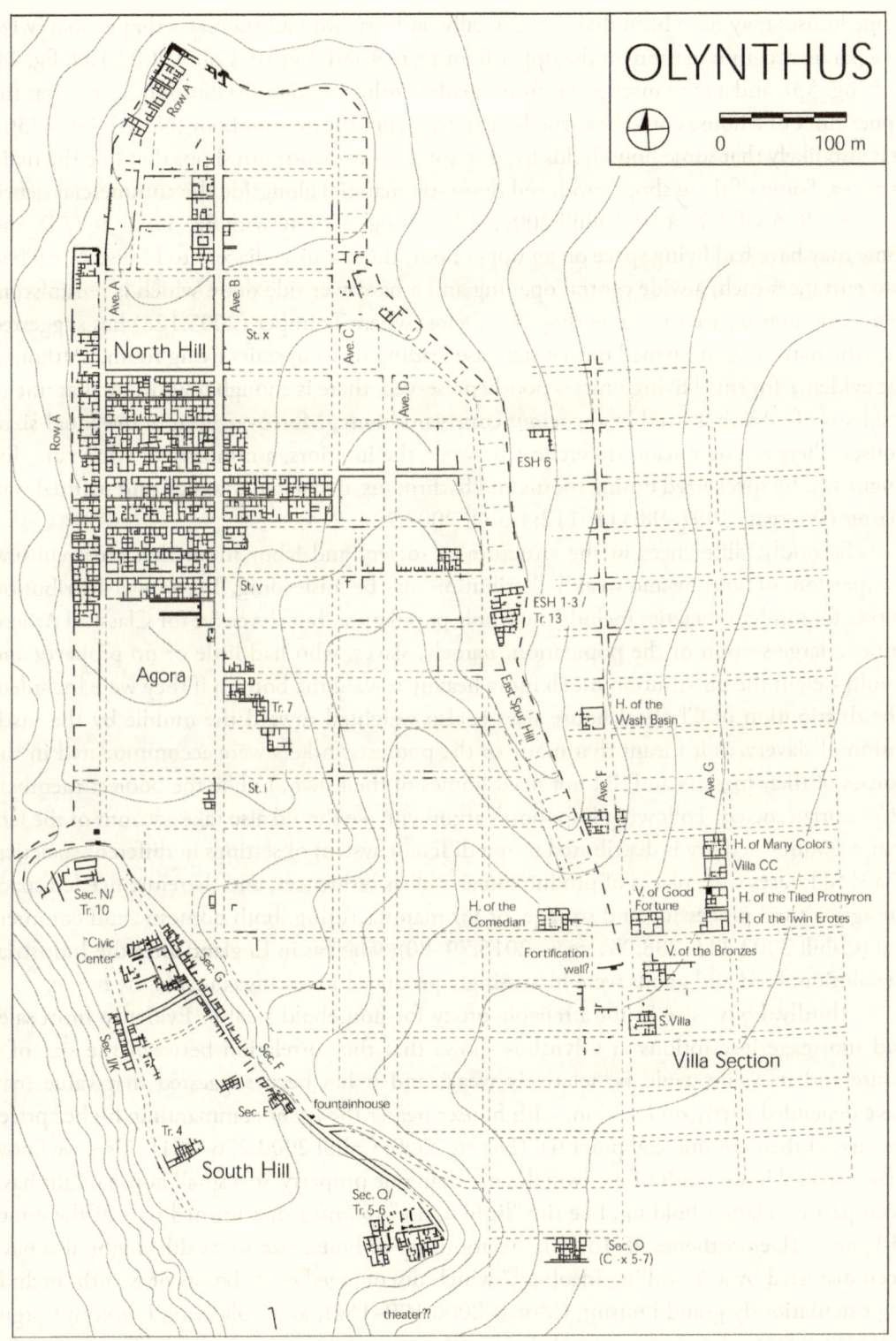

FIGURE 13.4. Olynthos (Cahill 2002:26, fig. 6; courtesy N. Cahill).

Some houses may have been divided vertically: at least two had staircases that probably led to separate accommodation on the upper floor (A iv 9 and A vi 10: Cahill 2002:109, fig. 24; 245, fig. 53), and a sales inscription from nearby Stolos (modern Kellion) indicates that the upper story of a house could be owned separately from the ground floor (Nevett 2000:336). It is also likely that some households lived in the one- or two-room shops that line the main avenues. Some of these shops produced domestic material alongside the commercial debris (e.g., A v 9, A vii 9, B vi 10: Cahill 2002:117 with fig. 25; 246 with fig. 35; 273–274), and some may have had living space on an upper floor: three shops adjacent to House A iv 9 had two entrances each, a wide central opening and a narrower side door, which is reminiscent of a configuration seen in some shops on Delos, where Trümper (2005:122) has suggested that the narrow door opened onto a staircase leading to an upstairs living room.[8] Although the evidence for small living units is poorly preserved, there is enough to indicate that not all residents of Olynthos lived in a spacious courtyard house. Moreover, even in the equal-sized houses, there are significant differences between the interiors, a minority of which are distinguished by specialized dining rooms and bathrooms, decorated mosaics, and painted wall plaster (Westgate 1997–98:111–112; Cahill 2002:204–214).

Secondly, differences in the structure of society and labor mean that cross-cultural comparisons of housing and wealth distribution may be misleading. The wealth distribution curves for modern societies include the whole population, but the curve for Classical Athens omits a large section of the population, namely, slaves, who had little or no property and would weight the distribution much more heavily toward the bottom if they were included. The distribution of Classical house sizes is also weighted toward the middle by the institution of slavery, as it meant that many of the poorest workers were accommodated in the houses of their masters and did not need homes of their own, unlike the poorest members of Victorian society. Following Rapoport's argument, we should also take account of the fact that economic activity is distributed over a different system of settings in different societies. Classical houses were places of production as well as residences, and therefore needed space for agricultural processing and storage, or for manufacturing, both domestic and commercial (Cahill 2002:223–288; Westgate 2015:79–80); whereas in England after the Industrial Revolution, food and goods were increasingly produced in settings outside the home.

Thirdly, house size is not a reliable proxy for household wealth. Evidence from sales and mortgage inscriptions at Olynthos shows that the correlation between the size of a house and its value could be relatively weak, and it has been suggested that value may have depended partly on location, with houses nearer the *agora* commanding higher prices because of their commercial potential (Nevett 2000; Cahill 2002:276–281). Also, we know that Classical households often owned more than one property, so a small house might have been part of a larger holding, like the "little house" (*oikiske*) that formed part of the estate of Komon (Demosthenes 48.13). The relationship of house size to wealth might also have been distorted by a "middling ideology," which discouraged overt boasts of wealth, including ostentatiously grand housing (Morris 2000:109–154), and, following Duplouy's argument, by people choosing to spend their resources on other means of gaining prestige: for example, in Athens there was clearly an expectation that the rich should spend their wealth for the benefit of the community through the system of liturgies, rather than on impressive private houses. Thus, although there must be some connection between house size and wealth, using house areas as an index of economic equality is potentially misleading.

The differentiation observed in Classical houses is also likely to relate to inequality in social status. Even in Athens, despite the ideal of political equality, there were still status distinctions. People who did not need to work for a living sneered at those who did (e.g., Demosthenes 57.30–31, 35–36, 45), and people who knew how to behave at social occasions such as symposia mocked those who did not (e.g., Aristophanes, *Wasps* 1208–1217). The increase in investment in houses, especially in the later part of the period, suggests that there had been a shift in the strategies by which people were competing for status: in Duplouy's terms, the house had become a means of social recognition. It is significant that many of the elaborations seen in Classical houses are connected with the prestigious activity of the symposium, notably specialized dining rooms with mosaics and other decoration (Westgate 1997–98:94–104). Lynch (2007) has argued that as sympotic-style drinking was taken up by a wider section of the population, the elite needed to find new ways of differentiating themselves, and one way of doing this was to create more impressive and exclusive settings for their symposia. Increased spending on houses may also be seen in Rapoport's terms, as evidence for a change in the system of settings that made up the activity system. The house might have become more important as a setting for social networking in this period, complementing or replacing other venues such as sanctuaries or gymnasia; holding social occasions in a private house rather than a public setting was perhaps another way of making them more exclusive.

Finally, although Hoepfner and Schwandner's theory linking standardized housing to democratic ideals of equality is problematic for various reasons,[9] a connection between inequality in housing and political inequality was certainly recognized at the time. In the fourth century, Demosthenes repeatedly compares the grand homes of contemporary politicians with those of the great men of the past, who were "careful to obey the spirit of the constitution" by living in houses that were "not a whit more splendid than those of their neighbors" (3.25–26; also 13.28–29; 23.206–208). Even if he is exaggerating the contrast, this suggests that his audience were aware of widening inequality in housing and that it could be seen as a threat to the political equality that underpinned Athenian democracy.

However, if we consider the case of Classical and early Hellenistic Crete, it becomes clear that there is not always a direct relationship between inequality in housing and inequality in social status and political power. Cretan houses of this period seem much more equal than those in Athens and elsewhere in the Aegean (Westgate 2007b). The range of sizes is relatively narrow: at Lato and Trypetos, for example (Figure 13.5), the largest houses are no more than four to five times the area of the smallest (c. 40–150 m² and 2–6 rooms at Lato), and even the largest known house, at Phaistos, only covers c. 300 m², many times smaller than the largest contemporary houses elsewhere.[10] There is also very little architectural elaboration or decoration to differentiate between houses: no peristyles, no specialized dining rooms, no decorated mosaics, and only scraps of painted plaster. But Cretan cities were not egalitarian in either political or social terms. They were ruled by narrow oligarchies, whose

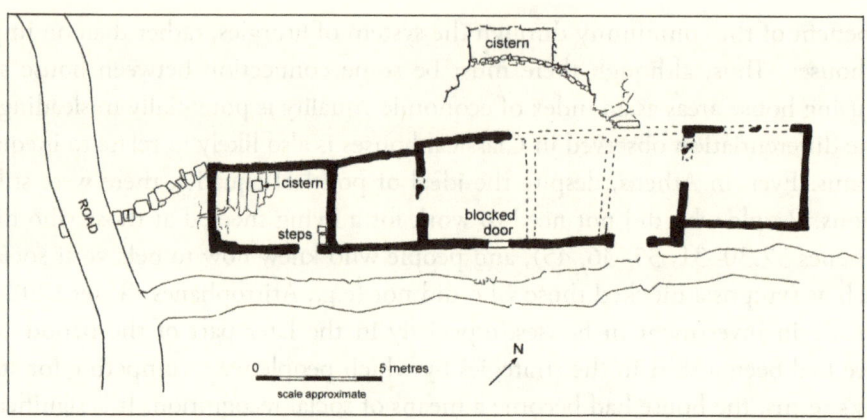

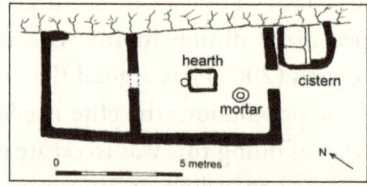

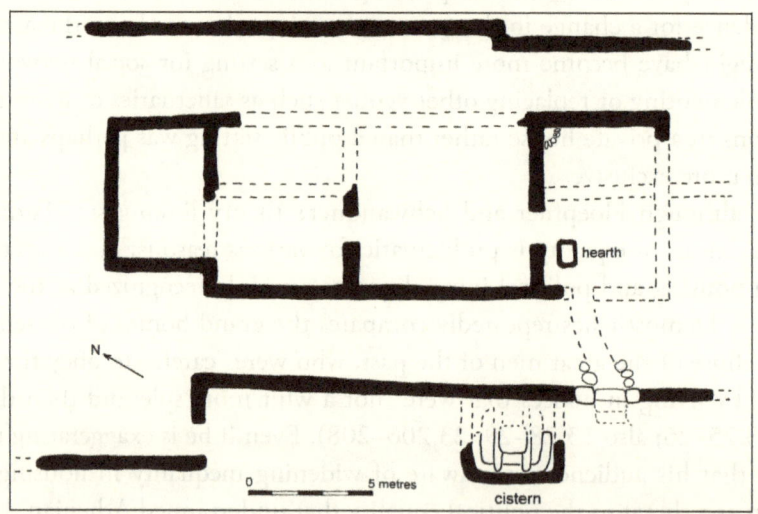

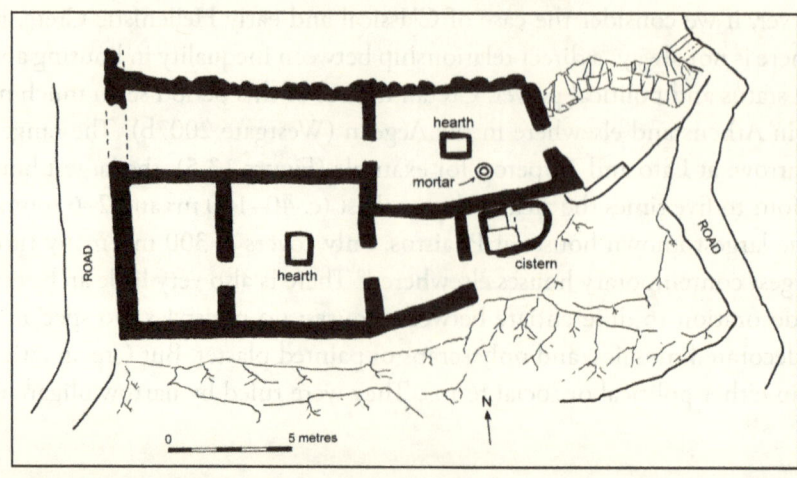

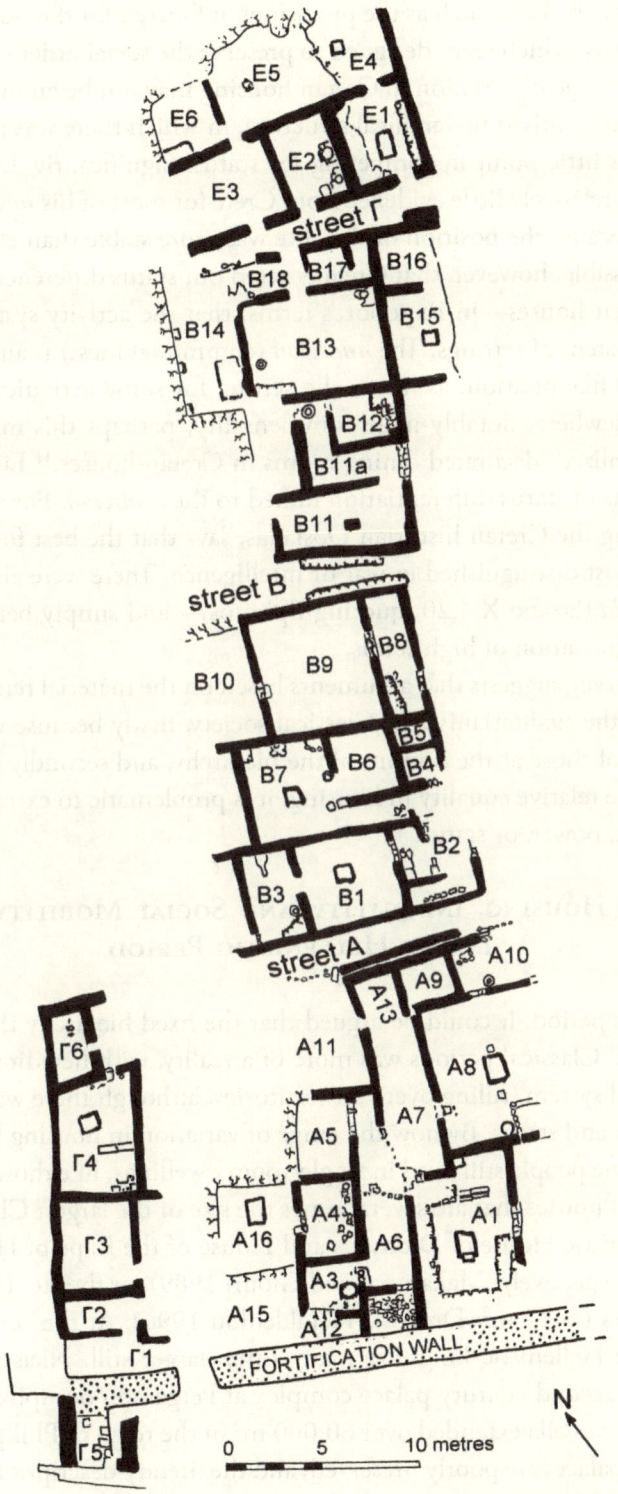

Figure 13.5. Late Classical–Hellenistic houses on Crete (drawings by H. Mason © Cardiff University): a. (opposite top three) Lato, Houses A, Δ, E, and (opposite bottom) two houses north of the Prytaneion (approximate scales); b. (above) Trypetos.

status was protected by laws, such as the provisions at Gortyn for the transmission of wealth between generations, which seem designed to preserve the social order (Whitley 2009:291). Thus, the limited range of variation in Cretan housing may not be an indication of equality, but of the opposite—a rigid hierarchical structure, in which there was limited potential for mobility and thus little point in competing for status. Significantly, Duplouy (2006:280) notes that there is relatively little evidence from Crete for most of his *modes de reconnaissance sociale*, perhaps because the position of the elite was more stable than elsewhere.

It is also possible, however, that Cretans acted out status differences in other contexts, rather than in their houses—in Rapoport's terms, that the activity system was distributed over a different system of settings. The *andreion* (communal mess) is an obvious alternative arena for status differentiation, as it was the setting for some activities that took place in private houses elsewhere, notably male commensality; perhaps this meant that there was no need for specialized, decorated dining rooms in Cretan houses.[11] Literary sources mention various means of status differentiation linked to the *andreion*. For example, Athenaeus (IV.143d), quoting the Cretan historian Dosiadas, says that the best food was given to the men who were most distinguished in war or intelligence. There were also contests between and within *andreia* (Strabo X.4.20, quoting Ephoros)—and simply being a member of an *andreion* was an indication of high status.

This brief survey suggests that arguments based on the material remains of houses may tend to overstate the egalitarianism of Classical society, firstly because we might be unable to see the homes of those at the bottom of the hierarchy, and secondly because even where there appears to be relative equality in housing, it is problematic to extrapolate from that to equality in wealth, power, or status.

HOUSING, INEQUALITY, AND SOCIAL MOBILITY IN THE HELLENISTIC PERIOD

By the Hellenistic period, it could be argued that the fixed hierarchy that Duplouy denies in the Archaic and Classical periods was more of a reality, with hereditary monarchs at the top of the political system, ruling over vast territories, although there was still intense competition for power and status. By now the range of variation in housing had increased enormously. While some people still lived in single-room dwellings, like those at Delos discussed below, we know of houses that are several times the size of the largest Classical houses, such as the early Hellenistic House of Dionysos and House of the Rape of Helen at Pella (3160 m^2 and 2350 m^2 respectively: Makaronas and Giouri 1989), or the late Hellenistic "palatial" complex at Rhodes (4412 m^2: Dreliossi-Herakleidou 1996). At the very top of the range, the palaces of the Hellenistic kings are many times larger still: Nielsen (1999:266, 271) estimates that the second-century palace complex at Pergamon occupied an area of 30,000 m^2, and the palace at Pella extended over 60,000 m^2 in the reign of Philip V (221–179 BC). Most of the royal palaces are poorly preserved, and the literary descriptions are a reminder of a critical problem with ranking houses on the basis of archaeological evidence: they mention a wealth of exotic woods, precious metals, rare stones, jewels, and sumptuous textiles, all of which are now lost without trace. However, some decorative features such as paintings and mosaics do survive, and it is clear that the introduction of new materials, styles, and techniques had increased the range of decorative options, and thus the potential for differentiation between houses (Westgate 1997–98:104–115, 2000, 2010:512–517).

This increased variation can be related to the growth of all three types of inequality. The gap between the richest and the poorest was probably wider than ever before, as the greater scale and complexity of the Mediterranean economy and the exploitation of conquered territories had expanded the possibilities for acquiring wealth; there are indications that economic activity intensified in this period, especially in the last two centuries BC (de Callataÿ 2005). Inequality in Hellenistic housing is also clearly linked to widening political and status inequality, and in particular to the institution of monarchy. Although the position of the kings was inherited and relatively formalized, they still needed to act out their power and status in relation to other kings and rivals, as well as their own subjects, and huge, lavishly decorated palaces were an integral part of their performance, especially the many spectacular spaces for receiving guests and entertaining them in suitably regal style. However, the vast size of the palaces was not merely a symbol of the kings' dominance, but also played a practical part in it, as they needed space for political and administrative functions that did not take place in houses in earlier periods: an activity system that had previously been spread across a range of public and private settings was now concentrated into a single complex, and thus into the control of a single individual.

The most promising site for assessing inequality in this period is Delos, where about 90 houses and numerous smaller residential units survive from the late second and early first century BC. The houses range in area from 53 to 866 m^2 (Trümper 1998:166–168), although some of the largest structures might be clubhouses rather than residences. About half of the houses fall in the range 100–200 m^2, and there are only seven with ground areas over 500 m^2; the top end of the range known elsewhere in the Hellenistic world is not represented here. This has been seen as evidence for a relatively egalitarian distribution of wealth compared to Pompeii and later societies, though less egalitarian than Olynthos (de Callataÿ 2012:73–74; Kron 2014:134–135). Once again, however, these analyses do not take into account a large number of smaller residential units, which are easier to identify on Delos than elsewhere because of the good preservation of the site (Figure 13.6: Trümper 2003; 2005). They include more than 500 one- or two-room shops or workshops, many of which were probably inhabited, and a variety of small complexes that combined shops/workshops with modest accommodation. Trümper (2005:122–128) discusses 13 such units, ranging in area from 47 to 208 m^2 (including the shops; 36–130 m^2 without the shops), but notes that there are many more that are unpublished or incompletely excavated. It is also clear that the upper floors of many houses were occupied by separate apartments (Trümper 1998:92–106), which must have been smaller than the ground-floor accommodation, as they did not have courtyards and often only extended over part of the house below. If these small living units were included in the analysis, they would weight the distribution of house sizes more heavily toward the smaller end and

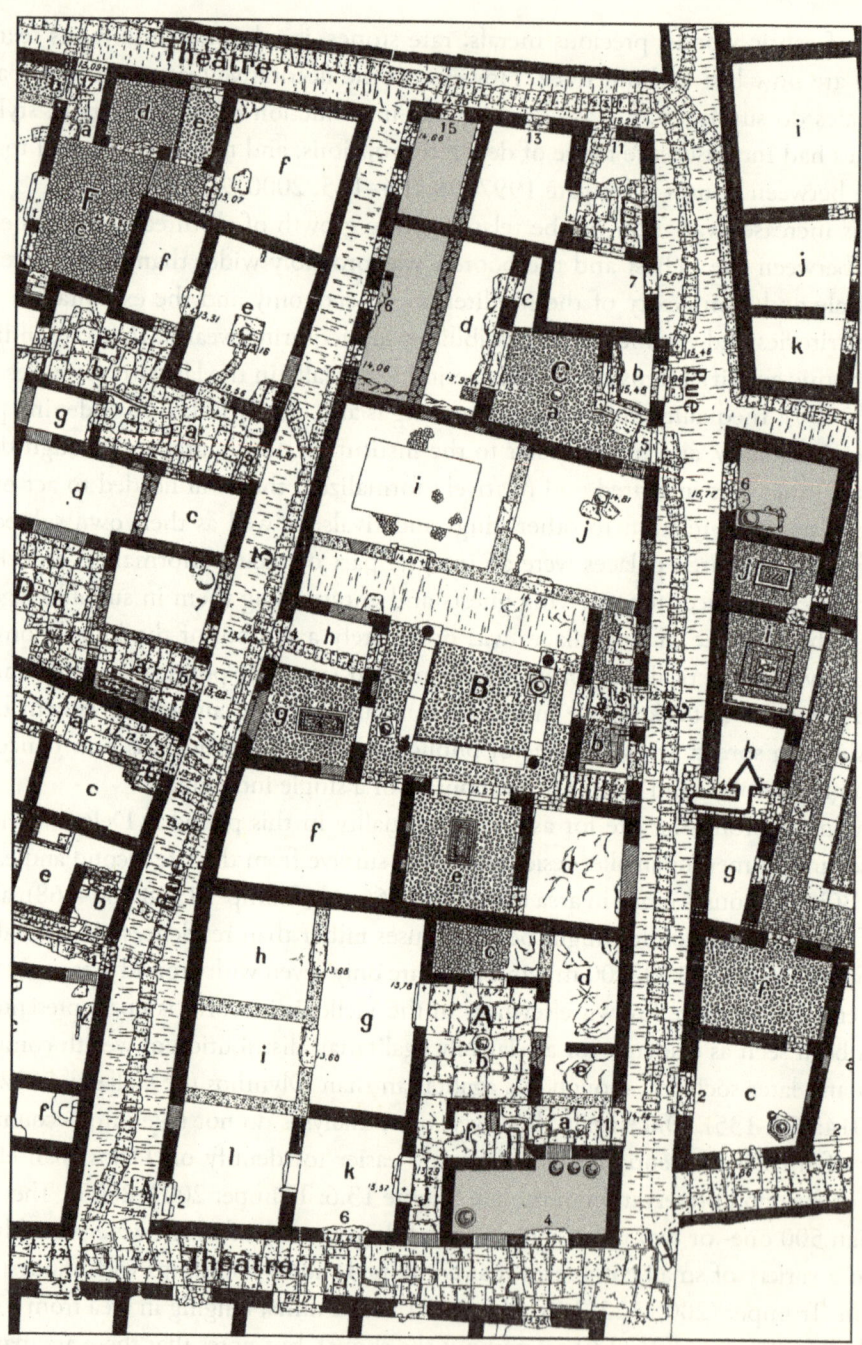

Figure 13.6. Delos, Insula IV of the Theatre Quarter, showing residential units of different sizes (after Chamonard 1922–24: pls. III–IV; courtesy École française d'Athènes). Shaded areas are shops that are only accessible from the street. A and B = houses (133 and 246 m² respectively, not including shops k, l, and 4 in House A); C = small residential unit (59 m² including shop 6); rooms 7-11-13[-15?] = unit with two or three shops, a courtyard, and stairs to the upper floor (47 m² including shop 15). The arrow shows the entrance to an upstairs apartment over rooms i, j, and 6 in the neighboring Insula II.

make it look distinctly less egalitarian. However, it is impossible to know how far this is typical of the period, as Delos might have been unusually densely inhabited because of its status as a free port, which encouraged people from all over the Mediterranean to crowd into its narrow streets to take advantage of the economic opportunities that it offered.

Although the houses and apartments on Delos are at the small end of the range of housing attested in the Hellenistic period, they are differentiated by an impressive array of features, including columns and other architectural elaborations such as wall-niches and ornate window frames, luxurious facilities such as sweat baths, and lavish interior decoration, including painted and molded wall plaster and mosaics of various types and degrees of complexity (Trümper 1998:30–80; Westgate 2000, 2010:504–512)—one of the largest concentrations of domestic decoration found anywhere in the Mediterranean at this date, including almost half of the known decorated mosaics. In contrast, many Hellenistic sites have produced no mosaics at all. This illustrates once again the point that different prestige strategies operated in different places and at different levels of society. The concentration of luxury features on Delos is partly down to the accidents of preservation and excavation, but it is also a product of specific local factors, both practical and social. The dense occupation and limited space on the island may have made it difficult to stand out by having a larger house, only a more elaborate one. Also, the residents of Delos were competing for status within a specific community, with its own values; given the commercial nature of the settlement, perhaps wealth and the display of wealth were particularly important as the basis of the social hierarchy. In other communities, houses and their decoration may not have been so important as a means of social recognition, because status was negotiated by other means or in other settings. Moreover, the social hierarchy on Delos may have been unusually fluid, because of the exceptional mobility and heterogeneity of the population, which included traders from all over the Mediterranean, many of whom were former slaves. The residents might therefore have felt the need to project their status more strongly than the inhabitants of more settled communities (Westgate 2010:511), generating a high level of competitive display, which is reflected in the frequent upgrading of the houses (Trümper 1998).

Although Delos is probably an extreme case, the increase in differentiation between houses—whether through size, architectural elaboration, or decoration—is mirrored at many other Hellenistic sites. While it undoubtedly relates to growing inequality, it is difficult to separate the effects of inequality from the effects of social mobility, in a world where the movement of people and the growth of new communities had undermined the certainties of earlier times.

CONCLUSIONS

This paper has revealed three major problems that we face when attempting to use variation in housing as evidence for inequality in wealth, power, or social status. Firstly, assigning value to houses is difficult, not only because so much is missing—especially the upper stories and any valuable or perishable materials—but also because we do not know the relative value attached to different qualities such as location and decor: was a floor mosaic more or less prestigious than a wall painting, and were either as highly valued as the lost furnishings in precious metals, expensive woods, and fine textiles?

Secondly, we have seen that attempts to assess inequality through statistical analysis of house sizes tend to exaggerate the egalitarianism of Greek communities because dwellings at the lower end of the range are underrepresented in the archaeological literature. This is partly because of archaeologists' tendency to focus on the larger, more impressive houses, and partly because of the difficulty of identifying poorer dwellings in the archaeological record. Although it is unlikely that any Greek settlement ever approached the density of population seen in Rome or the cities of nineteenth-century England, in every period there were probably households living in small units that we do not easily recognize as houses, such as the shops and modest house-cum-workshops on Delos, or in apartments or subdivisions of apparently "normal" houses, or even in structures built from perishable materials that have left no archaeological trace at all.

Finally, even if we could quantify inequality in housing accurately, its relationship to inequality between households is not straightforward. The house was just one of many possible means by which social recognition could be achieved, and one of many settings in which inequality might be expressed. Although increasing wealth between the Archaic and the Hellenistic period made it possible for the range of variation in housing to increase, it was not the determining factor: in some periods and places, people might have chosen to spend their wealth elsewhere. Moreover, in communities where inequality was entrenched, there may have been little to gain by investing in a large and ostentatious house; differentiation in housing might be as much a product of the potential for mobility within the social or political hierarchy, as of inequality itself.

ACKNOWLEDGMENTS

I would like to thank the conference organizers for offering me the opportunity to take part in such a stimulating and enjoyable event, and the other participants and James Whitley for their helpful comments on this paper.

NOTES

1. For a discussion of the issues raised by the term, see Kamen 2013:1–3. Social status could cut across legal status distinctions: for example, metics (resident foreigners) in Athens could enjoy high social standing despite their legal disabilities, like the family of the orator Lysias, who mixed in the highest social circles.

2. This assumes that the complex extended as far as the southwest corner of H29. Another complex, though smaller in area, has 11 rooms (J3-J4-J5-J6-J8-J9-J10-J11-J12-J21-J22), but it is not certain that they all belonged to the same house.

3. Sources for these "invisible" status markers include Anakreon, fragments 397, 415, 434 (Page 1962); elegy 2 (Athenaeus XI.463a); Alkaios, fragments 322, 346, 362 (Lobel and Page 1955); Xenophanes, fragment 1 (Diels and Kranz 1951). For the status implications of the game of *kottabos*, see Kurke 1999:278–283.

4.   The late-fourth-century palace at Vergina is much larger, c. 12,500 m² and more than 50 rooms according to the latest reconstruction (Kottaridi 2011), but this was a product of the very different social and political conditions in Macedonia; palaces will be discussed below, in the context of the Hellenistic period.

5.   E.g., the "Priest's House" at Cape Zoster, 325 m²; Dema House, 355 m²; House C/D in the Industrial Quarter, period 2, over 400 m²; House 1 at Thorikos, first phase, c. 450 m² (rough estimates from Young 1951; Jones 1975; Mussche 1998:fig. 93; Nevett 1999).

6.   There are several units of 140–160 m² where standard plots have been divided into two (A iv 7, A v 8, A viii 10). The largest completely excavated house is the Villa of Good Fortune, at 442 m².

7.   Hoepfner and Schwandner 1994:110–112, fig. 88; this is questioned by Cahill, according to Ault 2005:144, n.5.

8.   Robinson and Graham 1938:85–86, 211–213, plates 23, 92, 93; they interpret the wider doors as shop windows. The ground floor of each unit covered 22.5 m².

9.   See Westgate 2007a, where I suggest that the plans and arrangement of houses in Classical cities might have reflected the ideal of political equality in more abstract ways.

10.   Figures from Westgate 2007b. The scales in Figure 13.5a are approximations, because the measurements given in the original publication of the houses are inconsistent. Very few Cretan houses have been completely excavated or published, and the best evidence comes from relatively minor settlements.

11.   However, there is evidence of formal drinking in houses (Westgate 2007b:430, 446). The relationship between the *andreion* system and the unusual form of Cretan houses is plausible but elusive (Westgate 2007b:450–453).

REFERENCES

Alexandri, O. 1967 Μενάνδρου 9. *Archaiologikon Deltion* 22 *Chronika*:98–100.

Alexandri, O. 1975 Ὁδός Μενάνδρου 7. *Archaiologikon Deltion* 30 22 *Chronika*:24–27.

Ault, B. A. 2005 Housing the Poor and the Homeless in Ancient Greece. In *Ancient Greek Houses and Households: Chronological, Regional, and Social Diversity*, edited by B. A. Ault and L. C. Nevett, pp. 140–159. University of Pennsylvania Press, Philadelphia.

Boardman, J. 1967 *Excavations in Chios 1952–1955: Greek Emporio*. BSA Supplementary Volume 6. British School at Athens, London.

Cahill, N. 2002 *Household and City Organization at Olynthus*. Yale University Press, New Haven.

Cambitoglou, A. 1972 Ἀνασκαφὴ Ζαγορᾶς Ἄνδρου (1971). *Praktika*:251–273.

Cambitoglou, A., A. Birchall, J. J. Coulton, and J. R. Green 1988 *Zagora 2: Excavation of a Geometric Town on the Island of Andros. Excavation Season 1969; Study Season 1969–1970*. Βιβλιοθήκη τῆς ἐν Ἀθήναις Ἀρχαιολογικῆς Ἑταιρείας 105. 2 vols. Archaeological Society of Athens, Athens.

Cambitoglou, A., J. J. Coulton, J. Birmingham, and J. R. Green 1992 *Zagora 1: Excavation of a Geometric Town on the Island of Andros. Excavation Season 1967; Study Season 1968–1969*. Βιβλιοθήκη τῆς ἐν Ἀθήναις Ἀρχαιολογικῆς Ἑταιρείας 105. Reprinted. Originally published 1971. Archaeological Society of Athens, Athens.

Chamonard, J. 1922–24 *Exploration archéologique de Délos VIII: Le Quartier du Théâtre. Étude sur l'habitation délienne à l'époque hellénistique*. De Boccard, Paris.

de Callataÿ, F. 2005 The Graeco-Roman Economy in the Super-Long Run: Lead, Copper, and Shipwrecks. *Journal of Roman Archaeology* 18:361–372.

de Callataÿ, F. 2012 Le retour (quantifié) du "miracle grec." In *Stephanèphoros: de l'économie antique à l'Asie Mineure. Hommages à Raymond Descat*, edited by K. Konuk, pp. 63–76. Ausonius, Bordeaux.

Diels, H., and W. Kranz 1951 *Die Fragmente der Vorsokratiker*, vol. I. 6th ed. Weidmann, Berlin.

Dreliossi-Herakleidou, A. 1996 Späthellenistische palastartige Gebäude in der Nähe der Akropolis von Rhodos. In *Basileia: Die Paläste der hellenistischen Könige*, edited by W. Hoepfner and G. Brands, pp. 182–192. Von Zabern, Mainz.

Duplouy, A. 2006 *Le prestige des élites. Recherches sur les modes de reconnaissance sociale en Grèce entre les Xe et Ve siècles avant J.-C.* Les Belles Lettres, Paris.

Hoepfner, W., and E.-L. Schwandner. 1994 *Haus und Stadt im klassischen Griechenland*. Wohnen in der klassischen Polis 1. 2nd ed. Deutscher Kunstverlag, Munich.

Jones, J. E. 1975 Town and Country Houses of Attica in Classical Times. In *Thorikos and the Laurion in Archaic and Classical Times*, edited by H. Mussche, P. Spitaels, and F. Goemaere-De Poerck, pp. 63–140. Miscellanea Graeca 1. Belgian Archaeological Mission in Greece, Ghent.

Kamen, D. 2013 *Status in Classical Athens*. Princeton University Press, Princeton.

Kassel, R., and C. Austin 1991 *Poetae Comici Graeci*, vol. II. De Gruyter, Berlin.

Kottaridi, A. 2011 The Palace of Aegae. In *Brill's Companion to Ancient Macedon*, edited by R. Lane Fox, pp. 297–333. Brill, Leiden.

Kron, G. 2011 The Distribution of Wealth at Athens in Comparative Perspective. *Zeitschrift für Papyrologie und Epigraphik* 179:129–138.

Kron, G. 2014 Comparative Evidence and the Reconstruction of the Ancient Economy: Greco-Roman Housing and the Level and Distribution of Wealth and Income. In *Quantifying the Greco-Roman Economy and Beyond*, edited by F. de Callataÿ, pp. 123–146. Edipuglia, Bari.

Kurke, L. 1999 *Coins, Bodies, Games, and Gold: The Politics of Meaning in Archaic Greece*. Princeton University Press, Princeton.

Lang, F. 1996 *Archaische Siedlungen in Griechenland: Struktur und Entwicklung*. Akademie Verlag, Berlin.

Lobel, E., and D. Page 1955 *Poetarum Lesbiorum Fragmenta*. Clarendon Press, Oxford.

Lynch, K. M. 2007 More Thoughts on the Space of the Symposium. In *Building Communities: House, Settlement, and Society in the Aegean and Beyond*, edited by R. Westgate, N. R. E. Fisher, and J. Whitley, pp. 243–249. British School at Athens Studies 15. British School at Athens, London.

Lynch, K. M. 2011 *The Symposium in Context: Pottery from a Late Archaic House near the Athenian Agora*. Hesperia Supplement 46. American School of Classical Studies at Athens, Princeton.

Makaronas, Ch., and E. Giouri. 1989 Οἱ Οἰκίες Ἀρπαγῆς τῆς Ἑλένης καὶ Διονύσου τῆς Πέλλας. Βιβλιοθήκη τῆς ἐν Ἀθήναις Ἀρχαιολογικῆς Ἑταιρείας 109. Archaeological Society of Athens, Athens.

Mazarakis Ainian, A. 1997 *From Rulers' Dwellings to Temples: Architecture, Religion, and Society in Early Iron Age Greece (1100–700 B.C.)*. Studies in Mediterranean Archaeology 121. Paul Åströms Förlag, Jonsered.

Mazarakis Ainian, A. 2007 Architecture and Social Structure in Early Iron Age Greece. In *Building Communities: House, Settlement, and Society in the Aegean and Beyond*, edited by

R. Westgate, N. R. E. Fisher, and J. Whitley, pp. 157–168. British School at Athens Studies 15. British School at Athens, London.

Morris, I. 2000 *Archaeology as Cultural History: Words and Things in Iron Age Greece*. Blackwell, Oxford.

Morris, I. 2004 Economic Growth in Ancient Greece. *Journal of Institutional and Theoretical Economics* 160:709–742.

Morris, I. 2005 Archaeology, Standards of Living, and Greek Economic History. In *The Ancient Economy: Evidence and Models*, edited by J. G. Manning and I. Morris, pp. 91–126. Stanford University Press, Stanford.

Mussche, H. F. 1998 *Thorikos: A Mining Town in Ancient Attika*. Fouilles de Thorikos II. Belgian Archaeological School in Greece, Ghent.

Nevett, L. C. 1999 *House and Society in the Ancient Greek World*. Cambridge University Press, Cambridge.

Nevett, L. C. 2000 A Real Estate "Market" in Classical Greece? The Evidence of Town Houses. *Annual of the British School at Athens* 95:329–343.

Nevett, L. C. 2009 Domestic Façades: A "Feature" of the Urban Landscape of Greek Poleis? In *Inside the City in the Greek World: Studies of Urbanism from the Bronze Age to the Hellenistic Period*, edited by S. Owen and L. Preston, pp. 118–130. Oxbow, Oxford.

Nevett, L. C. 2010 *Domestic Space in Classical Antiquity*. Cambridge University Press, Cambridge.

Nielsen, I. 1999 *Hellenistic Palaces: Tradition and Renewal*. 2nd ed. Aarhus University Press, Aarhus.

Ober, J. 2010 Wealthy Hellas. *Transactions of the American Philological Society* 140:241–286.

Ober, J. 2015 *The Rise and Fall of Classical Greece*. Princeton University Press, Princeton.

Page, D. L. 1962 *Poetae Melici Graeci*. Clarendon Press, Oxford.

Rapoport, A. 1990 Systems of Activities and Systems of Settings. In *Domestic Architecture and the Use of Space: An Interdisciplinary Cross-Cultural Study*, edited by S. Kent, pp. 9–20. Cambridge University Press, Cambridge.

Reber, K. 1998 *Eretria, Ausgrabungen und Forschungen X: Die klassischen und hellenistischen Wohnhäuser im Westquartier*. Éditions Payot, Lausanne.

Robinson, D. M. 1946 *Excavations at Olynthus, Part XII: Domestic and Public Architecture*. Johns Hopkins University Press, Baltimore.

Robinson, D. M., and J. W. Graham 1938 *Excavations at Olynthus, Part VIII: The Hellenic House*. Johns Hopkins University Press, Baltimore.

Shear, T. L. 1975 The Athenian Agora: Excavations of 1973–1974. *Hesperia* 44:331–374.

Thompson, H. A. 1959 Activities in the Athenian Agora: 1958. *Hesperia* 28:91–108.

Trümper, M. 1998 *Wohnen in Delos: Eine baugeschichtliche Untersuchung zum Wandel der Wohnkultur in hellenistischer Zeit*. Internationale Archäologie 46. Marie Leidorf, Rahden.

Trümper, M. 2003 Wohnen und Arbeiten im hellenistischen Handelshafen Delos. In *Wohnformen und Lebenswelten im interkulturellen Vergleich*, edited by M. Droste and A. Hoffmann, pp. 125–159. Peter Lang, Frankfurt.

Trümper, M. 2005 Modest Housing in Late Hellenistic Delos. In *Ancient Greek Houses and Households: Chronological, Regional, and Social Diversity*, edited by B. A. Ault and L. C. Nevett, pp. 119–139. University of Pennsylvania Press, Philadelphia.

Walter-Karydi, E. 1994 *Die Nobilitierung des Wohnhauses. Lebensform und Architektur im spätklassischen Griechenland*. Xenia 35. Universitätsverlag Konstanz, Konstanz.

Wason, P. K. 1994 *The Archaeology of Rank*. Cambridge University Press, Cambridge.

Westgate, R. 1997–98 Greek Mosaics in their Architectural and Social Context. *Bulletin of the Institute of Classical Studies* 42:93–115.

Westgate, R. 2000 Space and Decoration in Hellenistic Houses. *Annual of the British School at Athens* 95:391–426.

Westgate, R. 2007a The Greek House and the Ideology of Citizenship. *World Archaeology* 39:229–245.

Westgate, R. 2007b House and Society in Classical and Hellenistic Crete: A Case Study in Regional Variation. *American Journal of Archaeology* 111:423–457.

Westgate, R. 2010 Interior Decoration in Hellenistic Houses: Context, Function, and Meaning. In *Städtisches Wohnen im östlichen Mittelmeerraum, 4. Jh. v. Chr.–1. Jh. n. Chr.*, edited by S. Ladstätter and V. Scheibelreiter, pp. 497–528. Archäologische Forschungen 18. Austrian Academy of Sciences, Vienna.

Westgate, R. 2015 Space and Social Complexity in Greece from the Early Iron Age to the Hellenistic Period. *Hesperia* 84:47–95.

Whitley, J. 2009 Crete. In *A Companion to Archaic Greece*, edited by K. A. Raaflaub and H. van Wees, pp. 273–293. Wiley-Blackwell, Chichester/Malden, Massachusetts.

Young, R. S. 1951 An Industrial District of Ancient Athens. *Hesperia* 20:135–288.

CHAPTER FOURTEEN

Mapping Inequality in Ancient Greece

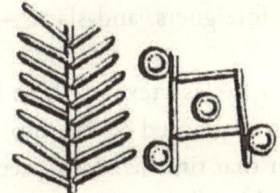

Rachel Zelnick-Abramovitz

Abstract   *This paper tries to "map" inequality in ancient Greece by tracing the situations where categories of noncitizens would be, and are mentioned, and the boundaries delineated thereby between statuses. This is done by looking at allusions to noncitizens (slaves and free noncitizens) in literary and epigraphic sources and comparing the picture emerging from this inspection with images of noncitizens (especially slaves) in vase painting and statues. It is argued that while in the visual arts it is often difficult to tell slaves and free noncitizens from citizens and slaves are often depicted as an integral part of the life of the polis, in literary and epigraphic sources the status of a person can hardly be mistaken: we recognize inequality because it is opposed to the dominant group.*

SURVEYING THE SURFACE: LINES AND BLURS

Sometime between 403 and 386 BC, an Athenian citizen prosecuted Pankleōn on an unknown charge before the Polemarch, the archon responsible for receiving and dealing with prosecutions against metics, namely, free noncitizen residents.[1] Pankleōn reacted by counterprosecuting the Athenian in an *antigraphē* (a special plea), on the grounds that the latter's action was inadmissible since he, Pankleōn, was no metic but had Athenian citizenship on account of his being a Plataean: in 427 BC, after the destruction of their city by Thebes, refugees from Plataea who chose to remain in Athens had received Athenian citizenship. This case is known to us from the defense speech written by the orator Lysias for the Athenian citizen in answer to Pankleōn's *antigraphē* (Lysias, Oration 23, *Against Pankleōn*). The Athenian recounts how he made inquiries in order to verify Pankleōn's claim that he had citizen, not metic, status; instead, he found out that two different people asserted that Pankleōn was their slave and tried to seize him and carry him away.

This case seems to convey two contradictory things. On the one hand, statuses in classical Athens were demarcated by clear-cut boundaries. We see this manifested in the reference to Athenian-born citizens, to naturalized citizens (the Plataeans), to metics, and to slaves. These statuses have different rights, as the classification of judicial proceedings shows, and slaves are sharply contrasted to free people by being subject to abduction.[2] On the other hand, in a relatively big city such as Athens a person's status might appear ambiguous, and he or she could be regarded by others as a metic, a citizen, or a slave.

Pankleōn's case, like other such cases (see below), raises one of the thorny questions regarding ancient Greek society: Were there clear status boundaries in classical Athens? That is, were citizens distinguished from noncitizens—metics, visiting foreigners, and slaves— and if so, how?

Prima facie, the answer to this question seems obvious from Lysias's text itself: as I noted, since the speaker mentions citizens (whether Athenian-born or granted citizenship), metics, and slaves, these three statuses at least must have existed at that time as recognized and applied categories, each with its individual set of privileges and liabilities. One way of reading this oration is to draw attention to the speaker's attempts to verify Pankleōn's actual status and point to the importance attached to legal status by the Athenians and their political and legal institutions: metics were judged by different law courts from those for citizens; citizenship was a hereditary privilege or one granted by the Athenian people; slaves had no legal personality and could be seized and dragged away, or else needed a citizen to assert their free status. Hence, it was important to ascertain one's status. But it is also possible to read this oration as demonstrating the fuzziness of status boundaries and as divulging the fact that in daily life legal status played a minor role, and people of different statuses mingled and worked together in shared spaces or spheres of activities.

These two readings reflect two approaches in modern scholarship. One approach, based on statements by the ancient Greeks themselves, emphasizes legal differences, and its proponents usually speak of three distinct legal statuses: citizens, metics, and slaves;[3] the other approach argues for the existence of a greater variety of statuses and puts more weight on the vagueness of legal boundaries and on the interaction and collaboration among statuses.[4] If the former reading should guide us, what should we make of such cases as that of Pankleōn? If the other reading is correct, how was it possible to tell citizens, metics, and slaves apart? How can we, today, perceive inequality in ancient Athens and elsewhere in the Greek world?

I shall return later to Pankleōn's case and the legal position of noncitizens. But it should be stated at the outset that different sources of information give different pictures of noncitizens' position in society, in Athens as well as other poleis. It will be argued here that status boundaries are clearer in literary and epigraphic sources than in material evidence or, for that matter, in reality.

THE VISUAL ARTS: PORTRAYING STATUSES

Looking at vase paintings, gravestone reliefs, and statues, we are seldom able to tell noncitizens from citizens. Scholars have suggested markers that might help us to identify slaves in Greek art. For example, Kelly Wrenhaven lists small size, nakedness, and barbarian features—sometimes combined with certain activities, which were conceived as servile or lowly (Wrenhaven 2012:43–89). Ingomar Weiler draws attention to the fact that in classical art and literature representations of slaves are an inversion of the characteristics that those who generate the evidence see as socially ideal. Since the identification of the free citizen was with the adult male Greek speaker, the warrior and the athlete, the slave was depicted as ugly or even deformed (slaves were excluded from the gymnasium). Slave status was believed to be accompanied by physical, and by implication also moral, inferiority (Weiler 2002). Sandra Karlsson takes for granted that figures expressing grief on grave reliefs are more likely to be representations of slaves or servants, especially since these figures have smaller stature (Karlsson 2014:50, 208, 211, 217).

But, as Sean Lewis cogently comments, such lists of status signifiers are rather misleading: small size might signify other low statuses or even children. Depictions of activities might also mislead: manual labor can signify slaves—and metics—but also citizens of low economic class. Certain garments were thought typical of slaves, but were also worn by free country people. Although sometimes people depicted on vases can be identified as slaves by their physical attributes (for example, tattoos for Thracians), these too cannot serve as unequivocal indicators of status (Lewis 1998/9:77–83).[5] Moreover, slaves are also often depicted as an integral part of the life of the polis—sometimes even heroized. Categories of status are thus blurred. The only safe indicator is when the artist labels a figure as slave—as attested on a late-fourth-century red-figure *krater*, describing the killing of Thersites.[6] Here, the inscription *dmōs*, a Homeric term for household slaves, above a naked figure is a safe indication that this figure represents a slave. Wrenhaven, who discusses this vase painting, nonetheless identifies other details in it that contribute to the identification of this figure as a slave: vulnerability expressed by his nakedness, lack of a weapon (in contrast to the other figures in the scene), and his stature, which she interprets as expressing fear (Wrenhaven 2012:78–79 with Fig. 2). But she recognizes that these markers are not always reliable signs and that some slaves are depicted in a more idealizing light, reflecting their benefit to their masters or accentuating the high social position of the latter (Wrenhaven 2012:62–63, 77–78).

In contrast, literary and epigraphic sources usually make a clear distinction between statuses. Habitually, slaves and free noncitizens are identified as such or presented as distinct groups, as against citizens. Hence, the status of a person mentioned in written texts can hardly be mistaken: we recognize inequality because it stands out in opposition to the dominant group and its ideology.

EPITAPHS: EQUAL IN DEATH?

The following example is an epitaph from Athens, engraved on a tombstone erected by Hippostratē in honor of her former wet nurse, Melitta:

IG II[2] 7873; Attica, after mid-fourth century BC:
>   Melitta, the daughter of Apollodorus the *isotelēs*.
>   A wet nurse.
> Here the earth covers the good (*chrēstē*) wet nurse of Hippostratē, and now she longs for you.
> I have loved you while you were alive, (my) wet nurse, and now—though you are beneath the

> earth—I still honor you, and will honor you as long as I live. And I know that even beneath
> the earth, if there is reward for the good—to you, nurse, as the first and foremost, honors are
> reserved by Persephonē and Plouto.

Now, Melitta's father, Apollodorus, is here described as *isotelēs*, literally: "paying equal taxes." This was a clear indication of his—hence, also her—status as a privileged metic, to whom the polis has granted the privilege of paying the same taxes as citizens.[7] In practice, this meant that he was exempt from paying the *metoikion,* a tax imposed on metics in Athens.[8] Hence, being granted the status of *isoteleia* was a token of honor, and those who became *isoteleis* made a point of noting their privileged status on their tombstones, as did Apollodorus, Mellita's father. On the other hand, this term also announced to the world Apollodorus's noncitizen status. Despite the warm feelings, which Hippostratē evidently had for Melitta, the latter's occupation[9] and her father's status are clear signifiers of her noncitizen status. If it hadn't been for her father's status, we might even consider the possibility that she was a slave, because of her description as *chrēstē* ("good" or "useful")—an epithet frequently applied to slaves in grave inscriptions.[10]

In fact, although wet nursing was not an occupation confined to slaves, most—if not all—women identified on tombstones as wet nurses probably were slaves.[11] But even as metics, that is, *free* women, wet nurses were inferior to women of citizen status, who themselves were inferior to men. Moreover, free women of citizen status who worked outside the home were typically of low economic class and were driven by poverty to help support their families. This was the case described by Euxitheos, who delivered a defense speech written for him by Demosthenes against the charge of pretending to be an Athenian citizen. One of the allegations hurled at Euxitheos as a proof of his noncitizen status was that his mother was a wet nurse and a ribbon seller (Dem. 57.44–45). Euxitheos claims that although wet nursing is a lowly occupation, free people are often compelled by poverty to do lowly and *servile* acts:

> For, as I am informed, many women have become nurses and laborers at the loom or in the
> vineyards owing to the misfortunes of the city in those days, women of civic birth, too; and
> many who were poor then are now rich.[12]

Wet nursing being considered a low profession, relatives of deceased women of citizen status would hardly be likely to note it on their tombstones as their occupation (Wrenhaven 2012:94). Moreover, many of those who are so identified on their gravestones bear foreign names. Therefore, such descriptions must be seen as referring to women of noncitizen status. Still, the ambiguity concerning their exact status—slaves or metics—again shows that status boundaries were blurred. Melitta's epitaph is unique in stating her father's legal status, but even in her case doubts exist.

But except for clear-cut cases like that of Melitta, it is not easy to distinguish foreigners with metic status from other noncitizens. Grave inscriptions, from many parts of the Greek world, often consist of only the name of the deceased, without any further status indication such as patronymics or ethnics. In such cases it is difficult to tell citizens, free foreigners, and slaves apart. It has been suggested that simple graves belonged to the less well-to-do, but these could be citizens or noncitizens.[13] Sometimes, however, epitaphs do impart clear information. The two epitaphs below, for example—one found in Epidauros, the other in Phistyon (Aetolia)—commemorate *apeleutheroi,* freedmen:

> a. *IG* IV² 1, 357; Epidauros, after ca. 200 BC:
> Iason, the freedman (*apeleutheros*) of Kallikon.

> b. *IG* IX, 1² 1:114; Phistyon, undated:
> Euporos, the freedman (*apeleutheros*) of Epinikos, 53 years old, farewell.

These epitaphs, like others commemorating freedmen, show that *apeleutheroi* constituted a distinct legal category. The term informed passers-by that the person buried there was once a slave, now free, yet not a citizen and often legally inferior to metics. The more orthodox view is that upon manumission slaves entered the metic status and there was no difference between the two groups.[14] Yet inscriptions like those quoted above make it quite clear that being described as *apeleutheros* indicated a separate legal category.

But unlike Melitta's father, whose status as an *isotelēs* was a mark of honor, hence worth advertising on his daughter's gravestone (and probably on his own), it is less clear why those erecting the gravestones of freedmen considered it important to do so, with this attesting to the deceased's former servile status. One possible explanation is that the deceased themselves, or their relatives, wished to broadcast the fact that they were slaves no longer; but this term also declared one's servile origin. Another possibility is that these gravestones were set up by the former masters of the deceased, who by noting the latter's status indicated their ongoing relationship with their former slaves—either affectionate gratitude to a loyal slave or a sign of continuing obligations due from the freedman to their ex-owner (Zelnick-Abramovitz 2005:117–119).

Public Inscriptions: Publicizing Inequality

Inscriptions often are our evidence for the social and legal stratification of the population in a given polis. For example, in early third-century BC Coresia, on the island of Ceos, regulations were set up regarding public sacrifices and feasts organized for the polis by benefactors. An inscription names the groups that may take part in the sacrificial feast:

> *IG* XII(5), 647 (= Sokolowski, *LSCG* 98), lines 9–11:
> And the citizens and those whom the polis invited will partake of the feast, and also the metics and *apeleutheroi* (freedmen), as many as pay taxes in Coresia.

Although people of all the named categories—citizens, metics, and *apeleutheroi*—were equally invited to take part in the feast, the careful listing of the various statuses attests to clear legal divisions and implies that in other, not festive, circumstances metics and freedmen were considered unequal to citizens.

Such status distinctions in seemingly equalizing occasions were also maintained later, as we see in two inscriptions from Sillyon in Pamphylia (Asia Minor) commemorating the donations given by the wealthy woman Mēnodōra, daughter of Megakles. Mēnodōra belonged to a prominent family. In the first inscription, probably from the third century AD, the Council of Elders and the Demos honor Mēnodōra, listing her titles and services to the polis, and then enumerate the donations by her and the groups that are to benefit:

> IGRR III, 801, lines 19–22:
> [T]o each citizen nine denarii, to *vindictarii* and *apeleutheroi* and *paroikoi* three denarii each.

The beneficiaries in this inscription include citizens; *vindictarii*, that is, slaves manumitted by the Roman mode of manumission called *vindicta*;[15] *apeleutheroi*, that is, slaves manumitted the Greek way; and *paroikoi*—residents without citizenship.

The second inscription, of approximately the same period, lists citizens, graded according to age and political position, women of citizen status, *vindictarii*, and *apeleutheroi* as the beneficiaries of money distributions:

> IGRR III, 802, lines 20–26:
> [A]nd to each old man 81 denarii and one measure of grain, and to each member of the *ekklēsia* 78 denarii and one measure of grain, and to their wives three denarii each, and to the *vindictarii* and the *apeleutheroi* four denarii each.

In both inscriptions donations are graded according to status.

We see similar classification and legal definitions, but in a different context and for different reasons, in an inscription from Pergamon, dated to 133 BC. Following the death of Attalus III, king of Pergamon (who bequeathed his kingdom to Rome) and the revolt of Aristonicus, a claimant to the throne, the polis Pergamon issued a decree granting citizenship to several groups of noncitizens "for the common safety":

> OGIS 338 (= *I. von Pergamon* 249), lines 10–25:
> With good fortune, it is resolved by the people to grant citizenship to those mentioned below: to those registered in the lists of the *paroikoi*, to the soldiers who are settled in the city and in the countryside, and likewise to the Macedonians and the Mysians and to the *katoikoi* (settlers) who are registered in the citadel and in the old city, and to the Masdyeni and to . . . guards and the other mercenaries who are settled or own property in the city or the countryside, and likewise to their wives and children. The freedmen *(exeleutheroi)* and the king's slaves will be transferred to the status of *paroikoi* . . . and similarly the public slaves.

The population of Pergamon is seen to have been very heterogeneous, consisting of various statuses: citizens, free noncitizen foreigners of different kinds, including soldiers (*paroikoi, katoikoi,* specific ethnic groups, and mercenaries), freed slaves (*exeleutheroi*), and slaves—themselves classified as private, royal, and public. All these statuses are mentioned in an official document because it was decided to upgrade them in face of the military danger.

Likewise, an inscription from Ephesos, dated to 86 BC, records an appeal to the noncitizen population to enroll and fight for the polis on the side of the Romans and against Mithridates VI king of Pontus, who had conquered Asia Minor. In return for joining the citizens in fighting, they were promised citizenship.

Syll.[3] 742 (= *I. Ephesos* 8), lines 44–46:
And also the *isoteleis,* the *paroikoi,* the *hieroi,* the *exeleutheroi,* and the *xenoi,* as many as will take up arms and enlist with the leaders, all of them will be citizens on equal terms . . .

Five categories are mentioned here: *isoteleis,* who—like Melitta's father mentioned in the Attic grave inscription cited above—were probably privileged metics; *paroikoi,* who seem to have been the free rural population with some political rights; *hieroi,* possibly, but not certainly, free inhabitants who farmed the sacred land of Artemis; *exeleutheroi,* the freedmen; and *xenoi,* alien residents in Ephesos.[16]

As in the above-cited inscription from Pergamon, the precise and detailed classification of the population of Ephesos derives from military needs and the pressing circumstances: each volunteer was to register with the leaders, thus had to declare his legal status; hence, we may assume that this information was checked—probably against lists recording the names of citizens and noncitizens in Ephesos. So this inscription provides us with striking evidence about the social and legal stratification in first-century BC Ephesos and, perhaps, also about existing registers of residents of Ephesos.[17]

LAWS AND REGULATIONS: UNEQUAL PENALTIES

Social differentiation is also patent in punitive clauses of laws and regulations. Citizens and noncitizens were liable to different penalties. A very fragmentary inscription from Athens attests to the flogging of defaulting metics and slaves, whereas citizens seem to be liable to monetary fines.

IG II[2] 380, lines 34–43 (Piraeus, 320/19 BC):
No one is allowed to throw out earth or anything else whatsoever, nor dung . . . anywhere in the *agora* or in the streets. And should anyone do any of these things, if he is a slave or a metic he will receive [—] lashes; if free (citizen?) [. . .].

A fourth-century BC text ascribed to Aristotle lists separate legal procedures for noncitizens in Athens:

[Aristotle], *The Athenian Constitution,* 57.3; 58.2–3:
Trials for deliberate murder and wounding are held in the Areopagus . . . whereas involuntary homicide and plotting to murder, and murder of a slave or a metic or foreigner *(xenos),* come before the court at the Palladium. . . . Only private lawsuits are brought before him (that is, the Polemarch) in which metics, *isoteleis,* and foreign consuls *(proxenoi)* are concerned. (Trans. H. Rackham)[18]

Likewise, a small tablet (undated) from Lamia in Thessaly that warns against trespassing establishes different penalties for different statuses.

IG IX(2) 1358:
No one is allowed to pass through the stadium, nor drive a beast of burden. Penalty—10 drachmae; for a slave—a flogging.

Literary Texts: The Reality of Everyday Life

I began this paper by citing Oration no. 23 of Lysias and the case of Pankleōn, and I would like to return to the issues it raises. As we saw, Pankleōn was considered a citizen, a metic, and a slave. We may never know what his status really was, but this speech makes clear, on the one hand, that statuses in classical Athens were explicitly demarcated and that metics and slaves had no equal share in citizens' political and legal rights. Since the defendant thought that Pankleōn was a metic, he prosecuted him before the court of the Polemarch, which dealt with *non*citizens; people who claimed that Pankleōn was their slave exercised physical force in an attempt to drag him away—an action he could prevent only by the intervention of a citizen on his behalf who would assert his free status.[19] On the other hand, this speech, like many other literary texts, reveals that in reality it was often difficult to distinguish a citizen from a slave or a metic, and that one's status in Athens was often challenged.

In another forensic speech, Aeschines, prosecuting Timarchos in 346 BC (Oration no. 1), narrates events connected with Pittalakos, a man he describes as a public slave; but this public slave is also said to have brought an action against two citizens—an act denied him as a slave. One of these two citizens he prosecuted retaliates by claiming that Pittalakos is his *private* slave. In response, Pittalakos procures the help of a third citizen who asserts his freedom. If we are to understand this speech literally, Pittalakos was living and working in Athens as a public slave but conducted himself as a free man, while at the same time he was claimed as a *private* slave. This confusing situation and Pittalakos's uncertain status have bewildered generations of scholars, some seeing this case as proof of slaves' power in Athens (Cohen 2003 [2000]:130–141) or their social integration (Vlassopoulos 2007:35; 2009:351–352), others pointing out the vagueness with which orators referred to statuses (Todd 195:193–4) or the way orators deliberately referred to freed slaves as still being slaves (Kamen 2009). It is nevertheless obvious that the Athenians were familiar with such unclear situations.

A famous condemnation of this blurring of status boundaries is voiced by the so-called Old Oligarch, in a text probably written in mid-fifth century BC Athens:

> "The Old Oligarch," *Constitution of the Athenians*, 1.10:
> Now, among the slaves and metics at Athens there is the greatest uncontrolled wantonness; you can't hit them there, and a slave will not stand aside for you. . . . If it were customary for a slave (or metic or freedman) to be struck by one who is free, you would often hit an Athenian citizen by mistake on the assumption that he was a slave. For the people there are no better dressed than the slaves and metics, nor are they any more handsome. (Trans. E. C. Marchant)

In Athens, argues the author, a citizen is easily mistaken for a slave because physical appearance and attire are no firm signifiers (Vlassopoulos 2007:34–35; Vlassopoulos 2009:357)! Yet, the fact that such statuses are mentioned indicates that in the context of law, there were clear status definitions with their known liabilities and rights, as is also made clear by other texts (for instance, Thucydides 1.143.1, Isokrates 8.21 and 53, and Andokides 1.144).

CONCLUSIONS: DRAWING THE MAP

This brings us back to representations of slaves and metics in the visual arts. If these do not allow an easy distinction between statuses, the reason perhaps is that in daily life, metics, slaves, and citizens worked side by side and often shared similar concepts and beliefs (Vlassopoulos 2007; 2009). This must have been true not only in Athens, for which we have the testimony of the Orators and the "Old Oligarch." In large commercial and cultural centers such as Pergamon and Ephesos, with their manifold fabric of population, citizens, free noncitizen residents, freed slaves, slaves, and other shades of statuses undoubtedly worked together and interacted on a daily basis.

In his article on Aristotle's *Politics* and Athenian citizenship, Charles W. Hedrick soundly observes:

> The society of the ancient Greek polis is dominated by the citizen, the politēs. . . . Other statuses of the person within the state, judged against this great autonomous standard, are peripheral, contingent, imperfect, defective. Their qualities are not characterized as positive and inherent—in a word, autonomous—as are those of the citizen but are typically defined in negative terms: they are as a group, to use a common modern term, "noncitizens." At the same time, however, the identity of the citizen is bound up with the exclusion and domination of noncitizens: citizens are defined in opposition to those who are not citizens, so their very self-conception, their freedom and equality, is at stake when the social discrimination between citizen and noncitizen is violated. Noncitizens are necessary to citizens because they are the immediate and specific manifestation of what citizenship is not. (Hedrick 1994:293)

So in the daily life of Athens, and probably of other big cities, people of all statuses formed "mixed and interacting cultures in collaboration and conflict," made possible by the existence of "free spaces" in democratic Athens;[20] and sometimes it was hard to tell a slave or a metic from a citizen. Nevertheless, status distinctions, which were the manifestation of inequality, did exist and were exhibited and actuated when needed.

To see and map out inequalities, then, we must look at the "sites" where these are likely to be revealed and emphasized: political decisions, laws, regulations, grave inscriptions, literary texts, including drama, where people are differentiated by their legal status. In short, we must look at situations where noncitizens are contrasted with citizens or—as in the case of donations made to the whole population—where noncitizens are exceptionally and temporarily put on par with citizens because of a special event.

To demonstrate this mixture of strict status definitions with the everyday loosening of boundaries we should look at the official Building Accounts of the Erechtheion in Athens. These are long inscriptions, listing the kinds of work done, the workers, and the money paid to them by the state officials. There we find citizens, metics, and slaves working together, often doing the same work (cf. Epstein 2010).

IG I^3 476, lines 159–162, 205 (Athens, 408/7 B.C.):
Phyromachos of the deme kephisia—the youth near the corslet: 10 dr.

Praxias, who resides in the deme Melita—the horse and the figure striking it from behind: 120 dr.
. . . .
Sosandros, who belongs to Simias: 10 dr. and 5 obols.

Although the workers' statuses are nowhere named, other signifiers are at play: citizens are described as *members* of a deme (for example, Phyromachus *of* the deme Kephisia); metics as *residing* in a deme (for example, Praxias *residing* in Melita); and slaves as *belonging* to their owners (for example, Sosandros *of* Simias). Epigraphic and literary texts thus stick to formal, legal distinctions; the visual arts may reflect everyday practices.

NOTES

1.   Metics were free immigrant foreigners. In Athens, metics were liable to a special tax (the *metoikion*) and had to be represented by an Athenian citizen; they were barred from participation in the political institutions; their private suits were overseen by a special magistrate, and the murder of a metic was considered as second-degree murder; they could not own houses or land, except as a special grant of privilege. On metics in Athens see Whitehead 1977; Patterson 2000; Niku 2007; Blok 2017, 265–275.

2.   On the statuses and legal procedures involved in the case described by this oration, see Todd 1993, 167–170. When a person's free status was challenged, he could have been subject to abduction; in such a case a procedure called *aphairesis eis eleutherian* ("taking away to freedom") was available to him or her, whereby a citizen asserted his or her free status by a symbolic act of dragging away the contested person and defending this action in court; see Harrison 1968, 178–179; Todd 1993, 187, 192; Zelnick-Abramovitz 2005, 292–300; and see also below.

3.   Hansen 1991, 116–120; Todd 1993, 170–200; Hedrick 1994:298–301 lists slaves, women, and metics as the major categories of noncitizens in Athens, though he recognizes the existence of some "less prominent others." See also Ober 1998, 301–309 on those excluded from citizenship according to Aristotle's *Politics*.

4.   Westermann 1945, and, more fully, Finley 1960 and 1964, argued for a spectrum of statuses. See also Bearzot 2005. A recent full discussion of the variety of statuses in relation to Athenian civic ideology is Kamen 2013. Vlassopoulos 2009 argues that citizens, metics, and slaves in Athens formed mixed and interacting cultures in collaboration and conflict. Cf. Taylor 2017, 240.

5.   See also Karlsson, 220, acknowledging that it is often difficult to distinguish children from figures of servile status in grave reliefs, but claiming that in reliefs from Smyrna and Kyzikos these two statuses are easily distinguishable.

6.   The *krater* (now in the Boston Museum of Fine Arts, 03.804) is attributed to the Varrese Painter, ca. 340 B.E. It presents a different version of thersites's story: Achilles killed him for having torn out the eyes of the Amazon Penthesilea, whom the hero had just killed in combat.

7.   On the privilege of *isoteleia* see Whitehead 1977, 11–13; Niku 2004:80–85.

8.   On the *metoikion* see Whitehead 1977, 75–77; Niku 2004:79–80.

9.   Wet nurses were often slaves, but when manumitted they may have practiced their former occupation. See B. MacLachlan 2012, 75–76; Wrenhaven 2012, 93–100.

10. It is, of course, possible that Melitta's father was a former slave and that she had been manumitted later than her father. On the epithet *chrēstē* as signifying slaves see Kosmopoulou 2001, 290–291; Taylor 2017, 227–229.

11. On wet nurses on tombstones and in Athenian art and their status see Kosmopoulou 2001, 285–292; Wrenhaven 2012, 92–100; Taylor 135–140.

12. Demosthenes 57.45 (translated by Norman W. DeWitt and Norman J. DeWitt). The speaker probably refers to economic troubles in Athens after the Peloponnesian War. On women forced by poverty to work outside the home see also Aristophanes, *Thesmophoriazusai*, 446–449. Xenophon, *Memorabilia*, 2.7.1–12 is often presented as another such example, but there Arsitarchos uses his female relatives' weaving skills to earn a living by making them work at home.

13. See Fraser 1957; Fraser 1977, 46–56; and Fraser 1995, on graves of noncitizens, including slaves and metics (some of whom may have been freedmen). See also Nielsen 1989; Bäbler 1998, 55–66, on burials of slaves.

14. For the orthodox view see, e.g., Clerc 1893, 286–288; Beauchet 1897, 480–481; Calderini 1908, 307; Whitehead 1977, 16–17; Todd 1993, 174. That freed slaves and metics constituted separate statuses is argued by Harrison, 1968, 181, 187–188 (with some reservations); Zelnick-Abramovitz 2005; Bearzot 2005; Dimopoulou-Piliouni 2008.

15. *Manumissio vindicta* was one of the two formal modes of manumission at Rome that led to the slave becoming a citizen, with some limitation (the other mode being by testament). This mode of liberation entailed the fictitious assertion before a magistrate of the slave's freedom (*vindicatio in libertatem*), followed by a symbolic act where some citizen (*adsertor libertatis*) touched the slave with a stick (*vindicta*), and said that the slave was a free man.

16. See Herz 2001, 185–207; he argues that the *exeleutheroi* were descendants of freedmen.

17. Describing the battle between the Alexander the Great and the Thebans, Diodorus Siculus recounts how the Thebans stationed their freed slaves, the refugees, and the metics to face those who assailed the wall (17.11.2). For other examples of status distinctions see *IG* XII(5) 721 from Andros (first century B.C.), lines 17–19, 25–29, mentioning *paroikoi*, *apeleutheroi*, and passing foreigners. Also, in a papyrus from Oxyrhynchus in Egypt (*P.Oxy.* III 480, lines 11–13; A.D. 132) a distinction is made among foreigners (*epixenoi*), Romans, citizens of Alexandria, Egyptians, and freedmen (*apeleutheroi*). Plutarch, in *Quaestiones Graecae* 49, recounts a story how most of the women in Chalcedon were forced to consort with freedmen and metics because there was a great scarcity in the city of men lost in war.

18. See also Plato, *Laws*, 914a, b.

19. On this action, called in Greek *aphairesis eis eleutherian* ("taking away for the purpose of freedom"), see n. 2 above and Zelnick-Abramovitz 2005, 292–300.

20. This is the term used by Vlassopoulos 2007, borrowing the expression from S. M. Evans and H. C. Boyte, *Free Spaces: The Sources of Democratic Change in America* (New York, 1986), to describe areas of activity that brought together citizens, metics, slaves, and women; they "created common experiences and interactions, and shaped new forms of identity" (38). Such spaces were the agora, the workplace, the tavern, the house, the trireme, and the cemetery. On the important role of women in Athens, see Blok 2017, Chapter 5.

REFERENCES

Bäbler, B. 1998 *Fleissige Thrakerinnen und wehrhafte Skythen. Nichtgriechischen im klassischen Athen und ihre archäologische Hinterlassenschaft*. B.G. Teubner, Stuttgart and Leipzig.

Bearzot, C. 2005 Né cittadini né stranieri: apeleutheroi e nothoi in Atene. In *Il cittadino, lo straniero, il barbaro, fra integrazione ed emarginazione nell'antichità*. Atti del I Incontro Internazionale di Storia antica, Genova, 22–24 maggio 2003. Serta Antiqua et Mediaevalia, VII, edited by M. G. Angeli Bertinelli and A. Donati, pp. 77–92. Giorgio Bretschneider, Roma.

Beauchet, L. 1897 *Histoire du droit privé de la république athénienne, Vol. II*. Chevalier-Marescq, Paris.

Blok, J. 2017 *Citizenship in Classical Athens*. Cambridge University Press, Cambridge.

Calderini, A. 1908 *La manomissione e la condizione dei liberti in Grecia*. U. Hoelpi, Milano.

Clerc, M. 1893 *Les métèques athéniens*. Thorin, Paris.

Cohen, E. 2003 *The Athenian Nation*. Princeton University Press, Princeton.

Dimopoulou-Piliouni, A. 2005 Apeleutheroi: Metics or Foreigners? *Dike* 11:27–50.

Epstein, Sh. 2010 Attic Public Construction: Who Were the Builders? *Ancient Society* 40:1–14.

Finley, M. I. 1981 The Servile Statuses of Ancient Greece. In *Economy and Society in Ancient Greece*, edited by B. D. Shaw and R. P. Saller, pp. 133–149. Chatto and Windus, London.

Finley, M. I. 1981 Between Slavery and Freedom. In *Economy and Society in Ancient Greece*, edited by B. D. Shaw and R. P. Saller, pp.116–132. Chatto and Windus, London.

Fraser P. M., and T. Rönne 1957 *Boeotian and West Greek Tombstones*. C. W. K. Gleerup, Lund.

Fraser, P. M. 1977 *Rhodian Funerary Monuments*. Oxford University Press, Oxford.

Fraser, P. M. 1995 Citizens, Demesmen, and Metics in Athens and Elsewhere. In *Sources for Ancient Greek City-State*, edited by M. H. Hansen, pp. 64–90. Munksgaard, Copenhagen.

Hansen, M. H. 1991 *The Athenian Democracy in the Age of Demosthenes: Structure, Principles, and Ideology*. Translated by J. A. Crook. Basil Blackwell, Oxford.

Harrison, A. R. W. 1968 *The Law of Athens. Vol. I*. Second Edition. Gerald Duckworth, London.

Hedrick, C. W. 1994 The Zero Degree of Society: Aristotle and Athenian Citizen. In *Athenian Political Thought and the Reconstruction of American Democracy*, edited by J. P. Euben, J. R. Wallach, and J. Ober, pp. 289–318. Cornell University Press, Ithaca.

Herz, P. 2001 Das Bürgerrechtsdekret von Ephesos: Inschriften von Ephesos 8. Gedanken zur Gesellschaft im spatrepublikanischen Kleinasien. In *Fünfzig Jahre Forschungen zur antiken Sklaverei an der Mainzer Akademie, 1950–2000, Miscellanea zum Jubiläum*, edited by H. Bellen and H. Heinen, pp. 185–207. F. Steiner, Stuttgart.

Kamen, D. 2009 Servile Invective in Classical Athens. *Scripta Classica Israelica* 28:43–56.

Kamen, D. 2013 *Status in Classical Athens*. Princeton University Press, Princeton.

Karlsson, S. 2014 *Emotions Carved in Stone? The Social Handling of Death as Expressed on Hellenistic Grave Stelai from Smyrna and Kyzikos*. Dissertation Submitted to the University of Gothenburg.

Kosmopoulou, A. 2001 "Working Women": Female Professionals on Classical Attic Gravestones. *Annual of the British School at Athens* 96:281–319.

Lewis, S. 1998/9 Slaves as Viewers and Users of Athenian Pottery. *Hephaistos* 16/17:71–90.

MacLachlan, B. 2012 *Women in Ancient Greece: A Sourcebook. Bloomsbury Sources in Ancient History*. Continuum, London.

Nielsen, T. H., et al. 1989 Athenian Grave Monuments and Social Class. *Greek, Roman and Byzantine Studies* 30:411–420.

Niku, M. 2004 When and Why Did the Athenian μετοικία System Disappear? The Evidence of Inscriptions. *Arctos* 38:75–93.

Niku, M. 2007 *The Official Status of the Foreign Residents in Athens, 322–120 B.C.* Finnish Institute at Athens, Helsinki.

Ober, J. 1998 *Political Dissent in Democratic Athens. Intellectual Critics of Popular Rule.* Princeton University Press, Princeton.

Patterson, C. 2000 The Hospitality of Athenian Justice: The Metic in Court. In *Law and Social Status in Classical Athens*, edited by V. Hunter and J. Edmondson, pp. 93–112. Oxford University Press, Oxford.

Sokolowski, F. 1969 *Lois sacrées des cités grecques.* Éditions E. de Boccard, Paris.

Taylor, C. 2017 *Poverty, Wealth, and Well-Being: Experiencing Penia in Democratic Athens.* Oxford Scholarship Online. DOI: 10.1093/oso/9780198786931.001.0001.

Todd, S. C. 1993 *The Shape of Athenian Law.* Oxford University Press, Oxford.

Vlassopoulos, K. 2007 Free Spaces: Identity, Experience, and Democracy in Classical Athens. *Classical Quarterly* 57(1):33–52.

Vlassopoulos, K. 2009 Slavery, Freedom, and Citizenship in Classical Athens: Beyond a Legalistic Approach. *European Review of History* 16(3):347–363.

Weiler, I. 2002 Inverted Kalokagathia. In *Representing the Body of the Slave*, edited by T. Wiedeman and J. Gardner, pp. 11–28. Frank Cass, London.

Westermann, W. L. 1945 Between Slavery and Freedom. *American Historical Review* 50:213–227.

Whitehead, D. 1977 *The Ideology of the Athenian Metic.* Cambridge University Press, Cambridge.

Wiedemann T., and J. Gardner (eds.) 2002 *Representing the Body of the Slave.* Frank Cass, London.

Wrenhaven, K. L. 2012 *Reconstructing the Slave: The Image of the Slave in Ancient Greece.* Bristol Classical Press, London.

Zelnick-Abramovitz, R. 2005 *Not Wholly Free. The Concept of Manumission and the Status of Manumitted Slaves in the Ancient Greek World.* Brill, Leiden.

CHAPTER FIFTEEN

Inequality in Republican Rome

Short-term and Long-term Effects of Warfare on the Distribution of Wealth

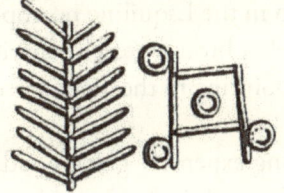

Luuk de Ligt

Abstract   *From the late eighth century BC large discrepancies in wealth, income and political power were hallmarks of Roman society. During the first 250 years of the Roman Republic many of the tensions that resulted from these discrepancies found expression in the so-called struggle of the orders. In this period nonelite citizens obtained some important concessions, such as better legal protection and limited access to newly conquered land, in part by agitation but also because poor and moderately well-off citizens cooperated with wealthy plebeians who were excluded from the highest magistracies. In the long term, however, externalizing social and economic problems through successful warfare proved to be the most effective way of defusing tensions within the citizen body. Large numbers of citizens who had fought in the legions received substantial plots of land in newly conquered territories, and debt-bondsmen of citizen status were replaced by enslaved war captives. Still, members of the economic and political elite consistently managed to capture the lion's share of the spoils of war. We are therefore dealing with a society in which warfare resulted both in a temporary alleviation of economic and social tensions and in a dramatic increase in levels of economic and social inequality.*

INEQUALITY IN REGAL AND EARLY REPUBLICAN ROME

In his account of the events of the year 458 BC, Livy relates how an invasion of Roman territory by the Aequians prompted the Senate to summon Lucius Quinctius Cincinnatus to assume the dictatorship. When envoys were sent to inform Cincinnatus of this decision, they found him working his small farm which consisted of only four *iugera* (1 hectare).

Wiping the sweat from his hands and face, he put on his *toga* and went to the city to assemble an army. Within fifteen days the Aequians were defeated, after which Cincinnatus returned to his ploughing (Livy 3.26.7–10).

Roman authors and readers of the late republican and early imperial periods relished stories about the simple lives some of the most distinguished generals of the early and middle Republic were supposed to have led. In reality, there are strong indications that regal and early-republican Rome was characterized by a high degree of inequality in terms of wealth and income. During the final decades of the eighth century BC, ostentatious burials begin to appear in the cemeteries of Northern Latium, not only at Osteria dell'Osa (c. 18 km east of Rome) and Castel di Decima (c. 18 km south of Rome) but also in the Esquiline necropolis at Rome. The richest graves at Castel di Decima contain jewelry, bronze vessels, chariots, and armor. These finds have convincingly been interpreted as pointing to the emergence of a dominant aristocracy (Holloway 1994; Bietti Sestieri 1997).

In the course of the sixth and fifth centuries, tombs containing expensive grave-goods disappeared. Excavations carried out under the direction of Carandini, however, have revealed that the final decades of the sixth century witnessed the appearance of spacious town houses on the northern slope of the Palatine. These houses clearly were part of a fashionable quarter of the city which was inhabited by elite families (Carandini 1990).

Simultaneously, large rural dwellings begin to appear in the archaeological record. In 1996, deep excavation work for the construction of a new concert hall (the Auditorium) in Rome resulted in the spectacular discovery of an extramural building complex that occupied 330 m^2 in the mid-sixth century BC. In the early fifth century a much larger structure was erected at the site, consisting of a farmhouse occupying 338 m^2 and another complex with coarser walls, which occupied 240 m^2. The latter building has been identified as the "servile quarters" of the farmhouse, but its exact function remains a matter of dispute (Capogrossi Colognesi 2006:575).

Both the sixth-century building and its fifth-century successor are much larger than ordinary rural dwellings of this period and are also of much better quality. The closest parallel for the complex unearthed at the Auditorium site in its second phase is a rural structure that was discovered a bit farther to the north, at Grottarossa. This structure occupied 300 m^2. Its dating is not entirely clear, but some of the associated material belongs to the sixth or fifth century BC (Terrenato 2001). In any case, the rural complexes at the Auditorium site and at Grottarossa can confidently be identified as elite residences.

These recent discoveries strongly support the theory that the disappearance of ostentatious graves during the sixth and fifth centuries reflects a change in funerary practices rather than any decrease in social inequality. From the early sixth century, aristocratic funerals became public rather than private commemorations, causing expenditure to be concentrated on banquets and entertainments rather than on grave-goods (Cornell 1995:108). The Law of the Twelve Tables (450 BC) regulates the conduct of funerals, but contains only one provision concerning grave-goods, namely, a ban on putting gold on the funerary pyre or in the grave (Crawford 1996:710). In all likelihood grave-goods received little attention in these laws because they had become a marginal element of funerary practice.

Various indications contained in the literary sources suggest that in the regal period a small number of aristocratic families, known as the *patres* ("fathers") or "patricians," played a key role in electing a new king after the death of the reigning monarch, although some kind of popular approval seems to have been necessary (Mitchell 2005:134–135). After the expulsion of the last king in around 510 BC, these aristocratic families initially supplied most of the consuls and after 445 BC they monopolized this office completely for more than a century. Exactly how they managed to do this remains unclear. During the Middle and Late Republic the consuls were elected by the *comitia centuriata,* a popular assembly consisting of five property classes. In this assembly, the first class controlled 80 (later 70) votes (out of 193) and the largely aristocratic cavalry another 18.[1] However, up until the final decade of the fifth century BC there seems to have been only one undifferentiated *classis,* composed of those able to afford heavy body armor.[2] It has been speculated that during the first century of the Republic, the Senate, a council dominated by the patricians which functioned as an advisory board for the consuls, preselected the highest magistrates through an internalized process and that in this early period "election" by the *comitia centuriata* meant little more than an act of acclamation (Mouritsen 2015:148). In such a system it would have been relatively easy for the patricians to monopolize access to the consulate.

There can be no doubt that the more developed *comitia centuriata* of the fourth and third centuries was a real "voting assembly."[3] However, since the highest property class, many of whose members must have been patricians, controlled a disproportionate number of votes, this assembly continued to elect patrician consuls until 342 BC (cf. below). Exactly what the *comitia centuriata* looked like during the early decades of the fourth century BC cannot be determined, but in the early third century BC the thresholds for membership of the first to fifth classes were 10,000, 7,500, 5,000, 2,500, and 1,100 bronze coins (*asses*) each of which weighed 324 grams.[4] According to some literary descriptions of the *comitia centuriata,* those whose assets fell short of the threshold for membership of the fifth class, the proletarians, were more numerous than any of the other groups, or even than all the other groups taken together.[5] Yet these poor citizens were given just one vote.

SOCIAL TENSIONS IN EARLY REPUBLICAN ROME, I: LEGAL PROTECTION AND ACCESS TO LAND

Livy's account of the history of early republican Rome is packed with references to tensions between various social groups and to the political conflicts fueled by these tensions. In the scholarly literature, these tensions and conflicts are often grouped together under the somewhat misleading umbrella term "the struggle of the orders."

The surviving sources present the "struggle of the orders" as a conflict, or series of conflicts, between patricians, the hereditary aristocracy of early republican Rome, and "plebeians." Modern scholarship is divided over whether or not the latter term was used to refer to all nonpatricians or to those nonpatricians owning insufficient property to qualify for service in the heavy infantry.[6] The former view seems more likely. If we accept it, the "plebeians" were a heterogeneous group, which included peasants rich enough to equip themselves as hoplites, cottagers owning too little land to support their families, craftsmen, but also some wealthy landowners who did not belong to the hereditary aristocracy.

During the first half of the fifth century the main issues in the conflict of the orders seem to have been the creation and acknowledgment of plebeian magistrates capable of protecting the nonpatrician citizens from arbitrary decisions or actions taken by their social superiors and the creation of written laws defining clear procedures for dealing with various kinds of legal problems, including those arising between creditors and defaulting debtors.

The first aim was achieved in two steps. In 494 BC the plebeians got their own magistrates (the *tribuni plebis*), and in 471 BC a plebeian assembly for electing plebeian officials (the *concilium plebis*) was created (Livy 2.23–33 and 2.54–58). The second objective was realized in 450 BC, when the Law of the Twelve Tables codified some important legal principles and procedures.

From the mid-430s BC the Romans slowly began to expand their territory. In 435 BC the city of Fidenae was besieged and captured, and between 415 and 404 Bola, Ferentinum, Carventum, and Artena fell into Roman hands (Livy 4.49, 4.51, 4.53, 4.61). It cannot be a coincidence that exactly in this period the *concilium plebis* began to pass a series of laws calling for the distribution of newly conquered land (Cornell 1995:269–271). During the early and middle Republic, the Roman government was in the habit of confiscating a certain proportion—sometimes amounting to a full 100 percent—of the lands that had belonged to defeated enemies. In principle, the confiscated land was added to the *ager publicus* (state-owned land), and this type of land could be occupied by any Roman citizen wishing to do so. The ownership of this land continued to rest with the Roman people (*populus Romanus*), but in practice the occupants exercised full control over their allotments and were allowed to pass them on to their heirs (Roselaar 2010). The existence of this practice allowed the patrician elite to establish control over a large proportion of the newly conquered territories. The agrarian laws of the late fifth century BC should be seen as an attempt to give plebeian citizens a larger share in the expanding *ager publicus*.

Since any law passed by the *concilium plebis* needed the senate's confirmation in order to become binding on all Roman citizens (including the patricians), the wave of legislation that can be observed after 424 BC initially produced few results. In 418 BC, however, the Senate decided to forestall agrarian agitation by sending out 1,500 settlers to the territory of Labici. Each settler was given two *iugera* (half a hectare) of land.[7]

In 396 BC, the Romans almost doubled the size of their territory by capturing the neighboring city of Veii. The free inhabitants are said to have been sold into slavery, with the exception of those who had thrown in their lot with the Romans before the fall of the city (Livy 5.22.1 and 6.4.4). Following this success (in 395 BC), the Senate tried to appease social unrest by proposing the settlement of 3,000 colonists on land captured from the Volscians. This time each settler was to receive three and seven-twelfths *iugera* (*c.* 0.85 ha) of land (Livy 5.24).

According to Livy, this proposal did not defuse the situation, since it left the more extensive and more fertile territory of Veii undivided. After further agitation, the Senate gave in (in 393 BC), passing a decree that gave each plebeian, including any children still subject to *patria potestas*, seven *iugera* (1¾ ha) in the newly conquered *ager Veiens*. In his *Universal History*, written between 60 BC and 30 BC, the Greek historian Diodorus reports that the settlers received either four *plethra* or 28 *plethra* (corresponding to four or 28 *iugera*?), without mentioning children as recipients. He must have drawn on other sources, and some specialists think the figure of four *plethra* is more plausible for the early fourth century than the more generous scheme described by Livy.[8] Despite these discrepancies, there can be no doubt that in 393 BC large numbers of nonpatrician citizens benefited from a land distribution scheme that was carried out in the former territory of Veii.

In 385 BC, 2,000 Roman citizens were dispatched to set up a colony at Satricum, where each of them received two and one-half *iugera* (0,63 ha), and two years later commissions were set up to divide the newly conquered *Ager Pomptinus* and to establish a colony at the formerly Etruscan city of Nepet (Livy 6.16 and 6.21).

Another important milestone in the struggle over access to *ager publicus* was the passing of the *Lex Licinia* of 367 BC. This law declared it forbidden for any Roman citizen to "have" or to "possess" more than 500 *iugera* (125 ha) of land. It is not entirely clear whether this law is to be interpreted as referring exclusively to public land or as prescribing a maximum for landholdings of any type (cf. below). On any view, its principal aim must have been to give plebeian citizens a larger share in the spoils of war by preventing the patrician elite from monopolizing access to the expanding *ager publicus*.

Distributions of newly conquered land as well as colonial foundations multiplied during and after the Latin War of 341–338 BC. In 340 BC, Roman citizens were settled on land confiscated from various Latin cities and from Capua, with allotments varying from two to three *iugera* (Livy 8.11.13–14). In 338 BC, more land was distributed in the confiscated parts of the territory of Velitrae (Livy 8.14.7). After the conquest of Sabinum (in 290 BC), the area received an influx of Roman settlers, each of whom is said to have received seven *iugera*.[9] The period between 340 BC and 260 BC also witnessed the foundation of 19 Latin colonies (Cornell 1995:381). The territories of these colonies were not regarded as belonging to the territory of the city of Rome, and those Roman citizens participating in the foundation of Latin colonies lost their Roman citizenship. Interestingly, they received much larger allotments than citizens who were resettled within Roman territory.[10] Part of the explanation must be that assigning large allotments to Latin colonists did not result in any increase of the membership of the third or fourth property classes of the *comitia centuriata*, which remained the most important Roman assembly in this period.

SOCIAL TENSIONS IN EARLY REPUBLICAN ROME, II: ACCESS TO THE CONSULSHIP AND PROTECTION OF DEBTORS

Livy reports that in 376 BC two tribunes of the *plebs*, Gaius Licinius Stolo and Lucius Sextius Lateranus, proposed three laws. The first dealt with debt, and stipulated that debtors should be allowed to subtract from the capital they had borrowed the sums that had been paid as interest, after which they would pay off the remainder in three annual instalments. The second law forbade Roman citizens to possess more than 500 *iugera* of land. The third abolished the election of military tribunes (instead of consuls) and provided that one of the two consuls should be plebeian (Livy 6.35.3–5). According to Livy, the patricians persuaded some of the other tribunes to veto these laws, after which Licinius and Sextius blocked all attempts to elect military tribunes. We are told that the resulting crisis lasted until 367 BC, when the patricians gave up their opposition and the three laws were passed. It is generally agreed that many details of Livy's account (including his claim that the crisis lasted a decade) are fictitious, but the historical reality of the three laws to which he refers is widely admitted.

The exact content of the law dealing with the election of consuls cannot be recovered, but it cannot have stipulated that one of the consuls had to be a plebeian. From the evidence supplied by Livy himself it appears that patrician candidates continued to monopolize the office until 342 BC. Only from that year onward at least one of the consuls was always a plebeian. Perhaps the law of 367 BC provided only that plebeian candidates *could* be elected to the consulship, without specifying that at least one of the consuls had to be a plebeian (Cornell 1995:338).

Interestingly, the precise content of the law that introduced a maximum amount of land a Roman citizen could possess is also open to debate. Since the plebeians had been struggling to gain better access to public land, it seems logical to assume that the maximum of 500 *iugera* applied to holdings of *ager publicus,* and indeed this is how the law was interpreted by at least some authors who lived in the imperial period.[11] On the other hand, some modern scholars have maintained that the upper limit of 500 *iugera* seems excessively high for a period when the city of Rome controlled only about 1,500 square kilometers of territory, most of which must have been private rather than state-owned land. One possible way out is to assume that, at least in its original form, the maximum introduced in 367 BC applied to both public and private land.[12] Regardless of which interpretation is opted for, the ban on holdings larger than 500 *iugera* was clearly intended to make it impossible for a small group of elite families to monopolize access to newly conquered land.

The first of the three laws mentioned by Livy alleviated the problem of widespread indebtedness, but only temporarily. Under the year 357 BC, Livy reports that a law was passed that set one-twelfth (8 1/3%) as the maximum monthly (!) rate of interest (Livy 7.16.1.; Andreau 1999:91). A law of 347 BC lowered this rate to four and one-sixth percent. In 342 BC a *lex Genucia* (which later fell into disuse) prohibited interest-bearing loans altogether. Finally, a *lex Poetelia* of 326 BC declared it illegal for lenders and debtors to enter into an agreement obliging the debtor to pay off his loan by working as the creditor's debt-bondsman (*nexus*).[13]

Despite these measures, the problem of debt resurfaces in literary accounts of the background to the passing of the *Lex Hortensia* of 287 BC which made it possible for the *concilium plebis* to pass laws that were binding not only on the *plebs* but on the entire citizen population without obtaining the Senate's approval. It has long been suspected that the Hortensian Law was introduced precisely with the aim of freeing the way for new legislation settling the problem of widespread indebtedness.[14]

How Did the Plebeians Achieve Their Aims?

More than two centuries passed between the election of the first popular tribunes in 494 BC and the introduction of the *Lex Hortensia,* which traditionally is seen as marking the end of the "struggle of the orders."[15] This basic fact shows that plebeian attempts to break the patrician hold on the highest political offices and to improve the juridical, economic, and political conditions of the poorer sections of the citizen population met with fierce opposition. Yet in the long run the plebeians managed to achieve all of their objectives: access to the consulate, better legal protection, large-scale distributions of newly conquered land, debt relief, the end of voluntary debt-bondage, and even the right to pass laws that were binding on all Roman citizens. How can these successes be explained?

According to Livy (2.32.3), the office of *tribunus plebis* was created when the plebeians, or a large group of plebeians, withdrew from the city and occupied the Sacred Mound (*Mons Sacer*), a hill overlooking the Tiber.[16] In practical terms, this meant that they sought to achieve their political aims by refusing military service. Livy reports that the *pleb*s not only elected the first plebeian tribunes but also provided them with authority by declaring that anyone who should harm them became "accursed" (*sacer*), meaning that such a person could be killed with impunity. This sanction has appropriately been described as "lynch law disguised as divine justice" (Cornell 1995:260).

Further "withdrawals" of the *pleb*s are reported to have taken place in 449 BC, when the board of Ten Men who had drawn up the Law of the Twelve Tables was forced to step down from office, and in 287 BC during the crisis which ended with the passing of the Lex Hortensia.[17]

Other unorthodox measures were used to force the patricians to agree to the three laws that were passed in 367 BC. Livy reports that when the patricians refused to make any concessions, the tribunes of the *pleb*s responded by vetoing all attempts to elect new magistrates as well as all military levies, except during a major military emergency, which occurred in 370 BC (Livy 6.35.8–10).

Basing himself on these and other instances, Finley argued that "it would not be far from the truth to say that the Roman *populus* exercized influence not through the formal machinery of government, through its voting power, but by taking to the streets, by agitation, demonstrations and riots" (Finley 1983:91). This may be going one step too far. As has already been explained, the plebeian movement was headed by wealthy plebeians who resented their exclusion from the consulate. For all their obvious shortcomings, the literary sources suggest that these men were prepared to champion the economic interests of the poorer sections of the Roman population whose support they needed to achieve their political aims. The converging interests of various subgroups among the plebeian population are clearly reflected by the three laws of 367 BC, which addressed a variety of plebeian grievances.

Other things being equal, the opening up of the consulship to plebeian citizens and the gradual co-optation of wealthy plebeians into the political elite might have made it more difficult for less well-off plebeians to obtain alleviation of their remaining economic problems, such as the inadequate size of many peasants' holdings and the never-ending problem of rural indebtedness. In reality, the second half of the third century BC witnessed the foundation of eight Latin colonies, large-scale distributions of newly conquered land on an individual basis, a reduction of interest rates and the abolishment of debt bondage (cf. above). In the first decades of the third century BC nonelite citizens benefited from further land distribution schemes, for instance, after the conquest of Sabinum, and from another round of colonial foundations.

Some of these schemes, such as the foundation of Latin colonies, and perhaps also some of the noncolonial distribution programs, seem to have targeted veterans, who by definition must have owned sufficient property to qualify for military service.[18] If most of those citizens who received allotments under such schemes were already moderately well-off, or at least not very poor, this might help to explain why the problem of indebtedness kept resurfacing during this period.[19] Nonetheless, it cannot be denied that a very considerable proportion of the Roman citizen body benefited from these very extensive land distribution programs.[20]

Why was the Roman elite prepared to share some of the spoils of successful warfare with large numbers of nonelite citizens? As we have seen, the literary sources suggest that in the late fifth and early fourth centuries BC land division programs were implemented only after considerable social pressure or agitation. However, as the pace of Roman expansion accelerated, ever larger amounts of newly conquered land became available, making it easier for the Roman elite, now consisting of patricians and wealthy plebeians, to give veterans, and in some cases even some of their really destitute fellow citizens, a slice of the much larger cake. An important reason to do so was that colonial foundations and other land distribution schemes helped the Roman government to strengthen its grip on newly conquered territories. At the same time, such schemes had the effect of enlarging the number of adult men of citizen or allied status owning sufficient property to qualify for service in future wars. Thirdly, since colonial foundations and other land distribution schemes tended to be carried out in recently conquered peripheral regions, they resulted in a substantial level of emigration from the Roman heartland in Central-Western Italy, thereby making it easier for members of the elite to expand their rural properties in this area (Cornell 1995:393–394).

Military expansion also paved the way for the abolition of contractual debt bondage in 326 BC. It is true that very little is known about the organizational aspects of Roman farming in the Early Republic, but the few snippets of information that are available suggest that debt bondage was an important source of dependent labor in this period. However, as the pace of Roman expansion increased, an alternative supply of dependent laborers became available in the form of enslaved war captives (de Ligt 2015:370–372). Viewed in this light, the abolishment of debt bondage was hardly a significant concession on the part of the political, social, and economic elite.

The most important conclusion that emerges from this brief analysis is that successful warfare made it possible for Rome's political elite to provide large numbers of Roman citizens with substantial amounts of farmland and to replace debt-bondsmen of citizen status with enslaved outsiders. In other words, military conquest made it possible for the Roman elite to *export* some of the social and economic problems lying behind many episodes of the many-faceted "struggle of the orders."

Given the vast scale of the colonial ventures and land distribution programs of the fourth and early third centuries BC, there are strong reasons to think that the descendants of the citizens of the fifth century were, on average, considerably better off than their ancestors. As we have seen, however, the bill for these improvements was footed by those members of other Italian communities who lost large amounts of land and often ended up as slaves in the households, or on the expanding farms, of wealthy Roman citizens.

A LONG-TERM PERSPECTIVE ON INEQUALITY IN REPUBLICAN ROMAN SOCIETY

So far it has been argued that successful warfare enabled the political elite of republican Rome to alleviate various social and economic problems arising from the high degree of inequality that characterized early Republican Roman society. However, Rome's remarkable success in solving some of its internal social problems at the expense of outsiders by no means implies that the Roman citizen body became less stratified in terms of wealth and income.

In theory, the second law of 367 BC, which declared it illegal for a Roman citizen to possess more than 500 *iugera* of (public?) land, should have made it impossible for individual citizens to accumulate large amounts of newly conquered land which had not been used for colonial foundations or other land distribution schemes. According to various literary sources, however, this law was soon evaded or ignored, and in any case those citizens who were sent out to colonies or benefited from other land distribution schemes received allotments that were much smaller than 500 *iugera*.[21] After the conquest of Sabinum (290 BC) some of the newly conquered territories were distributed among nonelite Romans, but we also read about plots of 50 *iugera* being sold off to wealthy buyers (Roselaar 2010:125). According to Fabius Pictor, the first Roman historian (c. 200 BC), it was the conquest of the Sabine land which gave the Romans their first taste of "wealth" (*ploutos*).[22]

The sources suggest that Roman generals were not allowed to keep war booty captured during successful campaigns for their personal use, but they were permitted to use part of this booty for games, for distributions to their staff and soldiers, to erect new public buildings, or to make gifts to temples. During the second and first centuries BC several generals were accused of having retained a considerable proportion of war booty as their personal property (Churchill 1999).

During the second century BC provincial administration became an important source of income for provincial governors and their staff, and after the kingdom of Pergamon had been incorporated as the province of Asia, other members of the elite began to make huge profits from tax-farming and by lending money to provincial communities at extortionate rates of interest.[23]

As countless studies have shown, some of this new wealth was used to build and decorate large town houses, to acquire additional land, to buy more slaves or for various kinds of conspicuous consumption. In 182 BC, only a few years after the successful conclusion of the eastern campaigns of the early second century BC, which had resulted in the defeat of Philip V of Macedon and of the Seleucid king Antiochus III, the first of a long series of sumptuary laws (*leges sumptuariae*) was issued. Most of these laws tried to curb expenditure on private dinners, and from this it has been inferred that their principal aim was to prevent those elite Romans who had suddenly become much wealthier than their social peers from extending their social and political networks at the expense of other elite Romans.[24]

While many members of the Roman elite became richer, other groups in Roman society also reaped some of the material benefits of conquest. After Roman control had been reimposed on the region between the Apennines and the river Po large numbers of Roman citizens (as well as a smaller number of allies) were settled in colonies or in areas where noncolonial allotments were distributed. Allotments assigned to Roman citizens sent out to Latin colonies ranged from 15 *iugera* to 50 *iugera* for foot soldiers and from 30 *iugera* to 140 *iugera* for horsemen.[25] In addition, soldiers who had participated in successful campaigns often received cash grants. Between the early second and mid-first centuries BC the size of these grants increased quite dramatically (Hopkins 2007). While these benefits accrued only to those citizens who had served in the legions, all Italian landowners of citizen status benefited from the decision, taken in 167 BC, to suspend the collection of *tributum,* a land tax levied to cover the costs of military campaigns (Plutarch, *Life of Aemilius Paullus* 38.1; Pliny the Elder, *Natural History* 33.56). In 123 BC Roman citizens living in Rome were given the opportunity to buy wheat at a heavily subsidized price. From 58 BC, this wheat was distributed without charge (Garnsey 1988:182, 213–214).

While various sections of the Roman citizen population (as well as some Italians who did not have Roman citizenship) benefited from military conquest, there can be no doubt that differential access to the proceeds of victory resulted in Roman society becoming progressively more unequal in terms of wealth and income. In the course of the third century BC the thresholds for membership in the propertied classes of the *comitia centuriata* (cf. above) were doubled, with the exception of that for the fifth class. In all likelihood, this was done because prices had roughly doubled. In around 140 BC, however, the thresholds for membership of classes one to four were raised again, this time by 150 per cent, while the threshold for membership of the fifth class was either left unchanged or even lowered (Rathbone 1993). If the former view is correct, the threshold for membership of the first class now was more than 60 times higher than that for the fifth (100,000 sesterces against 1,600 sesterces).[26] In this period the minimum requirement for membership in the inner elite from which members of the Senate were recruited stood at 400,000 sesterces, 250 times higher than the minimum property qualification for military service (Nicolet, 2000:163–187).

According to various literary sources, a growing proportion of Roman citizens did not even own enough property to qualify for membership in the lowest property class, thereby causing a shortage of adult male citizens qualifying for service in the legions. This was the problem Tiberius Gracchus tried to solve by introducing a law prescribing that holders of public land that had been occupied in previous centuries or decades were to be deprived of any land possessed in excess of the old maximum of 500 *iugera* and that the land retrieved by the Roman state was to be distributed to poor Roman citizens (de Ligt 2012:158–171).

During the first century BC, the trend toward greater inequality intensified, in part because new conquests created fresh opportunities for elite enrichment and also because certain individuals did well out of the civil wars of the early and late 80s BC. In a speech against a land bill proposed by the tribune Servilius Rullus (in 63 BC), Cicero noted that the territory of the city of Praeneste, where Sulla had settled large numbers of veterans after defeating his last opponents in 81 BC, had fallen into the hands of "a few men."[27] In the late 50s BC, Marcus Licinius Crassus, a former supporter of Sulla, owned property worth about 170 million sesterces, enough to cover the annual subsistence costs of between 485,000 and 725,000 people.[28] A few years later (in 46 BC), Cicero noted that his rural estates yielded an annual income of 100,000 sesterces, enough to cover the subsistence costs of between 285 and 425 people, whereas a comfortably rich man could count on an annual income that was six times higher (Cicero, *Stoic Paradoxes* 49).

As in earlier periods, various other groups in Roman society reaped some of the benefits of continuing military expansion and increased levels of elite expenditure. Veterans who benefited from various distribution schemes carried out in Italy by Caesar and Octavian are known to have received allotments ranging from 25 to 66 and two-thirds *iugera*. Any farm belonging to the upper half of this range could not be worked by one family alone (de Ligt 2012:274–275). In Rome and other Italian cities merchants dealing in imported craft goods, raw materials, or food items, as well as many workshop owners, craftsmen, and other specialists producing goods or services for the growing urban markets became moderately prosperous, and at least some of them acquired substantial fortunes, giving rise to the *plebs media* ("the middling people") of the first century AD.[29] Despite these developments, there can be no doubt that differences between rich and poor citizens in wealth, income, and lifestyle became much wider in this period.[30]

Even from this very brief and simplifying account it should be clear that during the more than 450 years that elapsed between the expulsion of the last Roman king and the end of the Republic (in 27 BC) the profits of military conquest took many different forms. At the same time, the ways in which these profits were distributed through various groups in Roman society evolved over time. Yet at the most basic level some important continuities can be observed. From the fifth century onward, the political elite of Republican Rome managed to capture a very large proportion of the material benefits of conquest, in the form of land, slaves, metals, and other types of plunder or through more sophisticated forms of exploitation, such as extortion or tax-farming. During many periods of republican history the proceeds of war were large enough to provide large numbers of less well-off Roman citizens with some of the land, cash, or grain that had been captured, or levied as tax, from various groups of outsiders. As long as the political elite of Rome stuck to this policy of distributing the spoils of war, it was able to alleviate many of the tensions resulting from the highly unequal distribution of wealth and income that characterized Roman society throughout the republican period.[31] In the long run, however, the most striking outcomes of this traditional policy were the emergence of a superrich elite and a dramatic increase in levels of economic and social inequality.

NOTES

1. Forsythe 2005:111–113, based on Livy 1.43.
2. Cornell 1995:184, based on Gellius, *Attic Nights* 6.13.
3. It has often been suggested that the differentiated *comitia centuriata* was created in 406 BC, when the introduction of *stipendium* (military pay) for soldiers taking part in the siege of Veii made it necessary to levy *tributum* according to wealth. But throughout the fifth century BC some form of taxation must have been necessary to provide provisions and military supplies, and the multiple-class system might have been introduced in 443 BC, when the first censor was appointed. See, for instance, Northwood 2008:265–266. The fact that the Roman army could still be referred as "the *classis*" in 426 BC (Livy 34.6–7; Cornell 1995:189; Forsythe 2005:113) need not rule out the existence of a differentiated assembly. Sage 2008:23–24.
4. Rathbone 1993. The sole surviving manuscript of Cicero's *The Republic* (2.40) gives 1,100 *asses* as the threshold for membership of the fifth class. The figure of 11,000 *asses* given by Livy 1.43 must be the same figure expressed in terms of the much lighter *asses* of the early second century BC, though at this time the threshold for membership of the fifth class actually stood at 4,000 *asses*.
5. Cicero, *The Republic* 2.40; Dionysius of Halicarnassus, *Roman Antiquities* 4.18.2 and 7.59.6.
6. Building on the ancient formula *populus plebesque*, Momigliano 2005:174, argues that originally the term *plebs* was used to refer to those citizens too poor to serve as heavy infantry. Drummond 1989:166, sees *populus* and *plebs* as overlapping categories. Forsythe, *A Critical History*, 180–182, argues that the distinction between *populus* and *plebs* was military versus civilian, with each term referring to the entire citizen body. The last of these theories sits uneasily with the ban on marriages between patricians and plebeians contained in the Law of the Twelve Tables (Crawford, *Roman Statutes*, vol. II, 712; cf. Livy 4.4.5), which strongly suggests that the term *plebeians* did not refer to the entire citizen population. Forsythe's solution (2005:168–169 and 225–230) is to reinterpret the term *patres* as referring exclusively to priestly senators and the provision of the Twelve Tables as prohibiting marriages between plebeians and holders of hereditary priesthoods, but there are no reliable indications that all patricians were priests.
7. Livy 4.47. In all likelihood, this land was assigned to individual settlers who were not organized as a self-governing colonial community. See Pelgrom 2012:90.
8. Diodorus Siculus 14.102.4:4 *plethra* or 28 *plethra*. Jones and Last 1928:538, argued that the figure of seven *iugera* mentioned by Livy reflects land division practices of the early third century BC and that a size of four *iugera* is more realistic for the early fourth century BC.
9. Valerius Maximus, *Memorable Doings and Sayings* 4.3.5; Columella, *On Agriculture* 1 *praef.* 14.
10. Since there is no evidence regarding the size of allotments given to Latin colonists in the fourth or third centuries BC, this statement is based on sources relating to the early second century BC. See final section.

11. E.g., by Appian, *Bella Civilia* 1.8.

12. Rich 2008; Cornell 1995:329 argues that a ban on individual holdings of public land exceeding 500 *iugera* fits the conditions of the 360s BC.

13. For these laws, see Cornell 1995:332–333.

14. von Ungern-Sternberg 2005:19–320; Forni 1953:203, speculates that the primary aim of the law was to free the way for legislation prescribing the distribution of newly conquered land (in *Sabinum* and the *Ager Praetuttianus*) to individual settlers.

15. von Ungern-Sternberg 2005, argues that some of the political conflicts of the period between 287 BC and the start of the Second Punic War can be seen as continuations of this struggle.

16. Livy 2.32.2. Many ancient historians regard the first withdrawal as a literary invention designed to explain the origin and nature of the plebeian tribunate. See, for instance, Forsythe 2005:172–174.

17. Livy 3.52 and the summary of his lost eleventh book.

18. Càssola 1988 followed by Erdkamp 2011.

19. Of course, colonial schemes and land division programs for veterans would have prevented downward social mobility of legionaries belonging to the fifth property class and their families. Citizens owning too little property to qualify for legionary service seem to have benefited from the foundation of a series of small number of "maritime colonies" along the Italian coast. See de Ligt 2014:106–121.

20. Between 334 BC and 263 BC, approximately 70,000 Romans and men belonging to allied communities received land in Latin colonies. See Cornell 1995:381. If about half of the settlers were Roman citizens and if there were approximately 300,000 adult male Roman citizens in this period, roughly 10 per cent of Roman citizens would have benefited from these schemes.

21. Appian, *Civil Wars* 1.8. For the size of allotments given to Roman citizens sent out to Latin colonies, see final section. The highest figure recorded (for horsemen) is 140 *iugera*, twice as high as the next-highest figure.

22. Fabius Pictor as quoted in Strabo's *Geography* (5.3.1).

23. Tax-farming: Merola 2001. Money-lending to provincial communities: Andreau 1999.

24. Bigger and more lavishly decorated houses: Hales 2013:57–58. More slaves 1978. Sumptuary laws: de Ligt 2015:379–381.

25. See, for, instance, Brunt 2007:150; Rosenstein 2004:68–69, 236 n. 82, suggests that the size of the allotments assigned to Latin colonists gives a good idea of what average-sized holdings in Roman Italy might have looked like, but this optimistic assessment takes no account of the fact that these settlers were compensated for losing the Roman citizenship. Colonists sent out to "citizen colonies" (*coloniae civium Romanorum*) received smaller allotments, but were allowed, and expected, to occupy plots of *ager publicus*.

26. In this period, a *sestertius* was worth 2½ *asses*. The *asses* of the mid-second century BC were five times lighter than those of the early third century BC.

27. Cicero, *On the Agrarian Law* 2.78: *agrum Praenestinum a paucis possideri*.

28. Plutarch, *Life of Crassus* 2: 7,100 talents = 42.6 million drachms/*denarii* = 170.4 million sesterces. For annual subsistence costs, see de Ligt, *Peasants, Citizens, and Soldiers*, 197n13.

29. On the *plebs media* see Veyne 2000; Mayer 2012.

30. Kron 2008 argues that large numbers of Roman peasants enjoyed high standards of living and that the mean body height of Italians in the Roman period exceeded that of

the populations of the European *ancien régime*. In my view, there can be no doubt that a considerable number of nonelite people in Roman Italy, including sections of the rural population, were reasonably well-off, but recent studies have revealed that the mean height of Italians declined in the Roman period (in part because of increased exposure to various infectious diseases) and that the nutritional status of many inhabitants of Roman Italy was quite bad. See, for instance, Paine, Vargiu, Signoretti, and Coppa 2009 and Gowland and Garnsey 2010.

31.   The social crisis and recruitment problems that prompted Tiberius Gracchus to launch his agrarian reforms were intensified by the near-cessation of colonial foundations and other land distribution schemes after 173 BC. See, for instance, de Ligt 2012:168.

REFERENCES

Andreau, J. 1999 *Banking and Business in the Roman World*. Cambridge University Press, Cambridge.

Bietti Sestieri, A. M., A. de Santis, and L. Salvadei 1997 The Iron Age Cemetery of Osteria dell'Osa (Rome): An Integrated Anthropological and Cultural Study. In *Demographie der Bronzezeit, Paläodemographie: Möglichkeiten und Grenzen,* edited by K.-F. Rittershofer, pp. 258–271. Verlag M. Leidorf, Westfalia.

Broadhead, W. 2004 Colonization, Land Distribution, and Veteran Settlement. In *A Companion to the Roman Republic,* edited by P. Erdkamp, pp. 148–163. Wiley-Blackwell, London.

Brunt, P. 1971 *Italian Manpower 225 B.C.–A.D. 14*. Oxford University Press, Oxford.

Capogrossi Colognesi, L. 2006 La villa dell'Auditorium interpretata. In *La fattoria e la villa dell'Auditorium nel quartiere Flaminio di Roma,* edited by A. Carandini, M. T. d'Alessio, and H. di Giuseppe, pp. 559–610. Bretschneider, Rome.

Carandini, A. 1990 Domus aristocratiche sopra le mura e il pomerio del Palatino. In *La grande Roma dei Tarquini,* edited by M. Cristofani, pp. 97–99. Bretschneider, Rome

Càssola, F. 2011 Aspetti sociali e politici della colonizzazione. *Dialoghi di Archaeologia*, 3(6.2):5–17.

Churchill, J. B. 1999 Ex qua quod vellent facerent: Roman Magistrates' Authority over *Praeda* and *Manubiae*. *Transactions of the American Philological Association* 129:85–116.

Cornell, T. J. 1995 *The Beginnings of Rome. Italy and Rome from the Bronze Age to the Punic Wars (c. 1000–264 BC)*. Routledge, London.

Crawford, M. (ed.) 1996 *Roman Statutes*, volume II. Institute of Classical Studies, School of Advanced Study, University of London, London.

de Ligt, L. 2012 *Peasants, Citizens, and Soldiers. Studies in the Demographic History of Roman Italy 225 BC–AD 100*. Cambridge University Press, Cambridge.

de Ligt, L. 2014 Livy 27.38 and the *Vacatio Militiae* of the Maritime Colonies. In *Roman Republican Colonization. New Perspectives from Archaeology and Ancient History,* edited by T. D. Stek and J. Pelgrom, pp. 105–121. Palombi and Partner, Rome.

de Ligt, L. 2015 Production, Trade, and Consumption in the Roman Republic. In *A Companion to Greek Democracy and the Roman Republic,* edited by D. Hammer, pp. 368–385. Oxford University Press, Oxford.

Drummond, A. 1989 Rome in the Fifth Century I: The Social and Economic Framework. In *The Cambridge Ancient History*, VII.2: *The Rise of Rome to 220 B.C.,* edited by F. W. Walbank and A. E. Astin, pp. 113–171. Cambridge University Press, Cambridge.

Erdkamp, P. 2011 Soldiers, Roman Citizens, and Latin Colonists in Mid-Republican Italy. *Ancient Society* 41:109–146.

Finley, M. I. 1983 *Politics in the Ancient World.* Cambridge University Press, Cambridge.

Forni, G. 1953 Mario Curio Dentato uomo democratico. *Athenaeum* 31:170–240.

Forsythe, G. 2005 *A Critical History of Early Rome. From Prehistory to the First Punic War.* University of California Press, Berkeley.

Garnsey, P. 1988 *Famine and Food Supply in the Graeco-Roman World. Responses to Risk and Crisis.* Cambridge University Press, Cambridge.

Gowland, R. and P. Garnsey 2010 Skeletal Evidence for Health, Nutritional Status, and Malaria in Rome and the Empire. In *Roman Diasporas. Archaeological Approaches to Mobility and Diversity in the Roman Empire,* edited by H. Eckardt, pp. 131–156. Journal of Roman Archaeology Supplementary Series, Portsmouth, Rhode Island.

Hales, S. 2013 Republican Houses. In *A Companion to the Archaeology of the Roman Republic,* edited by J. D. Evans, pp. 50–66. Wiley-Blackwell, London.

Holloway, R. R. 1994 *The Archaeology of Early Rome and Latium.* Psychology Press, London.

Hopkins, K. 1978 *Conquerors and Slaves.* Cambridge University Press, Cambridge.

Kron, G. 2008 The Much Maligned Peasant. Comparative Perspectives on the Productivity of the Small Farmer in Classical Antiquity. In *People, Land, and Politics. Demographic Developments and the Transformation of Roman Italy, 300 BC–AD 14,* edited by L. de Ligt and S. Northwood. Brill, Leiden.

Mayer, E. 2012 *The Ancient Middle Classes. Urban Life and Aesthetics in the Roman Empire 100 BCE–250.* Harvard University Press, Cambridge.

Merola, G. D. 2001 *Autonomia locale, governo imperiale. Fiscalità e amministrazione nelle province asiane.* Edipuglia, Bari.

Mitchell, R. E. 2005 The Definition of *Patres* and *Plebs*: An End to the Struggle of the Orders. In *Social Struggles in Archaic Rome* expanded and updated edition, edited by K. A. Raaflaub, pp. 128–167. Blackwell, Malden, Massachusetts.

Momigliano, A. 2005 The Rise of the *Plebs* in the Archaic Age of Rome. In *Social Struggles in Archaic Rome,* expanded and updated edition, edited by K. A. Raaflaub, pp. 168–184. Blackwell, Malden, Massachusetts.

Mouritsen, H. 2015 The Incongruence of Power: The Roman Constitution in Theory and Practice. In *A Companion to Greek Democracy and the Roman Republic,* edited by D. Hammer, pp. 146–163. Wiley-Blackwell, Malden, Massachusetts.

Nicolet, C. 2000 Le cens senatorial sous la République et sous Auguste. In *Censeurs et publicains. Économie et fiscalité dans la Rome antique.* Fayard, Paris.

Northwood, S. 2008 Census and Tributum. In *People, Land, and Politics. Demographic Developments and the Transformation of Roman Italy, 300 BC–AD 14,* edited by L. de Ligt and S. Northwood, pp. 257–270. Brill, Leiden.

Paine, R. R., R. Vargiu, C. Signoretti, and A. Coppa 2009 A Health Assessment for Roman Imperial Burials Recovered from the Necropolis of San Donato and Bivio CH. *Journal of Anthropological Sciences* 87:193–210.

Pelgrom, J. 2012 *Colonial Landscapes. Demography, Settlement Organization, and Impact of Colonies Founded by Rome (4th–2nd centuries BC),* unpublished PhD thesis, Leiden.

Rathbone, D. 1993 The Census Qualifications of the *Assidui* and the *Prima Classis.* In *De Agricultura. In Memoriam Pieter Willem de Neeve (1945–1990),* edited by H. Sancisi-Weerdenburg et al., pp. 121–152. J. C. Gieben, Amsterdam.

Rich, J. 2008 *Lex Licinia,* lex *Sempronia*: B. G. Niebuhr and the Limitation of Landholding in the Roman Republic. In *People, Land, and Politics. Demographic Developments and the*

Transformation of Roman Italy, 300 BC-AD 14, edited by L. de Ligt and S. Northwood, pp. 519–572. Brill, Leiden.

Roselaar, S. T. 2010 *Public Land in the Roman Republic. A Social and Economic History of Ager Publicus in Italy, 396–98 BC*. Oxford University Press, Oxford.

Rosenstein, N. 2004 *Rome at War. Farms, Families, and Death in the Middle Republic*. University of North Carolina Press, Chapel Hill.

Sage, M. M. *The Republican Roman Army. A Sourcebook*. Routledge, London.

Scheidel, W. 2007 A Model of Real Income Growth in Roman Italy. *Historia* 56:322–346.

Stuart Jones, H., and H. Last 1928 The Making of a United State. In *The Cambridge Ancient History, vol. VII. The Hellenistic Monarchies and the Rise of Rome*, edited by S. A. Cook, F. E. Adcock, and M. P. Charlesworth, pp. 519–553. Cambridge University Press, Cambridge.

Terrenato, N. 2001 The Auditorium Site in Rome and the Origins of the Villa. *Journal of Roman Archaeology* 14:5–32.

Veyne, P. 2000 La "plèbe moyenne" sous le haut-empire romain. *Annales: Économies, Sociétés* 55:1169–1999.

von Ungern-Sternberg, J. 2005 The End of the Conflict of the Orders. In *Social Struggles in Ancient Rome*, expanded and updated edition, edited by K.A. Raaflaub, pp. 312–332. Blackwell, Malden, Massachusetts.

CHAPTER SIXTEEN

Slave Spaces

Housing Dependent Workers at Villa Magna

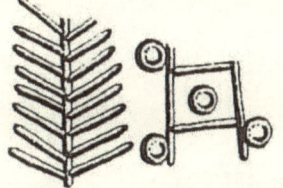

Elizabeth Fentress

In the very unequal Roman world there is no doubt that slaves were more unequal than anyone else. An exception can be made for some household slaves in the aristocratic *domus,* but even there it is likely that they were among the last to be considered in terms of food and lodging. Their strength, if it can be described as such, lay in their numbers, but even their numbers would have created pressure for equal rather than hierarchical treatment. Attempts to examine the world that the Roman slaves made are seriously hampered by the lack of identifiable slave quarters excavated with any precision. Our expectations are conditioned by what we know of the housing on American plantations, but we have no such parallels for large urban households, and it is frequently argued that household slaves at least slept where there was an available corner, in kitchens, corridors, and vestibules (e.g., Marzano 2007:145–153). Without going to the extremes of some recent literature, which denies the existence of purpose-built slave quarters, it is clear that there is no universally accepted model for the building type, if one exists (George 1997; Marzano 2007; Joshel 2013). Cases where we may be certain that we are dealing with slave quarters, the *cellae familiae* of Cato, Varro, and Columella,[1] are few, except in the case of the Pompeian villas and some Roman houses. What I want to do here is to propose an example of a mid-Roman slave barracks from the imperial villa of Villa Magna, near Anagni,[2] and then compare it to some earlier structures, examining the differences between them.

THE BARRACKS AT VILLA MAGNA

Excavations at Villa Magna, which took place between 2006 and 2010, revealed three major structures dating to the imperial period: the imperial residence, a large and magnificently appointed winery, and the building under discussion today, a slave barracks (Figure 16.1).

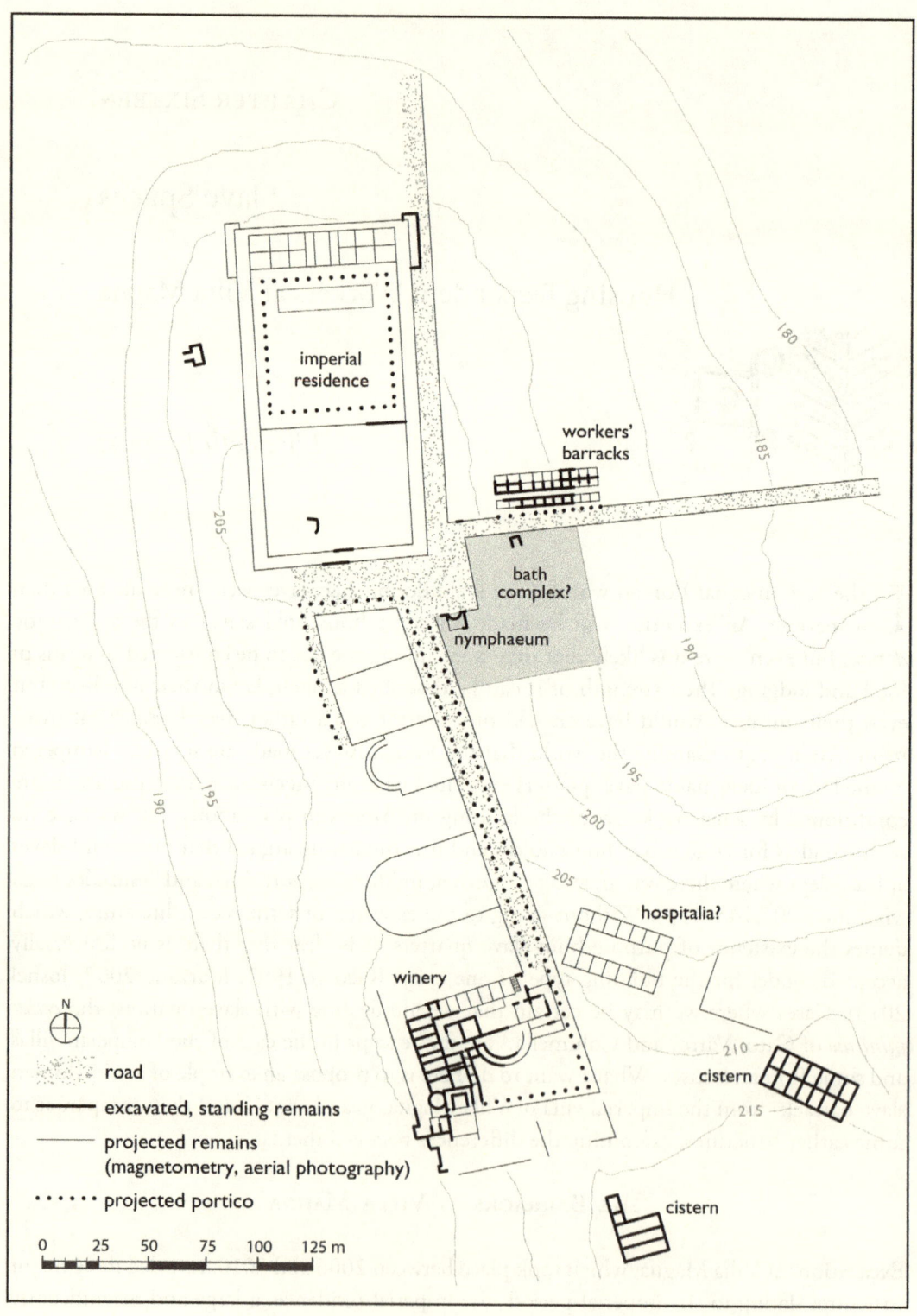

FIGURE 16.1. The plan of the villa in the early third century BC (J. Andrew Dufton).

The villa was built at the end of the reign of Trajan or the beginning of that of Hadrian, and was certainly the property from which Marcus Aurelius wrote two well-known letters to Fronto (IV.4 and IV.5). It was probably the site of an annual festival which marked the beginning of the vintage in Latium, and it certainly produced large quantities of wine (Fentress and Maiuro 2011). We know nothing of the rest of the *pars rustica* for the first hundred years of the life of the villa, and thus do not know whether the slave barracks replaced an earlier structure or were a way of augmenting the available space.

THE PLAN OF THE BUILDING

The building lies to the north of an access road leading up to the main buildings of the villa, around 20m. from the imperial residence. It is characterized by two structural blocks separated by an alley (Figure 16.2). The plans of these two structures can be reconstructed almost in their entirety. The southern block comprises a portico on its south side, facing the road, and, behind it, a row of ten small rooms facing north onto an alley (Figure 16.3). The northern block is composed of two rows of ten rooms, whose plan mirrors the northern row of rooms in the southern block.

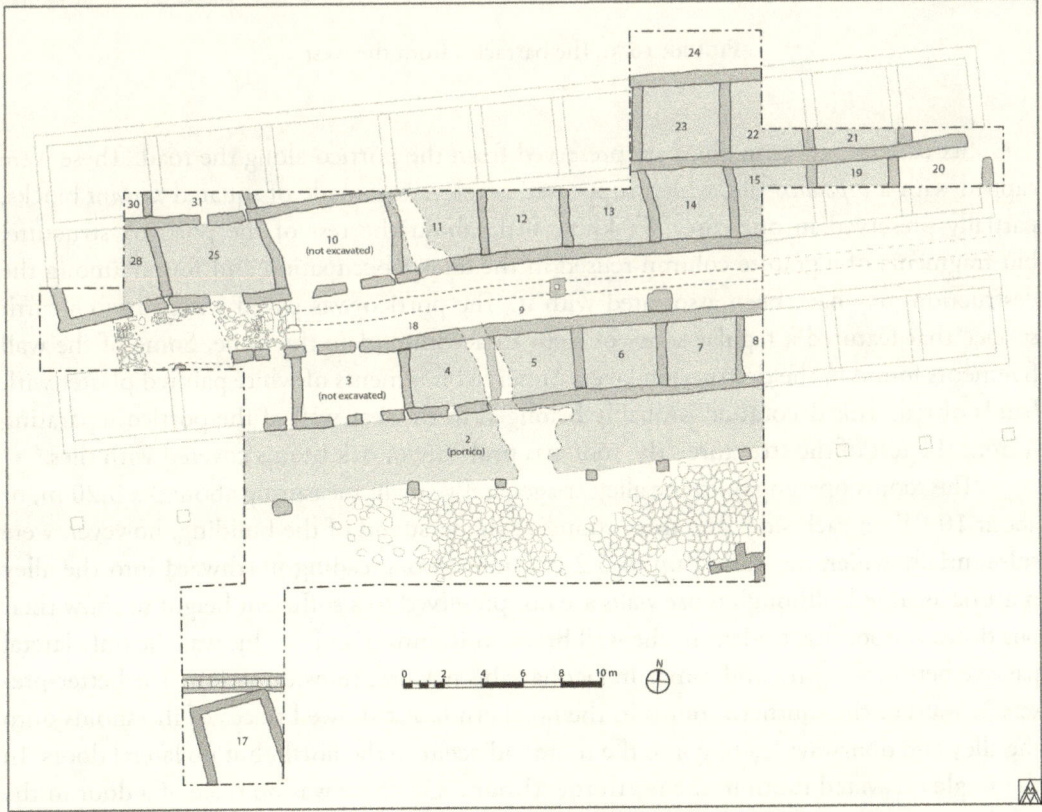

FIGURE 16.2. The plan of the barracks (J. Andrew Dufton).

FIGURE 16.3. The barracks, from the west.

Six concrete column bases are preserved from the portico along the road. These were capped with a *bipedalis* tile, which supported an elevation made of squared *tartara* blocks, partially preserved in one case. We know little about the rest of the portico's structure, but fragments of a granite column reused in the later reoccupation and found among the destruction may have been associated with it. The portico was paved with a beaten-earth surface that featured a regular series of steps to accommodate the slope. Some of the wall fragments found in the destruction layers preserved fragments of white painted plaster with bands of red. This decoration probably belonged to the rear wall of the portico separating it from the rest of the structure. The roof was probably of oak beams covered with tiles.[3]

The rooms opening onto the alley are generally small, measuring about 3 x 3.20 m, or about 10 RF on each side. The three rooms at the west end of the building, however, were substantially wider, measuring up to 5.2 m wide. Doors leading northward into the alley must be assumed, although those walls are not preserved to a sufficient height to show their positions. A door was evident in the wall between Rooms 3 and 4. This was the only lateral passage between rooms, and it may in fact have been a later transformation. The better-preserved walls of the southern rooms in the northern block showed traces of thresholds onto the alley and doorways leading into the rooms adjacent to the north, but no lateral doors. In the single excavated room in the north row (Room 23), there was no trace of a door in the northern exterior wall, suggesting that the rooms of the northern structure communicated only with the alley to the south of it.

The alley dividing the two structural blocks was about 3 m wide and paved in beaten earth. It is difficult to know whether its ends were closed by doors. The exterior wall of Room 28, at the western entrance to the alley, is thickened at the corner by a semicircular protrusion, which may represent a pilaster and thus a formal entrance, but it does not necessarily suggest a door. Indeed, no evidence for a hinge or post was found, perhaps making an open entrance more likely.

A drain ran down the center of the entire length of the alley. At least three construction phases were evident for the drain, and each seemed to correspond to principal stages in the life of the building as a whole. The earliest phase, dateable between the beginning of the third and the middle of the fourth century AD,[4] showed careful construction, with masonry sides and a tile base. *A cappuccina* drains connected to this phase of the drain led from Rooms 5 and 12. The second phase of construction cut into the fill of the first and was characterized by a lining employing reused materials—paving stones and fragments of marble revetment probably deriving from other structures. To this second phase also belong two mortar structures inserted at points along its length, each roughly square with the top half of an amphora inserted into a central hole. These probably served as recipients for water falling from gutters or spouts from the roofs of the surrounding structures.

The final phase, best-preserved in the western half of the alley, consists of a regular cut lined with reused marble and a covering of reused marble and paving stones. The pavement of the drain in this phase indicates that it was probably related to the area outside Room 25, interpreted as a washroom, which also featured an extensive pavement of reused marble slabs. The two later phases date toward the end of the occupation of the building, with the second phase belonging to the second half of the fourth or the early fifth century AD and the latest, third phase to the middle of the fifth century. No material dating to later than the third quarter of the fifth century AD was found in it.[5]

The building was almost certainly two stories high, as the extent of the collapsed remains of the western wall of Room 10 (Figure 16.4) showed. A square slab of concrete abutting the north wall of the southern block in the alley can be interpreted as the base of a wooden stair that would have led to a balcony running along the perimeter of the building and partially covering the alley. This would have further restricted the amount of light and air entering the rooms. Within the rooms, the floors were consistently beaten earth, compact and almost without inclusions, made from the clay of the hillside. In Rooms 5, 7, 8, and 11, a slab of *opus signinum* covered the center of the floor. The remnants of ash and traces of burning on top and around them suggest that they served as bases for hearths.[6] Querns and hearths were found in several of the rooms on the south side, along with small pits that might have held jars containing foodstuffs (Figure 16.5). Substantial *dolia* were also present in many of the rooms, partially sunk into the ground. These are interpreted as storage for grain, which would seem to have been rationed to the inhabitants of each room. Otherwise, there was no trace of furniture, except, in room 13, for two blocks against the west wall that may have served as supports for a bench, and, in room 23, for the creation of what seems to have been a storage cupboard, built in a second phase, and possibly replacing the *dolium* in that room.

FIGURE 16.4. The east wall of room 10, collapsed.

FIGURE 16.5. Room 6, from the north.

The two blocks of the buildings might have had different functions. The distribution of *dolia* and hearths shows that all of the rooms in the southern block had both features, but their distribution in the northern block is different. No obvious accommodations for *dolia* were found in the southern row of rooms, while Room 23 in the northern row contained one in the northeastern corner. On the other hand, all of the southern rooms that were fully excavated had hearths, while Room 23 did not. This distribution, together with the doors between the northern and southern rows, suggests that the northern building was organized in two-room suites.

Infant Burials

A striking feature of the later occupation of the building is a series of infant burials.[7] There are eight in all, of which six can be attributed to the fifth-century AD occupation. In Room 13, two infant skeletons filled a cut against the east wall. The cut was floored with tile, but otherwise unlined. The uppermost infant was covered with a thick layer of tiles. The whole tomb was then covered by the last beaten earth floor of the room, which shows that the burial took place during the occupation of the building. The room to the west, 23, contained fully four infant burials, three buried one on top of the other in a single, constructed tomb along the west wall, and one in the northeastern corner, over the backfilled remains of the *dolium* pit. The constructed tomb was lined with tile and thin slabs of white marble. It was reopened for the second deposition, which was covered with tiles, while the third deposition was dug down from the floor surface and simply placed on the tile covering. The backfill was then leveled to the surface. Again, these seem to have been contemporary with the use of the room, although they were not covered by a subsequent floor.

In both cases, then, we seem to be seeing members of the same family returning to the same tomb to bury a new child. Strikingly, all of the infants were afflicted with pathological lesions characteristic of vitamin and mineral deficiencies.[8] Although the patterns of porotic hyperostosis on the Area D babies could indicate three different disorders—anemia, rickets (vitamin D deficiency), and scurvy (vitamin C deficiency) (Ortner 2003), given the very young age of most of these children, Samantha Cox argues that it is most likely that these children suffered from a genetic anemia, probably thalassaemia, a disease that spreads in reaction to the presence of the more deadly malaria *falcipara*.[9] This would, in itself, argue for an allochthonous origin for the people of the barracks, as the area around Villa Magna, separated from the coast by the high wall of the Monti Lepini, has never been malarial, and none of the medieval burials exhibit similar symptoms. Transmitted within one or two families on site (it is striking that almost all of the infants suffered from it), it shows them as foreign, at least to the immediate area. The under-floor burials, in carefully stacked tombs, are also eloquent: the practice of burying children under the floors of inhabited rooms was extremely rare in Roman Italy.[10] Whatever the belief system this form of burial implies, it is not one that is common in Italy and, again, suggests a more distant origin for the family in question.

THE SMALL FINDS

Within the rooms and, particularly, the drain, were found a reasonably large number of small finds—the distribution of the most common are found in Figure 16.6. There were numerous costume elements, generally devoid of any trace of decoration and reduced to the purely functional—keeping hair in place and clothes on—and a certain number of tools, largely related to textile working. The finds are generally of fairly modest quality, and largely domestic in character. This fits well with the interpretation of the building as housing for dependent labor of both sexes, either free or slave. Although our inclination is toward the latter interpretation, it should be admitted that slave collars and chains, or even the iron rings associated with slaves, are no more evident than military equipment in the finds.[11] An exception might be a bronze leaf-shaped pendant (Figure 16.7) found in the destruction layer of the building. This has a large, circular attachment for suspension. It is identical in shape to an inscribed pendant from the Antiquarium Comunale in Rome, which reads "*Tene me ne fugia(m) et revoca me at (=ad) ni(m)feu(m) Alexandri*" ("Stop me from running away and return me to the Nymphaeum of Alexander").[12] There are, to my knowledge, no other examples of uninscribed pendants for slave collars, but the similarity in shape is telling: the pendant is very heavy, and would have been uncomfortable to wear, while the large attachment hole suggests an equally heavy collar.

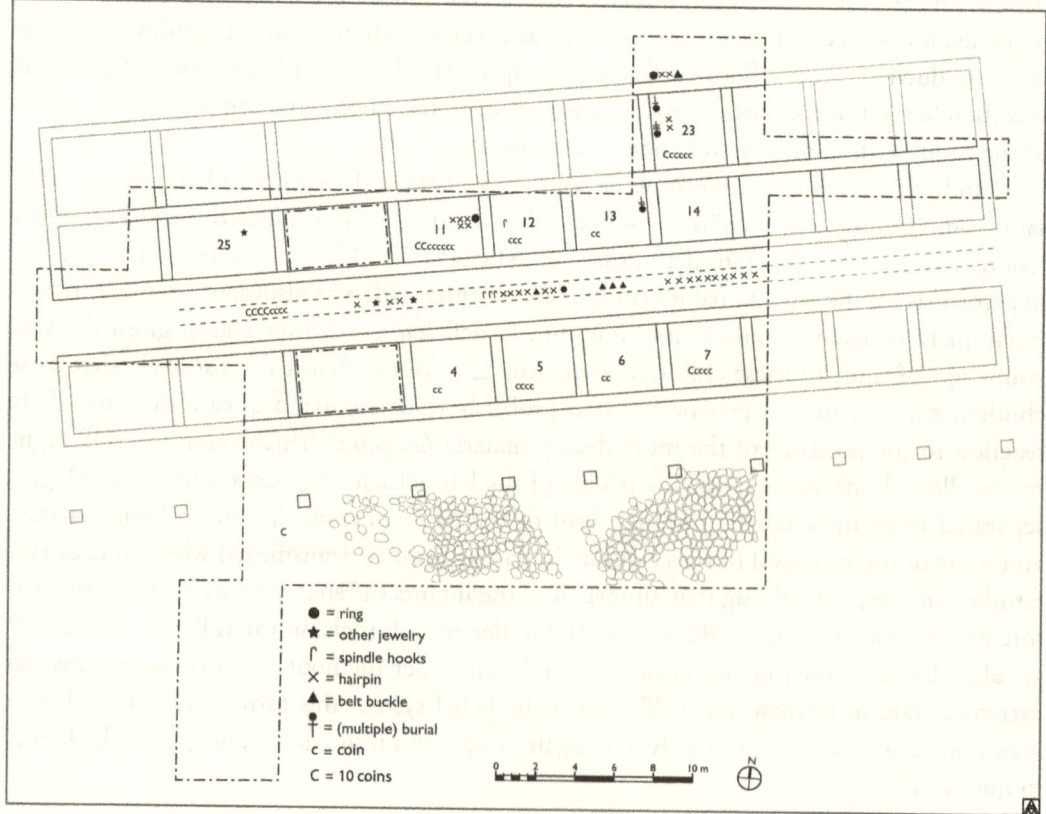

FIGURE 16.6. The distribution of coins and small finds (Margaret Andrews).

FIGURE 16.7. Bronze pendant from the destruction of the building.

The distribution of objects with some gender specificity—hairpins, pins, jewelry apart from rings, needles (all of which can be reasonably assumed to be used by women), and rings and belt elements (probably used by men) shows some significant variation. The vast majority of these finds come from the central drain, and may result in casual loss or breakage occurring in any part of the structure. However, it may be significant that all of the other finds except for coins come from the rooms on the north side of the building. It might be suggested from this that that side of the building, with its two-room suites, was reserved for families, rewarding the production of children, while the single rooms were occupied by single males: it is significant that all of the southern rooms contained *dolia* and hearths, which would have allowed these groups to store their grain rations in the *dolium*, grind it with the querns, and cook or warm up their meals over the hearth, which would also have served for heat.

The clearly larger rooms that are present at the western end of the building are noteworthy, but we have few clues, apart from their size, about what made them distinct from the others. Room 25, which contained a large sink with a drain, was certainly designed as a washroom, probably for all the inhabitants of the building. There is no trace of a latrine.[13] This might have been found in Room 31 to the north of Room 25, although there is no apparent door between them. It is possible the central drain in the alley was used for this purpose, although flotation did not reveal any mineralized material.[14] The large rooms at the end of the corridor might have housed personnel of a higher rank, on analogy with the centurion's quarters that occupied the ends of the rows of *contubernia* in army barracks. A three-room suite for a *monitor* might have comprised Rooms 28, 30, and 31, an arrangement which would have given access to Room 31.

If this disposition of the rooms is accepted, it is possible to estimate, at least roughly, the number of people the building contained. If the single rooms of the southern block measure roughly 12 m^2, and some of the area was occupied by the *dolium,* they could each have held a maximum of five individuals if they were no more densely packed than auxiliary barracks. We might put a similar number in the two-room suites to the north. At this density there would have been a maximum of 90 on the lower story and a similar number on the upper story, giving c. 180 in all. Lower figures are possible, of course, but it is hard to imagine that a building this size contained fewer than 100 workers.

DISCUSSION

The building is very unusual, at least in the context of a villa, although, as we shall see, some comparisons exist. Its similarity to imperial army barracks is evident. These were generally long buildings placed back to back, with a portico open onto a road on one side and an alley on the other. Rooms within these structures were modular, and the blocks one or two rooms deep.[15] They might have housed civilians, *immunes,* or soldiers, but they were characteristic of army camps. The size and proportions of our structures would fit well in to the range characteristic of auxiliary forts.[16] However, the only soldiers one might expect at an imperial villa, a detachment of the praetorian guard, would seem to require far more luxurious accommodations.[17] The poverty of the construction, with its pavements in beaten earth, the absence of marbles or even wall plaster, the quantity of domestic pottery, the relative absence of amphorae, and the *dolia* in each of the southern rooms argues against this interpretation, as do the multiple objects belonging to women. Further, military equipment among the finds is notable by its absence, with the exception of a couple of buckles.

The disposition of the structure, with its very limited access and equal cells—with the single exception of the larger room at the top of the alley, probably that of a *monitor*—certainly argues that it was designed for a constrained labor force. The fact that it looks almost identical to army barracks, although significantly more closed in, simply speaks to the penetration of the military model into every sphere of society. The walls were rough and unplastered and, except on the side facing the street, inaccessible to the inhabitants. The only common space in the building appears to be a room with facilities for washing. As we have seen, the idea that the northern side of the building with its two-room suites was used for families is reinforced by the finds of objects associated with women exclusively on that side of the building, as well as the infant burials. There was, then, much less space for the community than at the earlier villas, but slightly greater space, and privacy, for families. This would fit in with a policy that encouraged the production of children to provide replacement labor on the estate (Roth 2007:39–52; Columella *Rust.* I, 19).

As noted above, both the condition of the infants and the nature of their burial argue for a foreign origin for the people housed in the barracks. This persistence of foreign-born workers on the estate as late as the first half of the fifth century also seems to argue for the presence of slaves into that period, a conclusion that is striking, at least for the fifth century, but hardly impossible.[18] The situation of the imperial properties would in any case have been unique, as the emperor would have had privileged access to war captives and, indeed, any slaves being sold, while never lacking the capital available for their purchase. The essential requirements for plantation agriculture, an intensive, market-oriented crop and an assured supply of slaves, continued to be met here.

The pottery from the third century shows significant shortages in vessels for food preparation and a total lack of an oven or other cooking facilities. Mihaela Ciausescu, in her study of the pottery, argues that this might point, in this period at least, to a provision of bread from a central kitchen and the arrival of rations on a daily basis, for simple food preparation on site.[19] Curiously, none of the vessels in ceramics or glass could have been used for drinking, a fact that probably implies the use of wooden beakers, perhaps carved on the site. Imported wine, as must be expected, was available only rarely, as the prevalence of amphorae used to carry foodstuffs suggests. Lamps, of which 150 were found in the assemblage, are hardly plentiful when compared to the amount of rooms to be lit, and when one considers the two and a half centuries of occupation. Glass lamps do not fill the gap, as only one of these was discovered in the late-fifth-century fill of the drain, and none in the other Roman contexts. Coins, almost absent in the third century AD, became far more numerous in the fourth century, dominated by the standard mid-century issues such as GLORIA EXERCITUS. Many of these were found in the drain, but there is a scatter in almost all of the rooms, showing some access to coinage and the market in this period. Finally, we must remember that passage between the rooms of the barracks and access to the outside took place through a narrow alley, with what became an open drain running down the middle, the probable destination of all of the sewage. Life in the barracks throughout the Roman period was thus uniformly grim: dark, smelly, and, probably, very crowded (Figure 16.8).

FIGURE 16.8. Reconstruction of the barracks building (Dirk Booms).

SLAVE BARRACKS ELSEWHERE

Exact parallels to the Villa Magna barracks, are few. A close comparison comes from Tiberius's villa at Sperlonga, where a row of fourteen small rooms opens on to a corridor blocked at the end by a door (Cassieri 2000). A stair base shows that here as well there were two storys. At the end of a corridor, a bread oven suggests that cooking was communal, and confirms the domestic use of the space, placed just behind the quarters of the praetorian guard (Figure 16.9a). A more compact block of small rooms giving onto what were probably alleys is found at the second-century villa at Tor Marancia near Rome, where there appear to have been several two-room suites (Figure 16.9c. De Franceschini 2005:202–204n.72). Finally, a building from the site of Torre di Palma, in Spain, in the context of a large villa built in the late first or second century AD and probably owned by an Italian, bears a strong resemblance to the Villa Magna plan (Figure 16.9b. Maloney and Hale 1996:280–284). The Italian identity of the original owner is suggested as much as anything else by the very classic atrium plan of the main building in its first phase. The subsidiary building had nine small rooms arranged on either side of what was probably a long, open courtyard. Around it on three sides was a portico, the roof of which could have been reached from a staircase, and which would have served for circulation on the upper story. Again, the structure was paved with beaten earth, with the exception of the central court and one of the rooms on the ground floor, which were floored with *opus signinum*. There was a single hearth, of brick.

These rather tightly constrained buildings are in strong contrast with what we find at earlier villas, particularly in the area of Pompeii, where a courtyard model appears to have been fairly generalized. The arrangement of small rooms around a courtyard is apparent in a number of buildings in the area of Vesuvius and, where finds have been recorded, they point to a domestic occupation rather than the alternatives of stables and storage. A good example comes from the small villa of T. Claudius Eutyches, where the eastern block of the building comprises a generous, rectangular courtyard with a portico, onto which open a line of 9 *cellae*, again on two levels, together with a significantly larger pair of rooms for a *monitor* (Figure 16.10: Della Corte 1922; Rossiter 1978:40–48). The upper story was reached from a staircase, whose base survives, and a balcony running along the front of the rooms. Each room had a beaten-earth floor, and a hearth toward the front. Stabling is apparent in the corner of the courtyard, where positions for four horses are signaled by mangers. In contrast to those of Villa Magna, the finds from the individual *cellae* were remarkably rich, including bronze candelabrae, while one room contained a hoard of intaglios, coins, cameos, and a gold ring, together with the dice and gaming pieces with which they might have been won.

Finds from another villa at Gragnano were less rich, but there, too, the courtyard was substantial, and surrounded by eleven rooms (Della Corte 1923). A kitchen with an oven showed that food production was centralized. Other villas in the area of Vesuvius have even larger courtyards surrounded by *cellae,* such as that lying southeast of the peristyle in the Villa Ariadne at Stabia, where there are, suggestively, again two different-size modules for the rooms. Although they were uniformly poorly plastered, one had a floor in white mosaic, and the finds, detailed by Weber, are again strikingly rich, with coins, numerous small

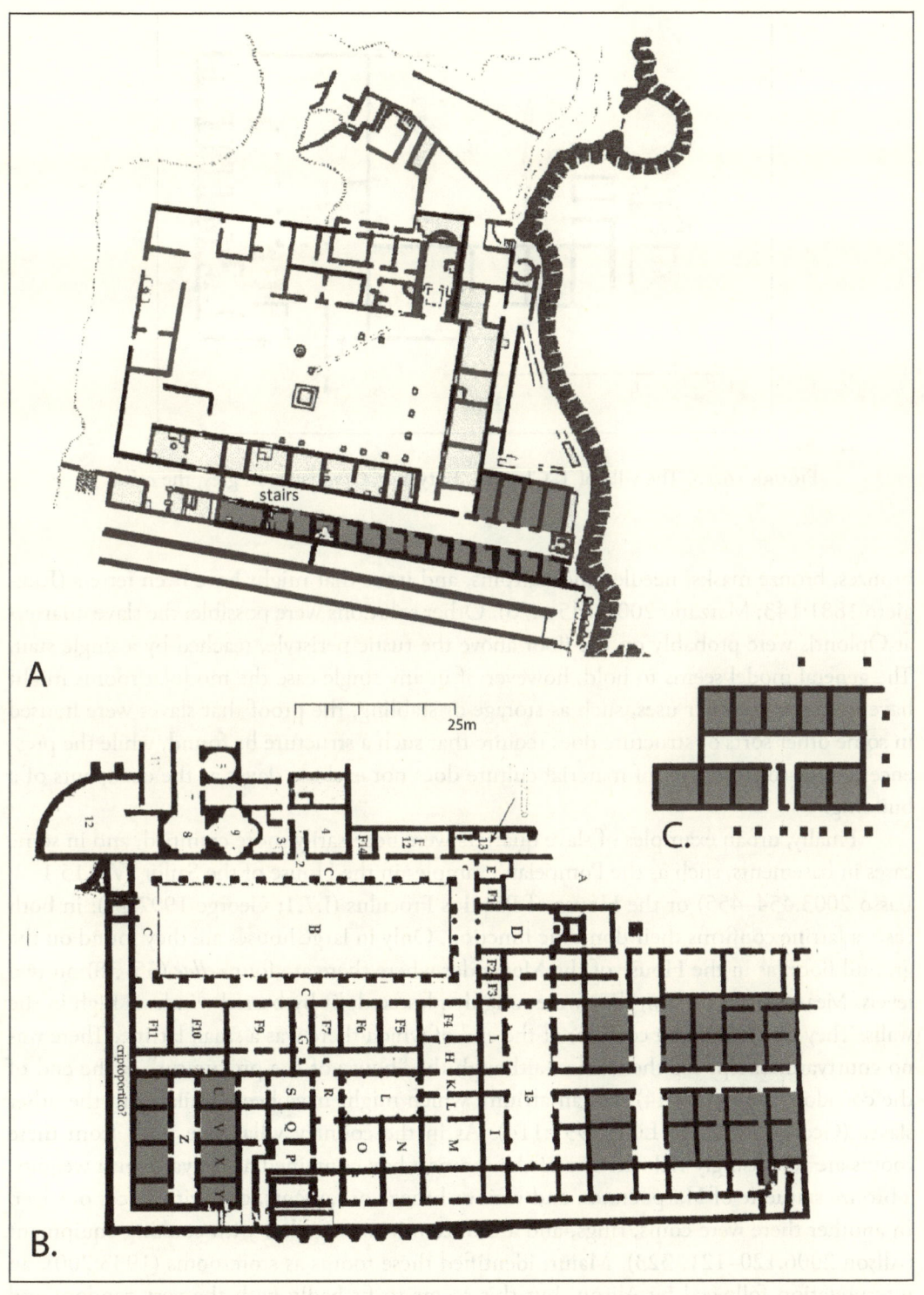

FIGURE 16.9. *Cellae* (in grey) at a. Sperlonga, b. Tor Marancia, Rome, c. Torre di Palma (Alto Alentejo) (redrawn by Elizabeth Fentress).

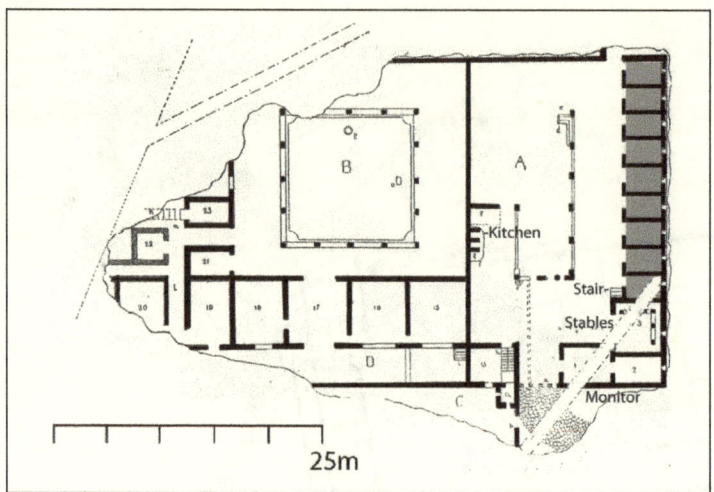

FIGURE 16.10. The villa of T. Claudius Eutyches, Gragnano. In grey, the *cellae*.

bronzes, bronze masks, needles and hairpins, and irons that might have been fetters (Ruggiero 1881:143; Marzano 2007:145 n.76). Other solutions were possible: the slave quarters at Oplontis were probably on the floor above the rustic peristyle, reached by a single stair. The general model seems to hold, however: if in any single case the modular rooms might have been put to other uses, such as storage or stabling, the proof that slaves were housed in some other sorts of structure does require that such a structure be found, while the presence of a reasonable level of material culture does not exclude slaves as the occupants of a building.[20]

Finally, urban examples of slave quarters were necessarily more cramped, and in some cases in basements, such as the Pompeian examples in the House of the Sailor (VII,15.1–2; Basso 2003:454–455) or the House of Paquius Proculus (I.7.1; George 1997:19): in both cases a latrine confirms their domestic function. Only in large houses are they found on the ground floor, as in the House of the Menander where there are four *cellae* (35–38) on two levels. Measuring 3 x 3.2m, they were roughly plastered, lit by barred windows high in the walls. They opened onto a corridor at the end of which there was a small latrine. There was no courtyard, except for the stables, although the "house of the procurator" at the end of the corridor (rooms 41–44) had an atrium, which might have been available to the other slaves (George 1997:18; Ling 1997:114). As in the country villas, the finds from these rooms are surprisingly rich. In one of the rooms a box contained a steelyard with weights, a bronze statuette of Harpocrates, and various bronze ornaments, one with traces of silver. In another there were coins, rings, and a bronze mirror, together with cooking equipment (Alison 2006:120–121, 323). Maiuri identified these rooms as storerooms (1933:200), an interpretation followed by Alison, but this seems to fit badly with the very random and highly personal items found there.

In Rome, slave quarters are regularly found in basements, and can be clearly articulated, if regularly fairly cramped. Examples come from the houses of Cn. Domitius Calvinus and Q. Lutatius Catullus (Carandini 2010:33–35, 121) The supports for beds, like those of some of the 60 *cellae* in the basement of the House of Aemilius Scaurus, show that the cells were intended for individuals, granting much more privacy than we have seen elsewhere (Carandini 2010:105; Basso 2003:448). The walls, too, were plastered and painted, and the basement was provided with a *lararium* and a small bath. The pottery from the structure, which was sealed during Nero's fire, was almost exclusively of *terra sigillata italica,* which led Maria Antonietta Tomei to argue that it served as a *lupanar,* though it is hard to imagine a senatorial residence on the Palatine with a brothel in its basement (Tomei 1995).

Again, these structures all date from the Republic or the early years of the Empire. In the city we are certainly dealing with household slaves, who would have been in frequent contact with their owners. Not altruism, but practical considerations would have made it advantageous to house them properly: the prestige of a household was also based on the well-being of its slaves. Such considerations would not always have applied in the country-side, unless visits from the owner were frequent, as in the case of Villa Magna in the first century of its existence (Fentress and Maiuro 2011).

In all of these examples we are looking at complex and articulated structures whose owners seem to have invested in the space in order to keep their workforces relatively comfortable, and thus productive. Indeed, Columella recommends that *cellae familiae* face south, so as to be as salubrious as possible, before discussing various stratagems for keeping up the morale of the slaves (*Rust.* 1.6): The courtyard structures offer a sharp contrast with the more cramped, and barracks-like, spaces that we have seen at the two imperial villas—to which could be added the 150 units of the *cento camerelle* at Hadrian's Villa at Tivoli (Salza Prina Ricotti 2001:163; Sgalambro 2010). Here, noncommunicating cells opened onto wooden balconies on four levels. Capable of housing up to 1,500 slaves, they were plastered and painted with red stripes on a yellow ground, and were roughly south-facing, with light and air coming from the door and the window above it. A latrine with 30 seats was found on the third floor, next to the staircase. Again, there are two modules, one significantly larger than the other. Clearly the huge number of slaves required for Hadrian's villa could hardly be housed in courtyard structures, but the plan and its articulation may have served as a template for later solutions.[21]

The contrast between the courtyard accommodations of the late Republic and Early Empire and the slave barracks from the imperial villas of Tiberius, Hadrian, and the Severan phase at Villa Magna suggests a genuine worsening of the conditions of slaves over time. Gone are the courtyards, along with subsidiary structures like infirmaries. The finds, when they were recorded, are far richer in the Vesuvian villas of Gragnano and Stabia, or indeed in the *domus* of Aemilius Scaurus, than those recovered at Villa Magna. The sample is small, and the reasons for this change unclear; it seems that those owners who were still using a slave labor force were principally interested in exploiting it to the full, without any particular consideration for its welfare. The fact that the barracks at Villa Magna were masked from the street by a painted portico that provided some decorum, at least from the point of view of the visitor, does not mitigate the squalor that lay behind it.

The reasons for this increase in slave inequality are not obvious—especially in a landscape where ever more agricultural labor was being carried out by tenants, *coloni,* who were able to live in their own houses and manage their own agriculture (Vera 1992). One tentative suggestion comes from the very particular nature of the imperial villas, for which there were at least two levels of administration, a regional procurator and a *vilicus* charged with the management of the individual estate, not to mention eventual *dispensatores* and *actores* (Carlsen 1995; Camodeca 2005).[22] While following the older model of slave-worked estates, the system had become more top-heavy, and further removed from the owner. It is hardly likely that the emperor, the largest landholder in Italy, would have been directly concerned with the construction of housing for slaves.[23] It seems possible that such a management structure, where the well-being of the estate workers was of less concern to the manager than it would have been to an owner, led to a greater degree of mistreatment on the part of the manager. A parallel comes from the Hadrianic legislation of the imperial estates in Africa. Although these were very differently run, it is clear that the *conductores,* who took out fixed-term leases on the property, were abusing the rights of the *coloni,* who appealed to the emperor for justice.[24] At Villa Magna, if the slaves were being abused, they would have had no such right of appeal, and any woes would have been smothered in the vast apparatus of the administration of the *res privata.* A desire to extract a maximum of labor for a minimum of investment, combined with the multiple layers of management that separated the imperial slaves from their master, must both have figured in what can only be seen as an increase in inequality, from the top levels of the imperial household down through multiple layers of slave labor.

NOTES

The final version of this article was submitted in 2016. Since then there has been new bibliography, not taken into account here, of which the most important is Molina Vidal, J., I. Grau Mira, F. Llidó López, and J F. Álvarez Tortosa, 2017 "Housing slaves on estates: a proposed ergastulum in a semi-basement at the Villa of Rufio (Giano dell'Umbria)" Journal of Roman Archaeology 30, 387–406: note an enlarged list of proposed slave quarters on p. 403. See also for France C. Gaston, 2018 'Le logement servile dans la demeure en Gaule romaine,' Archéopages, 46, 44–47.

1.   Cati *De Agri* XIV; Varro *Rust.* 1.13; Columella *Rust.* 1.6.3; Note that I am not discussing the question of *ergastula,* where chained slaves slept (Columella *Rust.* 1, 6, 3, for which Étienne 1972). One case of such a structure, confirmed by the presence of a chained slave, is the Villa of the Columns in Mosaic, outside Pompeii (Basso 2003:455).

2.   For a general discussion of the villa see Fentress and Maiuro 2012, and Fentress, Goodson, and Maiuro 2016:123–136, where the barracks building is published by Margaret Andrews and Serena Privitera. I am grateful to both for their work on the building. The excavation was co-sponsored by the Soprintendenze alle belle arti of Lazio, the University of Pennsylvania and the British School at Rome.

3.   Charcoal identification by Robyn Veal, in Fentress, Goodson, and Maiuro 2016:79.

4.   The contents of this layer date from the beginning of the third century AD (fragments of Dressel 43 and Leptiminus 1 amphorae) to the first half of the fourth, with fragments of Keay 25.3 (Africana 3B).

5.   The pottery is studied by Mihaela Ciausescu in Fentress, Goodson, and Maiuro 2016:147–171.

6.   These simple structures compare well with similar structures in the villa of the Auditorium: Carandini et al. 2007:15, fig. 8.

7.   These are discussed by Margaret Andrews in the publication.

8.   A detailed report on the osteology of the infant skeletons is published by Samantha Cox, in Fentress, Goodson, and Maiuro 2016.

9.   Ibid.:183–187.

10.   While infant burial in villas or residential spaces during the fourth and fifth centuries was fairly common, the vast majority of known examples, particularly those from sites within the Italian peninsula, have been found within rooms or areas of a structure or site that were clearly abandoned or used only for refuse disposal: Di Gennaro and Griesbach 2003.

11.   Plin. *NH* 33.23; Plin. *Ep.* 8.6.4.

12.   Trimble, 2016: Antiquarium Comunale, n. 239.

13.   Latrines are notably absent from army barracks as well: Davison 1989:236. Note that there are no latrines in the slave quarters at Settefinestre: Carandini 1985:20.

14.   A comparison comes from Brough on Humber, where the eavesdrop channel was used as a latrine, see Davison 1989:236.

15.   For further discussion see von Petrikovits 1975; Davison 1989.

16.   Davison 1989:6. At 43 x 8.10 m, both blocks fall into the second size-range, from 30–52 x 4–13 m, a size characteristic of auxiliary forts in all periods. The equally sized rooms of the north block mirror the *arma* and *popilio* of the *contubernia* of his type B.

17.   See, for example, the fine mosaic floors at the *Castrum praetorium* (Busch 2011:65, fig. 26). However, the floors of the barracks in the *Castrum Albanum* were of beaten earth, although the walls were plastered and far better constructed (Aglietta and Busch 2011).

18.   For the continuity of slaves in Late Roman agriculture, Harper 2011:151–200. For the use of slaves in the traditional, plantation way rather than as tenants, and a view as to their rarity in this period, Wickham 2005:262, 268, and 276, where he denies the existence of slave plantations except in the Aegean after AD 300: see also on this (pro) Whittaker 1987 and (contra) Vera 1992.

19.   Fentress, Goodson, and Maiuro 2016:171–174.

20.   The model large, courtyard slave barracks at Settefinestre and Lucus Feroniae have both been the subject of controversy. The first is rejected by Marzano on the grounds that it could have been a stable, in that horses could fit through the doors, in spite of the absence of mangers. She proposes that slaves were housed elsewhere, in structures of perishable materials, which would be very curious in an area where all rural construction was of *pisé de terre* on a stone socle, and would rather defeat the purpose of keeping the workforce under close control. We might not accept the definition of the various rooms—indeed, the single two-roomed suite would seem more appropriate for a monitor than for an infirmary (*valetudinarium*)—but there is no doubt that the arrangements seem more suitable for people than for horses. The second, Lucus Feroniae, is rejected on the grounds that its huge courtyard is simply too grand, and the *lararium* too beautiful for slaves—in spite of the regularity with which *lararia* were found in the service areas of Pompeian houses, where the *vilica*, the *vilicus,* and the *familia* could join in the worship of the household gods (Cato *de Agr.* 143.2), often feasting after the sacrifice (Kolendo 1993:273). Manacorda 1982:62 and De Franceschini 2005:284 suggest respectively that the courtyard was used for storage and for *nundinae,* while Marzano argues for its use as an inn: 2007:146.

The standard plan is found as far north as Friuli:where recent excavations have revealed a large, porticoed building, apparently of the first century AD, with at least nine square or rectangular rooms aligned in a row with a portico in front of it opening onto what is apparently a large open space or courtyard (Ventura and Rigoni 2011).

21.   Salza Prina Ricotti 2001:165 lists the various interpretations as housing for the Praetorian Guard or storage, which she dismisses. It seems, however, not impossible that the bottom levels, opening onto the road, were used for storage.

22.   One such figure would be M. Aurelius Sabinianus, a freedman and probably an imperial procurator, known from Anagni: *CIL* X.5917 (AD 161–192).

23.   On the extent of the imperial properties in Italy, Maiuro 2012.

24.   On the agrarian legislation from Roman North Africa, Kehoe 1988, with previous bibliography.

REFERENCES

Aglietti, S., and A. Busch 2011 Dalla villa imperiale ai Castra Albana: le nuove ricerche del DAI sull'accampamento della legione II Parthica e sui suoi dintorni. In *Lazio e Sabina* 7, edited by G. Ghini, pp. 259–67. Quasar, Rome.

Alison P. 2006 *The Insula of the Menander at Pompeii v.III, the Finds, a Contextual Survey.* Oxford University Press, Oxford.

Basso, P. 2003 Gli alloggi servili. In *Subterraneae Domus. Ambienti residenziali e di serviziio nell'e-dilizia privata romana,* edited by P. Basso and F. Ghedini, pp. 443–459. Cierre, Caselle di Sommacampagna.

Busch, A. 2011 *Militär in Rom. Militärische und paramilitärische Einheiten im kaiserzeitlichen Stadtbild* (*Palilia* 20). Reichert Verlag, Wiesbaden.

Camodeca, G. 2007 La proprietà imperiale in Campania. In *Le proprietà imperiali nell'Italia romana. Economia, produzione, amminjistrazione.* Atti del Convegno Ferrara-Voghiera 304 giugno 2005. Edited by D. Pupillo, pp. 143–167. Le Lettere, Florence.

Carandini, A. 2010 *Le case del potere nell'antica Roma.* Laterza, Rome.

Carandini, A. (ed.) 1985 *Settefinestre. Una villa schiavistica nell'Etruria romana.* Panini, Modena.

Carlsen, J. 1995 *Vilici and Roman Estate Management until AD 284.* Analecta Rommana Instituti Danici Supp. XXIC. L'Erma de Bretschneider, Rome.

Cassieri, N. 2000 *La Grottta di Tiberio e il Museo Archeoogico Nazionale di Sperlonga.* Istituto poligrafico e Zecca dello Stato, Rome.

Carandini, A., M. T. D'Alessio, and H. Di Giuseppe 2007 *La fattoria e la villa dell'Auditorium* (*BCAR Supplement* 14). Bretschneider, Rome.

Davison, D. 1989 *The Barracks of the Roman Army from the 1st to 3rd Centuries A.D.: A Comparative Study of the Barracks from Fortresses, Forts, and Fortlets with an Analysis of Building and Construction, Stabling and Garrisons.* British Archaeological Reports International Series 472. Oxford University Press, Oxford.

De Franceschini M. 2005. *Ville dell'Agro Romano.* Bretschneider, Rome.

Della Corte, M. 1922 Pompei: Scavi eseguiti da private nel territorio di Pompei *Notizie degli Scavi di Antichità* 1922:459–478.

Della Corte, M. 1923 Villa rustica esplorata dal sig. Cav. Carlo Rossi-Filangieri in un fondo del sig. Comm. Agnello Marchetti. *Notizie degli Scavi di Antichità* 1923:375–380.

Di Gennaro, F., and J. Griesbach 2003 Le sepolture all'interno delle ville con particolare riferimento al territorio di Roma. In *Suburbium. Il suburbio di Roma dalla crisi del sistema delle ville a Gregorio Magno*. Collections de l'École Française de Rome 311, edited by P. Pergola, R. Santangeli Valenzani, and R. Volpe, pp. 126–66. École Française de Rome, Rome.

Étienne, R. 1972 Recherches sur l'ergastule in Actes du Colloque 1972 sur l'esclavage. *Annales littéraires de l'Université de Besançon* 163:49–266.

Fentress, E., M. Maiuro, C. Goodson, M. Andrews, and J. A. Dufton (eds.) 2016 *An Imperial Estate and Its Legacies: Villamagna, near Anagni*. Supplement to the Papers of the British School at Rome, Rome.

Fentress, E., and M. Maiuro 2011 Villa Magna near Anagni: The Emperor, his Winery, and the Wine of Signia. *Journal of Roman Archaeology* 24:333–369.

George, M. 1997 Servus and Domus: The Slave in the Roman House. In Domestic Space in the Roman World: Pompeii and Beyond. *Journal of Roman Archaeology* suppl 22:15–24.

Harper, K. 2011 *Slavery in the Late Roman World. AD 275–425*. Cambridge University Press, Cambridge.

Joshel, S. 2013 Geographies of Slave Containment. In *Roman Slavery and Roman Material Culture* Phoenix Supplementary Volumes 52, edited by M. George, pp. 99–128. Toronto University Press, Toronto.

Kehoe, D. 1988 *The Economics of Agriculture on Roman Imperial Estates in North Africa* Hypomnemata 89. Vandenhoeck u. Ruprecht, Göttingen.

Kolendo, J. 1993 La religion des esclaves dans le *De agricultura* de Caton. In *Religion et anthropologie de l'esclavage et des formes de dépendance, Le ville romane della X regio*: Centre de Recherches d'Histoire Ancienne 133, edited by J. Annequin and M. Garrido-Hory, pp. 267–274. Presses Universitaires Franche-Comté, Paris.

Ling, R. 1997 *The Insula of the Menander at Pompeii. The Structures*. Clarendon Press, Oxford.

Maiuri, A. 1933 *La Casa del Menandro e il suo Tesoro di argenteria*. Libreria dello Stato Rome.

Maiuro, M. 2012 *Res Caesaris: ricerche sulla proprietà imperial nel Principato* Pragmateiai 23. Edipuglia, Bari.

Maloney, J. J., and J. R. Hale 1996 The villa of Torre di Palma (Alto Alentejo). *Journal of Roman Archaeology* 9:275–294.

Manacorda, D. 1982 Il frantoio della villa dei Volusii a Lucus Feroniae. In *I Volusii Saturnini. Una famiglia romana della prima età imperiale*, pp. 55–82. De Donato, Bari: Rome.

Marzano, A. 2007 *Roman Villas in Central Italy: A Social and Economic History*. Brill, Leiden.

Ortner, D. J. 2003 *Identification of Pathological Conditions in Human Skeletal Remains*. 2nd ed. Academic Press, San Diego.

Rossiter, J. 1978 *Roman Farm Buildings*. British Archaeological Reports 52. Oxford University Press, Oxford.

Roth, U. 2007 *Thinking Tools. Agricultural Slavery between Evidence and Models*. Institute of Classical Studies, London.

Ruggiero, M. 1881 degli Scavi di Stabia dal MDCCXLIX al MDCCLXXXII. ipografia dell'Academia reale delle scienze, Naples.

Salza Prina Ricotti, E. 2001 *Villa Adriana. Il sogno di un imperatore*. Bretschneider, Rome.

Schumacher, L. 2001 *Sklaverei in der Antike. Alltag und Schicksal der Unfreien*. C. H. Beck, Munich.

Tomei, M. A. 1995 Domus oppure Lupanar? I materiali dallo scavo Boni della "casa repubblicana" a ovest dell'arco di Tito. *Mélanges de l'Ecole française de Rome. Antiquité* 107:549–619.

Trimble, J. 2016 The Zoninus Slave Collar and the Archaeology of Roman Slavery. *American Journal of Archaeology* 120(2):447–472.

Ventura, P., and A. N. Rigoni 2011 Abitari e lavorare in villa: Torre di Pordenone. *Histria Antiqua* 20:257–268.

Vera, D. 1992 Schiavitù rurale, colonato e trasformazioni agrarie nell'Italia imperiale. *Scienze dell'antichità* 6–7:291–339.

von Petrikovits, H. 1975 *Die Innenbauten römischer Legionslager während der Prinzipatszeit*. V. S. Verlag für Sozialwissenschaften, Opladen.

Whittaker, C. R. 1987 Circe's Pigs. *Slavery and Abolition* 8:88–122.

Wickham, C. 2005 *Framing the Middle Ages*. Oxford University Press, Oxford.

CHAPTER SEVENTEEN

Inequality and Roman Imperial Properties

A Case Study

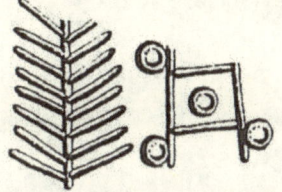

Myles McCallum

Abstract *The following paper presents some ideas about how archaeologists might measure inequality in the Roman countryside of Italy based on the evidence for imperial estates, with particular attention paid to the site at San Felice/Vagnari, a site where I have directed excavations since 2006 (Figure 17.1). The topic is a broad and daunting one, but, based on the potential social significance of imperial properties within the Italian peninsula, any study of inequality in rural Italy must take them into account. As such, this paper presents potential avenues of inquiry based on reference to extant archaeological datasets, rather than a definitive statement on how imperial estates structured economic and social opportunity in the Roman countryside.*

ROMAN IMPERIAL ESTATES

Roman imperial estates, quite sensibly, begin with the end of the second triumvirate and the foundation of the Principate (post 31 BC), and continue until the end of the Roman empire in the west (AD 476), although elements of the institution continue in some form into the sixth century AD under the reign of the Ostrogothic kings of Rome, and along the Adriatic coast and in southern Italy under Byzantine rule (Maiuro 2007b; Volpe 1998:332–338).

Imperial estates are properties owned by the *princeps/dominus* (emperor), and according to Lo Cascio, are to be considered part of the imperial *patrimonium Caesaris* (land-holdings), and a central concern of imperial *fiscus* (finances, here concerned with revenue and capital) (Maiuro 2012:18–19; Lo Cascio 2000:111–120; Kehoe 1988:220–223). These

FIGURE 17.1. Map showing location of imperial property at San Felice/Vagnari.

properties were associated with the office of emperor rather than the individuals who served as emperor, and so passed from ruler to successor.

The first such properties belonged to Augustus and included lands he inherited from Julius Caesar, lands acquired through confiscations, and properties given to the emperor both as legacies and gifts (Lo Cascio 2000:130; Maiuro 2012:38–88). By the second century AD, this came to include all the former *ager publicus* or public lands that had once been confiscated from Rome's Italian enemies/allies, previously controlled by the Senate (Lo Cascio 2000:115–117). As Lo Cascio and Maiuro have demonstrated, there was a constant fluctuation in the status of imperial properties: emperors frequently sold imperial lands to cover debts, or gave them as gifts to close Senatorial and Equestrian allies, the inner circle of the *amici Caesaris,* or the "friends of Caesar," who often returned them to the emperor as legacies in their wills (Maiuro 2012:88–109; Lo Cascio 2000:133–135). By end of the first century AD, these estates were collectively the most important element of public property in the empire. As such, they contributed to inequality in the Roman countryside, and the archaeological study of them is important for understanding critical elements of inequality and social hierarchy.

Such properties generated revenue and commodities used to support the imperial family and court, the imperial bureaucracy, and Rome's military, for the construction and renovation of religious and public structures, for the hosting of *munera* or games, and for the supply of the *annona* and *alimenta* (food distributions at Rome and in Italian municipalities), among other things. Consequently, these properties were an important element of the public sector of Rome's economy.

The imperial estates in Italy are known principally through textual evidence, much of it in the form of inscriptions. The most complete list of them has been compiled by Maiuro and includes discussion of the epigraphic or other textual data as well as, where possible, that of the archaeological remains (Maiuro 2012:241–348; Maiuro 2007a: Appendix C). These properties included land in every region of the peninsula and in the Po Valley, both large pleasure estates such as the imperial *villae* at Tivoli, Sperlonga, and on Capri, former Senatorial properties in the Roman campagna, and smaller, principally productive properties like the one discussed below at San Felice/Vagnari.

What is known about the management of these estates comes principally from the epigraphic record of North Africa, on which the historian Dennis Kehoe has published widely, and Egypt, on which Parrasoglou, Bagnall, and others have commented over the past three decades (Kehoe 2007, 2006, 1988; Parrasoglou 1978). In essence, their administrative structure is based on the experience of wealthy private landowners during the late Republic that evolved through practice and experience during the Imperial period. It is likely that such properties were managed indirectly by the *fiscus* through a series of leasehold agreements, negotiated and overseen either directly between an imperial agent (*actor?*) and *coloni* (tenant farmers), or indirectly between *conductores* (lessees) who engaged in lustral (five-year) leases with imperial representatives (*actores* or perhaps even *procuratores*) who, in turn, leased or managed imperial leasehold agreements with *coloni* (Kehoe 2007:48–52; 1988:78–88). Certainly, leasehold agreements and tenancy played a significant role in the management of large private estates and imperial properties, particularly from the start of the second century AD, and tenancy was typical of the management of imperial estates in North Africa (McCallum and vanderLeest 2014:133–134; Kehoe 1988:48). With respect to the archaeological evidence for imperial estates, it is possible that imperial agents, *conductores,* or the agents of *conductores* were resident on such sites, either full- or part-time. To further complicate matters, it is also possible that the leasehold arrangements of imperial properties were multiple and included both long-term leases to *coloni* and short-term leases to *conductores.*

Turning to the limited but growing body of archaeological evidence, it is now clear that the reality of imperial estates in Italy was complex. Certainly, the best known such properties are those that served as imperial residences including the estates of Tiberius at Capri and Sperlonga, the massive complex constructed by Hadrian at Tivoli, or the palatial country residence of Maxentius just outside of Rome on the Via Appia. While archaeologists have typically concerned themselves with the architectural and decorative elements, including mosaics and sculpture, of these structures as part of imperial self-display and construction of ideology, we also know that these properties were revenue-generating productive estates. At the same time, based on the rather small sample size of imperial properties about which we possess detailed knowledge, it is unclear to what extent these properties represent the norm in Italy and, therefore, to what extent their careful archaeological study can reveal elements of inequality in the Roman countryside more generally.

More recently, a few archaeological projects in Italy have been dedicated to the investigation of the productive elements of larger imperial properties and the examination of smaller such estates. These include the excavations at Villa Magna in the province of Frosinone (see Fentress in this volume) (Fentress, Goodson, and Maiuro 2016; Fentress and Maiuro 2011), at Colle Plinio in the Tiber Valley near *Tifernum Tiberinum* (Città di Castello) in Umbria (Braconi and Saez 1999), at San Giusto in the province of Foggia (Volpe 1998), and excavations of multiple sites that form a part of the imperial estate at San Felice/Vagnari in the province of Bari (McCallum and vanderLeest 2014; Small 2011; McCallum, vanderLeest et al. 2011; Prowse, Barta, von Hunnius, and Small 2010; Small and Small 2007), among others.

In total, Maiuro identifies dozens of potential imperial estates within Italy including the Po River Valley, which, he freely admits, is only a small portion of the total that must have existed (Maiuro 2012:241–346; 2007:496–515). The ownership histories of imperial estates, which move in an out of the control of the imperial *fiscus,* further complicate the issue. As a result, is often impossible to assign archaeological data from excavated imperial estates with specific periods of imperial control. Finally, the sample presented by Maiuro is quite small and we are left to wonder the extent to which it is representative of all the estates that may once have existed in Italy (Maiuro 2012:159–169). Consequently, subsequent discussion is restricted to potential avenues of investigation indicated by these data sets and what these data suggest about the possible role of imperial estates in perpetuating a system of inequality in the Roman countryside.

Two possible avenues of inquiry:

1. Inequality within the imperial estate/property itself:

    A. Architectural elaboration/spatial differences/access.

    B. Functional areas.

    C. Artifactual assemblages and environmental data.

2. Inequality between Imperial Estates and other estates:

    A. Spatial distribution of Imperial estates compared to other estates.

    B. Access to resources and markets.

INEQUALITY WITHIN IMPERIAL ESTATES

Historically, Classical archaeologists have focused on architectural design and decorative elements, in part because a number of ancient Latin texts present discussions of Roman architecture and vivid descriptions of elite residences (Vitruvius *de Arch* 6.5–6; Pliny the Younger *Ep* 2.17). As a consequence, Roman archaeologists and art historians have identified a suite of indicators to identify and understand elements of differential social access to architectural spaces. One of the best-known presentations of this approach is Andrew Wallace-Hadrill's study of space and society at Pompeii and Herculaneum (1994), and his approach has been refined and applied to other similar datasets over the past 15 years (Özgenel 2007; Ellis 2007).

Based on studies of architectural data and their associated decorative elements, it is possible to examine the divisions of space within the grand imperial properties at Tivoli, Sperlonga, and on Capri in a rather gross manner. Based on the excavation histories of these properties, it must also be noted that this can at present only be done for the residential and reception areas of these properties, that is, spaces occupied by the emperor and his retinue during visits to these properties. At Tivoli, this includes areas such as the Maritime Theatre and the Hall of the so-called Winter Palace (MacDonald and Pinto 1995:186–197). We can also identify some areas inhabited by household servants and slaves, such as the barracks area and the Praetorium (MacDonald and Pinto 1995:183–192). These spatial data indicate that those areas reserved exclusively for the residence and other activities of slaves or servants represent a relatively small proportion of the entire property, although it is quite possible that certain elements of the staff were housed at some distance from the villa proper, possibly in Tivoli, while other members of the staff must have been employed only during imperial visits and entertainments (MacDonald and Pinto 1995:185–186). At the same time, it should also be stressed that in the execution of their daily duties, these individuals penetrated residential areas reserved for the imperial family and their guests (Wallace-Hadrill 1994:38–44, 57–60), which makes such studies of relatively limited utility in understanding inequality within the structures themselves. It also seems unlikely that the unequal access to space seen in an imperial property was much different from what one might have encountered at any large, private rural estate.

There has been only limited investigation of the industrial or agricultural areas associated with these properties, which were also venues for the activities of those of lower social rank. Consequently, there are relatively few studies that address the humbler aspects of these monumental properties. For Tivoli, there are a handful of articles by Jansen looking at social distinctions and issues of privacy in the toilets at Hadrian's estate that draw clear distinctions among various social groups (2007; 2003).

New datasets and a reconsideration of seldom-considered data are now addressing this bias. The Villa Magna excavations demonstrate that architectural evidence can provide clear guidance to spatial divisions based on status and rank, and afford insight into how these divisions might change over time in relation to localized events and more general histories (Fentress, this volume). To this we can add a new project directed by Franco de Angelis and

Marco Maiuro at Tivoli, which is focused on the study of the more humble aspects of the imperial property. Unfortunately, we will have to wait to draw on their results.

Turning to the imperial property at San Felice/Vagnari, we can evaluate the various categories of archaeological evidence with respect to identifying social inequality. The property is located in the Basentello Valley of modern Puglia, within the territory of the town of Gravina in Puglia (province of Bari). The estate has been the subject of archaeological investigation since the late 1990s when the two primary sites that comprise the property were identified during regional field survey (Small and Small 2005). Since then, excavations at the site of Vagnari, located on a relatively flat plain at the base of a large plateau, and at San Felice, situated on a natural terrace of this plateau approximately 900 meters to the southeast, have generated a range of relevant data.

Epigraphic and archaeometric data indicate that they are two parts of a single imperial property, a very early addition to the imperial *patrimonium* during the first quarter of the first century AD (Small, Volterra, and Hancock 2003; McCallum, vanderLeest et al. 2011:24–26). Taken together, the sites appear to have functioned as a residential villa (San Felice) and its associated workers' village (Vagnari), which shows evidence for iron working, tile making, and agricultural processing (Small 2011:26–28, 279–286). Both the village and the villa were constructed during the second half of the first century BC (McCallum, vanderLeest et al. 2011:36; Small 2011:18–20). The villa at San Felice existed throughout the first century AD but the structure was destroyed during the second century AD, after which the site was used for artisanal activities (McCallum, vanderLeest et al. 2011:64–69). Renovations and activities at the site can be divided into three phases of occupation and a postoccupational phase (Table 17.1). The village at Vagnari was occupied continuously until the sixth or early seventh century AD (Small 2011:371).

Since archaeological investigations of the two sites began, there has been clear evidence for a degree of social and economic inequality between them. The surface scatter at San Felice contained colorful fragments of wall plaster (Figure 17.2), column bricks, and

TABLE 17.1.
PERIODS OF OCCUPATION AT THE IMPERIAL ESTATE OF SAN FELICE/VAGNARI

San Felice (Villa/Residence)	Vagnari (Village)
Pre-Roman Occupation: Second Century BC?	Pre-Roman Occupation: Second Century BC?
Phase 1: Last ¼ of 1st Century BC to First ¼ to ½ of 1st Century AD	Phase 1: Last ¼ of 1st Century BC to First ¼ to ½ of 1st Century AD
Phase 2: Mid1st Century AD to Late 1st/ Early Second Century AD; Destruction of Villa/Residence	Phase 2: Mid1st Century AD to Mid 2nd Century
Phase 3: Re-use of site? Late 2nd Century AD	Abandonment: 6th Century AD

FIGURE 17.2. Painted wall plaster recovered from surface survey at the site of San Felice.

what appeared to be *suspensurae,* while that at Vagnari contained none of these items (Small 2011:53–72; McCallum, vanderLeest et al. 2011:29–32). The initial hypothesis of excavators working at both locations was that the site at Vagnari was the location of a workers' village and associated artisanal area, while the site at San Felice was home to a residential villa occasionally occupied by the landowner (McCallum and vanderLeest 2014:132–133; McCallum, vanderLeest et al 2011:99–101; Small 2011:26–27). Much of our initial investigation of the site at San Felice was concerned with testing this hypothesis through excavation to understand if this degree of material inequality between the surface assemblages was indicative of social inequality.

The question of who was resident in the villa both before and after it became an imperial property is of significance to our discussion of inequality. There is no evidence to indicate the identity of the villa's owner and residents, but, based on what is known about rural properties throughout Roman Italy in the late republic and early empire, a bit can be said about the status of the owner and those with whom he shared his rural residence. Presumably the structure, based on its size, the level of decoration, and the investment in productive infrastructure, may have belonged to someone of the local or regional elite, rather than the elite at Rome.

Once the property was transferred to the imperial fisc, the status of those resident at San Felice doubtless changed. The property might have been managed directly by the imperial fisc, in which case we might expect an *actor* and his staff to be resident in the structure and to have been responsible for overseeing leasehold agreements between the fisc and local *coloni*. Alternatively, the property might have been leased to *conductores,* individuals of some wealth and status in a position to enter into contracts with the imperial fisc, who maintained a representative resident on site to oversee the management of the estate and deal directly with the *coloni* who in turn leased parts of the estate, productive infrastructure, or grazing rights from the *conductores* (McCallum and vanderLeest 2014:132–133). Based on what has been noted about the transformation of the *pars urbana,* it seems unlikely that the individuals resident within the villa at this time were of high social status or rank.

Architectural Evidence

Architecturally, there is also a noticeable distinction between the two sites. The structure excavated at San Felice is clearly that of a small to mid-sized courtyard villa (at least 1,200 square meters), with a west-facing loggia, similar to others excavated throughout Basilicata and northwestern Puglia (Figure 17.3) (McCallum, vanderLeest et al. 2011:26–27; Di Giuseppe 2008 and 2007; Gualtieri 2008). There is no evidence to indicate a second story. Decorative elements within the western range of rooms are consistent with a residential or reception function during the first phase of occupation at the site (Table 17.1) (McCallum, vanderLeest et al. 2011:98–99). With respect to these decorative elements, they include relatively simple frescoes (Figure 17.4) and painted concrete floors, similar to those found at other nearby Hellenistic and Republican rural structures in Apulia and Lucania (McCallum, vanderLeest et al. 2011:100; Russo 2006:108). This level of decoration would seem to indicate an owner of relatively modest means rather than a member of Rome's senatorial or Equestrian elite (for example, Settefinestre, Carandini, and Filipi 1985; Ossaia in the Valdichiana, Fracchia 2006; and the villa of Pliny at Tifernum Tiberiunum, Braconi and Saez, 1999; Braconi, 2008).

The area around the small peristyle or large *impluvium* is of unknown function; there is some red painted wall plaster, but the floors are beaten earth with river cobbles, and the working part of the structure, including a wine- or oil-pressing facility (or both), is immediately adjacent (Figure 17.5) (McCallum, vanderLeest, and Hyatt 2014:339; McCallum and vanderLeest 2014:129–130).

The pressing facility, which represents a significant capital investment, is perhaps indicative of commercially oriented surplus agricultural production at San Felice. Such villa infrastructure is seen throughout Italy starting in the late Republic (Marzano 2013; Foxhall 1990; Carandini and Filippi 1985). While the example at San Felice is relatively small in comparison to contemporaneous sites excavated elsewhere in Italy (for example, the villa at Settefinestre, Carandini and Filippi 1985), the villa itself is not large, so its size is a function of appropriate scale. The revenue generated through the production and sale of oil and wine

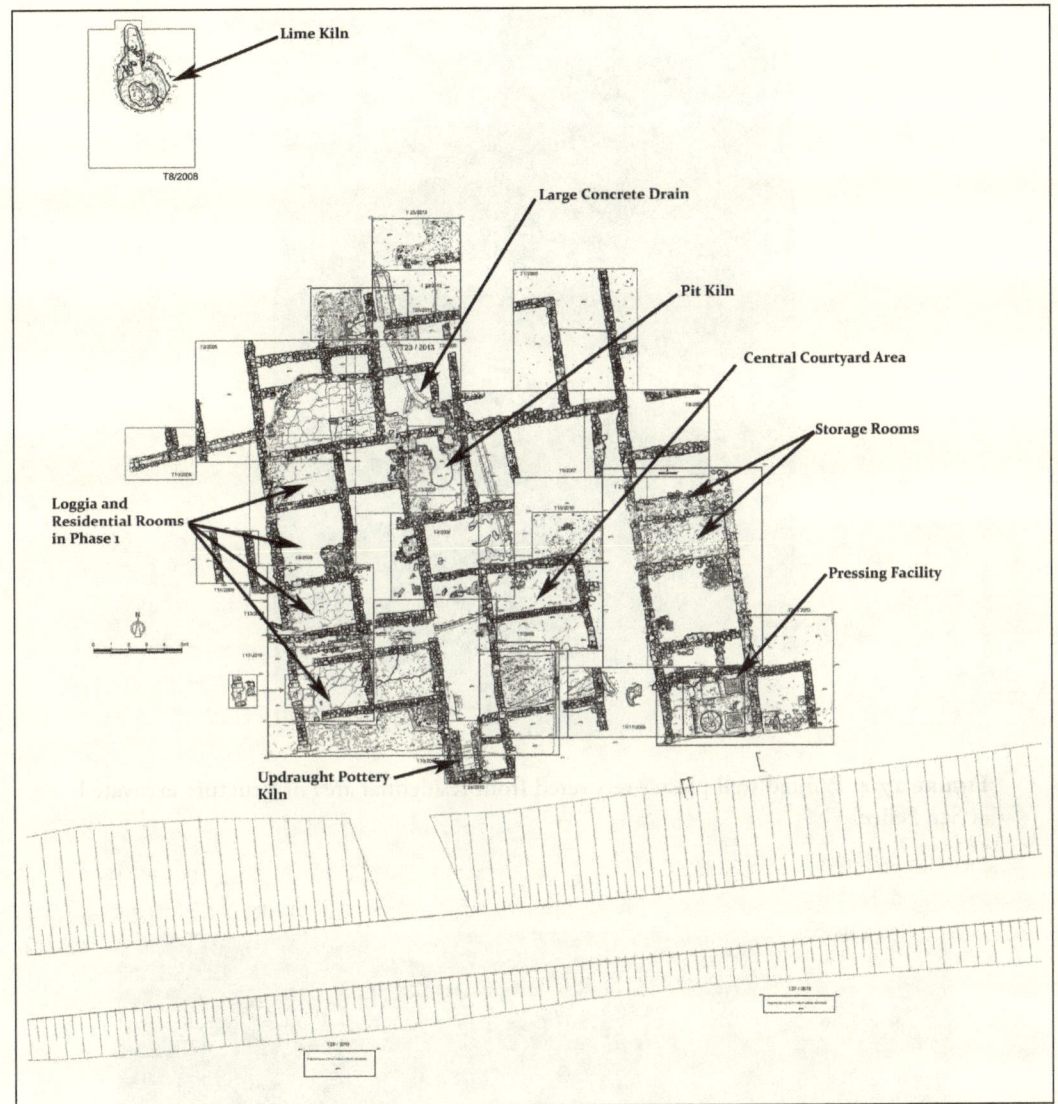

FIGURE 17.3. Plan of Roman structure excavated at San Felice.

might have created a degree of social and economic inequality between the residents of the villa at San Felice and those of the so-called workers' village at Vagnari. Prior to the transfer of these properties to the imperial fisc, this inequality would have represented that between the estate owners and those who worked and leased their land.

At Vagnari, excavations of structures associated with Periods 1B, 2, and 3A span the transition of the property from a private to an imperial estate (Table 17.2). Excavation has revealed an orthogonal plan with a internal road "network," at least one metal-working area, storage areas, a market area, a small residential area, and two tile kilns, hence the inter-

FIGURE 17.4. Painted wall plaster recovered from residential area of structure excavated at San Felice.

FIGURE 17.5. Pressing facility at San Felice.

TABLE 17.2.

PERIODS OF EARLIEST OCCUPATION/ACTIVITY AT THE SITE OF VAGNARI

Period of Activity at Vagnari	Date Range
1B	Second to First Centuries BC
2	First Century AD
3A	End of First and the Second Century AD

pretation of the site as a workers' village or *vicus* (Small 2011:21–29). The architectural differences between San Felice and Vagnari are quite striking. The single structure at San Felice is more than twice as large as the largest building excavated at Vagnari. Also, there is no evidence for the same level of spatial differentiation as at San Felice (i.e., it is difficult to identify the separation between residential and productive spaces; the floor surfaces are beaten earth and river cobbles, rather than painted concrete; there are no frescoes) (Small 2011:21–29). The inference drawn from this is that in the village there was little separation of residential from productive space (except, perhaps, with respect to the tile kilns) and that there were no contemporaneous spaces identifiable as the loci of social receptions.

Once the villa and village become imperial possessions in the early first century AD, it is more difficult to find good evidence for social or material inequality between the two sites. The western range of rooms at the villa continue to have wall plaster and decorated concrete floors (save for one), but it is not clear how many of them continue to have a residential and reception functions. At least one of these rooms appears to have been converted to a working area, and the communication between two other rooms is interrupted when a secondary drain for the courtyard is inserted into a long corridor between them (Figure 17.6) (McCallum, vanderLeest et al. 2011:46–47). This would have changed traffic patterns within the structure and possibly altered the performance of social rituals (i.e., *cenae*). Also, the central courtyard/peristyle appears to be converted into a large basin (Figure 17.7), exact function unknown, although the presumption is that it may be associated with productive activity such as wool or agricultural processing. The oil/wine-pressing area continues in use during this period. It is, however, difficult to know the extent to which those resident in the formerly private villa residence would have benefited economically from the presence of the wine- and oil-making facility and if the presence of this facility can be seen as an indicator of continued economic and social inequality.

In Phase 3, the structure at San Felice appears to lose its residential function. The basin goes out of use and is filled by garbage (a large number of butchered animal bones, large pieces of pottery, including several complete or nearly complete vessels, broken window glass, and a variety of broken metal objects), the rooms to the east of the peristyle are subdivided into smaller spaces, at least one of which becomes a storeroom. This also appears to indicate a marked change in fortune of those resident or employed within the structure, and provides no clear evidence for social inequality with respect to those resident or employed at Vagnari.

FIGURE 17.6. Drain inserted into corridor at San Felice.

ARTIFACTUAL AND ENVIRONMENTAL DATA

The principal difficulty when comparing the artifactual and environmental data sets from the two sites is that the first-century-BC through early second-century-AD layers at Vagnari present the smallest amount of archaeological data from the excavation, while those at San Felice produce the vast majority of the archaeological data. Most of the data from Vagnari pertain to the third through fifth centuries AD (Small 2011:28–34), while the site at San Felice is not used beyond the late second/early third century, and then only at a much reduced level (McCallum and vanderLeest 2014:127). Also, the nature of the deposits at both sites renders comparison difficult. Most of the first-century-AD archaeological contexts at Vagnari are small construction trenches associated with wall building and renovations (Small 2011). Some of the material related to the first century AD at San Felice, however, comes from transposed primary depositions, in this case fills that are the equivalent of middens and contain whole or almost complete artifacts (McCallum, vanderLeest et al. 2011:54–59). Consequently, these datasets can only be compared cautiously on a presence/absence basis.

FIGURE 17.7. Corner of basin excavated in 2009 showing height of wall built on top of original stone socle.

Despite the reduction in the residential and reception areas of the villa at San Felice once it becomes an imperial property, the artifactual evidence indicates continued residence in certain areas. The related contexts contain large amounts of cookware, including *clibani* or cooking covers, toiletry items, including a leaded mirror, red and yellow glass vessels, two bronze lamps and the remains of a candelabrum, a marble tabletop (Figure 17.8), a wide array of bone hairpins, bone *styli* (for writing), items of tack and harness, including bronze spurs and several fragments of bronze bits, bronze and bone furniture fittings, objects associated with the production of textiles (loom weights and distaffs), and a host of tablewares associated with the storage and consumption of food and drink (McCallum, vanderLeest et al. 2011:70–83).

While the pottery assemblage from both sites is essentially the same, including slipped tablewares, cookwares, lamps, and storage vessels, the contemporaneous artifactual assemblage from Vagnari is missing some elements that might be of significance. For example, there are no artifacts associated with spinning or weaving, no carnelian intaglios, no leaded mirrors, no marble tabletops, no bronze lamps or candelabra, no *styli*, and no red and yellow glass vessels.

At first glance, then, it seems that the material standard of living of those resident at San Felice at this time was higher than that of those resident and employed at Vagnari. The artifactual record would seem to be a potential indicator of inequality between the two parts

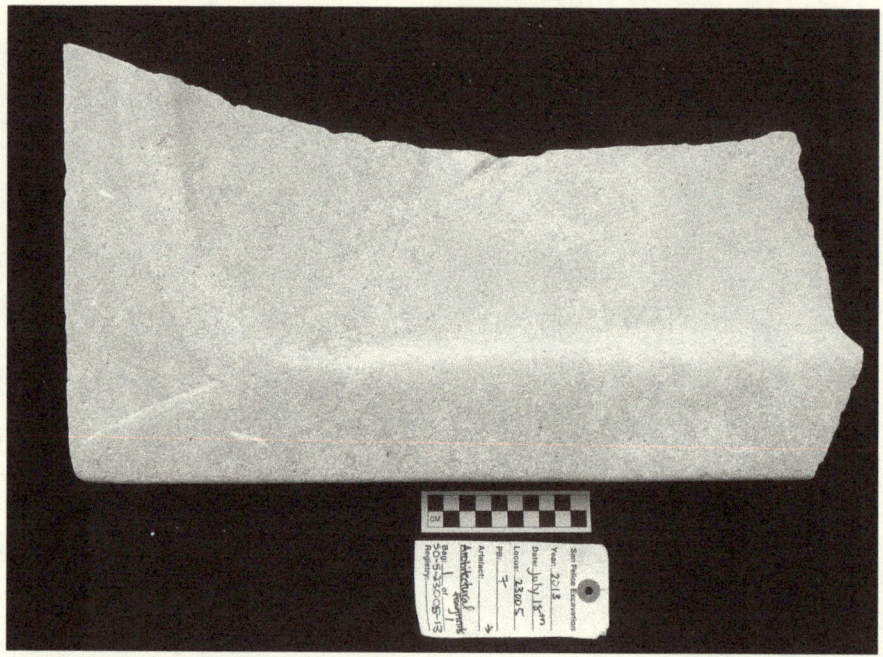

FIGURE 17.8. Marble tabletop recovered from fill layer at San Felice.

of this single estate. If this is true, it is also evidence for the continuation of the system of unequal consumption and a differential standard of living present when the property was in private hands.

A more careful consideration of this data suggests that the artifactual assemblage may not be a robust indicator of inequality. First, the Phase 2 material found in contexts created after the probable transfer of ownership includes a high percentage (23 percent) of residual pottery produced from the last half of the first century BC to the early decades of the first century AD. While it is not possible to accurately date many of the other artifacts noted above—such as loom weights, the mirror, or the candelabrum—one can imagine that a number of these artifacts also predate the transitional event. In short, much of the artifactual assemblage may already have been present on the site prior to its transfer to the imperial fisc. It is quite possible to imagine a situation in which the transfer of such a private estate into public hands might include a significant amount of *instrumentum domesticum* present already. If this is the case, then the artifacts deposited in fills associated with renovations during this phase of occupation may provide less information about the contemporaneous level of material wealth at the site. While *instrumentum domesticum* was not automatically included in the sale of property (*Digest* 19.17), in the case of items of relatively limited monetary value, such as pottery, one wonders to what extent a wealthy owner of multiple properties would be interested in maintaining possession of these *instrumenta* after the sale of the property in which they were housed.

Also, pottery is not a good indicator of economic disparity. As a consumer good, it was of relatively little economic value, particularly in comparison to other materials such as metalware and textiles. Just as survey archaeologists no longer take the presence of slipped finewares (Black Gloss, Terra Sigillata, or African Red Slip) in surface scatters as indicative of the status of a particular settlement, so it is doubtful that pottery in and of itself can be used as an indicator of economic and social inequality.

The archaeobotanical data from the two sites are also quite similar. In short, there is evidence for cereal agriculture in all phases at both sites, and no discernible difference in the types of grains consumed (McCallum, vanderLeest et al. 2011:84–90; Fiorentino, Primavera, Dand and Monkton 2011). The aforementioned production of wine and oil at San Felice is not well attested in the archaeobotanical record—there are a couple of grape pips and a couple of olive pits—so the archaeobotanical dataset may not be entirely representative. Still, there are no glaring differences that might indicate differences in diet related to social status or rank.

The faunal remains show a greater variety in the types of meats consumed at San Felice, including more species of game (deer and boar in particular), and more pork (McCallum vanderLeest et al. 2011:99–101), which may be a more robust indicator of status. At the same, time, the Phase 2 assemblage from San Felice includes a relatively large midden that contains more animal bones (1600 MNI) than are present at Vagnari during all phases (MacKinnon 2011:321–322), so it is difficult to determine the degree to which the assemblages may be compared.

The charcoal data suggest that macchia, small pieces of quick-growing wood, was commonly used as a wood fuel at both sites, although the industrial activities at Vagnari required charcoal and some larger pieces of wood (McCallum vanderLeest et al. 2011:95–98; Fiorentino, Primavera, Dand, and Monkton 2011). This may indicate that the populations were not affluent in the same manner as residents of the coastal areas of west central Italy, for which many more charcoal datasets exist. It is also quite possible that this is simply an indicator of a regional strategy of resource exploitation necessitated by climate and vegetation.

These combined datasets indicate that the degree of inequality between the two parts of this imperial property is difficult to estimate. The consumption of meat appears to have been generally similar at both sites, with possibly more pork and a game consumed at San Felice. The ceramic assemblage is essentially identical and does not indicate differences between food preparation and consumption. While there appear to have been some items of higher value—the red and yellow glass vessels, the bronze lamps, and the marble table—it is difficult to assess their significance with respect to inequality.

Overall, the data seem to indicate a continued level of inequality between the residents of both sites after the estate becomes an imperial property, although at a reduced level compared to what existed previously. This may indicate the residence, either part or fulltime, of some sort of estate manager in the villa structure. The status of this manager is not known. Based on evidence for such estates in North Africa, we should expect some low-level imperial official to coordinate both with those who leased imperial property and with the office of the territorial or regional imperial *procurator* who oversaw many such properties. Possible candidates include a *vilicus,* a lower-level clerical grade charged with the oversight of a single villa or property, or a *tabularius,* an intermediate clerical grade frequently charged with overseeing the operations of leaseholders.

The evidence for inequality derives from a wide array of archaeological evidence, any single category of which would likely be insufficient on its own to demonstrate inequality conclusively. When compared to the architectural data that we encounter at places such as Tivoli, Sperlonga, or Capri, it is clear that at primarily productive, small imperial properties, there was likely a much less significant social divide between management and workers. It is important to note, however, that this inequality was structured by a set of relationships between representatives of the fisc and lessors; in this sense, a pervasive institution such as imperial estates must have been seminal in the construction of inequality, even in places of what appears to be marginal significance, such as San Felice/Vagnari in the early imperial period.

INEQUALITY BETWEEN IMPERIAL ESTATES AND OTHER PROPERTIES

The spatial distribution of imperial estates throughout Italy is perhaps the most important category of evidence for determining how imperial estates structured inequality throughout the Italian countryside. Such data are suggestive of differential access to both resources and markets, which is, of course, an important factor in establishing and perpetuating inequality. Maiuro has recently published on this topic, concluding that the privileged economic importance given to imperial estates within Italy by Roman historians is exaggerated. He calculates that in total imperial estates represented only 5 percent of all productive land (2012:143–145). Maiuro's calculations, which are based mostly on epigraphic data, might underestimate the amount of fiscal land in Italy, particularly in regions where the epigraphic habit was not strong, or after the second century AD when there is a reduction in the number of inscriptions across Italy as a whole. His suggestion that imperial estates, and those estates controlled by Rome's senatorial elite, represent a small minority of productive Italian land appears to be a valid observation. More importantly, however, the distribution of these properties with respect to valuable resources, quality land, transport corridors and infrastructure, and, by extension, markets, indicates that they had an outsize economic significance.

Maiuro notes this phenomenon in his discussion of imperial estates and an associated port northwest of Rome along at the Tyrrhenian coast at Centumcellae (Figure 17.9). He suggests that the port site, which was large and evidently unique, was involved in the shipment and transshipment of both fiscal and private cargoes, thus functioning as one of Rome's feeder ports (Maiuro 2012:260–262). If this is so, then the surrounding imperial properties were in the best position to take advantage of this transport infrastructure and their produce had privileged access to the Roman market. Also, nearby private estates would have relied on the presence of the imperial port and relations with the management of the associated imperial estates for marketing their produce at Rome. The port's possible role with respect to transshipment further extends imperial economic influence to cargoes traveling long distances and the *negotiatores* (shippers) responsible for them.

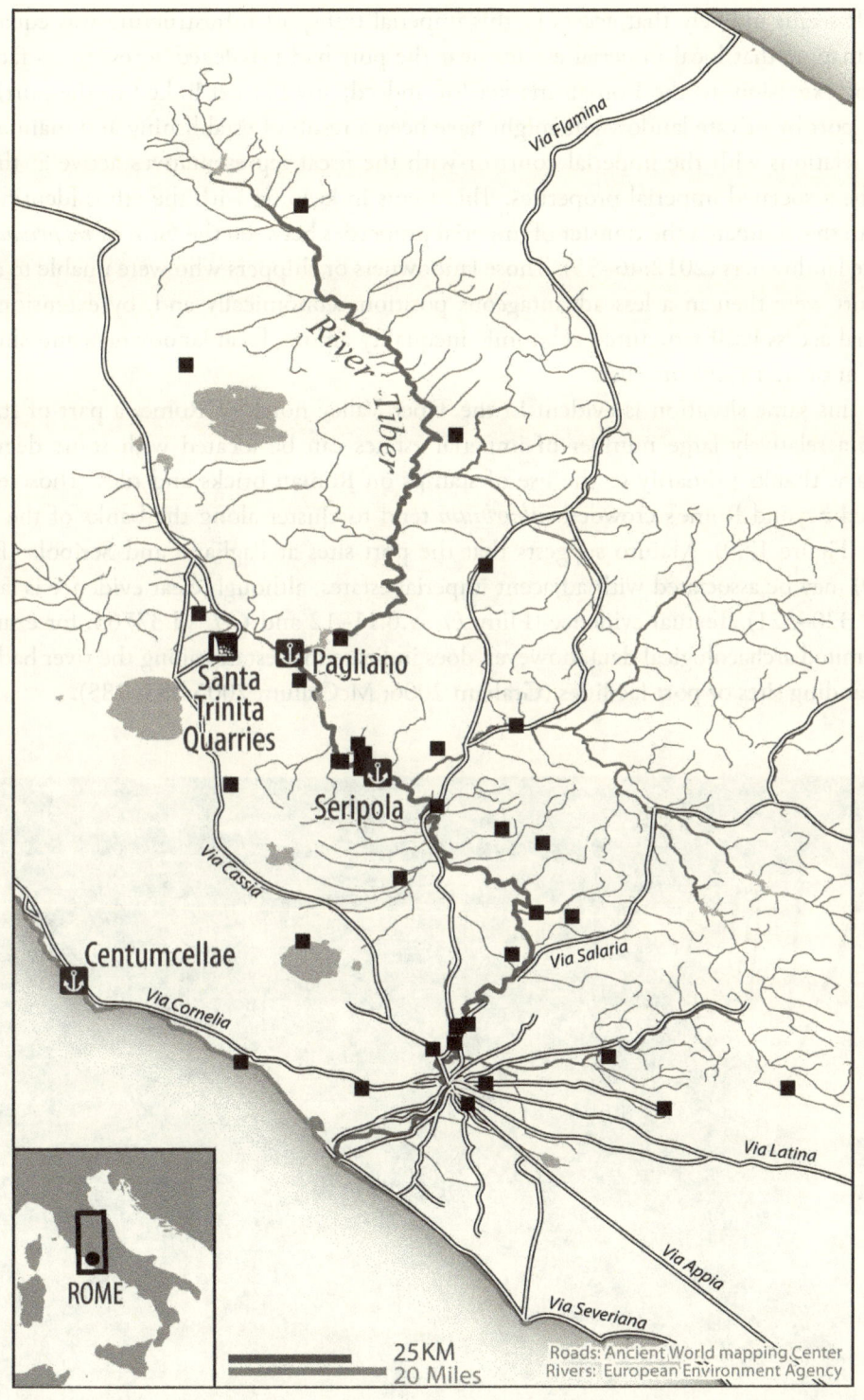

FIGURE 17.9. Map of West Central Italy showing conjectured locations of imperial properties, port sites, and road network. Map prepared by William Flanagan, Saint Mary's University.

It seems unlikely that access to this imperial transport infrastructure was equal. We may imagine that local imperial estates near the port had privileged access to its facilities and, by extension, to the Roman market (or, indeed, any market linked to the port). Use of the port by private landowners might have been a result of establishing and maintaining good relations with the imperial court or with the fiscal representatives active at the site and the associated imperial properties. This seems in keeping with the ethos identified by Maiuro that animated the transfer of imperial properties between the *fiscus* or *res privata* and private landowners (2012:46–55). Those landowners or shippers who were unable to access the port were then in a less advantageous position economically and, by extension, this unequal access itself structured economic inequality among local landowners and shippers active at or near Centumcellae.

This same situation is evident in the Tiber Valley north of Rome, a part of Italy in which a relatively large number of imperial estates can be located with some degree of accuracy, thanks primarily to the use of stamps on Roman bricks and tiles. Those estates situated beyond Rome's crowded *suburbium* tend to cluster along the banks of the Tiber River (Figure 17.9). Maiuro suggests that the port sites at Pagliano and Seripola (Figure 17.10) may be associated with adjacent imperial estates, although clear evidence is lacking (2012:320–321). Textual evidence (Pliny *Ep.* V.6.11–12 and *CIL* VI.37763, for example) and limited archaeological data, however, does indicate that estates along the river had their own landing sites or port facilities (Graham 2006; McCallum 2005:283–285).

FIGURE 17.10. View of possible storage area, Roman river port on the Tiber at Seripola.

Estates located along the banks of the Tiber, or within easy reach of the river, would have had privileged access to the most important transport corridor in west central Italy. Indeed, there is no known imperial estate farther than 10 km from the river once one reaches the town of Orte (ancient *Horta*), and most appear to include land along the river's banks. This suggests that such estates were positioned to take advantage of commercial connections with Rome, the largest market center in Italy, and any other market served by merchandise transported on the Tiber. The elevated value of these estates, noted by Cicero in his *Pro Roscio* (VII.20), corresponds to their productivity and ease of transport to the Roman market (McCallum 2005:284).

From a variety of archaeological and textual datasets, we know that productive estates within the Tiber basin, including imperial properties, were responsible for supplying the city of Rome with building materials (bricks and tiles) (Graham 2006; McCallum 2005:204–209; DeLaine 1997:126; Setälä 1977:19–20), foodstuffs (wine, oil, and grain) (Marzano 2013; McCallum 2005:141–187; De Sena 2005; Rizzo 2003; Peña 1998; Panella 1994), fuel (McCallum 2005:209–215; Delaine 1995), timber (Diosono 2008; McCallum 2005:209–215), pottery (Bergamini 2014; Rizzo 2003; Peña 1998), and millstones (McCallum 2010:89; Peacock 2014:86–88). As already noted in our discussion of the estate at San Felice/Vagnari, the production of these materials involved a number of different economic actors. The legal, epigraphic, and textual sources indicate that most of the imperial estates of the early and middle empire leased land to tenants as part of a system to reduce financial risk on the part of the owner, the best example of this being the leasing of vineyards by Pliny the Younger on his Tiber valley estate at Tifernum Tiberinum (Pliny *Ep.* 8.2; Kehoe 1997:197–199; McCallum 2005:245–248). The production of brick and tile on imperial estates was also the result of *location-conductio* leasehold agreements between estate managers and brick and tile makers (Setälä 1977:222–224; Helen 1975:82–83). Access to these productive lands, their resources, and the markets they served was controlled by those who managed them. Based on the example of the aforementioned imperial port at Centumcellae, it is also likely that access to elements of transport infrastructure—river ports and access roads—was frequently controlled or mediated by the managers of imperial properties in the Tiber valley.

Moreover, these imperial estates were not isolated. Members of Rome's Senatorial and Equestrian elite, as well as the wealthiest imperial freedmen, owned adjacent, high-value land along the Tiber River (McCallum 2005:120–131; Vera 1995:204). Survey data generated for Rome's hinterland indicates that more modest properties existed alongside these large estates (Witcher 2008:478–483). It is possible to imagine a situation in which the most economically productive land, that which was best positioned with respect to the Tiber, was principally controlled by the imperial fisc and Rome's economic elite (McCallum 2010:89–90; McCallum 2005:95–96; Dyson 1992:97), and that access to the resources and transport infrastructure associated with these properties by actors of lower socioeconomic status or rank was mediated through leasehold or tenancy agreements with private and public fiscal estate managers.

The same appears to be true in southern Italy, where Small has plotted the find spots of the inscriptions associated with the presence of imperial estates in ancient Apulia, Calabria, and eastern Lucania (Small and Small 2005). These properties are clustered along the region's trunk roads. There are likely two reasons for this: first, many of these properties were involved in the production of wool (combined with cereal agriculture, thanks to a system of long-distance transhumance), and the Roman trunk roads worked in combination with drove roads to move flocks to and from the Apennine mountains (Small and Small 2005:898–899); second, the lack of navigable water courses in Apulia, Calabria, and Lucania made overland transport the only option for the movement of commodities from agricultural estates to market. Corbier, based in large part on her interpretation of the famous Saepinum inscription, *CIL* 9.2438, has suggested that imperial flocks and their handlers had privileged access to the region's drove roads (2007; 1983). Alongside this pastoral activity, environmental and archaeological data suggests that this pastoral activity was integrated with cereal agriculture. Consequently, unequal access to the region's road system would have privileged the marketing of products produced on imperial properties throughout the region. Those who wished to have similar access would have had to lease property (pasture, agricultural land, or infrastructure) from the imperial *fiscus*.

Returning to the industrial and agricultural village at Vagnari, it is an excellent example of the economically privileged status of imperial estates in southern Italy. The excavation data indicates an expansion of the village in the fourth century AD that may be a direct consequence of its location in the Basentello/Bradano valley and the newly renovated port at Metapontum, allowing it to export grain during a period of increased cereal agriculture production in south Italy (fourth through mid-fifth century AD) (Small 2011:29–33). Survey and excavation results in other parts of the Bradano/Basentello watershed suggest an increase in the number of sites and the size of many rural sites with easy access to roads leading to Metapontum during the period, a phenomenon that doubtless includes both private and imperial estates (Small 2011:29–33; Lapadula 2011; De Siena and Giardino 2001:162;).

The principal axis of inequality in all of these cases is the access to commercial markets. We might also presume that the access to resources is also a measure of inequality among imperial properties, rural productive properties owned by members of Rome's Senatorial and Equestrian classes, and those owned by members of the lower juridical orders. In this scenario, fiscal and senatorial properties likely possessed better soils, more trees for timber and fuel, higher-quality pasture, accessible mineral resources (via quarrying or mining) (McCallum 2010:80–81).

Conversely, based on the conjectured management structure of the estate at San Felice/Vagnari, participation by Roman leaseholders, in this case *coloni* (Small 2011:25–26), might represent improved access on the part of average Roman farmers to markets, drove roads, and resources. Or, if in this leasehold system we see a continuation of such arrangements between wealthy landowners and farmers of lesser means, then this system of differential access mediated to a certain extent through legal contracts continued under the imperial system.

The current evidence points in the direction of this interpretation, indicating that imperial properties, alongside large private estates, were an essential element structuring inequality in the Italian countryside. This role is directly related to the presence, productive activities, and management of imperial properties, and their interaction with private rural economic actors.

With respect to the overall goals of this conference, to come to a better understanding as to how we all might approach the issue of inequality from an archaeological perspective, using archaeological data and material culture studies to inform issues of social hierarchy and differential rank, there are some circumscribed but potentially significant observations to be made. First, while architecture and decorative elements immediately after their construction or creation may offer some insight into spatial differentiation related to status/rank, this is not always true after renovations. A residential or reception room with frescoes may be reutilized as a workspace with little or no alteration to the decorative elements. The same is likely true of spaces with mosaics or *opus sectile* floors. Second, artifactual data from most fill and dump deposits is also of relatively limited use for identifying inequality, at least based on current approaches taken by most Classical archaeologists. Pottery, which as a rule is the most common element in any Roman-period archaeological deposit, is not a clear indicator of social status or rank. There is hardly any first-century-AD site in Italy that would not produce red-slipped tablewares and un-slipped finewares associated with food consumption and storage, and residential sites in the countryside will doubtless produce cookwares associated with food preparation, including cooking covers or *clibani*. Those materials that were possessed by, and formed the social identify of, members of higher rank, such as metals, both precious and non-precious, or textiles are rarely found in the archaeological record of a rural villa, or at least not to the extent that they will allow us to say much about the status of the people living there during any given occupational period. Third, environmental data has the potential to contribute to understanding social differentiation and the presence of inequality. Diet and access to resources is likely much more indicative of inequality than the possession of African Red Slip pottery. With improvements to environmental data collection, the integration of this activity with overall research goals, and the dissemination of the data among Classical archaeologists, there exists the possibility of a radical improvement in our understanding of social inequality both within imperial estates and between imperial estates and other types of rural settlements throughout Roman Italy.

REFERENCES

Bergamini, M. 2014 *Scoppieto 4.1, I materiali, terra sigillata decorate a rilievo*. All'Insegna del Giglio, Florence.

Braconi, P. 2008 La villa di Plinio il Giovane a San Giustino. Il monumento e il suo contesto. In *Mercator placidissimus. The Tiber Valley in Antiquity. New Research in the Upper and Middle River vValley*, Atti del Convegno, Rome, British School at Rome, 27–28 febbraio 2004, edited by F. Coarelli and H. Patterson, pp. 105–121. Quaderni di Eutopia, 8, Quasar, Rome.

Braconi, P., and J. Uroz Saez 1999 *La villa di Plinio il giovane a San Giustino: primi risultati di una ricerca in corso*. Quattroemme, Ponte San Giovanni, Perugia.

Carandini, A., and M. R. Filippi 1985 *Settefinestre: una villa schiavistica nell'Etruria romana, 1*. Panini, Modena.

DeLaine, J. 1997 *The Baths of Caracalla: A Study in the Design, Construction, and Economics of Large-scale Building Projects in Imperial Rome*, Supplement 25. Journal of Roman Archaeology, Portsmouth, Rhode Island.

DeLaine, J. 1995 The Supply of Building Materials to the City of Rome. In *Settlement and Economy in Italy: 1500 BC to AD 1500*, edited by N. Christie, pp. 555–562. Oxbow Books, Oxford.

Dyson, S. 1992 *Community and Society in Roman Italy.* Johns Hopkins University Press, Baltimore.

De Sena, E. 2005 An Assessment of Wine and Oil Production in Rome's Hinterland: Ceramic, Literary, Art Historical, and Modern Evidence. In *Roman Villas around the Urbs. Interaction with Landscape and Environment Proceedings of a Conference at the Swedish Institute in Rome*, The Swedish Institute in Rome, Projects and Seminars, 2, edited by B. Santillo Frizell and A. Klynne, pp. 135–149. Swedish Institute in Rome, Rome.

De Siena, A., and L. Giardino 2001 Trasformazioni delle aree urbane e del paesaggio agrario in età romana nella Basilicata sudorientale. In *Modalità insediative e strutture agrarie nell'Italia meidionale in età romana*, edited by E. Lo Cascio and A. Storchi Marino, pp. 129–167. Pragmateiai, 7, Edipuglia, Bari.

Di Giuseppe, H. 2008 La villa romana di San Pietro di Tolve dalla proprietà senatoria a quella imperial. In Felicitas temporum: *dalla terra alle genti: la Basilicata settentrionale tra archeologia e storia*, eited by A. Russo and H. Di Giuseppe, pp. 354–391. Soprintendenza per I Beni Archeologici della Basilicata, Potenza.

Di Giuseppe, H. 2007 Proprietari e produttori nell'alta valle del Bradano. *Facta* 1:157–182.

Diosono, F. 2008 Il commercio del legname sul fiume Tevere. In *The Tiber Valley in Antiquity, New Research in the Upper and Middle Tiber Valley*, edited by F. Coarelli and H. Patterson, Mercator placidissimus, pp. 251–283. Edizioni Quasar, Rome.

Ellis, S. 2007 Shedding Light on Late Roman Housing. In *Housing in Late Antiquity: From Palaces to Shops*, edited by L. Lavan, L. Özgenel, and A. Sarantis, pp. 283–304. Brill, Leiden.

Fracchia, H. 2006 *The Villa at Ossaia and the Territory of Cortona in the Roman Period.* Syracuse, Lombardi.

Fentress, E., and M. Maiuro 2011 Villa Magna near Anagni: The Emperor, his Winery and the Wine of Signia. *Journal of Roman Archaeology* 24:333–369.

Fentress, E., Goodson, C., and Maiuro, M. 2016 Villa Magna: An imperial estate and its legacies: Excavations 2006-10. *Archaeological monographs of the British School at Rome*, 23. The British School at Rome, London.

Fiorentino, G., M. Primavera, A. Dand, and S. Monkton 2011 L'analisi dei resti vegetali carbonizzati. In *Vagnari: il villaggio, l'artigianato, la proprietà imperiale = The Village, the Industries, the Imperial Property*, edited by A. Small, pp. 329–344. Edipuglia, Bari.

Foxhall, L. 1990 The Dependent Tenant: Land Leasing and Labour in Italy and Greece. *Journal of Roman Studies* 80:97–114.

Graham, S. 2006 Ex figlinis: *The Network Dynamics of the Tiber Valley Brick Industry in the Hinterland of Rome*. John and Erica Hedges, Oxford.

Gualtieri, M. 2008 La villa di Masseria Ciccotti di Oppido Lucano: fase edilizi, architettura, mosaic. In Felicitas temporum: *dalla terra alle genti: la Basilicata settentrionale tra archeologia e storia*, edited by A. Russo and H. Di Giuseppe, pp. 264–287. Soprintendenza per i Beni Archeologici della Basilicata, Potenza.

Jansen, G. 2007 Toilets with a View: The Luxurious Toilets of the Emperor Hadrian at his Villa near Tivoli. *Babesch* 82(1):165–181.

Jansen, G. 2003 Social Distinctions and Issues of Privacy in the Toilets of Hadrian's Villa. *Journal of Roman Archaeology* 16:137–152.

Kehoe, D. 2007 *Law and the Rural Economy in the Roman Empire*. University of Michigan Press, Ann Arbor.

Kehoe, D. 1997 *Investment, Profit, and Tenancy. The Jurists and the Roman Agrarian Economy*. University of Michigan Press, Ann Arbor.

Kehoe, D. 1988 *The Economics of Agriculture on Roman Imperial Estates in North Africa*. Vandenhoeck u. Ruprecht, Göttingen.

Lapadula, E. 2011 Imperial and Late Roman Settlement in the Metapontino. In *The Chora of Metaponto 3: Archaeological Field Survey Bradano to Basento*, edited by J. Carter and A. Prieto, pp. 1137–1146. University of Texas Press, Austin.

Lo Cascio, E. 2000 *Il princeps e il suo impero: studi di storia amministrativa e finanziaria romana. Studi di storia amministriva e finanziaria romana. Documenti e studi. Collana del Dipartimento di Scienze dell'antichità dell'Università di Bari Sezione storica 26*. Edipuglia, Bari.

MacDonald, W., and J. Pinto 1995 *Hadrian's Villa and Its Legacy*. Yale University Press, New Haven.

MacKinnon, M. 2011 The Faunal Remains. In, *Vagnari: il villaggio, l'artigianato, la proprietà imperiale*, edited by A. Small, pp. 305–328. Edipuglia, Bari.

Marzano, A. 2013 Agricultural Production in the Hinterland of Rome: Wine and Olive Oil. In *The Roman Agricultural Economy: Organisation, Investment, and Production* Oxford studies on the Roman economy, 3, edited by A. K. Bowman and A. I. Wilson, pp. 85–106. Oxford University Press, Oxford.

Marzano, A. 2007 *Roman Villas in Central Italy: A Social and Economic History*, Columbia studies in the classical tradition, 30. Brill, Leiden.

McCallum, M. 2010 The Supply of Stone to the City of Rome: A Case Study of the Transport of Anician Building Stone and Millstone from the Santa Trinità Quarry (Orvieto). In *Trade and Exchange: Archaeological Studies from History and Prehistory*, edited by C. White and C. Dillian, pp. 75–94. Springer, New York.

McCallum, M. 2005 Tiberis navigabilis: *Commercial Activity between Rome and the Middle Tiber Basin during the Roman Period*. PhD dissertation, University at Buffalo, State University of New York.

McCallum, M., and A. Hyatt 2104 A View of Vagnari from across the Basentello: Initial Results from the BVARP Survey, 2012. In *Atti, Beyond Vagnari Conference, University of Edinburgh, October 26—28, 2012*, edited by A. Small, pp. 169–180. Edipuglia, Bari.

McCallum, M. and H. vanderLeest 2014 Research at San Felice: The Villa on the Imperial Estate. In *Atti, Beyond Vagnari Conference, University of Edinburgh, October 26—28, 2012*, edited by A. Small, pp. 123–134. Edipuglia, Bari.

McCallum, M., H. vanderLeest, and A. Hyatt 2014 San Felice and the Basentello Valley Archaeological Research Project, July—August, 2013 (Comune di Gravina in Puglia, Provincia di Bari, Regione Puglia). *Papers of the British School at Rome* 82:338–343.

McCallum, M., and H. vanderLeest 2013 San Felice and the Basentello Valley Archaeological Research Project, July–August 2012 (Comune di Gravina in Puglia, Provincia di Bari, Regione Puglia). *Papers of the British School at Rome* 81:371–374.

McCallum, M., H. VanderLeest, R. Veal, A. Taylor, L. Cooney, L. Brown, and M. Munro 2011 The Roman Villa at San Felice: Investigations, 2004–2010. *Mouseion* 11(1):25–108.

Maiuro, M. 2012 Res Caesaris. *Ricerche sulla proprietà imperial nel Principato*. Edipuglia, Bari.

Maiuro, M. 2007a *La proprietà imperial in Italia: un'interpretazione storica*. PhD Dissertation, Trieste-Clermont Ferrand.

Maiuro, M. 2007b Archivi, amministrazione del partimonio e proprietà imperiali nel *Liber Pontificalis*: la redazione del *libellus* imperial copiato nella *Vita Sylvestri*. In *Le proprietà imperiali nell'Italia romana. Economia, produzione, amministrazione*. Quaderni degli Annali dell'Università di Ferrara, Sezione Storia, 6. Le Lettere, Firenze:235–258.

Özgenel, L. 2007 Public Use and Privacy in Late Antique Houses in Asia Minor: The Architecture of Spatial Control. In *Housing in Late Antiquity: From Palaced to Shops*, edited by L. Lavan, L. Özgenel, and A. Sarantis, pp. 239–282. Brill, Leiden.

Panella, C. 1994 Produits agricoles transportes en amphores: l'huile et surtout le vin. *CEFR* 198:145–65.

Peña, J. T. 1999 *The Urban Economy during the Early Dominate: Pottery Evidence from the Palatine Hill*, BAR international series, 784. Archaeopress, Oxford.

Rizzo, G. 2003 Instrumenta Urbis I, *Ceramiche fini da mensa, lucerne ed anfore a Roma nei primi due secoli dell'Impero*. Ècole Française de Rome, Rome.

Russo, A. 2006 *Con il fuso e la conocchia*. Ministero per i beni e la attività culturali, Dipartimento per i beni culturali e paesaggistici, Rome.

Small, A. 2011 *Vagnari: il villaggio, l'artigianato, la proprietà imperial*. Edipuglia, Bari

Small, C., and A. Small 2008 Archaeological Field Survey at San Felice in Apulia. *Mouseion*, 7(2):101–122.

Small, C. and A. Small 2007 Excavation in the Roman Cemetery at Vagnari in the Territory of Gravina in Puglia. *Papers of the British School at Rome* 75:123–229.

Small, C., and A. Small 2005 Defining an Imperial Estate: The Environs of Vagnari in South Italy. In *Papers in Italian Archaeology VI. Communities and Settlements from the Neolithic to the Early Medieval Period*, edited by P. Attema, A. Nijboer, and A. Zifferero, pp. 894–902. Archaeopress, Oxford.

Vera, D. 1995 Dalla "Villa Perfecta" alla villa di Palladio: sulle trasforazioni del sistema agrario in Italia fra Principato e Dominato, prima parte. *Athenaeum* 83(1):189–211.

Volpe, G. 1998 *San Giusto: la villa, le ecclesiae : primi risultati dagli scavi nel sito rurale di San Giusto, Lucera* (1995–1997). Edipuglia, Bari.

Wallace-Hadrill, A. 1994 *Houses and Society in Pompeii and Herculaneum*. Princeton University Press, Princeton.

Witcher, R. 2008 The Middle Tiber Valley in the Imperial Period. In *The Tiber Valley in Antiquity, New Research in the Upper and Middle Tiber Valley*, edited by F. Coarelli and H. Patterson, Mercator placidissimus, pp. 467–485. Edizioni Quasar, Rome.

CHAPTER EIGHTEEN

Countering Inequality through Organized Collective Burial in Imperial Rome

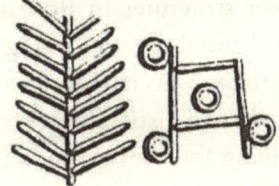

Dorian Borbonus

Abstract *Inequality was not perceived as an injustice in classical antiquity, but it still presented stumbling blocks to social mobility. The question taken up in this chapter is how social outsiders could have addressed their exclusion. My argument is that one way to do so was organized collective burial, which presented numerous opportunities for interaction. This is illustrated through the activities of associations that buried their members, but also organized different kinds of convivial meetings. Their atmosphere of solidarity is reflected in the columbarium tombs of early Imperial Rome, which united large burial communities and visually emphasized the unity of all of their members. Organized collective burial parallels other ancient and modern responses to inequality that did not outright reject the established social order and its associated ideology and culture, but instead addressed contradictory social experiences.*

As various other contributions in this volume have already shown, the distribution of authority and the allocation of social privilege were decidedly asymmetrical in ancient societies. However, and in contrast to most contemporary reactions, systemic inequality was not typically perceived as a sign of injustice.[1] This is, perhaps, one of the biggest dilemmas in studying inequality in antiquity, since modern moral dispositions that are brought to bear on the evidence present both the opportunity to enable new and productive lines of inquiry, but also the risk of framing the analysis in terms of modern concepts of what constitutes justice. Not only would such an approach be anachronistic, but it entails the risk of an overly deterministic narrative that overstates the blatant inequality in "primitive" societies in order to celebrate "advanced" mechanisms that aim at broad participation.[2] The political debates about the historical trajectory and acceptable degree of social inequality in modern societies doubtlessly establish the relevance of the topic and offer a timely occasion to reflect on the history and roots of the phenomenon in ancient societies. The cautionary point I would like to add is that this line of inquiry needs to recognize the fundamental differences between modern and ancient responses to inequality. Contemporary responses tend to entail systemic critiques (or defenses), whereas ancient responses were more pragmatic and aimed at resolving the contradictory effects of asymmetrical power relations on individuals.

Countering the effects of social inequality must have been critical in imperial Rome, where a dramatic disparity of social privilege was institutionalized legally, ideologically, and culturally (Osborne 2006; Morley 2006). The asymmetrical power structures in Roman society presented persistent stumbling blocks to social mobility and sustained an ideology that defined worth so narrowly that it excluded even those—or perhaps especially those—who attained a certain amount of agency. The mechanisms that upheld and justified this system are well known through textual sources that illustrate the evolving (but never abating) prerogatives of social elites, the ideals that informed social ambition, and the practices and symbolism that articulated and reinforced social differences (Gleason 1999; Eck and Heil 2005; Rosenstein 2010; Flower 2011). The ancient literature thus provides a relatively clear picture about the prevailing sensibilities regarding the social order. The problem with these texts is that they circulated, by and large, among the intellectual and political elite, which obscures the experiences, interests, and ambitions of social outsiders. Simply assuming that everyone embraced this normative system clearly does not do justice to the complexity of Roman society.[3] This is where material culture offers an opportunity by complementing the perspective that permeates ancient texts. The voices of the intellectual elite are still important because they furnish the immediate historical context in which inequality was upheld and exploited. However, as I hope to show, material culture can reveal the responses of marginalized populations in this system and, hence, offer a glimpse into their experiences and tactics.[4]

The particular question that I take up in this chapter is how those who were outside of the self-defined elite countered social exclusion, especially if such exclusion contradicted successes in their lives. My focus is on the city of Rome, because it presents unique evidence but also special conditions. Social inequality existed in the countryside, but the contradictions between success and exclusion tend to intensify in urban environments in which relatively able and connected populations possessed a certain amount of autonomy while being subject to persistent social distinctions.[5] In the city of Rome, the contrast was especially dramatic for the often highly skilled professionals with contacts in the epicenter of the imperial system who nonetheless remained in relationships of dependency and became the target of suspicion and derision. Many of them were slaves and freed slaves whose autonomy was limited by their dependence on current or former owners.[6] Such populations often produced cultural responses that are both assertively innovative and deferentially traditional, especially so in the case of unusually successful groups such as Augustales, vicomagistri, *apparitores,* or Imperial freedmen.[7] Their unique position results from the fact that they were neither completely exploited nor solidly participant, but situated somewhere between privilege and marginalization. This is the reason that their social tactics did not neglect a system from which they benefited (to an extent), but they also did not embrace it in its entirety.

The link between contradictory social positions in Roman urban populations and their distinctive cultural responses is a methodological opportunity, because it makes social inequality archaeologically visible. Thus, it enables the exploration of material culture that is demonstrably deployed in a context of unequal social relations. The potential downside of this reasoning is its dependence on concrete identifiers of social status. In the case of the abovementioned successful freedmen, this information stems from inscriptions and visual clues in standardized imagery. In other words, the evidence is the product of cultural choices that are perpetuated through modern analysis, at the expense of those who could not or would not participate in the practices that generate permanent evidence. The same dependence on concrete signs of underprivileged populations also characterizes the material basis of my case study: the distinctive form of burial that I describe below can be associated with slaves and freed slaves only on the basis of funerary epitaphs. This dependence demonstrates the need to address the dilemma of archaeological visibility and to explore ways to reveal silenced perspectives and historical change.

ORGANIZED COLLECTIVE BURIAL

My case study focuses on a powerful form of community building: organized collective burial. I use this term to refer to burial and commemoration in communities that extend beyond relationships of family or direct dependency and that exhibit some level of formality, administration, and monumental unity. Organized collective burial was practiced in a wide variety of ancient historical contexts, such as Greek war memorials or Roman catacombs.[8] The vast historical and pragmatic differences between such disparate scenarios make any direct comparison difficult, but a few fundamental observations seem to hold true across time and space. First, organized collective burial delineated a group, whether intentionally or not, by including some people and excluding others. The significance of this group and the strength of its cohesion varied dramatically between different contexts and even between individual members of the group, but unified burial nonetheless created a social space. Second, this social space comprised a behavioral component (of common rituals) but also a physical manifestation (of common burial grounds or monuments). These immaterial and material components reinforced each other, especially if the burial site was used for repeated burial and commemoration for a duration of time: physical proximity in the confined environment of common burial locales created opportunities for social interaction and, conversely, common rituals such as processions, cremations, meals, or commemorative gatherings could prompt the inclusion of the appropriate functional features in the physical setup.[9]

The basic distinction between the immaterial and material dimensions also informs the following discussion of organized collective burial in the Roman world. First, the operations of formal societies that buried their members (*collegia*) illustrate the formal organizational structures that developed around the practice. Secondly, collective tombs, exemplified here by columbarium tombs that accommodated up to several hundred burials in the early Imperial period, represent the tangible material evidence. In combination, these two aspects show that community building in general, and organized collective burial in particular, countered systemic inequality by creating communities that offered an intimate atmosphere internally while consolidating social relationships externally. Organized collective burial offers an instructive case study because it enables a reconstruction of ancient social behavior but also an exploration of the material conditions that shaped—and that were shaped by—this practice.

The structures and activities of domestic, religious, and professional associations (*collegia*) illustrate community building, because they offered occasions for social networking between members and with respect to patrons. *Collegia* often assumed responsibility for the burial of their members or provided financial assistance and logistical support for funerals, a function that highlights the close connection between such associations and organized collective burial.[10] The burial activities of associations feature prominently in the scholarly debate, because they are documented in the inscribed legal documents of associations from the first and second centuries AD. These inscriptions also illustrate the membership of such associations, which centered on nonelite urban populations but probably did not include the destitute because modest (but not negligible) contributions were required (Patterson 1992:21; Delaine 2000:121; Ebel 2004:50; Graham 2006:46). Even though the evidence is limited to a few inscriptions from different places and different times, what comes through clearly in these documents is the centrality of collective action, their internal hierarchical structure, and their fundraising strategy.

The fullest manifestation of these characteristics comes from the first-century-AD charter of the familia Silvani near Rome (Figure 18.1) and the second-century-AD charter of the *cultores Dianae et Antinoi* ("worshippers of Diana and Antinous") from Lanuvium.[11] Both inscriptions outline the operation of the association and specify recurring occasions for meetings between association members. In Lanuvium, the purpose of these meetings ranges from recreation to formal matters. There were purely convivial gatherings, especially the banquets that were celebrated on the birthdays of the society's patron and his family members. At these dinners, the elected "directors of dinners" (*magistri cenarum*) had to supply wine, water, bread, sardines, and couches (II.11–16).[12] The society's president (*quinquennalis*) performed religious rituals in white clothes and, on the birthdays of Diana and Antinous, he provided oil for all members to attend the public baths before the banquet (II.28–32). Such meetings arguably expressed and reinforced the horizontal bonds in the association. They provided regular occasions for social interaction among members but also showcased the collegium publicly through the collective use of the bathhouse.[13] The banquets were explicitly distinguished from business meetings (*conventus*), at which any complaints should be voiced and any other formal business could be conducted.[14] Aside from banquets and business meetings, the *cultores* also convened for the funerals of their members. The charter specifies that fifty sesterces were to be distributed at the pyre (I.25–26), presumably in order to ensure a well-attended funeral. Furthermore, the regulation that an

FIGURE 18.1. Rome, Via Salaria, Lex Familiae Silvani, Museo Nazionale Romano alle Terme di Diocleziano, Inv. # 108767-8 (su concessione del Ministero dei beni e delle attività culturali e del turismo—Soprintendenza Speciale Archeologia, Belle Arti e Paesaggio di Roma, photograph: author).

imaginary funeral (*funus imaginarium*) was to be held for slaves whose body could not be obtained (II.4–5) suggests that the gathering to commemorate a fellow group member was as important as the actual burial.

The special obligations of the collegium president indicate the existence of a social hierarchy within the association, which reveals that conviviality and cooperation do not necessarily imply equality within the group. The obligations came with privileges, such as exemption from membership dues during the period of tenure (II.17–18) and higher ratios at banquets during the period of tenure and after its successful completion (II.18–19, 21–22). These privileges extended to other officials besides the president: the inscription of the *cultores* specifically mentions *scribae* (secretaries) and *viatores* (messengers or, perhaps, agents). Such exemptions were also commemorated on funerary inscriptions, most prominently in the Columbarium of Livia on the Via Appia in Rome, where numerous individuals recorded their immunity or honored status (Borbonus 2014:131–132). It is not always clear how they achieved this position but in analogy with the *cultores Antinoi et Dianae* it may have had something to do with their official capacity within the association. In fact, collegium officials often emphasized their formal designation on funerary inscriptions, similar to the way in which privileged status was commemorated. The range of positions extends from *curatores* (commissioners) and *decuriones* (board members) to *sacerdotes* (priests) and *quaestores* (treasurers). These opportunities could absorb the ambition of more successful members in the group and translate it into social privilege.

Another characteristic that the charter reveals is the fundraising strategy of the association, which combines collective access to personal patronage with a revenue stream from individual members. Regarding the former, the charter commemorates an endowment that the society's self-described patron donated to the *cultores*. Gifts from patrons to associations were common and an Antonine inscription commemorates a similar endowment to the *collegii Aesculapii et Hygiae* in Rome.[15] At the same time, all association charters are concerned with membership dues and they record entry fees, monetary contributions, donations in kind, and fines.[16] A similar financial strategy was sometimes used for major investments, such as the construction of a tomb monument. Several inscriptions from Rome commemorate associates who united to pool their financial resources for this purpose.[17] The combination of maintaining relationships to affluent patrons while regulating the collection of individual contributions not only illustrates the financial strategy of associations, but it reveals one of the major benefits of associations for their members. The financial burdens and any obligations attached to the endowments were minimized through their distribution among numerous members. At the same time, the dual strategy aimed at securing the financial viability of the association, thus providing some measure of predictability to individual members who counted on accessing its resources at some point.[18] It was thus an ideal solution for those who could not bankroll an entire burial monument individually, but had sufficient means to meet the shared obligations imposed by collective organization.

The collective rituals surrounding burial, commemoration, and conviviality thus integrated individual members into communities of social peers. They provided an environment of solidarity at an especially traumatic juncture, but also a measure of financial autonomy and opportunities for relative social privilege. Associations mitigated unequal social relations externally and internally. Externally, they consolidated collective access to patronage, and internally they provided paths to social prestige for an internal leadership circle in the form of official roles in the collegium's administration.[19] An interesting modern parallel for this sort of community building are the *landsmanschaftn* of New York City. These benevolent societies provided Eastern European Jews with a convivial atmosphere at social events such as dances and picnics, but they also provided tangible benefits, such as basic insurance and burial. Like many Roman associations, *landsmanschaftn* typically maintained communal burial plots that were fenced off from larger surrounding cemeteries (Figure 18.2). These burial grounds illustrate a spatial configuration that must have reinforced the functions of the organizations. Internally, the burial ground provided opportunities for regular meetings between group members and may have become a site of shared identity. Externally, the elaborate gates and inscriptions represented the public face of the *landsmanschaft*. It is precisely those two functions that also characterize Roman columbarium tombs.

FIGURE 18.2. Burial plot of *landsmanschaft* in Washington cemetery, Brooklyn, New York (Courtesy of Dr. Steven Lasky, www.museumoffamilyhistory.com).

THE MATERIAL DIMENSION OF COLLECTIVE BURIAL

Columbarium tombs are the most important physical manifestation of organized collective burial in Rome. In fact, there are epigraphic hints that many of them were administered by formal associations (Cf. Borbonus 2014:130–132). Columbarium tombs concentrate on the city of Rome, where numerous examples were excavated between the seventeenth and twentieth centuries, but similar monuments also existed in other central Italian cities, most importantly the port cities of Ostia and Puteoli.[20] The columbarium tombs in Rome (Figure 18.3) are underground burial chambers that accommodate up to several hundred burials in cinerary ash urns that are immured into the wall and accessible through little arched openings. The result is a more or less regular grid of semicircular niches that are usually arranged in several rows and often (but not always) accompanied by inscriptions that record the names of one or more occupants. The interior walls are plastered, and, sometimes, painted decoration has been added between the niches or in continuous friezes between the rows. Like the burial plots of *landsmanschaftn,* columbarium tombs united a burial community and gave a visual articulation to its size, cohesion, and internal dynamic.

Columbarium tombs were first built in Rome during the reign of the first emperor Augustus (27 BC–AD14) and the novelty of their architectural blueprint becomes appar-

FIGURE 18.3. Rome, Via Aurelia, Columbarium "of Scribonius Menophilus" (su concessione del Ministero dei beni e delle attività culturali e del turismo—Soprintendenza Speciale Archeologia, Belle Arti e Paesaggio di Roma, photograph: author).

ent when comparing them with other Roman tomb monuments. Most importantly, the internal orientation of columbarium architecture reverses the representative nature of contemporaneous tombs such as the pyramid of Cestius (Figure 18.4). Here, the buried individual was represented publicly through large inscriptions that faced two major extra-urban roads to boost their visual impact. In contrast, the burial chamber was originally inaccessible (Ridley 1992; Neudecker 2005). The subterranean location of columbarium tombs probably gave them a more unassuming exterior appearance, even though the shortage of aboveground remains prevents detailed reconstructions. The lack of exterior façades highlights the interior design of columbarium chambers that maximized their capacity and accessibility while providing equal burial spots to individuals. All the burial niches were typically visible from any point in the burial chamber and they arguably provided a visual snapshot of the burial community. The homogeneity does not necessarily indicate equality between those buried in the collective monument. Rather, the visual parity suggests that the emphasis within the group was not placed on highlighting any differences. The internal design of columbarium tombs thus visually underscores the collegiality within the communities that used them.

FIGURE 18.4. Rome, Via Ostiense, Pyramid of Gaius Cestius (photograph: author).

Aside from the visual impression of columbarium architecture, its interior focus surely affected interactions within the group. The sheer scale of the monuments with up to several hundred niches will have resulted in regular meetings at the tomb site. On the recurring commemorative festivals, such as the *rosalia* or *parentalia,* that prompted visits of the burials of relatives, a collective monument must have been bustling with visitors, even if only a fraction of burial niches was actively commemorated.[21] Other encounters must have been planned, most importantly a funeral, which entailed the cremation (a burial custom that was shared by everyone in the tomb) and deposition of cremated remains in the collective tomb, and may have brought together a subset of the burial community. Purpose-built facilities for planned gatherings have not survived in any of the extant columbarium tombs in Rome, but they are attested epigraphically in Rome and archaeologically at Ostia and other sites.[22] Both planned and accidental encounters must have visibly outlined the membership of the burial community that used the same tomb. The reconstruction of the interaction within the group admittedly remains hypothetical, but it is likely that collective burial monuments constituted social spaces in which rituals of burial and commemoration intersected with the dynamic of the community that shared the same burial spot.

This community also constituted the primary audience for commemorative displays inside the burial chamber. Two kinds of commemorative displays exist: decoration and epitaphs. Most of the decoration on columbarium walls constitutes comprehensive decorative schemes that divide niches vertically or underline the horizontal rows with moldings or painted friezes. There are, however, cases, in which this decoration applies to a subgroup of niches or even individual ones (Figure 18.5). The decoration could, thus, be used to either beautify the entire tomb chamber or to isolate and distinguish some niches over others.[23] Epitaphs always identified individual niches, but they are brief and formulaic (Figure 18.6). As a result, they do not provide any real impression of the deceased beyond a few facts of

FIGURE 18.5. Rome, Via Appia, Columbarium 2 in the Vigna Codini (su concessione del Ministero dei beni e delle attività culturali e del turismo—Soprintendenza Speciale Archeologia, Belle Arti e Paesaggio di Roma, photograph: author).

FIGURE 18.6. Rome, Via Appia, Columbarium 1 in the Vigna Codini, epitaph of Publius Cornelius Theopropus and graffito of Corin(eli?), CIL 6.4932 (su concessione del Ministero dei beni e delle attività culturali e del turismo—Soprintendenza Speciale Archeologia, Belle Arti e Paesaggio di Roma, photograph: author).

life, such as name, legal status, age, or profession. The repetitive vocabulary commemorated individuals but it did so in standardized terms. Every individual received a comparable amount of information, the nature of which ranged from common elements such as a name to more exceptional ones, like the individual's official position in a collegium. The nature of this vocabulary thus matches columbarium design: it suggests that the visual cohesion embedded in that design extended to the behavior of individuals in the burial community who composed epitaphs that reflected their common background.

Because of their brevity and formulaic vocabulary, columbarium epitaphs can only be used for demographic reconstructions within limits. They do, however, reveal that columbarium tombs were used by Romans outside the political elite, and a majority of them were freed slaves or slaves that often belonged to aristocratic households like that of the Statilii Tauri.[24] This distinctive "user profile" suggests that the key to understanding the phenomenon of collective burial in Rome lies in the social experience of this group. During the short time when columbarium tombs were built, starting in the reign of the first emperor Augustus and continuing for a few decades, the social experience of slaves, freed slaves, and other nonelite urban residents was inconsistent. On the one hand, the operation of the imperial capital attracted (or forcibly relocated) talent and offered new opportunities for professional careers. On the other hand, the reactionary social legislation of the Augustan period reinforced the boundaries between formal orders and legal status groups, which might have presented stumbling blocks to the autonomy of freed slaves.[25] The tension between opportunities for success and persistent social exclusion arguably produced a status inconsistency. Collective burial could have addressed such a status inconsistency because it embedded individuals and families in a wider community that was held together by frequent encounters, a shared burial custom, and a communal funerary monument, in which each individual was treated equally.

Organized collective burial—in associations and in columbarium tombs—is a particularly tangible and easily documented aspect of community building. It provided means to counter social inequality, especially for populations that were not entirely marginalized but that had some access to social privilege while being locked in asymmetrical power relationships or various states of dependency. The social exclusion they experienced was counterbalanced in burial communities that were strengthened through frequent interactions between peers and visualized through the homogeneous layout of columbarium chambers. At the same time, the special responsibilities and privileges of collegium officials and the commemoration of leadership roles on columbarium epitaphs are hints of internal hierarchies that separated regular members from a distinguished subgroup. This leadership cadre could absorb the social ambition of the more successful members of a burial community. Aside from these group dynamics, burial communities also provided a measure of security and autonomy through their financial strategy, which relied on individual contributions, but also on collective access to patronage. While this strategy was limited to funerary matters and social events, it provided certainty at an especially traumatic time when a death in the community could have had numerous unpredictable consequences for those in positions of social dependency.

Despite its apparent benefits, organized collective burial in columbarium tombs was a short-lived phenomenon. A few decades after their first appearance during the Augustan reign, different architectural designs started to be used for newly built tombs, and existing ones started to be modified. The endpoint of the development was a new type of tomb, the aboveground columbarium (Figure 18.7) that still presented the characteristic cremation burial niches, but accommodated much smaller burial communities, featured a hierarchical architectural design that distinguished between regular and visually enhanced burial spots, and presented a representative façade toward the outside. The precise reasons for this development are not easy to determine, but my theory revolves around the generational turnover from freedmen to their descendants who were not subject to the same legal restrictions as their parents' generation and whose interests aligned more fully with the ideals of mainstream society.[26] Intriguingly, the same development can be observed in the aforementioned *landsmanschaftn,* the burial plots and financial viability of which also started to decline two

FIGURE 18.7. Rome, Via Ostiense, Sepolcreto Ostiense, Columbaria 7 and 8 (photograph: author).

or three generations after they were first established, when the descendants of Jewish immigrants assimilated more fully into mainstream society.

CONCLUSION

The short-lived popularity of columbarium tombs indicates that organized collective burial is a pragmatic method to counter the effects of inequality, rather than a sustained critique of its basis. Despite their innovative design, columbarium tombs also embraced aspects of Roman culture, such as the quintessentially Roman burial custom of cremation or the practice of commemoration through monumental writing that also characterized the contemporaneous cityscape.[27] The lack of a philosophical stance against inequality may be one element in a general theory of inequality in antiquity.[28] Perhaps, we can go even farther and conclude that the sort of collective action that I have described in this case study only existed because it was tolerated as a sort of social pressure valve. Contrary to my reconstruction, it has recently been suggested that Roman associations were not social networks that helped escape the discrimination of Roman society, but tools of subjection that reinforced status differences by allowing organization on an ultimately inconsequential level (Perry 2011:511–512). In this sense, it might be that inequality could only be countered in a very limited sense whereas the systemic inequalities of Roman society and the ideology on which they were based remained in place. This plausible alternative is a vivid reminder of the risk to exaggerate the similarities between responses to inequality in antiquity and contemporary parallels.

Despite this caveat, the case study of organized collective burial and of columbarium tombs demonstrates that material culture can refine our understanding of responses to inequality in two ways. The first contribution that material culture offers pertains to the dimension of time: even though material culture tends to paint a less specific picture than written sources, the ability to date material remains, even if only vaguely, allows analyzing changes diachronically. In the case of columbarium tombs, the evolution of architectural remains thus enables us to trace the social dynamic of a distinct population from the moment that it comes into view to the point when it dissolves into mainstream society. If the material record can be successfully tied to the analytical categories of disparity and differentiation, these analytical categories can be traced as historical phenomena with greater consistency than possible with more anecdotal conventional texts. The result is that many contributions in this volume document long-term changes and chart the processes by which inequality was created, justified, upheld, and countered.

The second contribution that material culture offers relates to the perspective it reveals, in the sense that it complements the conventional source material and reveals the interests, ambitions, and fears of population groups that are often silenced in the written record (and in historical practice). In the case of organized collective burial, the inscribed records of associations, and the built environment of columbarium tombs, the narrative shifts from a Roman obsession with social hierarchy to a more collegial environment inside burial collectives. Material culture also adds a tangible dimension that highlights the emotive and embodied experience in burial communities. In columbarium tombs, this experience is conveyed through the visual uniformity of the burial chambers, which provides a "visual snapshot" of the burial community, both in antiquity and today.[29] At the same time, written materials are still indispensable. Funerary inscriptions are crucial to map the material culture onto demographic realities and to identify slaves, freedmen, and anybody else in a socially dependent or otherwise marginal position.[30] Literary sources, even though they present an elite perspective, are necessary to identify the mainstream social values, according to which systematic inequality would not necessarily be interpreted as a sign of injustice.

The ever-looming dilemma that archaeologists keep facing when seeking and exploring social inequality is the one of imperfect archaeological visibility when it comes to underprivileged populations. This poor visibility is, in part, a result of past archaeological strategies and has even been used as a justification to further silence such groups in historical reconstructions (Webster 2005). The dilemma of identifying inequality in the archaeological record remains, however, and I can see two ways to address it. My case study has focused on a situation in which slaves and freed slaves are identifiable in the material record because of their funerary inscriptions. Monumental writing and other written words from known contexts have the definite advantage of unmistakably linking status differences with the physical environment in which they operated. One potential downside of this approach is a dependence on written information that limits the analysis to a small number of fortunate cases that may not be the most typical ones. Another recent approach is to bypass the problem of archaeological identification and to assume an omnipresence of social inequalities in the ancient world. This approach allows reading the material world as a context for the inequalities that we know to have existed (from textual sources). The potential downside of this approach is the risk of overemphasizing social dichotomies and overlooking cases of symbiotic cooperation.[31] Both approaches gain strength from a robust theoretical framework, however, and this is where the analytical concept of inequality may help to avoid overly simplistic binaries such as free and enslaved, elite and nonelite, male and female, or urban and rural.

NOTES

1. One of the most sustained arguments for the necessity of systematic inequality stems from Aristotle's *Politics*. In the ideal polis, inequality in kind between rulers and ruled (and on the household level between master, wife, children, and slaves) is necessary to produce unity, because the natural differences in capacity for virtue produce an exchange that constitutes the good life (Deslauriers 2013). Aristotle's ideal polis is entirely theoretical, but references of Greek orators and comedians also emphasize the difference in kind between free and slave that justified their differential treatment (cf. Dover 1994:283–288).

2. Even though he does not contrast it with modernity, Mattingly stresses the need to emphasize "ugly" sides of Roman rule in order to achieve a more balanced narrative (2001:22–26). The need for such a balanced narrative is surely justified, but I would caution that the method to emphasize "ugly" aspects does not control against overcorrection.

3. Bell and Ramsby describe the hostile characterization of freed slaves (2012:4–10).

4. I take the notion of "tactics" from Joshel and Petersen who, in their analysis of Roman slave experiences, distinguish between "master strategies" and "slave tactics" (2014:8–17). This distinction has the advantage of recognizing the constraints in slave regimes, which makes it more subtle than my own earlier concept of "social strategies" (Borbonus 2014:139–142).

5. On inequality in the countryside, see McCallum, this volume.

6. The continued dependence of freedmen has most recently been described by Mouritsen (2011:36–65).

7. The literature is vast, but important starting points are: Laird (2015) on *Augustales* (cf. review by MacLean 2016), Lott (2004) on *vicomagistri*, Purcell (1983) on *apparitores*, Leppin (1996) and MacLean (2012) on Imperial freedmen, and Borg (2012) on freedmen. This culture has led Mayer to identify an ancient middle class with a unique behavioral and representational culture (2012), a concept that Mouritsen judges as "too modernizing to be really convincing" (2012) while Wallace Hadrill judges Mayer's use of the concept of "class" to be too rigid (2013, furthering an earlier argument of Harris 1988).

8. On the Athenian war memorials, see most recently, Arrington 2015, and on Christian collective burial Rebillard 2006.

9. See below in note 22.

10. While burial was a service that many associations provided, it probably does not isolate a separate type of "burial association" or even burial insurance. This latter idea is the asser-

tion of Theodor Mommsen (1843), who coined the term *collegia funeraticia* based on the legal regulations surrounding formal associations. Scholarly opinion about the functions of associations has shifted significantly over time and the current consensus characterizes *collegia* as multifunctional social organizations (Ausbüttel 1982; Perry 2011; Tran 2006 and 2011; Verboven 2007 and 2011). The collective burial of *collegium* members is a practice that stretches across associations of all types (domestic, professional, religious).

11. The most recent translation and analysis of this inscription (*CIL* 14.2112 = *ILS* 7202) has been provided by Bendlin (2011) who cites all earlier literature.

12. The references in parentheses refer to the lines in columns I and II, in which the relevant information appears.

13. The charter emphasizes the goal of celebrating banquets "undisturbed and cheerfully" (*quieti et hilares,* cf. CIL 14.2112: II.23–24), which implies a desire for unanimity in the group.

14. The inscription records that the association's patron Lucius Caesennius Rufus promised to provide a generous endowment during a *conventus* that he himself had called (*CIL* 14.2112: I, 15). Other tasks that presumably also took place during the business meetings were the determination and exaction of fines (II.25–28), the admission of new members (I.20–22), the disbursal of funerary funds (I.24–26), the formation of committees for distant funerals (I.27–30), and the collection of membership dues (I.14).

15. *CIL* 6.10234 = *ILS* 7213. The symbiotic relationship between associations and their sponsors is reminiscent of Hellenistic cities where a similar phenomenon has been documented by Gabrielsen (1994, 2001).

16. A particularly detailed inscription is the one of the familia Silvani (AE 1929, 161) that specifies thorough procedures to discipline shortcomings of regular *collegium* members and the leadership group through fines (Buonocore and Diliberto 2002–03, esp. 380–387).

17. Examples include the famous tomb of the 36 *socii* on the Via Latina (*CIL* 6.11034), a tomb monument on the Esquiline that was financed by 13 associates (*CIL* 6.6150), and the Colombario Maggiore near the Via Aurelia that apparently used a similar mechanism (*CIL* 6.33292-3).

18. This fundraising strategy could also fail, as shown by the example of a Dacian *collegium* that was dissolved in AD 167 because it was not financially viable anymore (Ebel 2004:46–48).

19. For another example of differentiation within social groups, see Westgate, this volume.

20. Heinzelmann has treated the columbarium tombs at Ostia most comprehensively (2000). For Puteoli see the various reports of Gialanella (1991, 2003:64–79, Gialanella and Di Giovanni 2001).

21. On the *rosalia* and *parentalia* generally, see Toynbee (1971:63–64).

22. Epigraphically attested convivial facilities are dining halls (*CIL* 6.4305, 4710, 4711, cf. Braune 2008:200–207, Gee 2008), solaria, and benches. A particularly well-preserved tomb complex at Ostia that features a dining hall, well, hearth, crematorium, and terrace is VL E4 (Floriani Squarciapino et al. 1958:124–125, Heinzelmann 2000:270–272).

23. The decoration of columbarium tombs has been described by Lugli (1921), Bendinelli (1941), Borda (1948), Cappelli 1998, Feraudi-Gruénais (2001), and Fröhlich (2008).

24. The reliability of epigraphic statistics has been questioned (Maier 1954; Clauss 1973; Eck 1988), in part because "inscribing a tombstone was a ritual action" (Morris 1992:58) and their messages were carefully constructed (Alföldy 2002; Barrett 1993). On the Statilii: Mouritsen 2013; Hasegawa 2005.

25. Professional opportunities concentrated on the imperial household (Weaver 1972) but new social roles are also implied by the new college of Augustales (Laird 2002), neighborhood presidents (Lott 2004), and firefighters (Taylor 2000). The purpose of Augustan social legislation is a controversial subject, but it is fairly clear that it could limit social mobility (see Treggiari 1996, with older bibliography).

26. D'Onofrio (this volume) also uses a "generational model" to trace change over time.

27. For cremation, see Morris (1992). On the epigraphic culture of Augustan Rome, see Alföldy (1991).

28. More generally, it is not clear if such a critique ever existed in antiquity, since even accusations of excessive *luxuria* and idealizations of bucolic simplicity were often calculated public messages rather than genuine social critiques.

29. With regard to slavery, Marshall has highlighted the potential of material culture to "reveal the embodied experience of enslavement" (2015:2).

30. On the difficulty of identification, see also McCallum in this volume.

31. This approach has been developed and applied with respect to Roman urban and villa slaves by Sandra Joshel and Lauren Petersen (2014: esp. 4–6).

References

Alföldy, G. 1991 Augustus und die Inschriften: Tradition und Innovation. Die Geburt der imperialen Epigraphik. *Gymnasium* 98:289–324.

Alföldy, G. 2003 Die Repräsentation der Kaiserlichen Macht in den Inschriften Roms und des Imperium Romanum. In *The Representation and Perception of Roman Imperial Power*, edited by L. De Blois, P. Erdkamp, O. Hekster, G. De Kleijn, and S. Mols, pp. 3–19. J. C. Gieben, Amsterdam.

Arrington, N. T. 2015 *Ashes, Images, and Memories: The Presence of the War Dead in Fifth-Century Athens.* Oxford University Press, Oxford.

Ausbüttel, F. M. 1982 *Untersuchungen zu den Vereinen im Westen des Römischen Reiches.* M. Lassleben, Kallmünz.

Barrett, J. C. 1993 Chronologies of Remembrance: The Interpretation of Some Roman Inscriptions. *World Archaeology* 25:236–47.

Bell, S. and T. Ramsby 2012 Introduction. In *Free at Last! The Impact of Freed Slaves on the Roman Empire*, edited by S. Bell and T. Ramsby, pp. 1–23. Bristol Classical Press, London.

Bendinelli, G. 1941 *Le pitture del colombario di Villa Pamfili.* Istituto Poligrafico dello Stato, Rome.

Bendlin, A. 2011 Associations, Funerals, Sociality, and Roman Law: The *collegium* of Diana and Antinous in Lanuvium (CIL 14.2112) Reconsidered. In *Aposteldekret und antikes Vereinswesen. Gemeinschaft und ihre Ordnung*, edited by M. Öhler, pp. 207–296. Mohr Siebeck, Tübingen.

Borbonus, D. 2014 *Columbarium Tombs and Collective Identity in Augustan Rome.* Cambridge University Press, Cambridge.

Borda, M. 1948 La decorazione pittorica del colombario di Pomponio Ila. *MemLinc* 8:359–83.

Borg, B. E. 2011 What's in a Tomb? Roman Death Public and Private. In Mors omnibus instat. *Aspectos arqueológicos, epigráficos y rituales de la muerte en el Occidente Romano*, edited by J. Andreu, D. Espinosa, and S. Pastor, pp. 51–78. Liceus, Madrid.

Braune, S. 2008 Convivium Funebre. *Gestaltung und Funktion römischer Grabtriklinien als Räume für sepulkrale Bankettfeiern.* Olms, Hildesheim.

Buonocore, M., and O. Diliberto 2002–3 L'*album* e la lex della *familia Silvani* di *Trebula Mutuesca*. Nuove considerazioni. *Rendiconti della Pontificia Accademia Romana di Archeologia* 75:327–93.

Cappelli, R. 1998 Il fregio dipinto dell'Esquilino e la propaganda Augustea del mito delle origini. In *Palazzo Massimo alle Terme*, edited by A. La Regina, pp. 51–58. Electa, Milan.

Clauss, M. 1973 Probleme der Lebensalterstatistik aufgrund römischer Grabinschriften. *Chiron* 3:395–417.

DeLaine, J. 2000 Building the Eternal City: The Construction Industry of Imperial Rome. In *Ancient Rome: The Archaeology of the Eternal City*, edited by J. Coulston and H. Dodge, pp. 119–141. Oxford University School of Archaeology, Oxford.

Deslauriers, M. 2013 Political Unity and Inequality. In *The Cambridge Companion to Aristotle's Politics*, edited by M. Deslauriers and P. Destrée, pp. 117–143. Cambridge University Press, Cambridge.

Dover, K. J. 1994 *Greek Popular Morality in the Time of Plato and Aristotle*. Hackett, Indianapolis.

Ebel, E. 2004 *Die Attraktivität früher christlicher Gemeinden: die Gemeinde von Korinth im Spiegel griechisch-römischer Vereine*. Mohr Siebeck, Tübingen.

Eck, W. 1988 Aussagefähigkeit epigraphischer Statistik und die Bestattung von Sklaven im kaiserzeitlichen Rom. In *Alte Geschichte und Wissenschaftsgeschichte. Festschrift für Karl Christ zum 65. Geburtstag*, edited by P. Kneissl and V. Losemann, pp. 130–139. Wissenschaftliche Buchgesellschaft, Darmstadt.

Eck, W., and M. Heil (eds.) 2005 *Senatores populi romani. Realität und mediale Präsentation einer Führungsschicht*. Franz Steiner Verlag, Stuttgart.

Feraudi-Gruénais, F. 2001 *Ubi diutius nobis habitandum est. Die Innendekoration der kaiserzeitlichen Gräber Roms*. Reichert, Wiesbaden.

Floriani Squarciapino, M., I. Gismondi, G. Barbieri, H. Bloch, and R. Calza 1958 *Scavi di Ostia* 3.1, *Le necropoli: Le tombe di eta repubblicana ed augustea*. Libreria dello Stato, Rome.

Flower, H. I. 2011 Elite Self-Representation in Rome. In *The Oxford Handbook of Social Relations in the Roman World*, edited by M. Peachin, pp. 271–285. Oxford University Press, Oxford.

Fröhlich, R. 2008 Il grande colombario di Villa Doria Pamphilj. Architettura e pittura. In *Ut rosa amoena. Pitture e iscrizioni del Grande Colombario di Villa Doria Pamphilj*, edited by C. Caruso, pp. 22–51. Electa, Milan.

Gabrielsen, V. 1994 The Rhodian Associations Honouring Dionysodoros from Alexandria. *Classica et Mediaevalia* 45:137–60.

Gabrielsen, V. 2001 The Rhodian Associations and Economic Activity. In *Hellenistic Economies*, edited by Z. H. Archibald, J. Davies, V. Gabrielsen, and G. J. Oliver, pp. 215–244. Routledge, London.

Gee, R. 2008 From Corpse to Ancestor. The Role of Tombside Dining in the Transformation of the Body in Ancient Rome. In *The Materiality of Death. Bodies, Burials, Beliefs*, edited by F. Fahlander and T. Oestigaard, pp. 59–68. Archeopress, Oxford.

Gialanella, C. 1991 Via Cupa Cigliano—Via Vecchia Vigna. *Bollettino di Archeologia* 11/12:175–80.

Gialanella, C. 2003 *Nova Antiqua Phlegrea. New Archaeological Treasures from the Phlegrean Fields*. Soprintendenza archeologica di Napoli e Caserta, Naples.

Gialanella, C., and V. Di Giovanni 2001 La necropoli del suburbio orientale di Puteoli. In *Römischer Bestattungsbrauch und Beigabensitten in Rom, Norditalien und den Nordwestprovinzen von der späten Republik bis in die Kaiserzeit*, edited by M. Heinzelmann, J. Ortalli, P. Fasold, and M. Witteyer, pp. 159–168. Reichert, Wiesbaden.

Gleason, M. W. 1999 Elite Male Identity in the Roman Empire. In *Life, Death, and Entertainment in the Roman Empire,* edited by D. S. Potter and D. J. Mattingly, pp. 67–84. University of Michigan Press, Ann Arbor.

Graham, E.-J. 2006 *The Burial of the Urban Poor in Italy in the Late Roman Republic and Early Empire.* Archeopress, Oxford.

Harris, W. V. 1988 On the Applicability of the Concept of Class in Roman history. In *Forms of Control and Subordination in Antiquity,* edited by T. Yuge and M. Doi, pp. 15–26. Brill, Leiden.

Heinzelmann, M. 2000 *Die Nekropolen von Ostia. Untersuchungen zu den Gräberstaßen vor der Porta Romana und der Via Laurentina.* Pfeil, Munich.

Joshel, S. R., and L. H. Petersen 2014 *The Material Life of Roman Slaves.* Cambridge University Press, Cambridge.

Laird, M. L. 2015 *Civic Monuments and the "Augustales" in Roman Italy.* Cambridge University Press, Cambridge.

Leppin, H. 1996 Totum te Caesari debes: Selbstdarstellung und Mentalität einflußreicher kaiserlicher Freigelassener im frühen Principat. *Laverna* 7:67–91.

Lott, J. B. 2004 *The Neighborhoods of Augustan Rome.* Cambridge University Press, Cambridge.

Lugli, G. 1921 La decorazione dei colombari romani. *Architettura e arti decorative* 1:219–41.

MacLean, R. B. 2012 Cultural Exchange in Roman Society: Freed Slaves and Social Values, PhD Dissertation, Princeton University.

MacLean, R. B. 2016 Review of Laird 2015, *Bryn Mawr Classical Review* 2016.06.22; http://bmcr.brynmawr.edu/2016/2016-06-22.html.

Maier, F. G. 1954 Römische Bevölkerungsgeschichte und Inschriftenstatistik. *Historia* 2:318–51.

Marshall, L. W. 2015 Introduction: The Comparative Archaeology of Slavery. In *The Archaeology of Slavery. A Comparative Approach to Captivity and Coercion,* edited by L. W. Marshall, pp. 1–23. Southern Illinois University Press, Carbondale.

Mattingly, D. J. 2011 *Imperialism, Power, and Identity: Experiencing the Roman Empire.* Princeton University Press, Princeton.

Mommsen, T. 1843 *De collegiis et sodaliciis Romanorum.* Libraria Schwersiana, Kiel.

Mayer, E. 2012 *The Ancient Middle Classes: Urban Life and Aesthetics in the Roman Empire, 100 BCE–250 CE.* Harvard University Press, Cambridge.

Morley, R. 2006 The Poor in the City of Rome. In *Poverty in the Roman World,* edited by M. Atkins and R. Osborne, pp. 21–39. Cambridge University Press, Cambridge.

Morris, I. 1992 *Death-Ritual and Social Structure in Classical Antiquity.* Cambridge University Press, Cambridge.

Mouritsen, H. 2011 *The Freedman in the Roman World.* Cambridge University Press, Cambridge.

Mouritsen, H. 2012 Review of Mayer 2012, *Bryn Mawr Classical Review* 2012.09.40; http://bmcr.brynmawr.edu/2012/2012-09-40.html.

Neudecker, R. 2005 Die Pyramide des Cestius. In *Meisterwerke der antiken Kunst,* edited by L. Giuliani, pp. 94–113. Beck, Munich.

Osborne, R. 2006 Introduction: Roman Poverty in Context. In *Poverty in the Roman World,* edited by M. Atkins and R. Osborne, pp. 1–20. Cambridge University Press, Cambridge.

Patterson, J. R. 1992 Patronage, *Collegia,* and Burial in Imperial Rome. In *Death in Towns. Urban Responses to the Dying and the Dead, 100–1600,* edited by S. Bassett, pp. 13–27. Leicester University Press, Leicester.

Perry, J. S. 2011 Organized Societies: Collegia. In *The Oxford Handbook of Social Relations in the Roman World*, edited by M. Peachin, pp. 499–515. Oxford University Press, Oxford.

Purcell, N. 1983 The *Apparitores*: A Study in Social Mobility. *Papers of the British School at Rome* 51:125–73.

Rebillard, É. 2006 Chrétiens et formes de sépulture collective à Rome aux IIe et IIIe siècles. In *Origine delle Catacombe Romane*, edited by V. F. Nicolai and J. Guyon, pp. 41–47. Pontificio Istituto di Archeologia Cristiana, Vatican City.

Ridley, R. T. 1992 The Praetor and the Pyramid. The Tomb of Gaius Cestius in History, Archaeology, and Literature. *Bollettino di Archeologia* 13:1–29.

Rosenstein, N. 2010 Aristocratic Values. In *A Companion to the Roman Republic*, edited by N. Rosenstein and R. Morstein-Marx, pp. 365–382. Wiley-Blackwell, Malden, Massachusetts.

Taylor, R. 2000 *Public Needs and Private Pleasures. Water Distribution, the Tiber River, and the Urban Development of Ancient Rome*. Bretschneider, Rome.

Toynbee, J. M. C. 1971 *Death and Burial in the Roman World*. Cornell University Press, Ithaca.

Tran, N. 2006 *Les membres des associations romaines. Le rang social des* collegiati *en Italie et en Gaules, sous le Haut-Empire*. École Française de Rome, Rome.

Tran, N. 2011 Les collèges professionnels romains: "clubs" ou "corporations"? L'example de la vallée du Rhône et de *CIL* XII 1797 (Tournon-sur-Rhône, Ardèche). *Ancient Society* 41:197–219.

Treggiari, S. 1996 Social Status and Social Legislation. In *The Cambridge Ancient History. Volume X, The Augustan Empire 43 BC–AD 69*, edited by A. K. Bowman, E. Champlin, and A. Lintott, pp. 873–904. Cambridge University Press, Cambridge.

Verboven, K. 2007 The Associative Order: Status and Ethos among Roman Businessmen in Late Republic and early Empire. *Athenaeum* 95:861–93.

Verboven. K. 2011 Professional Collegia: Guilds or Social Clubs? *Ancient Society* 41:187–195.

Wallace Hadrill, A. 2013 Trying to Define and Identify the Roman "Middle Classes." *Journal of Roman Archaeology* 26:605–609.

Webster, J. 2005 Archaeologies of Slavery and Servitude: Bringing "New World" Perspectives to Roman Britain. *Journal of Roman Archaeology* 18:161–179.

PART IV

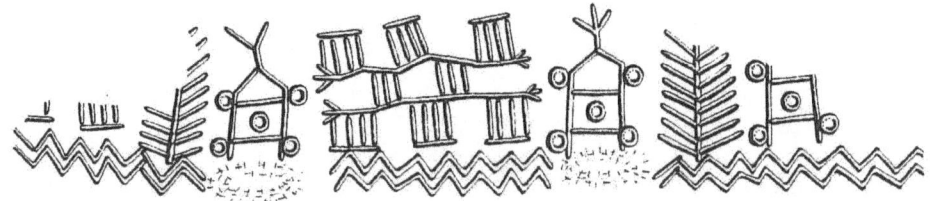

Bioarchaeology of Historical Inequality

CHAPTER NINETEEN

A Bioarchaeology of Inequality

Lessons from American Institutionalized and Anatomical Skeletal Assemblages

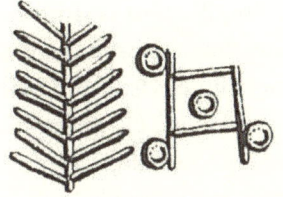

Jennifer L. Muller

Abstract   *Physical manifestations of social inequalities in skeletal remains are most likely to be evident under circumstances in which disparities are normalized within political, economic, and social structures. The physiological responses associated with the various environmental and cultural stressors of inequity may be literally embodied in human skeletal tissue. Bioarchaeological analysis of inequalities in two skeletal assemblages from the nineteenth- and twentieth-century United States are discussed here—the Erie County Poorhouse Cemetery, Buffalo, New York, and the W. Montague Cobb Human Skeletal Collection, Washington, District of Columbia. This research illustrates that studies of inequality in the past must carefully contextualize the multitude of cultural and temporal transitions that might impact individuals within their lifetime. In addition, it demonstrates that the mortuary context itself may be indicative of processes related to inequity and structural violence.*

Martin and colleagues (2013:1) provide a succinct definition of bioarchaeology as

> the study of ancient and historic human remains in a richly configured context that includes all possible reconstructions of the cultural and environmental variables relevant to the interpretations drawn from those remains.

As such, bioarchaeology does not focus solely on the study of skeletal and mummified human remains, but also on their contextualization which may be achieved through critical analysis of mortuary context, ancient texts, documentary archives, and ethnographic data. Bioarchaeology has contributed to scholarly investigations of inequality and social stratification in the past. Oftentimes, such research includes the observation of patterns and disparities in human skeletal assemblages as they relate to skeletal growth and development, markers of activity, pathologies, and traumatic injuries (Martin et al. 2013). The exploration of the economic and political variables that lead to the creation and the maintenance of inequalities in human groups, which may be embodied in the human skeleton, is achieved through the incorporation of multiple sources of data.

Inequities have the potential to impact the physiology of the human body through the introduction and/or perpetuation of various environmental and cultural stressors. In some cases, these physiological consequences and/or attempts to adapt to these stressors may be literally embodied in skeletal remains. It is the human skeleton's incredible elastic and plastic properties that allow it to respond to environmental and cultural stressors. However, it is also plasticity that permits the carving of lived experiences into and onto osteological material. Physical manifestations of social inequalities in skeletal remains are most likely to be evident under circumstances in which disparities are normalized within political, economic, and social structures. Studies of structural violence (Galtung 1969), harm to particular segments of society that is socially sanctioned by those in power, has recently been embraced by bioarchaeologists (e.g., Klaus 2012; Nystrom 2014). Public health scholars argue that the impacts of this structural violence in modern populations are most readily witnessed in the slow, continued, and oftentimes intergenerational suffering of the poor (e.g., Farmer 2004; Krieger et al. 2012; Krieger et al. 2003).

To what extent is it possible to assess past human archives (Watkins and Muller 2015) for the impacts of inequalities resulting from structural violence? Inequalities in two distinct groups of impoverished and marginalized peoples within the United States historical record are discussed here. This includes infant skeletal remains from the Erie County Poorhouse Cemetery, Buffalo, New York, and individuals from the W. Montague Cobb Human Skeletal Collection, Washington, District of Columbia. Both of these skeletal assemblages are associated with a wealth of documentary archival data. These data suggest that investigations into inequality in the past must carefully contextualize the multitude of cultural and temporal transitions that may impact individuals within their lifetime. In particular, this chapter discusses the impacts of changing ideologies related to social identities and migration on the assessment of inequality. In addition, the mortuary context itself might be indicative of processes related to structural violence.

TOWARD A BIOARCHAEOLOGY OF INEQUALITY

For nearly 60 years, bioarchaeologists have used the biocultural paradigm in their interpretations of the interactions between past social and natural environments and human biologies (Mays et al. 2017). One of the many benefits of this approach is that it permits the integration of the subdisciplines of anthropology (Zuckerman and Armelagos 2011). Since the critical contextualization of skeletal remains may require inclusion of theoretical and methodological considerations from all four subdisciplines of American anthropology, the biocultural paradigm has dominated much of bioarchaeological research.

Building a New Biocultural Synthesis, edited by Goodman and Leatherman (1998) promoted an approach to bioarchaeology (and human biology) that emphasized the impacts of local, extralocal, and global variables on the creation of inequalities, as well as their potential contributions to health disparities in both current and past populations. Biocultural models address the means by which cultural and environmental stressors interact with and lead to biologies. Bioarchaeologists may use these models to assess the social conditions that relate to the physiological stress responses observable in bone. The human adaptability and political economy model, presented by Thomas (1998), complicated previous ideas regarding inequality and human variation by including agency in the model. Individuals were not solely viewed as the recipients of nonegalitarian resource allocation, but adjusted or attempted to adjust behaviorally, biologically, and psychologically to stressors. Depending on the very specific set of circumstances, such adjustments could impact biologies positively and/or negatively or not at all.

Mays and colleagues (2017:4) discussed that although the biocultural paradigm has long framed hypothesis-driven and population-based bioarchaeological research, engagement with social theories has been a fairly recent development. Agarwal and Glencross's (2011) edited volume *Social Bioarchaeology* reinvigorated new developments in the biocultural synthesis (Martin et al. 2013). Since the publication of this volume, a proliferation of bioarchaeological research that incorporates social theories have been produced. Among the recent catalysts for such publications is Springer's *Bioarchaeology and Social Theory* series, edited by Debra Martin (Mays et al. 2017).

Research focusing on the concept of structural violence seeks to inform our understanding of the socially sanctioned oppressive forces that negatively impact human agency. As such, this concept is extremely helpful when incorporated with biocultural perspectives on inequality. Structural violence, a term first used by Johan Galtung (1969), *forms* social inequalities and these have the potential to alter human biologies, especially in cases when resources are unevenly distributed. Studies focusing on the impacts of structural violence on living human populations have been given substantive attention by the work of public health scholars, for instance, Paul Farmer (2004). Although public health research is focused on living human groups, Farmer (2004) advocates for the examination of the dead and those left for dead in order to understand how suffering is muted altogether. In what Farmer (2004) refers to as "compounding axes of discrimination," the differing and cumulative effects of cultural marginalization on specific subsets of the population is accompanied by a very particular set of stressors. These same forces will also impact individual and group agency. The compounding axes of discrimination associated with social identities such as age, sex, gender, race, nativity, perceived disability, and sexual orientation might have a profound influence on the biological outcome of poverty and political exclusion for particular individuals within the archaeological record. Engaging concepts, such as structural violence, and social theories, such as intersectionality, disability theories, feminist theories, and political economy enhance the utility of the biocultural model to bioarchaeological investigations.

A study of the biologies of inequality has emerged, focusing on both present-day bodies and those from archaeological contexts. Current research within bioarchaeology that focuses on inequality is decidedly more integrative, incorporating social theories, historical narrative, and ethnographic study of the biological and social body (Byrnes and Muller 2017; de la Cova 2014; Geller 2017; Harrod et al. 2012). Bioarchaeological assessment of structural violence and its relationship to inequality requires investigations of normalized disparities in resource allocation. For bioarchaeologists who specialize in the analysis of pathological conditions and traumas among impoverished and marginalized groups, much research interrogates the inability to effectively buffer environmental stressors due to the suppression of agentive decisions that accompanies structural violence.

All societies both past and present possess inequities, even those labeled as egalitarian. But in examining the bioarchaeological record in antiquity, when do we actually begin to see the biological consequences associated with inequity? Some of the complexities associated with making such observations have been summarized by Robb (2014). The first being that inequality, in and of itself, is extremely complicated. There is a distinction among those societies that possess inequalities and those that normalize distribution of and access to resources within a strict hierarchical framework. In order to address this in the past requires an analysis of the human archive (Watkins and Muller 2015) as interpreted through all available sources of information: documentary archival, archaeological, and osteological. The second reason is that inequities do not necessarily lead to negative, or even positive, consequences in health. The assumption that inequity in antiquity impacts biology is partly the result of our ethnocentric viewpoint. We can very clearly see signs of how impoverishment and marginalization *today* impact human biologies *today*. However, as Robb (2014) asserted, environmental variables and resources that currently impact human biologies, such as medical care, presence of specific infectious disease vectors, the variety of foods available, and contamination of water, might not have even existed or been associated with differential distribution/access in antiquity. As argued by Klaus (2012), responses to structural violence will not always lead to osteogenic and/or destructive changes in bone. However, differences in resource distribution *must* lead to physiological changes that manifest themselves in bone in order for bioarchaeologists to study resulting inequalities in human skeletal remains. Even with these limitations, it *is* possible that social inequities may manifest themselves in human biologies, with both positive and/or negative outcomes.

Erie County Poorhouse Infants

Within the past decade, bioarchaeological research focused on children has increased significantly (Mays et al. 2017). Children contribute immensely to society, partially through the social identities assigned to them, but also through their work, play, and their transmission of cultural values (Ellis 2010; Mays et al. 2017; Muller 2017). Cultures respond to the very specific role of children through investment in institutions and practices that change and/ or adjust their environments (Ellis 2010). Ellis has discussed that these, in turn, may impact the adaptability of the child in coping with environmental, biological, and cultural stressors.

Careful historical contextualization of New York State's poorhouses reveals that government policies, such as the Children's Law of 1875, and additional practices pertaining to the removal of "healthy" infants and children from the poorhouse may further complicate our understanding of those buried within associated cemeteries (Muller 2017). As discussed here, social attitudes regarding impairments and society's disabling of these children may further compound their experiences with inequity (Muller 2017). The intersecting identities and potential axes of discrimination (Farmer 2004) based on impoverishment and disability clearly impacted the lived experiences of these children.

The poorhouse system, adopted in the United States during the nineteenth century, was designed to provide "indoor relief" for the poor and destitute (Katz 1983). "Outdoor relief" in the form of charitable efforts to provide food, firewood, and other essentials, was not able to meet the demands of the increasing impoverished populations of New York State. Improving the health of poorhouse inmates was never truly the impetus for indoor relief. The poorhouse, instead, was designed to serve as a deterrent to poverty and its causing of idleness, laziness, and immorality (Higgins 1998). It was hoped that institutionalization would optimize the effects of the government's financial contributions in preventing death from homelessness and starvation (Katz 1983). The poorhouse would not positively impact the lives of the poor, nor would it serve as a buffer against disease, malnutrition, and several devastating epidemics (Higgins 1998).

From 1851–1926, the Poorhouse was in operation in what was then referred to as Buffalo Plains. Rather than a singular building, the poorhouse is more accurately defined as a complex. It would serve as a poorhouse, an insane asylum, an orphanage, and a hospital, including a maternity ward and a tuberculosis ward (Raines 2014). The demographic profile of the poorhouse would change significantly over its years of operation due to changing social ideologies and a series of laws and cultural practices. The poorhouse would eventually transition from an institution that accepted entire families to one that primarily cared for the elderly and disabled (Katz 1983).

One dramatic shift took place with the passage of *An Act to Provide for the Better Care of Pauper and Destitute Children*, also known at the New York State Children's Law (Olmstead 1888). Prior to this law, it was common for infants to be removed from their pauper parents and placed in religious and public institutions, bound out as laborers or apprentices, or "adopted" by more well-off couples and families. Even though children were kept separate from the rest of the residents, the poorhouse was deemed to be an inappropriate place for them. As detailed in an annual report of the New York State Commissioners of Public Charities (1874), it was believed that the conditions of the poorhouse morally and physically corrupted the child. Under such conditions, it was feared that children were likely to continue the cycle of poverty and crime.

Children with mental and/or physical impairments, as well as a variety of illnesses, would not be the recipients of care by private and religious charitable institutions. In nineteenth-century New York State, the compounding axes of poverty and disability led to inequities in the treatment of children dependent on this social welfare system. As stated in the Children's Law, a child between the ages of three and 16 was to be removed from the poorhouse "unless such child be an unteachable idiot, an epileptic or paralytic, or be otherwise defective, diseased or deformed, so as to render it unfit for family care" (*An Act To Provide for the Better Care of Pauper and Destitute Children* 1875)

Bioarchaeology of the Erie County Poorhouse

Between 2008 and 2012, major infrastructure changes at the State University of New York at Buffalo's (UB) South Campus necessitated the salvage excavation of human skeletal remains associated with the Erie County Poorhouse and Hospital cemetery (Hartner 2012). The primary goal of the salvage excavation was the respectful and complete disinterment of all skeletal remains impacted by the construction area (Perrelli and Hartner 2014). Therefore, a small portion of the cemetery was excavated. An analysis of burial documents associated with the poorhouse complex (Higgins et al. 2014) suggested that the excavated portion represents a very small percentage of the estimated 3,105 individuals buried within the Erie County Poorhouse cemetery. The documentary archive, associated artifacts, and skeletal demographics also suggests that this portion of the cemetery was likely in use from the 1870s to as late as 1913 (Higgins et al. 2014).

UB's Archaeological Survey excavated the remains of 377 individuals. Sixty-seven of these were children (59 infants and eight children between the ages of two and 16). Infants are defined here according to the cultural parameters of the time period. The Children's Law, which initially stipulated that children between three and 16 years of age should be removed from the poorhouse, was amended to include children between the ages of two and 16. There is no separate burial location for infants and children. Most children were placed in their own coffins. However, there are a few instances of child coffins being placed inside of, or on top of adult coffins.

Establishing the demographic profile of children from the bioarchaeological record is an essential part of understanding the influences on their short lives. Bioarchaeological and clinical research indicate that there are two major peaks in mortality rates among children. The first is the period at and just following birth; the second occurs during weaning, and in terms of life history theory, is the terminus for the infancy period (Halcrow and Tayles 2011; Lewis 2007). It was hypothesized that prematurity and neonatal death are very high among the poorhouse infants. Age at death was estimated using measurements associated with deciduous dentition, cranial, and postcranial skeletal elements (Muller 2016). While social age categories were used to define children as infants, it is not possible to determine social age from this skeletal archive. Results do indicate a peak in age at death in premature infants and neonates, with 75 percent of all children analyzed as being between 25 gestational weeks and 3.0 months old.

Macroscopic analysis of infant remains does not provide clear evidence for severe congenital conditions or, of course, mental illness. However, it does suggest that a number of infants suffered from physiological stress. Evidence of the macroscopic changes among the skeletal remains, for example, flared metaphyses and bowing; grooved teeth and destructive lesion in the palate; expansion of the diaphysis; extensive porosity to the bones of

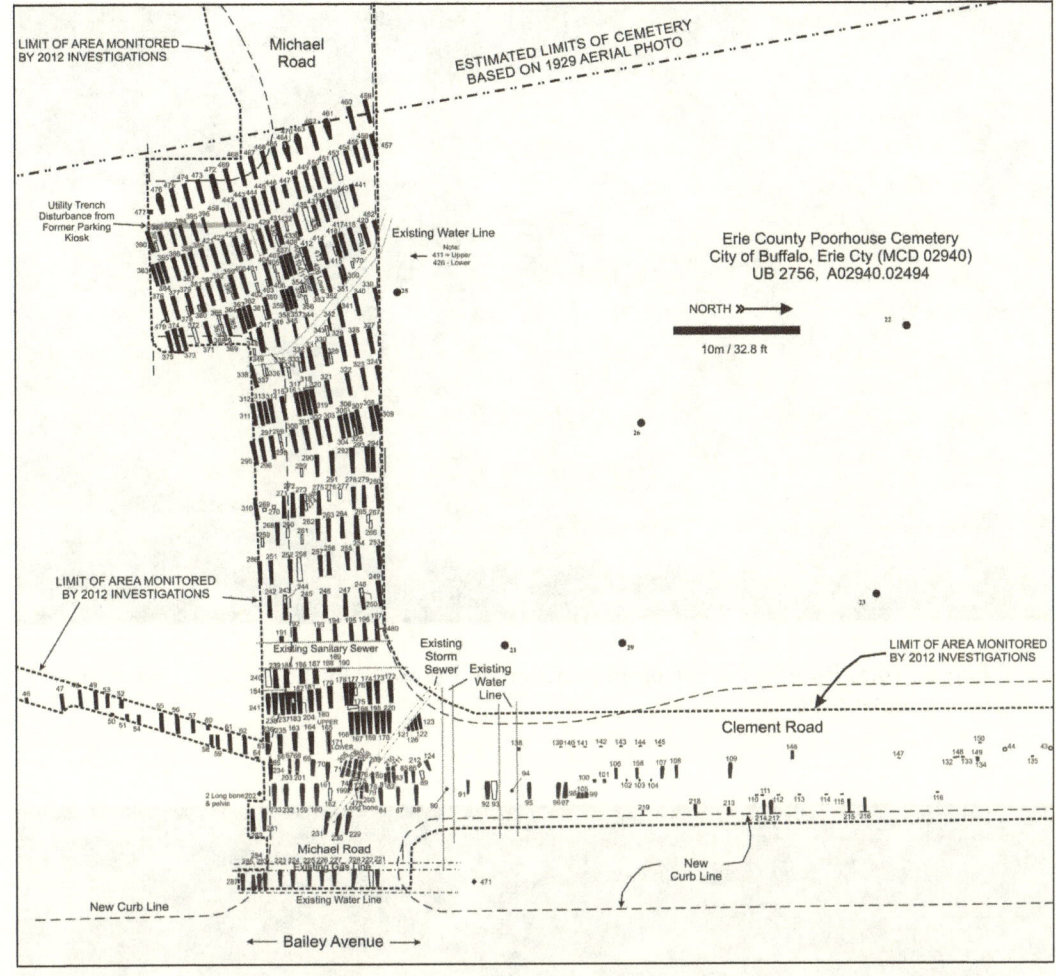

FIGURE 19.1. Map of Erie County Poorhouse cemetery with child burials outlined black with white fill. Base map was created by James Hartner (2012), Manuscript on File, SUNY Buffalo Archaeological Survey, Department of Anthropology, used by permission.

the cranium; and callus formation indicate that several infants suffered from infectious disease, malnutrition, that is, scurvy and rickets, and trauma. Given the synergistic relationship between malnutrition and disease, it is highly probable that the infants suffered from comorbidities o`f malnutrition and these diseases and conditions.

There is a significant amount of historical documentation associated with New York State poorhouses. Intake Records, or the Census for Almshouse Inmates in New York, is publically available via ancestry.com. These documents contain information regarding age, sex, nativity, and reason for entry in the poorhouse. In addition, the Reports of the Superintendent of the Poor, including Keeper's Reports, provide details on the number of inmates, illnesses, causes of death, and purchase of supplies. While the documentary histor-

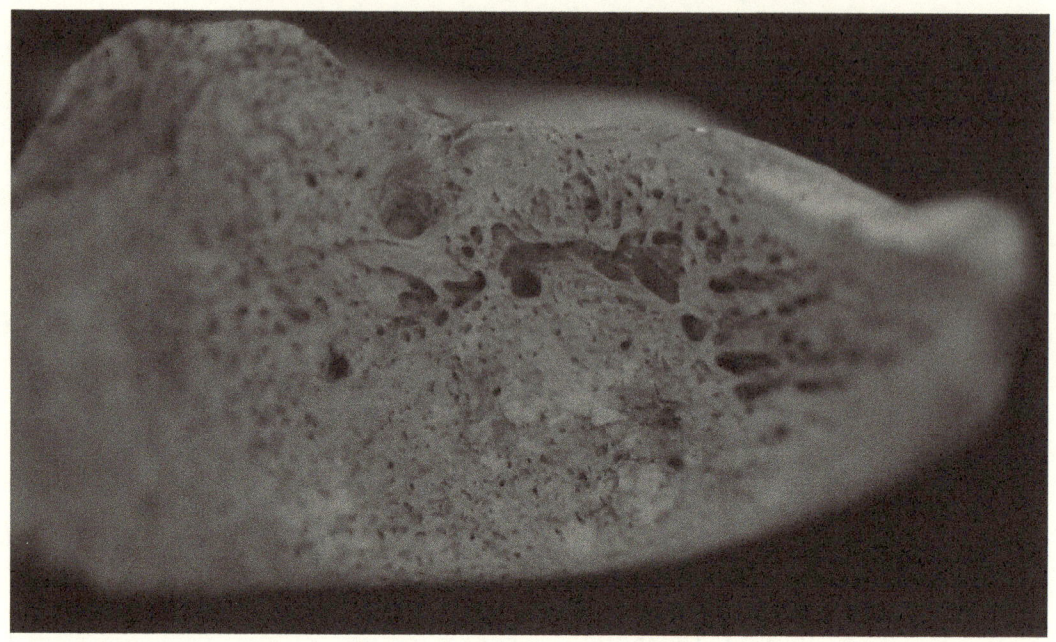

FIGURE 19.2. Pathological osteogenic reaction and porosity in the zygomatic bone of infant, burial #176.

FIGURE 19.3. Antemortem fracture in rib fragment, infant, burial #368.

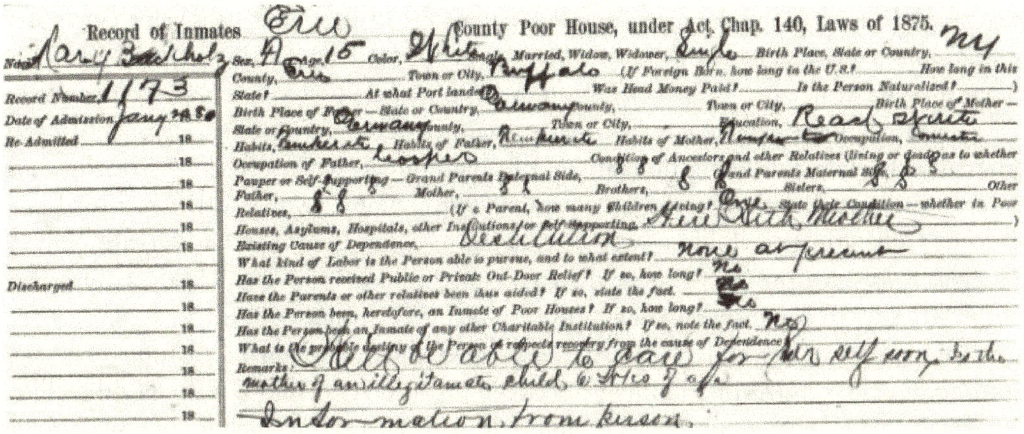
Record of Inmates Erie County Poor House, under Act, Chap. 140, Laws of 1875. NY

Name, Mary ... Sex, F Age, 15 Color, White Single, Married, Widow, Widower, Single Birth Place, State or Country, NY

County, Erie Town or City, Buffalo (If Foreign Born, how long in the U.S.? How long in this State? At what Port landed? Was Head Money Paid? Is the Person Naturalized?)

Record Number 1173

Date of Admission Jany 1880

Re-Admitted 18

Birth Place of Father—State or Country, Germany County, Town or City, Birth Place of Mother—State or Country, Germany County, Town or City, Education, Read & write

Habits, Intemperate Habits of Father, Intemperate Habits of Mother, Temperate Occupation, ...

Occupation of Father, Cooper Condition of Ancestors and other Relatives (living or dead) as to whether Pauper or Self-Supporting—Grand Parents Paternal Side, S S Grand Parents Maternal Side, S S Father, S S Mother, S S Brothers, S S Sisters, S S Other Relatives, S S (If a Parent, how many Children living? One. State their Condition—whether in Poor Houses, Asylums, Hospitals, other Institutions or Self-Supporting. Here with mother)

Existing Cause of Dependence, Destitution

What kind of Labor is the Person able to pursue, and to what extent? None at present

Has the Person received Public or Private Out-Door Relief? If so, how long? No

Discharged 18

Have the Parents or other relatives been thus aided? If so, state the fact. No

Has the Person been, heretofore, an Inmate of Poor Houses? If so, how long? No

Has the Person been an Inmate of any other Charitable Institution? If so, note the fact. No

What is the probable destiny of the Person as respects recovery from the cause of Dependence? Will be able to care for her self soon, is the

Remarks: mother of an illegitamate child 6 wks of age

Information from person.

FIGURE 19.4. Erie County Poorhouse Intake Record that describes a white female aged 15 years who was the mother of an "illegitimate" child, six weeks of age. Note that the record indicates that this woman's mother was also in the poorhouse.

ical archive indicates that poorhouse inmates and deceased hospital patients were buried in the poorhouse cemetery, both were subject to similar economic circumstances at the times of the deaths (Higgins 2014; Sirianni et al. 2014).

It is argued that bioarchaeological analysis of the infant, with their shortened life, can help researchers to understand the stressors associated with the immediate surroundings. Premature infants would have significantly reduced chances of survival. Premature and small-for-gestational-age infants with potentially underdeveloped lungs and immune systems are particularly vulnerable to disease (Ellis 2010). In addition, fetal programming variables, which are unobservable in the osteological record, are likely to have contributed to infant death (Perry 2006). It is all too often forgotten that environmental variables also include those in utero. The potential physiological impacts of in-utero environmental stressors do not only impact premature infants and newborns. In most cases, the developing fetus will take what they need from the mother, sometimes to the detriment of the mother's health. However, when the mother is unable to meet her minimum nutritional needs, the developing fetus might also be deprived with potentially significant consequences. Both clinical and anthropological research, mostly conducted in the medical anthropology and human biology subdisciplines, continue to address the importance of the in-utero environment and of fetal programming (Halcrow and Tayles 2011). The child's health is contingent on the mother's health. We are reminded that the body is both biological and social even before birth; possibly even before conception when one considers epigenetic change (Gowland 2015). The impacts of in-utero development do not just affect the child in infancy and adolescence, but may do so throughout their adult life, as suggested by the Developmental Origins of Health and Disease hypothesis (Gowland 2015).

Therefore, in order to truly understand the impacts of inequality and structural violence on the infant born into poverty, we must address the impact of structural violence on impoverished mothers. Intake records indicate that one of the many causes for entry into the poorhouse was pregnancy or recent birth coupled with destitution. The ill-health of infants, even those newly born, was most often attributed to the mother by those in authoritative positions in the poorhouse. Women engaging in employment outside of the home, neglectful behaviors and being illiterate and feeble-minded were seen as *the* contributing factors to the poor health of children (Higgins 1998). Women who worked as prostitutes and/or had "illegitimate" children were considered morally corrupt and among the least fit mothers (Olmstead 1888). Of course, there is no mention that poverty was the culprit that had forced many impoverished women into survival sex (Farmer 1997).

Compounding the biological issues associated with prematurity, malnutrition, and infectious disease is the distinction made between the impaired child and the healthy child. In some cases, the degree of perceived disability is made fairly clear; such is the case between teachable children and chronic unteachable idiot children (see Muller 2017 for discussion). These children were more likely to remain in the poorhouse, while others might have been removed from their mothers and placed in religious and charitable institutions, for instance, St. Mary's Asylum or the Syracuse Idiot Asylum, or 'adopted' by couples deemed appropriate by poorhouse officials. This differential treatment of children based upon their impairments and resulting disability further complicates the representativeness of the infant skeletons excavated from the cemetery to the overall poorhouse infant residents. The historical record suggests that structural violence resulted in the exclusion of impaired infants from adoption and other forms of placement. This resulted in an altered representation of poorhouse infants in the cemetery sample. In other words, these infants were likely those who died during childbirth, very shortly after childbirth as the result of acute disease, malnutrition, and/or fetal programming variables, or children who possessed manifestations of impairment that were perceived as disabling or unfit for care outside the poorhouse. Infants who were born healthy are more likely to have been removed from the poorhouse shortly after birth.

The very presence of these children's skeletons in the poorhouse cemetery is the result of socially sanctioned practices that increased the vulnerability of the poor and impaired child. The historical archive has revealed that children with impairments, both physical and mental, were treated quite differently by New York's historical welfare system (Muller 2017). To what extent the skewed representation of children in the cemetery leads to differences in skeletal manifestations of disease is unclear. However, the infants and children represented by the skeletal remains in the Erie County Poorhouse and Hospital Cemetery are not necessarily representative of all the children associated with the institution, but reflect social inequality.

THE W. MONTAGUE COBB HUMAN SKELETAL COLLECTION

The W. Montague Cobb Human Skeletal Collection, curated at Howard University in Washington, District of Columbia, is one of the largest documented skeletal collections within the United States. It includes the remains of more than 680 individuals as well as over 900 written records associated with the cadaver dissections from anatomy classes at the Howard University Medical School (Cobb 1936). William Montague Cobb, the first Black biological anthropologist, compiled this collection between 1932 and 1969. The collection is inclusive of a significant documentary archive, containing records with variable amounts of data including age, sex, ethnicity, occupation, nativity, cause of death, and morbidity. Several of these records also include photographs, drawings, measurements, and notes on specific medical conditions contributing to morbidity and mortality. Cobb's desire to establish Black scholars as authorities on human biology was the major impetus for commencing with the collection (Cobb 1936). Cobb focused his efforts on the impacts of environmental and cultural stressors on morbidity and mortality.

While Cobb collected the skeletal remains between the years 1932 and 1969, the skeletons actually represent individuals living from 1846 through 1969 (Muller et al. 2017). More than one hundred years seems like a potentially insignificant amount of time, given the vast archaeological record. However, the history of the period is defined by dramatic shifts in the social landscape of the United States. Collectively, these individuals experienced the Civil War up through the Civil Rights Movement. Individuals represented by the Cobb skeletal remains were subject to both inter- and intraracial discrimination. This discrimination led to inequalities that manifested themselves in several ways, including their living conditions and occupational opportunities.

The Cobb Human Archive (Watkins and Muller 2015) includes those individuals within the collection that are represented by skeletal remains *and* those whose information is in the documentary archive, but for whom we no longer have skeletons. The Cobb Human Archive consists of individuals who are representative of the poorest residents of the District of Columbia *at the times of their deaths*. The means of acquisition of Cobb individuals who would become cadavers, and then skeletons in the laboratory, does vary temporally. The vast majority of individuals were requested for District disposal due to the lack of financial means for burial or lack of next of kin (Muller 2006; Watkins 2003). In the case of the latter, unclaimed bodies were sent to District medical schools for dissection rather than buried or cremated at the expense of taxpayers (Muller et al. 2017). Some individuals had willed their bodies to the Howard University Medical School or to Cobb, himself. These "donated" individuals were not necessarily of better economic means, as this option was a less-expensive means of disposal of the decedent. Most individuals died in local hospitals and institutions. Approximately 17 percent of Cobb individuals died at the facility known through the years as Blue Plains, the Home for Aged and Infirm, and DC Village. The institution served as the District's poorhouse and eventually transitioned into a nursing home.

TRAUMATIC INJURIES IN THE COBB COLLECTION

Investigation of injury in skeletal remains is a major focus of research in biological anthropology (e.g., Glencross 2011; Judd and Redfern 2012; Martin 2012). Skeletal remains preserve evidence of injuries sustained by individuals throughout their lifetimes. Anthropological analysis of trauma is particularly informative as certain behaviors are known to influence fracture pattern and frequency (Lovell 1997). The majority of these impoverished individuals in the Cobb Collection were restricted in life to physically taxing occupations—basically, laborer for men and domestic for women. It was hypothesized that the added physical stress and dangers of their jobs would likely result in increased frequencies of trauma in their skeletons.

Macroscopic skeletal analysis of 205 Cobb individuals indicates a higher frequency of traumatic injuries when compared with many archaeological skeletal samples. In the Cobb Collection, 75 percent of males have fractures. Of particular interest is the resulting frequency of female fractures at 59 percent. The overall rate of injury to individuals represented by the Cobb Collection must have been very high, when one considers that skeletal evidence of injury is only one type of trauma. There are also lacerations, bruises, and burns that may not be evident in bone. The better preservation experienced by anatomical individuals may be partly responsible for the higher frequencies. However, that Cobb female fracture frequencies are much greater than for female frequencies in other skeletal samples cannot be explained by preservation issues alone. These results indicate that females are at a similar risk of fracture compared with their male counterparts, excepting for the fibula and cranium. This is not as frequently seen in historical samples and clinical studies, and it was not expected. There are also no statistically significant differences detected in the frequencies of males and females with multiple injuries. This is surprising given that males, working as laborers, were expected to have encountered much greater risk of injury working as laborers.

Although many fractures may be explained by simple accidents and occupational injuries, there is evidence to suggest that violence played a large role in the frequency and patterning of fracture in the Cobb Collection. Among the most compelling evidence includes fractures to the cranium. In U.S. clinical studies, the nasal region is the most frequently fractured element in violence-related incidents. Analysis of the Cobb Collection reveals that nasal bones are fractured in 40.82 percent. This is the most frequently fractured skeletal element in the entire sample. Chi-square analysis indicates there is no statistical difference in fractures to the right and left cranial elements. However, a trend for increased fracture prevalence to the left side is present. This would be an expected outcome of violence related trauma, given that 90 percent of people in the United States are right-handed. The majority of blows by a right-handed assailant in face to face altercations will affect the left side of the victim.

In order to truly understand injury in the collection, as well as potential sources of violence, we must delve much further into the complexities of the lived experiences of Cobb individuals. Until recently, there has been a tendency to treat people as temporally and spatially static entities in skeletal analyses (Watkins and Muller 2015). The Cobb Collection is often described as representative of the poorest of Black Washingtonians. However, the demography and lived spaces associated with the Cobb Collection is much more complex. There are many individuals in the collection who were born and who died in the District of Columbia. However, some lived there for 50 years, 20 years, in one case three days. Although the individuals comprising the collection died in the District of Columbia, the

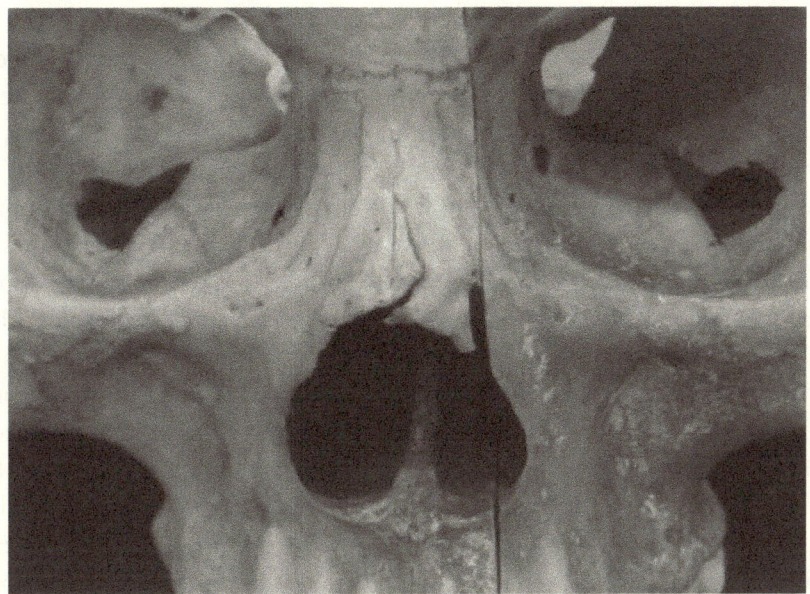

Figure 19.5. Fracture to the right nasal bone of an individual associated with the Cobb Human Archive.

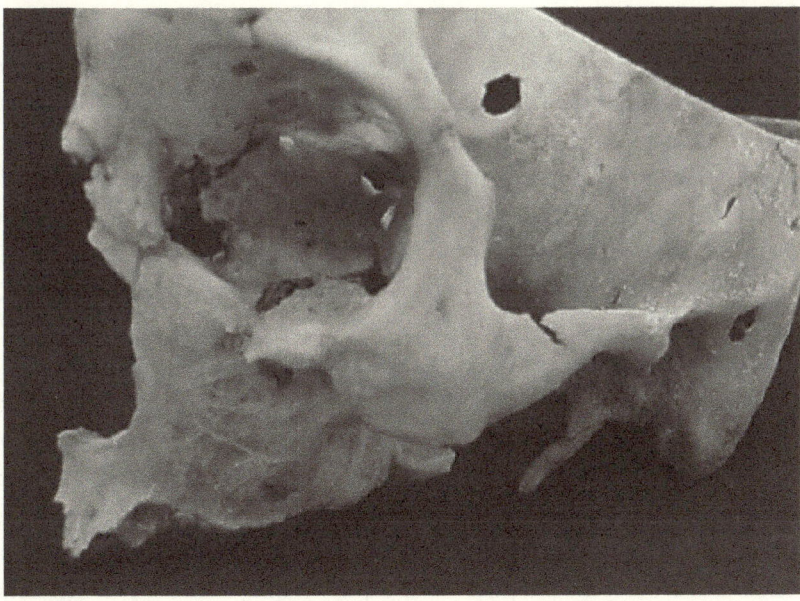

Figure 19.6. This individual from the Cobb Human Archive presents with multiple fractures to the left side of the cranium. These include a comminuted fracture (multiple fragments) of the nasal and maxillary bones. There is also an extensive fracture to the zygomatic bone (cheek bone), maxilla, and orbit which has resulted in the permanent displacement of the left zygomatic

vast majority were migrants. Many arrived in the District as part of the Great Migration (1910–1970) that included the relocation of more than six million Black people from the rural South to industrial centers in the urban Northern, Midwestern, and Western United States (Muller et al. 2017). This mass migration was attributed to several factors, including escape from racial violence, the negative consequences associated with Jim Crow violations, the sharecropping system of the rural South, as well as natural disasters that impacted crop production (Muller et al. 2017). Each of these meant a lack of political and economic opportunity for Black people living in the rural South. As a result, a large percentage of individuals in the Cobb Collection *might* have worked on a farm or plantation prior to their arrival in the District of Columbia. Their injuries may reflect agricultural hazards instead of industrial labor. Perhaps individuals in the Cobb Collection were victims of imprisonment or physical abuse related to the violation of Jim Crow laws, which demanded segregation in both public and private sectors. The social and physical environments of the District of Columbia may have had no impact at all on their lived experience. Therefore, the physiological responses to stress embodied in the skeleton *might* be telling us about the experiences of inequality in the spaces lived outside of the District. Therefore, we must be cognizant of the multiple spaces in which people live out their lives and how experiences of inequality may change temporally with physical movement of *individuals* (Watkins and Muller 2015).

Conclusion

As asserted by Larsen (2015), skeletal assemblages are biased for a multitude of reasons; many related to social identities. A required step in any bioarchaeological investigation is determining the representativeness of the skeletons to the population from which they are drawn. In terms of biological definition, neither the individuals in the Cobb Collection nor those associated with the Erie County Poorhouse and Hospital complex represent a population. Collectively, they represent many different populations, with significant variations in cultural systems and environmental stressors. It is this skewed demographic character that may provide insight into the social and political environment of the time (Watkins and Muller 2015).

Both assemblages consist of individuals who were impoverished and marginalized at the times of their deaths. The biological manifestations of their impoverishment are quite distinct, age-specific, and culture-specific. A critical and interdisciplinary bioarchaeological analysis of these particular subsets of society highlights the specific stressors encountered by these impoverished and marginalized groups. These documentary-rich skeletal assemblages provide lessons for bioarchaeologists of antiquity. Analysis of the W. Montague Cobb Collection illustrates how movement through multiple spaces can alter the experience of inequality within one individual's lifetime. Research on the infants of the Erie County Poorhouse reminds us that the social and biological body is the result of intergenerational experience. It also cautions that the experience of inequality might be influenced by society's perceptions of impairment and disability (Muller 2017).

The evolution of inequity is not restricted to the temporal changes associated with societal complexity. Change within individuals' lifetimes can dramatically impact experiences with inequity. Perhaps migration is one of the most obvious instigations of this change. Investigations of inequity's impact on biologies in antiquity must recognize the specific extralocal and local contextualization of the individuals and their movements throughout their histories (Watkins and Muller 2015). Having stated this, it is quite evident that this poses a significant challenge to many archaeologists. In instances in which significant documentation exists, bioarchaeologists should make efforts to unravel such complexities. Likewise, technological advances in isotope analysis may now permit bioarchaeologists to assess migration in antiquity. These recent developments hold significant promise in tackling the complex impacts of migration in understanding human lived experience with inequity. Given what we have learned from the bioarchaeological record, perhaps *local biologies* is not an appropriate term as it does not adequately convey the nonstatic nature of human lived experiences and the multitude of spaces and therefore environments and cultures in which they are embedded. People have always moved about, both historically and in antiquity. The health-inequality relationship is not fixed, but evolving (Robb 2014).

ACKNOWLEDGMENTS

I extend my gratitude to Joyce Sirianni and Doug Perrelli for the invitation to participate in the Erie County Poorhouse Project. I also thank Jennifer Liber Raines for sharing historical information regarding the Erie County Poorhouse children. I also wish to acknowledge Mark Mack (d. 2012), curator of the W. Montague Cobb Human Skeletal Collection (2001–2012) for his support and permission to work with the collection. A special thanks to the anonymous reviewers for their thoughtful comments, and to Orlando Cerasuolo for the invitation to contribute to this volume.

REFERENCES

Agarwal, S. C. and B. A. Glencross (eds.) 2011 *Social Bioarchaeology*. John Wiley & Sons, Oxford.

Blakey, M. L. 1998 Beyond European Enlightenment: Towards a Critical and Humanistic Human Biology. In. *Building a New Biocultural Synthesis: Political-Economic Perspectives in Human Biology*, edited by A. H. Goodman and T. L. Leatherman, pp. 379–405. University of Michigan Press, Ann Arbor.

Blakey, M. L. 2001 Bioarchaeology of the African Diaspora: Its Origins and Scope. *Annual Review of Anthropology* 30:387–422.

Brickley, M. and M. Smith 2006 Culturally Determined Patterns of Violence: Biological Anthropological Investigations at a Historic Urban Cemetery. *American anthropologist* 108(1):163–177.

Byrnes, J. F. 2015 "A Pauper's Shame": A Biocultural Investigation of Trauma, Impairment, and Disability in the Erie County Poorhouse Cemetery, 1851–1913. PhD Dissertation, University at Buffalo.

Byrnes, J. F., and J. L. Muller (eds.) 2017 Bioarchaeology of Impairment and Disability: Theoretical, Ethnohistorical, and Methodological Perspectives. Springer, New York.

Cobb, W. M. 1936 The Laboratory of Anatomy and Physical Anthropology, Howard University, 1932. 1936. Howard University, Washington, District of Columbia.

de la Cova, C. 2012 Trauma Patterns in 19th-Century-Born African American and Euro-American Females. *International Journal of Paleopathology* 2(2–3):61–68.

de la Cova, C. 2014 Controlled Lives, Impoverished Deaths: The Biological Stresses of Institutionalization. Paper presented as part of the "Embodied Politics of Inequality and Pain," symposium at the Society for American Archaeology 79th annual meeting, Austin, Texas.

Douglass, F. 1854 The Claims of the Negro. Ethnologically Considered: An Address, Before the Literary Societies of Western Reserve College, at Commencement.

Ellis, M. A. 2010 The Children of Spring Street: Rickets in an Early Nineteenth-Century Urban Congregation. *Northeast Historical Archaeology 39*.

Geller, P. L. 2017 The Bioarchaeology of Socio-Sexual lives: Queering Common sense about Sex, Gender, and Sexuality. Springer, New York.

Glencross, B. A. 2012 Skeletal Injury across the Life Course: Towards Understanding Social Agency. In *Social Bioarchaeology*, edited by S. C. Agarwal and B. A. Glencross, pp. 390–409. Wiley-Blackwell, Oxford.

Goodman, A. H., and T. L. Leatherman (eds.) 1998 *Building a New Biocultural Synthesis: Political-Economic Perspectives on Human Biology*. University of Michigan Press, Ann Arbor.

Grauer, A. L. (ed.) 1995 *Bodies of Evidence: Reconstructing History through Skeletal Analysis*. John Wiley and Sons, Oxford.

Halcrow, S. E., and N, Tayles 2008 The Bioarchaeological Investigation of Childhood and Social Age: Problems and Prospects. *Journal of Archaeological Method and Theory* 15(2):190–215.

Harrod, R. P., J. L. Thompson, and D. L. Martin 2012 Hard Labor and Hostile Encounters: What Human Remains Reveal about Institutionalized Violence and Chinese Immigrants Living in Carlin, Nevada (1885–1923). *Historical Archaeology* 46(4):85–111.

Hartner, J. E. and D. J. Perrelli 2014 Erie County Poorhouse Cemetery Site Artifacts and Material Patterns. In Forgotten People in Forgotten Places: the Archaeology, History, and Biology of the Erie County Poorhouse, Buffalo, New York. Annual Meeting of the American Association of Physical Anthropologists.

Higgins, R. L. 1998 *The Biology of Poverty: Epidemiological Transition in Western New York*, Doctoral dissertation, State University of New York at Buffalo.

Higgins, R. L., J. L. Raines, and N. L. Montague 2014 Confirming Burial Location in the Erie County Poorhouse Cemetery Using Death Certificates and Mortality Records from 1880–1913. In Forgotten People in Forgotten Places: The Archaeology, History, and Biology of the Erie County Poorhouse, Buffalo, New York. Annual Meeting of the American Association of Physical Anthropologists.

Farmer, P. 2004 An Anthropology of Structural Violence. *Current anthropology* 45(3):305–325.

Galtung, J. 1969 Violence, Peace, and Peace Research. *Journal of Peace Research* 6(3):167–191.

Gowland, R. L. 2015 Entangled Lives: Implications of the Developmental Origins of Health and Disease Hypothesis for Bioarchaeology and the Life Course. *American journal of physical anthropology* 158(4):530–540.

Halcrow, S. E. and N. Tayles 2011 The Bioarchaeological Investigation of Children and Childhood. In *Social bioarchaeology*. edited by S. C. Agarwal and B. A. Glencross, pp. 333–360. Wiley-Blackwell, Oxford.

Harrod, R. P. 2012 Centers of Control: Revealing Elites among the Ancestral Pueblo during the "Chaco Phenomenon." *International Journal of Paleopathology* 2(2):123–135.

Judd, M. A., and R. Redfern 2012 Trauma. In *A Companion to Paleopathology*, edited by A. L. Grauer, pp. 357–379. Wiley-Blackwell, Oxford.

Katz, M. B. 1983 *Poverty and Policy in American History*. Academic Press, New York.

Katz, M. B. 1986 *In the Shadow of the Poorhouse: A Social History of Welfare in America*. Basic Books, New York.

Klaus, H. D. 2012 The Bioarchaeology of Structural Violence. In *The Bioarchaeology of Violence*, edited by D. L. Martin, R. P. Harrod, and V. R. Perez, pp. 29–62. Bioarchaeological Interpretations of the Human Past: Local, Regional, and Global. University Press of Florida, Gainesville.

Knudson, K. J., and C. M. Stojanowski 2008 New Directions in Bioarchaeology: Recent Contributions to the Study of Human Social Identities. *Journal of Archaeological Research* 16(4):397–432.

Krieger, N. 2012 Methods for the Scientific Study of Discrimination and Health: An Ecosocial Approach. *American journal of public health* 102(5):936–944.

Krieger, N., J. T. Chen, P. D. Waterman, D. H. Rehkopf, and S. V. Subramanian 2003 Race/Ethnicity, Gender, and Monitoring Socioeconomic Gradients in Health: A Comparison of Area-Based Socioeconomic Measures–The Public Health Disparities Geocoding Project. *American journal of public health* 93(10):1655–1671.

Krieger, N., D. L. Rowley, A. A. Herman, and B. Avery 1993 Racism, Sexism, and Social Class: Implications for Studies of Health, Disease, and Well-Being. *American journal of preventive medicine* 9:82–122.

Larsen, C. S. 2015 *Bioarchaeology: Interpreting Behavior from the Human Skeleton*. Vol. 69. Cambridge University Press, Cambridge.

Laws of New York State. 1875 An Act To Provide For the Better Care of Pauper and Destitute Children.

Lewis, M. E. 2007 *The Bioarchaeology of Children: Perspectives from Biological and Forensic Anthropology* (Vol. 50). Cambridge University Press, Cambridge.

Little, M. A., and K. A. R. Kennedy 2010 *Histories of American Physical Anthropology in the Twentieth Century*. Lexington Books, Lanham, Maryland.

Lovell, N. C. 1997 Trauma Analysis in Paleopathology. *American Journal of Physical Anthropology* 104(S25):139–170.

Martin, D. L., N. J. Akins, A. H. Goodman, and A. C. Swedlund 2001 Harmony and Discord: Bioarchaeology of the La Plata Valley. *Totah: Time and the Rivers Flowing Excavations in the La Plata Valley* 242.

Martin, D. L., R. P. Harrod, and V. R. Pérez (eds.) 2012 *The Bioarchaeology of Violence*. University Press of Florida, Gainesville.

Martin, D. L., R. P. Harrod, and V. R. Pérez 2013 *Bioarchaeology: An Integrated Approach to Working with Human Remains*. Springer Science and Business Media, New York.

Muller, J. L. 2006 Trauma as a Biological Consequence of Inequality: A Biocultural Analysis of Washington DC's African American Poor. PhD dissertation. Buffalo, New York: Department of Anthropology, University at Buffalo.

Muller, J. L. 2017 Rendered Unfit: Defective Children in the Erie County Poorhouse. In *Bioarchaeology of Impairment and Disability: Theoretical, Ethnohistorical, and Methodological Perspectives*, edited by J. F. Byrnes and J. L. Muller. Bioarchaeology and Social Theory. New York: Springer.

Muller, J. L., K. Pearlstein, and C. de la Cova 2017 Dissection and Documented Skeletal Collections: Legalized Embodiment of Inequality. In *The Bioarchaeology of Autopsy and Dissection in the United States*, edited by K. C. Nystrom. Springer, New York.

New York State Commissioners of Public Charities. 1874 New York State Commissioners of Public Charities Annual Report.

Nystrom, K. C. 2014 The Bioarchaeology of Structural Violence and Dissection in the 19th-Century United States. *American Anthropologist* 116(4):1–15.

Nystrom, K. C. 2017 *The Bioarchaeology of Dissection and Autopsy in the United States*. Springer, New York.

Olmstead, F. L. 1888 *Hand-Book for Visitors to the Poorhouse*. Adopted by the State Charities Aid Association. GP Putnam's Sons, New York.

Perrelli, D. J., and J. E. Hartner 2014 Erie County Poorhouse Cemetery Site Excavation Methods and Results. In Forgotten people in forgotten places: The archaeology, history, and biology of the Erie County Poorhouse, Buffalo, New York. Annual Meeting of the American Association of Physical Anthropologists.

Perry, M. A. 2006. Redefining Childhood through Bioarchaeology: Toward an Archaeological and Biological Understanding of Children in Antiquity. *Archeological Papers of the American Anthropological Association* 15:89–111.

Raines, J. L. 2014 The Importance of Documentary Evidence in Understanding Demographic Patterns at the Erie County Poorhouse (1851–1926). In Forgotten people in forgotten places: the archaeology, history, and biology of the Erie County Poorhouse, Buffalo, New York. Annual Meeting of the American Association of Physical Anthropologists.

Rankin-Hill, L. M., and M. L. Blakey 1994 W. Montague Cobb (1904–1990): Physical Anthropologist, Anatomist, and Activist. *American Anthropologist* 96:74–96.

Robb, J. 2014 Retheorising Inequality and the Body. Paper presented as part of the "Embodied Politics of Inequality and Pain," symposium at the Society for American Archaeology 79th annual meeting, Austin, Texas.

Robb, J., R. Bigazzi, L. Lazzarini, C. Scarsini, and F. Sonego 2001 Social "Status" and Biological "Status": A Comparison of Grave Goods and Skeletal Indicators from Pontecagnano. *American Journal of Physical Anthropology* 115(3):213–222.

Sirianni, J. E., R. L. Higgins, and J. F. Byrnes 2014 Paleopathology and the Poor: Comparing Historical Records of Morbidity and Mortality to Skeletal Paleopathology in the Erie County Poorhouse Cemetery. In: Forgotten people in forgotten places: The archaeology, history, and biology of the Erie County Poorhouse, Buffalo, New York. Annual Meeting of the American Association of Physical Anthropologists.

Sofaer, J. 2006 *The Body as Material Culture: A Theoretical Osteoarchaeology*. Cambridge University Press, Cambridge.

Thomas, R. B. 1998 The Evolution of Human Adaptability Paradigms: Toward a Biology of Poverty. In *Building a New Biocultural Synthesis: Political-Economic Perspectives on Human Biology*, edited by A. H. Goodman and T. L. Leatherman, pp. 451–473. The University of Michigan Press, Ann Arbor.

Thompson, J. L., M. P. Alfonso-Durruty, and J. J. Crandall (eds.) 2014 *Tracing Childhood: Bioarchaeological Investigations of Early Lives in Antiquity*. University Press of Florida, Gainesville.

Tung, T. A. 2007 Trauma and Violence in the Wari Empire of the Peruvian Andes: Warfare, Raids, and Ritual Fights. *American Journal of Physical Anthropology* 133(3):941–956.

Walker, P. L. 2001 A Bioarchaeological Perspective on the History of Violence. *Annual Review of Anthropology* 30:573–596.

Watkins, R. J. 2007 Knowledge from the Margins: W. Montague Cobb's Pioneering Research in Biocultural Anthropology. *American Anthropologist* 109(1):186–196.

Watkins, R. J., and J. L. Muller 2015 Repositioning the Cobb Human Archive: The Merger of a Skeletal Collection with Its Texts. *American Journal of Human Biology* 27:41–50.

Zuckerman, M. K., and G. J. Armelagos 2011 The Origins of Biocultural Dimensions in Bioarchaeology. In *Social Bioarchaeology*, edited by S. C. Agarwal and B. A. Glencross, pp. 15–43. Wiley-Blackwell, Oxford.

Contributors

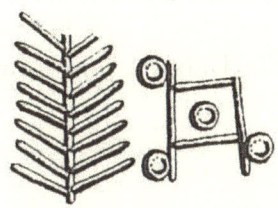

Giovanna Bagnasco Gianni, Department of Cultural and Environmental Heritage, Università degli Studi di Milano, Milan, MI 20122, Italy

Dorian Borbonus, College of Arts and Sciences, History, University of Dayton, Dayton, OH 45469, USA

Patrice Brun, Department of Art and Archaeology History, University Paris 1 Panthéon-Sorbonne, 3 rue Michelet, 75006 Paris, France

Orlando Cerasuolo, Department of Asia, Africa, and Mediterranean, Università degli Studi di Napoli L'Orientale, Naples, NA 80121, Italy

Simona Dalsoglio, Department of Asia, Africa, and Mediterranean, Università degli Studi di Napoli L'Orientale, Naples, NA 80121, Italy

Luuk De Ligt, Institute for History, Universiteit Leiden, Leiden, VL 2311, Netherlands

Anna Maria D'Onofrio, Department of Asia, Africa, and Mediterranean, Università degli Studi di Napoli L'Orientale, Naples, NA 80121, Italy

Elizabeth Fentress, Independent Researcher, Rome 00186, Italy

Bryan K. Hanks, Department of Anthropology, University of Pittsburgh, Pittsburgh, PA 15260, USA

Brian Hayden, Department of Archaeology, Simon Fraser University, Burnaby, B.C. V5A 1S6, Canada

Myles McCallum, Department of Modern Languages and Classics, Saint Mary's University, Halifax, Nova Scotia B3H 3C3, Canada

Jennifer L. Muller, Department of Anthropology, Ithaca College, Ithaca, NY 14850, USA

William A. Parkinson, The Field Museum, Chicago, IL 60605-2496, USA

Elisa Perego, Institute of Archaeology, University College London, London, WC1H 0PY, UK

T. Douglas Price, Department of Anthropology, University of Wisconsin-Madison, Madison, WI 53706, USA

Massimo Saracino, Museo Civico di Storia Naturale di Verona, Verona, 37129 VR, Italy

†Mario Torelli, Accademia Nazionale dei Lincei, Roma, RM 00165, Italy

Vicky Vlachou, Ecole Française d'Athènes, GR 106 80 Athens, Greece

Ruth Westgate, School of History, Archaeology and Religion, Cardiff University, Cardiff, CF10 3AT, UK

Lorenzo Zamboni, Department of Cultural and Environmental Heritage, Università degli Studi di Milano, Milan, MI 20122, Italy

Vera Zanoni, Guest Lecturer at Università di Pavia, Dipartimento di Studi Umanistici, C.so Strada Nuova 65, 27100 Pavia

Rachel Zelnick-Abramovitz, Department of Humanities, Tel Aviv University, Tel Aviv, 6997801, Israel

Index

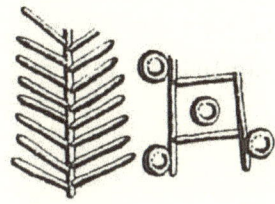